Suicide in the Entertainment Industry

Suicide in the Entertainment Industry

An Encyclopedia of 840 Twentieth Century Cases

DAVID K. FRASIER

Foreword by Kenneth Anger

McFarland & Company, Inc., Publishers

Jefferson, North Carolina, and London

The present work is a reprint of the illustrated case bound edition of Suicide in the Entertainment Industry: An Encyclopedia of 840 Twentieth Century Cases, *first published in 2002 by McFarland.*

LIBRARY OF CONGRESS CATALOGUING-IN-PUBLICATION DATA

Frasier, David K., 1951—
Suicide in the entertainment industry : an encyclopedia of
840 twentieth century cases / David K. Frasier.
p.   cm.
Includes bibliographical references and index.

ISBN 0-7864-2333-1 (softcover : 50# alkaline paper) ♾

1. Entertainers — Biography — Dictionaries.   2. Celebrities —
Biography — Dictionaries.   3. Entertainers — Suicidal behavior.
4. Celebrities — Suicidal behavior.   5. Entertainers — Death.
6. Celebrities — Death.   I. Title.
PN2208.F73   2005   791'.092'2 — dc21   [B]   2001045020

British Library cataloguing data are available

Manufactured in the United States of America

*McFarland & Company, Inc., Publishers
Box 611, Jefferson, North Carolina 28640
www.mcfarlandpub.com*

To my beloved son, Hayden —
my favorite production

ACKNOWLEDGMENTS

I wish to acknowledge and thank the following individuals and institutions without whose support this book could not have been written:

Kenneth Anger, film director and cinema historian, whose *Hollywood Babylon* books first fired the imagination of a teenager some thirty years ago. Thank you for the foreword and for the selfless friendship you have shown to me and my family throughout the years. Jeffrey Graf, reference computing coordinator, a colleague and dear friend whose taste and judgment I value above all others. In addition to providing expert computer support, Jeff was also my principal sounding board throughout every phase of the project. Michael Newton, author of *Encyclopedia of Serial Killers* and many other true crime books, whose friendship and support I now accept as a given in my life. Lee Harris and his wife, Jana Wells, Hollywood friends who photographed many suicide sites and show biz graves for this book. Michael Cavanagh, photographer at the Indiana University Art Museum, a longtime friend who, like the cavalry in a B Western, always arrives in the last reel to save my life.

I would also like to individually thank my colleagues in the Reference Department of the Main Library, Research Collections, at Indiana University–Bloomington. While the majority of them do not share my passion for the darker side of show business, to a person they recognized and supported my research. I name them here:

Ann Bristow, department head, who supplied letters of support on my behalf to various funding agencies within the library. When routinely asked during the course of my ongoing research into celebrity self-slaughter if she remembered so-and-so, Ann invariably replied (before quickly changing the subject), "No, but I'm sure they lived a long, happy life, and died peacefully surrounded by their loving family." Frank Quinn, associate librarian and assistant department head, who suggested cases and was a source of encouragement during the research and writing of this book. Jian Liu, associate librarian, whose expertise on the Internet greatly aided me. Anne Graham, senior reference associate and mother of Sean Egyhazi, the "little man," for her friendship and interest. Anne Haynes, associate librarian, for her friendship. Tom Glastras, associate librarian emeritus, for his gentle good humor and passion for living. Mark Day, associate librarian, a friend who finds my research interests as arcane as I do his. Celestina Wroth, assistant librarian and collection manager for history, a good friend. Mary Buechley, a former reference colleague whose departure from the department made my days a bit less entertaining and interesting. Gabriel Swift, office manager and senior reference associate, a new reference colleague who, when not imbibing massive quantities of designer water, is an acknowledged master of the pie chart.

My thanks are also due to the corps of student reference assistants (past and present) who have helped me throughout the years. Steve Duecker, now a reference maven at Ball State University, knows a lot about popular culture and suggested several cases to me. Other reference assistants to whom I owe a debt of gratitude: Gina Bush, Joe Tennis, Victoria S. White, Jennifer Heffron, David Gonsoroski, Sarah Hammill, Martha Lorber, Merlyne Howell, Caroline Seigel, Joshua Carson, and Rebecca Olson. This book could not have been written without the dedicated assistance of the Document Delivery Services department at Indiana University–Bloomington. Two respected colleagues and treasured friends, Rhonda Long and Ron Luedemann, deserve special thanks for borrowing at my request hundreds of reels of microfilmed newspapers from libraries throughout the world. Other noteworthy DDS staffers (past and present) include P. Gail McKenzie, Rita Rogers, and Elizabeth Knoerle. Diana Hanson, Marty Sorury, and Sherry Brookbank of the Microforms Department were instrumental in facilitating my research by making hundreds of photocopies from this microfilm.

I would also like to thank the following individuals and institutions, most notably for the information they supplied and their support. Geographically, they include:

CALIFORNIA: Russ Meyer, film director and head of RM Films International, a dear friend who generously showed me around Hollywood. Dace Taube, curator of the Regional History Collection at the University of Southern California, for her assistance in securing several of the photos in this book. Bill Margold, porn performer and historian.

ILLINOIS: C. Brian Smith, friend and reference librarian at Judson College–Elgin, who, while a student reference assistant at Indiana University, researched several cases. I miss seeing him on a daily basis.

INDIANA: This project was supported by an Indiana University Librarians Association Research Incentive Grant (2000) and an Indiana University Libraries Research Leave (1998). IU collection managers Robert U. Goehlert (Political Science, Economics, Criminal Justice), Nancy Boerner (Classical Studies, Germanic Studies, Comparative Literature), Murlin Croucher (Slavic Studies), and Marion Frank-Wilson (African Studies) were sources of support and helpful translators. Professor Murray Sperber, IU Department of English and American Studies, a hard-working source of inspiration. Emeritus professor Charles Forker, IU Department of English, for advice and support. Emeritus professor Robert H. Ferrell, IU Department of History, for his support and unfailing interest. Dr. John Walsh, IU Lead Electronic Text Specialist and leader of the Sinkholes, for suggesting entries and providing documentation in the area of popular music. Dennis O'Brien for suggesting entries in music and providing documentation. Friends Jimmie Onken and Hugh Barbry, IU Main Library mail room, for their encouragement and support. Ann Trisler, suggestions and friendship. Cynthia L. Stokes, assistant librarian, IU-PUI reference department, for her interest, research assistance, and support. The late Dan Etter, good guy and interested friend. "Skip" Bawel and Hugh Wittenbraker, voices from the past, for all the movies. Radha Surya, IU Electronic Text Support Specialist, for her friendship.

MICHIGAN: Dan Carmine, friend and case consultant.

NEVADA: Guy Rocha, archivist, Nevada State Archives, a man whose family has experienced the tragedy chronicled in this book.

OHIO: Beau David Case, head, Linguistics and West European Languages Library, Ohio State University, for suggesting numerous cases, providing documentation, and being a friend.

PENNSYLVANIA: Jack Widner, head of Instructional Services, Edinboro University of Pennsylvania, supplied me with several cases from the world of popular music.

VIRGINIA: Dr. Samuel Stetson, noted

authority on the history of "sex in the cinema" and a trusted friend for two decades.

Lastly, I would like to thank my wife, Mary, and son, Hayden, for their love, patience, and understanding. While only they know if my absence from home every weekend during the years spent writing this book was a hardship or a blessing, I want them to know that I deeply appreciate their sacrifice.

It was a great comfort to know that after a day spent plodding through a litany of broken lives all ending in self-inflicted death that I could return home to them … and life.

David K. Frasier
Bloomington, Indiana
Fall 2001

CONTENTS

"I don't know why she killed herself. She had hundreds of people around her. Maybe she died of loneliness." — Jay Kent, brother of Marilyn Monroe look-alike and suicide Kay Kent.

FOREWORD

"Always do what you are afraid to do." — Emerson

Lighten up. Each of us has at some point in our lives contemplated suicide. It's only human. The showfolk in this volume did more than contemplate a final curtain; they succeeded in carrying out the act. So you can consider these cautionary tales, on their own terms, as success stories. They wanted to bow out. Boy, they succeeded.

When Tom Mix died in a car crash I was just beginning to read, and as I had already decided Tom Mix was my favorite Western star, my eyes were drawn to the headline on the front page of the *Los Angeles Examiner*, "Tom Mix Dead!" I asked my grandmother, "What is dead?" She replied, "Death is sleep. Peace." Not a bad explanation to give a boy just learning to read, before he had personally experienced death. That came soon enough. Spot, the puppy I won as a prize conducting my Toy Orchestra, was poisoned by the gardener of the large estate across the street. Ground glass mixed in a ball of raw hamburger. (This gardener, a fanatical neatnik who hated all dogs as potential poopers on his manicured lawn, got away with the crime.) I buried Spot among the zinnias in our back yard, and I learned about death.

All creatures want to live. (As Susan Hayward screamed in the movie with the same title, *I Want to Live!*) Yet as that tarnished icon of the 20th century, Freud, pointed out, opposite Eros, the Life Instinct, lies the realm of Thanatos, the Death Instinct. Thanatos, brother of Eros, has his charms, fatal for the merry crew whose calculated conclusions make up the bulk of this book.

You will find in David Frasier's exhaustively researched compendium of cancelled careers some of the more emblematic suicides touched upon in my *Hollywood Babylon* books, such as the fatal plunge of Peg Entwistle from the top of the "Hollywood" Sign, or Lupe Velez's lurid final act on my street in Beverly Hills, North Alpine Drive, but you will find many more tragic tales of faces today forgotten, once famous and beloved, or the talented artists, the make-up geniuses who created those faces, and the creators of gowns that turned shopgirls into goddesses. All of these lives, and deaths, famous or obscure, retain our interest in Frasier's pithy and mordant portraits.

All major religions condemn the act of suicide, save one: Aleister Crowley's *Thelema*. In Crowley's credo, *Liber LXXVII*, also called *Liber OZ*, we discover these rules:

Man has the right to live by his own law —
to live in the way that he wills to do,
to work as he will,
to play as he will,
to rest as he will,
to die when and how he will.

1

Crowley died a natural death at the age of 72, and though the end was unpleasant — with crippling asthma attacks — he stuck it out to the bitter end. To each his own.

Are suicides cowards, as Mary Karr insists — newly converted to the Catholic Church and having survived an adolescent attempt of her own — or are they courageous, as Byron and Baudelaire make claim? Suicide is a ceremony in which the actor is both killer and victim — a truly juicy dual role. These actors choose to hang themselves, take poison, jump from high buildings, pierce their breasts with knives, slash their wrists with razors, shoot themselves, drown, die by every means imaginable.

These are those who actively woo death. This volume doesn't deal with the slow suicides — smoking and drinking — the chronic suicides that pursue a reckless and heedless lifestyle, that must include serial sexual encounters.

I count among my personal losses in the show business community my friend James Whale, the witty and brilliant director of *Frankenstein* and *The Bride of Frankenstein*; Fred Halsted, pioneer in gay erotica; Donald Cammell, another Brit who chose to die by the gun in the manner prefigured in his masterpiece *Performance*. Then there were a couple of screenwriters who gave up fighting the Hollywood machine, and my own cameraman for my film *Lucifer Rising*, the talented Michael Cooper. A near-loss was the singer and actress Marianne Faithfull, whom I caught in the act of slicing her wrists with a razor in Mick Jagger's bedroom on Cheyney Walk in London. I bound up Marianne's wrists with one of her deco-patterned scarves and I guess saved her for her latter-day career as a torch singer. Marianne gave me the scarf as a souvenir — mottled with rust-colored blood stains. She promised me she wouldn't be so foolish again.

As I actively intervened in saving the life of Marianne Faithfull from an ill-considered suicide, I would, if I could, intervene in many of the cases in this volume and try to dissuade them. There are ill-considered suicides, and there are considered suicides, such as Richard Farnsworth's choice of shooting himself to shorten the agony of terminal cancer, calling Prince Sirki, as Thanatos was called in *Death Takes a Holiday*, superbly portrayed by Frederic March.

I continue to live by Crowley's credo, which allows it is "OK" to take your own life if that is your will. Yet the loss of my friends haunts me still. I think it's probably true that the dead continue to live in us, in both negative and positive ways. Death is part and parcel of the Sweet Mystery of Life.

So, dear reader, this book is not for the tenderhearted. You have been warned.

This is a book for Brave Hearts — who can look life and death in the face. Brave Hearts, read on.

Kenneth Anger
"Tinseltown"
Hollywood, California
Spring 2001

PREFACE

I was 18 years old in 1969 when a club called The 13th Hour opened in the basement of the ABC discount center in Evansville, Indiana. The venue, what today is called an "all ages club," was what passed for psychedelia in southern Indiana in the late sixties. Remarkably, this small club was able to book bands like Jethro Tull, Blue Cheer, the Flock, and Iron Butterfly for a ticket price of $5.00. Like every other rock spot of its time, the Hour was decorated with anti-establishment posters and lit with blacklights.

On my first visit, I noticed an adult (anyone over 20 was so labelled) projecting a 16mm film on one of the blank walls off from the stage. The film, Douglas Fairbanks' 1924 silent classic *The Thief of Baghdad*, prompted me to speak to the projectionist, Leroy "Skip" Bawel. Skip, a knowledgeable film collector, was kind enough to take me and a friend, Hugh Wittenbraker, under his wing and help educate us about movies.

More importantly, however, Skip introduced me to a book that quite simply changed my life — *Hollywood Babylon*, Kenneth Anger's chronicle of Tinseltown foibles and tragedy. Years later I learned that the ratty paperback with the lurid photos that he loaned me was the pirated 1965 English language edition of *Hollywood Babylone*, originally published in Paris in 1959 by J. J. Pauvert. Anger's graphic description of Hollywood decadence, death, and scandal fired my imagination, deepened

my interest in movies, and helped form my own ambivalent thoughts about "show biz" and celebrity.

Ironically, I began a correspondence with Kenneth Anger while employed as a librarian at the Institute for Sex Research (since renamed the Kinsey Institute) on the campus of Indiana University in Bloomington. Anger, a personal friend of biologist and pioneer sex researcher Alfred C. Kinsey (1894–1956), was among the Institute's most celebrated supporters and devoted donors. Correspondence with Anger evolved into research assistance (*Hollywood Babylon II*, 1984), and ultimately into a lasting friendship that survived my departure from the Kinsey Institute in 1987.

In the ensuing years, Anger has played host to me during my frequent visits to Hollywood to research independent filmmaker Russ Meyer. Anger, a noted director and knowledgeable cinephile, escorted me on pilgrimages to many of the sites featured in this catalog of self-slaughter. For a devotee of show biz scandal these excursions with Ken into Tinseltown's underbelly was like being a physics student able to discuss the Theory of Relativity with Einstein.

Jump cut to 1993 when, in my duties as a reference librarian at Indiana University, I consulted the multi-volume *Variety Obits* to answer a question. Perusing the volumes, I was immediately struck by two facts. First, that the "bible of show business" did not limit its coverage of entertainment industry deaths to the so called "headliners." Instead, the publication chose to define "show business folk" as belonging to a vast international fraternity. In the pages of *Variety*, deceased big name stars of stage and screen are listed side by side with those of vaudeville house ticket takers, theatre managers, and others in even less glamorous show biz related occupations. Death, after all, is the great leveller. Second, the sheer number of suicides reported in the *Variety Obits* is impressive. The base set alone (1905–1978) contains more than 1,600 suicides. Add to this the hundreds more that I unearthed in other sources (see Bibliography) and it seems as though self-inflicted death in show business is an occupational hazard.

When I began this project in 1993, I naively envisioned an exhaustive encyclopedia that would include an entry for every person in the worldwide show business fraternity who intentionally took his or her life in the 20th century. After the first few years, I realized the impossibility of this task. In several instances, I was unable to obtain the newspaper coverage for many of the more obscure cases to be found in *Variety*. More often than not, the newspaper did not even report the death. Rather than merely paraphrase the *Variety* obits without further documentation, I chose to omit such entries.

I quickly learned that a large gray area exists in show business suicide, i.e., whether the suicide was accidental, suspected, or resulting from a lifestyle choice. On the whole, I have omitted accidentally self-inflicted deaths such as that of singer Russ Columbo (1934), Johnny Ace (1954), Chicago guitarist Terry Kath (1978), and television actor Jon Erik-Hexum (1984). A notable exception is thirties screen star Thelma Todd, found dead from carbon monoxide poisoning in a garage in 1935. Though Todd's death was ruled accidental, it is included here because her case continues to generate comment with current research strongly suggesting that "Hot Toddy" was murdered.

On the other hand, I have been forced to make judgment calls in several suspected cases.

Though, by and large, the deaths of celebrities like Margaret Sullavan (1960), Diana Barrymore (1960), Alan Ladd (1964), Gia Scala (1972), *et al.* were ruled as "probable accidents," I chose to include them because each manifested severe depression with concomitant life-threatening behaviors. More problematic are the "marquee cases" like Paul Bern (1932), George Reeves (1959), and Marilyn Monroe (1962). The truth surrounding the last moments of these celebrities' lives has been hopelessly obscured by studio cover-ups, possible conspiracies, police incompetence, and the inexorable passage of time. In the category of "death by lifestyle choice" I have chosen to include only one individual, Albert Dekker. His bizarre accidental death in 1968 today seems like a straightforward case of autoerotic asphyxiation.

What remains are 840 suicides taken from the ranks of vaudeville, film, theatre, dance, music, literature (writers with direct connections to film), and other allied fields in the entertainment industry (see Occupations Index) ending with the death of actor Rick Jason on October 15, 2000. Excluded are sports figures, except for professional wrestlers who seem to me to be entertainers first and athletes second. Selectively included here are the great, near great, has beens, and never weres, all members of the great show business fraternity who have chosen to dispatch themselves for whatever reason in a variety of creative ways (see Methods Index).

In the final analysis, are people connected with show business more likely to take their lives than those working in less ego-bruising professions? Not being a trained sociologist, psychologist, or psychiatrist, I would not presume to offer a "definitive" answer. However, after having spent seven years of my life in close proximity with the tragic people documented in this book, I can echo an observation made by comedian Richard Lewis on show business in general. Delivering the eulogy at a memorial service for his friend and fellow comedian Steven Lubetkin, who committed suicide, Lewis said, "The business, by and large, is made up of wallets, not hearts."

THE CASES

Abingdon, William L.

Abindgon (born William Lepper Pilgrim in Towcester, Northants, England, on May 2, 1859) made his first stage appearance in Belfast in 1881. On the London stage since April 26, 1886, the hard-working actor appeared in both English and American productions until his suicide in New York City on May 17, 1918. Late that night, Abingdon's wife, actress Bijou Fernandez, heard groans coming from the bathroom of their home at 235 West Seventy-sixth Street. Investigating, she found the 59-year-old actor bleeding copiously from safety razor slashes to his wrists and throat. Abingdon died an hour later in a private hospital. Friends of the dead actor noted that he had recently been brooding over the outcome of World War I and was gravely concerned over the safety of his two sons in the British military.

At the scene, a medical examiner found notes written by Abingdon concealed in a memorial service booklet distributed at the funeral of his longtime friend, actor William Terriss. Terriss had been murdered at the stage door of a theatre following a performance several years before. The notes read: "For some time I have been suffering from neurasthenia, melancholia, a desire to avoid people, and a lack of interest in anything and everything — Haven't been near the club in weeks. Hiding away in cheap picture shows or staying in the house. Even baseball has no attraction for me.

Everybody is against me. One more mistake and then — 'the great conundrum.'" Four hundred people in the theatrical profession attended Abingdon's funeral in Brooklyn's Evergreen Cemetery on May 19, 1918.

Acland, Christopher John Dyke

Acland (born September 7, 1966, in Kendal, Cumbria, England) enjoyed by his own account a charmed childhood as the son of an affluent executive at a local paper mill. In 1987, he met fellow English literature student and singer-guitarist Miki Berenyi at North London Polytechnic. Lovers for a time, Berenyi asked Acland to play drums in Lush, the band she formed with backing vocalist-guitarist Emma Anderson in 1988. The group signed with independent label 4AD and, though never commercially successful, were initially praised by critics as saviors of Britain's ailing indie pop scene. From 1985 through 1995 the group released four albums and played with some top American bands on the "Lollapalooza" tour while cementing their offstage reputation as hard core party people around London.

Following an exhausting and disappointing American tour, the depressed 30-year-old drummer returned to his family home in Kendal on October 12, 1996, to reassess his future with the band. Five days later, Acland's body was found by his father hanging from some scaffolding in an outhouse at the bottom of a garden behind the house. Acland's family established a fund in his memory to refurbish the music department at the Lake School in Cumbria where he learned to play drums.

Acord, Art

Born Arthemus Ward Acord to Mormon parents in Prattsville, Utah, on April 17, 1890, the celluloid cowboy star spent his early years as a working cowpoke and ranchman before becoming a professional stunt rider with various Wild West shows from 1909 to 1910. Filmdom's first "real cowboy," Acord had won several rodeo events before getting his first big movie break in 1913 in Cecil B. DeMille's early feature, *The Squaw Man*. Prior to this time, he had appeared in several one-reelers for Bison, Selig Polyscope, and Universal beginning in 1911 with *The White Medicine Man*. In November 1916, Acord signed a contract with the Fox Film Corporation and went east to work in their New Jersey studio. Acord enlisted in the military in 1918 and as an infantryman earned the French medal of valor, the Croix de Guerre. Discharged in January 1919, the actor returned to Hollywood and signed a three-year contract with Universal to appear in two-reel Westerns (*The Wild Westerner*, 1919; *The Kid and the Cowboy*, 1919; *A Ranch Romeo*, 1921) and serials (*The Moon Riders*, 1920; *Winners of the West*, 1921; *The Oregon Trail*, 1923).

Though never a box office star like Tom Mix or Buck Jones, Acord enjoyed a loyal small town following. By the mid-twenties, however, the actor's chronic alcoholism was destroying his career and personal life. A mean drunk, Acord went through three marriages, fought with fellow actors, and was often in trouble with the law. After making 14 five-reel Westerns under the "Blue Streak Western" label from 1925 to 1927 and six Poverty Row five-reelers for J. Charles Davis Productions in 1929, Acord's career was over. Unemploy-

able in the States, Acord drifted down to Mexico where his films were still popular, and his personal appearances earned him enough for drinking money. Following a failed mining venture, the 40-year-old cowboy star drank a fatal dose of potassium cyanide in his room at the Hotel Palacio in Chihuahua City on January 4, 1931. Legend holds that the dose was enough to have killed 2,500 men. The player in more than 100 films was buried with full military honors by the Veterans of Foreign Wars in Forest Lawn Memorial Park in Glendale, California.

FURTHER READING

McKinney, Grange B. *Art Acord and the Movies: A Biography and Filmography*. Raleigh, N.C.: Wyatt Classics, 2000.

Acosta, Peter

A Houston musician and plaster worker, Acosta, 56, murdered his estranged wife and daughter in Navasota, Texas, on October 18, 1971, following a failed attempt at reconciliation. After bludgeoning his 28-year-old daughter to death with a two-foot-long pipe in their home on 7110 Gainesville, Acosta sat for hours in a lawn chair in the back yard waiting for his wife and four children (ages 10–12) to return from a friend's birthday party. According to the children's account, when they arrived home at 12:10 A.M. Acosta shot their mother several times as she walked up the driveway. Fleeing the scene, Acosta phoned a son to report the murders. At 3:45 A.M., he fatally shot himself in the chin after his car was stopped on a dirt road by a Houston police officer.

Adams, Margaret

Grief stricken over the recent death of her sister from tuberculosis and lonely for her parents, the 21-year-old former hostess of a Broadway nightclub opened a gas jet in the wall of her furnished room on the second floor of a rooming house at 336 West Fifty-first Street in New York City on April 4, 1926.

ART ACORD—While Acord never attained the popularity of other celluloid cowboy stars like Tom Mix and Buck Jones, he did work steadily throughout the teens and twenties before a mean disposition and chronic alcoholism ended his career in 1929. On January 4, 1931, the 40-year-old veteran of more than 100 Westerns downed a fatal dose of potassium cyanide in his room at the Hotel Palacio in Chihuahua City, Mexico.

Adams, Nick

The son of immigrant parents from Ukraine, Nicholas Aloysius Adamshock was born in Nanticoke, Pennsylvania, on July 10, 1931. In his late teens, Adams hitchhiked to Hollywood with the dream of breaking into films. Unsuccessful, he enlisted in the Coast Guard in 1952, but kept knocking on studio doors. His persistence paid off. During weekend leaves and craftily arranged passes, Adams appeared in small parts in *Somebody Loves Me* (1952), *Mr. Roberts* (1955), *Picnic* (1955, original play written by fellow suicide William Motter Inge — see entry), and *Strange Lady in Town* (1955). Discharged from the Coast Guard, Adams played the role of "Moose" in the 1955 James Dean picture *Rebel Without a Cause*. In 1958, he scored a hit as Andy Griffith's bespectacled friend "Ben Whitledge" in *No Time for Sergeants*.

Other films of the period include *Teacher's Pet* (1958, costarring fellow suicide Gig Young — see entry), *The FBI Story* (1959), and *Pillow Talk* (1959). Adams is best remembered, however, as ex–Confederate soldier "Johnny Yuma" in the ABC television series *The Rebel*. While the show lasted only from 1959 to 1961, Adams had every reason to believe his "star" had finally risen. His follow-up series on NBC, *Saints and Sinners*, ran only during the 1962-1963 season. In 1963, Adams returned to the big screen with an Oscar nominated performance as Best Supporting Actor for his role as an accused killer in *Twilight of Honor*. Though campaigning vigorously for the award, Adams lost the Oscar to Melvyn Douglas in *Hud*. The remainder of "The Rebel's" film career was a depressing downslide marked by roles in increasingly low-budget schlock like *Young Dillinger* (1965), *Die, Monster, Die* (1965), *Invasion of the Astro-Monsters* (1965), *Frankenstein Conquers the World* (1966, Japan), *Don't Worry, We'll Think of a Title* (1966), *Fever Heat* (1968), and *Mission Mars* (1968).

Adams, depressed over his stalled career and ongoing marital problems, was prescribed paraldehyde, a sedative used in the treatment of nervous disorders and alcoholism. After failing to hear from his from his friend for two days, Adams' attorney, Ervin Roeder, went to the actor's modest Coldwater Canyon home at 2126 El Roble Lane around 8:00 P.M. on February 7, 1968. Entering through a rear window, Roeder found Adams' body in an upstairs bedroom in a sitting position on the floor propped against a bed, eyes wide open, clad in bluejeans, boots and a shirt. A briefcase containing $900 in cash was discovered near the body. The 36-year-old actor had been dead an estimated 24 to 36 hours when found. Dr. J. Wallace Graham, deputy county medical examiner, determined the "immediate cause" of the actor's death was "paraldehyde intoxication." Adams apparently took the drug in liquid form. Though assistant coroner Herb McRoy later noted the impossibility of determining whether "death was accidental or if Mr. Adams wanted to destroy himself," the amount of the dosage suggested that death might have been the intended result. The actor is buried in Saints Cyrils and Methodius Ukrainian Church Cemetery in Berwick, Pennsylvania, beneath a grave marker bearing the inscription "Nick Adams The Rebel" within a silhouette of the actor wearing his character's trademark Confederate cap.

Alban, Jean-Pierre

Alban (born Hans Peter Schaich in Cairo, Egypt, on November 14, 1932) studied ballet in Berlin and Paris before coming to Britain in 1956 as a guest with the London Festival Ballet. Invited to stay with the company, he became a principal dancer specializing in character parts. After 16 years with the ballet, Alban left on January 6, 1973, with plans to form his own company. On January 15, 1973, the 40-year-old former husband of heiress Barbara Hutton leaped to his death from the kitchen window of his fourth floor flat in Sloane Avenue, Chelsea, London. Alban left suicide notes.

Albertson, Arthur

The actor came to New York looking for work after the quick closing of the play *Black Belt* in Chicago. On October 20, 1926, Albertson, 33, was found lying on the floor of his room at the Times Square Hotel at Eighth Avenue and Forty-third Street with a bottle of Lysol close at hand. Although police ruled that Albertson swallowed the poison because of career difficulties, friends of the dead actor claimed that his death was accidental.

Alexander, Aleta Freel

Tired of hearing his 28-year-old wife complain about not finding acting work in Hollywood pictures, screen actor Ross Alexander angrily agreed with her that she should go back to her parents' home in Jersey City and return to the stage. Alexander told the coroner's jury that on the night of December 6, 1935, he lost patience with Aleta in their Los Angeles home at 7357 Woodrow Wilson Drive and shouted, "Well, for God's sake go on back and quit nagging me about it!" The failed actress stormed out of the room. Moments later Alexander and his butler heard two shots from the yard. Investigating, the actor found his wife of two years sprawled on the front yard gasping from self-inflicted gunshot wounds, a .22-caliber hunting rifle beside her. The actress known on the New York stage as "Aleta Freel (Friele)" died the following morning at Cedars of Lebanon Hospital. According to actor Henry Fonda's autobiography, *Fonda: My Life*, the actress took her life because of her husband's numerous infidelities. Apparently overwhelmed by guilt, Ross Alexander (see entry), killed himself on January 2, 1937.

FURTHER READING

Fonda, Henry, and Teichmann, Howard. *Fonda: My Life*. New York: New American Library, 1981.

Alexander, Ross

Alexander (born A. Ross Smith in Brooklyn, New York, on July 27, 1907) was 18 when he made his Broadway acting debut in *Enter Madame* with Blanche Yurka. According to Lawrence J. Quirk in his biography of Bette Davis, *Fasten Your Seat Belts*, the bisexual Alexander was seduced by older actors and kept by a series of wealthy men when not working. In the early thirties he married stage actress Aleta Freel and moved to Hollywood where he broke into movies with a small part in the 1932 Paramount feature *The Wiser Sex*. In 1934, Alexander signed a contract with Warner Bros. and that year appeared in *Flirtation Walk*, *Gentleman Are Born*, and *Social Register* on loan out to Columbia Pictures. Alexander's star was rising in 1935 with larger roles in *A Midsummer Night's Dream* ("Demetrius") and as "Jeremy Pitt" in the Errol Flynn classic *Captain Blood*.

Trouble, however, was brewing on the homefront. Aleta Freel Alexander, the Broadway-trained actress who had unselfishly promoted her husband's career at the cost of her own, learned that the days and nights he supposedly spent at the studio were in reality being spent with other women. On December 6, 1935, an argument between the couple at their home at 7357 Woodrow Wilson Drive in the Hollywood Hills ended tragically. Depressed over her stalled career and her husband's infidelity, the 28-year-old actress (see entry) shot herself in the head with a .22-caliber hunting rifle in the front yard of their home. She died the next day.

Alexander continued making films for Warner Bros. although the studio no longer considered him star material. During 1936, Alexander appeared in three films with starlet Anne Nagel: *Hot Money*, *China Clipper*, and *Here Comes Carter*. The couple married on September 16, 1936, and settled on a ranch at 17221 Ventura Boulevard in the San Fernando Valley. From the start the marriage was troubled by Alexander's odd behavior. According to servants, the actor spent hours moodily writing poetry before the fireplace. On December 6, 1936, the one year anniversary of his first wife's suicide, Alexander ordered his black valet, Cornelius Stevenson, to bring him a

.22-caliber target pistol to the barn behind the house. The actor told the skeptical servant that he wanted "to shoot some sparrows." Stevenson, carrying the bullets in his hand, brought the unloaded weapon to the barn. A scuffle ensued when Alexander attempted to snatch the gun and bullets away from his valet. Stevenson broke free with the gun, ran back to the house, and alerted Alexander's father who then looked after his hysterical son.

On January 2, 1937, Nagel and Alexander spent the early part of their evening taking down their Christmas tree at their home on Ventura Boulevard. The 29-year-old actor appeared to be in good spirits and happily spoke with Nagel about taking a honeymoon to New York City in the near future. Between 7:30 and 8:30 P.M., Alexander left his wife contentedly knitting in the house, collected a flashlight and the infamous .22-caliber target pistol, and walked to the barn. Inside, he crawled atop a chicken coop, placed the barrel of the gun in his mouth, and pulled the trigger. In his autobiography, *Fonda: My Life*, actor Henry Fonda, best man at the wedding of Aleta and Ross Alexander, poetically maintained that the actor killed himself with the very rifle that his wife had used to take her life. Alexander was buried on January 8, 1937, at Sunrise Slope in Forest Lawn Cemetery in Glendale, California.

FURTHER READING

Fonda, Henry, and Teichmann, Howard. *Fonda: My Life*. New York: New American Library, 1981.
Mank, Gregory William. *Women in Horror Films, 1940s*. Jefferson, N.C.: McFarland, 1999.
Quirk, Lawrence J. *Fasten Your Seat Belts: The Passionate Life of Bette Davis*. 1st ed. New York: Morrow, 1990.

Allard, Bob

Allard, a popular Twin Cities radio personality, began his career as a page at WCCO-AM in Minneapolis, and went on to announce for stations in north Minnesota, South Dakota, and Iowa. Shortly after learning that his late night talk show on WAYL-AM was

being dropped because the station was changing to an all-music format, the 55-year-old announcer stabbed himself in the abdomen moments before air-time. At the time, his family partially blamed the action on his diabetes. Three months later on May 30, 1982, Allard's mother found her son dead from carbon monoxide poisoning in his car parked in the garage of her home at 4043 Lyndale Avenue North in Minneapolis.

Allen, Chet R.

Allen was a 12-year-old soprano with the Columbus Boychoir when Gian Carlo Menotti chose him to sing the title role in the opera "Amahl and the Night Visitors" broadcast by NBC-TV in December 1951. On the strength of that performance, Allen was signed by Universal-International to co-star with Dan Dailey in the 1952 Douglas Sirk–directed musical *Meet Me at the Fair*. Unfortunately for Allen, when his voice changed to a baritone immediately after the film, it ended his singing and motion picture career. Depressed, the former child star returned to Columbus, Ohio, and held a variety of jobs including a ten year stint as a stock boy at a Lazarus department store. Through his own treatment for depression, Allen became involved with volunteer work at Town House, a "drop-in" center operated by a local community health center. On June 7, 1984, Allen took five times the lethal dose of an anti-depressant medication he had been secretly hoarding. The 44 year old died ten days later in Riverside Hospital. A family member summed up Allen's life, "He had a better singing voice than most of the people you see on television, but he wouldn't sing.... He couldn't reconcile himself to the use of his talent."

Anderson, Charles

Anderson, a musician and small time producer based in Chicago, travelled to Boston to plead with his wife of three years, Fay Norman, to give up her spot with the burlesque show *Hippity Hop*, currently playing in that city's Waldron's Casino. On February 18, 1924, Anderson appeared at the Commonwealth Hotel where his wife was staying and tried in vain to convince her to leave the show and return with him to Chicago. Dismissing his threat that he would kill himself should she refuse, Norman signed a contract with the show. Anderson produced a bottle of carbolic acid, drank from it, and died two hours later at the Relief Hospital. Norman missed a few performances, but rejoined the show in New York the next week.

Andre, Gwili

Born Gwili Andresen in Copenhagen, Denmark, on February 4, 1908, the striking blonde was a fashion model in Europe before coming to New York in the late twenties. In the center of U.S. fashion, Andre commanded $50 an hour as an artist's model, and earned $25,000 a year modelling gowns. Dubbed "America's most beautiful model," she routinely graced the covers of *Vogue*, *Harper's Bazaar*, and *Vanity Fair*. Andre was brought to Hollywood in 1932 by producer David O. Selznick, inked a contract with RKO–Radio Pictures, and was given the star treatment. Cast in the 1932 action-adventure film *Roar of the Dragon* opposite Richard Dix, the model was savaged by critics who complained that her looks did not translate well on screen and that she lacked animation. Andre failed to catch on and made only six other films before ending her career with a bit part in RKO's 1942 programmer *The Falcon's Brother*, starring fellow suicide George Sanders (see entry) in the title role.

The failed star was equally unfulfilled in her personal life. Two marriages (one to chess champion Stanislaws Miotkowski, the other to Beverly Hills realtor William Dallas Cross, Jr.) ended in divorce. The former actress had been living in lonely obscurity for years when firefighters were called to her small apartment at 2109-B Ocean Front in Venice, California, on February 5, 1959. There, according to Hollywood historian Kenneth Anger writing in

his classic tome, *Hollywood Babylon*, they found the 51-year-old Andre "burnt to a crisp in a funeral pyre of her useless publicity." Found among the scrapbooks and photos documenting her former successes was a card from an alcoholics' rehabilitation center. Questioned by authorities, neighbors of the former international beauty confessed, "We've been afraid something like this would happen. She drank a good deal."

FURTHER READING

Anger, Kenneth. *Hollywood Babylon*. San Francisco: Straight Arrow Books, 1975.

Andre, Rene

Andre (real name Everlyine Adams) was an exotic dancer for 20 years before disfiguring scars suffered in a botched skin rejuvenating treatment in Los Angeles ended her career in 1959. She moved to Chicago and purchased the Trius Restaurant at 6048 S. Ashland Avenue. On March 12, 1961, the former dancer's body was found seated in her car in a carbon monoxide–filled garage behind the restaurant. Only days before, Andre's niece had talked the 42 year old out of committing suicide.

Angeli, Pier

Angeli (born Anna Maria Pierangeli on June 19, 1932, in Cagliari, Sardinia) was a student in Rome when she was discovered in 1949 by director Leonide Moguy and cast in his film *Domani e troppo Tardi* (*Tomorrow Is Too Late*) opposite Vittorio de Sica. On the strength of her performance in the film and its 1950 sequel, *Domani e un altro Giorno*, the 5 foot tall, 100 pound beauty landed a contract with MGM. Brought to America with her twin sister, actress Marisa Pavan, Angeli debuted as the Italian war bride of a U.S. soldier played by Jon Ericson in director Fred Zinneman's 1951 film *Teresa*. In 1952, Angeli was selected as the first "MGM Star of the Future." The archetypal fragile heroine, Angeli never achieved the star status MGM envisioned for her

U.S.) and *White Slave Ship* (1962, Italy-France).

More memorable than any of Angeli's film roles, however, was her private life, which was played out under the unblinking stare of her mother. While dating Kirk Douglas during the making of *The Silver Chalice* on the Warners' lot in 1954, the 22-year-old actress met and fell in love with future film legend James Dean, 23. Angeli's devoutly religious mother bitterly opposed the relationship first, and foremost, because Dean was not a Catholic and secondly because she despised his rebel persona. Conversely, MGM frowned on an Angeli-Dean marriage out of fear that the union would damage his rebel image at the box office. For whatever reason, to placate her family or to punish Dean for being slow to ask her to wed, Angeli announced her intention to marry crooner and fellow MGM contract player Vic Damone in 1954. According to show biz legend (more

PIER ANGELI — Angeli, brought from Italy to Hollywood in 1951, co-starred in two Paul Newman films (*The Silver Chalice*, 1955, and *Somebody Up There Likes Me*, 1956), but failed to catch on with American audiences. Today, she is best remembered as the young actress who fell in love with screen legend James Dean, but was prevented from marrying him by her overly possessive, devoutly Catholic mother. Broke, unemployed, and afraid to turn 40, the 39-year-old actress took her life with barbiturates in Beverly Hills on September 10, 1971.

despite appearing in films like *The Devil Makes Three* (1952), *The Story of Three Loves* (1953), *The Flame and the Flesh* (1954), and two Paul Newman features (*The Silver Chalice*, 1955; *Somebody Up There Likes Me*, 1956). After starring in 1958 with Danny Kaye and fellow suicide Barbara Bates (see entry) in her final MGM film, *Merry Andrew*, the actress worked almost exclusively in European films like *Sodom and Gomorrah* (1959, Italy-France-

probably an overactive press agent's imagination), while the Damone-Angeli wedding ceremony was in progress at St. Timothy's Catholic Church in Westwood on November 24, 1954, Dean was across the street on his motorcycle gunning the engine (the actor was later killed in his Porsche Spyder just east of Paso Robles, California, on September 30, 1955). Though the marriage produced one child, Perry, on August 22, 1955, it was an unmitigated disaster. The couple divorced in 1958 with Damone pointing the finger at Angeli's domineering mother as the primary cause. For the next seven years Damone and Angeli carried on a very public and ugly custody battle over the child. In 1962, Angeli married Italian band leader Armando Travajoli, but they divorced the next year soon after the birth of their son.

By 1971, the 39-year-old actress was essentially through in the motion picture business and close to bankruptcy. A survivor of four previous suicide tries, she wrote to a friend in 1971: "I'm so afraid to get old — for me, being 40 is the beginning of old age…. Love is now behind me, love died in a Porsche." Angeli, attempting to revive her U.S. film career, was sharing an apartment with her drama coach, Helena Correll, at 355 South McCarty Drive in Beverly Hills. On September 10, 1971, Correll discovered Angeli dead there from an overdose of barbiturates.

FURTHER READING

Dalton, David. *James Dean: The Mutant King*. New York: St. Martin's Press, 1983.

Ardell, John E.

On April 26, 1949, police found the 68-year-old character actor dead from carbon monoxide poisoning in his car parked in front of his home at 1334 N. Cordova Avenue in Burbank, California. Ardell, never more than a bit player, had last appeared as a dice player in the 1947 film *T-Men*.

Argov, Zohar

Son of Yemen immigrants, the Israeli pop singer was credited in the late seventies with pioneering a type of music popular with both Israelis and Palestinians living together in occupied areas. Dubbed the "King of Mizrahi Music," the Israeli equivalent of Soul, Argov blended modern lyrics with the traditional music brought to Israel by Jewish immigrants from Arab countries. By 1987, Argov's rags to riches rise from ghetto streets to pop stardom had left him an alcoholic drug abuser. While on parole waiting to serve a six month sentence for a drug-related offense, Argov was arrested in connection with the alleged rape of a 19-year-old woman. On November 7, 1987, the 31-year-old singer used strips torn from a blanket to hang himself in a police cell in the central Israeli town of Rishon Lezion. In 1993, Israeli director Eran Riklis completed a film of Argov's life titled *Zohar: Mediterranean Blues*. In April 1994, Argov's 21-year-old son, Gilli, was arrested in Tel Aviv for allegedly holding five grams of heroin because he wanted to "experience what his father had felt."

Armendariz, Pedro

Armendariz (born May 9, 1912, in the Mexico City suburb of Churubusco) moved with his family to San Antonio, Texas, in 1918. While majoring in aeronautical engineering at the California Polytechnic Institute, the young student was drawn into amateur acting. Entering Mexican films in 1935 with roles in *Rosario Bordertown* and *Maria Elena*, Armendariz quickly became that country's top star. On the strength of standout performances in two internationally celebrated films, *Maria Candelaria* (1943) and a 1945 adaptation of John Steinbeck's novel *The Pearl*, the popular Mexican actor was signed in 1947 to appear in his first U.S. film, director John Ford's *The Fugitive*. Since then, Armendariz co-starred in more than 93 films, often directed by Ford and starring close friend John Wayne (*Fort Apache*, 1948; *Three Godfathers*, 1948). Armendariz was also featured opposite a badly miscast John Wayne as "Genghis Khan" in the 1956 box office bomb *The Conquerors*. Shot on location in Utah near an A-Bomb test site, to date nearly half the film's cast and crew have developed some form of cancer. Cast members Wayne, Susan Hayward, Dick Powell, and Agnes Moorehead all fell victim to the disease.

In 1963, Armendariz took ill while on location in London filming scenes for the

PEDRO
ARMENDARIZ y

AMANDA DEL LLANO

en

LA

CASA COLORADA

LA PELICULA QUE CONSAGRO
DEFINITIVAMENTE a PEDRO
ARMENDARIZ!

*LUCHANDO
Y AMANDO
COMO SOLO
EL SABE
HACERLO!*

Distribuida por
FILMS DE MEXICO   MONTERREY 101-701-MEXICO.D.F.

PEDRO ARMENDARIZ— Armendariz was a star in his native country of Mexico and well-known to U.S. audiences in the John Ford films *The Fugitive* (1947), *Fort Apache* (1948), and *Three Godfathers* (1948). Diagnosed with terminal cancer shortly after completing work as Turkish secret agent "Kerim Bey" in the 1963 James Bond film *From Russia with Love*, the 51-year-old actor smuggled a gun into the UCLA Medical Center and shot himself on June 18, 1963.

James Bond adventure *From Russia with Love*. Armendariz's scenes as the Turkish secret agent "Kerim Bey" were quickly wrapped and, back in the States, he was diagnosed with terminal cancer of the lymph glands in his neck. On June 12, 1963, the 51-year-old actor was admitted to the UCLA Medical Center in Los Angeles where his concerned wife was given permission to stay with him in a fourth floor private room. Unknown to her, Armendariz had smuggled a .357 Colt Magnum into the facility hidden in his luggage. On June 18, 1963, while his wife was at lunch, the pajama-clad actor fired a bullet through his heart that exited through his back and lodged in a door.

Armitage, Pauline

The Nashville, Tennessee–born actress appeared in several Broadway plays before accepting a role in a ten week roadshow production of *Naughty Cinderella* starring Irene Bordini. During the tour, the production's "script doctor," Wilson Mizner, became enamored of the 28-year-old Armitage, and apparently promised to marry her when the show returned to open in New York City's Lyceum Theatre in early 1926. Shortly after arriving in the city, however, Mizner broke off the engagement, and Armitage left the show at his request. Ten days prior to her death, a visibly shaken Armitage visited a friend at a newspaper and stood transfixed before the large presses. "Do you know my reaction to all this?" she asked her acquaintance. "I seem to see printed in great type across the front page of your newspaper, 'Pauline Armitage Commits Suicide.'" On the morning of February 16, 1926, Armitage was in the bedroom of her suite on the 14th floor of the Hotel Shelton at Lexington Avenue and Forty-ninth Street in New York City when the telephone rang in the sitting room. When the maid left the room to answer the phone, the nightgown-clad actress locked the door, leaped from the window, and fell with a crashing thud on the sidewalk below between two laundry truck drivers. Notified of the tragedy in Palm Beach, Florida, Mizner denied ever having been engaged to Armitage.

Arnold, Jess

Arnold, a foreign correspondent during the Spanish Civil War who once operated a two-man bureau with Walter Cronkite for the International News Service in El Paso, was a well-known and colorful figure in Texas. A novel based on his war reportage, *Reunion in Barcelona*, was serialized in *Cosmopolitan* magazine, and his short story "A Mission to General Houston" served as the basis for the 1949 Paramount film *The Eagle and the Hawk*, which starred John Payne and Rhonda Fleming. On January 3, 1964, Arnold's body was found at the Garza Ranch on Brodie Lane near Austin, Texas. The 46-year-old writer had fully dressed and packed a suitcase before firing one fatal shot into his chest with a British made .38-caliber pistol that he had asked a friend to sight for him a few days earlier. Several years before when he talked of living to be a hundred, Arnold wrote his own obituary, dated it March 11, 2016, and gave it to a friend for safekeeping. It read: "Jess Arnold, the centaur passed away today. The rootingest, tootingest, non-fightingest, runningest Texan that ever lived died quietly…. The Mighty Arnold died as he lived — with his boots off. He never wore a hat. The Mighty Arnold never wrote anything of note,

but did keep on living. He was always going to write a novel, but never got around to it…. 'Hell,' he would say, 'that takes work.'"

Ash, Ernest A.

Ash, 49, a socially prominent pianist and president of the Associated Music Teachers League, was found on the back seat floor of his car just inside the Ocean Avenue entrance to Prospect Park in Brooklyn, New York, on March 14, 1933. The music teacher's mouth and throat were coated with liniment taken from a bottle that lay on the floor. Ash's wife, who refused to accept the coroner's verdict of suicide, told police that her husband suffered from acute sinus trouble and used chloroform liniment to ease the pain. Ash operated a music school in Brooklyn and was known as the inventor of a silent piano keyboard designed for practice work that flashed lights instead of producing tones.

Auer, Norma

Barely one month after winning the right to retain custody of their two children following a rancorous divorce, the 36-year-old former wife of Russian-born screen comedian Mischa Auer asked him to take them back. On October 2, 1942, Beverly Hills police responded to an emergency call placed from the divorcee's home at 315 N. Doheny Drive. Auer explained to the officers that she had consumed a poisonous antiseptic mixture since "There's no reason for me to live and I just turned over the children to my former husband." Mischa Auer, recently remarried to radio singer Joyce Hunter, was at his ex-wife's bedside at California Hospital when she died later that day. Auer was buried at Forest Lawn Memorial Park.

Austin, Anne

The 32-year-old actress at one time appeared in a number of Broadway shows (*Oh, Boy!*, 1917; *Daddies*, 1918), but had recently been unable to find work. Austin's financial outlook momentarily brightened after signing a contract with a New York stock company, but the troupe lasted only a week before disbanding. Broke and suffering through a romantic breakup with a Brooklyn man named Emil Lawlo, Austin committed suicide in her apartment at 120 West Seventy-first Street in New York City on June 18, 1926. The actress first placed a mattress beside the stove in her kitchenette, but deciding gas was too slow, downed 25 bichloride of mercury tablets. When found, Austin resisted efforts by authorities to administer an antidote. She died an hour later. A letter in the actress' desk instructed that all her clothes be given to her black maid, and pointedly blamed "Emil (as) the cause of it all." Burial fees were paid for by the Actors' Fund.

Austin, John Van "Tex"

A colorful figure on the Santa Fe, New Mexico, social scene, "Tex" Austin gained international fame as a rodeo promoter whose gala events had entertained the king and queen of England. In September 1936, Austin stopped promoting rodeos, settled in Santa Fe, and with his wife opened the popular nightclub and restaurant Los Rancheros. After closing the restaurant shortly after 1:00 A.M. on October 26, 1938, Mrs. Austin returned to their home at 507 Camino del Monte Sol. In the attached garage, she found her husband's body propped up on two pillows in the back seat of his closed sedan. A hose connected to the exhaust pipe ran into the car through a back window. Inside the house, investigators found a signed note from the 50 year old pinned to a bureau in which he asked his wife's "forgiveness." At a subsequent coroner's inquest, witnesses testified that weeks earlier Austin had been advised by a physician that he would lose his eyesight in six months. The verdict: "Carbon monoxide poisoning, self-administered."

Aye, Maryon (Marion)

Born April 5, 1903, in Chicago, Illinois,

the stage and screen actress is best remembered as the female lead in a group of Western and dramatic silent films of the twenties: *Montana Bill* (1921), *The Vengeance Trail* (1921), *The Eternal Three* (1923), *The Meanest Man in the World* (1923), *The Last Man on Earth* (1924), *The Roughneck* (1924), and *Irene* (1926). The 48-year-old former actress was all but forgotten when, despondent over an attack of uremic poisoning suffered while house hunting in Culver City, California, she took poison on July 10, 1951. Aye died in LA's General Hospital on July 21, 1951. According to records, she had previously tried to take her life by poison in 1935.

Ayler, Albert

Ayler, considered by many jazz aficionados to be among the most influential saxophonists and composers of the sixties, never achieved commercial success. While his brand of "free" jazz with its trademark horn blasts marked him as an innovator, it also limited his appeal to mainstream listeners. Born July 13, 1936, in Cleveland, Ohio, Ayler studied saxophone with his father until the age of 10. For the next eight years he studied jazz with Benny Miller, a former sideman with Charlie Parker and Dizzy Gillespie, at Cleveland's Academy of Music. During his teen years, Ayler became well-known in rhythm and blues clubs in Cleveland and spent two summers while in high school touring with bluesman Little Walter. The black sax player's mastery of the bebop style earned him the nickname "Little Bird" (a reference to Parker). While serving in the Army from 1958 to 1961 Ayler was stationed in France where he was deeply influenced by expatriate bebop tenor saxophonists like Dexter Gordon and Carlos "Don" Byas. Ayler switched from alto to tenor sax and spent weekends and leaves playing in jazz clubs in Paris and Copenhagen.

Discharged in 1961, Ayler moved to Sweden in 1962, and the next year recorded his influential album *My Name Is Albert Ayler* in Copenhagen. Returning to the States, Ayler formed a quartet in 1964 with trumpeter Don Cherry, bassist Gary Peacock, and drummer Sunny Murray. The quartet afforded the saxophonist the freedom to create compositions that combined elements of New Orleans–style group improvisation with melodies from black spirituals. In 1965, Ayler formed a new group featuring his younger brother Don on trumpet, Murray on drums, and Lewis Worrell on bass. That same year they recorded the classic album *Bells* at a live concert in New York City's Town Hall. Ayler continued to record throughout the sixties (*Spirits Rejoice*, 1965; *Albert Ayler in Greenwich Village*, 1966–1967; *Love Cry*, 1967). Though respected by sax players like John Coltrane, Pharoah Sanders, and Archie Shepp, Ayler never achieved widespread popularity. As Ayler tried to become more commercial with albums like *New Grass* (1968), his personal life became increasingly bizarre. He spoke to friends of having "violent apocalyptic visions" where flying disks shot colors and the "devil's mark" was branded on people's foreheads. Shortly after returning from a European tour in 1970, Ayler was reported missing from his apartment in Brooklyn in early November. According to his companion, the 34-year-old jazz man blamed himself for the nervous breakdown and subsequent health problems suffered by his brother Donald. The trumpet player broke down after Ayler dissolved the band in 1968. Ayler reportedly boarded a ferry to the Statue of Liberty and jumped off before the vessel docked at Liberty Island. On November 25, 1970, some 20 days after he was last seen, Ayler's body was found floating in the East River near the Congress Street Pier in Brooklyn. The circumstances surrounding the saxophonist's disappearance and death remain unclear and some have advanced the theory that the police were involved. Albert Ayler is buried in Highland Park Cemetery in his hometown of Cleveland.

FURTHER READING

Lyons, Len, and Perlo, Don. *Jazz Portraits: The Lives and Music of the Jazz Masters*. New York: Morrow, 1989.

Aylmer, David

The son of the distinguished British stage actor Sir Felix Aylmer (1889–1979) was found dead in his London flat in Maryland Road on July 20, 1964. Aylmer, a 31-year-old supporting actor, broke into films in 1956 with *A Touch of the Sun*. The actor also appeared in Agatha Christie's play *The Mousetrap* as well as on several television shows. Police found an empty bottle of sleeping pills and a note near his body. Aylmer reportedly had been in ill health for the last two years.

Ayres, Dudley

Ayres (born in Iowa in 1890) acted in stock theatre and silent films (*The Uphill Path*, 1918), and was leading man at the Castle Square Theatre in Boston, the Majestic in Los Angeles, and for three years at the Alcazar Theatre in San Francisco. In June 1930, he became the director of speaking broadcasting at radio station KYA in San Francisco. Ayres, 40, specialized in delivering inspirational messages to the downtrodden, discouraged, and shut-ins in daily 15 minute "chatalogues" in the morning and on Friday evenings in a segment of dramatic sketches titled "The Voice and the Harp."

On the morning of September 5, 1930, Ayres arrived at KYA to prepare his morning message prophetically titled "It Can Be Done." After concluding his 15 minute show with a reading of Edgar A. Guest's inspirational poem "How do You Tackle Your Work," Ayres drove to the garage of his home at 655 Powell Street and shot himself in the head. His Chinese houseboy, hearing the car's engine running and noticing exhaust fumes issuing from the closed garage, investigated and found his employer dead on the car's front seat. Near the hand that still clasped a .38-caliber revolver was found a note to his third wife: "Marjorie, my dear — I'm afraid I'm losing my mind — and haven't the courage to go on. And I don't want to spoil your life, so am taking the coward's way out. Dudley." Scores of persons who had been touched by Ayres' daily inspirational messages filed past his bier in a Market Street funeral chapel before the body was sent to Los Angeles for burial.

Bacon, Faith

Voted the "most beautiful" girl on Broadway in 1931, Bacon had once been the top paid showgirl in *Earl Carroll's Vanities*, and was a contemporary of ecdysiasts Ann Corio, Gypsy Rose Lee, and noted fan dancer Sally Rand. Dancing with two fans in her act as early as 1930, Bacon once sued Rand for $300,000, claiming that the better known dancer had lifted the idea from her. In 1933 and 1934, the pair competed on the same bill at the Chicago World's Fair. Unlike her more famous "sisters in skin," however, the fan and bubble dancer was unable to continue working in the big time, and gradually her career deteriorated to the point where she was stripping in carnivals and dives. By September 26, 1956, the day of her death, Bacon (about 45) had been unable to find work for weeks and feared that she might have to leave Chicago and return home to Erie, Pennsylvania. As a female friend tried to stop her, the still shapely ex-showgirl jumped out of the third floor window of her room in the Alan Hotel at 2004 Lincoln Park West. A police inventory of Bacon's possessions listed "miscellaneous clothing," a white metal ring, a train ticket to Erie, and 85 cents.

Badfinger

The story of the English band Badfinger is perhaps the most tragic chapter in the history of rock 'n' roll. Victims of bad luck and criminally corrupt management, the group's two most talented songwriters, Pete Ham and Tom Evans, were literally driven to commit suicide amidst a swirl of seemingly endless litigation.

Peter William Ham (born in the "Town-hill" district of Swansea, South Wales, on April 27, 1947) began teaching himself guitar at age 12. Two years later, a youth club director gave the 14 year old his first guitar. Though an apprentice electrical engineer at a radio and television shop in Swansea, Ham was determined to make a career in music. While still in his mid-teens he formed the Wild Ones (formerly the Panthers, then the Black Velvets). In late 1964, the band changed its name to the Iveys and began to get noticed playing clubs in and around Swansea. By 1965, the Iveys were opening for groups like the Moody Blues, the Yardbirds, and The Who when they played the area. In April 1966, the Iveys were spotted by Bill Collins, a fiftyish "manager" with limited experience or expertise, who recognized the band's potential. Collins moved the group to London, installed them in a communal house in Golders Green at 7 Park Avenue near the Abbey Road recording studio, placed them on a tight allowance, and encouraged guitarist Ham to begin writing songs.

Like Pete Ham, Tom Evans (born in Liverpool on June 5, 1947) also loved music from an early age. After hearing The Beatles play at the Cavern Club in Liverpool in the early sixties, Evans dedicated himself to becoming a musician. The guitarist subsequently played in several bands (the Inbeatweens, the Calderstones) before joining the Iveys in 1967. Evans, moody, quiet and withdrawn, was the polar emotional opposite of Ham, the friendly, outgoing optimist who trusted everyone. Their vastly different temperaments, however, meant two songwriting points of view in the band and made for a productive collaboration.

On the strength of their demo tapes, the Iveys were signed by Apple Records, The Beatles' fledgling label, on July 23, 1968. The band's debut single, "Maybe Tomorrow," was released in November 1968, but failed to click as did the album of the same name released in November 1968. Reviews noted that the group's vocals bore an uncanny resemblance to The Beatles. To distance themselves from the failed record, the Iveys changed their name to Badfinger. Ham and Evans continued to write as internal squabbles among the various Beatles left Apple Records moribund. Badfinger was in limbo when Paul McCartney gave them his song "Come and Get It" in exchange for their promise to write two songs for the soundtrack of the 1970 movie *The Magic Christian* starring Ringo Starr, Peter Sellers, and Raquel Welch. McCartney produced the single and played piano on the song, which achieved Top Ten status on both sides of the Atlantic. Combined with the release of their album *Magic Christian Music* on March 28, 1970, the group achieved instant celebrity. The press, eager to find replacements for the imploding Beatles, focused their attention on the band's "sound-alike" protégé, Badfinger. On November 28, 1970, the album *No Dice* was released featuring the song "No Matter What." The single spent 12 weeks on the *Billboard* chart, peaking at Number 4. The first "true" Badfinger album, *No Dice* featured Evans' melodies balanced by Ham's introspection. One Ham-Evans collaboration on the album, "Without You," was covered by American singer Harry Nilsson and released as a single in December 1971. The tune was a Number 1 hit and has since been recorded by dozens of artists including a hugely successful cover by Mariah Carey in 1994.

While Badfinger's melodic sound was huge in America it was rapidly going out of style in post–Beatles England. Bill Collins decided to promote the group in the States and looked for U.S. representation. New York City businessman Stan Polley impressed Collins and the band as a man who could make good on his promise to make them all millionaires under his direction. Under the terms of an agreement with the group, Polley became the band's financial overseer and president of Badfinger Enterprises Incorporated. He would control all funds and distribute them to the band. Under Polley's direction, Badfinger was placed on a punishing, but seemingly lucrative, touring schedule that left them little time to record. *Straight Up*, the band's third album, was recorded in England during a break in touring and released on Christmas Day in

1971. Produced by Todd Rundgren and George Harrison, the album peaked at 31 and spawned the single "Day After Day." The Pete Ham tune reached Number 4, the highest charting single ever released by Badfinger. The album also produced another Top Twenty hit, "Baby Blue." The band's final album for Apple, *Ass*, was released on December 15, 1973. Released as Apple was going under, the album was not properly promoted and failed to crack the Top 100.

In 1974, Polley cut a six figure deal with Warner Records which, he assured the band, would soon make them millionaires. The group hurriedly released the eponymous *Badfinger* in March 1974 and continued touring; secure in Polley's promise that he was saving their concert fees and royalties. Placed on a $1,000 a month allowance, the band was forced to live frugally as they crisscrossed America playing almost non-stop. While Evans distrusted Polley, Ham had complete faith that the business manager was doing everything he could to promote the band. Amid growing discontent, the band released the album *Wish You Were Here* in November 1974. The album was selling 25,000 copies a week when Warners pulled it off the market after an audit of Badfinger Enterprises' account revealed $600,000 in advance money missing from an escrow account. Warners sued the band, claiming that its management had prematurely cashed in advances on the album. In effect, the band was sued for money that it had never received.

Badfinger never recovered from the pulling of the album and its subsequent hassle with its management. Ham was particularly shattered by the experience. Broke and with a pregnant girlfriend, Ham frantically tried to contact Polley. The business manager refused to return his calls. When Ham finally contacted Polley's assistant, he was informed that the band's earnings had vanished. What little remained was hopelessly tied up in litigation between Badfinger Enterprises and the record label. Apple, fearful of becoming a party in the suit, continued to pay old royalties into a suspended account that no one could touch. Unable to record because of outstanding contractual obligations with Warners, Badfinger was blocked from getting new management until their legal disputes were settled. As Badfinger's legal woes mounted, Ham, 27, fell into a deep depression fueled by alcohol. Badly overdrawn at the bank, the musician spent his days at his home in Weybridge, Surrey, with his pregnant girlfriend, Anne Ferguson, and her child from a previous relationship, Blair.

On the night of April 23, 1975, Ham and bandmate and neighbor Tom Evans went out to a local pub to discuss their problems concerning Stan Polley. After drinking the equivalent of ten scotches, Ham finally agreed with Evans that the band should break with its business manager. Early the next morning, Evans dropped Ham off at his home. As he was leaving, Ham assured his friend, "Don't worry, I know a way out." Anne Ferguson awoke alone in bed later that morning and went looking for Ham in the garage where he often stayed up all night working on his music. She discovered his body there hanging from a rope tied to a beam. An overturned stool and a half-empty bottle of wine was nearby. A handwritten note found in a songwriting notebook in the garage read: "Anne — I love you. Blair, I love you. I will not be allowed to love and trust everybody. This is better. Pete. P.S. Stan Polley is a soulless bastard. I will take him with me." Five weeks later, Anne Ferguson gave birth to Pete Ham's daughter. At the inquest, the time of Ham's death was put at between 3:00 and 7:00 A.M. on April 24, 1975. The songwriter's blood alcohol content at the time of his death was three times the legal limit for driving a car in Britain. Ham's body was cremated at the Morriston Crematorium in Wales and his ashes scattered in one of its gardens.

Warners eventually reached a settlement with Polley, but the surviving members of Badfinger (bassist Evans, guitarist Joey Molland, drummer Mike Gibbins) saw no money. The group disbanded in 1975, but was vari-ously reformed by Evans and Molland in 1978. In 1979, the reconstituted group released the lackluster album *Airwaves* for Elektra. The label dropped the band that same year. A March 1981 album on the Radio Records label, *Say No More*, was barely reviewed. The band disintegrated with Molland and Evans each taking rival Badfinger groups on the road. By 1983, Evans was in deep tax trouble and in constant litigation over songwriting royalties for "Without You." Moody, withdrawn, and manifesting increasingly erratic behavior, the 36-year-old songwriter was drinking heavily and bitterly depressed. Greatly affected by Ham's death, Evans began talking openly about suicide. At one point, he told his wife, Marianne: "I want to be there, where he is."

On the evening of November 18, 1983, Evans phoned Molland in America and engaged in a heated argument over the band's royalties from Apple. Marianne Evans and a friend, Kerstin Lorenzen, returned from a pub in time to hear the musician slam down the phone. Evans told his wife, "I'll be dead before I get the money." He stayed downstairs playing Everly Brothers records while his wife went upstairs to bed. The next morning around 8:45 A.M. Lorenzen saw his body hanging from a tree in the back garden. Evans left no note. His remains were cremated at the Woking crematorium in Surrey. An inquest determined that Evans' blood alcohol level at the time of his death was identical to that of Pete Ham's. In 1997 Rykodisc released the CD, *7 Park Avenue*, a previously unreleased collection of Ham's home demo recordings. The song "No More" is virtually a musical suicide note. In it, one of his last recordings, Ham wrote:

> "Drunken days, drunken nights
> Someone please turn out the light
> I can't face the mirror anymore...."

FURTHER READING

Du Noyer, Paul. "A Hard Day's Night." *Mojo*, 53:40–46, 48, 50–51, April 1998.
Matovina, Dan. *Without You: The Tragic Story of Badfinger*. San Mateo, Calif.: Frances Glover Books, 1997.

Bainbridge, Barton Leon

Barton Bainbridge was estranged husband of actress Evelyn Keyes, who played "Suellen O'Hara" in the 1939 MGM classic *Gone with the Wind*, and was the proprietor of an unsuccessful swimming pool corporation in Hollywood. Months before her husband's death, Keyes left the 32-year-old businessman when his drinking and violent behavior made her fear for her life. The actress consoled herself by beginning an affair with director Charles Vidor (later her second husband), and informed Bainbridge there would be no reconciliation. On July 19, 1940, Bainbridge met amicably with Keyes to announce that he was leaving the country to start a business in South America. After trading his blue Packard convertible for her old white Pontiac, Bainbridge told Keyes, "I will think of you, Evelyn, as long as I live." Later that evening, his body was found slumped behind the wheel of the coupe in an isolated area on Sherman Way, one-half mile east of Lankershim Boulevard in Sherman Oaks. Police theorized that the businessman had placed a shotgun between his knees and fired a blast into his heart by pulling the trigger with the thumb of his right hand. While press accounts claimed there was no note, Keyes writes in her autobiography that a note was found in which Bainbridge cited her leaving him as the reason for his suicide.

FURTHER READING

Keyes, Evelyn. *Scarlett O'Hara's Younger Sister: My Lively Life In and Out of Hollywood.* Secaucus, N.J.: L. Stuart, 1980.

Baker, James Robert

Baker (born in 1946 in Laguna Beach, California) attended UCLA film school where he won the prestigious Samuel Goldwyn Writing Award. In 1976 his film school project, *Mouse Klub Konfidential*, an underground movie about a Mouseketeer turned gay bondage pornographer, caused a sensation at that year's San Francisco Gay and Lesbian Film Festival. Baker's follow-up film, *Blonde Death*, featured parricide and teen rebellion in eighties Orange County. After working as a screenwriter for five years, Baker left the industry he hated to pursue writing full time. In 1985 writing as "Robert Dillinger" Baker published his first novel, *Adrenaline*, about two gay fugitives. The book introduced Baker's provocative writing style, which combined biting satire with graphic sex in what he described as "raunch with intelligence." Baker's other novels were *Fuel Injected Dreams* (1986), *Boy Wonder* (1988), *Tim and Pete* (1993), and *Right Wing*, a political parody written in 1996 and published on the Internet. On November 5, 1997, the 50-year-old filmmaker and novelist committed suicide (means unreported) in his home in Pacific Palisades, California. According to his companion, Baker suffered from long-term depression and was recently disheartened that he had not published since 1993.

Banks, Gladys Frazin *see* Frazin, Gladys

Bantchevsky, Bantcho

A well-known musical comedy performer in the thirties on "Bulgaria's Broadway," a theatrical section of Sofia, Bantchevsky left Bulgaria after it became a Soviet ally during World War II. He continued to perform as an actor and singer throughout post-war Europe before emigrating to the U.S. in the early 1950s with the dream of starring in American theatre. In New York, he supported himself as a singing coach, and by writing political satire for Radio Free Europe. A devoted opera enthusiast, Bantchevsky, 82, was a fixture at Metropolitan Opera House performances, and had cultivated friendships with many of its Bulgarian stars.

On the morning of January 23, 1988, Bantchevsky refused a friend's dinner invitation with the comment that he could not eat because "I'm going to die tonight." Attending the Met's matinee performance of Verdi's opera *Macbeth*, Bantchevsky seated himself in the "Family Circle," the fifth and highest balcony in the opera house where desks are provided for patrons to study the score during the performance. During the first intermission two ushers had to pull Bantchevsky away from the top railing where he was seated rocking slowly back and forth. Ten minutes into the second intermission, the singing coach plunged 80 feet from the top railing, bounced off a lower balcony rail, and landed on unoccupied seats ten rows from the back of the orchestra with a broken seat atop him. The rest of the opera, broadcast on nationwide radio over the Texaco Metropolitan Opera Network, was cancelled. Friends of Bantchevsky afterward said that the elderly man had recently suffered from poor health, and had constantly talked of suicide.

Baretti, Louis

On April 17, 1932, the former Broadway nightclub manager of the Embassy and the Atlantic Beach Club committed a suicide marked both by its methodical planning and consideration of others. Clad in pajamas, Baretti sat in his Manhattan apartment at 171 E. Sixty-fourth Street and penned six sealed notes, five of them to women. In a letter to his trust company, the dismissed manager gave instructions concerning the execution of his will. In another addressed to his landlord, he apologized to the woman for his act, and hoped that the $500 he left for her in his will would make up for any inconvenience. Baretti then locked the doors and windows of his bedroom, sealed off the crevices with folded newspaper, and turned on all the jets of a gas heater prior to retiring to bed. His action was attributed to the recent loss of both of his nightclub jobs.

Barnes, Frederick Jester

Once a well-known British music hall artist, Fred Barnes, 53, had degenerated from a comedic headliner to singing in saloons and passing the hat. On October 23, 1958, Barnes was found dead in his rented lodgings in St. Ann's Road at Southend-on-Sea, England. Dressed immaculately in a blue suit, overcoat, gleaming patent leather shoes, and a silk muffler knotted around his throat, the former vaudevillian was discovered in front of a gas ring in an upstairs sitting room. Told by his doctor that he had "three months to live — six months if you're careful," Barnes quipped, "I am 12 months up on that doctor so far, and I still feel pretty fit." An inquest verdict determined that death was due to coal gas poisoning.

Barnet, Boris Vasilievich

Russia's most renowned director of film comedy owed his non–Slavic surname to an English grandfather who settled in Russia in the 19th Century. Born in Moscow on June 18, 1902, Barnet studied painting at the Moscow School of Art and Architecture before leaving in 1919 to join the Red Army as a medic and physical training instructor. Following a stint as a professional boxer, he was signed by Soviet director Lev Kuleshov to act the role of "Jeddy," a cowboy, in the 1924 slapstick film satire *Neobychainye priklyuchneiya mistera Vesta v strane bolshevikov* (*The Extraordinary Adventures of Mr. West in the Land of the Bolsheviks*). Encouraged by the film's success, Barnet joined the Kuleshov workshop as a student and general handyman. In the mid-twenties, he acted in a few films before collaborating with Theodore Otsep in 1926 to co-direct the thriller serial *Miss Mend*. The next year, Barnet directed his first solo effort, the comedy *Devushka s korobkoi* (*The Girl with a Hatbox*). During the next few years, he established himself as the top Soviet film satirist while continuing to direct dramas like *Moskva v oktyabre* (*Moscow in October*, 1927) and *Lyodolom* (*The Thaw*, 1931). In 1933, Barnet directed his first sound film, *Okraina* (*Outskirts*). Considered by most critics to be his masterpiece, the film portrayed life in a small Russian town during World War I. Other films directed by Barnet include *U samogo sinego morya* (*By the Bluest of Seas*, 1936), *Stari nayezdnik* (*The Old Jockey*, 1940, unreleased until 1959 following its ban), *Podvig razvedchika* (*The Exploits of a Scout*, 1947), and *Borets i kloun* (*The Wrestler and the Clown*, co-directed with Konstantin Yudin in 1957). In 1963, Barnet directed his final comedy film, *Polustanok* (*Whistle-Stop*). The film's lack of commercial and critical success undermined the moviemaker's confidence and fueled his propensity for depression and alcohol. On January 8, 1965, the 62-year-old director hanged himself with fishing line in his hotel in Riga, Latvia, where he was at work on a scenario for the Russian studio Mosfilm. In his suicide note, Barnet wrote that he had lost the ability to make good films and with it, his desire to live.

Barraco, Paul

Barraco, 58, once owned the Best Theatre and several other neighborhood movie houses in Houston, Texas, before quitting show business to sell real estate. Despondent over financial losses and ill health, Barraco shot himself in the head with a revolver in the bedroom of his home at 2705 Louisiana Street on May 25, 1932. Two days before, he had remarked to several friends that he "was through."

Barron, Donna

Barron, 28, was a minor dancer in the stage shows *Rose Marie* and *Rio Rita* when she met wealthy, married stockbroker Edwin Page in Chicago in 1927. Page installed the young beauty as "Barbara Cole" (and other aliases) in various hotels in the city, but tired of his mistress after a couple of years. On the afternoon of June 5, 1929, the 47-year-old stockbroker confronted Barron in her 12th floor apartment at Canterbury Court at 1220 North State Parkway, and left thinking he had ended the affair. That evening, Page received a hysterical phone call from Barron in which she threatened to end her life. Dismissing the woman's bluff, Page hung up on her. Mo-

ments before taking the fatal plunge, Barron called the apartment's switchboard operator and announced, "This is Miss Cole. I am going to jump out of my window." The woman ran to the office window and saw Barron's broken body on the pavement. Under the white sweater worn by the dead woman, police found a photo of the stockbroker and a note: "I love Edwin Page, 1209 Astor Street. I tried to live and couldn't, I love him so much. I was mean to everyone. Barbara Cole."

Barry, Don "Red"

The veteran Western actor (born Donald Michael Barry De Acosta in Houston, Texas, on January 11, 1911), attended the Texas School of Mines before relocating to Los Angeles in the early thirties to work in advertising. A role in summer stock theatre led to the diminuitive actor's film debut in 1933 with a microscopic part in director Cecil B. DeMille's *This Day and Age*. His "official" debut as "Donald Barry" came in the 1936 RKO crime drama *Night Waitress*. Barry appeared in at least 18 other films prior to being cast in the title role of the 1940 Republic Studio Western *The Adventures of Red Ryder*, based on the exploits of Fred Harman's popular newspaper cartoon strip character. The role not only gave Barry his nickname "Red," but also established him as one of Republic's most durable Western stars. In the forties alone, Barry starred in 29 features for the studio, including *The Apache Kid* (1941), *Outlaws of Pine Ridge* (1942), *The Cyclone Kid* (1942), *The Man from the Rio Grande* (1943), and *Outlaws of Santa Fe* (1944).

Based on the financial success of these films Barry was consistently voted by the *Motion Picture Herald* as one of the "Top Ten Western Stars" from 1942 to 1944. He quit the studio in 1949 to produce and star in his own films, but never again achieved the success he enjoyed with Republic. Beginning in the early fifties, Barry appeared regularly in television, although he continued throughout the period and into the seventies to do supporting roles

Don "Red" Barry— Nicknamed "Red" after his title role in the 1940 Republic Studio feature *The Adventures of Red Ryder*, Barry was one of the most popular Western stars of the forties. Unwisely quitting Republic in 1949 to form his own production company, the veteran Western star continued to make films and to do guest appearances on television. On July 17, 1980, a domestic disturbance between the 69-year-old actor and his estranged third wife at their home in North Hollywood ended in tragedy when Barry shot himself in the head.

Known as one of filmdom's greatest lovers, "Red" Barry carried on celebrated dalliances with Hollywood stars Joan Crawford, Linda Darnell, Jill Jarmyn, Susan Hayward, and Ann Sheridan. Not surprisingly, Barry was married three times, divorced twice, and separated from third wife, Barbara, when domestic troubles escalated into tragedy. On July 17, 1980, Barbara Barry notified authorities after violently quarrelling with the 69-year-old actor at his North Hollywood home at 4729 Farmdale Street. Police arrived at the scene at 9:30 P.M., settled Barry down, and were in the process of leaving when the veteran actor emerged from the house onto the front porch brandishing a .38-caliber pistol. Ignoring their pleas to drop the weapon, Barry fired a single shot point-blank into his head. He was pronounced dead on arrival at Riverside Hospital. Barry is interred at Forest Lawn Cemetery in Los Angeles under a tree in the "Court of Liberty," Plot 5442.

in films. In the late fifties, the actor was briefly cast in the ABC western *Sugarfoot* starring Will Hutchins. During the 1960–1961 season of the ABC detective drama *Surfside Six*, Barry played the role of "Lt. Snedigar." The actor's last regular series work (1963–1964) was as "Mr. Gallo" in the short-lived NBC drama *Mr. Novak*. Barry continued to do guest shots on numerous television shows (*Rawhide, The Virginian, The Wild, Wild West, The Bionic Woman, Little House on the Prairie, Charlie's Angels*) until his death.

Barrymore, Diana (Blanche)

The daughter of legendary actor John Barrymore (1882–1942) and his second wife, poetess Michael Strange (Blanche Oelrichs), was born in New York City on March 3, 1921. Largely ignored by her famous parents, the young Barrymore was packed off to private schools in the United States and France. At 17 she was declared the "personality debutante" of the 1938–1939 social season. Strongly influenced by her family's acting tradition, Barrymore studied for two years at the American Academy of Dramatic Arts. In 1938, her family's illustrious name opened the door to a summer stock job at Maine's Oguinquit Playhouse. In 1940, she made her Broadway debut in *The Romantic Mr. Dickens*. Brooks Atkinson, drama critic of *The New York Times*, termed her performance "the best Barrymore debut for some time." On the strength of her reviews in this play and *The Land Is Bright* in 1941, the actress relocated to Hollywood in early 1942. After signing a $1,000 a week contract with Universal, Barrymore was proclaimed "The Most Sensational New Screen Personality of 1942" by the studio's publicity department. That same year she was cast opposite Robert Stack in director Arthur Lubin's World War II aviation drama *Eagle Squadron*. Barrymore's performance failed to impress reviewers as did her subsequent starring roles in films like *Between Us Girls* (1942), *Nightmare* (1942), and *Frontier Badmen* (1943). By 1944, she was reduced to a supporting role in *Ladies Courageous*. The film signalled an end to her Universal contract and Barrymore returned to New York hoping to find stage work.

As graphically detailed in her 1957 tell-all autobiography, *Too Much, Too Soon*, Diana Barrymore was a self-destructive alcoholic with a penchant for marrying the wrong men. Her first marriage to actor Fletcher Bramwell in 1942 ended in divorce in 1946. Barrymore quickly rebounded and married professional tennis player John R. Howard in January 1947. The union ended in just six months amid well-publicized drunken brawls and police arrests. Barrymore was doing summer stock when she married Robert W. Wilcox, an alcoholic bit actor in B films, in 1950. The death of Wilcox from a heart attack in 1955 left his wife broke, overweight, and unemployed. In 1956, the suicidally depressed actress voluntarily committed herself to a New York sanitarium to curb her alcoholism. Barrymore again made national news in 1957 with the publication of her autobiography and in 1958

when *Too Much, Too Soon* was filmed starring Dorothy Malone as the troubled actress. In the late fifties, Barrymore toured in various stock productions of Tennessee Williams' *A Streetcar Named Desire*, *Cat on a Hot Tin Roof*, and *Garden District*. Reportedly in love with the homosexual playwright, she was devastated when Williams rejected her for the 1959 London production of his play *Sweet Bird of Youth*.

On January 25, 1960, the nude body of the 38-year-old actress was found face-down on the bed in her second floor apartment at 33 East Sixty-first Street in New York City. According to press reports, bottles of tranquilizers and sleeping pills as well as several empty liquor bottles were found scattered throughout the $200 a month, two-and-a-half room apartment. An autopsy determined that death was caused "by an acute alcoholic intoxication enhanced by the effect of ingested barbiturates." Although the coroner generously ruled out suicide or foul play in the actress' death, Barrymore's history of acute depression, loneliness, and alcoholism made her a prime candidate for self-destruction. Eulogized by Gerold Frank, the co-author of her autobiography, as a "frightened and recklessly emotional woman" who worked ceaselessly to be a Barrymore, the actress was buried in the family plot next to her mother in Woodlawn Cemetery in the Bronx.

FURTHER READING

Barrymore, Diana, and Frank, Gerold. *Too Much, Too Soon*. 1st ed. New York: Holt, 1957.
Parish, James Robert. *The Hollywood Celebrity Death Book: From Theda Bara and Rudolph Valentino to Marilyn Monroe and James Dean*. Las Vegas, Nev.: Pioneer Books, 1993.

Barton, Arthur

A one-time motion picture press agent, Barton (real name Hartman) collaborated with Edward Chodorov in writing *Wonder Boy*, a play produced in 1931 by Jed Harris. Two years later he collaborated with Don Lochbiler on a play titled *Man Bites Dog*. On April 8, 1936, the 32-year-old playwright was found dead in his gas-filled two room apartment at 309 East Twenty-third Street in New York City. In a note scribbled in pencil Barton explained that he was losing his eyesight and found it difficult to "function as I should." At the time of his death, Barton was employed on a WPA project dramatizing a novel.

Bates, Barbara

Unable to achieve stardom despite being under contract to four separate studios during a nearly 30 year film career, Bates is undoubtedly best remembered for her role as "Phoebe," the aspiring actress who holds the Sarah Siddons Award in front of a three-way mirror, in the final shot of the classic 1950 film *All About Eve*. Born in Denver, Colorado, on August 6, 1925, Bates received early training in ballet, and by her mid-teens was modelling clothes for the Denver May Company. At 18, she won first prize in a local beauty contest: two round-trip tickets to Hollywood. Accompanied by her mother, Bates arrived in Los Angeles in early 1944. Two days before they were set to leave, she was "discovered" by Cecil Coan, a publicist for United Artists. Impressed by the young woman's Susan Hayward-like beauty, Coan landed Bates a contract with Universal Pictures in September 1944. Coan, 45 and recently divorced, secretly married his 19-year-old protégé on March 27, 1945. That same year, Bates made her screen debut in *Salome, Where She Danced*. As one of the "The Seven Salome Girls," Bates and six other studio starlets served as handmaidens to Yvonne De Carlo in the title role. Over the next couple of years, Universal cast Bates in small decorative parts in *Blonde Ransom* (1945), *Lady on a Train* (1945), *Easy to Look At* (1945), and *A Night in Paradise* (1946).

She left Universal in 1946 over a salary dispute and, based largely on her modelling work in various photography magazines, signed a contract with Warner Bros. on May 26, 1947. The studio gave her the standard ingénue build-up in such films as *That Hagen*

Girl (1947), *April Showers* (1948), and *Johnny Belinda* (1948). In 1948, the actress was given the title role in Warners' *June Bride* starring Bette Davis and Robert Montgomery, but the film did little to ignite her career. Her next big shot came in 1949 when Danny Kaye handpicked her to play his servant girlfriend, "Leza," in *The Inspector General* co-starring fellow suicide Walter Slezak (see entry). The film featured Kaye singing the tune "Lonely Heart" to Bates, but unfortunately the majority of her scenes wound up on the cutting room floor. Shortly afterward, studio head Jack Warner terminated Bates' contract after she refused to take part in a publicity tour to promote *The Younger Brothers*, a film in which she was not even cast.

In 1950, the actress signed a contract with yet another studio, 20th Century–Fox. That year, she appeared as one of the daughters of Clifton Webb and Myrna Loy in *Cheaper by the Dozen* and in director Joseph L. Mankiewiczs' masterpiece *All About Eve*. Yet another shot at stardom eluded Bates in 1952 when Charlie Chaplin picked her to star opposite him in *Limelight*. Fox, however, refused to permit her to appear in the film out of fear that any perceived association with Chaplin and his leftist political leanings would damage the studio. The role eventually went to Claire Bloom. Bates continued to work throughout the fifties (*I'd Climb the Highest Mountain*, 1951; *Let's Make it Legal*, 1951; *The Outcasts of Poker Flat*, 1952; *Belles on Their Toes*, 1952; *All Ashore*, 1953; *The Caddy*, 1953; *Rhapsody*, 1954) while awaiting a breakout role.

In a last ditch effort to make his wife a star, Coan, a British subject, signed a deal making Bates a contract player with J. Arthur Rank in England. Coan liquidated their Hollywood property and transferred to the United Artists London office as a publicity director. After making *Triple Deception* there in 1956, Bates reportedly suffered a nervous breakdown and attempted suicide after being cast with rising star Dirk Bogarde in *Campbell's Kingdom*. Actress Barbara Murray replaced her in the film. Returning to America following the cancellation of her Rank contract, Bates made the 1958 Western *Apache Territory* with Rory Calhoun. Shortly after the film's release, the actress announced that making movies no longer interested her although she did do some television work.

Unable to cope with Coan's terminal cancer, Bates slashed her wrists in the mid-sixties. She was devastated when he died on January 25, 1967. One week after Coan's death, she moved back to her hometown of Denver where by day she worked as a nurse's aide at the hospital where her mother worked and attended secretarial school at night. Bates appeared to be happy after marrying sportscaster and former childhood sweetheart William Reed in December 1968. After work on March 18, 1969, Eva Bates, mother of the 43-year-old former actress, returned home to discover her daughter's Volkswagen parked inside the locked garage. On closer examination, Bates was found dead on the front seat, a victim of carbon monoxide poisoning. She was reportedly pregnant. Bates is interred in the Crown Hill Cemetery and Mortuary in Lakewood, Colorado.

FURTHER READING

Crivello, Kirk. *Fallen Angels: The Lives and Untimely Deaths of Fourteen Hollywood Beauties.* Secaucus, N.J.: Citadel Press, 1988.

Bates, Edward

The 45-year-old orchestra leader for Boston's Shubert Theatre shot himself through the right temple with a revolver in his home at 39 Walnut Park in Roxbury, Massachusetts, on September 23, 1926. Pronounced dead on arrival at the City Hospital, Bates had recently been under observation for depression at a local mental hospital.

Battles, Marjorie Ann

On stage since the age of 6 months, the daughter of South Philadelphia restaurateur Don Battles studied drama at Carnegie Tech, and acted in several local theatre groups before getting her big Broadway break in 1965. Bat-

tles appeared in 650 performances of *Cactus Flower* as an understudy to lead Brenda Vaccaro, but in her regular role as "Botticelli's Springtime" spoke only 15 lines a performance. Quitting show business as an act of political conscience in 1968, the 27 year old became a Head Start teacher for black and Hispanic children on New York City's Lower East Side. Her return to acting in 1972, prompted by the belief that she could help more children were she famous, met with limited success. She had a bit part in the 1975 Liza Minnelli-Burt Reynolds flop *Lucky Lady* and appeared on various television shows, which included *Police Woman*, *Hawaii Five-O*, and *Quincy*.

In 1979, depressed and in the initial stages of mental illness, Battles returned to Philadelphia. She was living in a second floor apartment over a cleaners when she disappeared for several weeks in 1986. Her father ultimately found her living with a friend in New York. In Philadelphia on the morning of October 18, 1987, the 46-year-old actress jumped to her death in front of a southbound train at the Tasker-Morris Station on the Broad Street Subway. In a 1966 interview, Battles was quoted as saying, "Most of the fine, sensitive people leave (Broadway) ... they get beaten down.... In fact ... the whole Broadway bit isn't even much fun except for the few minutes I'm on stage.... Nobody knows exactly how it is unless they've been here."

Baucus, Frank M.

One hour before he was to be tried on a charge of grand larceny stemming from his alleged diverting of funds from a large estate left to him by a relative, Baucus, 52, swallowed poison in Troy, New York, on June 12, 1933. Well known in the East, Baucus was the former president of the Troy Auto Club and drum-majored that city's famous Oriental Temple band.

Baxter, Dale

The British-born Baxter (real name Baxter Pickering) had been a successful radio scriptwriter and emcee for the NBC quiz show *It's Up to You* (1939), and *Pictorial Paragraphs*, a series depicting New York scenes. In the months prior to his death, however, the 42-year-old scriptwriter had failed to sell any of his work to radio. On February 23, 1940, Baxter's wife dropped by her husband's one room, sixth floor apartment–writing studio overlooking New York's East River. A sign on the door warned, "Be careful, gas." Inside, Baxter lay dead with a tube leading from his mouth to the gas range. Clasped in his hand was a letter of rejection for his last radio script: "We have no client at the present time who would be interested in your show, 'Roll Call.' Several people have read it and the general consensus is that it is a program which we would not be interested in developing at present. I will be very happy to keep it in mind."

Beckett, Scott Hastings

Regarded by many *Our Gang* aficionados as the all-time most appealing member of the "Little Rascals," Scotty Beckett was born in Oakland, California, on October 4, 1929. Following his screen debut in the 1933 20th Century–Fox film *Gallant Lady*, the child was signed by producer Hal Roach in 1934 to appear in the *Our Gang* comedies. As Spanky McFarland's sidekick, Beckett (in an oversized turtleneck sweater and askew baseball cap) appeared in 15 *Little Rascals* adventures before leaving the series in 1935. Beckett's boyish appeal kept him working throughout the thirties and forties in films like *Pursuit* (1935, starring fellow suicide Chester Morris), *Dante's Inferno* (1935), *The Charge of the Light Brigade* (1936), *Conquest* (1937, with fellow suicide Charles Boyer), *Marie Antoinette* (1938), *My Favorite Son* (1940), *Kings Row* (1941), and *Ali Baba and the Forty Thieves* (1944, with fellow suicide Jon Hall). In 1946, Beckett was memorably cast as the young Jolson in *The Jolson Story*, arguably his last important screen role. Unable to make the transition from adolescent to adult actor, Beckett continued to work in mostly minor films until his last screen appearance in 1957, a 30 second walk-on, in *The Oklahoman*. In addition to films, Beckett also appeared onstage (*Slightly Married*, 1943), on radio (*The Life of Riley*), and as a regular ("Winky") on the syndicated television series *Rocky Jones, Space Ranger* (1954).

As his career waned in the late forties, Beckett's personal life began to spiral out of control. An arrest for drunk driving in 1948 signalled that the actor was having problems with alcohol and drugs. Two marriages ended in divorce. In 1954, Beckett was arrested for carrying a concealed weapon and passing a bad check. In 1960, he was placed in police custody for assaulting his stepdaughter with a crutch. Three years later, following an arrest for an assault with a deadly weapon, Beckett slit his wrists, but recovered. On May 10, 1968, the 38-year-old former child star intentionally overdosed on barbiturates in his room at the Royal Palms Hotel in Los Angeles. The contents of a partially written suicide note found near an empty pill bottle were not disclosed. Beckett is buried in the San Fernando Mission Cemetery in Mission Hills, California.

FURTHER READING

Maltin, Leonard, and Bann, Richard W. *Our Gang: The Life and Times of the Little Rascals*. New York: Crown Publishers, 1976.

Beecroft, A. A.

A former associate of David Horsley, an early motion picture producer, Beecroft served as the business manager of the movie trade magazine *Exhibitors Herald* for 20 years before it ceased publication in 1932. Despondent over the magazine's cessation and his separation from his wife, Beecroft, 56, hired a boat and rowed 100 yards off the beach in Mamoroneck, New York, on July 8, 1934. As hundreds of people on the shore watched and shouted "Don't do it!" Beecroft stood up, deliberately raised a .38-caliber pistol to his head, and pulled the trigger.

Begelman, David

The son of a Bronx tailor, Begelman began his career in Hollywood in the late forties as a talent agent. With longtime partner Freddie Fields, he formed Creative Management Associates in 1960 that represented such megastars as Judy Garland, Paul Newman, Fred Astaire, and Steve McQueen. The pair pioneered the "package deal" whereby the talent agency could attach stars, directors, and writers it represented to a single picture deal and, in addition to raking off their 10 percent agents' fee, pocket a hefty packaging fee as well. In 1973, Begelman left CMA to assume the presidency of financially ailing Columbia Pictures. Under his leadership, the studio enjoyed a string of successes with *Shampoo* (1975), *Funny Lady* (1975), and Steven Spielberg's 1977 hit *Close Encounters of the Third Kind.*

Begelman was at the top of his form and raking in a $300,000 a year salary plus stock options worth another $1.4 million when scandal toppled his career. In 1977, he admitted forging actor Cliff Robertson's name on a $10,000 check from Columbia. By the end of the police investigation, other company checks totalling more than $80,000 were found to have been forged by Begelman to cover gambling and drug debts. Columbia's board of directors tried to cover up the scandal, but failing, forced him to resign in 1978. Begelman never served a day in prison. The ex-mogul pleaded no contest to embezzlement charges, was fined $5,000, forced to surrender his stock options, entered a drug therapy program, and hired someone to make an anti-drug public service documentary to fulfill his community service sentence. Ultimately, Begelman's grand theft conviction was reduced from a felony to a misdemeanor.

In a turn of events that has since come to symbolize Hollywood corruption (see David McClintick's book, *Indecent Exposure*), actor Cliff Robertson was effectively blacklisted in the industry for having blown the whistle on Begelman, while the successful studio head was given control over another studio. In 1979, Begelman was named president and chief executive officer of MGM-UA. Proving, however, that Hollywood can forgive anything except failure, Begelman was forced out in July 1982 after the studio made the flops *Pennies from Heaven* (1981), *Buddy, Buddy* (1981), and *Yes, Giorgio* (1982). Later that year, Begelman joined Sherwood Productions, owned by sports mogul Bruce McNall. The duo formed Gladden Entertainment in 1984 and initially did well with *Mannequin* (1987), *The Fabulous Baker Boys* (1989), and *Weekend at Bernie's* (1989). In the nineties a run of box office losers like *Short Time* (1990) and *Mannequin Two: On the Move* (1991) led the company to declare bankruptcy in April 1994. McNall would later plead guilty to defrauding several banks of more than $236 million. Though Begelman remained above the legal fray, Hollywood analysts said that he had intimate knowledge of McNall's business dealings, and was scheduled to be a witness at his partner's sentencing hearing.

On the morning of August 7, 1995, the 73-year-old Beverly Hills resident checked into the Century Plaza Hotel & Tower in Century City under an assumed name. He spent the day making anguished phone calls to friends, one of whom called security at the hotel and requested that they check on him. At about 10:30 P.M., three security guards found Begelman's pajama-clad body sprawled across the bed, a .38-caliber pistol and a bottle of champagne by his side. Police estimated that he shot himself in the head sometime between 9:30 and 10:00 P.M. A one-line message written on a telephone note pad read, "My real name is David Begelman." Earlier in the day, Begelman had sent letters to friends asking them to look after his third wife, Annabelle. According to Hollywood publicist Warren Cowan, the ex-studio head had been "distressed and despondent" over a series of failed business deals.

FURTHER READING

McClintick, David. *Indecent Exposure: A True Story of Hollywood and Wall Street.* New York: Morrow, 1982.

Behrmann, Dimitri

After the 1994 release of *Law-Town*, an album based on his experiences in Lawrence, Massachusetts, the 25-year-old Haitian immigrant and aspiring rap artist told an interviewer that music served as an outlet for his anger as a black man. Recently, however, Behrmann had complained of insomnia and seemed depressed over his stalled music career. On June 5, 1998, the rapper picked up Beverly Cora, 27, at their apartment in Haverhill, Massachusetts. Cora, Behrmann's longtime girlfriend and mother of his 5½ year old son, appeared to be in good spirits as they left for a drive around 2:30 P.M. Less than an hour later as they were driving on Route 495 near the Route 13 exit in Methuen, Massachusetts, Behrmann fired a round from a 9mm Glock semiautomatic handgun into Cora's head before turning the gun on himself. The Toyota sedan veered off the road at 70 miles per hour, snapped a tree, and flipped over. Both victims were alive when rescuers arrived, but died after being taken to separate hospitals. Cora's parents, who loved Behrmann and refused to blame him for their daughter's death, asked that the pair be buried together.

Bell, Stanley

The 41-year-old British actor was a member of the Stratford-on-the-Sound Company in which he had performed the roles of "Escalus" in *Measure for Measure*, the "Duke of Venice" in *Othello*, the "Prince of Arragon" in *The Merchant of Venice*, and "Don Pedro" in *Much Ado About Nothing*. Prior to the start of the 1958 tour, Bell became emotionally unsettled after a young apprentice with the company was drafted into the army and sent to Germany. By the time the tour arrived in Washington, D.C., in February 1958, Bell's mental state had deteriorated alarmingly. The company's artistic director, John Houseman (later to win an Academy Award as "Professor Kingsfield" in the 1973 film *The Paper Chase*), considered replacing the actor, but kept him as the tour was almost over. The company's leading actress, Katharine Hepburn, also spoke with Bell and was convinced that he could continue acting.

However, during a performance of *Much Ado About Nothing* at the Shubert Theatre on February 15, 1958, Bell (as "Don Pedro") jumped from the stage during the first act, ran up the aisle, and exited the lobby into the streets of the nation's capital. A search for the actor revealed that he had gone directly from the theatre to a gas station across the street, changed his clothes in the men's restroom, asked the attendant to return his costume to the theatre, then drove off in a rented car with his two dogs. The next morning Bell turned up at Houseman's apartment in Boston and spoke with the artistic director's wife, Joan. Shortly after she phoned Houseman in Washington and relayed his assurances to the actor that he would not be reported to the stage union authorities, Bell disappeared. Houseman hurriedly took the train back to Boston where he received reports from friends in various parts of the city that Bell had dropped in to speak with them. An actor reported that Bell told him that he was going to Germany to be with his drafted friend. Bell, however, escaped with his dogs out of a back window and down a fire escape to the street. On February 17, 1958, Bell jumped to his death from the eighth floor of Boston's Hotel Touraine. The actor was killed instantly after landing on the marquee over the Boylston Street entrance to the hotel. At the conclusion of the tour, Katharine Hepburn donated her entire accumulated salary of $30,000 for a scholarship to be established in Bell's name.

FURTHER READING

Houseman, John. *Final Dress*. New York: Simon and Schuster, 1983.

Bellamy, Peter Franklyn

Bellamy (born September 8, 1944, in Bournemouth, Dorset, England) studied at the Norwich and Maidstone art schools before dropping out without a degree after becoming interested in folk music. In 1965, Bellamy co-founded the folk group Young Tradition with Royston Wood and Heather Wood. The popular trio, which featured a capella arrangements of traditional folk and American gospel songs, shared the bill with Janis Joplin at the 1968 Newport Folk Festival. In 1969, after cutting three highly influential albums with the group (*The Young Tradition*, 1966; *So Cheerfully Round*, 1967; *Chicken on a Raft*, 1968), Bellamy left the Young Tradition to pursue a solo career. With the release of *Oak, Ash and Thorn* in 1970, the singer-composer successfully added his own arrangements to the poems of Rudyard Kipling. Two additional albums of Kipling poetry set to music (*Merlin's Isle of Gramarye*, 1972; *Barrack Room Ballads*, 1974) served as the basis of Bellamy's one-man show, *Kipling's History of England*, which toured the U.S. and Britain. In 1977, Bellamy wrote the folk opera *The Transports*, which many critics consider to be his masterpiece. Selected Folk Album of the Year by *Melody Maker*, the double record told the true story of Henry Cabell and Susannah Holmes, the first Norfolk convicts transported to Australia.

In the eighties, a combination of throat problems and Bellamy's feeling that he was out of touch with the left wing political elements of the new wave of folk groups led to a serious curtailing his public performances. Disillusioned with the state and direction of English folk music, the depressed 47-year-old folk singer took a fatal overdose of tranquilizers and alcohol at his home in Keighley, Yorkshire, on September 24, 1991.

Benda, Marion

Benda (real name Marion Elizabeth Watson) was a former *Ziegfeld Follies* showgirl who was better known in later life as one of the "ladies in black," the women who made annual pilgrimages to mourn at the gravesite of silent film star Rudolph Valentino. Although she intimated that she was secretly married to the screen sensation, Valentino's family flatly denied the claim. Twice married to rich and influential men (Baron Rupprecht von Boecklin and Dr. Blake H. Watson), the statuesque redhead amassed a small fortune by divorcing them. Since 1945, however, Benda had lived in relative poverty, and was a familiar sight in Los Angeles area hospitals where she was routinely taken after numerous overdoses of sleeping pills. A week before her death, the 45-year-old ex-showgirl was found in her Hollywood apartment in a state of hysteria after swallowing a number of pills. On November 30, 1951, Benda finally succeeded in taking her life with sleeping pills. The empty bottle was found at her side. In an act of charity, police listed her suicide as "possibly accidental."

Benet, Brenda

The attractive actress (born in Los Angeles on August 14, 1945) was in the process of ending her nine year marriage to *The Incredible Hulk* television star Bill Bixby when a weekend vacation at Mammoth Lakes, a Sierra ski resort in California, with their 6-year-old son, Christopher Sean, ended in tragedy. Alone with his mother, the child contracted a rare throat infection called acute epiglottis. Christopher lapsed into a coma and died the next day, March 1, 1981, on the operating table. Benet and Bixby divorced that December. Benet, a cast member on the NBC soap opera *Days of Our Lives* since July 1979, continued her role as "Lee Williams" on the show while also doing guest shots on television programs like *The FBI*. On April 7, 1982, the 36-year-old actress locked herself in the bathroom of her Pacific Palisades home, knelt on the floor beside a lighted candle to meditate, then fired a single shot from a .38-caliber Colt Cobra pistol into her mouth.

Bengston, Elmer L.

A former production manager at radio station KLZ–Denver, "Benny" Bengston, 37, was free-lancing as a radio writer in Los Angeles. On September 27, 1938, he phoned a female friend prior to drinking poison in his apartment at 6018 Carlton Way. Hollywood police ascribed the act to despondency.

Bennett, Jill

The actress whose idea of heaven was "to be eternally rehearsing" was born in Penang, British Malaya, on December 24, 1931. Following her father's imprisonment by the Japanese during World War II, Bennett and her mother escaped to England. The teenager was sent to various boarding schools, but was repeatedly expelled for rebellious conduct. Discovering a love of acting, Bennett studied at the Amersham Repertory and the Royal Academy of Dramatic Art before turning professional in predominantly Shakespearean roles at Stratford-on-Avon in 1949. In 1950, the 19 year old made her London debut in the Laurence Olivier-staged production of the Denis Cannan play *Captain Carvallo*. Seven years later, Bennett gained critical attention as "Isabelle" in Jean Anouilh's *Dinner with the Family*. After her second marriage to playwright John Osborne in 1968 (her first, to playwright Willis Hall, ended in divorce after three years in 1965) Bennett appeared to strong notices in several of his plays, most notably *Time Present* (1968), *West of Suez* (1968), *Hedda Gabler* (1972, Osborne's adaptation of the Henrik Ibsen play), and *Watch it Come Down* (1976) for the National Theatre.

In 1951, Bennett began a film career that spanned nearly 40 years and more than 25 films with a small role in *The Long Dark Hall*. Other films included *Moulin Rouge* (1952), *Lust for Life* (1956), *Charge of the Light Brigade* (1968), *Julius Caesar* (1970), *For Your Eyes Only* (1981), and her final film, Bernardo Bertolucci's *The Sheltering Sky*, released after her death in 1990.

Bennett's personal life was inextricably linked with her profession. In 1949 she began a long relationship with stage actor Godfrey Tearle, 40 years her senior, documented in her book *Godfrey: A Special Time Remembered*. She lived with him for four years until his death in 1953. Marriages to playwrights Hall and

Osborne lasted three and nine years, respectively. While married to Osborne, Bennett suffered two miscarriages and was told by doctors that she could not carry a child to term. In 1987, Swiss-born multi-millionaire stockbroker Thomas Schoch left his wife and family for Bennett and lived with the actress in his fashionable home, Gloucester Walk, in the Chelsea area of West London. Though temperamental opposites (Schoch was described by friends as "stolid" while Bennett was demanding and subject to tantrums), the couple enjoyed a rich social life. In December 1989, however, Schoch informed Bennett that he would be spending the Christmas holidays with his wife and family. By mid–1990, the relationship had deteriorated to the point that Schoch, 52, was an infrequent visitor at the home he shared with Bennett.

On August 5, 1990, the 58-year-old actress was barely rescued after intentionally overdosing on drugs. Bennett emerged from the hospital even more depressed and often spent days in bed drinking half-bottles of champagne and watching videos of her and Tearle's old movies.

On October 5, 1990, Bennett washed down a lethal dose of quinylbarbitone tablets with champagne in the bedroom of Gloucester Walk. Authorities estimated that she had probably taken her life the day before. Unknown to Bennett, Schoch's solicitor had written asking when she planned to vacate the home. Though the contents of various notes left by Bennett were not officially released, an unnamed friend of the actress who read the final note she left for Schoch reported that she blamed the man. Bennett was cremated at the Putney Vale Crematorium after which, according to her wish, a champagne party was thrown for her friends at her own home in Britten Street. Upon learning that Bennett had left over £600,000 in her will to the Battersea Dogs' Home, John Osborne condemned his fourth wife for her "most perfect act of misanthropy," and regretted that he was "unable to look down upon her open coffin and drop a large mess in her eye."

FURTHER READING

Bennett, Jill, and Goodwin, Suzanne. *Godfrey: A Special Time Remembered*. London: Houghton and Stoughton, 1983.

Bennison, Louis

In films since 1914 (*Damaged Goods*), Bennison was a minor Western star in several programmers, including *Oh, Johnny!* (1918), while also appearing in the title roles of two 1919 features, *Sandy Burke of the U-Bar-U* and *Speedy Meade*. By the early twenties, however, Bennison's alcoholism had all but ended his film career. He appeared briefly on the New York stage in legitimate theater and vaudeville before travelling with a road company on a tour of Australia in the mid-twenties. In Australia, Bennison met the beautiful actress Margaret Lawrence, a stage veteran who had received excellent notices for her work in Chicago and Broadway. When the pair returned to New York City, they were already embroiled in a tempestuous love affair that estranged Bennison from his wife and child. Like Bennison, Lawrence also suffered from a drinking problem that affected her work. In the late twenties, the producers of the Broadway play *Possession* sued the actress when they suspected that she was a no-show at a performance because she was drunk. In March 1927, the lovers worked together in a play, *The Heaven Tappers*, which closed after a brief run. Another attempt to work together in a 1929 vaudeville sketch called "She Made Up Her Mind" was a similar disaster.

Compounding the disappointment and depression both felt in their stalled careers was Bennison's insane jealousy. The 40-year-old actress was still a strikingly handsome woman, and it maddened Bennison to see her talking with men in nightclubs. To placate the 45-year-old actor, they often stayed home together and drank in Lawrence's penthouse apartment on the roof of 34 East Fifty-first Street in New York City. On June 9, 1929, a concerned friend of Lawrence's dropped by the apartment to check on her. In a visit with the actress just a few days before, their conversation had been interrupted when Bennison stormed into the room waving a gun, yelling, "This will finish us both." Alarmed when no one answered the door, Lawrence's friend notified the police, who forced the door. Inside, the apartment was littered with 40 empty liquor bottles and several glasses. A note, scribbled on the back of an envelope and found pinned to the door leading from the living room to the kitchenette, read: "The sunset has a heart. Look for us up there." Signed "Tianna," authorities later determined the script had been written by Bennison. Another note written by Bennison on white correspondence paper read: "Please notify Mr. Mussen at the Lambs Club at once." In the bedroom, police found Lawrence's nightgown-clad body lying in bed with her arms folded across her breast, dead from a single gunshot wound to the chest. Sprawled on the floor in a half-sitting, half-lying position with his head resting on the side of the bed was Bennison, also dead from a similar wound. The pistol lay between them on the bed. Fully dressed, except for his shoes and socks, the actor was carrying $900 in cash.

Detectives theorized that a drunken Bennison shot Lawrence while she slept, then turned the gun on himself. An autopsy later confirmed that both victims had blood alcohol levels four times higher than the legal standard for intoxication. Interviewed at the Lambs Club, Mussen recalled that Bennison was subject to fits of depression, and that two years earlier at the club he had threatened to kill himself after a bout of heavy drinking.

Bergman, Mary Kay

An accomplished voice-over actress with more than 400 television commercial credits, Bergman was best known for supplying the majority of female voices for the hit Comedy Central cartoon *South Park*. Since the show's debut in 1997, Berman did the voices of "Ms. Cartman," "Wendy Testaburger," "Mrs. Broslovsky" (Kyle's Mom), "Mrs. McCormick" (Kenny's

Mom), "Mrs. Marsh" (Stan's Mom), "Mayor McDaniels," "Ms. Crabtree," "Principal Victoria," "Shelley Marsh," "Nurse Gollem," and others. In 1999 she was also heard in the films *South Park: Bigger, Longer and Uncut* and *The Iron Giant*. In addition to voice work for three Disney films (*Beauty and the Beast*, 1991; *The Lion King*, 1994; *Mulan*, 1998), Bergman was also heard on the 1999 *Star Wars: Episode I— The Phantom Menace* video game, and had inherited the role of "Daphne" in the new *Scooby-Doo* videos. At the time of her death, Bergman was also serving as the co-executive producer and the character "The Lady in Red" in husband Dino Andrade's independent film directorial debut *Bob's Video*.

Unknown to her friends, Bergman suffered from what Andrade termed "a progressive phobic disorder" and "was haunted by irrational fears that steadily grew." On November 11, 1999, the 38-year-old actress died instantly from a self-inflicted shotgun blast to the head in her apartment at 10853 Rose Avenue in the Venice area of Los Angeles. Andrade discovered the body at 10:18 P.M., some three hours after police investigators estimated that the troubled woman pulled the trigger. Bergman left two farewell notes (one to Andrade, the other to their friend, writer John Bell) saying she "could not handle the fear anymore." To honor his late wife, Andrade established the Mary Kay Bergman Memorial Fund at the Suicide Prevention Center of the Didi Hirsch Community Mental Health Center in Culver City, California.

Bern, Paul

On September 5, 1932, the nude body of MGM production supervisor Paul Bern was found dead from a supposed self-inflicted gunshot wound to the head in the home he shared with his movie star wife, Jean Harlow, in the Benedict Canyon section of West Los Angeles. Bern's death, shrouded in controversy and innuendo, stands with the 1935 suicide, accident, or murder of screen star Thelma Todd (see entry) as Hollywood's most enduring mystery.

Born Paul Levy on December 3, 1889, in Wandsbek, Germany, a suburb of Hamburg, the future film executive emigrated to America when he was 9 with his father Julius, a candy maker, mother, Henrietta, and his 17 siblings. Settling in New York City, the family endured continual financial hardships compounded by the death of Julius Levy in 1908. At 18, Paul Levy was forced to put aside his childhood dream of becoming a psychiatrist in order to support his family as a commercial stenographer. In September 1909, however, he was accepted in a two-year acting course at the prestigious American Academy of Dramatic Arts and Empire Theatre Dramatic School. Levy quickly changed his name to the less Semitic sounding "Paul Bern" and became an American citizen.

In February 1911, Bern made his acting debut onstage at the Empire Theatre in *Friends of Youth*. In the company was an attractive young actress named Dorothy Millette, with whom Bern lived in a common-law wife relationship for several years. Over the next decade, he developed a professional resume that made him an ideal candidate for the movie business. Bern acted on Broadway, toured with an East Coast stock company, wrote film scripts, and managed a movie theatre in Manhattan owned by Joe and Nick Schenk prior to their involvement in United Artists and Loew's. In 1920, Bern was living with Millette (registered as "Mrs. Paul Bern" in the Algonquin Hotel) and doing writing assignments for the Samuel Goldwyn Company, then making films in New York City.

Bern was in the initial stages of relocating to Hollywood when two tragedies delayed his plans. On September 15, 1920, his 72-year-old mother drowned herself. Though the death was ruled accidental, Bern confessed to friends that it was suicide. In 1921, Dorothy Millette suffered a mental breakdown and was institutionalized at the Blythewood Sanitarium in Greenwich, Connecticut. Advised by doctors that Millette's schizophrenia was irreversible, Bern made arrangements for her long-term care and moved to Hollywood in

In Hollywood, Bern's talent and versatility made him much in demand as a director (*Head Over Hills*, 1922; *Worldly Goods*, 1924; *The Dressmaker from Paris*, 1925; *Flower of Night*, 1925 with Pola Negri), scenario writer (*The Christian*, 1923; *Lily of the Dust*, 1924; *The Marriage Circle*, 1924; *The Great Deception*, 1926; *The Beloved Rogue*, 1927), and film supervisor (*Geraldine*, 1929; *Noisy Neighbors*, 1929; *Square Shoulders*, 1929).

While serving as a production supervisor at Pathé in 1926, Bern met Irving Thalberg, nicknamed the "Boy Wonder" at MGM where he served as that studio's highly successful vice-president and supervisor of production. Thalberg hired Bern that year as his personal production assistant (producer) and story consultant. While MGM producers were not given screen credit, Bern supervised the studio's productions of *New Moon* (1931), *The Prodigal* (1931), and *Grand Hotel* (1932). At MGM Bern's impeccable manners, taste, and compassionate treatment of others earned him universal respect and admiration. Known as "Hollywood's Father Confessor," the sensitive production supervisor was renowned for helping out anyone in need.

During his years in the entertainment capital, Bern had also earned a reputation as a ladies' man. In 1932, the 42-year-old producer fell passionately in love with 21-year-old actress Jean Harlow while pushing her for the sexy leading role in the film *Red-Headed Woman*. Harlow got the part and overnight became the biggest star on the MGM lot. Less than two weeks after the film premiered, Harlow married Bern on July 2, 1932, in a private ceremony attended by the top brass at MGM given at his Benedict Canyon home at 9820 Easton Drive. Bern gave his new bride the deed to the house as a wedding gift.

PAUL BERN—(pictured here in 1924) was a production assistant (producer) at MGM and largely responsible for bringing sex bomb Jean Harlow to the studio. The couple married on July 2, 1932, and appeared to be deeply in love. However, on September 5, 1932, the 42-year-old producer was found dead from a supposedly self-inflicted gunshot wound to the head in their home in the Benedict Canyon section of Beverly Hills. A cryptic suicide note found at the scene, MGM's subsequent smear campaign against Bern based on vicious sexual innuendo, and the revelation that the producer already had a common-law wife (who may have murdered him) continue to make this case one of Hollywood's most intriguing mysteries. (Courtesy of University of Southern California, on behalf of the USC Library Department of Special Collections.)

1922. Millette spent a year at the sanitarium then moved back into the Algonquin Hotel. Bern continued to support her with monthly checks of $350 channeled through his brother, Henry Bern.

Outwardly, the couple appeared to be blissfully happy. Bern maintained a dizzying work schedule while Harlow told a close friend that all she wanted to do was "sit at Paul's feet and have him educate me." Unknown to the glamorous superstar, however, her husband was maintaining Dorothy Millette, a.k.a. "Mrs. Paul Bern," in a hotel back East. Millette read of her common-law husband's marriage to Harlow in a fan magazine and began pressuring him to let her come to Hollywood. Bern played for time telling the mentally unbalanced woman that he was too busy to see her. Finally relenting, he had Millette installed at the Plaza Hotel in San Francisco on May 4, 1932. He was overseeing the production of *Red Dust* starring Harlow and Clark Gable when the complicated situation reached its crisis in September 1932.

While the truth of the matter can now never be known thanks to a possible studio cover-up, conflicting accounts of key events, and the accumulated force of innuendo built up over nearly 70 years, Paul Bern did die in his Benedict Canyon home on Easton Drive on Labor Day, September 5, 1932, days after he took out a life insurance policy on himself naming Harlow as the beneficiary. The evening before the tragedy, Bern and Harlow apparently argued. The blonde superstar chose to stay across town at her mother's, leaving Bern alone in the house. At 11:30 the next morning, the producer's butler, John Carmichael, arrived at the house and found Bern's naked body lying on the floor in a puddle of blood half out of a walk-in closet off the bedroom. A gaping wound in Bern's right temple two inches in front of his ear had been inflicted by a .38-caliber Colt revolver still clasped in his right hand. The gun was initially unseen by Carmichael because it was obscured under the right side of his employer's body. The bullet exited the left side of Bern's head and lodged in the wall of the closet.

Carmichael phoned Harlow's mother who (instead of notifying police) called MGM head Louis B. Mayer at his Santa Monica beach house. Acting quickly, Mayer contacted Whitey Hendry, head of MGM studio's police, and Howard Strickling, MGM's head of publicity who specialized in "fixing" personnel problems at the studio. They met at the death house shortly after noon and combed the house for clues before calling the police. On a table near Bern's body Strickling found a second .38-caliber revolver belonging to the dead man next to his morocco-bound guest book containing the names of several celebrities. On page 13 Strickling discovered a cryptic message written in Bern's hand that read: "Dearest dear, Unfortunately this is the only way to make good the frightful wrong I have done you and to wipe out my abject humiliation. I love you. Paul. You understand that last night was only a comedy."

Mayer wanted to destroy the note, but Strickling convinced him that without it Bern's suicide had no motive and Harlow might be suspected of killing him. Strickling replaced the book opened at page 13 on the table. At 2:30 P.M., four hours after the discovery of Bern's body, the police finally arrived at the scene after Irving Thalberg reported the death. Told of her husband's death, Harlow became hysterical and had to be sedated. When later questioned about the possible meaning of the reference to the "frightful wrong" committed against her by Bern, Harlow could provide no explanation. Mayer and the publicity machine at MGM, however, could.

Anxious to protect the studio's biggest star from any blame in the suicide and to ensure the public's sympathy for her, Mayer orchestrated a smear campaign against "Hollywood's Father Confessor." Studio doctor Edward B. Jones, conveniently unavailable for the subsequent inquest, issued a press statement in which he announced that Bern had a medical problem that caused him to be impotent. Dr. Jones later told the press that "Bern's suicide was due to an acute melancholia and nervous strain which developed into a mania." Fed by Mayer's publicity machine, it became common "knowledge" that Bern's genitalia were so undersized that he could not engage in sexual intercourse. The cryptic lines in Bern's suicide note referring to the "frightful wrong" and the mysterious "last night was only a comedy" could then be interpreted as guilt, embarrassment, humiliation, and frustration over his inability to sexually satisfy his wife, who also happened to be the sexiest woman in movies. Harlow, not Bern, was the offended party.

Several of Bern's former lovers, however, dismissed the vicious innuendo as patently untrue. Dr. Frank Webb, assistant autopsy surgeon of the coroner's office, testified at the inquest that Bern's "sexual organs were undersized, but not so much as to cause psychic melancholia or physical impotence." The coroner's official verdict: "Death by gunshot wound to the head, self-inflicted by the deceased with homicidal intent. Motive undetermined."

An alternative theory of the case, however, accounts for some of the facts initially told to the police by witnesses later hushed by MGM. In the early morning hours on the day Bern died, a neighbor reported seeing a woman being picked up by car at the death house. The woman was subsequently identified as Dorothy Millette. The night before, neighbors heard raised voices and Bern scream, "Get out of my life!" According to the "murder theory," Bern orchestrated an argument with Harlow to get her out of the Easton Drive house so that Millette could visit him. Millette arrived and Bern entertained her at the pool before the evening ended in a loud argument. Bern was removing his trunks in the walk-in bedroom closet when Millette picked up one of the two guns in the room and fatally shot him in the head at point-blank range. Appearing at the scene later, MGM security chief Whitey Hendry placed the gun in the dead man's hand to make the murder appear like a suicide. Murder, it seems, could hurt Harlow's career as much as suicide. A woman's wet bathing suit (not Harlow's) was found near the producer's body. The undated "suicide note" (positively identified as written by Bern) was in actuality an apology to Harlow for the reemergence of Millette back into

his life. The "comedy" of "last night" referred to the argument he staged in order to get her out of the house so that he could meet Millette. An MGM driver later told several people that he had driven a woman back to the Plaza Hotel in San Francisco. The charge for the trip was even billed to Bern's estate.

The next day, September 6, 1932, Millette checked out of the Plaza Hotel and purchased a round trip ticket on the *Delta King*, the overnight ferry to Sacramento. The press, informed of her existence by Bern's brother, Henry, was frantically searching for the woman when a Japanese fisherman found her badly decomposed body floating in the Sacramento River at the Georgiana Slough on September 14, 1932. The coroner's inquest determined that the "38-year-old Dorothy Millette came to her death on the 7th of September, 1932, by asphyxiation by drowning."

Jean Harlow reportedly paid the $250 needed to bury her dead husband's common-law wife in Sacramento's East Lawn Memorial Park under a headstone that read, "Dorothy Millette Bern." On September 9, 1932, 2,000 mourners and sightseers attended Paul Bern's funeral services at the Grace Chapel in Inglewood. Following the service, the much maligned suicide or murder victim was cremated and his ashes interred at the Golden West Mausoleum in Inglewood Park Cemetery. Jean Harlow died of uremic poisoning at the age of 26 on June 7, 1937.

FURTHER READING

Golden, Eve. *Platinum Girl: The Life and Legends of Jean Harlow.* New York: Abbeville Press, 1991.
Marx, Samuel, and Vanderveen, Joyce. *Deadly Illusions: Jean Harlow and the Murder of Paul Bern.* New York: Random House, 1990.
Shulman, Irving. *Harlow, an Intimate Biography.* New York: Bernard Geis Associates, 1964.
Stenn, David. *Bombshell: The Life and Death of Jean Harlow.* 1st ed. New York: Doubleday, 1993.

Best, Don

The British Broadcasting Corporation radio development and services manager was found dead in a fume-filled car on May 9, 1988, in London. Best (age unknown) left a note blaming himself for the outbreak of Legionnaire's disease at Broadcasting House.

Bettelheim, Spencer D.

"Spence," as he was widely known among theatre folk, was the treasurer of Sam H. Harris Productions, the lessee of the Lyceum Theatre, and president of the Lyco Realty Corporation, whose offices were located on the second floor above the Lyceum at 149 W. Forty-fifth Street in New York City. The Lyceum's production of *Having a Wonderful Time* had concluded on November 5, 1937, when Bettelheim's nephew found his uncle's body on the floor of the theatre man's office. A .38-caliber revolver still clutched in his right hand, Bettelheim, 43, had evidently fired two practice rounds into the floor before firing a bullet into his right temple. A decorated veteran of World War I, Bettelheim was gassed during the conflict and still suffered from a pulmonary infection. Weeks before his death, he intimated to friends that the agonizing pains around his heart had become nearly unbearable. In the absence of a suicide note, death was attributed to ill health combined with a heavy tax penalty levied against him by the IRS for accepting gratuities from ticket agencies. Accorded a military funeral with full honors, the Bettelheim burial cortege was routed past the Lyceum Theatre out of respect for his memory.

Beyfuss, Alexander

A 14 year veteran of the motion picture business, Beyfuss was the former manager of the Hollywood-based California Pictures Corporation, which was originally formed to produce a number of Bret Harte stories. Relocating East, he organized the Exceptional Pictures Corporation, although at the time of his death he had been inactive for two years. On January 8, 1925, the 35 year old took his life in a room at the Shelton Hotel at 549 Lexington Avenue in New York City. Beyfuss dressed himself, carefully shaved in front of a bathroom mirror, then used it to position a revolver against his right temple. His body was found by a maid when she entered to clean the room. A short note to his attorney found near the body offered no motive for the act.

Bing, Herman

Bing (born in Frankfurt, Germany, on March 30, 1889) played vaudeville and stock at 16 and toured Europe for several seasons as a circus clown. Learning the production end of motion pictures under famed German director F. W. Murnau, Bing accompanied the filmmaker to Hollywood in the twenties and served as his assistant on *Sunrise* (1927). Bing also worked as an assistant director with Hollywood heavyweights Frank Borzage and John Ford. A penchant for dialects, a doughy body, and an excitable manner served Bing well as comedic relief in a score of films in the thirties and early forties (*Footlight Parade*, 1933; *The Great Ziegfeld*, 1936). Bing's final film role, a minuscule bit part in *Night and Day*, the Warner Bros. bio-pic of popular composer Cole Porter, was in 1946.

Unemployed for more than a year, the 57-year-old comedian was living in the spare bedroom of his married daughter's home at 355 N. Almont Drive in Hollywood when depression proved too much for him to bear at 7:00 A.M. on January 9, 1949. Bing's daughter, Mrs. Ellen Young, was breakfasting with her husband and young child when a shot rang out. They found Bing's body on the floor of his front bedroom, a pistol still clutched in his hand, a gaping bullet wound in his heart. Two notes addressed to his daughter were found in or on separate envelopes near the body. One, dated January 8 with a signed check for $1,000 attached, read: "My beloved Ellen: Please forgive me! My nerves. Eternal love! Daddy. I tried so hard for a come-back!" A note on the back of the other envelope read, "Dear Ellen: Such insomnia! I had to commit suicide! Suicide! Your Daddy." Bing is buried in Hollywood Memorial Park.

Birdwell, Dorothy

Birdwell's promising Broadway dance career ended in 1928 after she sustained a serious head injury in an automobile accident. On December 29, 1930, Birdwell, 21, depressed over her failure to fully recover from the injury, seated herself on a tree stump beneath a bridge in the Mountain Creek district six miles west of Dallas, Texas, and fired a bullet into her heart. Her body was found the next day by highway employees who went under the bridge to get water for an overheated car engine. Hundreds of people filed past Birdwell's body at a local mortuary before she was positively identified by a neighbor.

Bishop, Robert Hamilton, III

In 1954, the Harvard-educated attorney organized Musicarnival, a summer tent show, with the purpose of bringing theatre to the Cleveland area. In addition to organizing and serving as the president of the Musical Arena Theaters Association, an organization representing more than 20 summer musical theatres across the country, Bishop was also a member of the national committee of the Metropolitan Opera Association. On December 11, 1963, the 47-year-old bachelor shot himself in the right forehead with a .22-caliber rifle in the bedroom of his three acre estate near Hunting Valley, Ohio. The contents of a note found near the body were not divulged. Bishop, however, had been a witness before a House subcommittee investigating racketeering and ticket prices on Broadway.

Blandick, Clara

The actress best known for her role as "Auntie Em" in MGM's classic 1939 film *The Wizard of Oz* was born aboard an American ship anchored in Hong Kong on June 4, 1880. Debuting on the Broadway stage in 1912, Blandick's motion picture career began in 1929, and encompassed some 41 films before ending with *Love that Brute* in 1950. On April 15, 1962, the 81-year-old actress, wracked by crippling arthritis and nearly blind, elaborately staged her death in her Hollywood apartment at 1735 N. Wilcox Avenue. Surrounded by Chinese antiques and memorabilia from her long professional career, Blandick carefully coiffed her hair, donned an elegant royal blue dressing gown, and reclined on a couch. After downing several sleeping pills she placed a plastic bag over her head. Blandick's landlady found the body the next day covered up to the shoulders with a gold colored blanket. A note on a nearby table read: "I am now about to make the great adventure. I can not endure this agonizing pain any longer. It is all over my body. Neither can I face the impending blindness. I pray the Lord my soul to take. Amen." Survived by a niece, Blandick was buried in Forest Lawn Memorial Park in Glendale, California.

Blaney, Mae

Blaney, 35, had been unemployed for seven months since last singing in the Chicago night spot The Parody Club. In the early morning hours of May 29, 1931, shortly after returning home to her apartment at the Maple Manor Hotel at 65 Maple Street from a night at the Club Le Claire, Blaney clasped a crucifix in her left hand and, holding a revolver in her right hand, shot herself in the head.

Blattner, Ludwig

Though born in Germany, Blattner spent the last 30 years of his life in England connected with the film industry. In 1920, he left the entertainment business in Liverpool to manage a circuit of small cinemas in Manchester. An innovator, Blattner turned the Gaiety Theatre into Manchester's first supercinema complete with short variety performances and the use of amplified gramophone records. Fascinated with the potential of sound in motion pictures, Blattner relocated to London, and in 1928 took a license on a magnetic recording machine devised and built by German inventor Kurt Stille. Named the Blattnerphone, the unwieldly machine magnetically recorded sound on steel wire. In May 1928, the businessman formed the Ludwig Blattner Picture Corporation at Boreham Wood, intending to use the Blattnerphone process to produce films with synchronized soundtracks. The venture was unsuccessful despite Blattner's sale of the experimental machines to the British Broadcasting Corporation in 1931. Blattner managed to survive financially until 1933 when he voluntarily liquidated his company. Broke and depressed over the poor health of his wife and daughter, the 54-year-old film pioneer was found hanging in a locked room at a country club at Elstree, Herts, England near his home on October 29, 1935.

Blood, Adele see Hope, Adele Blood

Bloodgood, Clara

Worn out by a long road tour of the South, and concerned about her physical and financial health, the 37-year-old actress shot herself in the mouth at the Hotel Stafford in Baltimore, Maryland, on December 5, 1907, as an expectant audience waited in the Academy of Music to see her perform in the Clyde Fitch comedy *The Truth*. Bloodgood, gowned only in a loose wrapper, was found lying on her back across the bed with blood flowing from her mouth. The actress had fired three shots. The first missed and lodged in the ceiling while another was never found. The death wound came from a round that passed through the roof of her mouth in front of the soft palate and into her brain. A few days before the incident, Bloodgood purchased a pistol, a .32-caliber hammerless double-action Smith & Wesson, and had even queried a bellboy at the Stafford on its use. A medical book containing marked sections outlining the parts of the brain was found in the room as was a tome titled *How to Shoot Straight*. The contents of a sealed letter addressed to her stockbroker husband located on a nearby table later

proved to have no bearing on the suicide. Onstage for nearly ten years, Bloodgood previously starred on Broadway in two of Fitch's plays (*The Coronet of the Duchess*, 1904; *The Girl with the Green Eyes*, 1904) before purchasing the rights to *The Truth*, and embarking on an exhausting 30 month road tour.

Bond, Graham

Largely unknown today, Bond was a major influence on British rhythm and blues. Born Graham John Clifton Bond on October 28, 1937, in Romford, Essex, England, he began playing alto sax with Don Rendell's quintet in 1961. That same year he was voted "Britain's New Jazz Star." In 1962, Bond met bassist Jack Bruce and drummer Ginger Baker while playing Hammond organ in Alexis Korner's Blues Incorporated. The trio left Korner the next year to form the Graham Bond Organisation. Behind Bond's gruff vocals and imaginative instrumentation, the group immediately distinguished itself as a pioneer of jazz, blues and R&B rock. An innovator, Bond was the first musician in Britain to record with the Mellotron synthesizer and to play his Hammond organ through a Leslie speaker cabinet. While commercially unsuccessful, the Graham Bond Organisation released two stunning albums in 1965 (*The Sound of 65* and *There's a Bond Between Us*) before Bruce and Baker left in 1966 to form Cream with guitarist Eric Clapton.

Unable to recreate his earlier musical success, Bond became disenchanted with the British scene and moved to America in the late sixties. There he recorded two albums in 1968 for the Pulsar label: *Love Is the Law* and *Mighty Graham Bond*. Bond returned to England in 1969 after the albums failed to find an audience. Deeply influenced by the thought of British occultist Aleister Crowley (1875–1947), Bond formed the Graham Bond Initiation with his wife Diane Stewart in September 1969 as a means to spread the teachings of the so-called "Great Beast." The band bombed as did a 1972 collaboration with lyricist Pete Brown. Other short-lived Bond–formed groups of the period included Air Force I and II (1970–1971), Holy Magick (1971) and Magus (1973).

By the early seventies, Bond was addicted to heroin and cough medicine, and was behaving strangely. After years of enduring Bond's physical abuse, Stewart left her husband in the autumn of 1972 taking their 14-year-old daughter, Erica, with her. Shortly after the break-up, Erica confessed to her mother that she had been undergoing sexual abuse by Bond since 1968. Following a marijuana bust in January 1974, Bond suffered a nervous breakdown and was briefly committed to a mental hospital.

On May 8, 1974, the shabbily dressed musician entered the Finsbury Park underground station in North London around 1:35 P.M. Bond, 37, bought a one-way ticket and walked down to the train platform. Three minutes later observers saw him run across nine feet of platform and dive headfirst with arms outstretched in front of an oncoming train. Thirteen pence, two marbles, a pink felt tip pen, a comb, a key, and London Transport ticket number 23118 were recovered from the dead man's pockets. At the time of his death, Bond was wearing a silver-colored five pointed star, the symbol of Crowley's "Ordo Argentei Astri" (Order Of The Silver Star). The musician was convinced that the talisman would afford him protection against the demonic spirits that he felt he was destined to battle in order to protect the world from evil. In the absence of a suicide note, the St. Pancras Coroner's Court declared an open verdict in Bond's death on June 27, 1974. Bond's body was cremated and the ashes scattered at a ruined mill located in Rocky Valley near Bocastle on the North Cornwall coast of England. Nearly 25 years later, British punk rocker Adrian Borland (see entry) took his life in an eerily similar manner.

FURTHER READING

Shapiro, Harry. *Graham Bond: The Mighty Shadow.* Enfield: Guinness Publishing, 1992.

Bondshu, Neil

On December 20, 1944, shortly before his dance band was to perform at San Francisco's famed St. Francis Hotel, the 28-year-old orchestra leader vanished. Bondshu's manager described him as "nervous and worried," and fellow band members recalled that their leader had been recently depressed over the break-up of his marriage to his wife, Vicki, and separation from his 7-year-old child, Diane. Three weeks earlier Bondshu had been arrested for breaking into his wife's home while she was out, but she dropped the charges. The focus of an all points bulletin, the missing band leader was found on December 22, 1944, across the Bay in Berkeley in a room in the Claremont Hotel he had reserved earlier for his mother. Near death from an overdose of sleeping pills, Bondshu was curled up in bed clutching a picture of his estranged wife and daughter. He died the next day in Berkeley General Hospital. Two days after Bondshu's discovery, hotel officials gave to police a suicide note found at the scene. Shakily written on hotel stationery with a room key dipped in ink, the note read: "Sorry, no pen. Vicki and mother, I'm sorry, but it's best this way."

Borland, Adrian

The singer-guitarist (born December 6, 1957) formed the British punk band The Outsiders with two school friends (Bob Lawrence, bass; Adrian James, drums) in 1976. In May 1977 they became the first punk group to produce a full-length album, *Calling on Youth*, on their own label (Raw Edge UK). The Outsiders released the album *Close Up* (1978) and the EP *One to Infinity* (1978) before Borland left in early 1979 to form The Sound with Dead Kennedys' co-founder Jello Biafra. The group signed with Korova Records and in 1980 released the well received album *Jeopardy* featuring the single "Heartland." Singles like "Heyday," "Sense of Purpose," "Hothouse," and the 1981 album *From the Lion's Mouth* established Borland as a creative and mature voice in the post-punk scene.

After the group broke up in 1987, Borland carved out a solo career that earned him a cult following in Europe. Backed by the Citizens, he released the solo album *Alexandria* on the Play It Again Sam label in 1989. Borland continued to record solo albums throughout the nineties (*Beautiful Ammunition*, 1994; *Cinematic*, 1996; *5:00 A.M.*, 1997) while also producing artists like the Servants, the Dublin group Into Paradise, the Australian punk band Celibate Rifles, and singer-songwriter Ana Christensen.

In April 1999 Borland was recording tracks for his new album when associates noticed that he was exhibiting signs of a longtime schizoid disorder. During the tapings the 41-year-old musician appeared agitated, confused, spoke in non sequiturs, and complained of hearing voices in his head. After promising friends that he would remain sober over the weekend, Borland (cf. entry on British rocker Graham Bond) jumped in front of a train in a London railway station on Monday morning, April 26, 1999. The Westminster Coroner's Court returned a verdict of "suicide while the balance of his mind was disturbed."

Borneman, Ernest

Born in Berlin on April 12, 1915, Borneman left Germany for England with many of his fellow Jews when Hitler seized power in 1933. At Cambridge University Borneman studied ethnology, concentrating on Afro-American music and jazz. Employed as a cameraman by the BBC in 1936, he filmed the network's first experimental television broadcast in 1939. In 1947, Borneman was named head of UNESCO's films division, a position he held until 1949. In 1954, he wrote the screenplay for the Carlo Ponti–produced film *Ulysses* starring Kirk Douglas and Silvano Mangano. Borneman's other screenplays include *Bang, You're Dead* (alternate title: *Game of Danger*, 1954), *Face the Music* (1954), *Double Jeopardy* (1956), and *The Long Duel* (1967). In 1961, he emigrated to Austria where he established himself as an eminent psychothera-

pist and sexologist in the Alfred C. Kinsey mold during the sexual revolution of the sixties. Dubbed the "Pope of Sex" by the media, Borneman wrote several academic books and published five English novels often using the pen name "Cameron McCabe."

In April 1995, the 80-year-old writer told an interviewer: "Whoever believes in life after death is crazy. When it's over it is—thank God—really over." At the time, his nine-year relationship with a German woman psychotherapist, more than 40 years his junior, was disintegrating. Borneman reportedly told the woman that he would take his life if she left him. Despite his warning, she walked out. On June 4, 1995, Borneman was found dead by his neighbors at his rural home near Linz, Austria. After leaving notes and a tape explaining that he could not live without his partner, Borneman downed a lethal cocktail of sleeping pills and cognac.

Bowers, John

Long regarded as the basis of the suicidal fading star "Norman Maine" in the 1937 Frederic March version of *A Star Is Born*, Bowers was born John Bowersox in Garrett, Indiana, on December 27, 1884. Entering films in 1915 with a supporting role in the Shubert Film Company production of *The Little Dutch Girl*, he developed into a capable leading man of more than 90 silent films. Among the best remembered are *The Sky Pilot* (1921), *Lorna Doone* (1922), *Richard, the Lion-Hearted* (1923), and *Chickie* (1925). While on location in Prescott, Arizona, shooting *When a Man's a Man* in 1924, Bowers met and later married his co-star in the picture, Marguerite De La Motte. They divorced years later. Following the advent of talking pictures in 1927, Bowers managed to find supporting roles in only two minor films (*Skin Deep*, 1929; *Mounted Fury*, 1931) before his movie career ended. As the acting assignments dried up Bowers developed into a hopeless alcoholic. After he went broke backing a flying school, and was turned down for a role in the Para-

JOHN BOWERS— The basis of the suicidal has-been actor "Norman Maine" in *A Star Is Born* (1937), Bowers was a leading man in over 90 silent films, but was unable to make the transition to sound. A hopeless alcoholic by the thirties, the 51-year-old actor rented a boat under an assumed name on November 15, 1936, and sailed into the Pacific Ocean off the Santa Monica pier. His drowned body was found two days later washed ashore near Los Flores, south of the Malibu Beach colony.

police that her brother was missing, and that he had told her that he was going to the beach. On November 17, 1936, the actor's body washed ashore near Los Flores, south of the Malibu Beach colony. The actor's death occurred just two weeks into the filming of *A Star Is Born*, lending credence to the widely-held notion that screenwriter Dorothy Parker used it as the prototype of Norman Maine's suicidal walk into the Pacific Ocean.

Boyce, St. Elmo

In recent months, the 31-year-old screenwriter (*The Wild West Show*, 1928) had been arrested five times for drinking and driving while intoxicated. In mid–October 1930, Boyce was scheduled to appear in court for drunk driving, a charge he confided to friends he would either beat or else take his own life. Concerned over his health, despondent over a broken romance, and above all fearful that he may have to do jail time, Boyce swallowed poison in the bedroom of his home at 532 North Edinburgh Street in Los Angeles on September 30, 1930.

mount film *Souls at Sea* (1937), Bowers told an old friend that he would just "sail away into the sunset."

On November 15, 1936, the 51-year-old actor rented a 16-foot sailboat from a concessionaire at the Santa Monica pier, scrawling an illegible name on the rental slip to conceal his identity. Hours later, the empty craft was found by lobster fisherman drifting a mile off the beach. The next day Bowers' sister notified

Boyce, Tommy

Born September 29, 1939, in Charlottesville, Virginia, Sidney Thomas Boyce first achieved musical success in 1959 when his song "Be My Guest" was recorded by Fats Domino on the Imperial label. The tune peaked at Number 8 on the *Billboard* chart. Though briefly pursuing a solo career during the early sixties, Boyce is best remembered for his collaborations with fellow songwriter Bobby Hart. In 1961 they penned two minor hits for Curtis Lee, "Pretty Little Angel Eyes" and "Under the Moon of Love," both produced by Phil Spector. The Boyce and Hart song "Come a Little Bit Closer" was recorded by Jay and the Americans in 1964 and rose to Number 3 on the pop charts. Number 1 status would be postponed until 1966 when producer Don Kirshner named the songwriting duo as musical directors for the NBC television program *The Monkees*.

A manufactured-for-television group, two of The Monkees (Davy Jones and Mickey Dolenz) had literally no musical experience. Nevertheless, the band's charisma combined with the songwriting talents of Boyce and Hart produced a series of *Billboard* chart topping hits. In addition to writing the show's theme song ("Hey, Hey We're the Monkees"), the team helped create The Monkees' sound with songs like "Last Train to Clarksville" (1966, No. 1), "(I'm Not Your) Steppin' Stone" (1966, No. 20), and "Valleri" (1968, No. 3). Before the show ended in 1968, Boyce and Hart were achieving success in their own right. In late 1967 their single "I Wonder What's She's Doing Tonight" peaked at Number 8. In 1975, the pair joined former Monkees Mickey Dolenz and Davy Jones to record the Capitol album *Dolenz, Jones, Boyce & Hart*.

Shortly after concluding a tour in support of the album, Boyce and Hart split up. Boyce moved to England in the late seventies and during the eighties produced tracks for Iggy Popp, Meatloaf, and some underground rock acts in London. Hart remained in the U.S. and worked for groups like the Partridge Family. On the morning of November 23, 1994, the 55-year-old songwriter shot himself in the head with a .38-caliber revolver in the home he shared with his wife in Nashville, Tennessee. The contents of several suicide notes found at the scene were not revealed by authorities. In all, Boyce and Hart are credited with having written more than 300 compositions.

Boyer, Charles

Boyer, the personification of Gallic charm in more than 70 motion pictures, was born in Figeac, France, on August 28, 1899. Educated at the Sorbonne in philosophy and in drama at the Paris Conservatory, he made his film debut in 1920 in director Marcel L'Herbier's *L'Homme du Large*. While continuing to make movies throughout the twenties, Boyer also appeared on the French stage. In Hollywood since 1931 (*The Magnificent Lie*), Boyer became the epitome of the "great lover" in a host of now classic films (*The Garden of Allah*, 1936; *Algiers*, 1938). Paired with some of the screen's most beautiful women (Loretta Young, Claudette Colbert, Marlene Dietrich, Greta Garbo, Hedy Lamarr), Boyer was an established star when World War II began in 1939. In an attempt to improve Franco-American cultural relations, the actor established the French Research Foundation in Los Angeles for which he was honored with a special Academy Award in 1942. In his career, Boyer was nominated for three Oscars (*Conquest*, 1937; *Algiers*, 1938; *Fanny*, 1961), received a special Tony Award in 1952, and in 1974 was voted Best Supporting Actor by the New York Film Critics for his performance in *Stavisky*. Throughout the fifties and sixties, Boyer acted on stage and in both U.S. and foreign films.

The actor was also among the first film stars to recognize the commercial and artistic possibilities of the new medium of television. In 1951 (with partners Dick Powell, David Niven, and Ida Lupino) Boyer co-founded Four Star Television and acted in many of the company's productions including *Four Star Playhouse*, and the NBC series *The Rogues* (1964–1965). Married to British-born actress Patricia Paterson since 1934, Boyer never recovered emotionally when their only son, Michael, committed suicide on September 23, 1965. On August 24, 1978, his wife of 44 years died at 67 of cancer in Scottsdale, Arizona. During her long decline, Boyer shielded Pat from the truth of her illness and was totally devoted to her. Two days after her death and two days before his 79th birthday, a despondent Boyer took a fatal dose of Seconal at a friend's home in Scottsdale on August 26, 1978. In a small private ceremony attended by industry friends John Forsythe, Loretta Young, and Irene Dunne, Boyer was buried next to his wife and son at Holy Cross Cemetery in Los Angeles.

FURTHER READING

Swindell, Larry. *Charles Boyer: The Reluctant Lover.* 1st ed. Garden City, N.Y.: Doubleday, 1983.

Boyer, Michael Charles

The only child of French actor Charles Boyer (see entry) and British actress Patricia Eliza Paterson was born on December 9, 1943. The elder Boyer, co-partner in the television production company Four Star Productions, hired his son as a dialogue director on his television show *The Rogues.* When it was cancelled in 1965, Michael Boyer became a promotion director for Valiant Records, a small firm owned by Four Star Productions. At his son's suggestion (and with Michael producing), Boyer recorded "Where Does Love Go?" for Valiant Records in early 1965. The famous actor was in Paris filming *Is Paris Burning?* when his wife phoned to tell him that their 21-year-old son had taken his life on September 23, 1965.

Michael Boyer, a gun collector with a history of playing Russian roulette, was at his Coldwater Canyon home at 1861 Heather Court when his fiancée, Marilyn Campbell, broke their engagement. According to Campbell, Boyer picked up a .38-caliber pistol and said, "I'm going to take care of something that has needed taking care of for a long time. I'm a loser and I always will be a loser. And I'm going to kill myself if I can't have you." Boyer left the living room and went alone into the den. Campbell related Boyer's threat to houseguest John Kirsch, who reassured her that his friend was "just acting." Moments later at 11:45 P.M., Boyer fatally shot himself in the temple.

FURTHER READING

Swindell, Larry. *Charles Boyer: The Reluctant Lover.* 1st ed. Garden City, N.Y.: Doubleday, 1983.

Boyle, Jack F.

Boyle, 40, had been out of vaudeville for nearly a decade when an auto accident two years before his suicide left him in constant pain. Two weeks prior to the act, Bobby Clark of the vaudeville comedy team of Clark & McCullough gave him $200 for an operation. Ironically, Paul McCullough (see entry) would fatally slit his throat and wrists in a Medford, Massachusetts, barber shop on March 23, 1936, shortly after being released from a mental institute. On May 26, 1930, Boyle knotted one end of a bed sheet around a bedpost in his room at the Hotel Endicott in New York City, the other around his throat, then rolled off the bed.

Bradbury, James, Jr.

In films since 1921 (*Bits of Life*), Bradbury was a supporting actor throughout the twenties and thirties. His credits include *Classmates* (1924), *The Little Giant* (1926), *Hellship Bronson* (1928), *Alibi* (1929), *The Rogue Song* (1930), *The Cisco Kid* (1931), *Gorilla Ship* (1932), *Helldorado* (1934), and *Mark of the Vampire*, director Tod Browning's 1935 remake of his silent classic *London After Midnight* (1927). In Los Angeles on June 21, 1936, the 41-year-old actor turned on the gas in a room he had rented for the day at 1008 West Eleventh Street and struck a match. Police found Bradbury in the hallway of the apartment house horribly burned about the face and body. According to authorities, Bradbury told them that a friend he had given $258 to for safekeeping had disappeared with the money. "It's a terrible way to commit suicide," he whispered to nurses moments before dying later that day at Georgia Street Receiving Hospital.

Brady, James Kelvin

Brady, an assistant business manager of the Paramount-Lasky Studios, endured a heart ailment for several years before deciding to end it all after a doctor informed him that he would be dead within 12 to 18 months. On May 9, 1929, the 41-year-old studio executive fired a bullet into his head at his home at 6276 Drexel Avenue in Los Angeles.

Brand, Marlon

Canadian-born actor Brand, 28, and his 25-year-old wife, Rebecca Jackson Mendoza, met in 1995 while auditioning for the Sydney, Australia-based production of *Miss Saigon*. They married the following year and had a daughter, but split up during a tour of Germany in 1997. Both continued to work together and were cast members of the *Show Boat* company when it began its Melbourne season at the Regent Theatre on December 30, 1998. Shortly after the show opened, Brand told management that he planned to quit the show and return to Canada with his 2-year-old daughter.

On January 25, 1999, the actor went to his wife's home in southeast Melbourne to discuss the matter. During the ensuing argument Brand stabbed her in the chest and fled the scene. Authorities, summoned by neighbors alarmed by Jackson Mendoza's cries for help, found the woman unconscious and bleeding from a partially severed carotid artery. Her life was saved by emergency surgery. Around 9:00 A.M. the next day, police found Brand's body hanging in a public toilet stall in Brady Road, Brantleigh, one kilometer from his wife's home in a park where he used to take his child to play.

Brando, Cheyenne

While in Tahiti filming the 1962 remake of *Mutiny on the Bounty*, screen legend Marlon Brando engaged in a highly publicized affair with Tarita Teriipia, a Polynesian beauty who appeared in the film. Their love child, Tarita Zumi Cheyenne Brando, was born in Tahiti on February 20, 1970. Three years later, Brando officially changed the girl's name to Cheyenne to underscore his lifelong interest in Native American culture. Cheyenne, largely neglected by her famous father whose contact

with her was limited to yearly visits, spent most of her childhood on the South Sea atoll of Teriaroa where Brando had large land holdings. Dropping out of school at 16 to become a model, the darkly sensual teenager was already a drug abuser and a fixture in the nightclub scene in Papeete, the capital of French Polynesia situated on the northwest coast of the island of Tahiti. While partying at a disco in Papeete, Cheyenne met and fell in love with Dag Drollet, a 23-year-old banker's son. The meeting ultimately set into motion a tragic chain of events that ended in Drollet's murder and Cheyenne's suicide.

Though Cheyenne eventually professed an undying hatred of her father, much of her life was spent in a desperate attempt to gain his attention. In 1989 Brando refused to let Cheyenne visit him in Toronto on the set of *The Freshman*. Hurt by Brando's neglect and still angry from a recent argument with Drollet, Cheyenne sped off in her brother's Jeep reaching speeds of 100 miles per hour on a Tahitian highway before slamming into a ditch. The high speed accident broke her jaw, partially ripped off an ear, and required 50 stitches to close other facial injuries. Brando brought her to Los Angeles for major reconstructive and plastic surgery. Afterward, Cheyenne recuperated in Tahiti with Drollet who, tired of his lover's jealous rages and drug abuse, sought to end the relationship even after learning that she was pregnant with his child. Not surprisingly, Cheyenne was briefly admitted to a psychiatric hospital and counseled on how to manage her "aggression and instability."

Concerned over his daughter's health, Brando convinced Cheyenne to have the baby in the United States. With a reluctant Drollet in tow, Cheyenne took up residence in her father's Mulholland Drive mansion in Los Angeles around May 1, 1990. Christian Brando, the actor's 32-year-old son by former wife Anna Kafshi, already shared the house with his father. In the early morning hours of May 16, 1990, a drunken Christian Brando confronted Drollet about the latter's habit of slapping around Cheyenne, now eight months pregnant. The argument ended abruptly when, after a brief struggle with Drollet, Christian fired a fatal pistol shot point-blank into the face of his half-sister's lover as she watched in horror. Marlon Brando, in another part of the house at the time of the shooting, attempted to resuscitate Drollet, but the young man was dead at the scene. Anxious to avoid being compelled to appear as a material witness against Christian at his murder trial, Cheyenne hastily returned to Tahiti. Severely depressed and addicted to drugs like LSD and Ecstasy, Cheyenne gave birth to Drollet's son, Tuki, one month after the murder. The infant was immediately sent to a detoxification unit.

Drollet's murder effectively shattered what little mental stability the young woman still possessed. As the international legal battle raged over her potential extradition to Los Angeles to appear at her brother's trial, Cheyenne overdosed on tranquilizers and antidepressants on November 1, 1990. While still recovering from the drug induced coma ten days later she tried to hang herself from a tree with a dog chain. After a judge on December 22, 1990, declared Cheyenne to be "mentally disabled" the prosecution cut a deal with Christian's attorneys in which he pled guilty to the lesser charge of manslaughter in exchange for a ten year prison sentence. Christian Brando was eventually paroled on January 10, 1996, after serving nearly five years in a California state penitentiary.

Drug addicted, chronically depressed, and unable to recover from the loss of Drollet, Cheyenne's subsequent life became a revolving door of psychiatric treatments in various mental health hospitals throughout the world. In April 1995, a court in Tahiti ruled the 25-year-old woman "mentally unfit" and awarded custody of her four-year-old son to her mother. On April 16, 1995, Easter morning, Cheyenne left the grounds of the Vaiami mental hospital to visit her family's compound eight miles away in Punaauia. She enjoyed a happy visit with her mother, brother, and son until they left the house to attend church ser-

vices and do errands. Alone in the home that afternoon, Cheyenne tied a rope around a ceiling beam in her bedroom, stepped up onto a chair, placed the noose around her neck, then kicked the chair away. Drollet's parents assumed custody of the orphaned child. In accordance with her final wishes, Cheyenne was interred alongside Dag Drollet in the family crypt in Faa'a, a small town outside Papeete.

FURTHER READING

Manso, Peter. *Brando: The Biography.* 1st ed. New York: Hyperion, 1994.

Brandstatter, Adolph "Eddie"

The film capital's most famous restaurateur, the foreign-born Brandstatter opened the famed Montmartre Cafe on Hollywood Boulevard near Highland Avenue in 1922. One of Hollywood's first night spots, movie people flocked to the trendy upstairs restaurant to see and be seen. Formerly employed in the famed restaurants of London, Paris, and New York before coming to Los Angeles, Brandstatter was the *maitre d'hotel* at the Victor Hugo around 1920 before opening Crillon Cafe near Eighth and Hill streets. A bad business investment in the late twenties closed the Montmartre Cafe, and shortly afterward the caterer was convicted of grand theft and placed on probation. Undaunted, Brandstatter and a partner opened yet another mecca for the film colony, Sardi's on Hollywood Boulevard near Vine Street. Stars and the fans who queued to see them packed the place until it burned down on November 1, 1936. Sardi's was rebuilt, but Brandstatter sold out his interest in April 1938. He dreamed of building a restaurant on Ventura Boulevard, the Bohemia Cafe, that would rival his past successes. The cafe never opened, but construction bills continued to pile up. Converting a former beauty shop on North Vine Street near Hollywood Boulevard into Brandstatter's Grill, he opened the modest restaurant shortly before the Christmas holidays in 1939.

On the night of January 17, 1940, Brandstatter complained of "not feeling well," kissed his wife, Helen, goodbye, and left the grill. At 3:30 the following morning, a restaurant employee drove Mrs. Brandstatter to her Moorish–style home at 4709 Norwich Avenue in Sherman Oaks. After a frantic search of the grounds failed to locate the missing 54-year-old Brandstatter, they checked the garage and found him still clutching the steering wheel of his car. He had placed a garden hose on the exhaust, ran its length up through the tonneau, and plugged up the window nearest him with his leather jacket. Authorities found numerous loan applications in the dead man's pockets.

Brannon, Robert R.

On April 1, 1962, the 33-year-old announcer–disc jockey for San Francisco radio station KYA was visiting his former wife and their three children in her home at 2205 Juniperberry Drive in Marinwood, California. A quarrel erupted after a few drinks, and Brannon pushed his ex-wife onto a bed and tried to choke her. He suddenly stopped, ran into the bathroom, and locked the door. When he failed to emerge, his former wife pried the door open with a kitchen knife and found him hanging by an electric wire from the rod on the shower door.

Breen, Benita

The 25-year-old vocalist (real name Mary Louise Breen) had been a featured singer with various "name" bands like Ted Weems, Henry King, and Bob Strong. On November 13, 1945, Breen's body was found in bed by her mother in their home at 915 Margate Terrace in Chicago. Police located an empty bottle of sleeping pills in the bathroom. While a coroner's jury was unable to determine whether the death was accidental or suicide, Breen had been treated for a nervous disorder five months before her death. Her father insisted that Breen had instead suffered from a heart condition.

Brennan, Louis Kelso

Passengers on the New York City subway at Seventy-second Street witnessed the 35-year-old vaudeville actor nervously pacing on an island platform prior to throwing himself in front of a northbound express train on September 22, 1916. Two cars passed over Brennan's body. Cards in the dead man's pocket led investigators to the Hotel Somerset where a friend who was waiting to pay Brennan a debt identified the mutilated body. Brennan, who had been in poor health, specialized in portraying Chinese characters.

Bridges, Florence see Southern, Dixie Lee

Bright, Oliver Jay

The sales manager for 23 years of the Levy-Page Company, a music equipment house in Norfolk, Virginia, Bright abruptly quit just weeks prior to the last day of his life, June 9, 1936. At 3:40 P.M. that day, Bright, 55, visited the City Hall Rifle Range in Norfolk, calmly asked for a .22-caliber target pistol, and announced to bystanders, "I want to see if I can shoot a bullseye." He fired two shots at the target then fired a third into his right temple. Bright died four hours later at St. Vincent's Hospital. In a note found afterward, the former sales manager explained that "business worries" had driven him to the act.

Brill, Peter

Brill, 24, was the manager of the Majestic Theatre in Fort Wayne, Indiana, before moving downstate to Gary two weeks prior to his death to assume similar duties in a theatre there managed by his brother. In the early morning hours of April 4, 1930, a quarrel between Brill and his wife Quillon, a 17-year-old burlesque dancer, erupted in her room at the Broadway Hotel that left the young woman wounded and her violent husband dead by his own hand. Confronted by Brill, who demanded to know her whereabouts following a performance two days before, Quillon informed her jealous husband that she was leaving him. Brill downed a glass of arsenic, pulled out a prop pistol reloaded with two live rounds, and shot his wife once in the leg. In their ensuing struggle over the gun, Brill discharged a fatal round into his chest.

Brody, Lee

Although appearing on Broadway (*Shoot the Works*, 1931; *The Straw Hat Review*, 1939), Brody was best known for her comedy stooge roles on radio programs like *The Danny Kaye Show* (where she was a cast member for a time), and as a sketch writer. Depressed over her divorce five years earlier from playwright John Murray, the 30 year old jumped to her death from her 15th floor apartment at 400 East Fifty-ninth Street in New York City on February 15, 1948. Contents of a suicide note were not released.

Brooke, Tyler

Brooke (born Victor Huge de Biere in New York in 1891) began his stage career there in 1912, and was the featured comedian in the 1925 production of *No, No, Nanette* at the Mason Theatre. In movies since 1927, the comedian notched up 39 films from 1931 to 1940, including appearances in the Ernest Lubitsch-directed *Bluebeard's Eighth Wife* (Paramount, 1938) and the 20th Century–Fox release *Alexander's Ragtime Band* (1938). Depressed over his failure to land studio work after several months of trying, the 52-year-old veteran actor asphyxiated himself in the garage of his Hollywood home at 4343 Laurel Canyon Boulevard on March 2, 1943. A suicide note directed Brooke's wife to the garage where she found her husband's body in a car rigged with a vacuum cleaner hose running from the rear exhaust pipe in through a window.

Brooks, Joseph

Perhaps best known for persuading General Lew Wallace to permit his novel *Ben Hur*

to be theatrically produced, Brooks, 67, was one of America's most successful and respected producers. In a career spanning 40 years, he personally managed some of the most famous actors of the American stage including Edwin Booth, Lillian Russell, Lawrence Parrett, and John McCullough. Suffering from depression and fearful of impending insanity, Brooks attempted to slit his wrists with a razor in September 1916. Less than two months later on November 27, 1916, the theatrical producer jumped to his death from the bathroom window of his eighth floor apartment at 140 West Seventy-ninth Street in New York City.

Brower, James "Jay" Delano

On June 21, 1943, the former band leader at San Francisco's El Capitan and Golden Gate theatres slashed an artery in his left arm with a razor blade in a hotel room at 1747 Cahuenga Boulevard in Los Angeles. The 46-year-old entertainer was apparently dejected over his recent discharge from the Navy. A suitcase filled with his press clippings was found near the body.

Brown, Susan

Financial worries prompted the 28-year-old cabaret singer to swallow a fatal dose of Lysol in her apartment at 1032 East Forty-third Street in Chicago on October 21, 1923.

Browne, John Barton

The advertising and promotion manager of the Ambassador Hotel in Los Angeles for 21 years, Browne is best remembered for co-writing (with H. Bedford-Jones) the *Saturday Evening Post* story "Garden of the Moon," which served as the basis for the 1938 Warner Bros. musical film of the same title directed by Busby Berkeley. It had been one year since he had retired from the Ambassador and only a month since his 37-year-old son had drowned in a pool accident in Hawaii when Browne, 55, ended his life. Returning home from a shopping trip on January 24, 1942, Browne's wife discovered her husband's pajama-clad body in the bedroom of their home at 2224 Ponet Drive in Los Angeles. Splayed across the bed, the writer held a .38-caliber revolver clutched in his right hand and a mirror in his left. Death came from a single shot through the mouth. A note addressed to his wife on a bedside table read: "I guess I skiied too hard for my age last Sunday because I feel pneumonia creeping on. But it was swell. Ask H. Bedford-Jones to finish our work. He will. Happily, I will leave enough to take care of all I care for despite taxes! Am badly choked up. Cheerio."

Bruckman, Clyde

In the early twenties, Bruckman (born September 20, 1894, in San Bernadino, California) was employed as a staff screenwriter at Warner Bros. when he met comedy genius Buster Keaton. The meeting began a long personal friendship and writing collaboration that produced some of the finest American comedy films of all time. With Keaton directing, Bruckman co-wrote the screenplays for *Our Hospitality* (1923), *Three Ages* (1923), *The Navigator* (1924), *Sherlock, Jr.* (1924), *Seven Chances* (1925), *The General* (1927, with Bruckman co-directing), and *The Cameraman* in 1928 directed by Edward Sedgwick. Bruckman solo directed his first film, the Monty Banks silent comedy *Horse Shoes*, in 1928. Based largely on his work with Keaton, Bruckman worked for some of the era's best film comics. He wrote the screenplay for Harold Lloyd's 1926 film *For Heaven's Sake*, and directed three of his features: *Welcome Danger* (1929), *Feet First* (1930), and *Movie Crazy* (1930). In 1935, Bruckman directed the W. C. Fields vehicle *The Man on the Flying Trapeze* for Paramount. Earlier in his career, he had directed Fields in the classic 1933 short *The Fatal Glass of Beer*. Bruckman also directed the Laurel & Hardy shorts *Putting Pants on Philip* (1927), *Call of the Cuckoos* (1927), and *Leave 'Em Laughing* (1928). His final directorial effort, *Spring Tonic*, was a 1935 screwball comedy starring Lew Ayres, Claire Trevor, and ZaSu Pitts.

From that date forward, Bruckman's alcoholism and deepening depression had reduced him to recycling gags to various studios that he had written for Keaton in the twenties. Just after Christmas in 1954, the 60-year-old former director borrowed a .45-caliber Colt automatic from Keaton on the pretext of using it for protection during an upcoming motor trip to Montana. At the time, Bruckman had been unemployed for a year since contributing gags to an Abbott and Costello feature. On January 4, 1955, he typed a note to his wife and drove to Bess Eiler's cafe on Wilshire Boulevard in Los Angeles. After finishing a meal for which he could not pay, Bruckman went into the men's room and shot himself in the head. In the note, he asked the "gentleman of the Santa Monica Police Department" to deliver his body to the Los Angeles County Medical Association or to a medical school for experimental purposes. "I have no money to pay for a funeral," the note read. In 1996, the television series *The X-Files* paid an homage of sorts to the veteran film man in an Emmy award winning episode, "Clyde Bruckman's Final Repose," starring Peter Boyle as an insurance salesman who could foresee the deaths of others.

Buchanan, Jack

The 6 foot, 4 inch contortionist was booked at the Cat and Fiddle at 1345 Central Avenue in Cincinnati, Ohio, when he committed suicide in his apartment next door to the nightclub on July 25, 1941. After Buchanan, 24, failed to appear for his show, the club's owner called and found the contortionist with his head covered in a blanket draped over an open gas range in the apartment. A note to the owner read: "Benny, I tried the bath tub, but it wouldn't work. Maybe I'll have better luck with the gas." In a separate note, Buchanan asked God's forgiveness for his act.

Buchanan, Roy

Buchanan, born the son of a Pentecostal preacher on September 23, 1939, in Ozark, Arkansas, was raised in Pixley, California, where he listened to gospel music at tent revivals and rhythm and blues on the radio. Encouraged by his father, Buchanan started taking guitar lessons when he was 7. By age 15, he left for Los Angeles to begin his musical apprenticeship with Johnny Otis, then with his own band, The Heartbeats. In 1957, Buchanan joined up with rockabilly artist Dale ("Suzie Q") Hawkins and made his record debut on Hawkins' single "My Babe." Buchanan left Hawkins in the late fifties and recorded with several groups (including the Hawks featuring future Band guitarist Robbie Robertson) before taking time off in 1963 to raise his family in Reston, Virginia.

After years of intermittently performing his brand of lightning fast country-blues on his Fender Telecaster in clubs around Washington, D.C., Buchanan rose to national prominence after *Rolling Stone* featured him in a 1971 article, and PBS aired a documentary on him called "The Best Unknown Guitar Player in the World." The publicity led to a record deal with Polydor, but after cutting five modestly successful albums for the company Buchanan remained dissatisfied with his recorded output. Though considered a "musician's musician" and lionized by musicians like Robertson, Eric Clapton, Jeff Beck, and John Lennon for his development of guitar harmonics, Buchanan never found his musical niche or achieved widespread popular appeal. By 1980, drugs and alcohol had begun to affect his work, and the guitarist dropped out of sight after drunkenly falling off a stage during a show in San Francisco. In 1985, Buchanan signed with independent label Alligator Records. Of the three albums he recorded for the label, *Dancing on the Edge* (1986) was considered the best.

Buchanan, 48, had performed at a free concert in New Haven, Connecticut, one week before when police in Fairfax, Virginia, responded to a domestic disturbance at his home on the night of August 14, 1988. Buchanan's wife, Judy, informed police that her husband, who had been drinking heavily, had just left the house. They picked up Buchanan several blocks away, and placed him under arrest after his wife admitted that she "could not handle him" in his present state. Booked into the Fairfax County Adult Detention Center on a charge of public drunkenness in the early morning hours of August 15, Buchanan appeared to be in good spirits. However, less than 45 minutes after his arrest, the guitarist's lifeless body was found suspended from the window bars of his cell by a noose fashioned from his own shirt. His larynx crushed, Buchanan failed to respond to attempts at resuscitation. Though his death was ruled a suicide, Buchanan's widow and close friends remain dubious that a large man like the guitarist would have taken his life in such a fashion. Buchanan was survived by his wife, seven children, and five grandchildren. The guitarist is buried at the Columbia Cemetery in Arlington, Virginia.

Buckland, Wilfred, Sr.

Born in 1866, Buckland was a stage director for David Belasco before entering films in 1914 as an art director for Famous Players–Lasky. As the first *bona fide* art director in the motion picture industry, he was credited with widening the scope of films by freeing them from the scenic limitations of the stage. An innovator, Buckland was the first to build architectural settings for films, and introduced artificial lighting into movies through the use of klieg lights. Buckland, often uncredited, served as the art director for several films directed by Cecil B. DeMille. These include: *The Squaw Man* (1914 and 1918 versions), *The Call of the North* (1914), *The Ghost Breaker* (1914), *The Virginian* (1914), *The Warrens of Virginia* (1915), *The Trail of the Lonesome Pine* (1916), *The Devil Stone* (1917), *We Can't Have Everything* (1918), *For Better, For Worse* (1919), and *Adam's Rib* (1923).

At 60, Buckland reached the pinnacle of his phenomenal career as "Hollywood's first art director" by creating the castle setting for the 1922 Douglas Fairbanks epic *Robin Hood*, directed by Allan Dwan. Buckland was 80 years old and in poor health when he decided that he could not chance leaving the care of his 36-year-old mentally ill son, Wilfred Buckland, Jr., to strangers. In 1940, shortly after the death of his mother, the younger Buckland suffered a mental breakdown. The next year, the one-time Princeton student was committed to the Camarillo State Hospital for the Insane. Discharged, he suffered a second breakdown in 1944. In early July 1944, Buckland, Jr., quit his job in a studio prop department because of "increasing nervousness."

On July 18, 1944, the elder Buckland entered his son's bedroom in the home they shared at 2035 Pinehurst Avenue in Hollywood, fired one shot from a .32-caliber Mauser automatic pistol into the sleeping man's head, then turned the gun on himself. The art director died in an ambulance en route to a hospital. In a note disposing of his possessions and naming William DeMille, the producer-brother of former colleague Cecil B. DeMille, as executor of his estate, Buckland wrote, "I am taking Billy with me."

Buckley, Helen Curry

Billed onstage and in the 1922 film *The Blue Flame* under her maiden name, Helen Curry, the actress married Frederick R. Buckley, then a reader at the Vitagraph studios, in 1916. In 1922, Buckley won the coveted O'Henry prize for his short story "Gold Mounted Guns," and from that date on made a lucrative living as a writer of Westerns. Sometime during the evening of November 14, 1931, while the couple was dining with friends, the former actress lifted her husband's .45-caliber automatic revolver out of his coat and hid it in their car. Seconds after they pulled into the driveway of their Newton Avenue home in Norwalk, Connecticut, around 2:00 the next morning, Frederick Buckley left the parked car to raise the garage door. Alone on the passenger's side of the front seat, the 35-year-old woman shot herself in the right temple, the bullet exiting the top of her head and tearing a hole in the roof of the car. As the

writer was at a loss to explain his wife's motive for suicide, the local chief of police ruled that the act was apparently done on the spur of the moment while she was in a melancholy mood.

Burton, Sam J.

On May 6, 1920, after taking three encore bows at Chicago's Studebaker Theatre for his two minute role as "Old Billiken" in the musical comedy *Sometime*, the 70-year-old veteran actor returned to his dressing room. In apparent ill health and frustrated over the increasingly smaller roles offered him, Burton knotted one end of the cord of his dressing gown around his neck, the other to a steam pipe, and stepped off a chair. A note in his vest pocket read: "If anything happens to me, please notify Mark Duncan. He is with the Chicago Talking Machine Company, 12 North Michigan Avenue." Known as "Si Perkins" in the late 1890s, Burton once headed up his own company and played opposite Lillian Russell. Days before taking his life, the actor had asked a friend if drowning was an easy death and was told no. Several thousands of dollars were found among Burton's effects.

Bustros, Dany

Lebanon's leading belly dancer, Bustros, 39, successfully combined traditional dance with Western dance forms such as modern and flamenco. Born in Beirut on October 8, 1959, she achieved acclaim for her dance revue "Boulevard de la Cite" in 1991. In 1993 she made her acting debut in the French play *Encore Une Minute*. Two years later, she starred in a musical with Lebanese singer-composer Melhem Barakat. In 1994, Bustros witnessed the drowning death of her 16-year-old son, George. Unable to emotionally recover from the tragedy and facing financial problems, the dancer twice tried to take her life. In the weeks leading up to her successful attempt, a close friend of the entertainer frequently saw her in church. When asked what was wrong,

Bustros replied, "I need God." Late in the evening of December 26, 1998, Bustros had an emotional fit, spoke of suicide, then locked herself in the bedroom of her home in the coastal town of Adma, 20 miles north of Beirut. Sometime later, Bustros' companion, Nasser Darrar, found her lying on the bedroom floor in a pool of blood from a gunshot wound to the head. The beloved dancer spent 21 hours in a hospital on life support before dying of a brain hemorrhage the next day.

Butterell, Sam

A philosophy student in Queens' College at Cambridge University, Butterell, 20, was a lighting technician with the Footlights student theatre group. Exhausted from working on the company's production of the pantomime *Peter Pan*, and worried about his studies and meager grant, Butterell attached wires to his chest and plugged them into a wall socket via a battery timer before going to sleep on November 25, 1992. The student was found the next morning fatally electrocuted when the timer engaged at 8:00 A.M.

Cady, Jerome

Cady (born in West Virginia in 1904) worked for several Los Angeles daily newspapers before becoming one of the top screenwriters at 20th Century–Fox. His screen credits include *Guadalcanal Diary* (1943), *The Purple Heart* (1944), *Forever Amber* (1947), and the classic James Stewart film *Call Northside 777* (1948). On November 8, 1948, less than one week after suffering a severe heart attack, Cady, 44, was entertaining some friends aboard his yacht, the *Harp*, moored in Avalon Bay off Santa Catalina Island in California. According to witnesses, Cady entered the cruiser's galley, poured sleeping pills into his hand, and gulped them down with a glass of water. As the dying screenwriter writhed in agony on his bunk, he kept moaning, "I did it. I did it. I did it." Shortly before dying Cady instructed a friend to call his wife and tell her that he had just committed suicide.

Calvert, Marguerite

Calvert, a popular 24-year-old vaudeville dancer and violinist, was married for less than a year to W. D. Harris, a New York-based automobile tire dealer, when she took her life in San Francisco's Palace Hotel on October 22, 1922. Days before arriving at the hotel following an exhausting cross-country car trip, the pair had visited the grave of Calvert's brother in Portland, Oregon. At the hotel, Calvert's depression and fatigue were exacerbated by a quarrel with her husband over his attentions to other women. Good-naturedly teased by another couple in attendance, Calvert burst into hysterics, threatened to take her life, seized a revolver, and locked herself in the bathroom. When a night clerk opened the door, the alarmed spectators found the violinist lying on the bathroom floor with the muzzle of the gun pressed against her heart. Ignoring their pleas not to harm herself, Calvert pulled the trigger.

Cammell, Donald Seton

Though Cammell directed only four films in a 26 year career, cinema historians have already begun to laud the visual complexity, radical editing style, and themes of human sexuality and identity that inform his work. The elder son of writer Charles Richard Cammell and Iona Macdonald, Cammell was born in Outlook Tower by the Edinburgh Castle in Scotland on January 17, 1934. Labelled an art prodigy at 3, he attended the Royal Academy School of Art on a scholarship and studied in Florence, Italy, with artist Pietro Annigoni. Upon returning to London in the fifties, Cammell set up a portrait studio in Flood Street, Chelsea, which soon became the center of salon life. There he met Greek actress Maria Andipa (*From Russia with Love*, 1963; *High Wind in Jamaica*, 1965) whom he later married and divorced. In 1967, Cammell wrote the screenplays for two forgettable British films, *The Touchables* and *Duffy*. However, in 1970 Cammell, with cinematographer Nicholas Roeg (*The Man Who Fell to Earth*,

1973), co-directed *Performance*. The film, starring Cammell's friend Mick Jagger, was praised by some as capturing the spirit of sixties counterculture.

After *Performance*, Cammell moved to Los Angeles where he wrote unproduced screenplays for seven years before directing his first Hollywood feature in 1977, *The Demon Seed*, starring Julie Christie as a woman impregnated by a computer. Cammell waited ten years to again direct. *White of the Eye*, a 1987 British film starring David Keith as a misogynist serial killer, was praised for its dazzling cinematic technique, but proved a box office disappointment. In 1995, Cammell completed his final film, *The Wild Side*, starring Christopher Walken and Joan Chen. The movie was never released theatrically, but without Cammell's consent was re-edited by the producers and shown on cable television sans his director's credit. Seemingly depressed over his career, the 62-year-old director shot himself in his Hollywood Hills home on April 24, 1996. At the time of his death Cammell was married to collaborator China Kong.

FURTHER READING

Chang, Chris. "Cinema Sex Magick: The Films of Donald Cammell." *Film Comment*, 32(4):14–19, 83, July–Aug. 1996.

Canada, Tressie J.

Canada spent 30 years touring and acting in stock and repertoire with her husband, Wilson R. Todd, before settling in Ashtabula, Ohio, around 1929. When the couple suffered financial reversals Todd left her, taking their young son with him. Destitute and depressed, the 52-year-old ex-actress travelled to Erie, Pennsylvania, where she asked an elevator boy to take her to the top of the Erie Trust building on May 29, 1934. Suspecting that she meant to harm herself, he refused. Undeterred, Canada registered at the Hotel Lawrence and, moments after being shown to her 11th floor room, plunged from the window, narrowly missing two men standing on the sidewalk

below. A note in the room addressed "Mr. Undertaker" read, "Please put me in the cheapest casket you have and my husband will pay for it when he comes." When he could not be located and her relatives were unable to pay funeral costs, friends of the dead woman took up a fund to prevent her from being sent to a potter's grave.

Canow, William

William B. Schultz, 55, was proprietor of an amusement park at Gardner Lake in Norwich, Connecticut, where 65-year-old William Canow had operated a concession for four years. The two men were on friendly terms, but on August 16, 1928, an argument between them in Canow's lakefront store led to murder-suicide. Canow, behind the store's counter, grabbed a single-barreled shotgun and shot Schultz in the stomach. He then went into a little room at the back of the store where he lived, reloaded the gun, and blasted off the top of his head. Schultz died hours later at the Backus Hospital in Norwich.

Capucine

Born Germaine Lefebvre in Toulon, France, on January 6, 1933, the actress known as Capucine rebelled against a stiflingly strict Catholic upbringing by running off to Paris at 17½ to become a fashion model. Renaming herself Capucine (French for "nasturtium"), she married an actor over her parents' objections, and divorced him after only eight months. While still a model, she made her screen debut in Jacques Becker's 1949 study of postwar Parisian youth, *Les Rendez-Vous de Juillet*. She also appeared in two other fifties French films, *Bertrand Coeur de Lion* and *Frou-Frou*. Capucine, a 5 foot, 7 inch beauty with facial features likened to those of an early Picasso, was earning the top modelling fee of $75 an hour in Paris when she moved to New York in the late fifties to improve her English and garner higher modelling fees. Film producer Charles K. Feldman discovered her in a restaurant and brought her to Hollywood for

CAPUCINE— A French model who took the name of a flower, Capucine made her Hollywood acting debut in *Song Without End*, a 1960 bio-pic of Hungarian composer Franz Liszt. In 1962 she played a New Orleans prostitute kept by lesbian bordello manager Barbara Stanwyck in *A Walk on the Wild Side*. In the seventies Capucine worked almost exclusively in European films. Following months of depression, the 57-year-old actress leapt from the window of her eighth floor apartment in Lausanne, Switzerland, on March 17, 1990.

a screen test. The test, directed by actor-director Gregory Ratoff, resulted in a $150 a week contract with the Famous Artists Agency. Intensive English lessons and drama classes with Ratoff prepared Capucine for her first Hollywood screen role as "Princess Carolyne" in *Song Without End*, a 1960 Columbia bio-pic of Hungarian composer Franz Liszt starring Dirk Bogarde. In quick succession she made *North to Alaska* (1960), *A Walk on the Wild Side* (1962), and *The Lion*, a 1962 British film starring William Holden shot on-location in Kenya. During the shooting, Holden fell in love with Capucine and left his wife, Brenda Marshall.

After appearing opposite Peter Sellers in the 1964 Blake Edwards comedy hit *The Pink Panther*, Capucine made another film with Holden that same year, *The Seventh Dawn*. Although the affair ultimately cooled, Capucine remained friendly with the actor, and was often bedside with him during his numerous hospitalizations for alcoholism. When Holden was found dead on November 16, 1981, the result of an alcohol-induced injury, he left her $50,000 in his will. From the mid-sixties through her final film in 1983, *The Curse of the Pink Panther*, Capucine worked primarily in Europe. Her European films include *Fellini Satyricon* (Italian/French, 1969), *Soleil*

Rouge/Red Sun (French/Spanish, 1971), *Rittrato di Borghese in Nero* (Italian, 1978), and *Da Dunkerque alla Vittoria* (Italian/French/Spanish, 1979). Seen occasionally on American television (*Murder She Wrote*), Capucine did a 1980 guest shot on the ABC television series *Hart to Hart* featuring Robert Wagner and Stefanie Powers as a husband and wife investigative team. Powers was Holden's last great love, and was also bequeathed $50,000 in his will.

Since finishing her last film in 1983, the 57-year-old actress had lived as a near recluse with only three cats for company on the eighth floor of an exclusive apartment house in Lausanne, Switzerland. Following months of depression, the actress jumped to her death from the window of her apartment on March 17, 1990.

FURTHER READING

Thomas, Bob. *Golden Boy: The Untold Story of William Holden.* New York: St. Martin's Press, 1983.

Carew(e), Arthur Edmund

Carew (born in Trebizond, Armenia, on December 30, 1884) came to America as a child and, after appearing on the stage for nearly a decade, came to Hollywood in 1919. In that year, he appeared in eight films including director Tod Browning's *Bonnie, Bonnie Lassie*, the Constance Talmadge feature *Romance and Arabella*, and *The World and Its Woman* starring fellow suicide Lou Tellegen (see entry). In the twenties and thirties, Carew's darkly intense features and suavely villainous demeanor made him a natural for melodramas and horror films. His performances in these genres included *The Ghost Breaker* (1922), *The Phantom of the Opera* (1925, as "The Persian"), *The Cat and the Canary* (1927), *The Claw* (1927), *Doctor X* (1932), and *Mystery of the Wax Museum* (1933).

Shortly after appearing opposite Warner Oland in *Charlie Chan's Secret* in 1936, Carew suffered a paralytic stroke and spent eight months recovering in a Los Angeles rest home.

On April 22, 1937, the 52-year-old actor took a taxi to an auto camp in Santa Monica and registered in a cabin there under the name "Harry Carter." Less than one hour later, Carew shot himself in the temple with a .45-caliber pistol. In separate notes, he asked the authorities not to seek to discover his true identity, and in another left $31 in cash to the camp owner in "payment for damages to the cabin."

Carlton, Rex

An independent producer-screenwriter of low-budget films (*The Brain That Wouldn't Die*, 1958; *Blood of Dracula's Castle*, 1967), Carlton, 53, was found by a neighbor dead of a gunshot wound in the water-filled bathtub of his West Los Angeles apartment at 8400 Sunset Boulevard on May 6, 1968. An Italian automatic pistol was found near the tub next to a handwritten suicide note. In the note, addressed to his brother, Carlton indicated that "things weren't going right" for him. The producer, who had been ill for some time, had made a previous attempt at suicide. At the time of his death, Carlton was a producer for East-West International Pictures, which had recently released the Broderick Crawford film *The Fakers*, and was president of Laurel Films in New York and Rex Carlton Productions in Los Angeles.

Carmall, Francis J.

Carmall, 60, had a magic act in vaudeville, but unable to find roles in the theatre, had in recent years taken work as a weaver in Worcester, Massachusetts. On April 14, 1926, the depressed former vaudevillian waited until his wife left their home at 521 Park Avenue and then turned on a gas range.

Carnevale, Luigi

A composer of 12 symphonies and symphonic poems, Carnevale, 39, organized the Pennsylvania Philharmonic Orchestra in 1940. Deeply distressed over a recent separation from his wife and two daughters, the conductor was visiting the Washington, D.C., home of a friend, Jerome M. Reimers, vice-president of the Columbia Opera Association, when he took his life on April 16, 1949. The two were preparing for a walk when Reimers noticed the kitchen door was closed. He opened it to discover Carnevale's body riddled with multiple self-inflicted stab wounds from a butcher knife lying on the floor in a pool of blood. In a note to his friend scribbled on a sheet of music paper, Carnevale wrote: "God forgive me for spoiling the Easter."

Carpenter, Donald Richard

Carpenter (born March 16, 1931, in Berkeley, California) published his first novel, *Hard Rain Falling*, in 1965 to wide critical acclaim. Characterized by uncompromising realism, Carpenter's novels were often set on the West Coast and peopled with social outcasts (*Blade of Light*, 1966; *Getting Off*, 1971). During a ten year period in the sixties and seventies, Carpenter worked as a television and movie scriptwriter while living intermittently at the Chateau Marmont hotel in Hollywood. In 1973, he co-produced and wrote the script for *Payday*, a highly regarded independent film directed by Daryl Duke that starred Rip Torn as a country singer. Carpenter used his experiences as a Hollywood insider to produce his most well known work, a triptych of novels about show business: *The True Life Story of Jody McKeegan* (1974), *A Couple of Comedians* (1979), and *Turnaround* (1981).

Productive during the eighties (he published three novels with North Point Press during the period), Carpenter's literary output ceased as the nineties began. Severely ill with diabetes and other health problems, the 64-year-old writer fatally shot himself in the chest with a 9mm pistol in his Mill Valley, California, home on July 27, 1995. Carpenter had recently finished a manuscript, *Fridays at Enrico's*, a semi-autobiographical novel about the lunches he shared with writers Richard Brautigan, Curt Gentry, and Evan S. Connell at the North Beach cafe in the mid-seventies.

Carr, Joseph L.

Carr, owner of the Montrose Theatre in Burbank, California, was found on the floor of one of its washrooms on July 19, 1930, shortly after swallowing a tumbler full of cyanide. In a note to his wife found on the 60-year-old theatre man's body, Carr blamed himself for being a failure, and gave directions for his funeral and suggestions for the future conduct of the theatre, which had reportedly just endured a financially ruinous season.

Carroll, James

A native of North Manchester, Indiana, Carroll performed in the band of the Dodson World Fair show when it played in Akron, Ohio, on July 14, 1938. That afternoon, the 39-year-old musician took a taxi to the High Level bridge located 20 miles north of Akron, asked the driver to wait, and leaving his glasses as security for the fare, walked out onto the bridge. A passing motorist witnessed Carroll jumping 90 feet to his death into the Cuyahoga River. The popular carnival musician was evidently depressed and upset over a letter he had received a few days before from his brother who was travelling with a circus in Tennessee.

Casady, Weir

A former theatre operator with Ackerman Harris and Charlie Thall, the 50-year-old Casady was employed as a Berkeley sales manager for a vacuum cleaner company when he shot himself through the temple in his home at 2464 Prince Street in Oakland, California, on August 21, 1932. He died shortly afterward at Alta Bates Hospital. According to a friend, Casady was despondent over ill health.

Cassady, Eddy

Cassady, once billed in vaudeville as "the Boy from Laughland," was an original member of Dumont's Minstrels, a show business institution in Philadelphia. Since the "death" of minstrelsy, however, the performer credited with having made the song "Pony Boy" a smash had fallen on hard times. On March 12, 1940, the caretaker of Cassady's apartment house smelled gas outside the locked door of the minstrel's fourth floor room while attempting to deliver a letter from the County Relief Board. The police were notified, forced the door, and entered the gas-filled room to find Cassady's body on the floor surrounded by pictures of the performer in his prime pasted on every wall.

Caux, Claude

A native of Abbeville, France, and a one-time colleague of mime Marcel Marceau, Caux, 57, taught drama for 17 years at the University of Houston where his works were performed at the Wortham Theater and at the Houston Ballet. On July 22, 1991, Caux and local actress Mary Avery Chovanetz quarreled in Memorial Park over her refusal to return his advances. The mime stabbed Chovanetz 15 times in the chest, abdomen, and legs as witnesses looked on. Caux then stabbed himself in the stomach and begged onlookers to "please let us die." Chovanetz died at the scene. The professor survived and was freed on $50,000 bond when he again attempted suicide on October 7, 1991. Caux's wife discovered him on the patio of their Houston home with a puncture wound in his stomach. A note written in French informing his family that he was going to kill himself was found at the scene. Caux again recovered. However, on January 10, 1992, Caux's body was found by his wife and son hanging from the staircase leading to the second floor of his condominium in the 5300 block of Richmond in southwest Houston.

Cavanaugh, Earl

Formerly of the vaudeville team "Cavanaugh and McBride," the 33-year-old comedian had been out of work for four months when, on September 16, 1926, he sent his wife and their 6-year-old daughter to a birthday supper at a local restaurant in the girl's honor. Alone in their apartment at the Hotel Alpine in New York City, Cavanaugh brooded over the fact that he did not have enough money to buy his daughter a present or to visit his dying mother in Chicago. When wife and child returned hours later, they found his pajama-clad body face down in bed. Cavanaugh had strangled himself by tying a valise strap around his neck and fastening the other end to the bedpost. Cavanaugh's wife denied that he had killed himself, insisting instead that the unemployed vaudevillian had died accidentally while rehearsing a new comedy skit called "Home Again!" in which an estranged husband tries unsuccessfully to hang himself with his belt.

Charle, Tamara

Charle, 26, a vivacious French-Russian nightclub singer also known as "Tamara Zoya" and "Tamara Stephan," appeared in Albany, New York, in the musical shows *The Cat and the Fiddle* and *Music in the Air*. On July 9, 1941, in that city, Charle shot her 4-year-old daughter (born after a separation from her husband) through the heart with a .22-caliber pistol in their room at the Ten Eyck Hotel. The child's body was later found on the bed surrounded by pillows and dolls. Foiled in the attempt to take her own life when the gun jammed, the despondent singer walked the streets of Albany for more than 12 hours before returning to the hotel, clearing the gun, then firing a bullet into her own heart. A note found at the scene read: "To Whom it May Concern — I wanted to go with the baby, but after the first bullet the gun jammed. I then bought potassium ferricyanide. That didn't work either. There is only one way." An autopsy revealed no trace of the poison. In a separate letter to her estranged husband apparently referring to a telephone conversation, the singer wrote: "I will not annoy you any longer after what happened last night."

Charters, Spencer

Charters (born March 25, 1875, in Duncannon, Pennsylvania) appeared in a total of 479 plays (including 11 years in George M. Cohan comedies) before trying his hand at film acting in 1923 with a role in *Little Old New York*. In 1930, Charters relocated to Hollywood to recreate on film his role in the Broadway smash *Whoopee*. During the next dozen years he appeared in character roles in some 150 movies including *Mr. Deeds Goes to Town* (1936), *Professor Beware* (1938), *The Hunchback of Notre Dame* (1939), and the 1941 Humphrey Bogart classic *High Sierra*. In ill health and despondent over the death of his wife the year before, the 66-year-old actor unsuccessfully tried to gas himself to death in the bathroom of his Hollywood home one week prior to actually taking his life on January 25, 1942. On that day, Charters' pajama and robe–clad body was found in the garage of his home at 1745 N. Vista Street lying near the exhaust pipe of his car. On the running board was a bottle of poison, and in the bathroom an empty bottle of sleeping pills.

Chavez, Dolores Lila Bettua

Chavez, a 24-year-old former cigarette girl and photographer at New York City's Club Zanzibar, had a stormy marriage with Eduardo Chavez, a nightclub orchestra leader at the China Doll on Broadway. In 1943, she stabbed the maestro and he languished for weeks near death in a New York hospital before recovering. On the afternoon of May 13, 1946, a bitter argument erupted between the pair in their ninth floor apartment at the Hotel St. James at 109 West Forty-sixth Street. According to the orchestra leader, he emerged from the bathroom to find Chavez perched on the window sill, but could not catch her as she fell to the courtyard below. A passerby told detectives that he saw the man attempt to pull the woman back into the apartment.

Chic, Charles J.

The Philadelphia-born Chic (real name Schick) came to Los Angeles in his youth, attended the University of Southern California, and began his motion picture career in 1918 as a prop boy at Universal. Serving his film apprenticeship as an assistant director under William Duncan and W. S. Van Dyke, he moved to Metro-Goldwyn-Mayer in 1927 and by 1938 had worked his way up the studio ladder to become a $1,000 a week production manager. Although active in his work, the 48 year old had recently worried over his poor health. On April 26, 1941, Chic's Japanese servant girl found a brief note addressed to her after arriving at her employer's Beverly Hills home at 151½ Bedford Drive. It read: "I have killed myself. First call Helen Lawson [his secretary]. If you can't get her call Rachel Chic [his ex-wife]. I thought that the garage would be too noisy, so I'm near the lot in Beverlywood." Police found the production manager's body under his limousine at a dead-end road at South Beverly Drive and Oakmore Street in Beverly Hills. Chic had fashioned a death mask out of a rubber hot water bottle by slashing its bottom and stretching the opening tightly over his face. Next, he fitted the funnel end of the container over the car's exhaust pipe after starting the motor.

Chubbuck, Christine

Eight days before Chubbuck, 29, earned the distinction of committing the first televised suicide, she told a colleague at WXLT-TV in Sarasota, Florida, that "I had this nifty idea. I thought I'd bring it [a gun] to work and blow myself away during my talk show." On July 15, 1974, the station's public affairs director and host of the daily morning news and talk program *Suncoast Digest* made good her threat. Moments after a mechanical problem prevented the running of a film clip during the morning show, the camera cut back to the broadcaster. Chubbuck looked into the lens and said, "In keeping with Channel 40's policy of bringing you the latest in blood and guts and in living color you are going to see another first — an attempted suicide." She drew a .38-caliber Smith & Wesson from a shopping bag behind her desk and shot herself behind the right ear. On Chubbuck's bloodstained desk colleagues found a dummy script written by her in the third person that began, "Today Chris Chubbuck shot herself during a live broadcast." The dummy script continued with a description of her ambulance trip to the hospital and a medical update on her condition. Chubbuck died 14 hours after the televised incident. According to the family, she had been terribly depressed and under the care of a psychiatrist.

Churchill, Frank E.

Churchill (born October 20, 1901, in Rumford, Maine) planned to study medicine before beginning his musical career at 15 as a professional piano player in Ventura, California. After working his way through the University of California by moonlighting with an orchestra, Churchill signed a contract with Walt Disney studios in 1930. During the remaining 12 years of his life he composed some of the best-loved and most enduring film music of all time. In 1933, Churchill wrote the music to "Who's Afraid of the Big Bad Wolf?" for the cartoon *The Three Little Pigs*. Though earning an Academy Award for his music in *Dumbo* (1941), the composer is best remembered for Disney's 1937 masterpiece *Snow White*, which featured Churchill's music to the songs "Someday My Prince Will Come," "Heigh-Ho," "Whistle While You Work," and "Silly Song."

Despondent over failing health, the 40-year-old composer committed suicide at his "Paradise Ranch" on U.S. Highway 99 near Castaic, California, in the pre-dawn hours of May 14, 1942. Churchill's body, shot once through the heart and lying on top of a hunting rifle and a rosary, was found by his wife and ranch manager after they were awakened by the gun's report. In a note to his wife, Churchill wrote: "Dear Carolyn — My nerves have completely left me. Please forgive me for this awful act. It seems the only way I can cure myself. Frank." Shortly after his death, the Disney film *Bambi* was released featuring Churchill's final work — the music to "Love Is a Song That Never Ends."

Clark, Frank

President of the music company bearing his name, Clark, 33, was best known on Tin Pan Alley as the song "booster" who made the George Meyer and Al Bryan tune "Brown Eyes" into a hit. The music publisher had been ill for several months and suffering from acute insomnia when, on April 13, 1926, he waited for his wife to leave her parents' Chicago home at 6367 Sheridan Road on an errand before shooting himself in the head.

Clermont, Hannibal N.

Clermont was formerly the head of Hannibal N. Clermont Photoplays, Inc., until a reorganization of the company on January 21, 1921, effectively removed him as president. Two days later, Clermont (age unreported) waited until his wife and 12-year-old son went to church before placing a revolver to the right side of his head and then pulling the trigger in the front room of their Hollywood home at 7159½ Sunset Boulevard.

Cobain, Kurt Donald

Cobain, guitarist and chief creative force behind the band Nirvana, has been called the "John Lennon of his generation" for his ability to seemingly read the minds of his disaffected Generation X listeners. The son of a cocktail waitress and an auto mechanic, Cobain was born in Hoquaim, Washington, on February 20, 1967. When he was 6 months old, the family moved to nearby Aberdeen, a logging town 70 miles southwest of Seattle. As a child, Cobain showed more interest in art and music than sports. This preference distanced him from a macho father while drawing him closer to the mother who nurtured these interests. Cobain was diagnosed as hyperactive and given the amphetamine Ritalin to control his behavior.

His parents' divorce in 1975 was a pivotal moment in the 8-year-old's life. As a custody battle raged, Cobain became increasingly antisocial and withdrawn. He wrote on his bedroom wall: "I hate Mom, I hate Dad, Dad hates Mom, Mom hates Dad, it simply makes you want to be sad." Cobain lived with his mother for a year, but she packed him off to stay with his father and new wife when she was unable to control the youngster. Cobain fared little better in his new environment. Pressured by his father to participate in school athletics, Cobain would purposely fail. Berated as a "faggot" by the school's jock population, he was routinely beaten. Cobain seldom fought back, but refused to back down. Rarely speaking, he started getting drunk in the seventh grade and began smoking pot in the ninth grade. As a teen, Cobain's rage expressed itself in vandalism. He was once arrested for spray painting cars with slogans like "Abort Christ" and "God is Gay."

Cobain's mother tossed him out of the house when he informed her that he had quit high school to pursue his music. The guitarist-songwriter stayed with friends and slept under bridges. In 1985, Cobain was playing in punk bands like Fecal Matter in Olympia, Washington, when he met bass player Chris (Krist) Novoselic. The duo formed a band called Stiff Woodies (later Skid Row) before settling on the name Nirvana in 1987. Now based in Seattle, Cobain, Novoselic, and various drummers recorded the songs that eventually became Nirvana's first album, *Bleach*. Recorded in six days at a cost of $606.17, *Bleach* was released to enthusiastic reviews in June 1989 on the Seattle-based independent label Sub Pop Records. Drummer Dave Grohl joined the band in the fall of 1990. The album's success, bolstered by nonstop touring, brought Nirvana to the attention of a major label, DGC, which signed them for $287,000 in 1991. The release of the album *Nevermind* in the fall of 1991 established Nirvana as *the* major alternative rock band. Be-

hind the hit single "Smells Like Teen Spirit" and its video played relentlessly on MTV, the album reached Number 1 on the charts and sold nearly ten million copies worldwide.

To Cobain's horror, the same people who used to beat him up in high school were now rabid Nirvana fans sporting the group's signature "grunge" look of flannel shirts and ripped jeans. Cobain was clearly uneasy with being "the voice of his generation." A manic depressive with a long history of chronic stomach pain, the guitarist became more deeply involved with drugs, especially heroin.

On February 24, 1992, Cobain married fellow addict Courtney Love, leader of the feminist punk-rock band Hole. Their daughter, Frances Bean, was born drug-free on August 18, 1992, amid allegations that Love had used heroin during her pregnancy. Rumors of Cobain's drug dependence were fuelled by the cancellation of the band's summer concert tour in 1992, although the guitarist asserted that he was suffering from recurring stomach pain. To sustain the band's momentum, DCG released *Insecticide*, a compilation of Nirvana tunes, in late 1992. The band's next album, *In Utero*, debuted at Number 1 upon its release in September 1993. Success, however, was beginning to wear on Cobain.

On January 8, 1994, Nirvana played the final show of their American tour at Seattle's Center Arena. Introducing the hit song "Smells Like Teen Spirit," Cobain told the sellout crowd: "We have to play this next song — it's in our contract. This is the song that ruined our lives and ruined Seattle and ruined your lives, too." In February 1994, Nirvana embarked on a disastrous European tour to promote *In Utero*. Depressed, drug addicted, and in constant stomach pain, Cobain was unable to sustain the rigorous tour schedule. The final dates of the tour were cancelled and he joined Courtney Love in Rome to rest. On March 4, 1994, Love found Cobain on the floor of their hotel room turning blue from a massive overdose of the tranquilizer Rohypnol. After penning a suicide note, Cobain had washed more than 50 tablets of the drug down with a bottle of champagne. He survived after spending more than 20 hours in a coma. The suicide attempt was officially ruled an "accident."

Following an argument with Cobain on March 18, 1994, at their $1.1 million home in the exclusive Seattle suburb of Madrona, Love called police after he locked himself in a room with four guns and 25 boxes of ammunition. Police confiscated the weapons and Love cancelled his credit cards and froze his bank accounts to prevent him from buying drugs. At the instigation of Love and friends, Cobain checked himself into the Exodus Recovery Center at Daniel Freeman Hospital in Marina Del Rey, California, on March 30, 1994. Before doing so, however, he had a friend, Dylan Carson, buy him a shotgun for "home protection." Cobain stayed at the facility for only 36 hours before bolting and placing a cryptic call to Love in Los Angeles. "No matter what, I love you," he told her. Love immediately notified Seattle police and hired a private investigator who checked the couple's home over the next few days. On April 4, Cobain's mother filed a missing persons report.

In Seattle, the rock star drifted from one drug shooting gallery to another before secretly returning to his home at 171 Lake Washington Boulevard East. Sometime on the late afternoon or early evening of April 5, 1994, Cobain retired to a bare apartment above the garage on the property, locked the door, and blocked it with a stool. With a red ballpoint pen, the 27-year-old "voice of his generation" wrote a suicide note to his wife and fans, tipped over a potted plant, and jabbed the pen through the note into a mound of soil. After injecting himself with a large dose of heroin and Valium, Cobain laid on the floor surrounded by a cigar box filled with his drug paraphernalia, a plaid hunter's cap, and his driver's license to identify the body. Cradling the stock of a Remington model 11 20-gauge shotgun between his legs, Cobain placed the barrel in his mouth, and pulled the trigger. On the morning of April 8, 1994, electrician Gary Smith found the musician's body while installing a new security system.

The next day, an estimated 5,000 people attended a memorial service for Cobain at the Seattle Center. Bereaved widow Courtney Love supplied an audiotaped message that was broadcast over loudspeakers to the assembled mourners. In it, Love read those parts of the suicide note not personally directed to herself or their child, often pausing to vent her heartbreak, rage, and frustration:

I haven't felt the excitement of listening to as well as creating music, along with really writing something, for too many years now. I feel guilty beyond words about these things — for example, when we're backstage and the lights go out and the roar of the crowd begins, it doesn't affect me the way in which it did for Freddie Mercury, who seemed to love and relish the love and adoration of the crowd. Which is something I totally admire and envy. The fact that I can't fool you, any one of you, it simply isn't fair to you or to me. The worst crime I could think of would be to pull people off by faking it, pretending as if I'm having 100% fun. Sometimes I feel as I should have a punch-in time clock before I walk out on stage. I've tried everything within my power to appreciate it, and I do, God believe me I do, but it's not enough. I appreciate the fact that I and we have effected [*sic*] and entertained a lot of people. I must be one of those narcissists who only appreciate things when they're alone. I'm too sensitive. I need to be slightly numb in order to regain the enthusiasm I once had as a child. On our last 3 tours I've had a much better appreciation of all the people I know personally, and as fans of our music, but I still can't get out the frustration to gather the empathy I have for everybody. There's good in all of us and I simply love people too much. So much that it makes me feel just too fucking sad. Sad little sensitive unappreciative Pieces.... I had good marriage, and for that I'm grateful. But since the age of seven, I've become hateful toward all human beings in general only because it seems so easy for people to get along that have empathy. Only because I love and feel for people too much I guess. Thank you all from the pit of my burning nauseous stomach for your letters and concern during the last years. I'm pretty much of an erratic moody person and I don't have the passion anymore. Peace, Love, Empathy, Kurt Cobain.

Love's final words to fans: "And just remember: this is all bullshit ... and I'm laying on our bed, and I'm really sorry. And I feel the same way you do. I'm really sorry you guys. I don't know what I could have done. I wish I'd been here. I wish I hadn't listened to other people, but I did."

Cobain's remains were cremated and his ashes distributed in various places (under a weeping willow tree outside his home, in an urn on a Buddhist altar kept by Love, in Washington's Wishkah River, and in India).

FURTHER READING

Azerrad, Michael. *Come as You Are: The Story of Nirvana.* 1st ed. New York: Doubleday, 1993.

Black, Suzi. *Nirvana Tribute: The Life and Death of Kurt Cobain, the Full Story.* London: Omnibus, 1994.

Clarke, Martin, and Woods, Paul, ed. *Kurt Cobain: The Cobain Dossier.* London: Plexus, 1999.

Sandford, Christopher. *Kurt Cobain.* 1st Carroll & Graf ed. New York: Carroll & Graf, 1996.

Thompson, Dave. *Never Fade Away: The Kurt Cobain Story.* St. Martin's paperback ed. New York: St. Martin's Paperbacks, 1994.

Codona, Alfredo

Codona, born in Laredo, Mexico, in 1895 to trapeze star parents, was once considered to be among the world's top trapeze artists. His first wife, Danish aerialist Lillian Leitzel, died in a fall in Copenhagen in 1931 during a performance of "The Flying Codonas." Vera Bruce joined the act and he married her the next year. Codona's career was cut short in 1933 when he missed a triple somersault and fell 60 feet from a flying trapeze during a performance of the Ringling Bros. and Barnum & Bailey Circus at New York's Madison Square Garden. When the aerialist's shattered shoulder failed to heal, he became the manager of the troupe and travelled for a year with Tom Mix's Circus as an executive to the cowboy star.

In 1937, Codona purchased a garage in Long Beach, California, and was working there when his wife was granted a divorce on July 1 on grounds of mental cruelty. On July 30, 1937, the Codonas, with Vera Bruce's mother, were in an attorney's office in Los Angeles discussing the division of household effects when Codona, 42, asked the lawyer to leave for a few moments. After he did, Codona calmly lit his wife's cigarette, locked the door, then said, "Vera, this is all you've left for me to do." Pulling an automatic pistol from his pocket, Codona pumped four rounds into his ex-wife before killing himself instantly with a head shot. Vera Bruce, 32, died the next day.

Cohen, Herbert

Son of independent film producer Maurice Cohen, the 28-year-old assistant producer of short subjects for RKO–Radio Pictures had long suffered from ill health and fits of melancholia. On the night of June 14, 1939, Cohen's body, clad only in a tee-shirt and underwear, was found dangling from a water pipe by a doubled length of cord in a vacant office a few doors from his own in the Director's Building on RKO's Gower Street studio.

Cohn, Richard

The Viennese-born pianist was the pupil of Theodor Leschetizky (1830–1915) before coming to the United States in 1905 to continue his education under Rafael Joseffy (1852–1915). In 1926, Cohn became the pianist and orchestral leader of the Vanderbilt Hotel in New York, but lost the position in 1932. For the next two years, Cohn barely survived by giving private lessons until he was forced to sell his piano. Deprived of a means of earning a living, the 53 year old gassed himself to death in his studio room at 74 East Ninety-second Street on March 28, 1934.

Collins, Etta Stewart

Surrounded by relics of her stage successes in such Broadway plays as *Red Mill*

(1910), *The Merry Countess* (1912–13), and *Buster Brown*, the 45-year-old leading lady committed suicide in her furnished room at 260 West Forty-sixth Street in New York City on April 23, 1929. Neighbors of the former actress called police after smelling illuminating gas coming from her apartment. Authorities forced open the door to find Collins fully dressed and lying on her bed with gas escaping from a heater.

Collins, Sid

In radio since 1946, Collins was widely known as the "Voice of the Indianapolis 500," a race he had called on Indianapolis radio station WIBC since 1952. Eleven days after being diagnosed with terminal amyotrophic lateral sclerosis at the Mayo Clinic in Rochester, Minnesota, the 54-year-old WIBC sports director hanged himself with a necktie in the closet of his apartment at 3832 Rue Delacroix in Indianapolis on May 2, 1977.

Combs, Raymond Neil, Jr.

The popular game show host was born the son of a steelworker in Hamilton, Ohio, on April 3, 1956. A former Mormon missionary, Combs was earning $150,000 a year as a furniture salesman in Indianapolis and doing stand-up comedy at night when he decided to risk everything to become a comedian. Depositing his wife, Debbie, and their children in Hamilton, Ohio, the 26-year-old hopeful moved alone to Los Angeles in 1983. Combs landed an emcee spot at the Ice House Comedy Club and quickly established himself as one of the town's top comic headliners.

The comedian was doing audience warm-ups for the NBC sitcom *Amen* in 1986 when talk show host Johnny Carson invited him on *The Tonight Show*. On October 23, 1986, Combs earned one of the few standing ovations ever given on the program. The entertainer's big break, however, came in 1988 when he was picked to replace *Family Feud* host Richard Dawson on the renamed *The*

New Family Feud. Combs scored a hit on the show, but invested much of his nearly $1 million a year salary in two ill-fated comedy clubs in Cincinnati. Both clubs lost large sums of money and were ultimately closed. In 1994, Combs unceremoniously lost his job on the *Feud* when Dawson was brought back to host the program.

Career and family problems were compounded by a near-fatal multi-car accident on the Ventura Freeway in 1995. The comedian suffered a broken neck and was a quadriplegic when first brought into the emergency room. Given large amounts of drugs to ease the swelling, Combs spent months in intensive rehabilitation sessions prior to being released. Though able to resume normal activities, Combs was in constant physical pain and hooked on Valium. Family and friends began to notice that he was always tired, overly emotional, subject to fits of tears, and spoke often about suicide. On the homefront, Combs' 17-year marriage to his childhood sweetheart was in trouble. In 1996, Debbie Combs was granted a court order banning her husband from their home and giving her temporary custody of their six children, aged 18 to 5.

In the summer of 1996, Combs taped a season of *Ray Combs' Family Challenge* for the Family Channel, but the comic's irregular work habits prompted the show's producers not to rehire him for the next season. Only days after learning of their decision from his agent, Combs was also informed that he was being dumped from another game show called *Satellite Bingo*, shot in Las Vegas.

On June 1, 1996, the hysterical comedian made a threatening phone call to his wife from his apartment. She called 911 and paramedics rushed him to a medical center where he was treated for an overdose of Valium. Later that morning as Debbie was driving her husband home from the hospital, Combs jumped out of the car at a red light and disappeared into the neighborhood. Hours later he showed up at the family home in Glendale and began shouting at the family and behaving irrationally. When police arrived, they found the

40-year-old entertainer on the front steps bleeding from the head. He told authorities that he fell in a jacuzzi. Combs became violent in the emergency room of the Glendale Adventist Medical Center and was placed on a 72-hour suicide watch in the hospital's psychiatric ward. The committal was the culmination of a two week stint of increasingly bizarre behavior during which the confused television star had twice tried to kill himself and had been observed repeatedly battering his head against walls.

Shortly after 4:00 A.M. on June 2, 1996, Combs' body was found by an orderly in the closet of his private room hanging by a bedsheet attached to a faulty clothes rod designed to break away under pressure. The game show host left his family $500,000 in debt and was buried without a headstone in Greenwood Cemetery in his hometown of Hamilton, Ohio. Responding to a fundraiser for the dead comedian's family, Johnny Carson quietly wrote a check for $25,000. Combs' gravemarker features his smiling portrait and reads: "Beloved Son, Brother, Father — Always Loved, Never Forgotten."

Common, Tommy

A boy soprano, the Toronto-born singer made his radio debut at age 8. In 1955, Common first appeared on television on the CBC show *Pick the Stars*. He later became a regular on a number of Canadian variety shows including *Country Hoedown, Don Messer's Jubilee*, and *It's a Musical World* (1973) in which he alternated hosting duties with Irish singer Tommy Makem.

Common's alcoholism, however, destroyed his show business career. Turning to politics, the divorced father of four worked as a senior aide to Liberal Senator H. A. ("Bud") Olson, but lost the position when Olson was dropped from the cabinet after John Turner became party leader. In 1984, Common unsuccessfully sought the federal Liberal nomination in the Calgary area of Bow River. Ironically, the 51-year-old former singer was the

coordinator of Calgary's vandalism prevention program when he was charged with breaking and entering into the northeast Calgary home of his former girlfriend, Suzanne Bensler, on June 3, 1985. According to Bensler, Common smashed a window and climbed inside the house while his 17-year-old daughter hid in a closet. "Then he made threats that he would burn the house down and that he'd burn the pet dog and scatter the ashes around the house," Bensler told authorities.

On August 14, 1985, the day he was scheduled to appear in Provincial Court for a preliminary charge of breaking and entering stemming from the incident, Common was found dead from a gunshot wound in a pickup truck parked outside Bensler's house.

Cooksey, Curtis

The veteran Shakespearean actor (born December 9, 1891) last appeared onstage in a 1953 production of *Mr. Roberts* at the Biltmore Theatre in Los Angeles before cancer forced him into retirement. On April 19, 1962, the 70-year-old actor's body was found lying on a sheet and pillow on the kitchen floor of his Hollywood home at 622 S. Serrano Avenue. Cooksey shot himself through the right temple with a .32-caliber revolver.

Cooper, Courtney Ryley

Cooper (born in Kansas City, Missouri, in 1887) began a lifelong love affair with the circus at 16 when he ran away from home to become a clown in the Cook & Barret travelling show. He later worked as a newspaper reporter for *The Kansas City Star, The New York World*, and *The Chicago Tribune*. Around 1912, Cooper began contributing articles to magazines, ultimately writing some 500 stories on circus and animal life. Many of his short stories served as the basis for films ("Land of the Lost" for *Step on It!*, 1922, and, "Crossed Wires" for *The Fast Express*, 1924). Cooper also wrote more than 30 novels including *Memories of Buffalo Bill* (1919), *Under the Big Top* (1923), *The Jungle Behind Bars* (1924), and *The*

Challenge of the Bush (1929). In 1917, Cooper was credited with "picturizing" the Norma Talmadge vehicle *The Secret of the Storm Country* while in 1934 he wrote the dialogue and narration for the Frank Buck film *Wild Cargo*, a sequel to the big game hunter's 1932 hit *Bring 'Em Back Alive*.

Unable to withstand the lure of the big top, in April 1940 the best-selling author accepted a salary of one cent a year to become the press agent and feature writer for the Ringling Bros. and Barnum & Bailey Circus. On September 27, 1940, the 53-year-old writer checked into a two-room suite at the Park Central Hotel in New York City under the name "C. R. Cooper" of Sebring, Florida. Cooper, who owned an estate in Sebring near the winter quarters of the famous circus, was seemingly suffering from nervous exhaustion brought on by overwork. Two days later on September 29, Cooper's body was found hanging from a steam pipe in a clothes closet in his room. He had been dead between ten and 11 hours. An unsigned note found at the scene read: "I am leaving $43 in my clothing. Pay $32 to the hotel, which I believe I owe."

More than 150 mourners, including FBI head J. Edgar Hoover, actor Fred Stone, and restaurateur Vincent Sardi attended the October 1, 1940, funeral service held at the Universal Funeral Chapel in New York City. Cooper's remains were subsequently cremated in Union City, New Jersey.

Corbaley, Maxine Castleton

Corbaley, 38, a former movie singer and a performer in the Jones Beach operettas under her maiden name of Castleton, gassed herself to death in the kitchen of her New York City apartment at 156 East Thirty-seventh Street on October 30, 1938. The singer's cat and Pomeranian were nearly overcome with gas and had to be removed to the hospital of the A.S.P.C.A. A farewell note to her husband offered no reason for the suicide.

Cory, George

Although Cory wrote more than 200 songs in collaboration with lyricist Douglass Cross, he is undoubtedly best remembered for the 1954 pop classic "I Left My Heart in San Francisco" recorded by Tony Bennett in 1962. In 1969, Frisco's Board of Supervisors unanimously adopted the song as the city's official anthem. Twenty-three years after it was written, the 55-year-old composer was still making $50,000 a year from sheet music and record sales. Depressed over failing health, Cory had not been seen for several days when a concerned business associate dropped by his fashionable Nob Hill apartment at 18 Pleasant Street on April 11, 1978. He found Cory's lifeless body on a couch in the apartment. A victim of an overdose of medication, the songwriter had been dead for an estimated 48 hours. Contents of a handwritten suicide note were not divulged by the coroner. Cory never married.

Cotton, Lucy

Cotton (born in 1891 in Houston, Texas) began working on Broadway in the mid-teens as a chorus girl in *The Quaker Girl* before graduating to larger roles in *Turn to the Right* (1916), *Lightnin'* (1918), and *Up in Mabel's Room* (1919). In films, Cotton had bit parts in *Divorced* (1915) and *Life Without Soul* (a 1915 version of *Frankenstein*) before receiving co-star billing in *The Prodigal Wife* (1918), *The Sin That was His* (1920), and the 1921 George Arliss vehicle, *The Devil*.

Cotton's personal life, however, was her greatest role. Married five times, her first in 1924 to Edward Russell Thomas, publisher of *The New York Morning Telegraph*, left her a multi-millionaire when he died two years later. In 1927, she married Colonel Lytton Ament. They divorced in 1930, and a year later she married Wall Street broker Charles Hann. The union ended in divorce in 1932, and the next year she married William M. Magraw, a former newspaperman. When this marriage ended on May 4, 1933, she married

Prince Vladimir Eristavi-Tchitcherine at Key West, Florida, on the same day. She divorced the exiled Russian prince in 1941 charging "extreme cruelty." The divorce decree gave her the right to retain the title of princess.

At 9:00 A.M. on December 12, 1948, the 57-year-old owner of the beachfront Macfadden-Deauville Hotel was found in a coma by the butler in her palatial home at 943 Venetian Way in Miami Beach, Florida. A note asking that a Miami doctor be called and an empty bottle of sleeping pills were found on a bedside table in her room. Princess Lucy Cotton Thomas Ament Hann Magraw Eristavi-Tchitcherine died hours later without regaining consciousness at St. Francis Hospital.

Cozad, Andrew M.

Cozad adopted the name "Norris" after founding the Norris & Rowe Circus in 1882 and managed the attraction for 16 years before selling his interest to a family member in 1898. At the time of his suicide, the 45-year-old former circus owner was a travelling liniment salesman. In ill health for the past five years and despondent over the death of his wife the previous year, Cozad was living with his parents in Santa Cruz, California. On December 5, 1907, he retired to his room after eating dinner, pressed the muzzle of a .32-caliber Smith & Wesson revolver above his right ear, and pulled the trigger, sending the bullet out the top of his skull into a wall. In a note addressed to his mother found at the scene, Cozad wrote: "Life is no longer worth living in my present frame of mind. It has the best of me. I hope you will forgive me. I wish to be buried alongside of my wife, and ask that you divide what little property I have with my brothers and yourself...."

Crandall, Harry M.

Impressed by the success of the nickelodeons in New York City, Crandall opened the 80–seat Casino Theatre at Fourth and East Capital streets in Washington, D.C., in 1911. Over the next several years, the impresario opened the Airdrome, Apollo, Metropolitan Avenue Grand, Central, Colony, Home, Savoy, Avalon, Tivoli, York, and several other theatres. His flagship theatre, the Knickerbocker, was erected in 1917. On the night of January 28, 1922, the roof of the theatre collapsed under a heavy blanket of snow, killing 98 and maiming a hundred others. While Crandall was exonerated of blame, the theatre's architect, Reginald Wyckliffe Geare, and four others were indicted on manslaughter charges. The District Supreme Court later dismissed the charges as "too vague."

Unemployable and wracked by guilt, Geare gassed himself to death on August 20, 1927 (see entry). Crandall successfully defended himself against 70 lawsuits stemming from the catastrophe and managed to amass a sizable fortune before selling his local theatre interests for $2,250,000 and stock options to Warner Bros. in 1929. Financially secure, but unhappy out of the theatre business, Crandall exhibited a panorama painting of the World War in Chicago and Washington in 1934. On February 26, 1937, the 58-year-old ex-theatre magnate was found dead from gas poisoning in his ninth floor room in the Parkside Hotel in Washington, D.C. Crandall, who owned a mansion across town, engaged the hotel room six months before with the express purpose of committing suicide there. A farewell note addressed to "The Newspaper Boys" read: "Please don't be too hard on me, boys, not for my sake, but for those I am leaving behind me. You don't have to look for the cause of me taking my life. I'll tell you that I have not committed any crime. Have no love affairs. Not insane. Have very good health. No. None of these are the reasons. Only it is I'm despondent and miss my theater, oh, so much. I have tried to get back in the game, but no luck. Boy, I never did any harm to anyone in my life and I don't crave headlines. So just a few lines on an inside page. What do you say, boys? Kind regards, H. M. C."

A second note read: "If anything happens to me tonight, I am going to try to make something happen, please notify —(name deleted by police). P.S. I turned out the light in the icebox because I don't want to blow up anyone upstairs. I am going to turn on the gas at 3 A.M., and if I am not found by 5 A.M. don't have the gas squad and others here. It will just cause a scene. It is now 2:45 A.M., and I am still myself, and I hope to go through with it. H. M. Crandall."

Crane, Vincent

Born Vincent Cheesman in Reading, Berkshire, on May 21, 1943, Crane grew up in Battersea, South London. A self-taught pianist by age 15, Crane studied classical music at the Trinity College of Music in London and graduated in 1964. Already known as a blues and jazz player at the Marquee and 100 Club, Crane joined The Crazy World of Arthur Brown in 1965. Two years later, he co-wrote the band's best known song, "Fire," and toured America with the group before leaving amid management and contractual problems. After the split, Crane was hospitalized in the U.S. for depression. Returning to Britain in 1969, the organist formed Atomic Rooster with drummer Carl Palmer and bassist Nick Graham. A progressive-rock group, the band's debut album, *Atomic Rooster*, reached Number 49 in the U.K. in June 1970. After the departure of Palmer and Graham, Crane retained the band's name, recruited other players, and released *Death Walks Behind You* (1970), *In Hearing Of* (1971), and *Made in England* (1972). Crane continued to front other lineups of Atomic Rooster until the band officially disbanded in 1982. In February 1984, Crane joined Dexy's Midnight Runners for their album *Don't Stand Me Down* and the group's subsequent tour. Crippled by chronic depression, the 45-year-old musician swallowed 288 Anadin tablets at his home in Maida Vale, London, on February 14, 1989.

Crash, Darby

Crash (real name Jan-Paul Beahm) grew up in West Los Angeles where he fantasized about fronting a band while still a student at University High School. In April 1977 he formed the punk band The Germs; so named because the group made people sick. Their first gig was opening for The Weirdoes at L.A.'s Orpheum in 1977. In true punk fashion, the singer-lyricist's stage antics were flamboyant and shocking. Known for covering his body with sticky red licorice, Crash would often fall flat on the stage, rip off his shirt, and let audience members draw swastikas and write obscenities on his writhing body with a magic marker. Clubs like the Troubador and Starwood quickly banned the group. In October 1979 the group released an untitled album (later named *G.I.*) on Slash Records that sold nearly 10,000 copies. However, by the summer of 1980 when Crash returned from London sporting a foot-high Mohawk haircut, the LA punk scene was in its death throes. The 22-year-old punk rocker renamed the group the Darby Crash Band and played a few badly received shows. On December 3, 1980, The Germs' reunion show in Los Angeles flopped. Four days later on December 7, 1980, Crash showed up at girlfriend Casey Hopkins' home on Fuller Avenue in the city's Wilshire District with $400 worth of heroin to consummate their suicide pact.

Crash wrote a note bequeathing the leather jacket he was wearing to a friend along with other undisclosed thoughts, then took ¾ of the heroin and gave Hopkins the rest. She survived, he died. Friends of the singer noted that his suicide was at least partially inspired by the overdose death of former Sex Pistols bassist Sid Vicious on February 2, 1979.

Summing up Crash's death, L.A. rock critic Richard Meltzer observed "[that] what seemed like a viable anarchist scream in the lyrical message now seems not so much anarchy as an indication of a bottomless sadness." The Germs can be seen performing in Penelope Spheeris' 1981 documentary on the LA punk rock scene *The Decline of Western Civilization*. Two of their songs, "Going Down" and "Lion's Share," are included in the soundtrack of the 1980 Al Pacino film *Cruising*.

FURTHER READING

Atkinson, Terry. "Punk Rocker was the 'Other' Death." *Los Angeles Times*, sec. IV, pp. 5, 9, December 13, 1980.

Creelman, James A.

Creelman, 40, a writer of several unproduced plays, had only recently returned to New York from Hollywood where he had also struck out as a film scenarist. In the early morning hours of September 9, 1941, Creelman entered the apartment building at 325 East Seventy-second Street where he was temporarily living with his mother and sister in their sixth floor digs. Instructing the elevator operator to take him to the 18th floor roof garden, the failed playwright jumped to his death in an inner courtyard 20 minutes later.

Criss, William "Sonny"

The jazz alto saxophonist (born October 23, 1923, in Memphis, Tennessee) first rose to prominence in Los Angeles in the mid-forties playing with Howard McGhee, Gerald Wilson, Johnny Otis, and Billy Eckstine. After touring the U.S. with the bands of Stan Kenton and Buddy Rich throughout the fifties, Criss relocated to Paris in 1961 and for three successful years worked in European radio, television, and nightclubs. Returning to Los Angeles in 1974, the musician suffered a nervous breakdown, but upon recovery worked extensively with disadvantaged children, the needy, and drug and alcohol abusers. On November 19, 1977, the 54-year-old exponent of bebop tinged with the blues was found shot to death in his home in the Wilshire district of Los Angeles. Police strongly suspected suicide. An LP released shortly before his death, *The Joy of Sax*, had been well received.

Crockett, Clarence

Crockett, a member of the radio hillbilly act known as the Crockett Family, was found by his father on August 19, 1936, lying unconscious across a bed with a bullet wound in his temple in his Santa Monica, California, home at 2627 Fifth Street. The 30-year-old entertainer died two hours later at the Santa Monica Hospital. Crockett's wife told police that he had been drinking heavily and had threatened to kill her before turning the gun on himself. Family members maintained that Crockett's death was accidental since he often playfully held a revolver to his head and bluffed suicide.

Crofoot, Alan

The East York, Ontario-born tenor made his debut with the Canadian Opera in 1956 followed by appearances in the United States and at the Glyndebourne Festival in England. Crofoot sang on Broadway in *Oliver!* and on British television in *Man of La Mancha* before appearing in the role of the "Circus Master" in Smetana's *The Bartered Bride* during the Metropolitan Opera's 1979 season. On March 5, 1979, Crofoot (accompanied by his fiancée) was in Dayton, Ohio, to direct his first full-scale opera, Richard Strauss' *Salome*. At 2:23 that morning, the 49-year-old tenor jumped to his death from a fifth floor window of the Dayton Downtown Sheraton Hotel. Jacobo Kaufmann, director of the Jerusalem Opera, was subsequently named to replace Crofoot as director of the Dayton Opera production.

Croft, Lee D.

Croft, a brother of the treasurer of West Coast Theatre, Inc., was assistant manager of the Criterion Theatre in Los Angeles when he became infatuated with Frances Turney, a pretty cashier who worked there. Though married, the 30-year-old Croft continued to ply Turney even after he was transferred to the Long Beach Theatre as a manager in September 1925.

Learning that the young woman was keeping company with another married man, wealthy Fullerton businessman T. K. Doyer, a drunken Croft confronted Turney at the Criterion on November 18, 1925. The woman refused to accompany Croft in his inebriated condition and had theatre employees send him away. Croft waited in his car as Doyer arrived at the theatre to drive Turney home. The jealous manager followed the couple to Turney's home at 1221 West Fifty-ninth Street and confronted the pair as they sat in Doyer's car. Croft forced Doyer out of the vehicle, fired two errant pistol shots at the man, then drove off in his rival's car with Turney on the front seat beside him sobbing hysterically. As Croft drove recklessly through the streets of Los Angeles threatening to kill Turney, the young woman prayed and begged for mercy.

The wild auto ride ended at Seventy-ninth Street and Western Avenue when Croft punctured the front tires against a curb. Croft ordered Turney out of the car and into a nearby vacant lot where a passing motorist tried to intervene, but was warned off by the theatre manager. According to Turney, Croft screamed, "Get down on your knees and make your peace with God! I'm going to kill you!" As the terrified woman knelt before him, Croft fired a shot that struck him in the foot. Moments later, Croft turned away from Turney and shot himself in the head. He died several hours later in the Receiving Hospital.

Crosby, Dennis Michael

The second son of megastar Bing Crosby and his first wife, jazz singer Dixie Lee, was born with twin brother Phillip in Los Angeles on July 13, 1934. The most reserved of the Crosby sons, Dennis was never interested in a show biz career although initially he half heartedly pursued one. In the late fifties and early sixties he joined his brothers in a nightclub act billed as the Crosby Boys. In films, he appeared with his brothers in the 1945 movie *Out of This World*, played himself in *Duffy's Tavern* (1945), and had a bit part as "Private Page" in *Sergeants Three* (1962) starring Frank Sinatra and his fellow "Rat Pack" cronies Peter Lawford, Dean Martin, Joey Bishop, and Sammy Davis, Jr.

After leaving acting, Dennis worked in a production capacity for his father's company,

Bing Crosby Productions. Like brothers Gary and Lindsay, he suffered from manic depression and alcoholism although he periodically achieved stints of sobriety through Alcoholics Anonymous. Unlike his brothers, however, Dennis downplayed the allegations of physical and emotional abuse made against their father by Gary Crosby in his 1983 tell-all book *Going My Own Way*. While admitting that older brother Gary was the prime target for their father's harsh discipline, Dennis added: "I was happy to be who I was even if I had the hell kicked out of me."

Professional and personal problems continued unchecked throughout Dennis' life. Shortly after his father's death in 1977, Dennis and his brothers learned that they would not immediately benefit from the crooner's demise. Instead, Crosby had set up a blind trust that was untouchable until his sons reached the age of 65. In December 1989, the brothers were informed by attorneys that the monthly four figure check each of them had received for years from a trust fund established by their late mother, Dixie Lee, was gone, wiped out by falling oil prices on the world market.

Eleven days after learning that there would be no more monthly checks, Dennis' favorite brother, Lindsay (see entry), fatally shot himself in the head on December 11, 1989. On May 4, 1991, two weeks after officially ending his 27 year second marriage, the 56 year old followed suit. Late that night, a roommate discovered Crosby's body lying on a couch in the living room of their modest home on Murphy Lane in the Black Point area of Novato, California. Depressed over finances, Lindsay's death, recurrent bouts of alcoholism, and a recent breakup with a girlfriend, Crosby had shot himself in the head with a 12-gauge shotgun. The weapon was found lying at his feet beside the couch. Dennis Crosby was cremated and his ashes spread in the Novato area.

FURTHER READING

Crosby, Gary, and Firestone, Ross. *Going My Own Way.* 1st ed. Garden City, N.Y.: Doubleday, 1983.

Crosby, Lindsay

The youngest of crooner Bing Crosby's four sons by his marriage to jazz singer Dixie Lee (real name Wilma Wyatt) was born in Los Angeles on January 5, 1938. Lindsay first appeared on film with brothers Gary, Dennis, and Phillip as audience members in the 1945 movie *Out of This World* featuring his famous father. In 1957, he made his television debut on *The Edsel Show* with his father and Frank Sinatra. A nightclub act with his three brothers called the Crosby Boys ran until 1959. Never steadily employed, Lindsay read scripts for his father while trying to carve out a place for himself in films. However, the best he could do was to land bit parts in low-budget biker, exploitation, and horror films like *The Girls from Thunder Strip* (1966), *The Glory Stompers* (1967), *Scream Free!* a.k.a. *Free Grass* (1969), and *Bigfoot* (1970). He also briefly appeared in two seventies films (*The Mechanic*; *Live a Little, Steal a Lot*, 1972) before making his final film, *Code Name: Zebra* in 1984.

Lindsay was 14 when his mother died in 1952. A trust fund set up by Dixie Lee based on then booming oil investments yielded each of them a monthly four figure check. Bing Crosby married actress Kathryn Grant in 1957 and was happily raising a second family when he died of a heart attack at age 73 on October 14, 1977, on a golf course in Madrid, Spain. If the sons were expecting to immediately inherit their father's considerable fortune they were soon disappointed. Perhaps he knew them too well. Lindsay, like older brother Gary, was an alcoholic and manic depressive who had suffered a nervous breakdown in 1962. In addition to several arrests for drunken driving and battery, Lindsay had also logged an arrest on indecent exposure charges in Durango, Colorado, in 1977 for running naked around a motel pool. The boys were shocked when they learned their father had left them money in a blind trust that could not be touched until they reached age 65.

In 1983, Gary Crosby published a memoir, *Going My Own Way*, in which he described in excruciating detail their father's physical and psychological abuse. Lindsay corroborated his brother's portrait of Bing Crosby as an emotionally distant father who wreaked emotional violence on his sons. On December 1, 1989, attorneys managing Dixie Lee's trust fund informed the brothers that the recent glut in the world's oil markets had wiped out their investments. Eleven days after learning that there would be no more monthly checks forthcoming, Lindsay Crosby took his life on December 11, 1989.

The 51 year old was staying in an apartment in Las Virgenes in the 26300 block of Bravo Lane while undergoing treatment for alcoholism at a center in nearby Calabasas, California. Crosby was set to return home for the weekend to his second wife and family in Sherman Oaks when a friend found him on the floor of his den dead from a single gunshot wound to the head. A small caliber rifle lay close by. Marilyn Reiss, spokeswoman for Lindsay's older brother, Gary, offered this explanation for the act: "You're dealing with a 51-year-old man who finds himself with a wife and four kids living in a fairly expensive home. He's under treatment for alcoholism, he's a manic depressive and then you throw a bomb at him. The one thing he could depend on was his mother, even when she wasn't alive. Then it (the inheritance) was gone.... Poof, it's gone." Older brother Dennis Crosby (see entry) took his life in an eerily similar fashion on May 4, 1991.

FURTHER READING

Crosby, Gary, and Firestone, Ross. *Going My Own Way*. 1st ed. Garden City, N.Y.: Doubleday, 1983.

Cudahy, John P.

The son of a wealthy Chicago meatpacker, Cudahy inherited a half-million dollars from his father's death as well as $100,000 a year from a trust fund. In addition to other business endeavors, Cudahy promoted the Monroe Salisbury Players' stage production of *The Barbarians* in which his two children performed. Ten days before his death, the

43 year old apparently attempted suicide by swallowing a non-fatal dose of bichloride of mercury. On April 21, 1921, Cudahy was recuperating in his palatial mansion at 7269 Hollywood Boulevard in Los Angeles when he received a letter from a Chicago trust company informing him that they would not loan him $10,000 without his sister's endorsement of the note. She had previously refused her brother's plea for financial assistance. Ill and facing possible bankruptcy, Cudahy blew off the top of his head with a Winchester shotgun in his bedroom while his wife and children were elsewhere in the house.

Cuneo, Lester H.

Cuneo (born either in Indian Territory, Oklahoma, or Chicago, Illinois, on October 25, 1888) carved out a niche as an actor in independent Westerns beginning in 1921 with a starring role in the Capital Film Company five-reel silent *The Ranger and the Law*. His other films include *Blazing Arrows* (1922), *Silver Spurs* (1922), *Fighting Jim Grant* (1923), *Ridin' Fool* (1924), *Western Grit* (1924), *Range Vultures* (1925), and *Two Fisted Thompson* (1925).

The Western star had been drinking heavily for several weeks when he returned to his Hollywood home at 1741 Crescent Drive to visit his estranged wife and two young children. A few days earlier, Cuneo's wife had filed for divorce, charging that her husband of five years had slapped her, and called her a "grafter and a thief." After heatedly arguing with his wife on November 1, 1925, the 37-year-old actor picked up his children and kissed them goodbye, telling them, "Daddy's going away." Cuneo then pulled a revolver from a closet, barricaded himself in the bedroom, and blew his brains out.

Curtis, Ian

On December 9, 1976, Ian Curtis (born July 15, 1956, in Manchester, England) and friends Bernard Albrecht and Peter Hook were in the audience at a Sex Pistols show at Manchester's Lesser Free Trade Hall. Shortly afterward they formed the band Stiff Kittens with Curtis writing and singing, Albrecht on guitar, and Hook on bass. Tony Tabac was brought in to play drums. Changing their name to Warsaw (inspired by the David Bowie tune "Warszawa"), they played their first gig at Manchester's Electric Circus in May 1977. Tabac left the group after five weeks and was replaced by Steve Brotherdale, who in turn was replaced by Stephen Morris in August 1977. To avoid confusion with another punk band named Warsaw Pakt, the group changed its name to Joy Division in late 1977. In Karol Cetinsky's dark World War II novel, *The House of the Dolls*, "joy division" was slang for the concentration camp units in which women prisoners were forced to have sex with their Nazi officer captors. Joy Division played their first gig on January 25, 1978, and that June released the EP *An Ideal for Living* on their Enigma label. The group's post-industrial punk sound featured Curtis' tortured lyrics in which he expressed his bleak vision of human existence.

Fascinated by tragic rock characters like Doors lyricist and singer Jim Morrison, Curtis was seemingly drawn to the idea of death in rock as symbolized in songs like David Bowie's "Rock and Roll Suicide." Onstage, the front man's jerky movements and manic performances quickly earned the group a devoted following. On December 27, 1978, Curtis suffered an epileptic seizure while travelling in the group's van after a London show. The phenobarbital prescribed to control his condition left Curtis prone to wild mood swings. As the singer's health steadily deteriorated, the band's fortunes rose. With the release of *Unknown Pleasures* on the Factory label in April 1979, the group cemented their critical position as one of the top post-punk bands in Britain.

The subsequent tour in late 1979, however, blurred the line between Curtis' illness and his wild stage antics. One critic wrote, "He'll suddenly jerk sideways and, head in hands, he'll transform into a twitching, epileptic-style mass of flesh and bone." Curtis' health forced the cancellation of several shows during the European leg of the tour. Offstage, the singer's affair with a Belgian woman, Annik Honore, threatened to end his nearly five year marriage to wife Deborah (Woodruffe), and estrange him from his newborn daughter, Natalie.

On April 4, 1980, Curtis suffered an epileptic seizure at a show at the Finsbury Park Rainbow in West Hampstead and had to be carried off stage. Later that same night at a gig at the Moonlight Club he suffered another fit five songs into the set. Three days later, the 23-year-old Curtis intentionally overdosed on Phenobarbitone, a drug prescribed to control his seizures. Fearful that the number of pills he took would not prove fatal, but leave him brain damaged, Curtis phoned his wife, who rushed him to the hospital to have his stomach pumped. On the evening of May 18, 1980, days before Joy Division's upcoming debut tour of America, Curtis was alone at his home at 77 Barton Street in Macclesfield, England. His estranged wife and child were living with her parents. Curtis watched Werner Herzog's *Stroszek*, a 1977 German film whose theme of an artist unsuccessfully attempting to choose between two women in his life reflected his own predicament. After the film, he placed Iggy Popp's album, *The Idiot*, on the turntable, drank some whiskey, then wrote a note to his wife, Deborah. In it, he declared his love for her despite his relationship with Annik Honore. The note also allegedly read: "At this moment I wish I were dead. I just can't cope anymore."

Curtis tied a rope to a clothes rack in the kitchen, fastened the other end around his neck, knelt on the floor, and leaned forward. When Deborah found his body the next day around noon, *The Idiot* was still spinning soundlessly on the turntable. In addition to Curtis' many apparent problems, Deborah intimated that he was also afraid of flying and anxious over how American audiences would react to his epilepsy. Curtis' body was cre-

mated on May 23, 1980. A grave marker in Macclesfield Cemetery is inscribed with his name, death date, and the inscription "Love Will Tear Us Apart," the classic Joy Division song that appeared on the band's second album, *Closer*, released to wide critical acclaim in 1980 after the singer's death. The surviving members of Joy Division formed the band New Order.

FURTHER READING

Curtis, Deborah. *Touching from a Distance: Ian Curtis and Joy Division*. London and Boston: Faber and Faber, 1995.
Flowers, Claude. *Dreams Never End: New Order + Joy Division*. London: Omnibus, 1995.
Johnson, Mark. *An Ideal for Living: An History of Joy Division: From Their Mythical Origins as The Stiff Kittens to the Programmed Future as New Order*. London and New York: Bobcat Books, 1986.
West, Mike. *Joy Division*. Todmorden, England: Babylon Books, 1984.

Cutts, Patricia

The daughter of British film director Graham Cutts (1885–1958), the actress also known as "Patricia Wayne" broke into films as a 6-year-old in *Self-Made Lady* (1932). Active in British and U.S. films in the forties and fifties, Cutts made only a handful of films in the sixties and was last seen in *Private Road* in 1971. The 49-year-old actress had been unemployed for several months when she landed a plum role as "Blanche Hunt" on *Coronation Street*, the long-running British television soap opera. Cutts had appeared in only two episodes of the hit series when her body was found by friends at her flat in Elm Park Gardens, Chelsea, on September 6, 1974. According to the coroner, the actress had taken 20 to 30 times the normal dose of barbiturate tablets.

Dailey, Daniel J., III

Shortly after asking directions to the emergency ward of St. John's Hospital in Santa Monica, California, in the early morning hours of July 1, 1975, the 27-year-old son of actor-dancer Dan Dailey (1914–1978) and his first wife, Elizabeth Hofert, shot himself in the right side of the head with a .22-caliber automatic pistol on the facility's front lawn. Contents of a suicide note found at the scene were not disclosed. Dailey is buried in Forest Lawn Memorial Park in Glendale, California.

Dalida

The internationally renowned singer was born Iolanda Gigliotti to Italian parents in the Shobra District in Cairo, Egypt, on January 17, 1933. Dalida's father, Pietro Gigliotti, was a violinist with the Cairo Opera. The statuesque 21 year old was employed as a secretary in an import company when she won the "Miss Egypt" beauty contest in 1954. Two years later she made her film debut in Egyptian director Niazi Mustapha's *Un verre, une cigarette*. Shortly afterward she moved to Paris to pursue a movie career. Frustrated by months of failing to land film work, Dalida was singing as an intermission act in the La Villa D'Este club when she was discovered by record industry executives Bruno Coquatrix and Lucien Morisse. Dalida married Morisse in 1961, but they divorced within a few months.

The Egyptian-born beauty's husky voice, blonde mane, and striking features quickly earned her a devoted following in France, Europe, and the Middle East. Her 1956 hit song "Bambino" was the first among several that included "Ciao, ciao bambina," "Gondolier," "Itsi bitsi petit bikini," "Darla Dirladada," and "Paroles, paroles" with French film star Alain Delon. In a career spanning more than 30 years, Dalida sold 85 million records. Her repertoire included more than 400 songs in French, 200 in Italian, and 200 in German, Spanish, Greek, and Arabic. As a film actress, Dalida appeared in *Rapt au deuxieme bureau* (1958), *Brigade de moeurs* (1959), *L'inconnu de Hong kong* (1963), and *Sixième Jour* (1986).

The singing star's personal life, however, was marked by tragedy. In 1967, she tried to kill herself with an overdose of sleeping pills after her close friend and singing partner, Italian singer Luigi Tenco (see entry), committed suicide at the 17th San Remo Song Festival in Italy. In 1970, ex-husband Lucien Morisse shot himself. A later companion, Richard Chamfray (a.k.a. "Comte de St. Germain"), gassed himself to death in 1983. On May 3, 1987, less than one week before she was scheduled to do concerts in Belgium and France, the 54-year-old singer was found dead from an overdose of sleeping pills in her apartment in the Montmartre Quarter of Paris. A suicide note read, "Life is unbearable, pardon me." French president François Mitterand offered his condolences in a telegram to Dalida's brother, Orlando Gigliotti: "Dalida will leave behind the memory of a great artiste who left her mark on the world of the french song, and also the memory of a generous and unhappy woman." The international singing star is buried in the Cimitiere de Montmartre in Paris.

Daly, Anna

Daly and friend and fellow suicide Olive Thomas (see entry) originally came together from hometowns in Pennsylvania to New York City via Pittsburgh in 1913 with the shared dream of taking Broadway by storm. Both young women modelled, but only Thomas landed a job with the *Ziegfeld Follies* and achieved international fame before dying a suspected suicide in Paris in 1920. Daly's theatrical aspirations never materialized and at the time of her death she was employed as a cloak model who occasionally posed for artists. On September 16, 1920, Daly's roommate, *Ziegfeld Follies* girl Betty Martin, found a note from the woman in their apartment at the Hotel Monterey. It read: "He doesn't love me anymore. I can't stand it any longer, and Olive is dead." The investigating detective noted that the physical description of the missing person matched that of a young woman who earlier in the evening had checked into a room at the Hotel Seville at Thirty-first

Street and Fourth Avenue under the name "Mrs. Elizabeth Anderson." The woman was found unconscious in the room after drinking a bottle of veronal and had died without regaining consciousness in Bellevue Hospital. A relative confirmed that the dead woman was Anna Daly.

Dandridge, Dorothy Jean

The first black actress to be nominated for an Oscar in a leading role, Dandridge was nonetheless not permitted to escape Hollywood's stereotyping of her as the sexual black temptress. Born November 9, 1922, in Cleveland, Ohio, Dandridge early experienced an unsettled family life. Her father, a Baptist minister, left shortly after her birth. Dandridge and older sister Vivian were raised by their mother, Ruby Jean Butler, a movie and radio comedienne. Under Ruby Jean's direction, the children toured the South for five years as the singing and dancing "Wonder Kids" performing their vaudeville-type act in black Baptist churches. In the early thirties, Ruby Jean moved the family to the Watts section of Los Angeles. There, she recruited another girl, Etta Jones, and transformed the "Wonder Kids" into the singing group the Dandridge Sisters. Through black casting director Charles Butler at Central Casting, Ruby Jean landed the Dandridge Sisters an unbilled appearance in Paramount's *The Big Broadcast of 1936* (1935). The Dandridge Sisters' big break came in 1937 when they appeared (unbilled) in the production number "All God's Chillun Got Rhythm" in the Marx Brothers film *A Day at the Races* for MGM. The Dandridge Sisters appeared in three other films (*It Can't Last Forever*, 1937; *Going Places*, 1939; *Irene*, 1940) before splitting up in 1940.

With the Dandridge Sisters the 18-year-old singer had already made her mark in nightclubs like the Cotton Club in Harlem and toured with black band leaders Cab Calloway, Duke Ellington, and Jimmy Lunceford. After playing stereotypical black bit parts in films like *Four Shall Die* (1941), *Lady from*

Louisiana (1941, with fellow suicide Ona Munson [see entry]), and *Bahama Passage* (1941), Dandridge married legendary tap dancer Harold Nicholas, of Nicholas Brothers fame, on September 6, 1942. From the start the marriage was doomed by Nicholas' womanizing, continual absences, and emotional distance from his 20-year-old bride. On September 2, 1943, Dandridge gave birth to their daughter, Harolyn. The child was later diagnosed with severe mental retardation likely caused by a lack of oxygen to her brain during the delivery. Dandridge severely cut back on her work schedule to take care of her young child. In 1948, Dandridge attempted to kill herself while accompanying the Nicholas Brothers on a European tour. Depressed over Harold's affairs, she took an overdose of sleeping pills in Sweden. Dandridge survived, but tried again weeks later in Switzerland. The couple divorced in October 1951.

Dandridge, forced to support herself and a handicapped daughter, dedicated herself totally to becoming an actress. To that end, she solidified her position as a top nightclub singer by appearing first with the Desi Arnaz Band and then as a solo performer at the Mocambo, Hollywood's top nightclub. Under the tutelage of her white manager, Phil Moore, Dandridge parlayed her stunning good looks into a sultry, sexy stage persona. Her triumphant appearance at the Mocambo in May 1951 led to appearances in London at the Cafe De Paris and helped open up nightclubs to other black entertainers. By November 1951, *Life* magazine was calling her the "most beautiful Negro singer to make her mark in nightclubs since Lena Horne."

After appearing in 1951 as "Melmendi, Queen of the Jungle" in Columbia's *Tarzan's Perils* starring Lex Barker, Dandridge was eager to appear in more challenging film roles. Years of expensive acting lessons paid off in 1953 when MGM production chief Dore Schary signed her to appear opposite black singer Harry Belafonte in *Bright Road*. Dandridge's appearance as a Southern schoolteacher in the film made her a star in the black community. The film, however, that established Dandridge's sexy and sultry screen persona was director Otto Preminger's 1954 black musical *Carmen Jones*, again co-starring Harry Belafonte. Over Dandridge's objections, opera singer Marilyn Horne was brought in to dub her singing parts in the title role. The shoot was further complicated by the love affair between the autocratic director and the vulnerable actress. Dandridge, who would later become pregnant with Preminger's child, had an abortion after he refused to jeopardize his career by marrying a black woman. *Carmen Jones* not only made Dandridge black Hollywood's greatest sex symbol, but also earned her an Oscar nomination for Best Actress. The 1954 nomination (the first ever in Academy history for a black in that category) coincided with the Supreme Court's landmark decision in *Brown vs. Board of Education*, which ruled that segregation in public schools was unconstitutional.

Dandridge's achievement as a black female in the white world of entertainment was equivalent to baseball legend Jackie Robinson's breaking of the color line in professional sports. Though Grace Kelly won the Oscar for *The Country Girl*, Dandridge had every reason to believe that her nomination would go far in convincing white Hollywood that she could transcend race-specific roles. It did not. While she played opposite white actors in films like *The Decks Ran Red* (1958) and *Tamango* (1958) it was still in temptress roles. Fearful of losing their Southern audiences, studios refused to let Dandridge kiss her white co-stars during their love scenes. In 1959, the actress was cast in the film version of *Porgy and Bess*, in essence a duplication of her role in *Carmen Jones*. Belafonte was cast as "Porgy," but flatly refused to do the film because he viewed it as an insult to blacks. A reluctant Sidney Poitier was substituted and Rouben Mamoulian was slated to direct. Weeks before the film was set to start shooting, however, Mamoulian was fired by producer Sam Goldwyn and replaced with Dandridge's ex-lover, Otto Preminger. According to fellow cast members, Preminger

treated the 35-year-old actress "like a dog" during the filming. Consequently, Dandridge failed to receive good reviews in the film and made only one more movie, *Malaga*, in 1960.

On June 23, 1959, Dandridge married white restaurateur and nightclub owner Jack Denison. A physically abusive drunk, Denison siphoned off much of Dandridge's earnings and sank them into a variety of dubious and failing business ventures. By the early sixties, their relationship had deteriorated to the point that he openly called her his "little *schwartze*" while Dandridge referred to him as her "headwaiter." What money Denison did not squander, Dandridge lost in a bad oil well investment. During this period, the actress began drinking heavily and taking prescription pills. Following a particularly abusive episode with Denison on October 23, 1962, Dandridge sought relief in the courts. On November 20, 1962, just after Dandridge's 40th birthday, Denison was ordered out of their house. That December Dandridge was awarded an interlocutory divorce decree on the grounds of "extreme cruelty."

The actress never recovered emotionally, professionally, or financially from her three-year marriage to Denison. Deeply in debt and hounded by the IRS, Dandridge was no longer a big enough draw to play the top nightclubs. In March 1963, the fading star filed bankruptcy. According to court documents, she owed more than $128,000 to some 77 creditors in the U.S. and Canada, and was involved in eight different lawsuits. Days after filing, the woman who took care of her daughter Harolyn returned her to Dandridge. Emotionally unable to care for a brain-damaged 20 year old who required around the clock attention, Dandridge was forced to place her daughter in the Camarillo State Hospital near Los Angeles.

Depressed and lonely, Dandridge upped the consumption of her favorite drink, a mixture of vodka and champagne, and increased her use of the prescription pep pill Benzedrine and appetite suppressants Dexamil and Dexedrine. The former Oscar-nominated actress even took to drinking with street people on a vacant lot near her home. Often drunk and disoriented, Dandridge began phoning friends late at night and talking for hours. Placed on the anti-depressant Tofranil, Dandridge was able to work in nightclubs throughout the world, but critics agreed that she lacked the spark that had once made her a top cabaret performer. Days before a scheduled engagement at a nightclub in New York, the 43-year-old performer fractured a small bone in her right foot during a gym workout. On the morning of September 8, 1965, Dandridge phoned her manager, Earl Mills, to ask him to reschedule a doctor's appointment for later that morning to have a cast put on her foot. Mills did so and last spoke with her shortly after 8:00 A.M. When he failed to hear from Dandridge by 2:00 that afternoon, he drove to her West Hollywood apartment at 8495 Fountain Avenue. Concerned when she did not answer his repeated rings at the door, Mills broke into the apartment with a tire iron. He found Dandridge's lifeless body on the bathroom floor naked except for a blue scarf on her head. She had apparently just bathed and powdered herself.

Sometime earlier she had left a note with Mills in a handwritten envelope marked "To Whomever Discovers Me After Death — Important." The note read: "In case of my death — to whomever discovers it — Don't remove anything I have on — scarf, gown or underwear — Cremate me right away — If I have anything, money, furniture, give to my mother Ruby Dandridge — She will know what to do — Dorothy Dandridge." "Carmen Jones" had also left notes scattered about the apartment directing how her death should be handled. At the time of her death, Dandridge had a bank account of $2.14. Initial published reports attributed the star's death as due to an embolism, a blood clot caused by the tiny fracture in her right foot. The Los Angeles County Medical Examiner later amended the report to show that she had died from an acute ingestion of Tofranil, the anti-depressant used to treat her depression. The coroner's office stated that it "would not attempt to determine whether the death was an accident or a suicide." To silence controversy surrounding the case, however, the Los Angeles County Coroner's Office appointed a three-man team of psychiatric consultants to conduct a "psychological autopsy." Friends and business associates of the dead actress were interviewed to determine her emotional state of mind prior to her death. The team's final ruling was that Dandridge's death had been a "probable accident." Many, however, who had often heard Dandridge speak of suicide disagreed. Filmdom's first black leading lady was cremated and placed in the Columbarium of Victory in the Freedom Mausoleum at Forest Lawn in Glendale, California. Her mother, Ruby Jean, joined her there in 1987.

FURTHER READING

Bogle, Donald. *Dorothy Dandridge: A Biography.* New York: Amistad, 1997.
Dandridge, Dorothy, and Conrad, Earl. *Everything and Nothing; the Dorothy Dandridge Tragedy.* New York: Abelard-Schuman, 1970.
Mills, Earl. *Dorothy Dandridge: A Portrait in Black.* Los Angeles: Holloway House, 1970 (Reprinted 1999).

Dane, Karl

Born Rasmus Karl Thekelsen Gottlieb in Copenhagen, Denmark, on October 12, 1886, Dane appeared onstage there before immigrating to Hollywood during World War I to make two anti–German propaganda features in 1918: *My Four Years in Germany* and *To Hell with the Kaiser*. Film stardom was deferred until 1925 when he appeared as the gangly, tobacco-chewing World War I doughboy "Slim" in director King Vidor's epic anti-war film *The Big Parade.* MGM signed Dane to a contract, and in 1927 paired him with Scottish comedian George K. Arthur in *Rookies.* Capitalizing on their physical disparity, (Dane was tall and skinny, Arthur small and ridiculous), the duo made a total of eight comedy features together between 1927 and 1929. Dane, a fine character actor, continued to make both comedy and dramatic films throughout the twenties (*Monte Carlo*, 1926; *Slide, Kelly, Slide*, 1927; *Baby Mine*, 1928; *Navy Blues*, 1929), and appeared ready to enjoy a long career in Hollywood.

With the advent of "talkies," however, his thick foreign accent became a liability. After making only a few films in the thirties (*The Big House*, 1930; *Free and Easy*, 1930; *Fast Life*, 1932), Dane was through in movies. Unable to act, he tried his hand as an auto mechanic and carpenter, and even suffered the indignity of opening a small hot dog stand outside MGM, the studio where he had enjoyed his greatest successes. Dane failed at every endeavor, and was reduced to borrowing rent money from his friends.

On April 14, 1934, the 47-year-old former actor's body was found by a friend, Frances Leaks, slumped in an armchair in his room at 626 Burnside Avenue in the Wilshire district of Los Angeles. Despondent and penniless, Dane had fired a .38-caliber pistol round into his head. Spread across a nearby table were his old film contracts, press clippings, publicity stills, and a note that read, "To Frances and all my friends — goodbye." For two days, Dane's body lay unclaimed in the L.A. County Morgue bearing the toe tag, "He may have relatives in Denmark … hold for a while." Finally, MGM saved their former star from a pauper's burial by paying for his funeral. Dane is buried beneath a simple marker inscribed with the legend "actor" in Hollywood Memorial Park.

Daniels, Roy G.

Failing in his bid to control all the popular priced vaudeville and picture theatres in Arkansas, Daniels, president of the Arkansas Amusement Company of Hot Springs, lost his business to creditors in 1909. In ill health and facing imminent financial ruin, he returned to Topeka, Kansas, where longtime residents remembered him as a wild young man who as a bartender in the 1890s beat a man to death with a beer mallet in a seedy dive. Tried for the murder, Daniels was acquitted in a contro-

versial verdict that had turned the town against him.

On October 4, 1909, the promoter (age unreported) took a room in the National Hotel and committed one of the most fastidious suicides on record. After writing notes to his mother, the press, the undertaker, and the coroner, Daniels removed pillows and a sheet from the bed, spread them on the floor and laid down to wait for the strychnine he swallowed to take effect. Fearful the poison would act too slowly, he shot himself once over the heart and in the side of the head with an old fashioned cap and ball revolver. The notes revealed Daniels' unusual attention to detail and a concern over how he would be remembered. In one he wrote: "This medicine is too slow. I have taken off the clothes I wish to be buried in, so as not to soil them." Another addressed to the newspapers begged: "Please be merciful…. I have been unsuccessful…. This and sickness has caused me to do this and for God's sake be merciful, this, the last, time." And to the coroner: "No investigation is necessary. I have done this myself owing to business failure, sickness and despondency."

Dannemann, Monika

On September 18, 1970, fabled rock guitarist Jimi Hendrix died of a drug overdose in Monika Dannemann's apartment in London. His death and allegations voiced by his former girlfriend, Kathy Etchingham, that Dannemann had delayed in calling an ambulance dogged the German-born former ice skating champion for 26 years. Etchingham, the inspiration for the Hendrix song "Foxy Lady," eventually married a doctor and raised two sons while Dannemann became a recluse and turned her thatched cottage in Seaford, East Sussex, into a Hendrix shrine. Paintings by Dannemann portraying the legendary guitarist as a young god come to earth adorned its walls. Though financially destitute, Dannemann's total devotion to Hendrix's memory led the artist to refuse an offer of $1 million to sell her dead lover's guitar.

Shortly after Hendrix's death, Danne-mann denounced Etchingham by repeating allegations made by the guitarist that she "would cheat and lie for money" and had stolen items from him while he was away on tour. In 1992 Etchingham sued her rival for libel, was awarded £1,000 in damages, and was granted the stipulation that Dannemann not repeat the allegations. However, Danneman referred to Etchingham as an "inveterate liar" in her 1995 book *The Inner World of Jimi Hendrix*. That same year, a Scotland Yard reinvestigation of Hendrix's death cleared Dannemann of any blame. Etchingham again sued and on April 3, 1996, Dannemann, 50, was convicted of contempt of court by a High Court judge. Ordered to pay court costs, the destitute woman escaped being sent to jail after medical reports deemed her too ill to serve prison time. Two days after the verdict, Danneman was found dead in her Mercedes sports car in the carbon monoxide fume–filled garage of her home in Seaford, East Sussex.

FURTHER READING

Dannemann, Monika. *The Inner World of Jimi Hendrix*. 1st U.S. ed. New York: St. Martin's Press, 1995.

Darvi, Bella

Born Bayla Wegier in Sosnowiec, Poland, on October 23, 1928, the future actress' parents immigrated to France in the thirties. Escaping a life of grinding poverty, Wegier ran away to Paris while still a teenager, and was in that city when it fell to the Nazis on June 14, 1940. The young girl was rounded up and shipped to Auschwitz for the remainder of the war. Demonstrating an ability to survive that would characterize the rest of her life, Wegier (by unknown means) managed to endure the horror of the concentration camp. By the late forties and early fifties, she had developed into a stunningly sexy young woman with the ability to speak four languages. A perennial at the Cannes Film Festival, Wegier was a fixture at the poshest parties and in the

top casinos on the Riviera, usually on the arm of some minor Italian, French, or English actor. Though still in her early twenties, the worldly young woman had already slept with most of the top critics and producers at the festival.

By the time 20th Century–Fox studio head Darryl F. Zanuck met her at Cannes in 1951, Wegier was known as a woman who borrowed money from her lovers to pay back gambling debts, but never repaid the loans. Zanuck, a notorious womanizer who conducted his numerous indiscretions in a bedroom behind his office at Fox, was nearly 50 when he and his wife of many years, Virginia, befriended the provocative beauty. While Mrs. Zanuck understood her husband's propensity to cheat, she permitted it as long as he exercised discretion and shielded the family from any potential fallout. Virginia Zanuck liked Wegier and encouraged her husband to give her a screen test should she ever come to Hollywood. She kindly offered to let Wegier stay in the beach house on the grounds of their home in Santa Monica until she could make other accommodations. Unknown to Virginia Zanuck, however, the studio head had already become sexually obsessed with the girl, and planned to bring her to Hollywood to continue the affair. Wegier arrived in Tinseltown at the end of 1952 and Virginia Zanuck put her up in the guest house in a room next to her 20-year-old daughter, Susan. Publicly, Zanuck kept his distance, but Wegier was a frequent visitor to the bedroom behind the studio chief's office.

Wegier was given a screen test at Fox that revealed to everyone (but the smitten Zanuck) that whatever sensual qualities she possessed in reality did not translate to the screen. At Virginia Zanuck's suggestion, Wegier was renamed "Bella Darvi," a combination of Darryl and Virginia. Given a huge publicity build-up by the studio, Darvi was assigned a small part in *Hell and Highwater* (1954), and the same year awarded the choice role of the seductive courtesan "Nefer" in director Michael Curtiz's film adaptation of Mika

Waltari's best-selling novel of ancient Egypt, *The Egyptian*. Budgeted at $4.2 million, the film bombed. *New York Times* reviewer Bosley Crowther charitably described Darvi's performance in it as "without charm or magnetism." Darvi's final film for Fox opposite Kirk Douglas, *The Racers* (1955), also lost money and received bad notices. Though Darvi was crushed by the bad reviews, Zanuck assured his lover that she would be a star.

Despite the critical condemnation of his "protégé," Zanuck might have continued to force Darvi on the film-going public had not an incident occurred that forced the aging studio head to send the actress packing. Virginia Zanuck had begun hearing rumors about their affair, but was content to do nothing as long as they were discreet. On the night of January 18, 1954, the Zanucks (with Darvi in tow) threw a huge welcome-back party at the Hollywood nightclub Ciro's for their daughter Susan, who had recently returned from entertaining the troops in Korea with the USO. At the party, a drunken Zanuck stripped off his shirt, and in the presence of 300 stunned party guests, attempted to do one arm pull-ups from a trapeze bar suspended over the stage. The embarrassing photo was later published full-page in *Life* magazine. Back home, Zanuck argued with his wife, then went to the guest house to be with Darvi, forgetting in his alcoholic haze that his returned daughter was back in her bedroom. Susan heard their lovemaking, told her mother, and Virginia Zanuck threw the pair off the property. That afternoon, Zanuck handed Darvi a first class plane ticket back to Paris and $2,000 in cash. Installed by her lover in a luxury apartment in Paris, Darvi enjoyed credit lines underwritten by Zanuck at the city's top clothiers and jewelers. She gambled with, and lost, vast sums of his money in casinos in Cannes, Nice, and Beaulieu. At one point, French authorities seized her passport and refused to let her leave the country until her gaming debts were settled. Zanuck paid them.

The affair finally ended at the Cannes Film Festival in 1955 after Zanuck learned that Darvi had taken a lesbian lover. After a couple of European flop films and a brief marriage to a French businessman, Darvi's life deteriorated into a series of suicide attempts brought on by depression and gambling debts. In August 1962, Darvi tried to take her life in Monaco. Attempt number two occurred at Roquebrune-Cap-Martin in April 1966. Darvi tried again in the Hotel Monte Carlo in June 1968 after the hotel confiscated her possessions for non-payment, and she had been slapped around on the streets by bill collectors. Zanuck bailed her out for the last time. On September 17, 1971, the 42-year-old actress' body was found in her apartment in Monte Carlo. Darvi had opened the gas taps on her cooking stove and then fell asleep. According to authorities, her body had been there for a week.

FURTHER READING

Mosley, Leonard. *Zanuck: The Rise and Fall of Hollywood's Last Tycoon*. 1st ed. Boston: Little, Brown, 1984.

Davidson, George A., Jr.

Davidson, a 28-year-old film test director for Fox studio, knew Constance Smith, a married mother of four children, for eight years before becoming hopelessly obsessed with her. Separated from actress-wife Thelma Roberts and struggling to pay a court judgment for her support, Davidson lived alone in a modest apartment at 7279 Fountain Avenue in Hollywood. On October 11, 1932, Davidson's repeated threats to kill Smith and then himself if she refused to marry him reached the flash point. That morning, the filmman phoned the 30-year-old woman at her home and threatened to come there and kill her if she refused his marriage demand. Fearful for her children's safety and with her husband out of town, Smith agreed to meet Davidson later that night at his apartment. When she arrived at 7:00 P.M., Davidson locked and nailed shut the front door, and for three hours brandished a .38-caliber revolver in her face all the while threatening to kill them both unless she relented. According to Smith, she had convinced Davidson to let her go when he suddenly fired two shots into his head.

At the scene, police found a note written by the woman to the dead man that read, "Georgie Darling: You are a very bad boy and I'm not going to love you anymore — love you enough now. How about a date tonight?" Smith maintained that Davidson had forced her to write the incriminating document during the three-hour ordeal. Davidson left two suicide notes. In one addressed to his boss at Fox studio, he wrote: "I have done this because it seems the odds are too much against me." To his mother, Davidson explained: "My mind has gone back on me. Thelma's … lawyer attached my salary and that, of course, broke me up, not having enough to take care of you…. I am perfectly sane and have planned this whole thing…. I love you and will always love you all. George."

Davies, Lynette

Davies, born the daughter of a customs and excise officer in Tonypady, Mid-Glamorgan, Wales, on October 18, 1948, turned to acting after growing too tall to be a ballerina. The striking blonde spent three years with the Royal Shakespeare Acting Company before landing the starmaking role of the sexy boardroom siren "Davinia Prince" in the smash BBC series *The Foundation* (1977–1978).

Davies complained of being typecast as bossy and bitchy in her subsequent television appearances in such shows as *Tales of the Unexpected* and *Inside Story*. After her stint on television, the actress returned to the stage, appearing in productions on the West End, New Zealand, Canada, and America. In the summer of 1993, Davies was touring with the Royal Shakespeare Company when the breakup of her second marriage prompted violent mood swings, depression, and stress. She voluntarily admitted herself to the Whitchurch Psychiatric Hospital in Cardiff where she responded quickly to treatment.

Soon after leaving the hospital, the actress was selected by writer Lynda La Plante to star in her nine-part BBC1 series *Lifeboat*, a chronicle of rescues at sea and drama on the shore of a coastal village in Wales. During the filming, police were called to the home of the 45-year-old actress and she was subsequently readmitted to Whitchurch under the Mental Health Act. When it became obvious that the depressed star would be emotionally unable to finish her assignment on the £4.5 million series, La Plante informed Davies that she had been replaced by actress Melanie Kilburn. Davies' scenes in seven of the nine episodes were scrapped and reshot with the new actress.

On December 11, 1993, just weeks after being dropped from *Lifeboat*, Davies was last scene getting off a bus in the seaside resort town of Penarth, South Glamorgan, Wales, after asking the driver, "Which way is it to the beach?" Sometime later, her partially clad, drowned body was found by a man walking his dog at the foot of cliffs on a deserted beach at Lavernock Point, one of the star's favorite childhood haunts near Penarth. The inquest at Cardiff returned an open verdict.

Davis, Peggy

Born Mary Margaret Laird in Birmingham, Alabama, circa 1894, the one-time *Ziegfeld Follies* beauty had a troubled history with men. At 12, she eloped with a military officer, but on the second day of their honeymoon he received a telegram from his true wife announcing that she had given birth to twins. The marriage was annulled, but three years later Davis married the son of a Pittsburgh millionaire. This time the honeymoon was four days old when Davis learned he was already married. Following the annullment, Davis travelled to New York City and established herself in the *Follies*. On April 2, 1925, she wed Australian millionaire David Townsend, retired from the stage, and with their young child, moved to the French Riviera in 1929. On the night of March 29, 1931, the 37-year-old beauty drove her car off a 200 foot cliff (known locally as a "suicide's leap") at a bend in the middle Cornice road near Eze, between Nice and Monte Carlo. A note found beside her crushed body read: "I hope my family will forgive me for the pain I am causing them. My only regret is leaving my little girl, but I am tired of life and I prefer to die."

Davis, Rose

Although crowned the champion cowgirl bronco rider at the Madison Square Garden Rodeo in 1938, success on the New York stage eluded the 25-year-old actress. By 1941 she had managed to snag only a handful of bit parts. Notified that her grandmother was near death in Fort Wayne, Indiana, Davis took an express train from New York to Chicago. On the night of January 7, 1941, as the train sped through the outskirts of New Brunswick, New Jersey, the bronco rider leapt to her death rather than face her family without having made her mark as a stage actress. Davis' broken body was found at the bottom of an embankment below the westbound tracks of the Pennsylvania Railroad. An illegible note scribbled in pencil on the back of a telegram and $1.35 were found in Davis' handbag near the body.

DeBerg, Adolph

DeBerg, who claimed to be a film director and misrepresented himself as a field man for Universal Film Corporation, was in the lower California town of Calexico to supposedly begin shooting a Spanish talking picture titled *Virgin Gold*. When the film fell through, he was subsequently wanted by police for passing two bad checks totalling $100. On August 4, 1930, the body of the "director" was found beside a shock of hay in a small pasture in Calexico, the victim of a fatal dose of self-administered ant paste. A note found on his body read: "I've studied myself all over, and I'm nothing but an unmitigated scoundrel. I've given myself a final trial and Judge Conscience, who is right always, has decreed the sentence of death. I'm going to the movies again and

then I'll end everything." In an added postscript to the note, DeBerg concluded: "The picture is over, and the lights are out for me."

Decker, Phelps

Variously identified by the press as a film editor for Universal, a scenarist, a researcher for D. W. Griffith and an advisor to Mary Pickford, Decker, 41, had long been unemployed when his wife found his lifeless body on February 5, 1928, slumped in a chair in front of a gas range with the jets and oven door open in the kitchen of their apartment at 35 East Thirtieth Street in New York City. Amid his wife's contentions that he had not committed suicide, Decker was subsequently cremated in Suffolk County.

Deckers, Jeanine

Better known as the "Singing Nun," Deckers scored an international hit in 1963 with her recording of "Dominique." Recorded while she was still a novice in the Dominican convent of Fichermont near Brussels, Belgium, "Sister Smile" (as she was called by the other nuns) did not learn of her fame until 1966 when MGM filmed a version of her life, *The Singing Nun*, featuring Debbie Reynolds in the title role. Unsure of her faith, Deckers left the cloister that year, but joined the Dominican Third Order, a group of lay members. Although "Dominique" was recorded more than 100 times by various artists, Deckers told an interviewer in 1978 that she had given all her royalties to the order and to Belgian tax collectors who claimed she owed $126,000. On the morning of April 1, 1985, police found the bodies of Deckers, 52, and a female friend in the home they shared in Wavre, Belgium. Both had taken fatal doses of sedatives. The women left a letter explaining the action and asking for discretion. Penniless at the time of their deaths, Deckers and her friend were known to have been despondent over the recent closure due to lack of funds of the institution they ran to aid handicapped children.

DeeJean, Delia

Famed throughout the Orient as a premier soprano, the 42-year-old opera star performed native India songs in costume at the Alexandria Theatre in San Francisco on December 12, 1923. Shortly before leaving for Australia on the first leg of a world tour, DeeJean became ill and was forced to remain in the city for weeks to recuperate. Despondent over her illness and the impending cancellation of the tour, DeeJean opened five jets on the gas range in her apartment at 765 Geary Street on January 9, 1924. A note to her sister pencilled on the back of an envelope found near the body read: "Florence, please send my things to babe (her daughter) and take care of her."

Dekker, Albert

A veteran character actor in more than 70 films and numerous stage plays, Dekker's accomplishments as an actor will forever be overshadowed by the bizarre nature of his death. Born Thomas Albert Ecke on December 20, 1904, in Brooklyn, New York, the future actor originally studied pre-med at Bowdoin College before an interest in student theatre prompted him to write a letter to famed stage actor Alfred Lunt. Through Lunt, Dekker found stage work in New York with the Group Theatre. In 1929, the same year he married actress Esther Guernini, Dekker made his stage debut in Eugene O'Neill's *Marco's Millions*.

A versatile character actor specializing in dialects, Dekker established himself on Broadway in plays like *Conflict* (1929), *Lysistrata* (1930), *The Passionate Pilgrim* (1932), *The First Apple* (1933–1934), *Fly Away Home* (1935), *Journey by Night* (1935), *Knock on Wood* (1935), and *Bitter Stream* (1936). In 1937, the 33-

year-old (billed as Albert van Dekker) came to Hollywood to appear in a small role in director James Whale's production of the *The Great Garrick* starring Brian Aherne in the title role. Whale (see entry), director of *Frankenstein* and *The Bride of Frankenstein*, later commited suicide in 1957. Dekker's stage training, imposing physical presence, and ability to do accents kept him in steady work in films throughout the late thirties and early forties. In his best remembered role, the 1940 Paramount sci-fi classic *Dr. Cyclops*, Dekker played "Dr. Thorkel," a mad scientist who shrinks people to doll-size.

Dekker's lifelong interest in liberal causes prompted the 39-year-old actor to run for and win a seat in the California State Assembly in

ALBERT DEKKER—Dekker established himself as a versatile character actor on Broadway prior to entering films in 1937. In a career spanning 40 years, he appeared in more than 70 films including a title role of the 1940 sci-fi classic *Dr. Cyclops*. Dekker's considerable accomplishments as an actor, however, will be forever overshadowed by the bizarre nature of his death in an apartment house in Hollywood in May 1968.

1944. Dekker, a Democrat, held the office for two years until running afoul of Senator Joseph McCarthy and his Communist witch-hunt in Hollywood in the fifties. An outspoken critic of McCarthy, Dekker was "graylisted" by the major studios and forced to support himself by doing dramatic readings at colleges, book societies, and literary groups. While the actor averaged at least four films a year in the forties, during the height of the McCarthy era Dekker made only one film in 1951 (*As Young as You Feel*), one film in 1952 (*Wait 'Til the Sun Shines, Nellie*), and no films during 1953–1954. Though continuing to act on Broadway and in touring companies, Dekker would not again actively enter films until 1955 with supporting roles in *East of Eden* and *Kiss Me Deadly*.

In the mid-sixties Dekker was on Broadway when he began taking "vitamin shots" for his throat problems. In actuality, the injections were liquid amphetamines which, while enabling the actor to stay up for days on end, quickly addicted him. Dekker was living in a modest apartment at 1731 N. Normandie in Hollywood after finishing his final movie, director Sam Peckinpah's 1967 Western *The Wild Bunch*. On May 2, 1968, Dekker, 63, and his longtime girlfriend, 45-year-old fashion model Jeraldine Saunders, returned to his apartment after attending the theatre. Saunders kissed him goodnight at the door and left. Dekker was never seen alive again. Unable to make contact with him for three days, a concerned Saunders arrived at Dekker's apartment building on May 5 and convinced the manager to open the actor's apartment.

What the horrified building super found ranks as either the most bizarre Hollywood suicide on record or the deadly aftermath of a solo sadomasochistic sex game gone horribly wrong. The dead veteran character actor was found in the bathroom crouching on his knees in the tub. Dekker, clad only in a negligee, had a rubber ball with a length of wire passed through it fastened in his mouth like a horse bit. Sexually charged words like "slave" were written all over his body in lipstick. "Whip" was scrawled on his buttocks. A leather strap, possibly a belt, was cinched around his neck. A rope tied to the shower head and pipe was fastened to the strap, passed down the length of Dekker's body, and secured his ankles together. Unlocked handcuffs hung from each wrist and two hypodermics were sticking out of his body. Police initially ruled Dekker's self-hanging as "quite an unusual case of suicide," but the coroner officially ruled it an accident caused by "suffocation and constriction of (the) neck by ligature." Today, Dekker's death appears to be a classic case of autoerotic asphyxiation.

De Lane Lea, William

De Lane Lea, a former colonel in the British Army, though universally known as the "Major," was chief engineer of the Record Company of America when he invented a system of synchronizing English dialogue to foreign films. Using the process, he dubbed the 1948 Italian film *Bitter Rice*. As managing director of De Lane Lea Purchases Ltd. of Moor Street, Soho, the film executive purchased several international movies, dubbed them, and exhibited the English language versions in Britain. These foreign films included three 1961 titles: *Carthage in Flames* (French/Italian), *Don Quixote* (Russian), *King in Shadow* (West German). In the mid-fifties, De Lane Lea suffered a serious heart attack that left him frail and depressed. On May 29, 1964, the 63 year old shot himself in the head with an Army revolver at his home in Charles Street, Mayfair. The coroner recorded that the Major took his own life while suffering from depression.

Desai, Manmohan

"The Miracle Man of Bollywood," or Bombay, capital of the Indian film industry, was born in that city on February 26, 1937. Son of director and studio owner Kikubhai Desai, he apprenticed with well-known director Babubhai Mistri in the late fifties. In 1960, at the age of 23, Desai made his directorial debut with *Chhalia* (*Tramp*). The movie was a moderate success and enabled the director to continue making small films. In 1977, Desai broke box office records with the blockbuster *Amar Akbar Anthony*. The film not only made Amitabh Bachchan one of India's biggest stars, but marked a radical departure in the way movies were made in the world's largest cinema industry. On average, India churned out 750 low-budget films a year on quick shooting schedules. Desai, following the traditional Hollywood model, spent money on lavish sets and took up to two years to make a film. Though never critical successes, the films appealed to the average moviegoer and made Desai India's most bankable independent producer-director.

After enjoying a string of nearly a dozen hits throughout the late seventies and mid-eighties, Desai became a victim of the public's changing taste in film. He quietly ended his collaboration with top actor Bachchan, and thereafter devoted much of his time to promoting the directorial career of son Ketan Desai. Forced into retirement in 1989 by severe backaches, Desai was depressed over his health and stalled career. On March 1, 1994, the 57-year-old showman jumped to his death from the roof of his three-story office building in Bombay.

Desmonde, Jerry

In his nearly 50 year show business career, British comedian Jerry Desmonde (real name James Robert Sadler) played the "stooge" in music halls to such famous comics as Sid Field, Norman Wisdom, Arthur Askey, and Bob Hope as well as appearing in some 19 films from 1946 (*London Town*) through 1965 (*Gonks Go Beat*). In the mid-fifties Desmonde guested on the BBC television program *What's My Line?*, and was emcee of the highly successful panel game *The 64,000 Question*, before being replaced in August 1957. On February 11, 1967, the 58-year-old comedian's son returned to their London flat in Eamont Street to find a suicide note in the living room.

Desmonde, dead from what a coroner later determined to be alcohol and barbiturate poisoning "self-administered while he was suffering from depression," was found in bed in his room. According to the son, Desmonde had been very upset by the death of his wife in November 1966.

Dewaëre, Patrick

Born Patrick Maurin in Saint-Brieuc, Brittany, on January 26, 1947, the popular French actor known for his aggressive, jumpy acting style once described himself as a "leftover from the May 1968" student revolution that nearly overturned the government of France. Debuting in Jean-Paul Rappeneau's 1970 film *Les Mariés de l'An II*, Dewaëre (with co-star Gerard Depardieu) shot to stardom in Bernard Blier's 1973 *Going Places*. Influenced by American actor Dustin Hoffman, Dewaëre essayed the roles of losers, outcasts, delinquents, and dreamers in more than two dozen films including *Get Out Your Handkerchiefs* (1978), *A Bad Son* (1980), and *Hotel of the Americas* (1981). After attaining stardom in 1973, the actor became a fixture in Left Bank sidewalk cafes and discotheques, despite being termed by friends a "solitary man" given to depression. In 1982, Dewaëre was at the height of his popularity when director Claude Lelouch signed him for *Edith and Marcel*, a film chronicling the relationship between French boxer Marcel Cerdan and singer Edith Piaf. On July 16, 1982, the actor appeared in good spirits at a photo session for the film conducted at the director's production office. One hour later, the blue-jean clad body of the 35-year-old actor was found on the floor of his townhouse in Paris' Montparnasse district. Dewaëre had shot himself in the mouth with a rifle, found at his side. Culture Minister Jack Lang issued this statement: "He knew how to translate the ambiguities and hesitations of a modern hero. Brutally interrupted, the career of Patrick Dewaëre will remain that of one of the great actors of French cinema."

Dimmitt, Charles Ridgley

Dimmitt, known in theatrical circles as "Ridge Waller," managed the Lafayette Theatre in Buffalo, New York, for ten years and was the editor of the theatrical publication *The Chorus Girl*. On April 13, 1909, the 47-year-old theatre manager entered the Greenmount Cemetery in Baltimore, Maryland, where his mother had been buried for 21 years. After paying the caretaker $3.00 for grave maintenance, Dimmitt proceeded to the grave, produced a pistol, and fired a shot into his mouth. He died hours later at St. Joseph's Hospital. Police recovered a gold ring, two brass buttons, and 16 cents from his pockets. Dimmitt was buried next to his mother.

Dimsdale, Howard and Dorothy

Logging his first screen credit for the 1942 Monogram comedy-thriller *The Living Ghost*, Howard Dimsdale wrote several other screenplays during the forties and early fifties. These include *Penthouse Rhythm* (1945), *Love Laughs at Andy Hardy* (1946), *A Lady Without a Passport* (1950), *Abbott and Costello Meet Captain Kidd* (1952), and *Captain Scarlett* (1953), which he also produced. However, after Dimsdale was identified as a Communist sympathizer by a "friendly" witness testifying before the House Un-American Activities Committee in 1950, he was blacklisted. Forced to work under the pseudonym "Arthur Dales," Dimsdale wrote the scripts for two British releases starring Kenneth More: *The Sheriff of Fractured Jaw* (1958) and *We Joined the Navy* (1962). In 1998, the Board of Directors of the Writers Guild of America voted to officially change the credits of these films to recognize Dimsdale's authorship. After Dimsdale returned to writing under his own name in 1971, he penned episodes for several television series including *Cannon*, *Executive Suite*, and *Medical Center*.

On August 27, 1991, Dimsdale, 78, and his wife of 30 years, Dorothy, were both found dead from an overdose of sleeping pills in their Hollywood Hills home. Dorothy Dimsdale, in her early sixties, had been suffering from Wegener's granulomatosis, a debilitating disease believed to be caused when the body attacks its own tissues. In a letter to their two children, Howard Dimsdale wrote: "Dorothy has gotten this really rotten disease. Treatment by chemotherapy is about as rotten as the disease.... At our age the road from here only goes downhill.... We got to this point together and we'll go together."

Dittrich, Frederick A.

Dittrich, the assistant manager of the Lyric and Ideal motion picture theatres in Endicott, New York, had been ill for several days, but his wife's nervous breakdown was credited with prompting him to commit suicide. On December 4, 1920, shortly after his wife had been removed to a hospital in Binghamton, the 44-year-old theatre manager entered the bedroom of his home in Hooper, New York, laid across the bed, and fired a bullet into his heart.

Dixon, Mort

Dixon, in collaboration with Harry Woods and Billy Rose, wrote the lyrics for such song standards as "That Old Gang of Mine," "Bye, Bye Blackbird," "I'm Looking Over a Four-Leaf Clover," and the thirties Tin Pan Alley sensation "The Lady in Red." On March 23, 1956, Dixon was found unconscious in his Yonkers, New York, home from an overdose of sleeping pills. The 64-year-old songwriter died hours later in Lawrence Hospital in nearby Bronxville. Yonkers police found two notes at the scene.

Dobritch, Alexander Anthony

A member of a European circus family, Dobritch was a producer of circus acts for the Las Vegas Circus Circus Casino. In November 1970 he was fired by Circus after being charged with the kidnapping and vicious pistol whipping of a longtime enemy and his girlfriend. Two days later, Dobritch was arrested on extortion charges for allegedly threatening to kill Strip entertainers if they did not kick back a portion of their earnings to him. When not engaged in protection racketeering, Dobritch worked free-lance booking circus acts for casinos and, at one time, for *The Ed Sullivan Show*. On March 11, 1971, Dobritch registered in the Mint Hotel under an assumed name, bolted the door of his 15th floor room, and 20 minutes later jumped from a window to his death, landing in the middle of First Street. Authorities, ruling out the possibility of a gangland hit in the absence of any signs of a struggle, theorized that the 56-year-old Dobritch may have become despondent over pending extortion trials.

Dolly, Jenny

The most popular vaudeville sister act of their day, Janszieka (Jenny) and Roszika (Rosa) Deutsch were born identical twins in Budapest, Hungary, on October 25, 1892. Known to American audiences as the Dolly Sisters, the pair were raised in Queens, New York, where by the age of 8 they were performing with an acrobatic troupe. In 1909, the dance team broke into vaudeville at B. F. Keith's Union Square Theatre. Shortly afterward, their month-long engagement at the Palace established a vaudeville record for a sister act. Their 1910 appearance in the musical comedy *The Echo* brought them to the attention of master showman Florenz Ziegfeld, who signed them for his 1911 *Follies*. In 1912, the sisters achieved headliner status with their dancing in Ziegfeld's *A Winsome Widow* and *The Merry Countess* for the Shuberts.

The next year, the sisters split after Jenny Dolly married Harry Fox and they formed their own vaudeville act. Although the childless marriage ended in divorce in 1921, Jenny Dolly had already reunited with her sister on Broadway in 1916 for *Her Bridal Night*. In 1918, the pair appeared as themselves in their only mutual film appearance, Metro's *The*

Million Dollar Dollies. In 1921, the Dolly Sisters scored a smash hit in London with their graceful synchronized dancing and eye-popping wardrobe in the Charles Blake Cochran revue *The League of Notions*. From 1922 until their official retirement from show business in 1927, the Dolly Sisters became recognized as international celebrities based on their highly successful appearances in music halls in London and Paris. In France, the pair lived like royalty and enjoyed a steady stream of wealthy suitors. Always fashion trendsetters, the sisters also introduced the Charleston and the Black Bottom into Parisian cafe society.

Jenny Dolly, a regular at casinos in France, was reportedly the first woman to break the bank at Monte Carlo. In 1929, Jenny adopted two Hungarian girls (Klari and Manzi) from an orphanage in Budapest. In 1933, while returning from a tryst with a lover, Jenny Dolly was severely injured in a car accident near Bordeaux when her chauffeur slammed into a tree going 75 miles per hour. Dolly sustained several broken bones, punctured lungs, and disfiguring facial scars that caused her to live as a recluse for three years while undergoing painful and expensive plastic surgery. Depressed, she later confided to a friend, "The doctors didn't do me any favors by saving my life." In 1935, she married Chicago attorney Bernard Vissinksy and he formally adopted her two girls. By mid–1941, Dolly had been separated from Vissinksy for six months and was living in Hollywood where her adopted teenaged daughters were trying to break into show business.

On June 1, 1941, the pajama-clad body of the 48-year-old dancer was found hanging by a rope improvised from two dressing gown sashes from a wrought iron curtain rod in the living room of her stylish Hollywood apartment at 1735 N. Wilcox Avenue. Two hours prior to the discovery of the suicide, Dolly had phoned her aunt, Frieda Bakos, to report that she "wasn't feeling well" since recently having a tooth removed. Concerned, Bakos rushed to Dolly's apartment, knocked on the door, but was answered from within only by the sounds of a whimpering dog. Summoning the manager, they opened the door to find Dolly's dog mewling beneath the suspended body of its owner. Dolly was buried at Forest Lawn Memorial Park.

In 1945, comedian George Jessel produced *The Dolly Sisters*, a 20th Century–Fox film based on the dancers' lives starring Betty Grable (Jenny) and June Haver (Rosa) in the title roles. Rosa Dolly died of a heart attack at the age of 77 in New York City on February 1, 1970. The Dolly Sisters are interred together in the Great Mausoleum in Forest Lawn Cemetery in Glendale, California.

Donley, Katherine

The wife of Robert Donley, former chief announcer at Pittsburgh radio station WCAE and currently with WINS in New York, was slowly driven to madness by her husband's application for divorce in April 1945. In court papers the announcer charged his 44-year-old wife with "cruel and barbarous treatment and with endangering his life with indignities." On November 7, 1945, the distraught woman checked into a 12th floor room of the William Penn Hotel in Pittsburgh with her 8-year-old son, James Patrick. Donley threw the boy out of the bedroom window and then plunged after him. Their shattered bodies were found 15 feet apart in a light well on the hotel's marquee three floors above street level. In two notes addressed to the dead woman's brother found in the room, Donley accused the 34-year-old announcer of being more interested in his career than family. One read: "My nervous system is completely shattered and I can't see my way — the financial insecurity and the worry and hurt over [son] Pat's predicament. His father hasn't inquired about him since last spring and saw him only once in the fall though we were 20 minutes by subway from where he was. Pat is bewildered, unsure, and afraid and I know I can't help him understand because I am in a worse state."

Donnelly, Cornelius

Appearing onstage as "Fred Arthur Walton," the 60-year-old actor was found dead in his one-room gas-filled furnished apartment at 317 West Fiftieth Street in New York City on August 8, 1938. Surrounded by photos of himself in various stage roles, Donnelly wrote two suicide notes (one bequeathing his clothes to the Actors' Fund of America), turned three gas jets on in a kitchen stove, and awaited death on his bed. Twenty-eight cents, the only cash found in the apartment, was also bequeathed to the actors' organization.

Doonan, Patric

Doonan, 31, had played the part of the detective-sergeant in Agatha Christie's long running play *The Mousetrap* at the Ambassador Theatre, London, for more than three years when he left the cast in late 1957 to take another part in a play, *Roseland*, which closed after just three nights at the St. Martin's Theatre. On March 10, 1958, the depressed actor was found dead in a gas-filled top floor room at his London home in Margaretta Terrace, Chelsea. According to the coroner, letters found after the actor's death showed that Doonan had suffered from a "certain amount of stress of mind." In addition to his theatrical work, Doonan had appeared in the British films *The Blue Lamp* (1950), *Appointment with Venus* (1951), and *The Gentle Gunman* (1952).

Dougherty, Virgil "Jack"

In movies since 1920 (*Neptune's Daughter*), the actor who made some 32 films is best remembered as the one-time husband of silent screen vamp Barbara La Marr, who overdosed on drugs in 1926. On the night of May 16, 1938, the 43-year-old actor's lifeless body was found slumped in the rear seat of his carbon monoxide–filled car parked at the corner of Woodstock and Willow Glen avenues in the Hollywood Hills. In one of the four suicide notes left by Dougherty the actor explained that he had recently passed several bad checks.

Douglas, Barbara L.

The wife of Alan Douglas, a popular Cleveland WEWS-TV personality, Douglas acted in the radio dramas *The Lone Ranger* and *The Green Hornet* under her maiden name of Barbara Lee DeWharton. In Cleveland area television, Douglas starred in a show called *Demitasse* (later renamed *Harmony Highway*) in which she sang and appeared in skits written by her husband. She retired from show business in 1966 following the birth of her son. On March 3, 1972, the 48-year-old entertainer left her home at 712 Tinkers Lane in the Sagamare Hills suburb of Cleveland after taking some Doriden sleeping pills. The next day at 9:30 A.M., a real estate agent, preparing to show an unoccupied new home three doors away from the Douglas house, opened the garage door and found the woman dead from carbon monoxide poisoning inside her car.

Dowling, Joan

A British actress born at Laindon, Essex, on January 6, 1928, Dowling was best known for her supporting roles in films like *No Room at the Inn* (1948) and *Women of Twilight* (1952). In 1951, Dowling married Harry Fowler, a cockney character actor she first met in 1947 when they were both filming *Hue and Cry*, in 1951. On March 31, 1954, the 26-year-old actress was found dead with her head in a gas oven in the kitchenette of her home in Farmer Street, Kensington, London. A subsequent inquest at Hammersmith ruled Dowling had taken her life "while the balance of her mind was disturbed." Responding to a question whether or not he and his wife were happy together, Fowler replied, "I do not think there was anybody as happy as Joan and I."

Drake, Nick

Though recording only three albums (31 songs) during a professional career that essentially lasted from 1969 to 1972, Drake's haunting blend of traditional British folk music with prevailing counterculture attitudes and lifestyle has deeply influenced contemporary artists such as Paul Weller, Peter Buck of R.E.M., Elton John, and others.

Born June 19, 1948, in Myanmar, Burma, where his father worked for a British timber company, Drake was 2 years old when the family returned to England and settled in the picturesque town of Tanworth-in-Arden, near Birmingham. After enjoying an outstanding public school career, Drake entered Fitzwilliam College, Cambridge, in October 1967 to study English. During the two years he spent there, Drake spent most of his time listening to Bob Dylan, practicing guitar, and writing poignant songs with themes of loneliness and introspection. Signed by Island after Fairport Convention bassist Ashley Hutchings saw him perform, Drake, 20, recorded his first album, *Five Leaves Left*, in 1969. Though critically well received, the album (often compared in mood to Van Morrison's classic *Astral Weeks*) sold only 5,000 copies. That same year, Drake quit school one year short of taking a degree, and moved to London. Intensely shy, Drake dreaded live appearances, and effectively ended his performing career in 1970 following a disastrous tour of student unions. In 1970, he recorded his second album, *Bryter Layter*, his most commercial venture. When it sold only 15,000 copies, Drake was cast into a spiralling depression.

Retreating from London to his parents' home in Tanworth-in-Arden, the musician became increasingly withdrawn, and spent hours staring out his bedroom window at the Warwickshire countryside. At the urging of family and friends, Drake visited a psychiatrist and was given a prescription for the anti-depressant Tryptizol. The medication evidently helped enough to enable Drake to return to the studio for two days in late 1971 to record the stark, acoustic album *Pink Moon*. Following the album's release in 1972, Drake did not record again until 1974 when he was coaxed back into the studio to lay down four tracks for an unreleased album. By that time, however, Drake's depression was out of control.

No longer bathing, increasingly uncommunicative, and subject to bouts of manic depression, Drake would often set off in his car to tour the surrounding countryside. Hours later, his parents would receive a call from their son asking them to come and get him. The car out of gas, Drake was emotionally unable to face the ordeal of stopping at a station to buy it.

On November 25, 1974, the 26-year-old musician was found by his mother lying dead on his bed from an overdose of Tryptizol. Though the coroner officially ruled the death a suicide, family and friends remain convinced that his death was accidental. A simple headstone in the graveyard of St. Mary Magdalene, the village church of Tanworth-in-Arden, reads "Nick Drake, 1948–1974."

FURTHER READING

Humphries, Patrick. *Nick Drake*. London: Bloomsbury, 1997.

Drew, Lillian

Known as "The Lily of the Essanay," the silent film star was born in Chicago, Illinois, in 1883. She received her early musical training in Chicago while appearing onstage there in various amateur productions. Turning professional, Drew became a leading woman in the Baker Stock Company of Portland and in San Francisco's Alcazar Stock Company. While appearing on Broadway, Drew married actor E. H. Calvert. In 1912, the pair joined the Essanay Film Manufacturing Company. With Calvert often directing, Drew appeared in at least 30 movies (often in vamp roles) made between 1913 and 1918. Drew's Essanay films include *The Lost Chord* (1913), *The Price of His Honor* (1914), *In the Palace of the King* (1915), *The Great Deceit* (1915), *His Moral Code* (1916), *The Wifeless Husband* (1917), and *Uneasy Money* (1918). With the decline of femme fatale roles, Drew's career nosedived in the early twenties. Among her last films was a small part in the 1923 Famous Players–Lasky six-reeler *Children of Jazz*. Now estranged from her actor-director husband, Drew suffered a nervous breakdown in 1923 while a modiste in New York. Emotionally spent and depressed over financial reverses, Drew spent the next six months recuperating in her mother's home at 4701 Winthrop Avenue in Chicago. On Saturday, February 2, 1924, the 41-year-old actress accidentally slipped and fell in the bathroom, striking her head against a radiator. To relieve the pain, Drew took a large dose of veronal. That afternoon after her condition became critical, the family registered Drew into the county hospital under the name "Helen Calvert." Drew, a probable suicide, died as the result of veronal poisoning on February 4, 1924.

Dreyfuss, Henry and Doris

The son of a theatrical costumer, Dreyfuss was born in New York City on March 2, 1904. At 17, he became an assistant to theatrical designer Norman Bel Geddes. Following a brief apprenticeship, Dreyfuss designed sets for the productions of *Hold Everything!* (1928), *The Last Mile* (1930), *Fine and Dandy* (1930), *The Cat and the Fiddle* (1931), and *Strike Me Pink* (1933). By the mid-thirties, Dreyfuss' interest had changed to industrial design where he distinguished himself as a top innovator. He designed the 20th Century Limited passenger train, the interior of the Boeing 707 airliner, and was the first to suggest putting swimming pools on the decks of ocean liners. In addition to designing everyday items like clocks, cameras, sinks, razors, and faucets, Dreyfuss also produced trademarks and revamped the formats of *Time*, *Life*, and *Reader's Digest*. On October 5, 1972, the bodies of Dreyfuss, 68, and his wife and partner of 42-years, Doris, 69, were found in a car in the carbon monoxide-filled garage of their home in South Pasadena, California. Authorities believed that the suicide pact was prompted by Doris' steadily declining health. An editorial in *The Los Angeles Times* characterized Dreyfuss as "a genius of creativity with the highest standards of taste and quality in every aspect of his life."

Duane, Ann

Unable to sustain herself by playing small roles like the maid in the vaudeville act "Cave-Man Love" at the Wintergarden Theatre in 1921, the 19-year-old actress ingested six bichloride of mercury tablets in the restroom of the Pennsylvania Station in New York City on July 3, 1922. When asked by a physician at Bellevue Hospital why she did not tell her friends at the scene of the poisoning, Duane replied, "When you have no money in the theatrical business you have no friends." Destitute, the actress had not eaten anything for four days at the time of her suicide attempt. Duane died on July 8, 1922. With monies jointly contributed by an actress-friend and the Actors' Fund, Duane was buried at the Evergreen Cemetery.

Duarte, Pablo

The dance team of "Ricardo and Georgianna" (Duarte, 41, and his 28-year-old wife) had danced in minor New York night spots, but were planning to return to their native Cuba when a deadly argument erupted in their one room ground floor apartment at 44 West Sixty-fifth Street on July 16, 1949. Later that day, Georgianna's brother arrived to help the couple pack and smelling gas, notified the building super and several neighbors. Breaking into the gas-filled apartment, the group found a classic scene of murder-suicide. Duarte, near death from the fumes, had fatally butchered his wife with an eight inch carving knife. Removed to Roosevelt Hospital, the dancer died three hours later.

Du Cello, Countess (Mary)

Friends assumed that the Englishwoman who called herself "Countess Du Cello" had once been married to a French count before coming to Los Angeles to recover from diabetes and heart disease. Her current husband, Christopher E. Bunting, lived in the Carleton Apartments in Buffalo, New York. In films as a supporting actress since 1916, Du Cello ap-

peared in at least 17 films for studios like Universal and Bluebird including *The Girl of the Lost Lake* (1916), *The Place Beyond the Winds* (1916, with Lon Chaney), *The Devil's Pay Day* (1917), *The Girl in the Checkered Coat* (1917, with Lon Chaney), *The Husband Hunter* (1918), and *Sue of the South* (1919). On the evening of November 20, 1921, neighbors heard choking groans issuing from the 60-year-old actress' room in the Bonnie Brier Hotel at 6806 Hollywood Boulevard in Los Angeles. Forcing the door, tenants found Du Cello writhing in agony on her bed next to an empty vial later determined to have contained morphine. Her doctor, L. R. Mace, was summoned, but was unable to save the woman. According to Mace, Du Cello had a history of nervous agitation and was subject to dramatic mood swings.

Duel, Peter

Born Peter Ellstrom Duell in Penfield, New York, on February 24, 1940, Duel (a.k.a. Deuel) graduated from the American Theatre Wing in New York City in 1961 and, following a tour in the national company of *Take Her, She's Mine* with Tom Ewell, arrived in Hollywood in 1964. A seriously trained actor, Duel's plan was simple: suffer through television work for five years then return to Broadway with enough clout to pick and choose stage roles. In 1965 he was a regular on *Gidget*, the ABC television series starring Sally Fields in the title role. When it ended in 1966, he landed a lead role in the ABC series *Love on a Rooftop*, which was cancelled in August 1967. That year, Duel signed a seven-year contract with Universal Pictures and was thereafter seen in guest shots on several studio-produced television series (*Ironside*, *The Name of the Game*) and made-for-TV movies (*Marcus Welby: A Matter of Humanity*, 1969). On film, Duel appeared in *Generation* (1969) and *Cannon for Cordoba* (1970).

While most actors welcome the professional security of a studio contract, Duel seemingly saw it as a prison sentence that

turning to New York City to become a "serious actor." Interviewed one month prior to his death, Duel described acting in a television series as "a big fat drag to an actor who has any interest in his work. It's the ultimate trap."

Unhappy in his profession, Duel suffered personal setbacks as well. In June 1971, an arrest for drunken driving (his second since 1967) resulted in a lost license, a two year suspension, and a promise extracted by a judge from the actor that he quit drinking. In November 1971, Duel lost a bid for an executive post in the Screen Actors Guild. Upset, he pinned the telegram notifying him of the defeat to a wall, and shot it. On December 30, 1971, the 31-year-old actor finished a day of shooting at the studio and returned for the evening to his two-bedroom home at 2552 Glen Green Terrace in the Hollywood Hills. There, Duel spent the evening drinking heavily and watching television with live-in girlfriend Diane Ray. After viewing an episode of *Alias Smith and Jones* and a Lakers game, the young woman retired to bed alone. She was awakened around 12:30 A.M. when Duel entered the bedroom, removed a snubnose .38-caliber revolver from a bedside drawer, and left saying, "I'll see you later." Moments later Ray heard the shot. Investigating, she found Duel's naked body underneath the Christmas tree, dead from a single wound to the right temple. The bullet that killed him exited the actor's head, went through a window, and landed on the floor of a carport across the street. Two empty shell casings were found in the gun — one from a bullet fired weeks before at the telegram, the other from the suicide shot. According to Duel's brother, the actor had recently spoken to him about being despondent over a drinking problem. Duel was buried in the Oakwood Cemetery in his hometown of Penfield, New York. Actor Roger Smith replaced Duel's character in the series, which ran until January 1973.

PETE DUEL— Unlike most actors who dream of landing a lucrative television series, Duel looked upon the work as a frivolous, but perhaps necessary step in realizing his true dream of stardom on the legitimate stage. Frustrated, the actor turned to political causes and alcoholism. After winning the role of "Smith" in the ABC Western series *Alias Smith and Jones* in 1971, Duel saw himself trapped in a hit series unworthy of his acting aspirations. On December 31, 1971, the depressed 31-year-old actor shot himself in his Hollywood Hills home following a night of heavy drinking.

prevented him from doing serious work. Duel turned to environmental activism and politics in the late sixties and was at Senator Eugene McCarthy's side during the 1968 riot-plagued Democratic Convention in Chicago. In 1971, Duel landed his third television series, *Alias Smith and Jones*, a lighthearted Western co-starring Ben Murphy. The show's popularity seemed to indefinitely delay his dream of re-

Duell, Joseph

Duell (born April 30, 1956, in Dayton, Ohio) and his older brother, Daniel, began dancing at an early age. At 15, he came to New York to attend the School of American Ballet's summer session and stayed on as a full-time scholarship student. Under the tutelage of famous choreographer George Balanchine, the young dancer joined the New York City Ballet corps in 1975. Driven by a desire to become a great dancer, Duell worked himself unmercifully to aspire to the level of his brother's dancing. At the time, he told an interviewer his goal was "to get better than my brother … if I could do that, I would get out from under." Advised by Balanchine to "Just live," Duell made a well-received choreographic debut with the company in 1982 and ultimately became the corps' principal dancer. Success, however, did not calm his personal demons and Duell, under the care of both a psychiatrist and a psychologist, had taken anti-depressant medication for years. On Sunday morning, February 16, 1986, Duell leaped from the fifth story window of his West Seventy-seventh Street apartment in New York City. He left no note. While friends noticed that Duell had seemed more depressed recently, none could point to a "final trigger" that drove the talented dancer to take his life.

Du Fragnne, Jacques

On January 2, 1931, the young French actor was at the Eagle Rock, California, home of Mrs. Ellis Timmons, a fellow thespian with whom he had appeared in the play *Gratuities, Please* at the Pasadena Community Theatre a few days earlier. Midway through a discussion of an upcoming play they planned to co-produce, Du Fragnne complained of being indisposed and went to the bathroom. He emerged moments later, staggered to a couch in an adjoining room, and asked Mrs. Timmons not to call a doctor. Hearing noises from the room sometime later, the woman entered to find the 28-year-old actor in convulsions. Du Fragnne died en route to a hospital. Police found an empty flask that had contained strychnine and a note addressed to a friend instructing that his former wife living in Oklahoma be notified of his death and be sent all his possessions.

Dunville, T. E. (Thomas Edward)

The Coventry-born Dunville (real name Wallen) came to London as a 17 year old in 1887 making his first regular stage appearance that year in pantomime. Following a brief interval on the legitimate stage, the comedian began his career in the music halls, where he remained a popular attraction for 25 years until motion pictures and a change in public taste limited his ability to get work. On March 21, 1924, the 54-year-old entertainer left his wallet containing some money and a note to his wife at the office of the York Hotel in London and disappeared. The next day, Dunville's fully clothed body was found floating in the Thames at Caversham Lock, near Reading, by two boys walking by the side of the river. The Reading Coroner returned a verdict of "Suicide while of unsound mind."

Dupree, Maida

On the evening of November 24, 1913, 20-year-old vaudeville soubrette Maida Dupree registered in Philadelphia's Hotel Vendig under the name "Elizabeth Daly." Sometime later, Dupree's agonized screams were heard by a floor matron who notified the house detective. Upon entering, he found Dupree semi-conscious after drinking carbolic acid. Rushed to nearby Medico-Chirurgical Hospital by taxi, Dupree died 20 minutes later. The soubret left no note, but authorities found jewelry in her room worth $2,000, a fur coat, a valise filled with clothing, and pawn tickets totalling $1,350.

Dusenbury, Will J.

On the morning of July 7, 1935, a woman witnessed the 70-year-old world traveller and prominent amusement park and theatre promoter walk onto the Town Street bridge in Columbus, Ohio, remove his coat and straw hat, and momentarily bury his face in his hands before climbing upon the railing and jumping into the Scioto River. Authorities dragged the river without success until early the next morning when George Sapp, a strolling singer and entertainer at a local beer garden, discovered the old man's body below the Rich Street bridge and, jumping into the Scioto, recovered it. Dusenbury, who with older brother Joseph had long been a fixture in Columbus entertainment circles, had been in ill health for several years.

Duval, Lillian Bell

Despondent over ill health and the separation from her husband, the 26-year-old vaudeville singer and dancer committed suicide in her Boston home at 396 Northampton Street on March 19, 1916 by opening up two cocks on her kitchen gas stove. Known on the stage as "Lillian Bell," the vaudevillian was barely alive when found on the kitchen floor and died shortly afterward in the ambulance en route to the hospital.

Eagels, Jeanne

Christened Amelia Jean at her birth in Kansas City, Missouri, on June 26, 1894, Eagels' acting career began at 7 when she played the role of "Puck" in a local production of Shakespeare's *A Midsummer Night's Dream*. The stagestruck adolescent spent several years touring with a repertory company in the Midwest before coming to New York City in the early teens to pursue her dream of Broadway stardom. After appearing in minuscule parts in plays like *Jumping Jupiter* (1911) and in *The "Mind the Print" Girl* (1912), Eagels gained critical notice as Alexander Hamilton's mistress in *Hamilton* (1917) and for her role in *The Wonderful Thing* (1920). In 1922, Eagels landed the star-making role of "Sadie Thompson" in *Rain*, the John Colton-Clemence Randolph play based on W. Somerset Maugham's short story. When the play closed in 1924 after two nearly sold-out years, Eagels continued the role with a touring company. During the play's Broadway run the actress had rarely missed a performance. On the road, however, Eagels developed the reputation of a prima donna, often failing to appear or petulantly walking off-stage if a scene failed to please her. Though Eagels did suffer from chronic upper respiratory and sinus problems, those close to the actress suspected that her erratic behavior was at least partially due to her drinking and drug-taking on top of her prescription medication.

While touring with *Her Cardboard Lover* in 1928, Eagels was suspended for 18 months by Actors' Equity for missing performances in Milwaukee and St. Louis. Banned from appearing in any stage productions, the actress turned to Hollywood where in 1927 she starred opposite John Gilbert in the MGM silent *Man, Woman, and Sin*. The movie received lukewarm reviews as did her final two films, *Jealousy* and *The Letter*, both Paramount Famous Lasky productions released in 1929.

After the suspension was lifted on September 1, 1929, Eagels returned to New York to begin preparing to reappear onstage. However, the actress' personal life was in ruins. On June 14, 1928, Eagels divorced her wealthy stockbroker husband of three years, Edward Harris Coy, on the grounds of physical cruelty. Almost immediately after arriving in New York, Eagels was operated on in St. Luke's Hospital for ulcers of the eyes caused by her chronic sinus infections. Some three weeks later on the night of October 4, 1929, the 35-year-old actress was taken by her maid to the Park Avenue Hospital where she had been receiving regular treatments from her personal physician, Dr. Edward Cowles. While being examined by his associate, Eagels went into a convulsion, collapsed, and died almost instantly. The initial cause of death, alcoholic psychosis, was changed after an autopsy revealed that the actress had died from an overdose of chloral hydrate, a nerve sedative and soporific. At a morning service conducted at the Campbell Funeral Church the next day,

3,000 friends, mourners, and curiosity seekers filed past her bier. That afternoon, her body was placed aboard the Twentieth Century Limited for Kansas City, Missouri. On October 7, 1929, thousands paid tribute to the memory of the dead actress in her hometown as her body lay in state at the St. Vincent de Paul Catholic Church prior to her internment in Cavalry Cemetery. In 1957, Kim Novak played the actress in the film biography *Jeanne Eagels*.

FURTHER READING

Doherty, Eddie. *The Rain Girl: The Tragic Story of Jeanne Eagels*. Philadelphia: Macrae Smith Company, 1930.

Eastman, George

Though George Eastman never wrote, directed, or starred in a motion picture, his contribution to filmmaking is perhaps unequalled. Born July 12, 1854, in Waterville, New York, Eastman was the only son of George Washington Eastman, founder of Rochester, New York's Eastman Commercial College. After the death of his father in 1862, Eastman was ultimately forced to leave school at 14 to help support his family as a messenger boy and office clerk. By the late 1870s Eastman was dabbling in the technical aspects of photography when not working full time as a bookkeeper in the Rochester Savings Bank. In 1877, he began experimenting in "dry plate" emulsion, a radical departure from the standard "wet plate" emulsions upon which most still photography was taken and then developed into prints. Eastman's search for a transparent, flexible film with a paper backing culminated in 1888 with the introduction of the Number 1 Kodak, a $25 box camera containing a 100 exposure roll of film.

It was not until 1895, however, that his dream of converting photography from the realm of the professional to that of a pastime for amateurs was realized with the production of the pocket Kodak camera, which cost around $5.00. Years before in 1889, Eastman's invention of a perforated celluloid film had enabled Thomas Alva Edison and W. K. L. Dickson to perfect their kinetograph, a forerunner of the modern motion picture camera. The Eastman Kodak Company, established that same year in Rochester and destined to employ some 20,000 workers, became the world's largest producer of raw film stock. The 35mm film size first manufactured by Eastman more than a century ago remains the standard today.

As a philanthropist, Eastman had few equals. It is estimated that during his life he gave away more than $75 million to the Massachusetts Institute of Technology (MIT), the Hampton and Tuskegee institutes, and in the establishment of the Eastman School of Music and the School of Medicine and Dentistry at the University of Rochester. Though Eastman's mind was still alert, years of poor health had forced him to assume a smaller role in his company. On March 14, 1932, moments after signing a new codicil to his will at his mansion on East Avenue in Rochester, New York, the 77-year-old unmarried industrialist and inventor excused himself to his attorney and doctor and went alone into his bedroom. Eastman stretched out on his bed, placed a wet towel on his chest to prevent powder burns, then pressed the muzzle of a Luger automatic to his chest. At 12:50 P.M. the film pioneer pulled the trigger. A suicide note written in ink on yellow-lined paper found on the night table read:

> "To my friends
> My Work is done —
> Why wait?
> GE"

A second Luger was discovered hidden in a bookcase in the room.

L. B. Jones, vice-president of the Eastman Kodak Company, put Eastman's suicide into perspective: "To those who knew the orderly working of his mind, his passion for being useful — always useful, his dread of an illness that might make him mentally, as well as physically inactive, his act can be understood. A great man. At the end of the chapter, he wrote his own *finis.*" Amid much pomp and circumstance, a funeral service was conducted at St. Paul's Church in Rochester on March 17, 1932. At 3:30 P.M. that afternoon all the lights in that town's movie houses were dimmed one minute out of respect for the man whose film had made motion pictures possible. Eastman was cremated the next day at the Mount Hope Chapel in Rochester, and the solid bronze urn bearing his remains buried at his parents' plot in Waterville, New York.

FURTHER READING

Brayer, Elizabeth. *George Eastman: A Biography.* Baltimore: Johns Hopkins University Press, 1996.

Eberhardt, Walter F.

A veteran exploitation publicist who worked for a number of film studios (Famous Players–Lasky, First National), Eberhardt joined Electrical Research Products, Inc. (part of Western Electric) in 1929 as director of publicity and advertising. In recent years, the executive had turned to mystery writing, producing the novels *Dagger in the Dark* (1932), *The Jig-Saw Puzzle Murder* (1933), as well as two film novelizations. For years Eberhardt had worn a glass eye, but shortly before his death feared that he was losing sight in the other. On October 26, 1935, the 44-year-old publicist took his life in the garage adjoining his home at 46 Walbrooke Road in Scarsdale, New York. Eberhardt's body was found slumped down in the front seat of his car with a rubber tube attached to the car's exhaust running up through the floor boards of the vehicle into his mouth. Three notes were located on the floor next to the body. In one, believed to be for his aunt, Eberhardt wrote: "I am sorry. I wanted to call you, but it was already too late. My abiding love. Walter."

Eccles, John B.

Eccles, the chief announcer for Detroit radio station WJR, worked his early shift on November 19, 1936, and was scheduled to broadcast again at 4:00 P.M. Shortly before air time, the ten year WJR veteran entered the basement of his home at 1558 Lawrence Avenue, wrote a farewell note to his wife, then placed a double barreled, 12-gauge shotgun in his mouth and fired. Eccles' wife found the body and the note he left her: "Mabel Darling—-This has been coming on for a long time. See Gene Weeks as soon as you can and have the insurance arranged. Believe it or not, I am very calm. I wonder if the B shot will do the job. 4's or 5's are better for geese. Hope I have the courage to shoot twice. God I hope you will forgive me — but why should you?"

Ecker, Murray

Ecker, a dentist of choice in theatrical circles, had suffered from a nervous ailment for some time when he plunged out of the eighth floor window of his ex-wife's apartment at 215 West Eighty-eighth Street in New York City on March 20, 1942. As the woman, her daughter, and Ecker's psychiatrist watched in stunned amazement, the 55-year-old dentist proclaimed, "Goodbye, I'm going," and jumped from the window before he could be restrained.

Eddy, Wesley

Eddy (real name Edward Gargiulo) was a versatile vaudeville and nightclub performer who gained renown as the one-time master of ceremonies at the Roxy Theatre in New York City as well as other large movie houses throughout the East. Subject to fits of despondency since the death of his mother in 1926, the 31-year-old emcee had flowers placed weekly on her grave in St. Michael's Cemetery in Stratford, Connecticut. During the night of September 16, 1934, Eddy visited the cemetery and shot himself once in the head over his mother's grave. While police initially suspected foul play when the gun was recovered partially buried in the ground some 20 feet from the body, they decided upon suicide when they found two notes at the scene.

In one addressed to his brother, Eddy wrote: "Please see that I am buried right away, next to our dear mother." Authorities reasoned that an individual found Eddy's body prior to the person who notified them and, because of religious scruples, attempted to bury the gun. The Bridgeport, Connecticut, medical examiner ruled the death a suicide.

Edwards, Darrell Darwin

A childhood friend of country legend George Jones, Edwards penned some 70 songs for artists like Johnny Cash, Willie Nelson, Conway Twitty, and Jerry Reed. Jones, who scored a Number 4 hit in 1955 with the songwriter's "Why, Baby, Why," ultimately recorded 24 songs written by Edwards. Among them were "What am I Worth?" (1956) and "Tender Years" (1961). Despondent after returning from an unsuccessful business trip to Nashville, the 56-year-old songwriter fatally shot himself in the garage of his brother's home in Beaumont, Texas, on June 10, 1975. Edwards was buried in Beaumont's Hooks Cemetery.

Edwards, Jeannie

Edwards, a 34-year-old actress who had been appearing for the last three days at the Grand Theatre in Raleigh, North Carolina, took an overdose of veronal in her room at the Capitol Inn on March 8, 1912. An empty pill vial and a note hastily penned on the back of her business card was found on a nightstand. The note read, "I leave everything to — " followed by some illegible names. Edwards died the next day at Rex Hospital after lying in a coma for 36 hours. A search of her effects revealed that she was also known as "Jennie McCann," an 1895 graduate of the Conservatory of Music of Boston who had appeared on both the dramatic and grand opera stages in that city.

Eichelberger, Ethyl

Born James Roy Eichelberger in Pekin, Illinois, on July 17, 1945, the flamboyant stage actor-playwright–performance artist legally changed his name to Ethyl Eichelberger in 1975. The son of Amish parents, he studied theater at Knox College in Galesburg, Illinois, before attending the American Academy of Dramatic Arts in New York. Eichelberger then acted for seven years with the Trinity Square Repertory Company in Providence, Rhode Island, under the direction of Adrian Hall. After coming to New York City with Charles Ludlam and the Ridiculous Theatrical Company in 1975, Eichelberger changed his first name to "Ethyl" and began perfecting his flair for comedy and wigmaking, which characterized his eccentric theatrical career. With the troupe, he appeared in *Caprice* (1976), *Der Ring Gott Farblonjet* (1977), and *Salammbo* (1985–86).

Known for performing both male and female roles with equal facility, Eichelberger was also a prolific playwright who created more than 30 plays, often zanily reinventing the classics. In *Leer*, his one-man condensation of Shakespeare's *King Lear*, the actor played the "King," the "Fool," and "Cordelia," while accompanying himself on the accordion and concertina. He gave similar treatments to the classics in *Dilbert Dingle-Dong* (an adaptation of Molière's *George Dandin*), *Hamlette* (a female version of Shakespeare's *Hamlet*), and *Das Vedanya Mama* (a variation on Chekhov's plays). On Broadway in 1989, Eichelberger performed opposite Sting in *The Three Penny Opera*, playing a crankbox and singing "Mack the Knife." Besides being an award winning stage actor (in 1982–1983 he won an Obie for his performance in *Lucrezia Borgia*), Eichelberger was also a master hairstylist who designed wigs for various productions of the Ridiculous Theatrical Company (*The Mystery of Irma Vep*, 1984–85; *Salammbo*, 1985–86; and *The Artificial Jungle*, 1986–87).

On August 12, 1990, the 45-year-old actor and AIDS sufferer slashed his wrists in his home in Staten Island, New York. Eichelberger's final performance was posthumous. He appeared as himself in Oliver Stone's 1991 film *The Doors*, unreleased at the time of his suicide.

Eisenberg, Emanuel

Eisenberg, 35, was a well-known theatrical press agent who was representing *Reunion in New York* at the Little Theatre in New York City when he apparently chose a most peculiar way to die on March 14, 1940. According to pilot Joseph Rosemarin, Eisenberg approached him at the Floyd Bennett Field in Long Island and asked him for flying lessons. The two were airborne in a two-seater Piper Cub monoplane equipped with dual controls when Eisenberg asked to fly over Broadway. As it was raining, Rosemarin refused. Eisenberg then tried to jump from the window of the plane and, when restrained by Rosemarin, grabbed the controls. During their fight, the plane lost altitude, finally pancaking into the waters of the New York Bay near the Statue of Liberty. Rosemarin was rescued by a passing tug, while Eisenberg's body remained undiscovered in the water for two days until it was located off Bayonne, New Jersey.

A friend later told authorities that on the morning of the fateful flight, Eisenberg told his work replacement, "I've got something big doing today." Known to be neurotic and moody, Eisenberg had recently suffered a career reversal when a publisher refused to publish his book on Harlem. Diagnosing himself with a brain tumor, the press agent failed to keep an appointment with a specialist arranged by his physician.

Ellison, Jim

When major label Mercury Records signed the Chicago rock band Material Issue in 1990, Ellison, the group's guitarist-singer-songwriter, had already spent years "selling" the band by plastering posters all over town and making contacts with local club owners. *International Pop Overthrow*, produced for a meager $5,000, was released by Mercury on February 5, 1991, and sold some 187,000 copies. A catchy collection of power-pop songs about girls containing such gems as "Valerie Loves Me" and "Diane," the album's success ushered in a Chicago rock renaissance. With Material Issue at the vanguard, such Chicago-based artists as Liz Phair, Smashing Pumpkins, and Urge Overkill all received national attention. However, when the group's next two albums (*Destination Universe*, 1992; and *Freak City Soundtrack*, 1994) experienced lackluster sales, Mercury dropped them at the end of 1994.

After trying repeatedly over several days to contact the 32-year-old musician by phone, Ellison's mother notified police. At 12:45 A.M. on June 20, 1996, authorities entered the garage at Ellison's home on the 2200 block of West Fletcher in the Chicago suburb of Lake View. They found a car running and Ellison's body slumped over the handlebars of a moped. In a suicide note found near the body, Ellison begged forgiveness from his friends and family, but stated that he just could not go on living in the aftermath of a recent breakup with his girlfriend. Though the rocker never abused drugs or alcohol, the medical examiner found a "very small amount" of cocaine in Ellison's blood that was probably taken two hours before he died.

Enslen, Neel B.

A graduate of the Eastman School of Music and the Bush Conservatory in Chicago, Enslen was an original member of that city's American Opera Company before coming to New York in 1929. Although lacking radio training, the baritone auditioned for the National Broadcasting Company and was hired as an announcer for the network's early morning and local programs.

On the afternoon of May 22, 1938, a tenant walking in the hall past Enslen's apartment at 80 Haven Avenue noticed a strong smell of gas coming from the announcer's room. A note found near his door warned, "Don't smoke cigarettes, don't light matches." Enslen, 45, was found asphyxiated on the kitchen floor of the apartment near a gas stove with five of its jets opened. Illness had recently forced him to take a two week vacation from work. Enslen's wife, the former musical comedy star Beatrice Kneale, was visiting friends at the time of the suicide.

Entwistle, Peg

Born Lillian Millicent "Peg" Entwistle in London, England, on February 6, 1908, the woman dubbed "the Patron Saint of Out-of-Work Actors" came from a show business family. Following the death of her actress-mother, Entwistle moved with actor-father Robert to New York where he appeared on Broadway. In 1925, the 17-year-old actress made her Broadway stage debut as a bit player in a production of *Hamlet*. The blue-eyed blonde ingénue worked in various stock companies while building her Broadway resume with small parts in two 1926 plays: *The Man from Toronto* and *The Home Towners*. In 1927, Entwistle earned

excellent reviews in the female lead opposite Sidney ("Charlie Chan") Toler in *Tommy*. That same year she married actor Robert Lee Keith, but the marriage ended in divorce in 1929 after Entwistle learned that her husband had been previously married. Ironically, Robert Keith's child, future actor Brian Keith of *Family Affair* television fame, would also fall victim to suicide in 1997 (see entry).

Entwistle continued to work on the New York stage throughout the late twenties and early thirties in *The Uninvited Guest* (1927), *Sherlock Holmes* (1929, opposite William Gillette), *She Means Business* (1931), playwright George Bernard Shaw's *Getting Married* (1931),

PEG ENTWISTLE— Peg Entwistle, the ultimate symbol of Tinseltown tragedy, was a moderately successful stage actress before coming to Hollywood in April 1932 to break into the movies. The best she could do, however, was to land a small part in the RKO feature *Thirteen Women*. Unable to find additional work, the 24-year-old actress became desperate. On the evening of September 18, 1932, Entwistle left this bungalow at 2428 Beachwood Drive in the Hollywood Hills where she lived with her uncle and walked the short distance to the "Hollywoodland" sign atop Mt. Lee. There, the failed actress gained an immortality of sorts by climbing to the top of the letter "H" and jumping to her death. *Photo 2000 by Jana Wells.*

Just to Remind You (1931), *Little Women* (1931), and *Alice-Sit-By-The-Fire* (1932). In 1932, the young actress supported Billie Burke in *The Mad Hopes*. For Entwistle, the play (which closed after a short run) represented the culmination of a promising acting career characterized by ever smaller roles in a series of theatrical flops. Entwistle, forced to leave the New York stage by the negative impact of the Depression and her waning reputation, relocated to Hollywood in April 1932 looking for a career in movies. While making the rounds in Tinseltown the 24-year-old actress stayed with her uncle, British actor Charles H. Entwistle, in his bungalow at 2428 Beachwood Drive just below the "Hollywoodland" sign on Mt. Lee. The sign, with its 50 foot high white block letters, was erected in 1923 to advertise a local real estate development. "Land" was dropped in 1949 long after the sign had become the most famous landmark in all of show business.

Entwistle quickly landed a familiar stage role supporting Billie Burke in the Los Angeles production of *The Mad Hopes*. The play closed in less than two weeks. Weeks later, RKO offered Entwistle an option contract to appear in *Thirteen Women*, a film based on Tiffany Thayer's novel. In a prophetic irony, the movie featured a young female character who commits suicide by jumping. In the film, Entwistle was listed ninth in the credits and portrayed the character "Hazel Cousins." Following a disastrous preview, the film was hastily recut by RKO and what would have been several minutes of screen time for the young Hollywood hopeful was reduced to a mere 15 seconds. *Thirteen Women* bombed and in July 1932 RKO did not pick up Entwistle's option.

Already shaken by a dismal Broadway season and further disheartened by a celluloid flop, Entwistle made the rounds of theatres and studios unsuccessfully looking for work. The young actress was even willing to swallow her pride and return to New York, but could not raise train fare. On September 18, 1932, Entwistle told her uncle that she

was going to walk to a nearby drugstore. Instead, she walked the short distance to the lighted "Hollywood" sign. Entwistle placed her black and tan silk jacket and a stylish purse containing a short, but poignant, suicide note at the base of the letter "H." While climbing up the 50 foot electrician's ladder on the back of the letter Entwistle lost one of her new shoes. Poised atop the glittering symbol of Tinseltown's hopes and dreams that overlooks Los Angeles, the failed actress jumped to her death. Early the next morning a hiker found the shoe, jacket, and purse containing the suicide note. The note read: "I am afraid I am a coward. I am sorry for everything. If I had done this a long time ago it would have saved a lot of pain.—P.E." Wishing to avoid publicity, the hiker left the material on the doorstep of the Hollywood Police Station and anonymously phoned in her discovery. Entwistle's mangled body was found a few hours later 100 feet down the side of a steep ravine.

Unable to identify "P.E.," authorities enlisted the aid of the press. On September 19, 1932, *The Los Angeles Examiner* ran a short piece titled, "Girl Ends Life in Hollywood Mountain Leap: Pretty Young Woman Jumps to Death from Top of Letter 'H' of Huge Sign; Initials 'P.E.'" Charles H. Entwistle, already vaguely concerned over his niece's mental state and alarmed by her failure to return home the night before, saw the article and positively identified Entwistle's body at the L.A. County Morgue. On September 20, 1932, the 24-year-old's body was cremated at the Hollywood Cemetery and the ashes shipped to the Oak Hill Cemetery in Glendale, Ohio, where they were interned in her father's grave. Despite the persistence of an urban myth to the contrary, Entwistle remains the only documented case of suicide connected with jumping off the "Hollywood" sign.

FURTHER READING

Golden, Eve. "Peg Entwistle: Falling Star." *Classic Images*, 204:57–59, June 1992.

Epic Soundtracks

Kevin Paul Godley (born March 23, 1959, in Leamington Spa, England) was 12 when he formed the influential avant-garde rock group Swell Maps with his brother Nikki Sudden in Solihull, England, in 1972. Upon joining the band, the drummer-keyboardist changed his name to Epic Soundtracks as an homage to renamed rockers like Iggy Popp (James Jewel Osterburg) and Alice Cooper (Vincent Damon Furnier). Swell Maps (named after the charts used by surfers to gauge the intensity of waves) released two albums, *Trip to Marineville* (1979) and *Jane from Occupied Europe* (1980), but experienced little commercial success. Now regarded as one of the pivotal bands of the New Wave, the group is credited with having influenced R.E.M., Pavement, Sonic Youth, and the Lemonheads.

After Swell Maps broke up in 1980, Soundtracks went on to perform with the Jacobites, These Immortal Souls, Crime and the City Solution, Red Krayola, Sonic Youth, and Pere Ubu. In 1993, he released his first solo effort, *Rise Above*, an album described by *Cake Magazine* as being "like the Carpenters for junkies and pillheads." Soundtracks' other solo albums are *Sleeping Star* (1994) and *Change My Life* (1996). On November 22, 1997, the 38-year-old musician was found dead after several days in his London apartment from an intentional overdose of anti-depressants. Epic Soundtracks was reportedly upset over the breakup with his girlfriend months earlier. Funeral services were conducted for Soundtracks in his hometown of Leamington Spa on December 1, 1997.

Erickson, Carl C.

A contract writer at Warner Bros., Erickson, 27, started as a reader at the studio in 1930 before collaborating on the screenplays of *Silver Dollar* (1932), *Mystery of the Wax Museum* (1933), *Easy to Love* (1934), *Sweet Music* (1935), and *Black Fury* (1935). On August 29, 1935, Erickson's body was found by two teenaged hikers slumped beneath a eucalyptus tree off Wonder View Place, a popular lover's lane area in the hills near Hollywood Lake overlooking the Warner Bros. studio. The writer had shot himself in the base of the skull just above the neck with a 2.9mm Luger automatic found under the body. The coroner estimated that Erickson had been dead about two days. In his home at 2139 Fairfield Avenue, detectives found an opened letter from an attorney in Reno, Nevada, informing Erickson that his wife had established residence there "for the purpose of securing a divorce on grounds of mental cruelty."

Ernst, Hugh (Bud)

Ernst, a radio producer and husband of Betty Furness, the actress who was then doing the Westinghouse commercials on the CBS television program *Studio One* (1948–1958), called a newspaper reporter on the afternoon of April 10, 1950, and told him that if he went to his room at New York City's Westbury Hotel at 15 East Sixty-ninth Street he would get a good story. The newspaper called Furness at her Park Avenue home and she went to the Westbury. While Furness waited in the lobby, a bellboy entered Ernst's room to find that the 39 year old had apparently placed a 20-gauge shotgun between his knees, closed his mouth over the barrel, and pulled the trigger. In a note addressed to Furness, Ernst claimed that he was "tired of everything."

Espe, Geraldine Soles

One day after a loan company repossessed the furniture in Espe's home in the Los Feliz section of Los Angeles, the 35-year-old secretary in the office of the Association of Motion Picture Producers loaded her toy fox terrier, "Junior Officer," and her ailing 60-year-old mother into her car and drove off. The next day, October 22, 1940, a private patrolman in the exclusive Hidden Valley area on the outskirts of the city near the secluded ranch of Will Hays, head of the national producers' group, found the dead trio in a small coupe on the side of the road. A rubber hose connected to the exhaust pipe led into the car. A note found in the glove box read, "Insurance policy at office; receipts in hat box in closet. Will take care of burial." In Espe's purse was a notice of judgment directing that the furniture be removed from their home.

Eustache, Jean

Eustache (born in Pessac, France, on November 30, 1938) fell in love with the movies as a child. In the late fifties he moved to Paris and haunted the offices of the influential film journal *Cahiers du cinéma* where his wife worked as a secretary. Eustache was already fluent in the literary and film works of various New Wave theorists and directors (Jacques Rivette, Claude Chabrol, François Truffaut, Jean-Luc Godard) before acting in, and serving as assistant director on, Paul Vecchiale's 1962 short *Les Roses de vie*. By late 1963, Eustache shot and directed his first short, the highly regarded 16mm project called *Les Mauvaises Fréquentations* (*Bad Company*). In 1965, he made his first 35mm film, the autobiographical short *Le Père Noël a les yeux bleus* (*Santa Claus has Blue Eyes*) produced by Jean-Luc Godard.

Fiercely independent, Eustache worked little in the sixties, and then only on projects that personally touched him, like "La Rosière de Pessac" ("The Virgin of Pessac"), a 1969 television documentary he directed about his native village. His other television documentaries include "Le Cochon" ("The Pig," 1970), "Numéro zéro" ("Number Zero," 1971), "Rosière de Pessac 79" (1979), and "Photos d'Alix" ("Alix's Photos," 1980). Though not widely known by the public in the early seventies, Eustache had earned the respect of several New Wave directors like Truffaut and film critics like André Bazin. With money borrowed from Barbet Schroeder, a friend from the Cinémathèque Française, Eustache spent three months writing *La Maman et la putain* (*The Mother and the Whore*). Released in 1973, the nearly four hour black-and-white motion picture won the Special Jury Grand Prize at the Cannes Film Festival (despite sharply divided critical opinion), and established Eustache as an important international filmmaker. Other films by the director include *Mes petites amoureuses* (*My Little Loves*, 1975) and *Une sale histoire* (*A Dirty Story*, 1977).

Injured in a fall in August 1980, Eustache rarely left his house during the remaining months of his life. On November 4, 1981, the depressed 42-year-old *auteur* shot himself in Paris.

Evans, Tom see Badfinger

Fabian, Abraham M.

The son of Jacob Fabian, vice-president and principal stockholder of the Stanley-Fabian Amusement Corporation and First National Pictures, Fabian, 31, had been the assistant treasurer of his father's corporation and an executive board member of First National before resigning due to ill health. Shortly after his marriage in September 1926, Fabian suffered a nervous breakdown on his honeymoon from which he never fully recovered. Fabian's wife obtained an anullment (no grounds cited) one month prior to his death. The elder Fabian purchased a country home on Norwood Avenue in Elberon, New Jersey, and there installed his son and a full-time nurse to look after him. In the early morning of June 1, 1927, Fabian stopped up the bathroom toilet with paper and called his nurse to unclog it. The 15 minutes she labored on the plumbing gave the deranged man more than enough time to enter the kitchen, lie on top of the stove, and asphyxiate himself with gas.

Fabris, Pasqual

Repeated career disappointments and the refusal of film star and vocalist Frances Langford to marry him prompted the 35-year-old violinist to run a length of fire hose from the exhaust pipe of his car into the closed compartment. On April 27, 1937, police in Los

Angeles found Fabris slumped in the seat of his car, the engine still running, a victim of carbon monoxide poisoning. A rambling 16 page note left in his apartment at 6326 Lexington Avenue listed a litany of professional and personal rebukes that had driven the mentally unbalanced musician over the edge.

Born in Dalmatia on October 28, 1901, Fabris had studied under the noted Viennese conductor Carl Flesch, made his concert debut in Berlin in 1924, and from 1927 to 1931 was first violinist with the Detroit Symphony Orchestra. In Los Angeles, Fabris' life began to fall apart. In 1933, Fabris failed to win the post of conductor of the Los Angeles Philharmonic Orchestra recently vacated by Artur Rodzinski. Afterward, a major studio's refusal of his offer to direct a cycle of Wagnerian operas was quickly followed by his dismissal from Raymond Paige's Orchestra, a position obtained through Frances Langford. The screen actress, however, delivered the final blow to the violinist's teetering sanity when she nixxed his marriage proposal and subsequent plan to retreat to Samoa where he planned to write a system of philosophy in which he heralded himself as a new Christ.

Falke, Charles H.

The 55-year-old burlesque manager-producer suffered a mental collapse after attending his mother's funeral four days before and, devastated by depression, walked off *The Sporting Duchess*, a burlesque show he was managing in Union City, New Jersey. Falke traveled to New York City and checked into a third floor room at the Forrest Hotel at 224 West Forty-ninth Street. On the afternoon of March 20, 1928, as a friend was knocking on his door to inquire about his health, the veteran burlesque manager leaped to his death. Falke barely missed actresses Miriam Hopkins and Frances Goodrich as they approached the stage door of the Ritz Theatre where they were appearing in the John McGowan comedy *Excess Baggage*. The hysterical women required medical attention. Falke died later that day at Bellevue Hospital from a compound fracture of the skull and other injuries.

Farnsworth, Richard

A favorite in Hollywood for his piercing blue eyes, floppy mustache, and gentlemanly Western-style demeanor, Farnsworth was a stuntman for nearly 30 years before getting his first big acting break at the age of 57. Born September 1, 1920, in Los Angeles, Farnsworth was 7 years old when his father died in 1927. At 15 he dropped out of school during the Great Depression to help support his family working as a $6.00 a week stable boy in a polo barn. His film debut came in 1937 as a steeplechase jockey in a race scene in the Marx Brothers feature *A Day at the Races*. Later that year he was working in the polo barn when scouts from Paramount came looking for mounts to use in the Gary Cooper film *The Adventures of Marco Polo* (1938). Asked if he could ride, Farnsworth pointed to his experience on the Marx Brothers film and was hired as a Mongolian horseman at $7.50 a day plus a box lunch.

For the next 30 years he rode horses and doubled for actors like Roy Rogers and Gary Cooper. As a stuntman Farnsworth appeared in more than 300 films including *Gunga Din* (1939), *Red River* (1948), *The Wild One* (1953), *The Ten Commandments* (1956, as a charioteer), *Spartacus* (1960, as Kirk Douglas' swordfighting double), *Texas Across the River* (1966), *Monte Walsh* (1970), and *Ulzana's Raid* (1972). In 1976, Farnsworth graduated from speaking a few lines in films to complete sentences with his performance as a stagecoach driver in *The Duchess and the Dirtwater Fox* starring George Segal and Goldie Hawn. The stuntman turned actor caught his big break in 1978 when director Alan J. Pakula cast the 57 year old in a supporting role in *Comes a Horseman* with Jane Fonda and James Caan. Farnsworth was nominated for an Academy Award as Best Supporting Actor, but lost to Christopher Walken in *The Deer Hunter*. In 1982, he was nominated for Canada's Best Actor Award for his portrayal of real-life stagecoach turned train robber Bill Miner in *The Grey Fox*. Other films in which Farnsworth acted include *The Natural* (1984), *Space Rage*

RICHARD FARNSWORTH—A Hollywood stuntman for 30 years, Farnsworth was 57 when he turned to acting. He received a Best Supporting Actor Oscar nomination in 1978 for his debut role in *Comes a Horseman*. Farnsworth, universally admired for his Western gentility and honesty, was secretly suffering from terminal bone cancer when director David Lynch lured him out of retirement in 1999 to star in *The Straight Story*. At 79, he became the oldest person ever to be nominated for an Academy Award in the Best Actor category. Unwilling to endure the pain any longer, Farnsworth, 80, shot himself at his ranch in Lincoln, New Mexico on October 6, 2000.

(1986), and *The Two Jakes* (1990). His television work includes numerous guest shots and the memorable role of "Matthew Cuthbert" in the made-for-television-movie *Anne of Green Gables* (1985).

In 1996, the 76-year-old actor retired to a ranch in Lincoln, New Mexico, a small town some 250 miles southeast of Albuquerque where outlaw Billy the Kid used to roam. Beloved in the town, Farnsworth was active in the community, lending his name to historic preservation and serving as spokesman for the annual Lincoln County Cowboy Symposium. Unknown to all but his immediate family, however, Farnsworth was suffering from terminal bone cancer. In 1999, director David Lynch persuaded Farnsworth to end his retirement with a starring role in *The Straight Story*, a true-life story of an elderly man who drove his lawnmower cross-country to see his dying brother. Farnsworth was in constant pain during the filming, but told cast and crew that the discomfort in his hip was from 30 years spent as a stuntman. He was honored as the Best Actor at Cannes and won the New York Film Critics Award. At 79, Farnsworth earned the distinction of being the oldest actor ever nominated for an Oscar in the Best Actor category for *The Straight Story*. He lost to Kevin Spacey in *American Beauty*.

By October 6, 2000, Farnsworth was unable to move his legs and enduring incredible pain. That evening around 5:30 P.M. the 80-year-old actor placed a shotgun against his head and pulled the trigger in the bedroom of his home in Lincoln, New Mexico. His fiancée, Jewel Van Valin, heard the shot from an adjacent bedroom and found the body. The actor's daughter, Missy Farnsworth, explained, "He had reached a level of pain that he was unable to get beyond."

Farnum, Jacqueline

Married to theatrical manager Nat Farnum for 14 years, the former vaudeville actress evidently became hysterical after drinking "tainted" liquor in their Hollywood, California, home at 1426 Sunset Boulevard on June 9, 1926. That afternoon, Nat Farnum returned home from a lunch at the Beverly Hills Hotel to find his 37-year-old wife running about the house and muttering incoherently. As he and his 16-year-old stepson discussed her condition, Farnum ran into the bathroom and shot herself in the abdomen with her husband's revolver. She died soon afterward in the Receiving Hospital without regaining consciousness.

Farrar, Margaret

Though described in a *Variety* obituary as a "screen actress," the 24-year-old woman was separated from her husband and running a beauty shop in Los Angeles when she drank poison in her apartment on August 1, 1925. Shortly before the incident, neighbors reported hearing the following telephone conversation coming from the woman's rooms: "I once loved you better than you will ever know. But it is too late now and everything is over." Farrar died in the Osteopathic Hospital eight days later.

Fay, Florence

On July 11, 1928, the domestic discord brewing between the 35-year-old former show girl (real name Vollbracht), her estranged husband, Robert Vollbracht, and her so-called lover, Frank McCoy, ended in tragedy in New York City. Weeks earlier, Fay's husband had instituted a divorce action after finding her in a room with McCoy. Although Fay insisted that their relationship was purely "companionate," Vollbracht moved out of their apartment at the Century Hotel at 111 W. Forty-sixth Street. On July 11, Florence Fay phoned a close friend to inform him that "I am going to end my life. Hurry here. When you arrive I will be dead." A hurried call to the hotel manager proved too late. Upon entering the ex-showgirl's room decorated with autographed photos of movie stars, he found Fay dead on the bathroom floor near an empty three ounce vial of Lysol. According to authorities, a newspaper clipping announcing a suit for divorce filed by her husband was found among her effects.

Felton, Earl

Crippled from childhood with polio, Felton (born in Cleveland, Ohio, on October 16, 1910) managed to walk with a crutch and a cane. After graduating from the University of Minnesota, Felton began his Hollywood screenwriting career with Warner Bros. in 1936. That year he either wrote the original story or screenplay for *Bengal Tiger, The Captain's Kid, Freshman Love,* and *Man Hunt* before leaving to free-lance for studios like MGM (*Bad Guy,* 1937), Republic (*Calling All Marines,* 1939), Universal (*Society Smugglers,* 1939), and Columbia (*The Lone Wolf Keeps a Date,* 1940). Felton's 50–plus screenwriting credits include *My Best Gal* (1944), *The Beautiful Blonde from Bashful Bend* (1949), *The Las Vegas Story* (1952), *Twenty Thousand Leagues Under the Sea* (1954), *Bandido* (1956), and *Killers of Kilimanjaro* (1959). On Sunday, May 2, 1972, the 61-year-old screenwriter shot himself in the head in his Studio City, California, home. One week before, Felton had told his attorney, "If I have to spend another Sunday alone I'll blow my brains out."

FURTHER READING

Fleischer, Richard. *Just Tell Me When to Cry: A Memoir.* New York: Carroll & Graf, 1993.

Ferrer, Nino

A popular French composer and singer for three decades, the gravelly voiced performer was born Agostino Ferrari to an Italian father and French mother in Genoa, Italy, on August 15, 1934. Strongly influenced by jazz in the fifties, Ferrer started out playing instruments before making his mark as a writer and singer in the sixties with hit songs like "Mirza," "Le Telefon," and "Les Cornichons." Though registering hits in the seventies with "Le Maison pres de la Fontaine" and "Le Sud," Ferrer walked away from show business in 1985 to devote himself to his family, nature, and painting. In an interview conducted at the time, the popular singer confessed, "I was all set to be a star, but in a few years I became totally disillusioned. I realized that it didn't fill my life." Ferrer was living in relative obscurity with his wife in Montouq, France, when his mother died at the beginning of the summer in 1998. On August 13, 1998, two days before his 64th birthday, the deeply depressed singer wrote a farewell letter to his wife, then drove to cornfield near the village of Saint-Cyprien. Laying down in the stubble, Ferrer shot himself with a hunting rifle.

Ferson, Earl H.

A former promotion manager for Albuquerque, New Mexico, radio station KOB and KOAT-TV, Ferson, 43, had been fined $10 in January 1963 for failure to yield the right-of-way in an accident that claimed the life of a 16-year-old boy. On December 1, 1963, in that city, Ferson fired a fatal shot into his head with a .38-caliber automatic pistol.

Fillmore, Russell

The former New York stage director of plays that featured ZaSu Pitts and Billie Burke was in Los Angeles to read *Until December,* a play written by Mae West's sister, when he suddenly disappeared. According to West, she last saw Fillmore on August 11, 1950, when he seemed to be elated at the prospect of producing the show on Broadway. Days later, his friends and associates filed a missing persons report after he failed to keep an important business appointment. On August 18, 1950, the 55-year-old director's body was found floating beneath a pier in Ocean Park, California. An autopsy revealed that Fillmore had slashed his wrists before hurling himself into the surf.

Finch, Mark

Between 1986 and 1990 Finch was head of film distribution for the British Film Institute (BFI) and co-programmer of the London Gay and Lesbian Film Festival. In 1990, he moved to San Francisco to work as distribution manager for Frameline, a nonprofit gay and lesbian arts organization. Finch briefly returned to the BFI in 1991 to launch the film-on-video label Gay Connoisseur. Back in San Francisco, Finch was credited with introducing the popular British television series *Absolutely Fabulous* to America. In 1992, he succeeded Michael Lumpkin as the exhibitions and artistic director of the San Francisco International Lesbian and Gay Film Festival. Under his auspices the event became the largest of its kind in the world, drawing 50,000 attendees in 1994. In addition to his programming duties, Finch also appeared in a cameo role as a newscaster in Gregg Araki's 1992 film *The Living End*, and, in Todd Verow's 1995 thriller, *Frisk*.

At 3:20 P.M. on January 14, 1995, Finch's leather briefcase was found by a bridge officer resting beside lamp standard No. 93 near midspan on the Golden Gate Bridge. In the case, a note was found that referred to ten suicide notes in Finch's office at Frameline. In the notes (some handwritten, some typed), the 33-year-old film programmer described his long battle with chronic depression and asked friends and colleagues not to blame themselves. In a letter to film producer Marcus Hu, Finch mentioned his "overwhelming loneliness." On February 23, 1995, a body found floating off the San Mateo County coast was positively identified as Mark Finch. According to Hu, "It didn't really surprise me. He must have been on that dark inescapable path and couldn't make that call for help. That's what tears you up about it — he had so many friends that would have run to help."

Finley, Ned

In films since 1912 (*The Curio Hunters*), Finley was once making $2,000 a week as head of Ned Finley, Inc. Dubbed the "Bill Hart" of his day, the actor was featured in the Western and frontier films *O'Garry of the Royal Mounted* (1915), *West Wind* (1915), *Britton of the Seventh* (1916, as "General Custer"), and *The Blue Streak* (1917). Finley lived for 17 years in the premier suite of New York's Hotel de France, but as acting and directing jobs became more scarce he was forced to move his wife and child to a modest room with bath. They abandoned him in 1919.

Forty-eight years old and with no prospects in sight, Finley spent his last dime buying cyanide from a local pharmacy on September 27, 1920. The druggist, alarmed over the actor's odd demeanor, substituted bicarbonate of soda for the deadly poison. Alone in his room, its walls covered with one sheets from his bygone film successes, Finley took the drug and recorded his final moments in a series of notes. "I have already taken what the druggist said was cyanide. I write this at 2:30 o'clock, ten minutes after taking the supposed fatal dose. I feel very much live — no bad effects." Minutes later in another note: "It is 2:45 A.M. I have some strychnine which I am going to give a try next. I will wait until 3 o'clock. I hope it will work. Goodbye, N.F." At 3 o'clock, a final note: "I have just taken the strychnine. Don't know much about it. The druggist said it would kill half a dozen dogs. The acid didn't work. I suffer no pangs of conscience. Don't believe I have any such thing. Hope this is goodbye. If it isn't I shall have to cut my throat." Hours later, a chambermaid found Finley dead from strychnine poisoning. A one cent piece, used as a paperweight, was found atop notes addressed to the hotel staff apologizing for any inconvenience and thanking them for their kindness to him over the years.

Finney, Frederic Norton

One of the best known newsmen in Tucson, Arizona, Finney scooped the nation's press when he reported on the capture of John Dillinger and his gang in that city in 1934. After an illustrious career with *The Los Angeles Mirror* and Tucson's *The Daily Reporter*, he joined radio station KTUC in 1952 and was news director there when he took his life on May 3, 1965. Suffering from asthma and other ailments, the 66 year old shot himself with a revolver in the bedroom of his Tucson home at 3003 E. 3rd Street. Finney left no note.

Fischer, Harry C.

On March 25, 1939, the 33-year-old engineer for St. Louis radio station KMOX descended into the basement of his home at 5803 Michigan Avenue and shot himself in the head with a revolver. Fischer's mother-in-law heard the shot and found him lying near death in a coal bin. The despondent engineer, who according to family members had often threatened to take his life, later died at City Hospital.

Fisher, Fred

Fisher (born to American parents in Cologne, Germany, on September 30, 1875) settled in Chicago in 1900 where he learned to play piano. Two years later, Fisher scored his first musical success with the hit "If the Man in the Moon was a Coon," which sold some 2½ million copies. Assuming the presidency of the New York City-based Fred Fisher Music Company in 1907, the songwriter wrote the music for "Peg O' My Heart" for the Broadway show of the same name in 1912, the lyrics to "Dardanella" in 1919, and the words and music for the classic tune "Chicago (That Toddlin' Town)" in 1922. Moving to Hollywood shortly afterward, Fisher began writing theme music for silent films and was well positioned when early talking screen musicals made their bow. In the 1928 film *My Man*, Fanny Brice sang the Fisher tune "I'd Rather Be Blue Over You." In all, Fisher collaborations were featured in more than 30 films. In 1949, actor S. Z. Sakall was cast as Fisher in the 20th Century–Fox film biography of the songwriter, *Oh, You Beautiful Doll*. Perhaps more impressively, during the 40 years Fisher ran his music company he wrote or published some 1,000 songs.

In declining health for several years, the 66-year-old songwriter was found suspended by an extension cord from the transom of his bedroom in his New York City penthouse apartment at 617 West End Avenue on January 14, 1942. On a bureau, Fisher left a note that said, "No one is responsible for my death." Five hundred persons, many of them his "Tin Pan Alley" colleagues, attended Fisher's funeral service.

Flanders, Edward Paul

Flanders (born in Minneapolis, Minnesota, on December 29, 1934) moved to San Diego, California, at 17 and began acting with the Globe Theatre Company there in 1952. Over the next 40 years, the versatile actor distinguished himself in almost every medium. In 1974, he won Tony and Drama Desk awards for Broadway's *A Moon for the Misbegotten*, also winning an Emmy in 1976 for a television production of the play. In 1977, Flanders received an Emmy as the outstanding lead actor in a drama or comedy special for his title role in *Harry S Truman: Plain Speaking*. As the kindly "Dr. Westphall" on the hit NBC series *St. Elsewhere* (1982–1988), Flanders received five Emmy nominations, winning as the outstanding lead actor in a drama series in 1983. In films since 1970 (*The Grasshopper*), Flanders also appeared in *The Trial of the Catonsville Nine* (1972, as "Father Daniel Berrigan"), *MacArthur the Rebel General* (1977, as "President Harry Truman"), *True Confessions* (1981), *The Exorcist III* (1990), and *Bye Bye, Love* (1995).

An alcoholic, the veteran actor had undergone rehab in the late eighties, but a series of personal calamities drove him to resume drinking heavily while living as a near recluse on his 190 acre ranch in Denny, California (population 30), some 280 miles north of San Francisco. In 1988, he was left in recurring pain after sustaining three crushed vertebrae in a car accident near the ranch. Six months before his death, Flanders underwent two cataract surgeries and feared losing his eyesight. Most affecting, according to friends, was the actor's 1991 divorce from his third wife, and separation from their son who lived with his mother in Eureka, California, some 80 miles from Denny.

On the morning of February 22, 1995, Flanders was alone in the house while the caretaker drove the 60-year-old actor's 8-year-old son back to his mother following a weekend visit to the ranch. Flanders went into the bathroom, sat on the toilet, placed the barrel of a Savage .30.06 rifle against his right ear, and pulled the trigger. He left no note. Flanders' body was cremated and the ashes spread along the Pacific coast.

Flather, Charlotte Carter

Once touted as "the best dressed girl in New York," Flather, 30, had acted on stage in *Turn to the Right* under the name "Charlotte Carter" before taking up scenario writing for the Famous Players–Lasky Corporation. She collaborated on the 1920 film *Devil's Garden* starring Lionel Barrymore. When her career as a scenarist fizzled, Flather turned to short story writing, but actually supported herself by working for the Features Syndicate, Inc., interviewing political leaders like Benito Mussolini and Georges Clemenceau. In 1921, the troubled woman attempted to end her life by drinking veronal laced with opium. Flather survived for another four years until bankruptcy, ill health, and the failure to find a publisher for a recently completed novel prompted her to try again. On March 13, 1925, the despondent writer penned eight notes, bathed and styled her hair, swallowed a dose of sodium cyanide, and peacefully crossed her hands and died in her New York City hotel room.

Fleck, Eugen

Fleck came to America from Germany in 1934 and became a member of the famous high wire aerial act the Flying Wallendas. In the act, the 31-year-old aerialist rode a unicycle on the high wire while carrying a girl on his shoulders. On March 29, 1938, as the troupe was preparing to leave their winter quarters in Sarasota, Florida, to begin touring with the Ringling Circus, Fleck's body was found along a lonely sand road outside of town. A coroner's jury determined that the performer had shot himself through the forehead with a .32-caliber pistol. None of the Wallendas could offer a reason for Fleck's action.

Fletcher, John W.

In 1912 the well-known palmist moved into a luxurious fourth floor suite in Boston's Hotel Pelham at 74 Boylston Street after a crusade against the practice drove him from New York City. Fletcher, 60, conducted discreet readings there until early 1913 when authorities received a rash of complaints from several young men who accused the seer of attacking them. An undercover officer managed to secure enough incriminating evidence to have an assault warrant issued against the palmist. On April 22, 1913, police served the warrant in Fletcher's suite. According to published reports, Fletcher turned white, moved hesitatingly towards a telephone, but instead of placing a call removed poison from the pocket of his vest and swallowed it. Seconds later he staggered across the room and fell unconscious to the floor. Fletcher died two hours later.

Fletcher, Stoughton J.

The Hollywood musician and nightclub entertainer billed as "Bruz," Fletcher, 28, was depressed over his inability to follow up on the rave reviews he won at the Club Bali. In a suicide unwittingly aided by a close friend, Fletcher took his own life on February 8, 1941. Staying at the home of motion picture set dresser Jack Sowden at 5847 Tampa Street in Tarzana, California, the musician decided to end it all following a night of partying there with friends. Sowden heard a car running in the garage and discovered Fletcher unconscious in the front seat. A handkerchief had been tied over the accelerator to keep the engine running. Thinking his friend only drunk, Sowden dragged him to bed. When the set dresser awoke the next morning "Bruz" was dead.

Flory, Regine

Days before leaving Paris, the 34-year-old French revue actress told friends that she would either obtain an engagement on the London stage or commit suicide. As Flory (real name Artaz) had tried two years before to take her life by throwing herself into the Seine, concerned friends hired a private detective to shadow the actress and keep her from harm. At 9:25 P.M. on June 17, 1926, Flory went to the offices of the Drury Lane Theatre to speak to Sir Alfred Butt, the managing director, about her desire to perform. By arrangement with Sir Alfred, the private detective was hidden in an adjoining room ready to intercede should the actress become agitated and suicidal. When the director regretfully informed the actress that no work was presently available, Flory produced a miniature silver-plated revolver with an ivory handle and fatally shot herself in the heart. Hearing the shot, the private detective burst into the room just in time to catch Flory's body as it slumped to the floor.

At the inquest, several telling details emerged. Flory, well-known on the French stage, was addicted to morphia and had taken the "cure" several times in Switzerland. Just weeks before embarking for London, Flory's affair with a married writer had ended badly. Days later, she bought a revolver, issued her "ultimatum," and travelled to London for her fateful appointment at the Drury Lane Theatre. Verdict: "Suicide while of unsound mind."

Fluellen, Joel

The Louisiana-born African-American actor came to Hollywood from the New York stage around 1940 and first appeared onscreen in the 1946 Mervyn LeRoy romantic-comedy *Without Reservations*. During the mid-forties when the National Association for the Advancement of Colored People was being critical of the motion picture industry for its stereotyping of blacks, Fluellen introduced resolutions to the Screen Actors Guild during 1946–1948 asking the group to "use all its powers to oppose discrimination against Negroes in the motion picture industry." SAG, under the leadership of guild president Ronald

Reagan, rejected the referendum that would have created a committee "to establish in the industry a policy of presenting Negro characters on the screen in the true relation they bear to American life." However, 23 years later, SAG formed the Ethnic Employment Opportunity Committee. In 1950, Fluellen caught his big film break as Jackie Robinson's brother in *The Jackie Robinson Story*. His other notable screen performances included the hired hand on Gary Cooper's farm in William Wyler's classic *Friendly Persuasion* (1956), the blind uncle in Gordon Parks' *The Learning Tree* (1969), and as James Earl Jones' boxing trainer in *The Great White Hope* (1970). On the small screen, Fluellen was featured in the two-part 1979 made-for-television movie *Freedom Road* starring Muhammad Ali, and appeared in episodes of *The Dick Van Dyke Show* and *Hill Street Blues*. In 1985, Fluellen was the first recipient of the Paul Robeson Pioneer Award from the Black American Cinema Society. Despondent in recent months over failing eyesight and other health problems, the 81-year-old actor shot himself in the head in his home in Los Angeles on February 2, 1990.

Flynn, J. Thornton

Nellie Gray, Flynn's actress-wife of four months, was talking on the telephone in their New York City room at 260 West Fifty-fourth Street when the 30-year-old vaudeville actor slashed his throat with a safety razor while shaving on May 20, 1925. He died in her arms before the doctor arrived. Depressed since the marriage, Flynn had earlier confided to the woman that he was in financial trouble.

Fonda, Frances Seymour Brokaw

The former Frances Seymour, product of a wealthy upper class New Jersey family, married millionaire George Brokaw in 1931. Brokaw, an abusive alcoholic, drowned in a sanitarium in 1934 leaving his widow with several million dollars. Actor Henry Fonda met the 27-year-old widow in 1936 while in

England shooting *Wings of the Morning*, the first British Technicolor film. Three months after the meeting, the pair married in New York City on September 16, 1936. Daughter Jane Seymour Fonda was born on December 21, 1937, with son Peter following on February 23, 1940. In 1948, the family moved into a 23 acre estate in Greenwich, Connecticut, so Henry Fonda could appear on Broadway in the title role of *Mr. Roberts*. While performing in the show, Fonda renewed his acquaintance with Susan Blanchard, the 21-year-old stepdaughter of lyricist Oscar Hammerstein. In the summer of 1949, the actor informed Frances that he was in love with Blanchard. That same year, Fonda left his family just before Christmas.

Concerned over her daughter's deepening depression, Frances' mother placed her under psychiatric treatment at the Austin Riggs Foundation in Stockbridge, Massachusetts. Diagnosed as a manic depressive, Frances was committed to Craig House, a sanitarium in Beacon, New York, on February 3, 1950. At the facility, her violent mood swings prompted doctors to place her under a suicide watch. By mid–March 1950, Frances' condition improved to the point that she was permitted, in the company of two nurses, to visit her children at their home in Greenwich. While alone in the bathroom there, the unbalanced woman hid a double-edged razor blade in the backing of a framed photo of Jane and Peter. Unaware of the hidden weapon, the nurses allowed their charge to take the framed photograph back to her room in Craig House. On April 14, 1950, her 42nd birthday, Frances slit her throat from ear to ear with the razor blade in her bathroom at the mental institution. Notes from the woman to various individuals expressed the same sentiment: "This is the best way out." Henry Fonda told Jane and Peter that their mother died of a heart attack, leaving them to find out the shattering truth on their own. Eight months after his wife's suicide, the 45-year-old Fonda married Blanchard, 22, on December 28, 1950. Of note, Henry Fonda's first wife, actress Margaret

Sullavan (see entry), died a possible suicide in 1960.

FURTHER READING

Collier, Peter. *The Fondas: A Hollywood Dynasty*. New York: Putnam's Sons, 1991.

Forman, Tom

A World War I veteran who entered the military as a private and was discharged a lieutenant in the flying corps, Forman acted in several motion pictures before turning to direction in 1920 with a pair of films for the Famous Players–Lasky studio: *The Ladder of Lies* and *The Sins of Rosanne*. From 1921 through 1926, the director helmed some 25 films including a 1923 version of the classic Western *The Virginian*, starring Kenneth Harlan in the title role. In early 1926, Forman suffered a nervous breakdown brought on by years of overwork. Separated from his wife and child, the 34-year-old director was recuperating at his parents' home at 26 Avenue Thirty-one in Venice, California. On November 7, 1926, one day before he was set to begin directing *The Wreck* for Columbia, Forman rose early and went into the bathroom to shave. His mother and father, cooking breakfast together in the kitchen, did not hear the shot. When Forman failed to answer their call, they found him lying full length on the bathroom floor with a .45-caliber revolver beside him. According to authorities, Forman had pressed the gun so tightly against his heart that there had been no sound of a report.

Fort, Garrett

Best remembered today for co-scripting the 1931 Universal horror classics *Dracula* and *Frankenstein*, Fort (born June 5, 1898, in New York City) also acted on Broadway before migrating to Hollywood during the silent era. Friends suspected nothing when the 45-year-old screenwriter informed them that "just in case something happens to me" he had recently made funeral arrangements and purchased a burial plot in a local Los Angeles cemetery. A week later on October 26, 1945, the manager of Fort's apartment house at 9764 Olympic Boulevard found him in his room unconscious from an overdose of sleeping pills. Fort died an hour later in the Beverly Hills Receiving Hospital. In a rambling four page note Fort blamed poor health and mental disturbance for his action.

Fox, Grace

Fox, known professionally as "Grace Morgan," was a former stock company actress before making the transition to radio following the decline of touring companies. According to her husband, the 32-year-old singer had recently complained of illness and remorse over her inability to appear on her show broadcast over radio station WJZ. On December 17, 1943, Fox leaped to her death from the roof of a 20 story New York City apartment house at 200 West Eighty-sixth Street where she lived.

Frazier, Brenda

Frazier, a 20-year-old Southern taxi dancer living in New York City, threatened suicide so often that her boyfriend, Edward Julian, no longer took her seriously. On March 17, 1940, Frazier finally made good her threat by turning on the gas in her apartment and drinking poison after having quarreled with Julian at a party earlier in the evening.

Frazin, Gladys

A stage and screen actress formerly married to Monty Banks, a comedian and associate producer for 20th Century–Fox in England, Frazin, 38, plunged from the window of her parents' New York City apartment at 562 West End Avenue on March 9, 1939. A note addressed to her parents asked their forgiveness and added, "I cannot suffer any longer." The four-time married actress was best known for her role as "Tondelayo" in the play *White Cargo*.

Freel, Aleta see *Alexander, Aleta Freel*

Freile, Aleta see *Alexander, Aleta Freel*

Freeman, Max

Known for a quarter of a century as the "Godfather of Comic Opera," the German-born Freeman was one of the leading stage directors, play adapters, and comic actors in America when, on March 28, 1912, a tenant at a hotel facing New York City's Hotel Grenoble saw the 60-year-old's body partially hanging out of one of its upper windows. Sick, unemployed, and financially ruined by a failed investment in a dramatic school, Freeman swallowed laudanum, then hanged himself with a fire escape rope. In accordance with his wishes, Freeman's remains were cremated. Leo Mars, a musical comedy actor and longtime friend of the dead director, suffered a nervous breakdown upon learning of Freeman's death. The 41-year-old actor died at a private sanitarium on April 7, 1912.

Friedman, Joel

Friedman, a 28 year veteran of NBC-TV, had recently been promoted from his previous post of manager of film coordination and film exchange to an executive vice-president's position as director of the network giant's program production services and videotape library. On May 14, 1980, within days of his appointment, the 54-year-old executive took his life (method unreported) in his ninth floor Rockefeller Center office in New York City. In notes to his wife and supervisor, Friedman identified a 1978 shake-up in NBC's top-level management combined with his fear of failure at running the tape library as causes for his action. Friedman's wife filed a death benefits suit against the company claiming that job-related stress drove her husband over the edge. NBC attorneys argued that Friedman's suicide had nothing to do with his job, but with an undiagnosed depression he had suffered for more than two decades. In 1992, the State Supreme Court Appellate Division upheld a $98,040 death benefit on behalf of Friedman, ruling that his suicide resulted from extraordinary stress triggered by job pressures that included incessant round-the-clock calls and beeper pagings from then network chief Fred Silverman. As Friedman's wife had died in 1990, it was unclear who would receive the compensation.

Fritz, Ward C.

With partner Betty Wetenkamp, Fritz (under his professional name "Paul Ward") was a well-known stage, ballroom, and nightclub dancer in Omaha, Nebraska. In 1937, the pair danced in a benefit for a "free shoe fund" sponsored by the local newspaper, *The World-Herald.* On May 15, 1938, the 22-year-old dancer left the home he shared with his parents in good spirits and took a taxicab to a nearby airfield, Dodge Park, in Council Bluffs, Iowa. Fritz bought a ticket for an aerial sightseeing tour, making a point to tell the pilot that he preferred to be the only passenger in the two-seater, open cockpit plane. The plane took off from the field and had reached its cruising speed of 100 miles per hour when, 2,000 feet up, the pilot noticed that Fritz had climbed out onto the lower wing of the biplane. Before the pilot could shout, the dancer jumped, hurtled through the air, and smashed face-up into the ground below just ten yards from a man working in his vegetable garden. The impact drove Fritz 18 inches into the ground, split his clothes up the back, knocked the heels off his shoes, and threw the watch he was wearing four feet away from the body. A woman sitting in her home 75 feet away reported that the body's impact jarred her entire house.

Fuller, Bobby

The rock star, born Robert Gaston Fuller on October 22, 1942, in Goose Creek, Texas (some sources report one year later in Baytown, Texas), made his first independent label recording, "You're in Love," in 1961. In the summer of 1963, the guitarist-vocalist moved from his homebase in El Paso to Hollywood, California, where the Bobby Fuller Four, with their fusion of rockabilly *a la* Buddy Holly with the newly emerging British sound, became a local sensation on the club scene. In January 1966, their cover of the Crickets' "I Fought the Law" on the Mustang Records label charted at Number 9 on the *Billboard* chart. When their follow-up single in April 1966, the Buddy Holly–penned "Love's Made a Fool of You," peaked at Number 26, everyone agreed Fuller was on his way to stardom. Despite the group's success, Fuller was moody and withdrawn. A perfectionist who oversaw every detail in the studio, Fuller, 23, was rankled that their biggest hit had not been written by him, and that he had yet to faithfully record the sound he heard in his head.

Despite Fuller's moodiness, however, few believed that he took his life. During the late afternoon of July 18, 1966, Fuller's mother, Lorraine, found her son's body lying across the bloodstained front seat of her car in a lot adjacent to the Hollywood apartment he shared with brother and bandmate Randy Fuller at 1776 N. Sycamore Avenue. The doors were unlocked, the windows closed, and no key was in the ignition. Fuller's friends and family later told authorities that the vehicle had not been parked there hours before when they searched the area for him. On the car's front floor, Hollywood police found a box of matches, and a gallon can of gasoline, with a plastic hose leading from it into the musician's hands. His hair and clothes reeked from gasoline which was also found in his body. Additionally, dried blood was detected on Fuller's chin and right eyebrow, and his chest and face exhibited bruises as though he had been beaten. Initially ruled a suicide, months later Bob Keane, owner and president of Mustang Records, persuaded authorities to change the report to "accidental death due to inhalation of gasoline." A rumor persisted that the insurance company would not pay off Fuller's $1 million life insurance policy if he had committed suicide.

At best, however, the subsequent police investigation was sloppy. The death car was never dusted for prints, and detectives at the scene inexplicably discarded the gas can into a nearby trash bin. In the years since his so-called "suicide," several theories have been advanced speculating on the actual cause of the rock 'n' roller's death. In one, Fuller is said to have been murdered on the orders of a jealous small-time club owner with gangland connections after he paid too much attention to the man's prostitute-girlfriend. In another scenario, Jim Reese, a guitarist with the band who died on February 1, 1985, is alleged to have killed Fuller out of professional jealousy motivated by the 75 percent royalty split enjoyed by the band's leader.

Furst, Anton

Born Anthony Francis Furst in Wendens Ambo, Britain, on May 6, 1944, the celebrated production designer studied four years at the Royal College of Art in London. An outstanding student, an early interest in the work of Professor Dennis Gabor, the inventor of holography, led him in the late seventies to design and stage "The Light Fantastic" laser shows featured by the rock band The Who. Furst co-founded the special effects company, Holoco, and designed television commercials before moving into feature films. Although the 1984 low-budget cult film *The Company of Wolves* was Furst's first solo production design effort, in 1969 he had worked on Stanley Kubrick's *2001: A Space Odyssey*. Kubrick was so impressed with Furst's work on *The Company of Wolves* that the director tagged him to design the film *Full Metal Jacket* in 1987. For the film, Furst created a Vietnamese town from an abandoned British gas work on the banks of the Thames. By the time Furst completed work on *High Spirits* (1988), he was universally recognized as a leading film production designer. In 1989, Jon Peters and Peter Guber selected Furst to design the Tim Burton film *Batman*. For his dark and brilliant vision of Gotham City as a gothic post-industrial New York, Furst was awarded an Oscar

for best art direction. He shared the 1989 award with set decorator Peter Young. In 1990 he designed the sets for the film *Awakenings*. Furst also designed the Planet Hollywood restaurant in New York City owned by actors Sylvester Stallone, Arnold Schwarznegger, and Bruce Willis.

At the height of his career, the 47-year-old father of two jumped to his death from the eighth floor of a parking garage in Los Angeles on November 24, 1991. At the time of his death, Furst and his partners had set up a company on the Sony Pictures Studios lot with an eye toward developing feature film projects that he would have designed and directed.

Gaby, Frank

The 49-year-old comedian and ventriloquist was stopping over in St. Louis between trains from New York to Oklahoma City en route to a two week USO engagement when a maid at the Manhattan Hotel found his body hanging from a clothes rack in his room on February 12, 1945. In Gaby's pocket was a contract to appear in two weeks of USO Camp Shows at $350 a week. A standard in vaudeville for many years, Gaby also appeared during the 1934 season at the Municipal Opera in St. Louis in roles in Sigmund Romberg's *East Wind* and Victor Herbert's *Sweethearts*.

Gardner, Frank

On May 10, 1948, a man registered as "George Grace" plunged to his death from the sixth floor of the Hotel Clinton in Philadelphia, Pennsylvania. A typed note and $32 in cash were found a few feet from the open window in his room. Addressed "To the authorities," it read: "In my room at 549 Dean Street, Brooklyn, N.Y., you will find a letter under my typewriter which will give full particulars.... I was unable to do it there because I was so closely watched. Frank Gardner." Gardner, a veteran vaudeville performer who once did a tramp characterization in an act billed as Gardner & Vincent, was reportedly despondent over the passing of the medium.

Garroway, Dave

Born the son of an electrical engineer in Schenectady, New York, on July 13, 1913, Garroway spent his early childhood on the road attending 13 elementary schools in his first eight years of education. He later said that during these years his "best friend" had been a set of encyclopedias that he read from cover to cover. After briefly attending Harvard, Garroway broke into show business as a $16-a-week page at NBC. He quickly enrolled in the network's announcer training school, and later landed a job as a special events director at Pittsburgh's KDKA. Following his return from naval service after World War II, the young announcer moved to NBC's Chicago affiliate, WMAQ. In 1949 he was hired as host for the free-wheeling variety show *Garroway at Large*. Based on its success, Garroway was noticed by the company brass and brought to New York in January 1952 to host a new morning news program, *The Today Show*. A radical programming concept (conventional wisdom held that viewers watched television only at night), *The Today Show* was given little chance to survive. In fact, it was failing until NBC executives decided to pair the easygoing 39-year-old announcer with the bow tie, horn-rimmed glasses, and professorial demeanor with a 10-month-old chimpanzee named "J. Fred Muggs." Ratings soared and remained constant even after the departure of the chimp four years later. By then, the show and Garroway's sign-off phrase, "Peace," had become a morning ritual for millions.

Suddenly Garroway was everywhere. On radio he hosted *Dial Dave Garroway*, and in October 1953 resumed his earlier show, *Garroway at Large*, this time originating the program from New York City. Paired opposite the ABC ratings winner *The Adventures of Ozzie and Harriet*, the show was cancelled in June 1954. On Sunday afternoons Garroway hosted the world news television show *Wide,*

Wide World. Overworked and stressed out, Garroway was fast approaching a career crisis when his second wife, the former Pamela Wilde, committed suicide in 1961. In July of that year, Garroway left *The Today Show*, telling viewers that he needed to take care of his children. Largely forgotten by viewers and colleagues alike, Garroway had been out of the national television spotlight for a decade when he launched an ill-fated comeback with the summer replacement variety show, *CBS Newcomers*, which premiered on September 6, 1971. A dismal flop, the program failed to discover any "new" talent and was cancelled on September 6, 1971. Garroway later told former *Today Show* colleague Frank Blair: "Nobody wants me anymore. I'm old shoe, old hat. Nobody cares for old Dave anymore." Thereafter, the former television star and amateur astronomer focused on his family and third wife Sarah Lee Lippincott, emeritus professor of astronomy at Swarthmore College and former director of the Sproul Observatory.

After a 1979 open heart surgery, his health steadily declined and, following a six week hospitalization in 1982, Garroway seemed fragile and depressed to friends. Shortly after his wife left their ranch style home on Cedar Lane in the Philadelphia suburb of Swarthmore at 8:45 A.M. on July 21, 1982, the 69-year-old broadcast pioneer shot himself in the head with a 12-gauge shotgun. His body was discovered at 9:20 A.M. by a houseman in a hallway between the study and the kitchen. Garroway is buried in the West Laurel Hill Cemetery in Bala Cynwyd, Pennsylvania.

Gary, Romain

Gary, born Romain Kacewgari in Vilna, Lithuania, on May 8, 1914, and made a French citizen in 1928, served with distinction in World War II, wrote several popular novels (*Les Racines du Ciel*, 1956, English translation *The Roots of Heaven*, 1958), directed two films (*Birds Come to Die in Peru*, 1968; *Kill! Kill! Kill!*, 1972), and served in the French diplomatic corps.

While acting as the French consul general in Los Angeles, Gary, 49, met actress Jean Seberg (see entry), the star of Otto Preminger's 1957 bio-pic of Joan of Arc, *Saint Joan*. The couple married in 1963 and had a son, but divorced in 1970 amid the controversy surrounding Seberg's involvement with black militants and Mexican revolutionaries in Hollywood. When the actress became pregnant in 1970, the FBI embarked on a campaign to destroy her reputation by spreading the malicious and untrue rumor that a member of the Black Panther Party had fathered the child. Soon after the press printed the FBI–planted story, Seberg's pregnancy ended with the premature birth of a baby girl who died soon afterward. Romain maintained that the Bureau's lies were responsible for the infant's death and Seberg's subsequent mental deterioration. "Jean became psychotic after that," according to Gary. "Each year on the anniversary (of the infant's death) she tried to kill herself." Seberg, 40, disappeared from her Paris apartment on August 30, 1979. Her partially decomposed body was found nine days later, September 8, wrapped in a blanket in the back seat of her car parked on the right bank of the Seine. A medical examiner determined that the actress had taken her life with an overdose of barbiturates and alcohol.

Seberg's unseemly death deeply depressed the writer-filmmaker who had remained close to her even after their divorce. "Having ceased to be my wife," he once said, "Jean became by daughter." After her death, Gary filled his villa in Spain with pictures of Seberg and spoke compulsively about her to his visitors. The 66-year-old writer had been under treatment for nervous strain when, on December 2, 1980, he walked into the bedroom of his apartment on the Left Bank of Paris, lay down on his back, placed the muzzle of a .38-caliber Smith & Wesson revolver in his mouth, then pulled the trigger. Gary left a note at the foot of his bed and mailed a copy to his publisher, Éditions Gallimard. It read: "No connection with Jean Seberg. Lovers of broken hearts are kindly asked to

search elsewhere. Obviously one could blame this on nervous depression. But then, one would have to admit that it had lasted since I reached manhood and had permitted me to carry on my literary work. Why then? Perhaps one must seek the answer in the title of my autobiography, *The Night Will Be Peaceful* (*La Nuit sera calme*). And in the last words of my last novel: 'Because it could not be said better.' I have explained myself fully."

FURTHER READING

Seinfelt, Mark. *Final Drafts: Suicides of World-Famous Authors*. Amherst, N.Y.: Prometheus Books, 1999.

Gaston, Rosamond Pinchot

Born in New York City on October 6, 1904, Pinchot (the niece of Gifford Pinchot, the former Governor of Pennsylvania) was discovered by stage director Max Reinhardt during a European ocean liner crossing. With no acting experience, Pinchot was cast by Reinhardt as "the nun" in *The Miracle*. The young actress performed the play in London and reprised her role when *The Miracle* opened in New York City at the Century Theatre on January 16, 1924. During the play's 300 performance run, Pinchot never missed a show while garnering praise from *The New York Times* for her "richly emotional" performance. Pinchot later appeared in *Danton's Tod*, as "Galatea" in W. S. Gilbert's *Pygmalion and Galatea* in 1926, and in *A Midsummer Night's Dream* at the Salzburg Festival in 1927. After marrying William Gaston in 1928, Pinchot retired from the stage to raise their two children. However, when the couple separated without a divorce around 1935, Pinchot returned to acting, appearing as "Queen Anne" in her only film, RKO's 1935 version of *The Three Musketeers*. In 1937, she appeared in her last stage role, "Bath-Sheba," in Max Reinhardt's production of *Eternal Road*.

Seemingly saddened by the failure of her marriage, the 33-year-old actress took her life at her rented estate on Valentine Lane and

Simondton Road in Old Brookville, Long Island, New York, on January 24, 1938. Clad in sport clothes, a sweater, woolen gloves, and bedroom slippers, Pinchot's body was found by a servant in the front seat of her car, the engine still running, in a closed garage. A garden hose attached to the car's exhaust and pushed through a rear window had flooded the vehicle's closed interior with deadly carbon monoxide fumes. A farewell note to her parents (not made public) was found at the scene. Following a service in New York City, Pinchot was buried in Milford, Pennsylvania, on January 26, 1938.

Gates, Ivan R.

Gates, founder of the Gates Flying Circus, was once among the most famous barnstorming aviators in the country. Learning to fly two years earlier, Gates toured the country alone in 1911 performing aerial acrobatics in his own pusher biplane. With the addition of fellow aviator-daredevils, the act grew into a circus featuring stunt flying and wing-walkers. Sensing that the rise of commercial air travel would lessen public interest in the attraction, Gates organized an aircraft company in 1928 that designed and built training biplanes for private fliers. The veteran aviator quickly sold his interests in the company and, following a series of business reversals, opened a museum in 1930 in New York City at Fifty-second Street and Broadway where "starving artists" exhibited their work.

In constant pain from past injuries and depressed over a bleak future, the 42 year old was with his wife in their sixth floor apartment at 220 West Twenty-fourth Street on November 24, 1932, when he announced, "I think I'll jump out of the window." To placate him, she suggested that he get something to eat and drink. After drinking a glass of warm milk, Gates dashed it to the floor, threw open the window, and with his wife attempting to restrain him, jumped to his death. Four days later, Gates' former flying comrades scattered his ashes over the Holmes Airport, Queens, where he had been the first pilot to land a plane.

Gatton, Daniel ("Danny"), Jr.

Called by *Guitar Player* magazine "The World's Greatest Unknown Guitarist," Gatton was so musically precocious that by the age of 10 a teacher told his parents that lessons were useless since the child had only to hear anything once to play it. In lieu of lessons, Gatton listened to the radio in the fifties absorbing and mastering every style of playing from blues, rockabilly, country, and jazz to Western swing. In various bands since the age of 13, the guitarist preferred solo work, moving effortlessly between different styles. Refusing to leave the Washington-Baltimore area and unwilling to travel extensively, the master guitarist built up a small, but intensely loyal following, composed in the main of other guitarists floored by his technical virtuosity. The Fender Company issued a Gatton signature model Telecaster, a distinction afforded only a handful of legendary guitarists. Though venerated by fellow musicians, widespread popular appeal eluded Gatton. In 1991, after a half dozen albums on small, independent labels, Gatton signed a seven-album deal with Elektra. The label dropped him in 1993 after two records (*88 Elmira Street*, 1991; *Cruisin' Deuces*, 1993) both sold poorly even though the 1991 album received a Grammy nomination for best rock instrumental performance.

By 1994, Gatton was living with his wife and 14-year-old daughter on their farm in Newburg, Maryland, and playing small club dates with his band in the Washington, D.C., area during the week. On October 4, 1994, the 49-year-old guitarist spent the day at his farm restoring a vintage car with his brother's help. Gatton spoke with his agent five times that day concerning his upcoming performance at a wedding in Arizona that promised a large fee plus expenses. Later in the evening, Gatton's wife and daughter returned from a school function to find him in an agitated state. Shortly after 9:00 P.M. he left the farmhouse muttering to himself, "I can't take this anymore." Gatton went to a nearby garage and shot himself in the head.

Geare, Reginald Wyckliffe

Geare was one of Washington, D.C.'s most promising architects when his career was destroyed on the snowy night of January 28, 1922. Ninety-eight people died and another hundred were injured when the roof of the Geare-designed Knickerbocker Theatre collapsed under the accumulated weight of a blinding snowstorm. Geare was indicted on manslaughter charges after a coroner's jury determined that the deaths had been caused by faults in the building's design and construction. Although Geare was subsequently exonerated by the District Supreme Court, which dismissed the charges as "too vague," his career was irretrievably ruined. Unemployable and haunted by the Knickerbocker disaster, Geare committed suicide in his home at 3047 Porter Street in Washington, D.C., on August 20, 1927. That morning, Geare's wife found her husband's lifeless pajama-clad body lying across the bed in a gas fume–filled attic bedroom. Harry M. Crandall (see entry), the former owner of the Knickerbocker Theatre, gassed himself to death on February 26, 1937.

Geng, Nian Mei

Geng met future husband Qian Ping Guo while they were still children studying ballet in their native China. Both learned European classical dancing and performed roles with the Liao-ning Ballet. Described as "a porcelain doll in pointe shoes," Geng competed worldwide and represented China at the International Ballet Competition in Bulgaria. The couple married in 1989. In 1994, the artistic director of the Ohio Ballet Company hired the principal dancers sight unseen after viewing a videotape of their performances with a ballet company in Eugene, Oregon. In the Akron-based company Geng danced principal roles in *Swan Lake*, *Le Corsaire*, and *Don Quixote*. In early 1996, however, Geng began missing performances and took a formal leave of absence. Unknown to everyone except her husband and company officials, the 32-year-old ballerina was suffering from severe de-

pression (possibly aggravated by her inability to adjust to American culture) and had made previous attempts to take her life. Guo took a leave of absence in early February 1996 to look after her. On February 25, 1996, Geng jumped to her death from a tenth floor balcony of the Highland Square Apartments in west Akron, Ohio.

Ghazal, Aziz

Ghazal (born in Israel in 1955) emigrated to California where in 1983 he became the stock room chief at the University of Southern California School of Cinema-Television. While working there in 1990, Ghazal produced the low-budget alternative film *The Natural History of Parking Lots*, which won critical raves. By 1993, the 38 year old was becoming noticed by industry power players hot to film a book property he had optioned, Gregory McDonald's *The Brave*, a novel about an unemployed father who agrees to let himself be killed for money in a "snuff" movie so that his family could get the profits. However, unknown to actress Jodie Foster's Egg Prods. and Touchstone Pictures, Ghazal had simultaneously signed legally binding deal memos with both companies for the same property. As the scheme unravelled, Ghazal was fired from USC in October 1993 following a dispute over a missing camera. Almost simultaneously, Ghazal's wife of 16 years, Rebecca, sued him for divorce, citing years of family and spousal abuse. In one documented incident, Ghazal arrived at his 13-year-old daughter's school and administered a brutal beating to her in front of dumbfounded classmates.

Armed with a restraining order against her volatile husband, Rebecca Ghazal and her three children were living in the couple's getaway home in the small California mountain town of Pine Cove, near Idyllwild in central Riverside County. On December 1, 1993, Ghazal arrived at the two-story cabin, bludgeoned his wife and daughter to death and, after torching the cabin with Molotov cocktails, fled the scene. His two sons were out of the house at the time of the slayings. Authorities discovered Ghazal's blood-spattered car stuck in mud some 300 yards from the house, but the aspiring producer's decomposed body was not found until January 9, 1994, when two hikers in a secluded area south of Mt. San Jacinto stumbled across the scene. A .380-caliber pistol was found near the body. Forensics suggested that Ghazal had probably shot himself within hours of killing his estranged wife and daughter. In notes penned three days before the tragedy found in Ghazal's Los Angeles residence, the producer had written, "I can't subject my kids to anymore of this," and "Please forgive me for what I am about to do."

Giaconni, Ernesto and Nellie

Baltimore, Maryland, authorities believed that Ernesto Giaconni, a buffo tenor with the Boston National Grand Opera Company, and his wife Nellie, a ballet dancer with the company, entered into a suicide pact because the singer's voice was deteriorating. On November 9, 1917, their bodies were found in bed at their rooming house, gas flowing from five of six jets in the room. Attempts to revive the pair with a Pulmotor failed and both died within hours of being discovered. The 47-year-old Italian-born singer's career extended over 36 years and included engagements with both the Metropolitan and Boston Opera companies as well as leading opera companies in Europe. In the absence of a note explaining their action, Max Rabinoff, the director of the company, insisted that the couple's death was accidental, claiming that he had just promoted a delighted Giaconni to the position of assistant stage director at a considerable raise in pay.

Gildo, Rex

Gildo (born Ludwig Alexander Hirtreiter on July 2, 1936, in the small village of Straubing, Bavaria) became one of Germany's most popular singers in the post-war era, selling more than 25 million albums. Making his singing debut in 1956 in the Munich Kam-

merspiele theatre, Gildo's striking good looks and resounding voice captivated an entire generation of German women. He became the greatest singer of Schlagers, a musical genre of syrupy, sentimental songs about innocent love that was hugely popular after the war. On the charts since 1960, Gildo recorded his first big hit, "Fiesta Mexicana," in 1972. Other hits followed including "Speedy Gonzalez" and "Hossa Hossa." Gildo's live shows, like those of Welsh singer Tom Jones, were marked with wildly enthusiastic female audiences who often threw their bras onstage.

Gildo's bronzed good looks and macho image made him a natural for movies and he was often cast opposite the current German sex symbols. His 30 films include *Hula-Hopp, Conny* (1958), *Mandolinen und Mondschein* (1959), *Schlagerparade* (1960), *Cafe Oriental* (1962), and *Unsere Tante ist das Letzte* (1973). The singing star's playboy image was further enhanced by tabloid coverage that routinely featured him coupled with beautiful women. It was all a lie. While Gildo's homosexuality was an open secret in the entertainment industry, it was kept carefully hidden from German society where homosexuality was illegal until 1974. The strain of maintaining a double life exacted a heavy emotional toll on the singer, who developed into an alcoholic and manic depressive.

Fearful that their star might lose his legion of female fans, Gildo's record company convinced him to marry his cousin, Marian Ohlsen. Though she walked out on the sham marriage in 1990, the charade of a happy home was maintained for the public. Shortly after Ohlsen's departure, the singer swallowed 40 sleeping pills in an unsuccessful suicide attempt. The singer's career, which peaked in the seventies, began to decline as the younger generation began to openly ridicule the treacly sentimentalism of Schlagers and Gildo himself as the genre's most ardent proponent. Attempting to revive his career, Gildo cut an album of ballads in the mid-nineties, but it flopped. By the end of the decade, the aging singer was performing at mall openings.

On the afternoon of October 23, 1999, Gildo, 63, performed before a crowd of 3,000 at the 20th anniversary of a furniture store on the outskirts of Frankfurt. After the performance, he was driven back to the Munich apartment he shared with his secretary and lover of seven years, Dave Klingeberg, 26. That evening, the pair argued about whether they should stay in the one-bedroom apartment or go to their country house. Klingeberg wanted to go, Gildo to stay. At about 8:15 P.M., Gildo locked himself in the bathroom and threatened to commit suicide. As Klingeberg pounded on the door and screamed, "No, no, don't do it!," the singer leapt from the second floor window of the apartment to the courtyard below. Paramedics called to the scene tended the groaning, semi-conscious Gildo for an hour until a specialist arrived to supervise his transport to the hospital. Three days later, October 26, Gildo died from his injuries while in a state of artificially induced coma. In an open letter released after his lover's death, Klingeberg wrote: "Rex, you could never accept what you really were. And I did not succeed in removing your eternal playboy mask. You simply could not part with it. No one really knew you. Do you actually know yourself who you were? Did you ever think of yourself? In love, your Dave."

Gillingwater, Claude, Sr.

Gillingwater (born August 2, 1870, in Louisiana, Missouri) had been onstage for 20 years (eight of them in plays produced by David Belasco on Broadway) when he entered motion pictures in 1921 with a lead role as the "Earl of Dorincourt" opposite Mary Pickford in the title role of *Little Lord Fauntleroy*. From that date through his last screen appearance in the 1939 Paramount feature *Cafe Society*, the veteran character actor appeared in more than 80 films. Among them were *Mississippi* (1935), *The Prisoner of Shark Island* (1936), and *Little Miss Broadway* (1938). Injured in February 1936 after falling from a five-foot platform at Paramount during the filming of the Jack Oakie comedy *Florida Special*, Gillingwater's

health began to steadily decline. On November 1, 1939, the 68-year-old actor's body was found in the closet of his bedroom in his home at 604 N. Bedford Drive in Beverly Hills, California. Gillingwater apparently entered the closet and shot himself through the heart with a .38-caliber pistol so that the report could not be heard by his chauffeur. A note found at the scene read: "To the police: I am ending my life because, in my advanced age, in my physical condition, there is no chance of ever being well again and I will not permit myself to become a helpless, lingering invalid. I alone am responsible for what I am about to do."

Gillott, Jacky

One of the first woman reporters on the British Independent Television News channel, Gillott left ITN in the late sixties (though she continued to appear on panels) to write novels. An early literary success with *Salvage* in 1968 was followed by *War Baby* (1971), *A True Romance* (1975), *Crying Out Loud* (1976), *The Head Case* (1979), and *Intimate Relations* (1980). On radio, Gillott hosted the BBC arts magazine *Kaleidoscope* while continuing to contribute articles and book reviews to a number of newspapers. On September 19, 1980, days before her 41st birthday, Gillott, a chronic insomniac and migraine sufferer, was found dead in the bedroom of the home she shared with her family at Stone Croft, Pitcombe, near Bruton, Somerset, England. At the inquest, it was determined that the novelist had taken more than twice the lethal dosage of aspirin and paracetamol. Letters found at the scene revealing Gillott's profound depression further bolstered the coroner's verdict of suicide.

Gleason, Russell

The son of beloved film star James Gleason and his actress wife, Lucille, Gleason was born on February 6, 1907, while his parents were appearing in a stock company in Portland, Oregon. On stage at three months and in films since 1929, Gleason appeared with

Phyllis Haver (see entry) that year in the Pathé Exchange feature *The Shady Lady*. On November 19, 1960, Haver took a fatal overdose of barbiturates at her home in Falls Village, Connecticut. Over the next sixteen years, the popular character actor appeared in more than 50 films including *All Quiet on the Western Front* (1930), *The Higgins Family* (1938, co-starring his parents), *Young as You Feel* (1940), *Fingers at the Window* (1942), and his final film, *The Adventures of Mark Twain* (1944). During World War II, Gleason, 36, was a sergeant in the Army Signal Corps Photo Center in New York City. At around 10:15 P.M. on Christmas Day 1945, the actor either fell or jumped to his death from his fourth floor room in the Hotel Sutton at 330 East Fifty-sixth Street.

Gloor, Kurt

Trained as a graphic artist, Gloor (born November 8, 1942, in Zurich, Switzerland) was inspired by the student movement in the sixties to make documentaries chronicling Swiss life. Beginning in 1967 Gloor made a few short films (*ffft*, 1967; *Hommage* 1968; *Mondo Karies*, 1968) before establishing his own documentary film production company in 1969. His German-language documentary films include *Die Landschaftsgärtner* (1969), *Ex* (1970), and *Die besten Jahre* (1973). In 1975, Gloor wrote, produced, and directed his first non-documentary movie, *Die Plötzliche Einsamkeit des Konrad Steiner* (1975), a fascinating account of an elderly shoemaker who was being forced into a retirement facility. Disillusioned with the lack of government support for the film industry, Gloor worked only for television after 1993. According to newspaper accounts, the 54-year-old Swiss filmmaker committed suicide (method unreported) in Zurich on September 20, 1997, prompted by a "deep depression from which he could not escape."

Gobets, Mary

Hours before gassing herself to death in her apartment at 60 West 104th Street in New York City on April 4, 1926, Gobets, a former dramatic singer, confided to her husband that she felt lonesome that her parents lived away from them in New Haven, Connecticut. At her request, he played several of her favorite songs on the piano while she vocalized before they retired to separate bedrooms. When neighbors on the upper floors smelled gas they awakened the man. He entered the kitchen to find his 30-year-old wife seated in front of an open gas range. An emergency crew from the Consolidated Gas Company worked over Gobets with a Pulmotor for 20 minutes before declaring her dead.

Goerlitz, Ernest

The German-born Goerlitz, 52, was the one-time general manager of the Metropolitan Grand Opera Company of New York and more recently an orange grower in Alta Loma, California. Broken by ill health and worried about his relatives in wartorn Germany, Goerlitz checked into the Hollenbeck Hotel in downtown Los Angeles on December 12, 1915, and took a large dose of cyanide of potassium before shooting himself in the head. Two friends found the former general manager's body in the bathtub. In two letters — one to his wife, the other unaddressed — Goerlitz explained that he did not want to be a burden to his family and directed that his body be taken to a named funeral parlor and cremated.

Gold, Cecil

On the afternoon of October 24, 1927, the management at the Brown Hotel in Des Moines, Iowa, forced entry into the 19-year-old chorus girl's room after a maid reported she could not gain entrance. Inside, they found Gold (real name Helen Smith) dressed in pajamas lying dead on the bathroom floor. Her head rested on a pillow and an empty glass was still pressed tightly to her lips. Two empty bottles that had contained chloroform were found in the room. A note addressed "To Whom It May Concern" read in part: "There is no one at fault. I just grew tired of it all. I am not a coward. If you grew tired of a show, would you not leave it? I am tired of life! I am not afraid. My conscience is clear."

A packet of love letters exchanged between Gold and Jack D. Mead, an actor in the Princess Stock Company, partially explained the young woman's actions.

A chorus girl in the Canadian Capers Company, Gold had played at the Capitol Theatre in Des Moines two weeks before her death. After the company disbanded following a brief run in Kansas City, Missouri, Gold returned to Iowa to be near Mead. In a letter written to Mead while she was still in Kansas City, Gold expressed her own insecurity at being only a minor player in the company: "I don't want you to think, 'Oh, I can't take her there because she's just a chorus girl and won't know how to conduct herself.' I can be nice and refined when I have to be." According to Gold's father, who claimed the body, he felt his daughter's suicide was prompted by her unsuccessful attempt to climb the social ladder and to realize her ambition to be a Broadway star.

Goldberg, Joseph E.

The Chicago native had been in film distribution since 1911 with various companies like Universal, Consolidated Film, and Fox–West Coast Theatres before becoming general sales manager of Columbia in 1931. Resigning from the studio in 1932, Goldberg embarked on a world tour with his wife and afterward returned to the U.S. to form Resolute Films. When the project failed, he hooked up with Jules Bachmann to form the independent film company Preferred Pictures. Though financially stable, Goldberg, 40, feared that he had an inoperable brain tumor. On December 12, 1933, Goldberg complained to his wife of a blinding headache and left their suite at the Hotel Biltmore in New York City to find relief in a Turkish bath. Instead, he went to a furnished room at 302 W. Fifty-first Street that he had engaged the night before. Goldberg's body was found at 4:00 A.M. the next morning when gas fumes alarmed the building's other tenants.

Goldsmith, Arthur

An 18 year veteran of the M. S. Bentham vaudeville booking office, Goldsmith, 35, quit the business in late August 1923 to recuperate from depression in a sanitarium. Deciding not to return to the booking firm following his release, he entered the auto business with his brother-in-law in September. On October 18, 1923, Goldsmith hanged himself with a rope in the washroom of his office at the Chevrolet Sales Corporation at 38 Westchester Square, the Bronx. In a note to his wife, Goldsmith described himself as an unambitious failure and encouraged her to find a man who would better suit her. Two other notes addressed "To Whom it May Concern" identified the deceased and his place of residence. Ironically, Goldsmith's father had committed suicide years earlier.

Gonzalez, Israel Chappa

Known as "Gargoyle" to his friends and associates in the porn industry, Gonzalez, 28, variously worked as a set designer, editor, and cameraman, and even performed onscreen sex under the "nom de porns" "Max DeNiro" and "Max Ren." Gonzalez joined Elegant Angel, a hard core video production company, in late 1996 after serving seven years as art director for porn director John T. Bone. During their relationship, Gonzalez shot and appeared in several amateur videos for the director. More recently, "Gargoyle" started Columns, Smoke, and Chains, a Glendale, California-based movie prop company outfitted from material he raided from the dumpsters of legitimate film studios.

On May 27, 1997, Mischelle Bowen told Gonzalez, her lover of eight years, that she planned to end their relationship. Gonzalez, already worried over a pending $10,000 tax bill, attacked Bowen with a taser gun, tied her up, stuffed a rag in her mouth to stifle her screams, and repeatedly slammed her head against the bathtub before leaving the scene. Acting on information supplied by the battered woman that Gonzalez often stayed in his loft office at the Elegant Angel warehouse located at 9801 Variel Avenue, just south of Lassen Street in Chatsworth, California, Glendale detectives Charles Lazzaretto, 30, and his partner Art Frank visited the warehouse later that night. As Lazzaretto, a ten year veteran and father of two small children, entered the darkened warehouse filled with porn movie props, Gonzalez fired a fatal shot into the detective's head. Throughout the night and early morning, Los Angeles police and a SWAT team exchanged gunfire with Gonzalez while periodically lobbing teargas and flash grenades into the building. Two LAPD officers were wounded attempting to rescue their fallen comrade.

At 6:00 the next morning, police entered the building after a lull in the gunfire and found the set designer dead from a gunshot wound. An autopsy later determined that Gonzalez had placed the muzzle of a semiautomatic handgun in his mouth and pulled the trigger. The act fulfilled "Gargoyle's" oft-repeated statement to friends that he wanted to "go out in a blaze of glory." More than 1,000 friends, fellow officers, and Glendale citizens attended Lazzaretto's funeral and donated more than $170,000 to his family.

FURTHER READING

Ross, Gene. "Elegant Angel 'Employee' Dies in Police Gun Battle." *Adult Video News*, 13(7):28, July 1997.

Goodbody, "Buzz" (Mary Ann)

Nicknamed "Buzz" by a brother because of her tremendous energy, Goodbody was only 24 when she became the first woman director ever engaged by the Royal Shakespeare Company. A Left Winger politically and a revolutionary in the theatre, the avant-garde director received critical acclaim for her work at RSC's experimental theatre in Stratford, The Other Place, where she had recently staged a modern day version of *As You Like It*. On April 11, 1975, one day after her production of *Ham-*

let opened in Stratford, the 28-year-old director retired to the bedroom of her home behind Arsenal Stadium in Highbury, London, N., to consider the impending government economy cuts that could end her career with the RSC. According to the coroner's verdict, Goodbody then took a lethal mixture of two sleeping tablets "while the balance of her mind was disturbed." Her body was found in bed the next afternoon beside two empty pill bottles and several notes. Shortly after Goodbody's death, the RSC released a statement to the press in which they maintained that the young director had been told that her position would not be affected by any budgetary cutbacks.

Goodman, Richard ("Dickie")

Goodman, with collaborator Bill Buchanan, pioneered the so-called "break-in" record, a novelty song based on topical issues that featured an interviewer whose questions were answered by snippets from hit records. The duo's first hit, "The Flying Saucer (Part 1)," reached Number 3 on the *Billboard* chart in 1956. Capitalizing on their initial success, they released "Flying Saucer (Part 2)" in 1957, which peaked at 18. Another 1957 novelty hit followed, "Santa and the Satellite (Parts 1 & 2)," with Goodman eventually going it alone on popular "break-in" records like "Mr. President" (1974) and "Mr. Jaws" (1975) based on the hit Steven Spielberg film *Jaws*. After cutting his final single, "Kong," in 1977, Goodman quit composing to write material for stand-up comedian Jackie Mason. During this period, he also headed up the music department at 20th Century–Fox and later wrote commercial jingles. On November 6, 1989, the 55-year-old fatally shot himself at his son's home in Fayetteville, North Carolina.

Goodrich, Joseph

Described in newspaper accounts of his death as a "Hollywood cameraman," Goodrich worked for Olive Thomas (see entry) shortly before she took her life in Paris on September 10, 1920. On November 20, 1925, the manager of the Elanore Hotel at 1057 North Vine Street in Hollywood smelled gas coming from the cameraman's locked room. Breaking down the door, he entered the gas-filled room to find Goodrich's lifeless body lying at the foot of a large photograph of Thomas personally inscribed to the cameraman. Propped against it was a farewell note addressed to a friend in which the dead man noted that he was penniless and dissatisfied over a recent business relationship, but did carry a life insurance policy for $2,000 with relatives as beneficiaries. In accordance with his wishes, Goodrich's body was cremated and the ashes scattered over the Pacific Ocean.

Goodwin, Denis

The British scriptwriter got his first break on the television show *Opportunity Knocks*, afterward joining with Bob Monkhouse to become one of radio and television's top comedy writing teams. At their height, they reportedly made £50,000 a year from personal appearances and churned out scripts for two television shows and three radio programs a week. As a solo, Goodwin wrote gags for 20 years for Bob Hope, contributed special material for Jack Benny when he played the London Palladium, and more recently wrote for David Frost. On February 26, 1975, the 44-year-old comedy writer was found dead at his London flat. Although no cause of death was reported, a suicide note was found near the body.

Gottlieb, Betty Montague

Gottlieb, a divorcee employed as a photo retoucher in Hollywood's Austin Studio and a sometime film extra, maintained a torrid 18 month affair with Herbert W. Mannon, vice-president of the Tec-Art Studios, before he tried to end the relationship in mid-1927. Although friends warned the film executive that the fiery 25 year old could be dangerous, he assured them, "Man is master of his destiny. Nothing can ever happen to me, for I will it otherwise. There is nothing to fear. I shall hold the thought that it is impossible for her to harm me." In the early morning of August 5, 1927, the pair were parked in a car near 1346 Formosa Avenue in Hollywood when Mannon, attempting to disentangle himself from Gottlieb, let her read a love letter from a woman he had become infatuated with during a recent trip to New York. According to the police reconstruction, Gottlieb handed the letter back to her lover, then slipped her left arm around Mannon, and asked for a goodbye kiss. As he leaned forward, the divorcee produced a small caliber pistol from her dress, pressed its muzzle against Mannon's ear, and fired an instantaneously fatal shot. Seconds later the woman who had spent the earlier part of the day reading Shakespeare's *Romeo and Juliet* shot herself in the head. Gottlieb lingered for several hours before dying.

Graham, Eddie

Known as violent, uncompromising, and nasty throughout his 22-year professional wrestling career, Graham (born Edward Gossett in 1930) teamed with several grapplers (Johnny Valentine, Sam Steamboat, Bob Orton, Jose Lothario, Dr. Jerry Graham) to hold various Southern tag team belts from the fifties through the seventies. In early 1973 the wrestler paired with his son Mike Graham to hold the NWA Georgia Tag Team Title. In 1976 they won the NWA Florida Tag Team Title. He retired from the ring in 1980.

Graham's professional persona as a "nasty" belied his humanitarian nature. In 1977, he donated $10,000 to the University of Florida to help equip a wrestling room named in his honor. Proceeds from a 1981 birthday roast of Graham were donated to the Leukemia Society of America. Early on the morning of January 20, 1985, the 55-year-old wrestler told his wife, Lucille, that he was not feeling well and was returning to bed. She left their home in Beach Park, Florida, to visit neighbors and returned shortly after noon to find that Graham had shot himself in the right temple with a large caliber revolver. He was pronounced dead at 10:03 A.M. the next day at St. Joseph's Hospital.

Graham, Juliann

In early 1934, Graham, 22, left her job at the public library in Sisterville, West Virginia. Armed with a "professional" résumé consisting of parts in amateur theatricals and a position in the local church choir, she went to Hollywood to realize her dream of stardom. Within days of her arrival Graham swallowed poison in a Hollywood hotel room on March 8, 1934, after failing to crash the gates at a major studio. When she recovered, Earl Carroll (then producing *Murder at the Vanities* at Paramount) took pity on Graham and convinced the studio to engage her on a week-to-week basis as a "bit" player. At the time, Graham warned other young girls to stay away from Hollywood until they were financially able to support themselves in town for at least six months. Despite Carroll's intercession, Graham again tried unsuccessfully to kill herself in September 1934 by ingesting a sleeping potion. On the morning of July 15, 1935, shortly after returning from a weekend spent on Santa Catalina Island with Ben F. Reynolds, a married motion picture cameraman, Graham went into the bedroom of his apartment at 2879 Sunset Place in Los Angeles while he slept in another room. Seating herself in front of a mirror, Graham placed a handgun against her left temple and pulled the trigger. Reynolds found her body slumped on the floor beneath the dressing table. Her one screen credit (as "Julia Graham") was as a waitress in the 1935 Paramount comedy *Love in Bloom* starring George Burns and Gracie Allen.

Grant, Arthur J.

Unrequited love for a Miss Lillian Stoll drove the 43-year-old former head cameraman at the Paramount-Lasky studio to hang himself with a bathrobe cord in his Hollywood apartment at 1735 North Wilcox Avenue on February 21, 1931. Three notes found near the body (apparently written by Grant at different times) contained rambling declarations of love for the woman he called his "darling Rose Girl," mentioned the name of a well-known Hollywood man that he perceived as his rival for Stoll's affections, and issued a threat that he would haunt the woman from beyond the grave.

Grant, Isabella

Grant, known on the German opera stage as "Belle Applegate," reached the pinnacle of her fame in 1909 when she became the mezzo soprano of the Stadt Theatre in Cologne. Once the toast of European opera houses, the diva's popularity waned throughout the war that claimed her husband. Returning to her hometown of Louisville, Kentucky, Grant continued to perform in "tribute concerts," but longed to return to the world of grand opera. On September 1, 1928, Grant travelled to the Windy City to audition for a small role with the Chicago Civic Opera. Becoming ill with high blood pressure in her room at the YWCA, the fiftyish singer was forced to enter the charity ward at St. Luke's Hospital, but pride prevented her from obtaining treatment.

On October 19, 1928, the former opera great was found near death in her room at the Evanston Hotel in that city from an overdose of poison. She died at the Psychopathic Hospital. Grant left seven notes. In one, addressed to the manager of the YWCA, she wrote: "The fates have played with me as if I were a wornout football and I can stand it no more. I did so want to sing for Mr. Johnson of the Civic Opera, and I would not have been brought to this extremity if I could have waited until I had had the audition, but what difference does it make anyhow? Even the Lincolns and Bismarcks and Napoleons are forgotten.... I can't help my deed — I am at the end of my rope. I long for peace — peace — you do not realize how I long for it. A small voice is whispering to me to go ahead and take my sleep. I am tired. Bless you dear friends. The end of an opera star. My blood be upon America for her treatment of the daughter of Kentucky pathfinders."

Grant, Shauna

Among the first of the hard core sex starlets to commit suicide (see entries Alex Jordan, Megan Leigh, Savannah), Grant's death in March 1984 was seized upon by the media to expose the corrupting influence of pornography. Born Colleen Applegate in Bellflower, California, on May 30, 1963, the future porn star moved in 1973 with her large family to Farmington, Minnesota (a small town 30 miles south of Minneapolis). Raised in a strong Roman Catholic environment, Applegate was a cheerleader and disinterested B student in high school. The teenager dreamed of leaving Farmington to become a Hollywood movie star. Upon graduating high school in 1981, Applegate's father got her a job as a repair clerk with the local phone company. That summer following an argument with her mother, Applegate attempted suicide by downing a bottle of prescription sinus pills. Unable to endure small town life, she and her high school boyfriend left Farmington for Hollywood in March 1982.

The 18 year old was out of work for a few weeks until she answered an ad from the World Modeling Agency for nude work. Applegate's 5'7" stature and wholesomely innocent Midwestern girl-next-door looks instantly made her the most photographed model in sex magazines. Soon she was earning $150 a day posing for *Velvet* and *Swank*, and up to $2,000 for layouts in *Hustler* and *Penthouse*. Two weeks after signing with the World Modeling Agency, Applegate's boyfriend left her, returned to Farmington, and told family and friends about her new life. By the fall of 1982, Applegate had made the transition from nude modelling to performing sex on-camera in a series of hard core shorts called "loops." As the money rolled in, the young girl began using cocaine for pleasure and to control her weight (cf. entry on Thelma

Todd). In late 1982, veteran porn producer Bobby Hollander (impressed by her work in the loops) became her manager and renamed her "Shauna (Shana) Grant." Grant parlayed her innocent looks into instant stardom in her first film, *Paper Dolls*. In 1983 she made some 30 X-rated films (*Virginia*, *Suzie Superstar*, *Nice Girls Do*), had an abortion, and contracted herpes, but was commanding $1,500 a day for celluloid sex. Of the estimated $100,000 she made that year, most of it went for cocaine, champagne, limousines, and stays in fine hotels.

In June 1983, Grant became involved with Jake Ehrlich, a 41-year-old alleged cocaine supplier, and moved into his home in Palm Springs, California. Apparently in love with Grant, Ehrlich tried unsuccessfully to wean her off cocaine and Quaaludes, got her out of X-rated films, and installed her as the manager of his leather goods store in Palm Springs. On February 21, 1984, Grant's newfound domesticity was shattered when Ehrlich was arrested and jailed for violating probation on a previous drug charge. The "retired" porn star attended an Erotic Film Awards show in Los Angeles on March 14, 1984, where she agreed to appear in a sex film, *Matinee Idol*, to be shot in San Francisco. One week later on March 21, an angry Ehrlich phoned his 20-year-old lover from Los Angeles and ordered her to leave his Palm Springs home immediately.

Later that day, Grant returned to Ehrlich's home in the desert and, as two houseguests were playing pool in another part of the house, lay on the bed, placed her ex-lover's .22-caliber rifle against her right temple, and pulled the trigger. Pronounced brain dead by doctors, Grant languished for two days in Desert Hospital before her family gave their okay to take her off life support. She was buried in Farmington, Minnesota, on March 28, 1984. According to one of Grant's porn friends who did not attend the funeral, "She was just an unhappy little girl with a big fantasy life." The 1988 CBS made-for-television movie *Shattered Innocence* was based on the porn star's life.

FURTHER READING

London, Michael. "Of Colleen." *Los Angeles Times*, sec. Calendar, pp. 1, 3–9, May 6, 1984.

Graves, Mina Rudolph

On November 27, 1936, the former singer of the San Toi Opera troupe of San Francisco and divorced wife of a wealthy San Francisco industrialist checked into the posh Beverly Wilshire Hotel in Beverly Hills where she requested "a room high up, where I can really rest." Graves was escorted to a room on the seventh floor. Minutes later hotel employees heard a muffled thud on a skylight over the ground floor. In the suicide's room, authorities found a note in that the 55 year old left all her possessions to another former husband and the postscript: "I don't want a minister, music nor praying at my funeral. Just one person to look at me...." See entry Rulolph, Mina.

Gray, Laurence

A vaudeville trouper for more than 20 years, the comedian-magician was billed with his singing wife as "Larry Gray and Carlotta." On March 5, 1951, three hours before a scheduled performance in San Francisco, the 52 year old shot himself in the head with a .38-caliber revolver a few doors down from their home in Oakland, California. A series of rambling notes found in a small suitcase near the vaudevillian explained that he "couldn't go on any longer." According to Carlotta, her husband was in excellent health, but depressed because he felt he was "washed up" in show business.

Greenacre, Fern

On July 17, 1938, 12 hours after kissing her husband goodbye as she was supposedly leaving for work in a local Detroit, Michigan, beer hall, the 25-year-old singer-dancer was found dead in a carbon monoxide–filled garage at the rear of their home on 457 Ledyard Street. The car's motor was running and a tube led from the exhaust into the vehicle. Beside the body was a note that read: "I've been so nervous lately that I can't stand it any longer."

Greene, Gilbert Clayton

Six hours after swallowing an arsenic-based weed killer, Greene, 38, died at Baptist Hospital in Nashville, Tennessee, on June 8, 1966. An announcer and on-air personality for Nashville television station WSIX, the former disc jockey was best known as the emcee of the station's Saturday wrestling show.

Greene, Winifred

The 21-year-old soubrette of the Ginger Girls Company had just completed singing an encore of "The Skeleton Rag" at Kansas City's Gayety Theater on February 24, 1912, when she rushed offstage to her dressing room and downed a bottle of carbolic acid. She died half an hour later at Emergency Hospital. A note to her husband, electrician for the company, was brief, but to the point: "Bert, if you go to heaven, I trust I may go to hell. — W.G." Moments before fainting at the hospital, the hysterical husband screamed, "I scolded her this afternoon for sending money home, but I wasn't harsh with her. I never would have thought she'd take it so to heart." In a separate note to her mother posted the night before, Greene apologized for killing herself.

Greenfield, Louis R.

The owner of two San Francisco theatres (the New Mission and the Fillmore) and the principal stockholder in the Consolidated Amusement Company of Hawaii, Greenfield opposed and bitterly resented talking pictures. On October 25, 1931, the 42-year-old businessman's financial worries apparently prompted him to hang himself from an interior door frame in his office at 109 Golden Gate Avenue.

Grey, Marion

Unemployed and unhappy, the 35-year-old stock company actress was found dead on July 17, 1930, of an overdose of poison in her northside Chicago apartment at 501 Deming Place. Grey, a 12 year veteran of stock theatre, had last worked in Terre Haute, Indiana.

Guthu, Harold

"Hal" Guthu, a talent agent who specialized in placing people in soft porn magazines and R-rated movies, established a large and devoted client base during his nearly 40 year career by treating everyone with honesty and respect in an industry not known for either virtue. He reportedly operated the camera on director Ed Wood, Jr.'s 1953 ode to angora, *Glen or Glenda*, and was cinematographer on the R-rated features *The Love Feast* (1969) and *Necromania* (1971). However, it was as the owner of the CHN International Agency at 7475 W. Santa Monica Boulevard in Hollywood since the sixties that Guthu was best known. Steering clear of hard core, Guthu snapped Polaroids of his clients and kept them in notebooks on his desk for potential employers in the soft core and bondage industry to consult.

On the afternoon of February 27, 2000, the 77-year-old talent agent's body was found in his fire-gutted office in West Hollywood. Death was attributed to a gunshot wound to the head. Initially investigated as a possible homicide, Guthu's death was later ruled a suicide after authorities found a suicide note in his car parked two blocks away from the death scene. The note reportedly mentioned problems with his health. Guthu was later determined to have been suffering from inoperable spinal cancer. Max, his beloved pet macaw, was found dead from smoke inhalation under some furniture in the office. Police theorized that Guthu removed all the valuables from the office, set it ablaze, then shot himself. On April 11, 2000, friends gathered at a memorial service for Guthu held in front of the old zoo at Griffith Park in Los Angeles. Seventy-seven doves, one for each year of his life, were released in remembrance of the man that everyone liked.

Hagel, Robert K.

A philosophy graduate of UCLA and a descendant of Nez Perce Indian Chief Joseph, Hagel joined Screen Gems, the television arm of Columbia Pictures, as a production executive for the programs *The Ugliest Girl in Town* (1968–1969) and *The Johnny Cash Show* (1969–1976). In 1972, Hagel, 31, became the general manager and chief executive for Burbank Studios, a joint venture by Columbia and Warner Bros. Under his direction, the company spent $10 million its first year modernizing the Warner facilities and adding eight state-of-the-art sound stages that attracted recording artists like Bob Dylan, Neil Diamond, and Barbra Streisand. After ten years with Burbank Studios, four as its president, ongoing back problems forced him to resign. On July 12, 1982, after being diagnosed with multiple sclerosis, the 41 year old took a fatal overdose of sleeping pills in his home in Sherman Oaks, California.

Hale, Dorothy

Still wearing the black velvet gown she had entertained friends in earlier in the evening prior to attending the theatre with Mr. and Mrs. J. Pierpont Morgan, Hale jumped from the window of her one-bedroom apartment on the 16th floor of Hampshire House at 150 Central Park South in New York City on October 21, 1938. According to authorities, after arriving home alone at 1:15 A.M. from the Twenty-One Club, the 33-year-old actress from an affluent Pittsburgh family spent the time until 5:15 A.M. typing notes and letters to family and friends before taking the fatal plunge. Actively pursuing an acting career since the age of 16, Hale landed a job in the chorus of *Lady, Be Good!* thanks to the assistance of family friends Fred and Adele Astaire. Following a brief marriage to industrialist Ty G. Thomas, Hale married noted mural painter Gardner Hale in 1927. Following his tragic death in a car accident in December 1931, she devoted herself full time to acting. A meeting with film producer Sam Goldwyn in 1932 led to minor movie roles in *Cynara* (1932) and *Catherine the Great* (1934). Upon returning to New York, Hale spent several seasons in stock theatre hoping to land a role on Broadway. Friends believe that it was her failure to realize this ambition that led her to suicide.

Hall, Jon

Born Charles F. Locher in Fresno, California, on February 23, 1915, the son of a Swiss ice skating champ and a native Tahitian mother was educated in Europe, although he spent much of his youth in Tahiti. Following a brief stage career, he began his film career in 1935 credited as Charles Locher in *Charlie Chan in Shanghai*. He changed his name to Lloyd Crane in 1936, before finally settling on Jon Hall in 1937. The handsome actor was an unknown $150-a-week contract player at Goldwyn Productions when he was cast opposite Dorothy Lamour in the 1937 South Seas epic *The Hurricane*, based on a novel co-written by his uncle, James Norman Hall. The film made him an instant star and thereafter the 6'2", 195 pound actor earned a comfortable living playing the bare-chested hero in a brace of films with romantic titles like *South of Pago Pago* (1940), *Aloma of the South Seas* (1941), and *On the Isle of Samoa* (1950). Hall also appeared in *Ali Baba and the Forty Thieves* (1944), *Cobra Woman* (1944), *The Prince of Thieves* (1948), *Hell Ship Mutiny* (1959), and his final film, *The Beach Girls and the Monster*, in 1965. On television, he played the title role in the enormously popular syndicated children's adventure show, *Ramar of the Jungle*, produced from 1952 to 1954. The 52 episode series was later re-edited and released theatrically in the late fifties and early sixties.

When film and television parts dwindled in the mid-sixties, Hall turned an interest in

JON HALL—In 1937, the athletic actor became a star opposite a sarong-wearing Dorothy Lamour in the hit film *The Hurricane*. Hall breezed his way through several "bare-chested" movie roles (*South of Pago Pago*, 1940; *On the Isle of Samoa*, 1950) and programmers like *Cobra Woman* (1944) and *Ali Baba and the Forty Thieves* (1944) before moving to television in the early fifties to star in the popular syndicated children's series *Ramar of the Jungle*. A millionaire inventor of optical equipment after leaving show business in the mid-sixties, the 63-year-old actor used a handgun on December 13, 1979, to escape from the pain of terminal bladder cancer.

underwater photography into several successful businesses. He designed and built the Scumpa, an underwater filming device for the Cinerama Company. Hall also invented a lens printing process that allowed the filming of distorted scenes. The process and lens were developed under Hall's Opti-Vision Equipment Company. In February 1979, the 63-year-old actor underwent surgery for incurable bladder cancer. In constant pain and weakened by ongoing chemotherapy treatments, Hall shot himself in the head with a handgun in the bedroom of his sister's home in Sherman Oaks, California, on December 13, 1979. The actor is buried in Forest Lawn (Hollywood Hills) in Los Angeles.

Hall-Davis, Lillian

In motion pictures since 1918, the elegant silent screen leading lady appeared in some 36 British films including *The Better 'Ole* (1918), *The Wonderful Story* (1922), *The Faithful Heart* (1922), *Roses of Picardy* (1927), and *The Farmer's Wife* (1928). Following her appearance in the 1931 talkie *Many Waters*, Hall-Davis contracted neurasthenia, was placed under a doctor's care, and was unable to work. Settling with her stage actor-husband, Walter Pemberton, and their 14-year-old son, Grosvenor, in a quiet house in Cleveland Gardens in the London suburb of Golders Green, N.W., the 35-year-old actress fell into an increasingly deep depression. Complaining to a neighbor that she felt "cut off" from all her theatrical associations and concerned that her nerves were not improving, she spoke openly of placing her head in a gas oven.

On the afternoon of October 25, 1933, Grosvenor returned home from school to find a note from his mother on a hall table informing him that the kitchen doors were locked and directing him to contact a neighbor. The home reeked of gas. Hall-Davis was found lying on the kitchen floor, her head placed inside a gas oven with the taps left open. In her right hand the actress clasped an old fashioned razor she had used to cut her throat. A coroner's inquest determined that she had died from the throat wound and not coal gas poisoning.

Seton Margrave, film correspondent for the London *Daily Mail*, wrote of the actress: "Miss Hall-Davis was a brilliant representative of typical English beauty. As a film heroine she played romantic parts with great intelligence, and infinite charm, and with that delightful whimsical sense of comedy which, with bet-ter fortune, would have made her one of the greatest stars of the talking-picture world."

Halsted, Fred

Halsted (born July 20, 1941, in Laguna Beach, California) was 3 years old when his father left for work and never came home. He moved around California with his mother doing agricultural work, ultimately opening a chain of nurseries. Selling the business in the spring of 1969, the 27 year old decided to become a gay porn star and without any film experience began scripting *L.A. Plays Itself*. Released in 1972, the hard core feature was a gritty tour through the homosexual sado-masochistic excesses of the City of Angels. It has since been placed in the permanent film collection of the Museum of Modern Art in New York City. Unlike many gay filmmakers at the time, Halsted was involved in every aspect of production including writing, directing, photographing, and editing. Halsted's other films (*Sex Garage*, 1972; *Truck It*, 1973; *Sextool*, 1975) all bear his distinctive cinematic touch of double exposures, narrative ruptures, and detached body parts. Seemingly depressed over his inability to move into mainstream films, the 47-year-old porno director died of an overdose of barbiturates in Dana Point, California on May 9, 1989.

FURTHER READING

Siebenand, Paul Alcuin. *The Beginnings of Gay Cinema in Los Angeles: The Industry and the Audience.* Thesis (Ph.D.): University of Southern California, 1975.

Ham, Peter William see Badfinger

Hamburg, Perke

On the morning of April 5, 1928, the musical director and composer checked into the Great Northern Hotel at 118 West Fifty-seventh Street in New York City. When Hamburg's bags failed to arrive by the evening, the management went to his fifth floor room to investigate. Hamburg was found lying across the bed dead from a single shot to the heart fired from a .22-caliber duelling pistol. No notes were found in the room, but there was an unsigned contract offering the 37 year old the musical directorship of a Joe Laurie musical comedy to be called *Is That Nice, Renee?* Hamburg would have received a down payment of $1,000 and a $500 weekly salary. Associates theorized that ill health prompted the suicide.

Hamer, Rusty

Hamer (born Russell Craig Hamer in Tenafly, New Jersey, on February 15, 1947) was the third son of a shirt salesman who was interested in community theatre. The family relocated to Los Angeles in 1951 where Hamer's parents took him to an open audition call for the role of comedian Danny Thomas' son in a new sitcom known first as *Make Room for Daddy* then *The Danny Thomas Show.* Thomas, impressed by Hamer's cuteness and talent, selected him from among 500 child actors. The popular show debuted on ABC in September 1953 and ran until September 1964. Hamer, as the precocious curly-haired "Rusty Williams," scored a big hit on the small screen. In 1956, he also appeared in the Abbott and Costello movie *Dance with Me, Henry.*

Hamer's early professional triumphs, however, were underscored by personal tragedy. Hamer's father died when he was 6, leaving the child actor his family's main financial support. Tutored on sound stages and educated in brief stays at Roman Catholic schools, the adult Hamer later complained that he received an inferior education that left him ill prepared to deal with the "real world." After the first series ended, Hamer came to two bitter realizations. First, fluctuating stock prices had wiped out most of his trust fund. Second, there was little professional work available for a grown-up child actor. In September 1970, friend and surrogate father

Danny Thomas cast the 23-year-old Hamer as a grown-up "Rusty Williams" complete with television wife and child in the ABC sitcom *Make Room for Granddaddy.* The show lasted one season. The demise of the series effectively ended Hamer's acting career although he occasionally showed up on nostalgia shows.

Tiring of working odd jobs in Los Angeles, Hamer moved in 1976 to the small southwestern Louisiana town of DeRidder about 40 miles north of Lake Charles. There, he worked sporadically at his brother John's restaurant and delivered newspapers. On January 18, 1990, the 42-year-old former child star fatally shot himself in the head with a .357-caliber revolver in his trailer in DeRidder, Louisiana. Hamer was cremated without services.

Hamilton, Harry Lud

A native of Maysville, Kentucky, Hamilton, 65, spent 43 years in theatrical work and served as a theatre manager of Gus Sun's vaudeville houses throughout Ohio. In his career, he was also an advance manager for stage productions, carnivals, and circuses, and business manager to former heavyweight boxing champion of the world Bob Fitzsimmons, and magicians Howard Thurston and Blackstone. The veteran showman, however, had been unemployed since the beginning of 1940 and living in a room at the Oxford Hotel in Cincinnati since June 4. Shortly after 7:00 A.M. on November 18, 1940, a passerby stopped to investigate a coat and hat hanging on the west wall of the Eden Park Reservoir in that city. Nearby, Hamilton's body was visible close to shore standing upright in some ten feet of water. Authorities found four cents and a note outlining his burial arrangements in the showman's pockets. Personal effects in Hamilton's hotel room included insurance policies and several notes. One to a hotel clerk read: "What is the use of fooling myself any longer. I will take the step that will part us. You will find my body over near the band stand in the park. I am going with my chin up. No regrets! Good wishes." Police determined that Hamilton probably drowned himself two days before he was found.

Hammell, John A.

Hammell, 57, quit his post as the head of Paramount Studio's Censorship Office in mid–1938 and travelled around the world before entering the Wilshire Hospital in Los Angeles on December 3, 1939, for a general checkup. The former circus worker was apparently in excellent spirits three days later when, clad only in a bed gown, he entered the washroom of his fourth floor room. When he failed to quickly return, a floor nurse entered the bathroom to find Hammel poised on a radiator near an open window. As she called out his name he jumped. Hammell left no notes, but was believed to have been in ill health since retiring from Paramount.

Hammond, Charles P.

Hammond (born in New York City on May 13, 1909) graduated from Cornell University in 1931, and worked on the editorial staffs of several newspapers before becoming a member of the National Broadcasting Company in 1943. In 1947 he was named NBC's vice-president in charge of advertising and promotion. Hammond had been missing for one day when his body was found on July 1, 1950, in the front seat of his car atop a hill in Chappaqua, New York, one mile from his home. A piece of garden hose connected to the exhaust pipe was run through the car's left front window. After examining two sealed notes (one addressed to his wife) found in the car, the Westchester County medical examiner stated that Hammond appeared to be despondent over "personal problems" and had committed suicide "while temporarily mentally disturbed."

Hancock, Tony

The most successful British comic of the fifties and sixties, Hancock failed, with tragic

results, to achieve his goal of international stardom. Born Anthony John Hancock on May 12, 1924, in Birmingham, England, he was 2 when his family moved to Bournemouth and purchased the Railway Hotel. Hancock's father, Jack, a semi-professional entertainer, turned the hotel into a mecca for many of the music hall artists of the day. Performers like Doris Walters befriended the young Hancock and often took him backstage during their shows. After leaving school, the 17-year-old Hancock billed himself as "The Confidential Comic" until joining the Air Force in 1942. He spent the remainder of World War II entertaining troops as part of Ralph Reader's *R.A.F. Gang Show*. Like most performers, Hancock found it difficult to re-enter show business after the war and supported himself working summer seasons in holiday resorts while waiting for a break. It came in 1948 when he was hired as a comedian for a six-week stint at the Windmill Theatre entertaining the audience between nude revues. Hancock caught the interest of the BBC and was offered a spot on the *Variety Bandbox* radio show in January 1949.

In 1951, the comedian gained national prominence after being added to the cast of the popular radio show *Educating Archie*. Simultaneously, Hancock lent his talents to *Happy Go Lucky*. The ill-fated comedy series introduced him to scriptwriters Ray Galton and Alan Simpson, two stellar talents who understood and shaped Hancock's comedic gifts. The pair wrote for the comedian's own radio show, *Hancock's Half Hour*, which debuted on November 2, 1954. The collaboration continued with great results when the program moved to television in 1956. When the series ended in 1960, Hancock decided to pursue his dream of becoming an international film star. In 1961, he starred in the comedy *The Rebel* (U.S. title, *Call Me Genius*). The film did good business in the United Kingdom and the Commonwealth, but bombed in America where Hancock desperately wanted it to succeed. *New York Times* critic Bosley Crowther savaged the film and described Hancock's performance as "a clumsy pretense of being funny." The comedian compounded this career mis-step by breaking with the writing team of Galton and Simpson. The pair went on to write the hugely successful television show *Steptoe and Son*, the basis for the hit U.S. series *Sanford and Son*. Hancock's follow-up film *The Punch and Judy Man* in 1963 was another flop. He appeared in smaller film roles with mixed results in *Those Magnificent Men in Their Flying Machines* (1965) and *The Wrong Box* (1966).

As his career waned, Hancock degenerated into a chronic alcoholic. In 1968, the 44-year-old entertainer was in Australia making a series of television programs for the world market when his drunkenness and inability to remember lines forced the show's producers to suspend production and order him to dry out at the Cavell House Pirvate Hospital in Rose Bay. On June 21, 1968, Hancock received word that his second wife, Freddie, had obtained an uncontested divorce on grounds of cruelty and adultery. His 15 year marriage to first wife Cicely Romanis had ended in 1965 after she could no longer tolerate his manic and wild mood swings.

On June 25, 1968, Hancock washed down a fatal overdose of tranquilizers with two bottles of vodka in the garden flat of 98 Birriga Road in the Sydney suburb of Bellevue Hill. The pen he used to write two suicide notes to Eddie Joffe, director of the television series, was still clutched in his hand. In one note, Hancock wrote: "Ed — Please send my mother this. I am sorry to cause her any more grief as she has already had enough but please pass on this message to her — that the soul is indestructable and so therefore Bill, who means nothing to you, will understand." The other read: "Dear Eddie — This is quite rational. Please give my love to my mother but there was nothing left to do. Things seemed to go wrong too many times." Fellow-comedian Spike Milligan said of Hancock's death, "One by one he shut the door on all the people he knew; then he shut the door on himself." The comedian's remains were cremated and his ashes committed at St. Dunstan's Church, Cranford, Middlesex.

FURTHER READING

Goodwin, Cliff. *When the Wind Changed: The Life and Death of Tony Hancock*. London: Century, 1999.
Oakes, Philip. *Tony Hancock*. London: Woburn Press, 1975.
Wilmut, Roger. *The Illustrated Hancock: With a Commentary*. London: Macdonald Queen Anne Press, 1986.
____. *Tony Hancock "Artiste": A Tony Handcock Companion*. London: Eyre Methuen, 1978.

Handley, Frank

The assistant manager of the Capitol Theatre for ten years, Handley, 37, started as an usher at the New York City movie house located at Broadway and Fifty-first Street when he 17 years old. Shortly after being declared unfit for military service, Handley began suffering from a nervous disorder. On the afternoon of October 24, 1943, he was found dead from a gunshot wound in an employee washroom on the ground floor of the theatre.

Hanley, Evelyn

In the five years they had partnered in the "Whirling Wonders" skating team, Hanley, 37, and her partner Clarence Anderson, 26, had appeared in both theatre and television. The pair had performed for nine weeks in the floor show at the Cafe Howard in Bridgeport, Connecticut, when a quarrel precipitated the skater's death. On February 19, 1947, one day after the argument, Anderson found Hanley's body in her room at the Howard Hotel. His partner swallowed an ounce of carbolic acid and, according to a medical examiner, died almost instantly from shock.

Hanley, Michael Edward

Broken in health by a three year period of illness that included a severe attack of shingles, neuritis, and a stroke that left the 84-year-old retired showman and theatre owner paralyzed on his right side, Hanley tried to discharge a .38-caliber pistol twice before fatally shooting himself above the left ear in his home at 1218 McClellan Street in Fort Wayne, Indiana, on June 18, 1942. Widely recognized as a producer of "clean" travelling shows, Hanley had been an intimate of Will Rogers and at the time of his death the one-time operator of a number of theatres in the Midwest still owned a movie house in Bluffton, Indiana. Relatives told authorities that during the last three years of his illness, Hanley often threatened suicide.

Hansen, Vern

Hansen joined the Washington, D.C., staff of CBS radio station WTOP in 1942, but left almost immediately to become a presentation editor with the Office of Strategic Services. There, he narrated the solider training film *Organization of the Army* before returning to WTOP in October 1943 and announcing assignments on programs like *The Factfinder, News at High Noon*, and the popular *Quizdown*. Hansen, 39, had been under a doctor's care for two weeks when his wife found him on September 30, 1950, hanging in the bathroom of his apartment at 1720 Queen Lane in Arlington, Virginia.

Harris, Walter Benjamin

On May 2, 1949, a little more than a month before he was to be married, the space buyer and assistant director of television programs for the advertising agency of Westheimer & Company fatally shot himself in the chest in the bedroom of his home at 5320 Waterman Boulevard in St. Louis, Missouri. Harris, clad only in his pajamas, used his U.S. Army issued .45-caliber pistol to inflict the deadly wound. The 26 year old's failure to land a job with a television station in New York City was believed to have been the impetus for the action.

Hartman, Brynn

Born Vicki Omdahl in Thief River Falls,

Minnesota, in 1959, the future wife of *Saturday Night Live* and *NewsRadio* star Phil Hartman dreamed of leaving the small Midwestern town for a career in Hollywood. Dropping out of high school, she quickly married and divorced Doug Torfin, a local telephone operator, while carving out a modest modelling career in Minnesota. Omdahl, moving to Hollywood in her 20s, changed her name numerous times (Vicki to Vicki Jo to Brindon to Brynn) and developed a major cocaine and alcohol addiction that lasted through most of the seventies.

While an acting career proved elusive, a reportedly drug-free Omdahl was working as a swimsuit model for the Catalina Sportswear Company when she met Canadian–born television star Phil Hartman on a blind date in 1986. The couple married on November 27, 1987, and produced two children, Sean and Birgen. Hartman, a gifted impressionist and actor, was hitting his comedic stride and was increasingly offered meaty roles in television and movies. In 1994, he left *Saturday Night Live* and moved to Los Angeles with his family. According to friends, Brynn was jealous of her husband's success and frustrated by her own inability to have a career. During Hartman's *Saturday Night Live* years the closest she came to appearing on the popular show was a brief shot of the back of her head in the opening credits. Brynn was the blonde sitting next to Hartman. In 1994, a bit part in Rob Reiner's flop film *North* failed to lead to any other acting assignments. She even failed to convince Hartman to get her a guest role on his series *NewsRadio*. Failing as an actress, Brynn with Sheree Guitar wrote the screenplay for the proposed film *Reckless Abandon*. The script was rejected by Showtime.

Brynn's lack of self-esteem prompted her to undergo a series of cosmetic surgeries in a confused attempt to become the perfect "Hollywood wife." By spring 1997, however, the troubled woman was again doing cocaine and receiving treatment in various drug rehabilitation centers. Her emotional insecurity fueled by substance addictions and jealousy over her husband's career led to frequent domestic quarrels. According to Hartman's ex-wife, Lisa Strain-Jarvis, Brynn routinely screamed at and slapped the actor during arguments. Hartman, the emotional polar opposite of his volatile wife, dealt with the situation by simply going to bed. This coping tactic failed in the early morning hours of May 28, 1998.

The evening before, Brynn, 40, had drinks with a female friend at a restaurant in Encino, California, a block from her home. Shortly after 10:00 P.M. she visited an old friend, Ron Douglas, at his home in Studio City. Sometime during the night, Brynn used cocaine and consumed more alcohol on top of the powerful prescription anti-depressant Zoloft she was taking. Studies suggest Zoloft, taken in concert with alcohol and drugs, can cause violent mania and blackouts.

At around 1:00 A.M. Brynn returned to the $1.4 million home at 5065 Encino Boulevard that Hartman had dubbed the "Ponderosa." Police theorize that she argued with Hartman while her children (son Sean, 9, and daughter Birgen, 6) slept in another part of the house. The 49-year-old actor, dressed in boxer shorts and a tee-shirt, ended the argument by going to bed. Around 2:00 A.M. Brynn removed a .38-caliber pistol from a locked safe and pumped three shots into her sleeping husband. Leaving her children asleep in the house, Brynn drove to Ron Douglas' home where she confessed the murder and then fell asleep. Douglas, though not initially believing Brynn's account, removed the pistol from her handbag. Shortly after 6:00 A.M. Brynn and Douglas drove back to the house on Encino Boulevard in separate cars. After confirming that Hartman was dead, Douglas called 911 to report the murder.

When a police SWAT teamed entered the house shortly after 6:20 A.M. to remove the children, Brynn had already barricaded herself in the bedroom containing Hartman's body. Moments before shooting herself in the head, Brynn called her sister with a message for her children: "Tell my kids that I love them more than anything and I always loved them, and Mommy doesn't know what happened, and she's just very sorry." After hearing the shot, police cautiously entered the bedroom to find Brynn, dressed in a two piece pajama outfit, in bed next to Hartman. Lying face-up in bed, her upper body was supported by pillows leaning against the headboard. The gun was still in her hand. Hartman, shot twice in the head and once in mid-torso, was found lying in a fetal position on his left side. A toxicology report verified that Brynn's body contained trace elements of cocaine and the antidepressant Zoloft, and registered a blood alcohol content of .12 percent. Under California state law a driver is considered to be under the influence with a blood alcohol level above .08 percent. In accordance with their wills, Hartman and Brynn were cremated. The comedian's ashes were scattered at Emerald Bay, Catalina Island. Custody of their children was given to Brynn's sister in Eau Claire, Wisconsin.

Hartman, Elizabeth

Mary Elizabeth Hartman (born in Youngstown, Ohio, on December 23, 1943) began acting in high school productions and won the Ohio Actress of the Year Award for her role in Tennessee Williams' *The Glass Menagerie*. After attending Carnegie Tech and working two summers with the John Kenley Players in Warren, Ohio, Hartman landed the ingénue role in a short-lived New York-bound production, *Everybody Out, The Castle Is Sinking*, which closed out of town. Her performance caught the eye of MGM scouts, and the 21-year-old actress was brought to Hollywood to audition for director Guy Green, who owned the rights to Elizabeth Kata's novel, *A Patch of Blue*. Hartman's sensitive portrayal of the film's blind heroine opposite popular actor Sidney Poitier garnered her an Academy Award nomination as Best Actress in 1965. While she lost to Julie Christie for *Darling*, Hartman won a Golden Globe in 1966 as the "New Star of the Year."

Despite the accolades, however, Hartman felt that the roles she was being offered lacked quality. Her popularity steadily waned throughout films like *The Group* (1966), *You're a Big Boy Now* (1967), *The Fixer* (1968), *The Beguiled* (1971), *Walking Tall* (1973), and *Full Moon High* (1981). In a 1971 interview, she blamed the studio: "I am the last product of the star build-up. But there was no follow-through. It got to the point where I died." In between film roles, Hartman periodically returned to the stage, and toured in company productions of *Becket* and *The Mad Woman of Chaillot*.

In 1982, she made her final film "appearance" as the voice of "Mrs. Brisby," a mouse character in the animated film *The Secret of NIMH*. Shortly afterward, Hartman moved from Los Angeles to Pittsburgh to be closer to her family. Hospitalized 19 times for depression, the actress spent the final years of her life medicated and subsisting on disability insurance, family handouts, and Social Security benefits. When not institutionalized, she passed her days at home listening to records or wandering alone through the Carnegie Art Museum. The 43-year-old actress was an out-patient at the Western Psychiatric Institute and Clinic in Pittsburgh when, on June 10, 1987, she phoned her psychiatrist and threatened to kill herself. He called police, but they arrived too late. Five years to the day after leaving the movies, Hartman had jumped to her death from the window of her fifth floor apartment. No one from the Hollywood or Broadway community was present at the actress' funeral in Boardman, Ohio.

FURTHER READING

Konte, Sandra Hansen, "The Short Life of Elizabeth Hartman." *Los Angeles Times*, sec. Calendar, pp. 3–4, November 22, 1987.

Harvey, Gerald

The vice-president of programming at the Z Channel, a popular Santa Monica, California-based pay television service, Harvey had been off of work for a week complaining of health problems when on April 10, 1988, he fatally shot his wife before turning a handgun on himself in their Westwood home in the 200 block of South Thurston Avenue. Though Los Angeles police said the 39 year old suffered from a "mental disorder," they could provide no motive for the murder-suicide. A public memorial service for the murdered woman, 39-year-old Frederica ("Deri") Rudulth, publisher of the *Westwood Insider*, was subsequently held at the Westwood Playhouse.

Hassall, Imogen

Born in 1942, the dark-haired supporting actress competently performed with the Royal Shakespeare Company, but could never escape her "pin-up" image in such films as *When Dinosaurs Ruled the Earth* (1970) and *Licensed to Love and Kill* (1979). Hassall also worked in commercial theatre and did guest shots on the British television shows *The Avengers* and *The Saint*. Continuing an ongoing pattern of trying to take her own life, the 38-year-old actress had survived an intentional overdose of sleeping pills just two weeks prior to November 16, 1980, when she was found dead in her bed from a large overdose of drugs at her home in Wimbledon, south London.

Hastings, Cuyler

Hastings, 50, once a leading actor for theatre impresario David Belasco, last appeared onstage in 1912 in the role of the reformer in *The Woman*, a Belasco production at the Republic Theatre in New York City. Earlier in his career, Hastings also starred in his own touring companies of *Sherlock Holmes* and *If I Were King*. In 1912 the actor suffered the first of two personal setbacks that ultimately led to his suicide. Hastings lost a large sum of money in a Wall Street speculation followed in the spring of 1913 by a stroke that left him partially paralyzed and unable to continue acting. On January 10, 1914, the veteran thespian shot himself in the head with a revolver in his room at 272 Fourth Avenue in New York City. Several notes found on a nearby table explained the deed.

Hathaway, Donny

Hathaway (born in Chicago, Illinois, on October 1, 1945) was raised by his grandmother, noted gospel singer Martha Pitts. Billed as Donny Pitts, "The Nation's Youngest Gospel Singer," Hathaway began performing in local churches at the age of 3. In the sixties, Hathaway was a straight A student at Howard University majoring in music theory, but left without graduating after joining the Rick Powell Group. Hathaway was already producing, conducting, or arranging sessions for Roberta Flack (a classmate at Howard), Aretha Franklin, the Impressions, and Jerry Butler when Atlantic Records signed him in 1970. His first single, "The Ghetto — Part 1," released in January of that year, established the singer as a major new force in Soul music. Hathaway undoubtedly, however, will best be remembered for his duets with singer Roberta Flack. Their first pairing in June 1972 produced the hit "Where is the Love," which peaked at Number 5 on the *Billboard* pop singles chart and won them a Grammy for Best Vocal Performance by a Duo or Group. They paired again in February 1978 with even greater success. Their "The Closer I Get to You" rocketed to Number 2 on the *Billboard* chart, and received a Grammy nomination. When not singing (he released four albums), Hathaway composed film scores (*Come Back, Charleston Blue*, 1972), wrote material recorded by Franklin and Butler, and produced the Staple Singers.

On January 13, 1979, the 33-year-old singer spent the day recording with Roberta Flack in a studio in New York City. According to his manager, Hathaway was in good spirits when they left Flack's Central Park West apartment following the studio session. Hathaway returned alone to his 15th floor room in the Essex House at 160 Central Park South, bolted the door from the inside, and jumped from the window, landing on a second floor ledge. According

to his estranged wife, the singer had been briefly hospitalized on two occasions in 1972 for emotional problems caused by his quick rise in the industry and the anxiety it produced.

Haver, Phyllis

Born Phyllis O'Haver in Douglas, Kansas, on January 6, 1899, Haver first appeared as a Mack Sennett Bathing Beauty in a series of

PHYLLIS HAVER— **A former Mack Sennett Bathing Beauty, Haver became typecast as the "bad girl" in several films like** *What Price Glory?* **(1926) and** *The Way of All Flesh* **(1927). In 1929 (after appearing in 50 features) she left films to marry into money. Divorced in 1945, Haver lived alone in Falls Village, Connecticut, until depression over the death of Mack Sennett prompted the 61-year-old ex-actress to take barbiturates there on November 19, 1960.**

comedy shorts shot in 1917–1918. By 1920, Haver's sex appeal led her typecasting as the "bad girl" in a number of "scarlet skirt" roles like "Shanghai Mabel" in *What Price Glory?* (1926), "The Temptress" in *The Way of All Flesh* (1927), and "Roxie Hart" in *Chicago* (1927). When Haver retired from films in 1929 to marry wealthy Manhattan businessman William Seeman, the popular sex queen had appeared in 50 features. After divorcing Seeman in 1945, she lived alone in Falls Village, Connecticut. On November 19, 1960, the 61-year-old former actress took a fatal overdose of barbiturates in the bedroom of her home. According to *Variety*, Haver was depressed over the recent death of Mack Sennett, the producer-director who had given her her start in films. Haver reportedly attempted suicide in 1959.

Hawke, Rohn Olin

A one-time movie actor in the late forties and former disc jockey on KOAT radio in Albuquerque during the fifties, Hawke, 43, was living in Santa Fe, New Mexico, and doing free-lance public relations for the State Corporation Commission when he shot himself between the eyes with a .38-caliber U.S. Army issue revolver in that city on February 15, 1967.

Hayes, Ray

Broke, unemployed, and with his wife of nine months soon to give birth to their first child, the 28-year-old Los Angeles musician and restaurant man leaped to his death from the seventh floor window of a Market Street hotel in San Francisco on February 14, 1932, after an initial attempt to kill himself with chloroform-soaked cotton failed. In addition to his baggage, an expensive saxophone, and $4.00 in cash, the police found four suicide notes in his hotel room. To his "Darling Mother," Hayes wrote: "Please try to understand and don't blame Peg for this. She has been the best friend I have ever had. There is to be a child. Try to see that she is cared for

through this because she will need you awfully. It will be your grandchild — we were married last June. I know I will see you in the time to come." In an open letter to the "Press," Hayes cited his reasons for the leap: "I could write volumes as to why I do this, but, after all, what good would it do? I can not get work and there is no one I can ask for help. I know my wife needs me, but under present conditions she will be better off without me. She is pure gold and not to blame for the condition I leave her in."

Heald, L. W.

On January 27, 1934, the 26-year-old accountant for Omaha, Nebraska, radio station KOIL was found in the bathroom of his lodging at 3926 Harney Street with his head near an open gas jet that had not been used for some time. An attempt to revive the auditor with an inhalator failed. Six weeks earlier Heald had reported sick to work from gas poisoning.

Heckler, Herbert

Throughout their two year engagement, Pearl Palmer, a 23-year-old prima donna best known for her role in Victor Herbert's opera *Princess Pat*, had delayed marrying Heckler, a 27-year-old opera singer from Chicago, in order to pursue a career. On September 26, 1915, Palmer was in her studio at the Conservatory Building at No. 240 West Seventy-second Street in New York City when a depressed Heckler arrived for a visit. Palmer complained of being ill and dispatched her beau to a pharmacy for medication. A friend who accompanied Heckler later told authorities that the singer had burst into tears when discussing his belief that Palmer no longer loved him. Returning to her studio, Heckler entered the room alone. Moments later, the sounds of a violent argument were heard followed by four gunshots in quick succession. When police forced the door they discovered Palmer unconscious, a bullet lodged in her head and two in her body. She died shortly afterward in the

Polyclinic Hospital. Heckler, the spurned suitor, lay dead in the center of the room, a gaping gunshot wound in his forehead.

Held, Lillian

Known outside show business as Lillian Bachman, the wife of a Manchester, New Hampshire, cigar manufacturer, the 41-year-old actress was formerly married to actor Frederick Russell. On the vaudeville circuit the duo were billed "Held and Russell." On July 31, 1920, Held's body was found across the bed of her room at 358 West Fifty-eighth Street in New York City. The windows were sealed and illuminating gas had flooded the room for hours. Several weeks before, Held had rented the room in the company of a man, signing the register as "Mr. and Mrs. Von Holding." The man, whose name was withheld, was later identified as a well-known musical director. In a brief note written on the back of a photograph of her deceased first husband, Russell, Held blamed the musical director for her death and requested to be buried by the side of her mother and her former vaudeville partner. In a separate note, Held identified the musical director by name and mentioned that he had threatened her life a few days before.

Hemingway, Ernest Miller

Commenting on how best a writer should deal with Hollywood, Hemingway suggested that the artist meet the producers at the California state line, then "throw them your book, they throw you the money. Then you jump into your car and drive like hell back the way you came." Despite having 15 films made (none of which he overly liked) from his books and short stories, Hemingway (born in Oak Park, Illinois, on July 21, 1899) visited Hollywood only once and then just to give a speech to raise money in support of the Republican side in the Spanish Civil War. In 1937, the writer's address to some of Tinseltown's wealthiest people was followed by a screening of Dutch filmmaker Joris Iven's doc-umentary *The Spanish Earth*. Hemingway, in his only original screenwriting, wrote and narrated the script for the film. Movies, however, made Hemingway among the wealthiest writers of his time. He received $80,000 for the screen rights to *A Farewell to Arms* (1932) and a whopping $150,000 for the 1958 screen adaptation of *The Old Man and the Sea*. Hemingway turned down a $300,000 offer from 20th Century–Fox for the film rights to *The Garden of Eden*, a novel in progress at the time of his death. The book was not published until 1986 and a film adaptation has not been made as of this writing.

The details of Hemingway's life rivalled those of any of his fictional creations and are chronicled in minute detail in dozens of critical biographies published since his death. An excellent "Hemingway Chronology and Dateline" is included in Charles M. Oliver's ambitious work *Ernest Heminway A to Z: The Essential Reference to the Life and Work* (1999). In 1952, Hemingway won the Pulitzer Prize for his novel *The Old Man and the Sea*. Two years later he was awarded the Nobel Prize for literature. The writer, however, was unable to attend the Nobel ceremony because of injuries sustained in back-to-back plane crashes while on safari in Africa in 1954. Hemingway suffered massive kidney damage which in turn led to high blood pressure. The drug prescribed to control the condition caused the writer to sink into a spiral of depression and may have been responsible for his wild mood swings. By the advent of the sixties, Hemingway suffered from depression, paranoia, hypertension, an enlarged liver, and high blood pressure.

Beginning in 1960, the literary legend underwent a battery of shock treatments at the Mayo Clinic in Rochester, Minnesota. The treatments often left him unable to remember his name. Following the procedure, Hemingway returned to his home in Ketchum, Idaho, to recover. The drug he took to control his high blood pressure inevitably led to another round of depression and more treatment. Physically, the electroshock took its toll on Hemingway. Weighing a muscular 220 pounds in his prime, he dropped to 160 pounds near the end of his life. According to his fourth wife, Mary Hemingway, the writer would get down on his knees and beg her not to send him back for more shock treatments.

On the morning of July 2, 1961, days after returning home from his 36th shock treatment, the 61-year-old writer retrieved a 12-gauge, double-barreled English shotgun from the basement storeroom of his home, and returning upstairs to the foyer, placed the gun's barrel against his head and pulled the trigger. Hemingway is buried between two pines in the Ketchum Cemetery in Ketchum, Idaho. Of note, suicide seems to run in Hemingway's family, having claimed his father, Clarence (1928), his two sisters, Marcelline (1963, suspected) and Ursula (1966), his brother, Leicester (1982), and his granddaughter, Margaux (1996, see entry).

Further Reading

Baker, Carlos. *Ernest Hemingway; A Life Story*. New York: Scribner, 1969.

Hemingway, Gregory H. *Papa: A Personal Memoir*. Boston: Houghton Mifflin, 1976.

Hotchner, A. E. *Papa Hemingway; A Personal Memoir*. New York: Random House, 1966.

Lynn, Kenneth S. *Hemingway*. New York: Simon and Schuster, 1987.

Mellow, James R. *Hemingway: A Life Without Consequences*. Boston: Houghton Mifflin, 1992.

Meyers, Jeffrey. *Hemingway, a Biography*. 1st ed. New York: Harper & Row, 1985.

Oliver, Charles M. *Ernest Hemingway A to Z: The Essential Reference to the Life and Work*. New York: Facts on File, 1999.

Hemingway, Margaux

Named after a bottle of Chateau Margeaux wine that her parents drank on the night of her conception, the model-actress was born Margeaux Louise Hemingway on February 16, 1954, in Portland, Oregon, the second of three daughters of Ernest Hemingway's son, Jack. The 6 foot tall, 19-year-old blonde left the family home in Ketchum, Idaho, in 1974 to pursue a modelling career in New York City. An instant success, the statuesque beauty graced the covers of *Vogue* and *Time*. In 1975 she landed the fashion industry's first million dollar model-spokesperson endorsement after signing with Fabergé to promote Babe perfume. In 1976 she made her film debut as a rape victim in *Lipstick*, which also featured her younger sister, Mariel. Critics savaged Hemingway's performance, but praised her 14-year-old sister as a promising actress. Mariel Hemingway would establish herself as a solid screen presence with such films as Woody Allen's *Manhattan* (1979), and *Star 80* (1983), Bob Fosse's bio-pic of slain *Playboy* centerfold Dorothy Stratten, while Margaux's acting career foundered in such bombs as *Killer Fish* (1979), the 1982 Kung-Fu parody *They Call Me Bruce?*, and *Inner Sanctum* (1991). By all accounts, an intense sibling rivalry existed between the pair that was slowly improving over time.

An early habitué of the trendy New York nightspot Studio 54, Hemingway's fast lifestyle led to two divorces, alcoholism, bulimia, and countless rounds of psychiatric counseling. In 1987 the actress nearly bit off her tongue during an alcohol-induced epileptic seizure. The next year she did a stint at the Betty Ford Center. In an attempt to jump-start her stalled career Hemingway posed nude for *Playboy* in May 1990. However, by the mid-nineties Hemingway was reduced to making infomercials, promoting the Psychic Hotline, acting in direct-to-video films, and hosting an upcoming wildlife television cable program. Weeks before her death, Hemingway began speculating to friends about "the other side." Days before the act she asked several acquaintances if they knew where she could get some phenobarbital capsules without a prescription. Although the actress came from a family where its most famous member, Ernest Hemingway (see entry), had taken his own life (as had his brother, sister, and father) friends were unconcerned. She had recently moved into a studio apartment near the beach in Santa Monica, California, and finally seemed happy.

The 42-year-old model-actress had not been seen for two days when on July 1, 1996, she was found dead lying in bed with her hands folded over her nightgown. Next to her was an empty bottle of phenobarbital. There was no note. An autopsy revealed that Hemingway had taken twice the lethal dosage of the drug, so much in fact, that she died before the pills could even digest in her stomach. The inscription on Hemingway's grave marker in the Ketchum Cemetery in Ketchum, Idaho, reads "Free Spirit Freed."

Hendon, Rigsby D.

The bedspread-wrapped body of the 42-year-old Hendon, owner of the Main Street Dance Hall in Houston, Texas, was found on the bedroom floor of his home at 1834 Hewitt Drive on September 6, 1956. Hendon had locked the bedroom door, taped the keyhole shut, then turned on a gas jet. Detectives found a note addressed to his wife in the house.

Henry, John

Henry (real name Norman Clapham) had been one of the most popular radio comedians in England, but his career was in rapid decline when he committed suicide in his London home on Holland Road, W., on May 14, 1934. The 52-year-old entertainer was found on the floor covered with an eiderdown blanket nestled on three pillows, clutching a photo of his beloved who had recently died and his head inside a gas oven. Letters found at the scene and earlier posted to friends by the dead man explained the act. Separated from his real wife, Henry had been living with Gladys Horridge, a featured player in his radio act whom he had been passing off as his wife. When Horridge died, weeks before he took his own life, Henry testified that she was his wife in order to spare her any embarrassment. When Henry's actual wife notified him that she was filing a lawsuit against him for support, he realized that he would not only be publicly embarrassed, but also face prosecution for giving false evidence at an inquest.

In the suicide note read at Henry's inquest, the comedian wrote: "I am going to join my girl. Please bury me with her and put her photo with me. She was good to me and without her life is not worth living. I am sorry to cause everyone trouble, but perhaps I have given a little happiness to others by the wireless. It will only require a few minutes after I turn on the gas. Hello everybody, John Henry. I am going to my girl. Goodbye everyone." Henry's funeral at the Streatham Park Cemetery was paid for by the Variety Artists' Benevolent Fund and attended by some 500 people.

Henshaw, Roger Dale

On April 3, 1938, the bodies of Henshaw, a 42-year-old film scenario writer and former Paramount Studios official, and his wife, the former singer-actress Miriam Christine Wills, 46, were found clasped in each other's arms in their automobile in the closed garage of their home at 10863 Blusside Drive in North Hollywood. A hose carrying carbon monoxide fumes from the exhaust into the car's interior had poisoned the couple and the small dog that lay dead at their feet. On the library table, authorities found a nearly completed scenario titled "Drinking and Dining With Hollywood," and two notes. One was a will; the other read in part: "We are both too tired, discouraged and ill to carry on. Today the last vestige of hope was dispelled. We have nothing to go on with, nothing in sight, so tonight we are going to sleep together, never to awaken."

Hero, Maria Iturbi

The 18-year-old daughter of famed Spanish pianist and symphony conductor Jose Iturbi (1895–1980) married violinist Stephen Hero in January 1936. The couple separated in August 1939 and the next year a settlement was reached giving the violinist custody of their two children for three months out of each year. In January 1941, the young woman was awarded full custody and officially sued Hero for divorce on November 13, 1942, alleging non-support. Jose Iturbi weighed into the legal fray on March 17, 1943, when he petitioned the Los Angeles Superior Court to grant him full custody of the little girls, claiming that his daughter was "not the proper person" to care for them. In an out-of-court settlement, Maria Iturbi Hero retained custody of the children, but they were ordered to live in her father's home at 913 N. Bedford Drive in Beverly Hills, California.

Around midnight on April 17, 1946, a dinner party had just broken up in Iturbi's home when he seated himself at the piano in the living room to practice. Seconds later, a pistol shot rang out from his daughter's second floor bedroom near those of her sleeping children. Iturbi entered the 28-year-old woman's room and found her on the floor, her hair ablaze, bleeding profusely from a gaping head wound. A .38-caliber pistol lay beside her. Iturbi extinguished the flames, called an ambulance, and was at his daughter's side when she died hours later at the Beverly Hills Emergency Hospital.

Higgins, Edgar

Higgins, 46, a writer for the DuMont Television Network show *Broadway to Hollywood* (1949–1954), died from an overdose of sleeping pills at his New York City home on 243 West Seventieth Street on August 25, 1951. A former newsman, Higgins had worked for the Associated Press, *The New York Journal-American*, and the National Broadcasting System before signing on to the magazine show that featured news, gossip, and quiz-related elements.

Hill, George William

Hill (born in Douglass, Kansas, on April 25, 1895) broke into pictures in 1908 as a prop boy for D. W. Griffith at the Fine Arts Studio. Evincing an interest in photography, he graduated to the position of first cameraman and shot several films in the teens including *The Sea Wolf* (1913), *Burning Daylight* (1914), *Buckshot John* (1915), *Polly of the Circus* (1917),

and *Turning the Tables* (1919). From the early twenties Hill turned to direction and made several well regarded films for MGM including *Tell it to the Marines* (1926), *The Cossacks* (1928), his 1930 masterpiece *The Big House*, and the classic comedy *Min and Bill* (1930) starring Wallace Beery and his dear friend Marie Dressler. In January 1930, the director married Frances Marion, his longtime scriptwriting collaborator, but the marriage ended in October 1933 amid charges of Hill's cruelty. Despite their estrangement, the pair continued to be amicable and were working together on the script of the MGM vehicle *The Good Earth*, which Hill was set to direct.

While preparing for the film in June 1934, Hill was seriously injured in a car accident when he swerved to avoid a group of children running onto Venice Boulevard. The director crashed into a telephone pole, crushing his chest and breaking several ribs. In constant physical pain following the accident, the man known to his friends as "the lone wolf" became even more withdrawn, morose, and moody. In the late afternoon of August 10, 1934, Hill returned to his spacious South Beach home at 5109 Ocean Front in Venice, California, after vacationing for several days at his cabin at Lake Arrowhead. To his valet, the 39-year-old director entrusted a tin box containing a .45-caliber pistol (a memento from Hill's days as a captain in the photographic division of the Signal Corps during World War I) with the instruction to "put it away." Hill then left and spent several hours with ex-wife Marion and studio officials on the MGM lot in a story conference concerning *The Good Earth*.

Shortly after 9:00 P.M., Hill returned home and phoned his valet to ask where he had placed the box containing the pistol. At 7:30 A.M. the next morning, the valet arrived at Hill's home to find the pajama-clad body of his employer dead in the second floor master bedroom clutching a pistol in his right hand. Sometime during the hours before, or, shortly after midnight, Hill had fired a practice shot into the ceiling, before laying in bed, placing

GEORGE WILLIAM HILL— Hill broke into films in 1908 as a prop boy for D.W. Griffith and during the teens rose to the rank of first cameraman. As a director he made *Tell it to the Marines* (1926), *The Cossacks* (1928), *The Big House* (1930), and *Min and Bill* (1930). In 1930, Hill married Frances Marion (pictured), one of Hollywood's highest-paid screenwriters and his frequent collaborator. Although their marriage ended in 1933, the pair were working together on the script of *The Good Earth*, which Hill was set to direct for MGM, when he was seriously injured in a car accident in June 1934. Unable to get beyond the pain, the 39-year-old director shot himself in the head on August 10, 1934, in his home in Venice, California. *Courtesy of University of South California, on behalf of the USC Library Department of Special Collections.*

the pistol in his mouth, and pulling the trigger. The bullet, passing through the director's skull, lodged in the headboard of the bed. While Hill left no note, he had drawn up a will days before the suicide in which he directed that his body be cremated immediately after the death certificate had been signed. By 4:00 P.M. the day he was found, Hill's body was cremated. Authorities speculated that Hill had either taken his life because of the car accident or his divorce from Frances Marion, or both.

Hilliar, William J.

The London-born Hilliar, 60, began in show business as a magician working with such greats as Harry Houdini and Thurston. In Chicago in 1902, he founded one of the first illustrated monthly magazines devoted to magic and magicians, *The Sphinx*, allied at the time with the Western Organ of the Society of American Magicians. Hilliar also wrote several books on the subject including *Magic Made Easy: Money Catching and 50 Other Tricks* (1902) and *Modern Magicians' Hand Book: An Up-To-Date Treatise on the Art of Conjuring* (1902). In addition to working on the staff of *Billboard*, the show business veteran also did publicity and press work for circuses and carnivals. On November 15, 1936, a cab driver picked up Hilliar in downtown Cincinnati and drove him to the magician's home at 1228 Iliff Avenue in the suburb of Price Hill. Telling the driver, "I'll be back in a minute," Hilliar went to the garage in the rear of the home and fired a bullet into his right temple.

Hoegler, Albert

On January 28, 1954, ten weeks after his contract was not renewed by the Standard Brewing Company, sponsor of the Cleveland Indians radio broadcasts on WERE, Hoegler, 30, a baseball statistician and co-announcer for the station, hanged himself in the basement of his home at 3025 E. 130th Street in Cleveland, Ohio. Hoegler's sister found her brother's body suspended from a clothesline tied to a ceiling water pipe.

Holland, Anthony

After graduating from the University of Chicago and studying acting with Lee Strasberg during the sixties, Holland became a member of the original Second City comedy troupe with Elaine May, Mike Nichols, and Alan Arkin. Holland's 1963 Broadway debut in Lillian Hellman's *My Mother, My Father and Me* was the first of several comedic and dramatic roles in an acting career that included regional theatre and off-Broadway productions. During the 1969–1970 theatre season, Holland won an Obie Award for his performance in *The White House Murder Case*, and another in 1986–1987 for his role in *The Hunger Artist*, Martha Clarke's adaptation of several stories by Franz Kafka. In addition to theatre work, Holland appeared in several television programs (*The Mary Tyler Moore Show*, *M*A*S*H*, *Cagney and Lacey*) as well as in films (*Klute*, 1971; *All That Jazz*, 1979). Terminally ill with AIDS, the 60-year-old actor used pills to take his life in his Manhattan apartment on July 10, 1988.

Hollenbeck, Don

Hollenbeck (born March 30, 1905, in Lincoln, Nebraska) attended the University of Nebraska, but left before graduating to work as a reporter for *The Nebraska State Journal*. During World War II, the newsman served with the Office of War Information in North Africa broadcasting reports on the occupation of Algiers and the Fifth Army's amphibious assault on Salerno. After the war, Hollenbeck joined the Columbia Broadcasting System where he distinguished himself as the host of the weekly program *CBS Views the Press* from 1947 until leaving in 1950 to become the commentator on the nightly news on WCBS-TV, New York. Tortured in recent months by severe stomach ulcers, Hollenbeck ended his life on June 22, 1954, by opening up all the gas jets on the kitchen stove of his Manhattan apartment at 148 East Forty-eighth Street.

Holliday, Frank, Jr.

Shortly after appearing on a radio program on August 3, 1948, the 35-year-old singer was arrested on suspicion of breaking into a service station on North La Brea Avenue and booked into the Hollywood Jail at 2:00 A.M. the next day. Although Holliday had a police record dating back to 1935, he had stayed straight ever since serving a year in County Jail for burglary in 1940. According to the officers who apprehended the singer fleeing from the service station, Holliday said: "I was walking around tonight, just looking around. I was broke and didn't have any place to go. I didn't plan to burglarize the service station. But I guess you fellows have caught me red-handed. I would appreciate it if you would give me a break. Would you be interested in $100 a piece to turn me loose and forget the whole thing? This is the first time I have ever been in trouble and under arrest." Less than an hour after being booked, Holliday used his belt to hang himself from a ceiling grille in his cell.

Holliday, Michael

Holliday (born Norman Alexander Milne in Liverpool, England, on November 26, 1928) began singing in the style of Bing Crosby while serving as a seaman in the Merchant Navy. Following his discharge, he sang in various holiday camps throughout Britain before signing with Columbia in 1955. Holliday specialized in covering several U.S. artists' hits before topping the U.K. charts with the Burt Bacharach-Hal David tune "The Story of My Life" in 1958. However, after scoring another Number 1 hit in England with "Starry Eyed," the singer was unable to sustain his chart success. In the sixties, Holliday appeared on British television in *Relax with Mike* and was paired opposite the comedy team the Crazy Gang in the 1962 film *Life Is a Circus*. On October 29, 1963, the 34-year-old Holliday took a fatal dose of Nembutal in his home at Addington, Surrey. In a note to his estranged wife, Holliday wrote: "The Income Tax want their money by Wednesday or else. I guess I ain't man enough to take it." According to her, the depressed singer been hospitalized twice in the past for drug overdoses.

Holman, Libby

One of the great white torch singers of the twenties and thirties, Holman's tragic personal life overshadowed her show business success. Holman was born Elsbeth (Elizabeth) Holtzman on May 23, 1904 (some sources report 1906), in Cincinnati, Ohio. Her father, a successful attorney, paid her tuition to the University of Cincinnati where she excelled in school theatrical productions while earning a bachelor of arts degree. In 1924 she made her stage debut in a short-lived touring production of *The Fool*. In New York in 1925, Holman auditioned for a singing role in the revue *Garrick's Gaieties* featuring songs written by Richard Rodgers and Lorenz Hart. Her star rose considerably with featured roles in *Greenwich Village Follies* (1926), *Merry-Go-Round* (1927), and *Rainbow* (1928).

In the fall of 1929, the 25-year-old performer scored a major hit in *The Little Show* starring Clifton Webb and Fred Allen. Holman's sexually charged rendition of "Moanin' Low" showcased the torch singer's sultry sensuality and smoky voice. In her career the singer known as "the dark purple menace" performed classic renditions of some of the most popular songs of the era including "Can't We Be Friends," "Body and Soul," "Something to Remember You By," "Am I Blue?" and "You and the Night and the Music." The new "It Girl" was earning $2,500 a week in *The Little Show* and developing a reputation as an uninhibited lover of both men and women.

A bisexual, Holman reputedly had sexual dalliances with actress and fellow suicide Jeanne Eagels (see entry), Tallulah Bankhead, black *Folies Bergère* star Josephine Baker, and Louisa Carpenter du Pont Jenney, heiress to part of the vast du Pont fortune. Smith Reynolds, the 18-year-old heir to the RJ Reynolds tobacco fortune, was immediately smitten with Holman after seeing her in *The Little Show.* Though married, he single-mindedly pursued the torch singer, constantly threatening to commit suicide should she not return his love. Holman finally relented and two days after Reynolds' divorce became final on November 23, 1931, secretly married the young heir. The marriage was in trouble from the outset. Holman, openly flirtatious with both sexes, repeatedly clashed with the insanely jealous and emotionally unstable Reynolds. At his request, she agreed to give up show business for a year and in early June 1932 took up residence with Reynolds in Reynolda, a thousand acre family estate on the outskirts of Winston-Salem, North Carolina.

On the evening of July 5, 1932, the couple was entertaining a small group of friends at Reynolda. As the moonshine flowed the party became wilder and an inebriated Holman began flirting with Ab Walker, a good looking childhood friend of Reynolds' who earned $125 a week as his personal secretary. Tension mounted between husband and wife culminating in a loud argument. Most of the embarrassed guests soon departed leaving Holman, Reynolds, and Walker alone in the house except for the servants. Shortly before midnight, a single gunshot rang out and Reynolds was found sprawled across a bed in a second floor sleeping porch bleeding profusely from a bullet wound in his right temple. He died the next morning at 5:25 at N.C. Baptist Hospital in Winston-Salem.

Holman's contention that her husband had taken his own life was supported by a doctor who hastily signed the death certificate listing the cause of death as "suicide." However, nagging questions persisted. Reynolds was left-handed, but the entry wound was on the right side of his head fired from a Mauser pistol determined to have been held 18 inches away from its target, an awkward way to commit suicide. The gun, missing after several initial searches of the room, was finally found an hour after the shooting on the floor three feet from the bed. Some of Holman's clothes were

also found in Walker's bathroom suggesting a romantic link between the two. Both were subsequently indicted on murder charges, but the case was quietly dropped when the tobacco family, fearing negative publicity, learned that Holman was pregnant with Reynolds' child. Christopher Smith, a son born seven months after his father's death, later died at the age of 17 in a climbing accident on Mount Whitney in August 1950.

In 1939, Holman married Ralph Holmes, who almost immediately went off to fight in World War II. Emotionally wrecked by his years in combat, Holmes agreed to a separation from his wife after returning from the war in 1945. On November 15, 1945, Holmes' underwear-clad body was found lying on a sofa in his New York City apartment at 340 East Sixty-sixth Street. An empty bottle of sleeping pills was found near the sofa. Authorities estimated that when found he had been dead for five or six days.

Holman, financially secure from a settlement with the Reynolds family, half-heartedly pursued a career. In between rare appearances in musicals, the torch singer caused a stir in the racially divided forties by performing with black folk singer Josh White in nightclubs. In the fifties she toured with a program concert act called *Blues, Ballads and Sin Songs.* Holman's personal life remained unsettled with her well-publicized friendship with troubled actor Montgomery Clift. A lifelong drug user, Holman was accused by many of supplying her lover Clift with various illegal substances. Married to Jewish artist Louis Schanker in 1960, Holman was devastated when Clift died in 1966 of a heart attack brought on by years of drugs and drinking. In the mid-sixties she worked little, occasionally giving folk concerts for charities while appearing in a pair of concerts for the United Nations Children's Fund.

On June 18, 1971, the 67-year-old torch singer's body (clad only in a bikini bottom) was found stretched out on the front seat of her Rolls Royce limousine parked inside the garage on her 112 acre estate, Treetops, in

Merribrooke Lane in North Stamford, Connecticut. The chief state medical examiner ruled the death a suicide due to acute carbon monoxide poisoning. Holman's remains were cremated and the ashes scattered over her estate.

FURTHER READING

Bradshaw, Jon. *Dreams That Money Can Buy: The Tragic Life of Libby Holman*. 1st ed. New York: W. Morrow, 1985.

Machlin, Milt. *Libby*. New York: Dorchester Pub. Co., 1980.

Perry, Hamilton Darby. *Libby Holman: Body and Soul*. 1st ed. Boston: Little, Brown, 1983.

Reynolds, Patrick. *The Gilded Leaf: Triumph, Tragedy, and Tobacco: Three Generations of the R. J. Reynolds Family and Fortune*. 1st ed. Boston: Little, Brown, 1989.

Hope, Adele Blood

The actress once called "the most beautiful blonde on the American stage" was born in San Francisco, California, on April 23, 1886. Billed onstage and in films as "Adele Blood," Hope was best known as a leading actress in travelling stock company productions of *The Unmasking*, *All Rivers Meet the Sea*, *The Picture of Dorian Gray*, and *Everyman* (in which she starred for five years). In films, Blood had leading roles in *The Devil's Toy* (1916), and the 1920 silent *The Riddle: Woman*, in which she ironically played a character who committed suicide with a gun. In the summer of 1936, the 50-year-old actress and widow lost an estimated $40,000 financing a stock company in which she, and her 17-year-old daughter, Dawn Hope, starred in dramas presented in the auditorium of the Bronxville High School.

On the evening of September 13, 1936, Hope entered the bedroom of her 12 room English–style house at 12 Griswald Lane situated on the grounds of the Westchester Country Club in Harrisonville, New York, and shot herself in the head with a .32-caliber pistol. She died hours later without regaining consciousness at the United Hospital in Port Chester, New York. Daughter Dawn subsequently sold her mother's possessions, including her pet Boston bull pup, Joy, at auction. Three years later on July 18, 1939, Dawn Hope (then married and known as Dawn Hope Noel) committed suicide in exactly the same fashion as her mother (see entry Noel, Dawn Blood).

Hopkins, Douglas

Hopkins, the lead guitarist and principal songwriter for the Tempe, Arizona-based rock band the Gin Blossoms, confided to his sister shortly before committing suicide that he had been "born unhappy." The Gin Blossoms, founded by Hopkins and bassist Bill Leen, played their first gig on Christmas Day in 1987 and slowly built a strong local following playing bars in Tempe. Based largely on the appeal of Hopkins' depressive lyrics set to an up-tempo pop sound, the group was signed by A&M Records on May 26, 1990.

While the band was in Memphis in 1992 recording their debut album, *New Miserable Experience*, Hopkins' lifelong battle with depression and alcohol reached a crisis. Unable to play lead guitar during the sessions, a drunken Hopkins asked the producer to replace him with another musician. In an April 1992 meeting, the other four band members voted to fire Hopkins when the album was finished. The split was rancorous. While Hopkins returned to Tempe and formed another band, the Chimeras, the Gin Blossoms launched a successful tour on the strength of two hit songs penned by Hopkins, "Hey Jealousy" and "Found Out About You." As the band became increasingly popular with fans and critics (one of whom wrote, "With music as exhilarating as this, misery has rarely sounded so good") Hopkins became increasingly depressed and drunken.

On December 3, 1993, two weeks after he had attempted suicide for the sixth time in his 32 year life, Hopkins purchased a .38-caliber pistol in a Tempe pawnshop. The next day, the musician laid across the bed in his apartment in the 500 block of West

University Drive, placed the gun's barrel in his mouth, then pulled the trigger. A friend, who earlier in the week had tried to dissuade the guitarist from committing suicide, recalled: "I wanted him to look at his life, and know that if he did kill himself, he would just be stereotyping the rock 'n' roll thing, you know? His response was that his life had been a stereotypical rock 'n' roll life and that's how he wanted it."

Hoppe, William H., Jr.

Hoppe, 49, began his theatrical career as an usher at the Skouras brothers-owned New Grand Theatre in Kansas City, Missouri, and later worked at the Missouri Theatre. A district manager for the St. Louis Amusement Company in the thirties, Hoppe resigned in 1939 to open a drive-in restaurant in Kansas City. Hoppe had been retired for a year and undergoing treatment for a nervous disorder when he entered the basement of his home at 6429 Murdoch Avenue on June 8, 1955, and fired a 12-gauge shotgun blast point-blank into his chest. He left two notes to his wife and two daughters indicating that he planned to kill himself.

Hopton, (Harry) Russell

A former stage actor, Hopton worked continuously as a bit player in films since 1930 often appearing as "low life" characters. His 80 plus films include *Call of the Flesh* (1930), *I'm No Angel* (1933), *Valley of Wanted Men* (1935), *The Saint Strikes Back* (1939), and his last role as a reporter in *Johnny Angel* (1945). Hopton also directed two 1936 features, *Black Gold* and *Song of the Trail*. In what may have been an accidental overdose of sleeping pills, the 45-year-old actor was found dead by his wife, Marjorie, in their home at 12415 Huston Street in North Hollywood, California, on April 7, 1945. A bottle still containing nine sleeping tablets was found in the kitchen sink. Hopton had been in poor health.

Horton, Murray

Arthritis and four years of personal turmoil marked by the death of his first wife, a divorce from his second, and the death of a daughter is credited with driving Horton, a former dance orchestra leader and assistant to the president of the Cincinnati local of the American Federation of Musicians, with swallowing a bottle of corrosive poison. The semiconscious musician was found in his room at the Broadway Hotel on April 1, 1940, after he phoned the president of the union. A quantity of chloroform was found near his body. Horton, 45, died as members of the Life Squad were moving him from his room to the General Hospital.

Houston, Elsie

Born in Brazil in 1902 and distantly related to Sam Houston, the liberator of Texas, the 40-year-old nightclub and concert singer was internationally acknowledged as the world's leading interpreter of Brazilian folk and voodoo songs. In 1928, Houston married French surrealist poet Benjamin Peret. Two years later she published a collection of Brazilian folk songs, *Chants Populaires du Bresil*, in Paris. The fiery singer had recently appeared in a young people's concert at New York City's Carnegie Hall when a friend found her fully-clothed body sans shoes on a bed in her apartment at 431 Park Avenue on February 20, 1943. An empty vial that had contained sleeping pills and two notes written in French (to her sister and a friend) were found on a bedside table. In the notes Houston wrote that she was "terribly upset" and pleaded, "Please don't let anyone know about this." According to friends, Houston had been worried over financial matters.

Howard, Andree

Howard (born in London on October 3, 1910) studied dance with Marie Rambert, and later in Paris with Russian emigré ballerinas Lubov Egorova, Mathilde Kshesinskaya, Olga Preobrazhenska, and Vera Trefilova. A member of the Ballet Rambert since its inception in 1930, Howard joined the Ballets Russe de

Monte Carlo in 1933, but was forced to drop out due to a heart condition. Later that year, Howard choreographed her first ballet, Resphigi's *Our Lady Juggler*, for the Ballet Club in London. Known for her ability to create and sustain a mood, the choreographer worked for many dance companies including the Ballet Rambert, London Ballet, Sadler's Wells Ballet, Turkish State Ballet, and the Fortune Ballet in Florence, Italy. In 1947, Howard created the first two-act British ballet, *The Sailor's Return*, for the Ballet Rambert. During a professional career that extended from 1927 through her final stage appearance in the Festival Ballet production of *The Nutcracker* in December 1967, Howard choreographed and designed more than 30 ballets. On April 8, 1968, the 57-year-old dancer-choreographer took an overdose of barbiturates in her home in Nugent Terrace, St. John's Wood, N.W., London. The Westminster coroner ruled that Howard had taken her life while suffering from depression.

Howard, George Fitzalan Bronson

Howard (born in Howard County, Maryland, on January 7, 1884) was already a successful playwright (*The Snobs*, 1911) and novelist (*God's Man*, 1915) when he volunteered for service in the British Army in 1915. Commissioned as a lieutenant in the Intelligence division, he was on active duty in France in 1916 when a mustard gas shell exploded near him. The writer spent five hours in the field before stretcher bearers could reach him. For the next 18 months Howard recuperated from the effects of the mustard gas poisoning in a British hospital. Though released, Howard's health was shattered and he was addicted to the drugs doctors had prescribed for his condition.

In Hollywood, Howard wrote the screenplays for *The Power of Evil* (1916) and *The Spy* (1917) while several of his stories were made into films (*Come Through*, 1917; *Queen of the Sea*, 1918; *Sheltered Daughters*, 1921; *Don't*

Shoot, 1922; *Borrowed Finery*, 1925). In 1922, Howard, 37, was working in Hollywood developing film stories for Universal while his estranged second wife and young child were living in Baltimore, Maryland. In the early morning hours of November 20, 1922, Howard and his secretary, J. C. Dubois, were working on a film treatment for Universal in the writer's apartment at 2500 Highland Avenue in Los Angeles. According to Dubois, Howard repeatedly questioned him about the effects of gas on the human body and how long it would take to die of gas poisoning. Dubois left the writer in apparent good spirits at 2:30 A.M.

Around 8:30 A.M. other tenants, alarmed by the smell of gas, entered Howard's fume-filled apartment through an outside window. Howard's body, dressed in pajamas and a bathrobe, was found in a small closet adjoining his bedroom. A long length of rubber tube clutched in his hand ran from under the closet door across the floor of the bedroom to an open gas outlet. Howard had sealed the window crevices with paper. A letter written in pencil to his wife, Jean Bronson, was found on a bedside table next to a copy of his novel, *God's Man*. In it, Howard cryptically referred to his drug addiction and his inability to send her money. It read (in part): "Jean — I got your unsteady and insulting letter. Now there is no use in writing me in such a crazy strain. I am going to send the baby $10 a week until I manage to get on my feet. Whenever I can I will try to send you some but after what has happened I think you have a nerve to expect me to send you anything.... Do you realize that the money I was sending you is being eaten up altogether by what I have to pay for what you know about? If you worry me too much, I will probably give up in disgust...."

Howard, Irma Kilgallen

In March 1916, the former Countess de Beaufort and daughter of Chicago millionaire steel magnate Michael Kilgallen married, over her father's strong objections, vaudeville star

Joseph E. Howard. The song and dance man's schedule left little time for a honeymoon with the result that by April 10, 1916, the newlyweds had only seen each other twice. On that day, Joe Howard was headlining at the Orpheum Theatre in Omaha, Nebraska, while his wife was registered across town in room 438 at the Fontenelle Hotel. Mrs. Howard was in a loud discussion with Clara Lamberti, the wife of one of the entertainers at the Orpheum, when she abruptly excused herself and went into the bathroom. A few seconds later, Lamberti heard the sharp report of a gunshot from behind the closed door. Alarmed, she summoned a bellboy and together they entered the room to find Mrs. Howard near death on the floor bleeding from the right temple. She died at the scene. A .22-caliber target pistol still bearing a price tag was found in the bathtub. Two handwritten suicide notes were also found. One, in the form of a will, left her husband a valuable necklace. The contents of the other, a note to her disapproving father, was not made public. Joe Howard, informed of his wife's death minutes before he was set to take the stage, remained true to the old show biz adage, "The Show Must Go On," and performed. Though accounts vary, it was generally believed that the young woman took her life because of her father's stand against the marriage or jealousy over her husband's possible involvement with another woman, or both.

Howard, Lisa

Howard (real name Dorothy Jean Guggenheim of Cambridge, Ohio) who was once referred to as the "Brenda Starr" of ABC television newscasters, worked previously for a decade as an actress in summer stock theatre. She chronicled her theatrical experiences in the 1960 novel *On Stage, Miss Douglas.* Hard-working and resourceful, Howard managed to conduct exclusive interviews with Fidel Castro, Nikita Kruschev, and President Kennedy. However, in September 1964, ABC suspended Howard, claiming that her active support of Republican Senator Kenneth B. Keating of New York violated the network's policy against staff political activity. The suspension prevented her from doing her daily news show, *Lisa Howard and the Woman's Touch.* Howard's subsequent $2 million suit against ABC was denied. Depressed over the loss of her child in a miscarriage three weeks before, the 35-year-old reporter was seen stumbling around a pharmacy parking lot in East Hampton, Long Island, on July 4, 1965. Friends drove her to a nearby clinic where she later died from an overdose of sleeping pills. Police said that Howard had altered a doctor's prescription for ten sleeping pills to 100.

Howden, Victoria

Pursuing her dream of an acting career, the attractive 26-year-old blonde left the British seaside resort of Torquay for Hollywood in 1990. In Tinseltown, the Devon native landed a single line appearance on a November 1990 episode of the NBC sitcom *Dear John*, but found steadier employment as a part-time stripper at private parties. Desperate to remain in America, Howden secured a Green Card by marrying Charles House in Las Vegas in December 1990. House, a 40-year-old former cop from Kentucky, was in training to become a police officer with the Los Angeles Unified School District.

On May 8, 1991, California Highway Patrol Officer Ronald Webb, 34, shot himself alongside a freeway in the San Fernando Valley after Howden refused to marry him. The next day, Howden went to the home of Webb's estranged wife threatening to commit suicide. She was subsequently held 72 hours for psychiatric evaluation. At 2:00 A.M. on June 10, 1991, neighbors heard a gunshot from House and Howden's apartment in the 4600 block of Willis Avenue in Sherman Oaks. Howden called a friend to report that House had shot himself, but when paramedics arrived they found her dead in the bedroom from a .357 Magnum shot to the chest. The gun and a note in which she both apologized for her death and requested to be buried next to Webb were found near the body. While police initially believed there had been a double suicide, the coroner's report and forensic evidence proved that Howden shot House in the head while he slept at the kitchen table, placed a phone call to her friend, then took her own life. Immigration authorities noted that Howden had been granted permanent resident status five days prior to the murder-suicide.

Hudson, Alfred, Jr.

Formerly with the Otis Skinner Company, the young stage actor had been unemployed for a month when he committed suicide on November 24, 1912, by inhaling gas in his room at 340 West Forty-fifth Street in New York City. His father, in an adjoining room, broke down the door but was unable (with the assistance of a gas company employee armed with a Pulmotor) to revive his son.

Huet, Jacqueline

Huet (born in Paris in 1929) trained as an actress at the Paris Conservatory and debuted in the 1946 film *L'Eventail*. The willowy blonde also appeared in *Mission à Tangier* (1949), *Porte d'Orient* (1950), *La Demoiselle et son Revenant* (1951), and *Mannequins de Paris* (1956) before making her name as one of the first female announcers ("speakerines") on French television (ORTF) from 1958 to 1975. She continued to act in films (*Les Hommes veulent vivre*, 1961; *De L'Assassinat considéré comme un des Beaux-Arts*, 1965) while also singing on two albums. Twice married and divorced, the 56-year-old television announcer had been suffering for weeks from a nervous breakdown when she was found dead from an overdose of barbiturates in the bath of her home in Paris on October 8, 1986.

Hughes, Adelaide

The 20-year-old nightclub dancer and *Ziegfeld Follies* girl took her life on August 19, 1937, by opening two burners in the gas range of her New York City apartment at 424 East Fifty-second Street. In a note, Hughes requested that her parents in Glendale, California, be told that her suicide was an "accident."

Hurst, Ronald S.

Formerly employed as a musician at the Boulevard Theatre in Los Angeles, Hurst, 30, married 18-year-old dancer Jinnette of the act "Carlos and Jinnette" in San Francisco in 1926. The marriage was subsequently annulled. Jealous over his ex-wife's interest in another man, Hurst ingested poison in a room of a downtown Los Angeles hotel at 813 South Flower Street on December 4, 1927. He left three notes on a dresser, one of which read, "I love you, Jinnette, honestly I do. Goodbye, Sweetheart, I adore you." Hurst died in General Hospital on December 12, 1927.

Hutchence, Michael Kelland Frank

Hutchence, Australia's answer to Mick Jagger and Jim Morrison, was born in Sydney on January 22, 1960, though he spent much of his early childhood in Hong Kong where his father ran an international trading company while his mother worked as a makeup artist. Returning to Australia in his late teens, Hutchence met Sydney high school classmate Andrew Farris and in 1977 began fronting the band The Farris Brothers, built around Farris and his two brothers, Tim and Jon. Throughout 1978, The Farris Brothers carved out a hard-won reputation playing the clubs in and around Perth before debuting as INXS (pronounced "In Excess") at the Oceanview Hotel in Toukley, NSW, in 1979. The band's first album, *INXS*, was released on Deluxe Records in 1980. Already known as one of the premier road bands in Australia, INXS established its fan base by averaging more than 250 live shows a year from 1979 to 1983. After releasing three additional albums in the early eighties, the band's fifth, *The Swing*, topped the Australian charts in 1984. On the strength of that album, INXS toured the U.S. for three months while MTV played their videos in heavy rotation. With the release of their 1985 album *Listen Like Thieves* with its Top Ten hit single "What You Need," INXS gained international attention. Their 1987 follow-up album *Kick* spawned three hit singles ("Devil Inside," "New Sensation," "Never Tear Us Apart") and sold 10 million copies worldwide.

As the band's fortunes rose fueled by hit singles, exciting videos, and sold-out world tours, Hutchence established himself as an international celebrity. In 1986 he appeared as a drugged out punk rocker in the Australian film *Dogs in Space* while in 1990 he played Percy Bysshe Shelley in director Roger Corman's *Frankenstein Unbound*. A staple of the tabloid gossip columns, Hutchence was involved in highly publicized relationships with Australian pop star Kylie Minogue and later supermodel Helena Christensen. In 1995, Hutchence fell in love with Paula Yates, a television presenter and wife of Boomtown Rats drummer and Live Aid organizer Bob Geldof, after she conducted an interview in bed with him for the British morning talk show, *The Big Breakfast*. Yates, married to Geldof since 1986 and the mother of his three daughters, divorced the rock star in 1996, the same year she gave birth to Hutchence's daughter, Heavenly Hiraani Tiger Lily. Hutchence and Yates spent much of 1996–1997 publicly fighting with Sir Geldof (knighted for his role in Live Aid) for custody of the three children. In September 1996, the couple was arrested on suspicion of drug possession, but the case was later dropped for lack of evidence. Concerned over the welfare of his daughters, Geldof pointed to the incident as proof that Yates should not be awarded custody.

As Hutchence's personal life deteriorated, the band's album sales continued to spiral, reaching an all-time low with the 1997 album release of *Elegantly Wasted*. Several rock critics had already written off INXS as an "eighties" group while Noel Gallagher of the band Oasis had openly called Hutchence a "has been." Expectations ran high as the band massed in Sydney, Australia to kick off its sold out 20th anniversary "Lose Your Head Tour" on November 25, 1997. Hutchence, 37, spent the evening of November 21 eating and drinking with family and friends before returning early the next morning to his fifth floor suite in the Ritz-Carlton Hotel in the affluent Sydney suburb of Double Bay. While details remain sketchy concerning the singer's final hours, Hutchence apparently called Yates in England to discuss Geldof's opposition to letting his two youngest daughters (ages 8 and 7) accompany their mother on the upcoming INXS tour. Hutchence allegedly told Yates, "I love you. I'm gonna ring Bob now and just beg him, just beg him to let the children come."

A person in the room adjoining Hutchence's suite told authorities that around 9:00 A.M. she heard the singer shout, "She's not your wife anymore! Stop interfering!" Geldof later confirmed that while he had received an hysterical call from Hutchence, he could not understand a word of it. At 11:55 A.M. on November 22, a maid entered suite 524 and found Hutchence's naked body hanging by a leather belt attached to a self-closing mechanism of the door to the room. Authorities later estimated that he had died between 10:00 and 11:00 A.M. When informed of the tragedy, Yates (who was set to marry Hutchence on the Tahitian island of Bora Bora in January 1998) immediately phoned Geldof and screamed, "You have murdered Michael as surely as if you'd strangled him yourself."

Authorities quickly dismissed the rumor that the singer's death had been an autoerotic sexual asphyxiation. Hutchence's father stated that his son had seemed worried over the custody issue at dinner and police had found a bottle of Prozac in the dead man's room. Overruling the objections of family, friends, and bandmates, Hutchence's mother permitted her son's November 27, 1997, funeral service at St. Andrew's Cathedral in Sydney to be televised. The singer's remains were cremated and divided into five equal parts between his father, mother, half-sister Tina, fiancée Paula Yates, and brother Rhett. His father, Kelland, scattered his portion of the ashes at his son's favorite spot by Sydney Harbour shortly after his death. Mother and sister retain his ashes in separate urns. Yates keeps the ashes she was given sewn into a pillow. In November 1999 Rhett Hutchence scattered his brother's ashes in a remote area of Tibet following a Buddhist ritual designed to let the dead man's spirit "move on" to the afterworld.

The coroner's report, issued on February 6, 1998, officially ruled the death a suicide. In addition, it determined that Hutchence's body was found to contain "alcohol, cocaine, Prozac and other prescription drugs." Under the terms of Hutchence's will made public in May 1999, Yates received $1.5 million of the singer's $16 million estate with the majority of the balance to be held in trust for his 3-year-old daughter, Tiger Lily, until she turns 25.

On September 17, 2000, the body of Paula Yates, 41, was found in the bedroom of her two-story home in London's Notting Hill district. An empty vodka bottle and a half-empty bottle of barbiturates were located nearby. A postmortem proved inconclusive as to the cause of death. On September 23, 2000, Yates was buried at the Church of Mary Magdalene in the town of Davington in Kent, southern England, in a private ceremony attended by former husband Bob Geldof, and celebrities including Eurythmics star Annie Lennox, U2 lead singer Bono, and British actor Rupert Everett. An inquest later (or subsequently) ruled her death was not suicide, but (rather) the result of "unsophisticated, non-dependent" heroin use.

FURTHER READING

Gee, Michael. *The Final Days of Michael Hutchence.* London: Omnibus Press, 1998.

Hutton, Leona

Hutton (real name name Mary Epstein) was a leading lady in silent films and starred in *The Typhoon* (1914) with Sessue Hayakawa and *The Market of Vain Desire* (1916) with H. B. Warner. Prior to her Hollywood career, she toured in stock companies as "Jane Whitman." Retired from acting, Hutton had resided in Toledo, Ohio, for 13 years, and was the president of the local chapter of the Women's Overseas Service League when a leg fracture in 1949 confined the former actress to her home at 1741 Evansdale Avenue for ten weeks. On March 31, 1949, Hutton informed her husband that she had taken an overdose of the painkilling drug codeine. She died 13 hours later in an iron lung at Maumee Valley Hospital. Hutton's death was ruled a suicide. Her niece and protégé, June Clyde, starred onstage and in British films (*Dance Band*, 1935; *Poison Pen*, 1939).

Hyde, George R.

Though known primarily as a veteran newspaperman in California, Hyde was formerly a press agent for evangelist Aimee Semple McPherson's Angelus Temple organization and for RKO at the Golden Gate theatre in San Francisco. Broke, depressed, and unemployed, Hyde swallowed poison in his room at 27 Monroe Street in San Francisco on July 28, 1932. In a note, Hyde said that suicide appeared "the only way out for him" and asked that his family be notified.

Hyman, Phyllis

Born in Philadelphia, Pennsylvania, on July 6, 1949 (some sources cite 1950), Hyman was raised in Pittsburgh where her vocal talent was noticed early and encouraged by an elementary school teacher. Though trained as a legal secretary at the Robert Morris Business College, the young black vocalist avidly pursued her dream of musical stardom. In the early seventies she toured with the group New Direction before forming her own group, Phyllis Hyman and the P/H Factor, in 1974. Nicknamed "the Nile" because of her vocal stylings, sultry beauty, and statuesque 6 foot,

1 inch physique, Hyman was already an established performer at the swank clubs on New York's Upper West Side when she caught the attention of noted music producer Norman Connors. On his 1977 album *You Are My Starship*, Hyman covered The Stylistics' hit "Betcha By Golly Wow." That same year she released her self-titled debut album on Buddha Records. In 1978, Hyman began a five-year association with Arista Records that produced five albums and three Top 15 R&B hits: "Somewhere in My Lifetime" (1979), "You Know how to Love Me" (1979), "Can't We Fall in Love Again" (1981). Hyman signed with Philadelphia International in 1986 and recorded *Living All Alone* (1986), *Prime of My Life* (1991), *I Refuse to Be Lonely* (1995), and the 1998 posthumously released *Forever with You*. In addition to her recording and touring schedule, the vocalist joined the cast of the Duke Ellington-inspired Broadway musical *Sophisticated Ladies*, earning a 1981 Tony nomination for her role as "Etta." On film, Hyman appeared in *Lenny* (1974), *The Doorman* (1985), director Spike Lee's *School Daze* (1988), and *The Kill Reflex* (1989).

Though supremely confident onstage, the jazz chanteuse's personal life was marred by personal and career self-doubt, alcoholism, drug addiction, manic depression, eating disorders, and financial problems. A brief marriage to her manager Larry Alexander in the late seventies ended in divorce. Hyman longed for a lasting relationship with a man, but was unable to establish one. The death of her mother and recent tax problems exacerbated her depression and fuelled her drinking. On June 29, 1995, the 45-year-old singer phoned her ex-boyfriend, Danny Poole, a real estate broker in Denver. During the conversation, Hyman told Poole that she planned to kill herself on July 6, her 46th birthday, adding that "I have no personal life and no energy." According to Poole, the singer (who first attempted suicide in Philadelphia three years before) ruled out jumping or shooting as a means of death. "I'm just going to take some pills and go to sleep." Poole was in the process of getting help for his ex-lover prior to her announced deadline when he learned of her premature death.

At 2:30 P.M. the next day, June 30, 1995, just hours before she was scheduled to perform at the Apollo Theatre, an unconscious Hyman was found lying face-up in bed surrounded by vials of sleeping pills in her West Fifty-sixth Street apartment in New York City. "The Nile" was pronounced dead at Roosevelt Hospital less than two hours later. A note found beside the body read: "I am tired. I'm tired. Those of you that I love know who you are. May God bless you." Hyman's remains were cremated. At a memorial service held at St. Peter's Lutheran Church in New York on July 6, Hyman's sister, Sakeema, told the congregation: "I'm going to tell the truth. She talked to me about dying and I told her to go to an AA (Alcoholics Anonymous) meeting. Some of you fed her the drugs that killed her. All I can think about is the pain and suffering my sister's been going through. Oh my God."

Hyson, Kevin Philip

On February 17, 1994, Hyson, a senior vice-president with Buena Vista International, was promoted to executive vice-president of theatrical marketing, largely as a reward for helping to set up Disney's autonomous overseas distribution network. In a statement released by the company, Hyson's marketing efforts for Walt Disney, Touchstone, and Hollywood Pictures were credited with the strong international box office showings of *Beauty and the Beast* (1991), *White Fang* (1991), *Aladdin* (1992), and *Sister Act* (1992). Less than three weeks later on March 6, 1994, a couple walking at 9:05 A.M. on a hillside in the 3100 block of Coldwater Canyon in North Hollywood noticed the 43-year-old executive leaning against a tree near a hiking trail gazing out over the valley. When they returned 25 minutes later, they found Hyson lying on his back with a bloodstained towel covering his face and a revolver beside him. A suicide note, which included instructions to his survivors, was discovered in Hyson's Bel Air home.

Inge, William Motter

Inge (born May 3, 1913, in Independence, Kansas) showed a theatrical flair at an early age. The son of a traveling salesman, Inge spent most of his childhood being raised by a doting mother who encouraged him to recite poetry at her ladies' club meetings. Attending the University of Kansas in Lawrence in 1930, Inge aspired to an acting career, but felt uncomfortable performing. After graduating with a bachelor of arts degree in 1935, he briefly taught high school drama in Columbus, Kansas, before earning a master's in 1938 from the George Peabody College in Nashville, Tennessee. That same year he began teaching English and drama at Stephens College in Columbia, Missouri. During the years he remained at Stephens (1938–1943) Inge acutely experienced the dual frustrations of wanting to write full time combined with the need he felt to conceal his homosexuality. Throughout his life Inge turned to solitary drinking as a means to relieve career and personal pressures.

In 1943 Inge left Stephens to temporarily fill in as a reviewer of plays, books, films, and records for the *Star-Times* in St. Louis. An interview with playwright Tennessee Williams in late 1944 prompted Inge to begin writing plays about what he knew best — life in the Midwest. His first two efforts, *Farther Off from Heaven* (1947) and *Front Porch* (1948) were poorly received and never performed in New York City.

Desperately unhappy, Inge returned to teaching and was soon hospitalized for exhaustion, alcoholism, and depression. Professionally, at least, Inge rebounded in the fifties, a decade in which he wrote the four plays that established his reputation as a major American playwright. In 1950, *Come Back, Little Sheba* earned the author the New York Drama Circle's "Most Promising Playwright" award. For his next play, *Picnic*, Inge was awarded the Pulitzer Prize in 1953. *Bus Stop* (1955) and the autobiographical *The Dark at the Top of the Stairs* (1957) were also hits. The sale of all four plays to the movies made Inge financially secure.

After the fifties, however, Inge was never again to enjoy critical or commercial success as a playwright. When his next play, *A Loss of Roses* (1959), lasted only three weeks on Broadway, Inge moved to Los Angeles and turned to screenwriting. His script for *Splendor in the Grass* earned him the Academy Award for Best Original Screenplay in 1961. Inge wrote the screenplay for *All Fall Down* (1962), and for the 1965 Ann-Margaret film *Bus Riley's Back in Town*. Inge had his name removed from the credits of this movie after the script was drastically changed to highlight Ann-Margaret's physique rather than the story's dramatic elements. He never again wrote for the movies. In 1966, Inge attempted to regain his Broadway success with the play *Where's Daddy?*, but bad reviews quickly closed it.

With film and the theatre seemingly barred to him, Inge turned to writing novels. His first effort, *Good Luck, Miss Wyckoff* (1970), sold only 11,677 hardback copies for Atlantic-Little, Brown. Inge's second novel, the autobiographical *My Son Is a Splendid Driver*, was published in 1971. Largely ignored by reviewers, the book sold a paltry 7,792 hardback copies. Inge's drinking, pill use, and depression intensified during this period. In late 1970 his sister, Helene Connell, moved into his Hollywood Hills home at 1440 N. Oriole Drive to look after him. The playwright now spent entire days alone in his room drinking and popping Valium while continuing to try to write. Several psychiatrists recommended to Helene that she institutionalize her brother, but she refused, citing a solemn promise she had made to him that she never would. In this atmosphere of declining physical and mental health, the 60-year-old writer finished the manuscript for his final novel, *The Boy from the Circus*, in 1973 and sent it off to an unnamed publisher in New York. Weeks before his death, Inge told an interviewer that he could no longer write, confessing that "It's a terrible thing to feel all used up."

On June 2, 1973, Inge was admitted to the UCLA Medical Center for psychiatric observation following an overdose of barbiturates. He signed himself out "against medical advice" three days later after arguing with his doctor. On June 10, 1973, the playwright's body was found by his sister behind the wheel of his Mercedes-Benz, its engine still running, in the closed garage of his home above the Sunset Strip. Although Inge left no suicide note, the unopened envelope from the publisher containing the rejected manuscript of *The Boy from the Circus* was found on a table in the living room. The LA coroner's Office officially ruled Inge's death a suicide by carbon monoxide poisoning.

FURTHER READING

Voss, Ralph F. *A Life of William Inge: The Strains of Triumph.* Lawrence: University Press of Kansas, 1989.
_____. "William Inge." In *American National Biography.* Vol. 11, pp. 644–645. New York: Oxford University Press, 1999.

Ingersoll, Fred

Since suffering a paralytic stroke the year before, Ingersoll, 52, had complained to friends and family that he "felt like he was on fire." On October 23, 1927, the lessee of Omaha, Nebraska's Krug Amusement Park could stand it no longer. The night before, Ingersoll left the family dwelling above the main office of the park and retired to a closed up concession stand where he sometimes slept. The amusement park manager tightly closed all the windows, disconnected a hose from the gas heater, and waited on a cot for death. He was found the next day by his daughter and an attorney in his employ who smelled gas outside the building.

Ingraham, Arthur P.

Depressed over his health, the 53-year-old musician was visiting his brother's home in Seattle on September 10, 1917, when he took advantage of his relation's temporary absence.

Ingraham went to the basement, spread newspapers out on the floor, placed a pillow under his head, then blew his brains out with a revolver.

Irene

Born Irene Lentz on her parents' ranch near Baker, Montana, on December 8, 1901, the future film clothing designer originally intended to become a pianist when she left home at 16 to study music at the University of Southern California. On a whim, however, she sat in on a clothing design class at the Wolfe School of Design, and was so impressed by the experience that she enrolled in the school. After graduating, the bargain dress shop she opened on campus became a mecca for style conscious coeds and Hollywood screen stars. As her reputation grew, Irene took charge of the custom salon at Bullock's Wilshire store in the early thirties, and began "unofficially" designing outfits worn in films by a star clientele that included Dolores Del Rio, Joan Bennett, Loretta Young, and Marlene Dietrich.

Though uncredited, her first film designs were worn by Ann Harding in the 1932 RKO picture, *The Animal Kingdom*, produced by David O. Selznick. In 1936, she married Hollywood writer Eliot Gibbons, brother of Cedric Gibbons the supervising art director at MGM. By 1942, when MGM selected her to replace chief costume designer Adrian, Irene was already an uncredited veteran of more than 25 feature films. Though overseeing a staff of 200, Irene personally designed clothes for the studio's "sophisticated women" (Barbara Stanwyck, Lana Turner, Claudette Colbert) and is generally regarded as the originator of the dressmaker suit. From 1942 through 1949, Irene was credited on more than 130 films including *The Palm Beach Story* (1942), *You Were Never Lovelier* (1942), *Gaslight* (1944), *The Picture of Dorian Gray* (1945), *The Postman Always Rings Twice* (1946), and *The Barkleys of Broadway* (1949). In 1949 she left MGM to devote herself full time to Irene, Inc., a company she had formed

IRENE— Irene (Irene Lentz), the chief costume designer at MGM from 1942 to 1949, checked into an 11th floor room at the Knickerbocker Hotel, 1714 N. Ivar, in Hollywood on November 15, 1962. After downing several drinks and attempting to cut her wrists, Irene leapt to her death. She originated the dressmaker suit worn by the studio's "sophisticated women" like Barbara Stanwyck, Lana Turner, and Claudette Colbert. The 60-year-old designer was depressed over her husband's death and worried about business problems. *Photo 2000 by Jana Wells.*

two years earlier to supply her designs and clothes to the nation's leading department stores. In the sixties, she briefly returned to films to "glamorize" Doris Day in *Midnight Lace* (1960) and *Lover Come Back* (1961).

Distressed over her husband's recent stroke and plagued by business problems, the 60-year-old designer jumped from the 11th floor of the Hollywood Knickerbocker Hotel at 3:20 P.M. on November 15, 1962. According to police, Irene had tried to cut her wrists before making the fatal plunge. Several notes were found in the room. One, apparently addressed to other guests in the hotel, read: "Neighbors: Sorry I had to drink so much to get the courage to do this." In another, she wrote: "I am sorry to do this in this manner.

Please see that Eliot is taken care of. Alden [Alden Olds, general manager of her firm] take over the business. Get someone very good to design and be happy. I love you all. Irene."

Israel, Richard

At one time the owner of a chain of small motion picture theatres that business reversals had recently forced him to sell, Israel, 42, checked himself into the Michael Reese Hospital in Chicago complaining of chronic laryngitis. On the morning of February 17, 1930, a nurse noticed Israel was missing from his bed and the window of his fourth floor room was open. The former theatre owner's broken body was found on the street below. An unsigned note found in the room read: "I am shocked at myself as much as the rest of the world. There is a God in heaven and one cannot break his laws and be unpunished."

Itami, Juzo

Itami, the son of director and film theoretician Mansaku Itami, was regarded as Japan's second-greatest living filmmaker after Akira Kurosawa. The future director began his career as an actor appearing under the professional name "Ichizo Itami" in English language films like *55 Days at Peking* (1963) and *Lord Jim* (1965), and later in Japanese pictures like *The Makioka Sisters* (1983) and *The Family Game* (1984). In the seventies, Itami wrote and directed television shows before scoring a hit in 1984 with his film directorial debut, *The Funeral*. With *Tampopo*, his 1986 parody of Westerns and other film genres, Itami became internationally recognized. Other films satirizing modern Japanese society directed by Itami include *A Taxing Woman* (1987) and *A Taxing Woman's Return* (1988), both starring his second wife, Nobuko Miyamoto.

In Tokyo on December 20, 1997, the 64-year-old director jumped to his death from the roof of the eight story office building where he worked after learning that *Flash* magazine was set to publish a report alleging his affair with a 26-year-old woman. In a note found at the scene, Itami wrote: "My death is the only way to prove my innocence. There was no other way I could prove it."

Jackson, Charles

Since first attracting attention in 1889 in the role of the "Jockey" in the Neil Burgess comedy *The County Fair*, Jackson had been a mainstay of New York theatre. Suddenly unemployed in 1907, the actor languished for eight months before landing the part of "Lew Ellinger," the chief comedy role in *The Witching Hour*, in January 1908. Although the managers of the show advanced Jackson money for living expenses, friends noticed that he was still depressed. On the evening of January 10, 1908, a dejected looking Jackson was spotted by an acquaintance sitting alone in a corner of the smoking room of the Lamb's Club. Asked what was wrong, the 45-year-old actor responded, "It's no use. I can't remember the cues or the lines, and I am done for. If I fall down on this it means the end, and I guess the only thing for me to do is to shoot myself." The next morning a maid at the Hotel Gerard on West Forty-fourth Street discovered Jackson's body hanging by a trunk strap from a water pipe in the top of the closet in his room. Pages filled with jumbled handwritten lines from the script Jackson had been unable to memorize were found littering the floor.

Jackson, Glenn E.

Known to radio fans in Lynchburg, Virginia, as the "Old Man With the Grey Whiskers," Jackson hosted a daily sports show and a popular hillbilly program. Less than four weeks after leaving his job of 12 years to become the commercial manager of radio station WCBG in Greensboro, North Carolina, Jackson was dead by his own hand. On April 9, 1942, two days after being arrested and booked on a drunk driving charge, the despondent 33 year old entered a small room at the WCBG extension on Ashe Street and fired a single .32-caliber round into his temple. He died shortly afterward at the Wesley Long Hospital.

Jacobs, David

One of the top show business solicitors in England, Jacobs at one time represented The Beatles, Judy Garland, Marlene Dietrich, Laurence Olivier, Shirley Bassey, and Liberace. On December 15, 1958, the 56-year-old bachelor was found hanging in the garage of his home in Prince's Crescent, near Hove seafront. Jacobs' brother stated that the attorney had recently suffered a nervous breakdown aggravated by a potentially costly tax audit. Scotland Yard detectives reported that in recent months a number of homosexuals had given statements about the activities of a blackmailer operating in Brighton and

London. Shortly before his death, Jacobs had made a long statement to police.

Jammer, Cal

Jammer (real name Randy Layne Potes) built sets for porno productions before stepping in front of the camera in 1989. Though never a top porn headliner, Jammer was a reliable performer in hard core videos like *Deep Throat 5*, *New Wave Hookers 2*, and many others. In January 1993, Jammer met future wife Adrianne at a Consumer Electronics Show in Las Vegas. They married that same year on Valentine's Day and, while Jammer dropped out of the business to build sets, Adrianne became a porn performer under various names (Seth Damien, Calista, Jill Kelly), the most widely known of which was Jill Roberts. Unable to make a living in construction, Jammer subsequently returned to porn with a role in director Mitch Spinelli's *Titanic Orgy*. By the fall of 1994, however, the pair had separated, and Jammer was the repeated subject of IRS audits. Perpetually insecure about his status in porn, Jammer began experiencing erectile problems on the set. He blamed his estranged wife. In the weeks before his death, Jammer became obsessed with the Simpson murder trial and told porn director Buck Adams that "I really want to kill my old lady. I think I know where O.J. must have got the idea."

On the rainy night of January 25, 1995, the 34-year-old porn performer finally snapped after months of attempts to reconcile with his wife. As he sped through the Hollywood Hills en route to her house, Jammer called his wife on his car cell phone to announce that he was coming to kill her. The terrified woman called friends and the police, then hid behind a shower curtain in an upstairs bathroom. After leaving a goodbye message on his answering machine, Jammer arrived at the house, but was unable to get Adrianne to answer the door. After hearing a loud "pop" at the front door, Adrianne went outside to investigate, and found her husband dead from a pistol shot to the head in the gutter at the bottom of the front yard stairs. Authorities found a suicide note in Jammer's left front pocket scrawled on the back of a sealed First Interstate Bank envelope containing five $100 bills. The note read: "Happy Birthday Big 24 — I Allway [*sic*] Love You — I [*sic*] sorry we didn't work out — Randy."

The transcript of Jammer's final phone message left on his answering machine included, in part: "Hello, if anybody is listening to this, this is Randy. I love everybody and uh.... Nobody wanted to help me so.... I knew I needed the help. There's $5,000, in the drawer right below underneath it in a manila folder, cash for my mother. I love you, mom and dad. I always loved you guys, and it's just these, all these audits and my wife is torturing me at work, and I can't get away from it and can't get another trade. I just can't take it. You guys are the best family you could ever have...." At his funeral, a tearful Adrianne eulogized: "You were the most beautiful person in the world to me.... I will always, always love you, and no one will ever take that away from me." She reportedly keeps her husband's cremated remains in a blue velvet box by her bed.

FURTHER READING

"Cal Jammer Kills Himself in Domestic Discord." *Adult Video News*, 10(3):128–130, March 1995.

Faludi, Susan. "The Money Shot." *The New Yorker*, 71(34):64–70, 72–76, 78–87, Oct. 30, 1995.

Janes, Luther C.

Janes came to Memphis, Tennessee, in 1921 and worked as an electrician at the Loew's State Theatre before joining the backstage crew at the Ellis Auditorium in 1930. During his 18 year tenure, Janes handled the lights for every performance to play the facility, eventually rising to the position of assistant stage manager and business agent for the Memphis stagehands' union. On the night of January 13, 1948, his unconscious body was found slumped over his desk in the Auditorium's electrical supply room. Despondent over failing health and marital problems (according to two type written notes addressed to his wife and an attorney), Janes had shot himself through the head with a pistol. The 55-year-old electrician died at St. Joseph Hospital without regaining consciousness.

Jarnegin, Jerry Overton

Jarnegin, a composer and pianist, was married to musical comedy star Irene Franklin and served as her accompanist in their touring vaudeville act. In 1934, three years after headlining in the Broadway production *Sweet Adeline*, Franklin and Jarnegin were living in

Los Angeles preparing to take screen tests at Warners for roles in a planned film of the musical. On the night of August 19, 1934, the couple hosted a dinner at their home at 3093 Lake Hollywood Drive in Toluca Lake to celebrate the upcoming marriage of Jarnegin's niece. In attendance were Franklin, Jarnegin, the engaged couple, and a family friend. Jarnegin appeared in good spirits as the group seated themselves at the dinner table, but soon excused himself from the room saying that he needed to "wash up."

A few minutes later the company heard what they thought was a car backfiring, but

JERRY JARNEGIN— On the evening of August 19, 1934, the popular composer-pianist and husband-accompanist of musical comedy star Irene Franklin excused himself during a dinner party at their home in Toluca Lake, California, went into another room, and fired a bullet into his head. While investigators initially questioned whether Jarnegin's death was a suicide after finding the weapon in a chair some six feet away from the dead man's body, a distraught Franklin admitted that she may have moved the gun. *Courtesy of University of Southern California, on behalf of the USC Library Department of Special Collections.*

paid no further attention to the muffled sound. When Jarnegin failed to return or answer their calls, Franklin left the table to search for her husband. She found the 41-year-old musician in the living room slumped in a chair, bleeding profusely from a gaping bullet wound just below his right ear. When police arrived at the scene, they found the pistol in the seat of another chair some six feet away from where the body lay crumpled. Franklin later intimated to detectives that she may have moved the gun when she found her husband's body. At the inquest, evidence was presented that suggested Jarnegin took his life because he was worried about financial troubles, and an impending trial involving a former servant who allegedly attacked the songwriter and his wife after they had recently fired him. Jarnegin's body was cremated and the ashes scattered over the Hollywood Hills. In 1936, four lines from a Jarnegin-composed song, "You Took Me from the Gutter," were used in the 20th Century–Fox musical *Song and Dance Man*.

Jason, Rick

Jason (born in New York City on May 21, 1926) refused to become a stockbroker like his father and enlisted in the Army Air Corps where he served from 1943 to 1945. After the war, the 6'4" veteran attended the American Academy of Dramatic Arts on the G.I. Bill. Jason worked as a hotel clerk, auditor, soda jerk, and riding instructor while doing occasional acting parts in summer stock and television. His theatrical break came in 1950 when director Hume Cronyn cast him in the play *Now I Lay Me Down to Sleep*. Jason won a Theatre World Award for his performance and quickly relocated to Hollywood and a film career. In 1953, he made his movie debut in *Sombrero* with Ricardo Montalban and Cyd Charisse. Other films of the period include *The Saracen Blade* (1954), *This Is My Love* (1954), *The Lieutenant Wore Skirts* (1956), *The Wayward Bus* (1957), and *Sierra Baron* (1958) co-starring fellow suicide Brian Keith (see entry). After appearing as a suave insurance

investigator with martial arts skills in the short-lived 1960 television series *The Case of the Dangerous Robin*, Jason landed his career-defining role as "Lt. Gil Hanley" on the ABC World War II drama *Combat!* The series ran from October 1962 through August 1967 and co-starred Vic Morrow as "Sgt. Chip Saunders." Morrow and two Vietnamese children were killed in 1982 by a helicopter during the filming of *Twilight Zone: The Movie*.

Although *Combat!* was cancelled after its fifth season, Jason continued to do guest shots on television up through the eighties. Semi-retired from acting, Jason and his wife, Cindy, moved to Moorpark, California, where the actor did voice-over work for commercials and operated The Wine Locker, a 4,000 square foot facility where customers could store their beverages under ideal conditions. Fan interest in *Combat!*, however, remained strong, bolstered by Internet sites and conventions. In early October 2000, the 74-year-old actor attended a three-day *Combat!* convention in Las Vegas where he was reunited with the surviving members of the cast.

At around 5:30 A.M. on October 15, 2000, Cindy Jason found her husband dead from a self-inflicted gunshot wound to the head in their home in Moorpark, California. There was no note. Jason's act was reportedly prompted by depression over personal matters.

FURTHER READING

Jason, Rick. *Scrapbooks of My Mind: A Hollywood Autobiography*. [Moorpark, Calif.?]: Argoe Publishing, 2000.

Jelin, Max J.

A former picture exhibitor in New Brunswick, New Jersey, Jelin moved to New York City in the forties to try his hand as a theatrical producer. The career change marked the beginning of a period of bad luck and shady financial dealings that left the producer one of the most despised men in theatre. Jelin leased the Belasco Theatre, presented flop after flop, and when pressed by the theatre owners for rent, filed numerous court actions to fight dispossession. The 40-year-old producer was finally ousted in October 1947, but had already leased the International Theatre. After two flops there, *The Magic Touch* and the short-lived black musical *Calypso*, Jelin was in serious tax trouble, owing the Internal Revenue Service some $140,000.

On January 22, 1948, four days after losing the lease on the International, Jelin was home alone in his 13 story apartment at 300 East Fifty-seventh Street when he opened four gas jets on the kitchen stove. The resulting blast instantly killed the producer and ripped out the walls adjoining two other suites in the new 18 story residential building. Jelin died owing $12,000 in back rent.

Jenkins, Jimmy

A jazz pianist and orchestra leader at the Black Sheep, a nightclub in London's West End, Jenkins, 32, was found dead by his dancer-wife in the gas-filled kitchen of his flat in St. John's Wood on August 11, 1960.

Jenkins, John Elliott

Jenkins, a broadcasting equipment manufacturer, wed the London stage star Alexandria Carlisle in 1924 soon after seeing her perform in *The Fool* at the Selwyn Theatre in Chicago. Once described by King George as "his actress," Carlisle was a former Gibson girl and the toast of the London stage from 1906 to 1914. Recently estranged, the pair was living in separate apartments in the same near north side building at 105 East Delaware Place in Chicago when Jenkins, 42, shot himself in the head on June 9, 1934. In a note addressed to his wife found next to the body, the radio engineer wrote: "This is my will. Not unmindful of my wife, Alexandria, I leave the wreck of my estate to my mother along with my deepest apologies. I hope my wife, or better, my widow, will pay my personal debts to Gene and Paul [business associates] out of my insurance, which she can collect from the Connecticut Mutual in time to go east next Monday. I wish her all the luck in the world." In a separate note, Jenkins left $17 in cash to be equally divided among the hotel bellboys whom in life he had been "unable to tip."

Jerome, Suzie

Known professionally as "Suzie Jerome" (real name Susan Willis), the 26 year old, 6 foot tall blonde English beauty appeared in the 1983 James Bond film *Octopussy*, in *Oh! Calcutta!* on the West End stage, and in television on *The Benny Hill Show*. Depressed over a failed relationship with actor Damien Thomas that had ended in an abortion, Jerome voluntarily admitted herself to a Gloucester mental hospital after slitting her wrists and taking a drug overdose. She told a psychiatrist there, "I have failed in my life. There is nothing to live for. I have no home, no career, no future." Shortly afterward, the troubled actress discharged herself and took a 250 mile taxi ride to Land's End, Cornwall. Fortifying herself with wine and brandy, Jerome visited the lonely cliffs during the height of a gale storm. Her body was found on a clifftop by a hiker on December 4, 1986, lying 12 feet away from a 300 foot drop. The local coroner ruled death was due to hypothermia, not the recently self-inflicted wrist wounds. In recording the open verdict, the official stated that the disturbed woman "just lay down and was eventually overcome by the weather, unable to save herself."

Johannesson, Cary Jon

Johannesson was a promising actor at the Valley Theatre in Woodland Hills, California, and the Encino Community Players when he was sentenced to life for the strangulation murder of his 15-year-old girlfriend, Phyllis Meltzer, in Reseda in 1958. In San Quentin, Johanneson (writing under the pseudonym "Jon Carey") was an award winning reporter for the prison newspaper and adapted scripts for the penitentiary theatre group. On August 28, 1966, the 27-year-old lifer used the earphone cord of a transistor radio to hang himself in his honor cell at the penitentiary.

Jones, Kenneth Bruce

Jones, 32, was a member of the Dallas, Texas, branch of the Screen Actors Guild and had appeared in television commercials and several local stage productions. On September 20, 1977, ten days before the air date of the ABC made-for-television movie *The Trial of Lee Harvey Oswald* in which he played a policeman, Jones phoned a friend at 2:00 A.M. to report, "I've done it. I have killed Myra and her blond-headed lover. Call the police because by the time they get here I'll be dead." Dallas police rushed to the apartment at 6402 Melody Lane of Jones' ex-wife, Myra Emmanuelli, and kicking in the front door, found Jones lying dead a few feet inside in a hallway. The gun he had used to shoot himself in the mouth was still clasped in his left hand. The nude bodies of Emmanuelli and her lover, 27-year-old local business executive Michael L. Crim, were found in a bedroom. Emmanuelli was shot in the face and chest and Crim in the head. The next day, the secretary whom Jones had been dating found a "farewell letter" from him in a satchel left on her doorstep.

Jordan, Alex

In porn movies since 1991, Jordan (real name Karen Elizabeth Hughes) was noted in the adult video industry for her athleticism and feral sexuality. Named "Best New Starlet" by *Adult Video News* in 1993, she was unable to parlay the award into feature film roles or the highly lucrative area of posing for video box covers. Frustrated by her lack of success, Jordan and her husband formed their own production company, Realistic Videos, in 1994. When their first release, *Interview with a Vamp* (starring Jordan in the title role), failed to click, the disappointed porn performer entered the world of fetish videos, perhaps the lowest rung on the hard core video ladder. Depressed over her career and physical appearance, the 31-year-old actress had recently made her "farewell appearance" in adult video with a scene in *Gang Bang Girl 16*. In the shot-on-video feature, Jordan skydived out of a plane and then had sex with ten men in the mud below.

Living alone in an apartment in Marina Del Rey, California, Jordan planned to relocate to Colorado to join her husband, who had moved there several months before to open a ski-related business. During this period, she confided to a business associate, "I don't feel like living anymore," a feeling aggravated by a phone call from her husband on July 27, 1995, informing her that their pet parrot had died. Blaming her husband for "killing the only living thing that mattered in her life," Jordan subsequently failed to show up for a striptease engagement in San Antonio, Texas. She was not seen alive again. Contacted by a concerned friend, fellow adult star Summer Knight, police entered Jordan's first floor apartment on the evening of July 2, 1995. They found the performer's fully-clothed body hanging from a clothes bar in a walk-in closet. Suspended by the neck with a tightly wrapped clothesline and a loosely knotted purple dress, Jordan had evidently ended her life by stepping off a clothes trunk. In a scene vaguely reminiscent of some of the bondage videos she had done for directors Bruce Seven and Ernest Green, a pair of handcuffs dangled from her left wrist. A suicide note was found on a bedroom stand. In all, Alex Jordan appeared in 166 adult videos from 1991 through 1995.

FURTHER READING

Ross, Gene. "Alex Jordan, Remembered." *Adult Video News*, 10(11):9, Sept. 1995.
_____. "No Foul Play Indicated in Death of Adult Star Alex Jordan." *Adult Video News*, 10(11): 22–23, 28, Sept. 1995.

Jorden, Albert Paul

Jorden, a Cincinnati-based trombonist with the Harry Rapp Orchestra, met and married future film star Doris Day when she began singing with the group in 1941. The union produced one child, Terry, but they divorced in 1943 when the singer could no longer tolerate Jorden's physical and verbal abuse. Terry later moved to California with his mother, took the last name of Melcher, and was the target of the Manson Family the night in 1969 when they invaded the record producer's home he had recently rented to actress Sharon Tate. Jorden was a staff musician with station WLW in the Cincinnati area from the late thirties through 1956. Months before his death, he opened a music shop and also worked with a local realty company. On July 5, 1967, the 50 year old fired a bullet into his right temple in his home in Delhi Township, a Cincinnati suburb.

Journee, Jeannette

The 30-year-old vaudeville dancer married Henri Journee, a foreign middleweight boxer, over the strong objections of her wealthy physician father in Noble, Illinois. Quitting their jobs to open a beauty parlor in the Bronx, the couple lost their life savings when the business failed. Financially ruined, the former fighter took a job as a hairdresser in a New York City beauty shop. Worried over their finances and distressed by her father's opposition to the marriage, Jeannette Journee became increasingly moody. At noon on August 3, 1931, Henri Journee returned to their basement apartment at 247 West Seventy-sixth Street to find the door chained and a strong smell of gas seeping from under the door. Fearing the worst, Journee got a policeman and together they forced the door of the apartment. Inside, they found the former dancer dead in a chair beside the kitchen range, with gas escaping from four open jets. Prior to taking her life, the woman had removed a pair of caged love birds, Jeannette and Henri, and Jimmy, a marmoset, into an adjoining sealed room to escape the fumes. In a note to her husband she wrote, "I have been bad luck to you, so I am leaving you never to return." In a separate note to her father, Journee berated him for opposing her marriage to the fighter.

Judd, Terence

One week before he was set to embark on a concert tour of Russia, Judd, one of the most successful young pianists in England, disappeared on the afternoon of December 16, 1979, after leaving his parents' home in Willesden, North London, to go for a walk.

Judd, 22, began playing piano at 5 and at 10 became the youngest winner of the National Junior Piano Competition. In 1978, the gifted musician won fourth prize in the Tchaikovsky International Piano Competition in Moscow.

On December 23, 1979, hours after his vanishing act forced the cancellation of his Russian tour, Judd's body was found at the foot of Beachy Head, East Sussex. In recording an "open verdict" on Judd's death, the East Sussex Coroner concluded: "Obviously a man of his profession would suffer a certain amount of [mental] strain with his ardent practising to keep him at the top. The country, particularly the musical world, is much the poorer with his passing."

Judels, Jules

Judels joined the New York Metropolitan Opera Company in 1891 as an assistant to his father (then master of rehearsals), eventually succeeding him in that position. By July 3, 1940, the 65 year old had spent 49 years at the Met persuading temperamental prima donnas and tenors to appear on time for rehearsals. On that date, Judels ended his life by inhaling illuminating gas amid some 300 pottery images and figures of cats that jammed his three room apartment at 35 Sutton Place. Awakened by the smell of gas, Judel's wife found him on the kitchen floor. In a note found near the body the "temperament tamer" wrote that he had fed their two cats before putting them outside of the apartment.

Julien, Pauline

The singer-activist known as the "Lioness of Quebec" was born May 23, 1928, in Cap-de-la Madeleine in the Trois-Rivières region of Quebec. Influenced by her father's belief that the English were "an alien force," Julien used her singing talent to promote political causes, most notably feminism and Quebec's separatist movement. Debuting as a singer in Paris in 1957, Julien returned to Quebec in the late fifties where she interpreted the music of Kurt Weill and the Quebec composer Gilles Vigneault. Shortly after her return, she fell in love with Québécois poet and journalist Gerald Godin and for the next 35 years they fought tirelessly for Quebec separatism. Though already an accompished cabaret singer, Julien's career was launched in 1962 when Jean Garron cast her as "Jenny" in *The Threepenny Opera*. In 1964, she made international headlines when she refused to sing for the queen. Five years later she disrupted a francophone conference in the Niger by shouting, "Vive le Quebec *Libre!*" Godin and Julien were both briefly jailed as terrorist sympathizers in 1970 during the height of the October Crisis when Prime Minister Pierre Trudeau deployed troops in the streets of Montreal in response to separatist violence. When Julien retired from performing in 1992, she had recorded 25 albums, appeared in several films, and had achieved the status of an institution in Quebec.

On September 30, 1998, the 70-year-old singer committed suicide (method unreported) at her home in Montreal after leaving a note with instructions not to revive her. According to a family member, Julien suffered from aphasia, a progressive cerebral affliction that prevented her from speaking and understanding words.

Jullion, M. Arthur

Known onstage as "Yvonnek," the French vaudevillian had become increasingly despondent since losing his voice two years earlier. On April 17, 1929, the 55-year-old singer of Breton folk songs leapt to his death from the window of his room in Paris.

Justice, Barry Norval Bannatyne

Though Justice had appeared in several West End productions (*Man and Boy*, 1962; *The Doctor's Dilemma*, 1966; *The Young Visitors*, 1968; *A Voyage Round My Father*, 1972), and in the 1964 Joseph Losey film *King and Country*, he achieved his greatest popularity in television as the ne'er-do-well "Burgo Fitzgerald" in the BBC series *The Pallisers*. Plagued with worry over his career, subject to binge drinking, and suffering from recurring bouts of tearful depression, the 39-year-old actor joined Exit, the voluntary euthanasia society, in July 1980. On August 6, 1980, Justice was found dead in his flat in South Kensington, London. A shotgun was at his side and a note stating that he had "exercised his inalienable right of choice." At the inquest, a spokesman for Exit testified that Justice was not a typical case and that the motive and method of his death had not been counselled by the group. Coroner's verdict: "Suicide while suffering from depression."

Jutra, Claude

The former medical student turned film director was best known for his classic 1971 movie, *Mon Oncle Antoine*, a cinéma vérité exposition of a boy's coming of age in rural Quebec that won best picture at the Canadian Film Awards that year. In 1985, an international film panel at the Toronto Festival of Festivals declared the motion picture to be the best-ever Canadian film. Other films directed by Jutra include *Kamouraska* (Cannes Prize winner in 1972), *For Better or Worse* (1975), *Surfacing* (1979), *By Design* (1980), and *La dame en couleurs* (1985). In addition to acting in films, Jutra also directed several television dramas for the Canadian Broadcasting Corporation and was a founding member of Quebec's Association of Professional Cineastes.

Depressed over the onset of Alzheimer's disease, the 56-year-old Jutra walked out of his downtown Montreal apartment on November 5, 1986, and vanished. Friends, fearing the worst, remembered a recent interview he had given in which he discussed the disease: "I can face death, but I cannot face watching myself disappear from within. Nowadays, when the world comes knocking at the door of Claude Jutra, there's no one home. I don't know who I am anymore." At his home, Jutra left notes to his friends stating that if he did not see them again soon, they would meet in the hereafter. On April 23, 1987, the filmmaker's body was found in the St. Lawrence River near Quebec City. A note written in French contained in a money belt said, "My name is Claude Jutra." The body, estimated to have been in the water for two to three months, was positively identified as Jutra's by dental records and a small tattoo found on the right arm. It is generally believed that Jutra leapt to his death from Montreal's Jacques Cartier Bridge soon after his disappearance.

Kaimann, William J.

Kaimann, 52, served as vice-president of Kaimann Brothers, Inc., a circuit of eight neighborhood movie theatres in St. Louis, under his 51-year-old brother, Clarence Kaimann, the company's president. Following a heated stockholder's meeting on January 26, 1944, Kaimann confronted Clarence in the basement office of their O'Fallon Theatre at 4026 West Florissant Avenue. After shouting, "You have cheated me again, " Kaimann cursed Clarence, produced an automatic pistol, and shot his brother four times. Though badly wounded, Clarence survived the attack. One hour later, William Kaimann's body was found in his parked car in nearby O'Fallon Park half dead from from a single self-inflicted gunshot wound to the head. He died in City Hospital 18 hours after the shooting without regaining consciousness. The surviving brother revealed that since threatening to fire Kaimann in 1941 he had received numerous death threats from him.

Kaliski, Louis

Kaliski, 63, was the former treasurer of the Fox Theatre in Detroit and the Detroit Opera House before becoming a member of the Theatrical Managers and Agents Union, AFL, in 1939. Earlier in his career, Kaliski was connected with the plays *Kiss and Tell* and *The State of the Union*, but had recently travelled to New York City from the West Coast for the revival of *The Desert Song*. On June 19, 1949, the manager was found dead from a self-inflicted bullet wound to the head in the shower stall of his room in the Great Northern Hotel.

Kappel, Adolph

The German-born actor played with the Pabst Theater company in Milwaukee from 1861 to 1870, toured Germany with his own company for ten years, and performed over the Lyceum Circuit from 1880 to 1890. Alone and longing for his glory days, the 70 year old had twice attempted to end his life before being successful on October 29, 1916. On that day, Kappel twisted a gas fixture loose in his Chicago home and laid on the floor until the escaping illuminating gas overcame him.

Kauter, William

Kauter, 47, was "Bill Cody" in the vaudeville dance team of "Cody and Cody" before a spine injury around 1919 forced him to retire. The former dance man opened a newsstand across the street from New York City's Palace Theatre where he had once shared bills with Raymond Hitchcock and George M. Cohan. Convinced that he was being "framed" by friends, Kauter often spoke of killing himself and had failed in an earlier attempt to slash his wrists. On November 9, 1934, Kauter stabbed himself 14 times with a pair of scissors in his home at 216 West Sixty-ninth Street.

Kean, Norman

Kean was the general manager of the original New York staging of Kenneth Tynan's controversial show *Oh! Calcutta!* when it first opened at the Eden Theatre on June 17, 1969.

That same year, he converted the ballroom in the Edison Hotel into a 499-seat playhouse, the Edison Theatre. The Edison Theatre opened in March 1970 with a poorly received production of *Show Me Where the Good Times Are*, a musical based on Molière's *The Imaginary Invalid*. In 1974, the theatre received critical success with the Tony Award winning bill *Sizwe Banzi Is Dead* and *The Island*, the first plays to depict life in Black South Africa to New York theatre-goers. On September 4, 1976, *Oh! Calcutta!* opened off Broadway at the Edison Theatre with Kean as its producer. Through his tireless efforts at promotion, the show took on the status of a New York tourist attraction and ultimately ran for 5,969 performances. In theatrical circles, however, *Oh! Calcutta!* was generally dismissed as a "nudie musical." The criticism stung Kean, who desperately wanted to be taken seriously as a top producer. In 1978, he produced *A Broadway Musical*. It flopped.

While *Oh! Calcutta!* continued to generate income, Kean's personal life was beginning to disintegrate. In the spring of 1987, Kean was dismissed as head of the theater advisory committee at the nonprofit John Drew Theater of Guild Hall in East Hampton, Long Island. At the same time, the 53-year-old producer learned that his wife, the former stage actress Gwyda DonHowe, was having an affair with an advertising executive. Kean and Don-Howe had met while doing summer stock in 1957, wed in 1958, and had one child, David. According to a friend, Kean's obsession with his wife throughout their 29 year marriage was "palpable." In an attempt to save his marriage, Kean spent more time at home, delegating business matters to deputies. In January 1988, however, he learned through a private investigator that Gwyda, 54, was still seeing the man.

Kean now applied the same compulsive attention to detail that characterized his success as a businessman-producer to planning the murder of Gwyda and his suicide. One week before the double tragedy, Kean instructed his attorney to draw up divorce papers. One day before she was to die, Gwyda confessed to a friend, "I want to be free as a bird." On the morning of January 15, 1988, Kean waited until their 14-year-old son left for school before entering the master bedroom of their luxury apartment on Riverside Drive in Manhattan. Sometime between 7:30 and 8:00 A.M. Kean stabbed his sleeping wife 60 times with a 6 inch kitchen knife. When the housekeeper arrived at 8:30 A.M., Kean instructed her not to awaken his usually late-sleeping wife. For the next several hours, the producer made business phone calls, left the apartment to drop off material at his attorney, and returned home around 3:00 P.M. After giving the housekeeper $150 in cash, three carboned letters, and a tape recording to place in his son's room, Kean went to the roof of the 15 story building, removed his glasses, and plunged 150 feet to his death into a back courtyard below.

David Kean discovered his mother's body when he returned home from basketball practice. He was later called on to identify his father's broken remains. Kean's notes (to police, his son, and housekeeper) contained references to his depression over Gwyda's drinking, the affair, and his love for her. In the audiotape, the producer told his son in a voice devoid of emotion that his college would be paid for and that what had just happened to his parents was better for him than suffering through a divorce.

Kearney, Patrick

Best known for adapting Theodore Dreiser's novel *An American Tragedy* to the Broadway stage in 1926, Kearney also dramatized the Sinclair Lewis novel *Elmer Gantry*, which had a brief New York run in 1928. In 1925, he wrote the successful play *A Man's Man*. Relocating to Hollywood in the late twenties, Kearney wrote the screenplays for two 1929 Paramount Famous Lasky Corp. productions: *Darkened Rooms* and *Fast Company*. The thirties, however, brought the writer nothing but disappointment. His play

Veiled Eyes was not produced while his adaptation of the German drama *Sickness of Youth* by Ferdinand Bruckner failed to reach Broadway. In 1932, Kearney filed bankruptcy after Universal released him as a scenario writer.

Once wealthy, the struggling writer had lost $250,000 during a two-year run of bad luck and, estranged from his third wife and their 4-year-old daughter, was living alone in a fourth floor furnished apartment at 348 E. Fiftieth Street in New York City. On March 28, 1933, Kearney was found lying on the floor with a rubber tube running from his mouth into an open gas jet.

Keats, Steven

The son of Jewish immigrants from Denmark, Keats was born in the Bronx in 1945, but grew up in Canarsie, Brooklyn. After graduating from the High School for the Performing Arts in Manhattan, he served in the Air Force in Vietnam during 1965–1966. Discharged, Keats turned his attention to acting and attended the Yale School of Drama and Montclair State College. He made his Broadway debut in 1970 in the second cast of *Oh! Calcutta!* In 1973, Keats acted in his first film, the gangster drama *The Friends of Eddie Coyle*. In a career lasting more than two decades, the actor appeared in more than 25 films including *Death Wish* (1974), *Hester Street* (1975), *Black Sunday* (1977), and *Turk 182!* (1985). Keats regularly did guest shots on several television series (*The A-Team, Kojak, Matlock, Law & Order*) and acted in several made-for-television movies (*The Story of Pretty Boy Floyd*, 1974; *The Last Dinosaur*, 1977; *Zuma Beach*, 1978; *The Executioner's Song*, 1982; *Lies of the Heart: The Story of Laurie Kellogg*, 1994). On May 8, 1994, the 48-year-old actor was found dead in his Manhattan apartment. Although the means of death was not reported, Keats' son, Thatcher, confirmed that his father had committed suicide.

Keegan, Terry

In 1960 Keegan began working as a page for NBC. By the end of a decade marked by various production jobs he had become director of West Coast live programming for the network. In the early seventies Keegan helped develop the popular ethnic humor-based sitcoms *Chico and the Man* (starring fellow suicide Freddie Prinze [see entry]) and *Sanford and Son*. Named vice-president of development, West Coast, in the mid-seventies, Keegan developed *Little House on the Prairie, Police Story, Police Woman*, and *The Flip Wilson Show*. He left NBC in 1975 to assume the position of vice-president of creative affairs at Paramount Television where he developed *Happy Days, Serpico, Laverne & Shirley*, and the miniseries *Shogun*. With fellow producer Arthur Fellows he formed The Fellows-Keegan Company in 1979 and produced the made-for-television movies *The Girl, the Gold Watch & Everything* (1980) and *One Shoe Makes it Murder* (1982). On January 29, 1993, the 59-year-old television producer took his life (method unreported) near Kingman, Arizona.

Keenan, Geraldine

The 22-year-old lovesick stenographer attempted suicide after learning that her employer at a downtown Cincinnati film exchange had lied to her about being unmarried. Heartbroken and disillusioned, Keenan dissolved five tablets of bichloride of mercury into a glass of water and downed the corrosive mixture in her apartment at 327 Broadway on September 1, 1919. A note found on the dying woman declared that "a certain young man" knew why she was taking her life. Keenan drifted in and out of consciousness for 19 days in the Queen City's General Hospital as family members maintained a bedside vigil, and doctors vainly administered a score of antidotes to counteract the poison. She died on September 19, 1919, after being unable to retain or assimilate nourishment. No prosecution was subsequently sought of the "man in the case."

Keim, Adrienne LaChamp

Keim, a 33-year-old Hungarian actress-singer-dancer, was one of the century's most prolific suicide note writers. On December 12, 1933, she leaped from a 15 floor window of the Lincoln Hotel in New York City, narrowly missing several pedestrians walking below on Forty-fourth Street. One of the two notes pinned to her dress read: "Please notify my mother, Mrs. A. LaChamp in Shanghai, China. Please, it is my wish to be buried untouched. I am sorry for the poor English." In the other, addressed to police, Keim wrote: "Please keep this out of the papers. This is just another funeral. Don't experiment on me and don't try to keep me alive." Six sealed notes, four addressed to the director of the St. James Theatre and the others to friends, were found in her rooms.

Keith, Brian

The son of Broadway stage and film actor Robert Keith (1896–1966) was born Robert Brian Keith, Jr., in Bayonne, New Jersey, on November 14, 1921. Keith was only 3 when he made his film debut in the 1924 Famous Players-Lasky silent *Pied Piper Malone*. The burly actor appeared in stock theatre and radio prior to serving four years as a machine-gunner in the Marine Corps during World War II. In 1953, Keith re-entered films with a role in *Arrowhead* opposite Charlton Heston. Several films later, Keith's career took off in 1961 when he was cast as the father to identical twins (played by Hayley Mills) in the Disney hit *The Parent Trap*. Equally at home in hardbitten, comedic, or sympathetic roles, Keith earned a reputation among directors as the consummate professional on such films as *The Russians Are Coming!* (1966), *Reflections in a Golden Eye* (1967), *With Six You Get Eggroll* (1968), *The Wind and the Lion* (1975, as Teddy Roosevelt), as well as some other 70 plus films.

BRIAN KEITH— Brian and Daisy Keith are interred next to one another in the Garden of Serenity (new Memorial Garden) in Westwood Memorial Park in Los Angeles. An actor's actor, Keith was the consummate professional in more than 70 films including *Arrowhead* (1953) and *The Wind and the Lion* (1975). It was, however, as "Uncle Bill" on the CBS comedy hit *Family Affair* (1966–1971) that the former Marine machine-gunner became a household name and face. Emotionally shattered by the suicide of his daughter Daisy in 1997 and suffering from terminal lung cancer and emphysema, the 75-year-old actor shot himself on June 24, 1997, at his home in Malibu, California. *Photo 2000 by Jana Wells.*

It is on television, however, that Keith is probably best remembered. His first important role came in 1953 in "Westward the Sun," a presentation of the *Motorola TV Theatre*, an anthology of hour-long dramas. From 1955 to 1956, the actor starred as freelance writer "Matt Anders" in the CBS series *Crusader*. His next series, *The Westerner* for NBC, was cancelled after a three month run in 1960. It was as "Uncle Bill," a swinging bachelor who took in the three orphaned children of his brother and sister-in-law on the hit CBS series *Family Affair*, that Keith won enduring television fame. The series ran from 1966 to 1971 and co-starred Sebastian Cabot (as "Mr. French"), Johnnie Whitaker (as "Jody"), Kathy Garver (as "Cissy"), and Anissa Jones (as "Buffy"), who died from a drug overdose in 1976 at the age 18. His three other series (*The Brian Keith Show*, NBC, 1972–1974; *Archer*, NBC, 1975; and *Hardcastle & McCormick*, ABC, 1983–1986) never achieved the same level of audience appeal or success.

In the later years of his life, the actor suffered greatly from terminal lung cancer and emphysema. Tired by chemotherapy treatments and depressed, Keith suffered an emotional blow from which he never recovered when, on April 16, 1997, his 27-year-old daughter, Daisy Sampson, committed suicide by shooting herself in the head. Shortly after 10:00 A.M. on June 24, 1997, the 75-year-old actor's body was found by family members dead from a self-inflicted gunshot wound to the head in his Malibu, California, home at 91A Malibu Colony Road in the 23000 block of the Pacific Coast Highway. In a handwritten note to his third wife and children found on a scrap of paper, Keith wrote: "The end is here. I'm finished. The pain is too much. Now it's time for me to join our little Daisy. She needs me. She didn't want to be without me here, so now she'll have me again over there. Don't be sad. This had to come soon." Keith's remains are interred above his daughter Daisy's in Westwood Memorial Park in Los Angeles.

"Kellee, Nancee" see *Van Dyke, Kelly Jean*

Kellin, Nina Caiserman

Amicably separated from television and film actor Mike Kellin, the 44-year-old former dancer with the Martha Graham Company and the New Dance Group disappeared from New York City on May 2, 1963, after posting a letter to her estranged husband indicating her deep depression. Kellin's body was subsequently found nine days later on a blanket in a wooded area near Warrensburg, New York. The coroner ruled the case a suicide, but the cause of death was unreported.

Kelly, Anthony Paul

A film scenarist since 1915 (*Body and Soul, The Builder of Bridges, The Great Divide*), Kelly is best remembered as the author of the play *Three Faces East*, first presented on Broadway at the Cohan & Harris Theatre on August 13, 1918. The successful mystery melodrama was filmed as a silent in 1926, and as a talking feature by Warner Bros. Pictures in 1930. Following the play's debut, Kelly enlisted in the Navy and served for the rest of World War I. Afterward, he returned to writing screenplays that include *Love's Redemption* (1921), *My Old Kentucky Home* (1922), *The Silent Command* (1923), and *The Scarlet West* (1925).

In 1932, Kelly received treatment for tuberculosis at a hospital in Mount Vernon, New York. Terminally ill, he left the facility and returned to his apartment at 410 W. 110th Street in New York City. On the morning of September 26, 1932, Anna Delaforce, a longtime friend of Kelly's, received a letter from the scenarist informing her that he intended to end his life. In it, he asked that she notify his brothers and other friends of his death. Delaforce immediately called police, who forced entry into the 35-year-old writer's apartment. Inside the gas fume-filled rooms, the lifeless Kelly lay on a couch, the floor around him littered with the manuscript of

Three Faces East and notes written to friends and the landlord. The writer left $27 to his landlord to cover any damage to the apartment. In an explanatory note addressed to police, Kelly wrote (in part): "Gentleman: This is a plain case of suicide. Having contracted an absolutely hopeless case of T.B. in both my lungs and intestines and since I have also contracted it in my throat, I can see no sense in prolonging this agony any longer. I thought I could endure it a little longer but I can't.... Give my belongings, such as they are, to the American Legion and kindly notify them that I requested that no religious services be held before my burial."

Kelly, George Augustus

Kelly, a native of Omaha, Nebraska, joined the U.S. Army at the outbreak of World War I, but transferred to the British Air Force where distinguished service in the sky over France gained him a captain's commission. Described as possessing a "magnetic personality," the handsome 30-year-old ex-flyer was acting as the manager of the Palais de Danse in Hammersmith when he met the attractive divorcee and dancer Sophia Erica Taylor, 29, there in 1920. Known as "Babs" to her friends, Taylor was a chorus girl at the Gaiety Theatre and Hippodrome and was notorious for making the rounds of London nightclubs to dance. The pair became lovers and dance partners, appearing in private exhibition dances in London though working principally in the suburbs. Their extravagant lifestyle coupled with Kelly's gambling and addictions to alcohol and drugs soon cooled the relationship. A violent pattern developed. Taylor, looking for a new benefactor, flirted with men while Kelly, drunk and insanely jealous, beat her. Weeks before the impending tragedy (during which time the ex-soldier would often disappear for days) the dancer confided to a friend: "I am very unhappy and Kelly is so strange. He has hit me many times, and threatened me. I do not know what to do." Taylor became intimate with Captain Allan Leslie, formerly in the Gordon Highlanders, and the two arranged to live together in Brighton.

Shortly after receiving a notice cancelling his appointment as manager for a circuit of suburban movie houses, Kelly entered Taylor's London flat at 8 St. James Street, Piccadilly, W., on December 17, 1920. In the presence of her maid, he attempted to strangle his former lover to death on her bed. The maid broke his grip, but Kelly fired a fatal shot into the fleeing Taylor before shooting himself in the head. Among items found on Kelly's body were a quantity of cocaine and notes to the dead woman in which he wrote: "Wish we could have fallen in love with each other as we have gotten along splendidly."

Kennedy, Kevin J.

Kennedy, a rock drummer who patterned his playing after The Who's Keith Moon, played with bands in Phoenix and Denver in the early eighties before moving to Omaha, Nebraska. In 1984, the drummer was in the band Ticket to Mars. Other local groups featuring Kennedy were On the Fritz, the Man's Band, the Doo-Rags, and T.D.K. Kennedy. Fascinated by Moon (who died of an accidental drug overdose in London in 1978), Kennedy sent Who guitarist and founder Pete Townshend a letter after the drummer's death asking for an audition. Townshend reportedly responded with a kind letter saying, "Thanks, but no thanks." A master's degree student in psychology at the University of Nebraska at Omaha, Kennedy was working on a thesis based on a case study of Moon's life and had begun contacting the drummer's family members to set up possible interviews. Around 10:00 P.M. on January 20, 1998, the 43-year-old musician jumped to his death from the sixth floor of the Doubletree Guest Suites at 7260 Cedar Street in Omaha.

Kennedy, Pat

The Irish tenor got his first big break in the "Roaring Twenties" as a singer with Ben Bernie's band. During that period, the

Pittsburgh orphan credited in press notices as being the person "who lifted Ben Bernie to fame" worked with celebrities like Al Jolson, Will Rogers, and Eddie Cantor. Kennedy stayed with the band until striking off on his own in the mid-thirties for a radio career in Chicago. Listeners, however, tired of the tenor's style and by 1939, following an unsuccessful turn with a band in Minneapolis, he was back in Pittsburgh driving a truck for his father-in-law's business and singing, and playing records in a bar in Crafton. After years of trying to make a comeback, the 50-year-old singer had had enough. On September 3, 1952, Kennedy took an overdose of sleeping pills in his room at the Fort Pitt Hotel. He died shortly afterward in Allegheny General Hospital. In a note to his estranged wife found at the scene, Kennedy wrote: "I am tired of living in a two-by-four room, so maybe you will understand. You have been a wonderful mother and God bless you but I just couldn't take it any longer. To all my would-be friends, always try to be at least on the level. When you are lonely and there is no one to talk to, remember that a friend in need is a friend indeed. Goodbye and God bless you all, Pat. P.S. You all thought I was clowning. So now you can talk about me seriously."

Kenney, Charles Elbert

In 1899, the 18-year-old New Albany, Indiana, native debuted with the Russell Minstrel Show in Lexington, Kentucky, and for several years was a member of the Keith Orpheum Circuit. From 1903 to 1905, Kenney played a lead role with the Red Feather Opera Company, but was best known onstage as "Blue Bert," and the blackfaced character "Nobody," which he originated in 1916. Kenney retired from the minstrel circuit in 1926, returned to live in New Albany, and from 1930 to 1935 broadcast baseball programs over radio station WAVE. He later presented a dog program over WHAS radio. At 4:30 A.M. on June 18, 1948, the 67-year-old former minstrel was found dead from a self-inflicted .32-caliber

pistol wound to the head in the kitchen of his hilltop cottage on Old Vincennes Road near New Albany. According to his brother, who found the body, Kenney had been in ill health.

Kent, Kay

As a teenager, the aspiring British model became obsessed with film star Marilyn Monroe (see entry), who overdosed on pills in her Brentwood, California, house on August 5, 1962. Kent repeatedly bleached her naturally brown hair until it became the same shade as Monroe's. Spare time was spent in her room practicing the dead film star's pout and perfecting her makeup. Finally, Kent spent $4,000 to have her breasts augmented to match Monroe's 38-inch bust. As a Monroe look-alike, she became a well-known face in British tabloids and television, and earned $90,000 annually impersonating the sex goddess in media advertising.

In early 1989, Kent's mother died of cancer and soon afterward the model broke up with her childhood sweetheart, 28-year-old rock singer Dean Hammond. On June 12, 1989, a tenant found the nude body of the 24-year-old Monroe impersonator dead on her bed in a row house in Chatham, England, some 34 miles southeast of London. Like her idol, Kent was found with an empty pill bottle beside her. Authorities reported that a half-empty vodka bottle and photographs of Monroe were strewn across Kent's bed. Movie stills of the actress, books about her, and Monroe recordings littered the room. A note addressed to her former boyfriend read: "Dear Dean, I love you so very much." Kent's older brother told a reporter: "She was so involved in her Marilyn image that she couldn't help herself from dying just like her idol. I don't know why she killed herself. She had hundreds of people around her. Maybe she died of loneliness."

Kibbee, Donald Guy, Jr.

On June 13, 1960, the son of veteran film character actor Guy Kibbee (1882–1956) was found by his mother in the bedroom of his home at 10527 Rochester Street in West Los Angeles, California. Kibbee, a 25-year-old student at UCLA, had shot himself in the head with a .32-caliber pistol. Although Kibbee left no note, his mother told authorities that her son had been morose and "unable to adjust to life."

King, Allyn

Born in 1900, King began working for Florenz Ziegfeld in 1915 in his *Midnight Frolic*, and was understudy for *Follies* star Ina Claire. The beautiful blonde became a principal in the *Follies* (1916–1918) and *Frolic* (1919–1920), but caused the greatest sensation in the "Arabian Nights" scene in the 1917 *Follies* when, as a provocatively attired Venus, she was lifted up against a backdrop of glowing beads in what appeared to be a giant bubble. Following her *Follies* career, King was featured in several plays and Broadway musical comedies including *Ladies' Night* (1920), Earl Carroll's *Florida Girl* (1925), *90 Horse Power* (1926), and *Pearl of Great Price* (1926). In 1923, she appeared in a bit part in her only film, *The Fighting Blade*, a romantic costume drama starring Richard Barthelmess.

In 1927, King's manager informed his client that her weight gain had made her unemployable on the stage. In an attempt to salvage her career, King embarked on a rigorous diet regimen supplemented with diet pills. Her health broken, the actress suffered a nervous breakdown and was institutionalized for two years in a sanitarium in South Norwalk, Connecticut. Released to an aunt's care in 1929, King still suffered fits of depression and could not meet stage friends without weeping. In an attempt to re-enter show business, the former Ziegfeld girl took voice lessons twice a week and was set to audition for a radio show. Though her condition was improving, King still needed constant attention, and was living in her aunt's fifth floor apartment at 116 Waverly Place in New York City.

At 9:00 A.M. on March 29, 1930, the 30-year-old former showgirl entered the kitchen alone to iron a dress for an audition. When King's aunt came looking for her moments later, she noticed an open window and heard crowd noises below. Looking down, she saw King splayed on the pavement of the courtyard. Still conscious and babbling incoherently, King was removed to Bellevue Hospital where she was diagnosed with two broken arms, two broken legs, and a skull fracture. After living for 19 hours, she died the next day. Although King had been unable to find work in the theatre, her funeral service was attended by some 200 stage celebrities.

FURTHER READING

Ziegfeld, Richard E., and Ziegfeld, Paulette. *The Ziegfeld Touch: The Life and Times of Florenz Ziegfeld, Jr.* New York: H. N. Abrams, 1993.

King, Edward L.

For many years, King, 50, had been the business agent of Local 38, the Detroit branch of the International Alliance of Theatrical Employees. In 1941, however, he was under investigation on a charge of payroll padding at the Michigan State Fair. According to authorities, King issued three checks totalling $178 to phantom employees, endorsed them, then collected the cash. King repaid the money and the charge against him was in the process of being dropped when he disappeared on October 21, 1941. The next day the union representative's body was found under his car with a hose attached to the exhaust on a lonely back road north of Starville, Michigan, in St. Clair County northeast of Detroit. A briefcase and a suicide note were beside the body.

King, Edwin

King (born Edwin Reinking) began writing songs in his 20s, often collaborating with Harry A. Carlson, head of Cincinnati, Ohio-based Fraternity Records. Together they penned "Cincinnati Ding Dong," "When I'm Alone," and "No One Lost More." It was as a free-lance songwriter in New York and Hollywood, however, that King was destined to garner his biggest hit with "Tennessee Polka" recorded by country singing star Red Foley in 1949. Under treatment for "mental depression," King slit his wrists in the bedroom of his home at 8631 Livingston Road in Groesbeck, Ohio, on May 2, 1960. The 42 year old had only recently finished his last work, "The Best Book on Earth."

Kinney, Anthony

The 40-year-old theatre manager had left a position in Stockton, California, two weeks before to manage the Santa Clara Theatre in the town of the same name when fellow employees, concerned when he failed to show up for work, discovered his body in a hotel room on December 18, 1938. Kinney, a photo of his 8-year-old son on the pillow next to his head, had shot himself through the heart with a .38-caliber pistol. A coroner placed the time of death at a day earlier. A superior court order instructing Kinney to pay $125 in attorney's fees and $25 a month upkeep for his son was found on a dresser. In three notes addressed to his ex-wife, his employer, and "To All My Friends," the theatre manager confessed that he "just couldn't take it any longer."

Klaw, Joseph

The son of the late Marc Klaw, a theatrical producer, and the manager of his father's theatre in New York City, was found dead in his car by a passing motorist in a secluded patch of woods on the outskirts of Douglaston, Queens, on September 22, 1937. Klaw, also the president of Ambrosia Chocolate, was discovered dead in the back seat of his car, the engine still idling, and a 12 foot length of rubber hose leading from the exhaust in through a slightly opened rear window stuffed with rags. His coat, vest, and raincoat were neatly folded on the front seat. Klaw left no suicide note, although it was generally believed that his act was precipitated by financial troubles.

Koenig, Frank

Depressed over the plight of his parents in Germany, Koenig, a 23-year-old acrobat, had tried on two previous occasions to take his life. On April 30, 1925, he finally succeeded by throwing himself in front of an automobile in Chicago.

Korsten, Georg (Ge)

Korsten, the popular singer who entertained South Africa's white Afrikaner community for more than 40 years, was born on December 6, 1929, in Rotterdam, Holland. The youngest of a family of eight, he relocated to South Africa with his family in 1936. Though trained as an electrical engineer in Pretoria, by 1957 Korsten's strong tenor voice began earning him a reputation in opera. Not limiting his career solely to opera, the singer also recorded 58 albums (20 earned gold record status) of Afrikaans folk music. Among South Africa's most honored entertainers, Korsten received six Sarie awards as best singer, won the MIDEM prize in 1976, and the Nederburg Prize for Opera in 1976. From 1985–1991, he held the position of chief director of the Cape Performing Arts Board. Korsten also appeared in several films including the 1967 musical *Hoor my Lied* (*Hear My Song*). On television he played a leading role in the South African soap opera *Egoli*. In 1987 he won the Artes Award for the most popular television personality of the year.

At 7:50 A.M. on September 29, 1999, one week after being voted *Keur* magazine's "Star of the Century," the versatile 69-year-old entertainer fatally shot himself in the head with a 7.65mm-caliber pistol in his home in Wilderness, South Africa. Curious about the noise, Korsten's wife, Elna, found her husband lying on his back in the kitchen. Thinking that he had only fallen, she ran to the neighbors for help. Upon their return to the scene, they discovered a bullet wound in the right side of Korsten's head and the pistol next to him.

Kortum, Lawrence

A failed songwriter whose only published piece was "The Night Is Made to Dance," [Kortum] shot himself between the eyes with a .22-caliber rifle in the early morning of August 9, 1938, in New York's Central Park about 500 feet from the Fifty-ninth Street and Seventh Avenue entrance. A briefcase found near the 28-year-old Montana native's body contained several of his unpublished songs and a note requesting that a relative be contacted. Police found 38 cents in Kortum's pockets.

Kosinksi, Jerzy

Jerzy Nikodem Kosinski was born the only child of well-off Jewish parents in Lodz, Poland, on June 14, 1933. When the Nazis invaded Poland in 1939 the 6 year old was sent to the countryside. Kosinski's novel *The Painted Bird* depicts in harrowing detail the maltreatment he suffered by Poles as a Jewish boy in the Nazi-occupied countryside. The 24-year-old Kosinski emigrated to the United States in 1957, was reunited with his family, and learned to write in English by listening to the radio and "living" in movie houses. He reportedly saw the 1954 Humphrey Bogart-Ava Gardner film *The Barefoot Contessa* more than 30 times. In 1965 Kosinski published *The Painted Bird*. Often called the finest piece of literature to emerge from World War II, the novel incited a firestorm of controversy in Poland where its graphic depiction of brutality against Jews was decried as slanderous. While Kosinski admitted that not every brutal event in the novel happened to him, he insisted that everything in the book was true. In 1982, the popular writer became the focus of a campaign to discredit him. Authors in a front page *Village Voice* article charged that Kosinski had hired editors to write his novels and that the Central Intelligence Agency had "apparently played a clandestine role" in the publication of his first two books. None of the charges were ever proven.

Kosinski's other novels include *Steps* (1968, winner National Book Award), *Being There* (1971), *The Devil Tree* (1973), *Cockpit* (1975), *Blind Date* (1977), *Passion Play* (1979), *Pinball* (1982), and *The Hermit of 69th Street* (1988). In 1979, he wrote the screenplay for *Being There* from his 1971 novel. The Peter Sellers film was a critical and commercial hit. In front of the camera, Kosinski played the role of the Bolshevik villain "Grigory Zinoviev" in his good friend actor-director Warren Beatty's 1981 account of the Russian Revolution, *Reds*.

A great favorite in New York society, the 57-year-old writer (with wife Katherina von Frauenhofer-Kosinski) attended a book party on the evening of May 2, 1991, at the home of friend and fellow author Gay Talese for Senator William S. Cohen, Republican of Maine, for his book *One-Eyed Kings*. Apparently cheerful and happy, Kosinski and wife Katherina returned home to their West Fifty-seventh Street apartment in Manhattan after midnight. He retired alone to his separate bedroom around 1:00 A.M. Later that morning Katherina von Frauenhofer-Kosinski found her husband's naked body in a half-filled bathtub with a plastic shopping bag twisted around his head. A note found in his office read: "I'm going to put myself to sleep now for a bit longer than usual. Call the time Eternity." The New York medical examiner concluded that a combination of drugs — alcohol and sleeping pills — not asphyxiation, caused the writer's death. A statement issued by Kosinski's widow explained the act: "My husband had been in deteriorating health as a result of a serious heart condition. He had become depressed by his growing inability to work, and by his fear of being a burden to me and my friends." Friend Gay Talese said: "He did something in the last minutes of his life that would have been unbelievable had it been performed by a character in one of his novels." Kosinki requested that no funeral services be held. His body was cremated.

FURTHER READING

Sloan, James Park. *Jerzy Kosinski: A Biography.* New York: Dutton, 1996.

Krause, Benjamin

Widely known in the South as the owner-operator of Krause Greater Shows, the 57-year-old veteran showman's business had all but been wiped out by a freak storm that struck the fair in the winter of 1936. On January 6, 1937, a depressed and suicidal Krause, accompanied by a concerned brother, was en route by train to a sanitarium in Philadelphia when he eluded his travelling companion at the Union Station in Savannah, Georgia. Earlier on the trip, Krause had twice tried to take his life, first by jumping off the train into a river and then later by breaking his glasses and attempting to slash his wrists. Ten hours after his brother reported him missing, Krause's body was found on the north bank of the Savannah River by blacks in search of driftwood. Burns on the showman's lips suggested that he had ingested a corrosive dose before jumping off the Atlantic Coast Line Railroad train into the river.

Ladd, Alan Walbridge

Though a major motion picture star at Paramount during the forties and fifties, Ladd is perhaps destined to be best remembered by the film-going public as the short actor (5'5") who was forced to stand on boxes and such to romance his taller leading ladies. Born September 3, 1913, in Hot Springs, Arkansas, Ladd was 14 when his father died. His mother, Ina Rawley, remarried three years later in 1920 and moved the family to North Hollywood, California. A standout athlete at North Hollywood High School, Ladd won the West Coast diving championship in 1931. He also landed a large role in the school's production of *The Mikado*. Based on his performance, Ladd and another discovery, Tyrone Power, were signed by Universal Studios. Both received acting lessons before being let go by the studio. In 1932, he appeared unbilled in the Universal film *Once in a Lifetime*, which featured fellow suicide Russell Hopton (see entry) in a bit part.

After graduating, Ladd landed a job in the advertising department of the *San Fer-nando Valley Sun-Record*, eventually working his way up to $35 a week as the newspaper's ad manager. His desire to become an actor, however, prompted him to work as a grip at Warner Bros. just to be in the movie industry. Ladd worked for the studio for two years until a bad fall forced him to leave. Undeterred, he enrolled in the Ben Bard School of Acting, but was still unable to land a role except for another unbilled appearance in the 1936 20th Century–Fox football comedy *Pigskin Parade*. That year in October, Ladd married Marjorie Jane (Midge) Harrold. Their one son, Alan Ladd, Jr., later became a successful film producer. Unable to break into movies, Ladd turned to performing in radio dramas in the Los Angeles area. In 1936, he was hired by KFWB radio to be the station's sole resident actor. At KFWB, Ladd was constantly on the air in capacities as diverse as acting and newscasting. In 1937, however, Ladd suffered a personal crisis that greatly affected the rest of his life.

His mother, Ina, was staying with him after the break-up of a love affair. A 49-year-old alcoholic prone to hysterical outbursts, the woman made the newlywed's life a living hell. On the night of November 29, 1937, Ina asked her son for a quarter so she could buy something "she needed" at a local store. Thinking that she meant booze, Ladd argued with the woman, but finally gave her the money. Ina purchased a can of arsenic-based ant paste at a night grocery and drank the lethal mixture in the back seat of Ladd's car.

Often supplying various voices in the KFWB programs, Ladd's vocal versatility brought him to the attention of Sue Carol, a former actress turned agent. Following their meeting in 1939, Carol devoted herself to finding him work. After appearing in various B films (*Rulers of the Sea*, 1939; the serial *The Green Hornet*, 1939; *Hitler, Beast of Berlin*, 1939), Ladd signed a $300-a-week contract with Paramount in 1941. Shortly after doing so, he divorced Harrold in July 1941 and married Carol on March 15, 1942. Their two children, David and Alana, both became

ALAN LADD—Ladd rocketed to stardom in 1942 playing a handsome cold-blooded killer in Paramount's *This Gun for Hire* and remained a top box office draw throughout the forties and early fifties with films like *The Blue Dahlia* (1946), *Captain Carey U.S.A.* (1950), and the classic 1953 Western *Shane*. At a height of 5'5", Ladd was among the shortest leading men in the films of his day and creative ways had to be found to photograph him with his taller leading ladies. As the popular actor's career faded in the mid-fifties, he continued to drink heavily and rely on sleeping pills. Though officially ruled "accidental," Ladd's drug and alcohol-related death at the age of 50 in Palm Springs, California, on November 29, 1964, is generally believed to have been a suicide.

actors. In 1942, Ladd's persistence finally paid off with a starmaking role in Paramount's *This Gun for Hire*, a gangster film based on British author Graham Greene's 1936 novel *A Gun for Sale*. Cast as the killer "Raven" opposite Veronica Lake and Robert Preston, Ladd created a new screen prototype — the handsome, sensitive tough guy who was also cold-blooded and unreachable. The movie transformed Ladd, described by reviewers as possessing the ethereal beauty of a "young Greek god," into an overnight star.

During the next decade he was consistently voted one of the nation's top ten movie stars. Ladd, a diminuitive 5'5", found the perfect leading lady in the 5'3" Veronica Lake. A popular screen team, they were paired in *The Glass Key* (1942), *The Blue Dahlia* (1946), and *Saigon* (1948). Ladd's other Paramount films include *The Great Gatsby* (1949), *Captain Carey U.S.A.* (1950), and the 1953 George Stevens–directed Western classic *Shane*. In 1953, Ladd left Paramount for Warner Bros. after completing the lackluster *Botany Bay*. The actor's inherent insecurities as a man and an actor were further fuelled by a series of bad notices in films like *Saskatchewan* (1954), *Hell on Frisco Bay* (1956), and *Santiago* (1956). That same year, Ladd made the worst career decision of his life. Begged by *Shane* director George Stevens to play the role of "Jed Rink" in *Giant*, Ladd turned down the part that eventually went to James Dean in the 1956 box office blockbuster because he would not accept a supporting role to rising star Rock Hudson. In 1957 Ladd was paired with Italian starlet Sophia Loren in *Boy on a Dolphin*, shot on location in Greece. The actor's ego, already bruised by a string of flops, was further battered by the indignity of being cast with a buxom leading lady who at 5'8" towered over him by three inches. In their scenes together, Loren was forced to stand in a ditch so as not to dwarf her costar.

By 1958, the depressed aging actor was drinking heavily and relying on sleeping pills. On November 1, 1962, Ladd "accidentally" shot himself in the chest with a .38-caliber

pistol. The bullet missed his heart by one-eighth of an inch. In 1964, Ladd returned to Paramount to co-star as "Nevada Smith" in director Edward Dmytryk's film adaptation of Harold Robbins' bestselling potboiler *The Carpetbaggers*. On January 29, 1964, the 50-year-old actor, clad in a pajama top and robe, was found in the bedroom of his home at 323 Camino Norte in Palm Springs, California. On the death certificate, the cause of death was officially listed as "Cerebral Edema due to Synergistic Effects of C.N.D. Chemical Depressants." The coroner's verdict: "Accident due to a reaction to a combination of Depressant and Ethanol," sleeping pills and alcohol. The official hour of death was set at 3:55 P.M. on November 29. In her biography of the actor, *Ladd*, Beverly Linet concludes, "The real mystery was — is — not in the facts of the cause of death, but rather whether it was 'accident,' as reported, or the decision of a man who had come to the end of his string." Ladd is buried in the Freedom Mausoleum, Sanctuary of Heritage, in Forest Lawn Cemetery in Glendale, California. *The Carpetbaggers*, Ladd's "comeback" film, was released in 1964 to uniformly scathing reviews.

FURTHER READING

Henry, Marilyn, and DeSourdis, Ron. *The Films of Alan Ladd*. 1st ed. Secaucus, N.J.: Citadel Press, 1981.

Linet, Beverly. *Ladd: The Life, the Legend, the Legacy of Alan Ladd*. New York: Arbor House, 1979.

Lafferty, Jeanette

Minutes after dropping her boyfriend off to meet a train at the Thirtieth Street Station in Philadelphia on August 14, 1950, the 24-year-old singer paid her toll at the Camden, New Jersey, bridge, drove 20 feet from the booth, and parking amidst bridge traffic, pressed the muzzle of a .22-caliber rifle against her left temple and pulled the trigger. Lafferty, an elementary school teacher in Woodbury, New Jersey, died in Cooper Hospital three and a half hours later. In the bloodstained car, authorities found five suitcases filled with clothes, and postcard sized photographic cards advertising the "Lafferty Sisters," Jeanette and her sister Beulah who, with a ventriloquist's dummy described as the "third member of the family," entertained on local radio and in private "Temperate Engagements Only." A note found in her handbag read: "I'm done living. God put me on earth. He is taking me off because I've failed miserably."

La Franie, Joseph

The 26-year-old stage actor had been drafted and was awaiting a call to go to camp when he travelled to Brooklyn, New York, to visit his aunt. On November 25, 1917, tormented by paranoid delusions, La Franie covered his head with towels and blankets in his second floor room and turned on the gas. A letter addressed to his relatives read: "I have been followed day after day by Secret Service men and police detectives, and I am in deadly fear of arrest as they think I am a German spy. Yesterday and today were something terrible, and I can stand it no longer. Good-bye and God bless you all for all that you have done for me. It is of no use while these fellows are after me."

LaGrange, Vivian

A poser in the vaudeville production *Patterson's Bronze Artists*, the attractive 25 year old had caused a minor sensation in Butte, Montana, when the show played at the Family Theatre during the week of November 16, 1908. After traveling with the show to Spokane, Seattle, and Vancouver, LaGrange returned alone to Butte and registered at the Northern Hotel on Front Street on February 15, 1909. Seemingly depressed over a broken love affair, LaGrange swallowed morphine two days later. She was discovered, and over her objections, nursed back to health. Less than a week after being pronounced well, the actress downed a large quantity of bichloride of mercury in her hotel room on February 21, 1909. She lingered for six days before dying at Butte's General Hospital.

Lake, Alan

Well known for playing heavies in British film and television, Lake earned a reputation equalling any of his acting roles. An alcoholic, he once served 18 months for maliciously wounding the manager of a pub. The hardbitten actor, however, softened after marrying U.K. sex siren Diana Dors in 1968, 18 months after they met. Utterly devoted to Dors, Lake was devastated by her death from cancer on May 4, 1984. He transformed their Sunningdale, Berkshire, home, Orchard Manor, into a shrine to her memory and largely cut himself off from family and friends. Those closest to Lake felt the actor was coming out of his grief when he put Orchard Manor up for sale. According to Lake, it was just too painful to continue living there. On October 10, 1984, the 16th anniversary of the day he met Dors, Lake, 43, was waiting to show the home to a prospective buyer. He went upstairs, pressed the barrel of a shotgun to his left temple, and pulled the trigger. While a deputy coroner rendered the official verdict that Lake took his own life while suffering a depressive illness, a neighbor's assessment of the act was, perhaps, more accurate: "He missed his wife so much. He was always crying for her. He just loved her so much that he couldn't carry on without her."

Lamont, Owen

The great-grandson of John Bigelow, author and Minister to France during the Abraham Lincoln administration, Lamont (real name Francis Poultney Clark) had appeared as the son in the play *Madame X* opposite Jane Cowl and toured in the production *Golden Wings*. On January 17, 1952, the 35-year-old actor's body was found in a locked closet of his two room suite at the Savoy-Plaza Hotel in New York City. Lamont left a note directing that the $700 found in his clothes be given to a person whose identity was not disclosed. The immediate cause of death was not known.

Lamy, Douglas Newland

Known in films as "Charles Drake" and "Johnny Mitchell" after the part he played in the 1944 Bette Davis vehicle *Mr. Skeffington*, the handsome former aviator had been depressed since his estrangement from his wife and children. On January 19, 1951, the 32-year-old actor was found dead in his mother's fashionable New York City apartment at 419 E. Fifty-seventh Street. Clad in a long sleeved red tee-shirt and riding breeches, Lamy's body was sprawled on a bedroom sofa surrounded by pictures of his wife and two children. Police reported that the actor had apparently placed a .22-caliber rifle between his knees, pressed his forehead against the muzzle, and pulled the trigger. Twice married, Lamy had a history of heavy drinking and spousal abuse.

Lancer, Martin

Hours after the Berlin Ballet launched the Israel Festival in Jerusalem on May 21, 1990, 25-year-old dancer Martin Lancer apparently jumped to his death from a sixth floor room at the Hilton Hotel. A police spokesman said that the Swedish national had been suffering from "deep depression."

Landis, Carole

Born Frances Lillian Mary Ridste of Polish-Norwegian parents on January 1, 1919, in Fairchild, Wisconsin, the future film actress and her family moved to California in 1922. At seven she was already performing in amateur nights and beauty contests. Married briefly to a writer at 15 (it lasted 25 days), she graduated from high school in 1936, and began working as a singer-hula dancer at the Royal Hawaiian nightclub in San Francisco. In 1937, choreographer-director Busby Berkeley noticed the shapely actress in a film walk-on appearance and changed her name to Carole Landis. Following small roles in a few films (*A Day at the Races*, 1937; *Four's a Crowd*, 1938) and the 1939 serial *Daredevils of the Red Circle*, Landis caught her big break in 1940

when Hal Roach cast her opposite rising star Victor Mature in the caveman saga *One Million B.C.* That same year Landis married a yacht broker, but the couple divorced five months later.

On the strength of her performance in *One Million B.C.*, 20th Century–Fox studio head Darryl F. Zanuck placed Landis under a studio contract. Like countless starlets before her, the actress touted as having the "best legs in town" was given the casting couch treatment by the studio mogul. Zanuck maintained a bedroom behind his studio office and every day at 4:00 P.M. the studio's business would stop while he entertained a potential screen hopeful. Landis' frequent visits to Zanuck's office earned her the title of "the studio hooker." After a series of mediocre films (*Moon Over Miami*, 1941; *My Gal Sal*, 1942), Fox dropped her contract. Though Landis continued to make films (*Four Jills in a Jeep*, 1944; *Having Wonderful Crime*, 1945), by the mid-to-late forties her career in Hollywood was over and she was forced to leave the country to find work.

In 1947, Landis was separated from her fourth husband and was in England filming *The Brass Monkey* when she renewed her acquaintance with Rex Harrison. The suave British actor was married to screen beauty Lilli Palmer (his second wife) and filming *Escape* for director Joseph L. Mankiewicz. The two began a tempestuous air that continued after Landis returned home to Hollywood with Harrison soon arriving in town to star in the aptly titled Preston Sturges comedy *Unfaithfully Yours*. While the affair was little more than a flirtation for Harrison, who had no intention of leaving Palmer, it became an obsession for the 29-year-old actress. Landis covered the walls of her house on Capri Drive in West Los Angeles with photos of Harrison and entertained him there nightly after he finished shooting for the day. Learning of the affair, Palmer and their child removed themselves to New York City. After completing the Sturges film, Harrison informed Landis that he would soon be leaving Hollywood to appear in a

CAROL LANDIS— Known for having the "best legs" in Hollywood, the curvaceous star of such mediocre films as *One Million B.C.* (1940), *Moon Over Miami* (1941), and *Four Jills in a Jeep* (1944) was almost unemployable in the States when she met British actor Rex Harrison in England in 1947. Landis became infatuated with Harrison and papered the walls of her home in West Los Angeles with his photos. The 29-year-old actress downed a lethal dose of Seconal with alcohol there on July 4, 1948, after Harrison informed her that he was going to New York to appear in a Broadway play. Rex Harrison's fourth wife, actress Rachel Roberts, washed barbiturates down with weed killer to end her life on November 27, 1980.

Broadway play. Unable to find film work in the U.S. and forced to put her house on the market, Landis was crushed by Harrison's impending departure.

After Harrison left her home at 9:00 P.M. on July 4, 1948, Landis collected all the personal items (letters, gifts, photos) that documented their intimate relationship, placed them in two small suitcases along with a note to the actor, and left them outside a friend's house where he was staying. Returning to Capri Drive, Landis went into her bedroom, wrote a note in pencil to her mother on monogrammed stationery, propped it among some cologne and perfume bottles, then went into the bathroom off the master bedroom. The next afternoon, Harrison found Landis' lifeless body on the floor. Her cheek rested on a jewel box while her left hand held a satin ribbon upon which the *Lord's Prayer* had been inscribed in gold lettering. On an envelope containing a single sleeping pill found under her right hand Landis had written: "Red — quick — 2 hours. Yellow, about 5. Can take two." An autopsy revealed that her body contained a lethal dose of Seconal and a high alcohol content. The suicide note read: "Dear Mommie — I'm sorry, really sorry, to put you through this, but there is no way to avoid it. I love you, darling, you have been the most wonderful Mom ever and that applies to all our family. I love you [and] each and every one of them dearly. Everything goes to you. Look in the files and there is a will which decrees everything. Goodbye, my angel. Pray for me — Your baby."

Harrison, with Palmer's support, insisted to the press that he and Landis had just been "good friends." On July 10, 1948, both were in attendance at Landis' funeral at the Church of the Recessional at Forest Lawn Memorial Parks in Glendale. Some 1,500 fans and friends filed past the open coffin where the actress lay dressed in her favorite strapless blue chiffon evening dress and clutching a matching blue orchid in her hands. Pallbearers included actors Cesar Romero and Pat O'Brien, her co-star in *Having Wonderful Crime.*

Bishop Fred Pyman's eulogy concluded, "She was a regular trouper and I don't think the Almighty would judge her too harshly." Nearly 32 years later, actress Rachel Roberts (see entry), Rex Harrison's fourth wife, washed down a fatal overdose of barbiturates with weed killer on November 27, 1980.

FURTHER READING

Moseley, Roy. *Rex Harrison: The First Biography.* Kent, England: New English Library, 1987.

Larkin, William

Larkin was an air traffic controller in Bakersfield and Santa Monica, California, in the early fifties when the jokes he occasionally submitted to Steve Allen landed him a full-time job as a gag writer on the comedian's television show. After writing for early television shows like *Mr. Peepers* and *Who Do You Trust?*, Larkin began a long term professional relationship with Bob Hope in 1953. The gag writer traveled with the comedian on his USO tours, scripted many of his specials, and ghostwrote two books of show biz anecdotes credited to Hope: *I Owe Russia $1200* (1963) and *Five Women I Love* (1966). Through Hope, Larkin supplied gags for the political speeches of then President Richard M. Nixon and Vice-President Spiro T. Agnew. Larkin's other television writing included work on *The Tonight Show*, several Academy Awards presentations, and *Archie Bunker's Place*. In failing health and in considerable pain, the 68-year-old veteran gag writer shot himself in the head in a garage next to his Marina Del Rey, California, apartment building on August 3, 1989.

LaSalle, Bob

LaSalle (real name Robert Wagner Hloucal), a disc jockey on radio station WRFD in Worthington, Ohio, took his life in that city on July 14, 1964. A neighbor found the 37-year-old's body on a living room couch in the announcer's home at 1423 Chesterton Square North shortly after 5:50 P.M. Shot once in the

183

forehead with a .45-caliber revolver, he still had the gun clutched in his hand. LaSalle left four notes indicating that he was driven to the act by family troubles.

Lashley, H. T. (Dick)

Known as "Mr. Theatre" to residents of Greenville, South Carolina, Lashley, 57, had seen more than 4,000 movies in a career in theatre management that spanned some 30 years. Lashley came to Greenville in 1930 to manage the Carolina Theatre and the Rivoli. Later, he became the city manager for Greenville Enterprises, a subsidiary of Wilby-Kincy Theaters, operators of the Carolina and Center theatres and the Skyland Drive-in. An early champion of "Sunday" movies, Lashley believed individuals should have a freedom of choice in deciding what to do on the "Lord's Day." On September 15, 1961, a maid found the theatre manager, dead from a .22-caliber rifle shot through the right temple, splayed across the bed in his Greenville home at 713 Crescent Avenue. The weapon lay near him on the bed. Lashley, in ill health for several months, did not leave a note.

Lassen, Elna

Lassen (born August 27, 1901, in Lyngby, Denmark) studied under dancer Valborg Borchsenius at the Royal Theater from 1909 to 1918. The ballerina danced at the Danish Royal Theater from 1918 to 1921 before relocating to the United States to study with Michel Fokine from 1921 to 1924. Returning to Denmark, Lassen scored a triumph as "Swanilda" in *Coppélia*. Her reputation as a strong technician was further assured by technically flawless performances as the "Ballerina" in Fokine's 1925 production of *Petrouchka*, and as the first Danish *Firebird* in 1928. In 1930, stage producer-director Max Reinhardt was so impressed with Lassen during a visit to Denmark that he created a waltz for her in his production of Strauss' *Die Fledermaus*. She performed the piece in Berlin on May 30, 1930, Reinhardt's 25th professional anniversary. On September

19, 1930, the 26-year-old premier *danseuse* of the royal Danish ballet was discovered dead in the bed of her Copenhagen apartment from a self-inflicted pistol wound to the heart. According to press reports, Lassen suffered from diabetes, but was also depressed over her rocky marriage to a medical doctor. Lassen's body was found by the man after he reportedly returned from a night out spent in the company of a Danish countess.

Laszlo, Lola

At 3:20 A.M. on December 16, 1939, the 21-year-old actress-dancer and stepdaughter of Hungarian playwright Aladar Laszlo leaped from the tenth floor window of the Hotel Gladstone in New York City's nightclub district. Earlier, Laszlo had visited the suite to talk to her paramour, German banker Baron Frederick von Oppenheim, who evidently informed her that he was married with three children. Clad in an evening dress and fur cape, Laszlo stepped from the window and fell to her death atop the marquee of the hotel. A note to her lover written in Hungarian read, "I lost my last orchid in you. Farewell." Representatives of the district attorney's office grilled the Baron for five hours, but he could offer no satisfactory explanation of the woman's death.

Laughlin, Leo C.

Recently fired from his post as the manager of the West Coast Mesa Theater in Los Angeles, Laughlin spent the evening of July 3, 1928, drinking whiskey in his home at 3331 West Fifty-fourth Street in the company of the theatre's assistant manager. When he left, the 35 year old waited for a call from his wife in San Francisco that never came. Shortly before midnight, Laughlin shot himself in the head with a .45-caliber revolver.

Lavrova, Vera

In the early evening of July 30, 1926, an unidentified young woman leaped to her death from the 19th floor of the Everglades apartment building on N.E. Biscayne Boulevard and Third Street in Miami, Florida. Moments after the suicide, an electrician found a white beaded handbag and a bag from a department store containing a few feet of electrical wire on the balcony of the second story of the building. A white handkerchief found in the handbag was stamped in red ink with the initials "B.R.G." The next day, Baron Royce-Garrett, a former officer in the Russian Army, was found hiding in a thicket near a rural bridge in the city. The seemingly dazed invalid told police that he was waiting for nightfall in order to join his wife, the Baroness Royce-Garrett, in death. His plans to hang himself from a tree were thwarted when he discovered that none would support his weight.

Days before taking the fatal plunge, the woman, a one-time diva known as Vera Lavrova in the Imperial Russian Opera, told her ailing husband that she could "not work or fight any longer." The couple, firm believers in reincarnation, decided to die together so that they could be reborn into a better world. The baron was enjoying his last day of life at a billiard parlor when he read in the newspaper that his 33-year-old wife had hastily preceded him in death. The baron's account was seemingly backed up by a suicide note found at their residence. Enclosed in an envelope bearing the words "From Us," the note written by Lavrova on a piece of white parchment paper read, "We die happily as we have lived, together. God bless all our friends. The Royce-Garretts."

While Lavrova initially earned $200 a week singing in New York and had planned vaudeville and cabaret engagements, she soon developed throat problems that left her unable to perform. On the advice of doctors, the Royce-Garretts moved to Miami, Florida, to reclaim their health. Financially ruined, the couple decided to die together rather than admit their poverty. Wealthy clubwomen in Coral Gables, Florida, established a burial fund for the opera star who would have been resigned to a potter's field. Lavrova's body was cremated, and on August 4, 1926, funeral services were conducted in the Coral Gables Congregational Church by members of the Coral Gables Theosophical Society.

Lawrence, Eddy

Lawrence, 50, was one of the most popular stage comedians and legitimate actors in San Diego, California, during the twenties. Universally liked and admired by the theatre-going public and his fellow actors, he began to openly speak about ending his life after the death of his wife and his ensuing financial troubles. Shortly before his death on December 5, 1931, the veteran actor again confided to friends that he planned to kill himself, but those with him at the time thought they had successfully dissuaded him. Hours later, police were called to his rooms at a Seventh Avenue hotel in San Diego when an employee smelled gas in the hall. Entering the room, authorities found Lawrence's fully-clothed body across the foot of the bed near a hose attached to an open gas jet. A terse suicide note requested that his body be delivered to the Benbough Mortuary.

Lawrence, Florence

"America's first movie star" was born Florence Annie Bridgwood on January 2, 1886, in Hamilton, Ontario, Canada. The daughter of a carriage builder and stage actress Lotta Lawrence (real name Charlotte Dunn), Lawrence began appearing in song and dance routines with her mother at age 3. Billed as "Baby Flo, the Child Wonder," she started touring as soon as she was old enough to learn lines. In 1907, Lawrence landed the small role of Daniel Boone's daughter in a one-reeler, *Daniel Boone; or, Pioneer Days in America*, shot at the Edison Studios in New York City. That same year she was cast as the female lead in a one-reeler for the Vitagraph Company, *The Shaughbraun*. Lawrence made 12 additional one-reelers for Vitagraph, a company that specialized in literary-type properties, before signing with the Biograph Company in mid–1908. At Biograph, Lawrence refined her acting skills under legendary director D. W. Griffith. In 1908 alone Griffith directed her in 36 one-reelers including *Betrayed by a Handprint*, *The Heart of O Yama*, *Mr. Jones at the Ball*, and *The Test of Friendship*. Also in 1908 Lawrence married Harry Solter, an actor with ambitions to direct, whom she had met at Vitagraph.

By 1909, Lawrence was becoming a recognizable star at Biograph, much to the displeasure of the studios of the day whose heads intentionally avoided publicizing actors out of fear that they would demand higher salaries. Solter and Lawrence were recuperating in Europe from the frantic two-film-a-week pace demanded of them at Biograph when the studio learned that the pair was planning to star in and direct their own films. Biograph summarily fired the couple and had them blacklisted among numerous other studios. In 1909, Lawrence and Solter joined the New York studios of the Independent Moving Pictures Company of America (IMP) (the forerunner of Universal) run by Carl Laemmle, Sr. To capitalize on Lawrence's fame as the former "Biograph Girl," Laemmle created an advertising campaign (the first in Hollywood history) to promote his new star. Thereafter, Lawrence's name was prominently featured in the publicity for her films (another Hollywood first). In 1910, Laemmle's new "IMP Girl — the Girl with the Dimples" starred in 39 short films directed by Solter (*Jane and the Stranger*, *The Eternal Triangle*, *The Irony of Fate*, *Pressed Roses*). That same year, however, Lawrence and Solter (claiming

FLORENCE LAWRENCE — In films since 1907, Lawrence became "America's first movie star" after studio head Carl Laemmle, Sr. began promoting his new star by name (a practice hitherto avoided by the fledging motion picture industry). An accident on the set of *The Pawns of Destiny* in March 1914 signalled the beginning of the end of her film career. After appearing in ever smaller parts in movies, her last credited role was in *The Hard Hombre* in 1931. In 1936, however, MGM placed Lawrence and several other former stars on the payroll as extras. On December 28, 1938, the 52-year-old "Biograph Girl" drank a mixture of cough medicine laced with ant paste in West Hollywood.

work-related exhaustion) broke their contract with IMP, and after some legal wrangling signed with the Sigmund Lubin film company. In 1911, Lawrence made 46 two-reelers directed by her husband for Lubin. Following a European vacation to soothe Lawrence's jangled nerves, the couple formed their own production unit, the New York City-based Victor Company, which shot many of its films in nearby Fort Lee, New Jersey. Between 1912 and 1915, Solter directed Lawrence in more than 40 films shot for the Victor Company and publicized and distributed by their old boss at IMP (then renamed Universal), Carl Laemmle, Sr.

In March 1914 an incident occurred during the filming of *The Pawns of Destiny* that irrevocably changed the life of Florence Lawrence. During the filming of a scene that required the 5 foot, 4 inch, 106 pound actress to carry her 178 pound co-star, Matt Morris, down a flight of stairs being consumed by fire, the actress severely injured her back, possibly fracturing vertebrae. Though contemporaneous news stories also reported that Lawrence sustained disfiguring facial scars in the blaze, there appears to be little evidence to support this myth. However, from November 1914 through April 1916, Lawrence did not work while recuperating from back surgery. By this time, Lawrence's marriage to Harry Solter was all but over, a victim of the director's depression and his wife's unstable temper and questionable mental health. In 1916, Lawrence attempted a comeback in her first full-length feature film, *Elusive Isabel*, directed by Stuart Paton for Universal. The film received lukewarm reviews and rather than risk being fired, the actress quit the studio. Lawrence, at one time a major star, was reduced to taking occasional small parts in films like *The Face on the Screen* (1917) and *The Love Craze* (1918).

Following the death of Harry Solter in 1920, Lawrence moved to Los Angeles and supported herself with stage work while mounting one final stab at a film comeback. In 1922, she starred in *The Unfoldment*, an Associates Exhibitors/Producers Pictures film directed by George Kern and Murdock MacQuarrie. The film's poor distribution combined with lukewarm reviews ended Lawrence's career as a lead. Following *The Unfoldment* the former star could only land sporadic bit parts in films like *The Satin Girl*

(1923), *Gambling Wives* (1924), *The Johnstown Flood* (1926), *The Greater Glory* (1926), and her final credited performance in *The Hard Hombre* (1931). Fortunately, Lawrence did not have to rely solely on film work to survive in Hollywood. Shortly after marrying Charles Bryne Woodring in 1921, the couple opened up Hollywood Cosmetics at 821 Fairfax Avenue, a store that sold Lawrence's own line of beauty products until it closed in 1931. After Lawrence and Woodring divorced in 1932, she hastily remarried a physically abusive alcoholic in 1933. The couple divorced in 1934.

In 1936, Metro-Goldwyn-Mayer, in an uncharacteristic act of charity, placed Lawrence and several other former silent screen stars on the studio payroll at $75 a week. The contract quaranteed the old stars a living wage while offering them first crack at extra and character roles in MGM movies. Lawrence appeared as an uncredited extra in several MGM films from 1936 to 1938 until illness made it impossible for her to continue. In mid–1937, the actress developed a possible case of myelofibrosis, a rare and acutely painful bone disease in which marrow is slowly replaced by collagen fibers.

At around 1:00 P.M. on December 28, 1938, the 52-year-old actress declined a telephone offer from MGM for extra work, telling the studio, "I'm too ill." Shortly afterward, the "Biograph Girl" swallowed a mixture of cough medicine laced with ant paste in the bedroom of her West Hollywood apartment at 532 Westborne Avenue off Melrose. She died an hour later at the Beverly Hills Emergency Hospital. A note found on a bedside table addressed to Bob, a studio employee who lived in the Lawrence house, read: "Call Dr. Nelson. I'm tired. Hope this works. Goodbye, my darlings. They can't cure me, so let it go at that. Lovingly, Florence. P.S. Bob — You've all been swell guys. Everything is yours. Florence Lawrence."

The former star was buried at the Hollywood Memorial (Hollywood Forever) Cemetery in Los Angeles in a modest grave paid for by the Motion Picture Relief Fund.

It lay unmarked and forgotten for more than 50 years until a British actor anonymously bought a bronze marker to commemorate it in 1991. The inscription (which incorrectly cites her birth date) reads, "Florence Lawrence, the Biograph Girl, The First Movie Star, 1890–1938."

FURTHER READING

Brown, Kelly R. *Florence Lawrence, The Biograph Girl: America's First Movie Star.* Jefferson, N.C.: McFarland, 1999.

Lazarus, Sidney

Lazarus, 43, came to Hollywood in 1927 as a scenarist for the Warners' silent *Patent Leather Kid* after enjoying a successful career on Broadway as the author of such plays as *Gabette, Come Along, Mandy,* and *Dixie to Broadway.* On December 2, 1933, the screenwriter and his wife, Maud, decided to end their years of ill health by dying together in a well-planned and touching suicide pact executed in their Beverly Hills home at 522 Palm Drive. The couple wrote and posted a letter to the manager of a Beverly Hills bank asking that he direct the police come to their garage. Later that afternoon they dropped off their dog at a friend's on the pretext that they were going away to a mountain resort for the weekend. Two days passed before the bank manager received the letter and notified police. Inside the garage, authorities found the car running and a rubber hose leading from the exhaust pipe up through the floorboard into the closed compartment. In the back seat, the asphyxiated couple sat side by side — he with with his arm draped tenderly around his wife while her head nestled on his shoulder.

Leavy, Adelaide M.

On November 27, 1931, two out-of-work chorus girls, Leavy, 25, and Jewel Warner, 20, were found lying side by side on a mattress alongside a gas stove with five open jets in the kitchen of their $150-a-month fourth floor apartment at the Parc Vendome at 353 West Fifty-sixth Street in New York City.

The pair, each dressed in silk pajamas, had stuffed the door and windows with paper and wet towels to keep the fumes from escaping into other units in the building. Authorities found an empty quart bottle of whiskey on top of the range and the walls of the three-room apartment plastered with framed photos of movie stars. One week before, the women had informed their maid that they could no longer afford her services. However, in a note from Leavy to her grandmother, the unemployed showgirl left her relative $1,500 in cash and her belongings.

Le Brun, Jean

Days after her married lover, pioneer aviator Leonard Bonney, died while piloting his experimental aircraft, Le Brun, a 35-year-old contralto who appeared in 1921 as the prima donna in *Lena Dailey's Burlesque Show* and later as a singer in Florida cabarets, joined him in death. On May 10, 1928, Le Brun's landlady smelled gas escaping from the singer's apartment on the second floor of a brownstone at 63 West Eighty-eighth Street in New York City. Authorities entered to find an automatic pistol on top of a table in the living room surrounded by live shells and newspaper clippings concerning the dead flier. Unable to disengage the gun's safety, LeBrun opted for gas. Forcing open the locked bathroom door, police discovered Le Brun's body face down on the floor. She had carefully stuffed every opening in the room with paper before opening two gas jets. Four neatly written notes explained the deed. To a brother she wrote: "My suicide is unavoidable. I cannot live any longer.... My sweetheart was killed in an aviation accident Friday and I cannot possibly live without him." Bonney's widow, denying that her husband ever knew Le Brun, asked, "Could you blame Rudolph Valentino, for instance, for all the silly women who killed themselves over him?"

Lee, Harry

Born William Henry Lee in Brooklyn, New York, on June 1, 1872, the future character actor attended Trinity Chapel School, New York, and Princeton University. Ironically, Lee broke into movies in the 1921 Selznick Pictures production *Bucking the Tiger*, a drama about five Klondike derelicts who plan to take out a large life insurance policy and collect the premium after one of them lost in a card game and committed suicide. Lee continued to work steadily onstage and in films (*The Wrongdoers*, 1925; *Sunny Skies*, 1930) until the early thirties when the Hollywood roles dried up. In desperation, the 55-year-old actor leaped from a fire escape of the Roosevelt Hotel at 7006 Hollywood Boulevard on December 8, 1932. His body landed on the roof of the third floor wing of the building. A note to his wife found in the dead man's pocket stated that she "would know the cause of his death."

Lee, Thomas Stewart

The wealthy son of automobile and communications magnate Don Lee, "Tommy" Lee was a pioneer in bringing television to Southern California. In 1931 he built the first transmitter in Los Angeles and later moved it in 1939 to the top of Mt. Lee in the Hollywood Hills. Known today as station KTSL, for years it was known only by its call numbers, W6XAO. In another first, Lee received the initial permit in the Southland for full commercialization of television programs starting July 1, 1941. As the result of a vertebra injury sustained in an automobile accident, Lee was declared mentally incompetent in a medical hearing on August 27, 1948. Ironically, the court-appointed guardian picked to oversee Lee's estimated $9,500,000 estate, Lewis Allen Weiss, a board member of the Don Lee Broadcasting System, would later commit suicide on June 15, 1953 (see entry). Less than a year after being declared incompetent, Lee's petition to terminate his guardianship was denied by a judge who personally interviewed him at a Pasadena sanitarium. On January 13, 1950, Lee flew in his private plane from Palm Springs to Los Angeles for a dental appointment in the Pellissier Building on 3780 Wilshire Boulevard. While his nurse and pilot parked the car, the 43 year old entered the building alone, made his way to the 12th floor, and after smoking part of a cigarette, jumped out of a fire escape window.

Lee, W. Albert

A pillar of the Houston, Texas, business community, Lee built the city's first television station, KLEE, in 1949. In addition to owning seven hotels in the area, the 59-year-old businessman also served as the rodeo and parade chairman of the Houston Fat Stock Show and Livestock Exposition. During his 12 year tenure, Lee was credited with bringing cowboy stars like Gene Autry, Roy Rogers, and William "Hopalong Cassidy" Boyd to Houston. In 1951 Lee began suffering from a nervous ailment that periodically caused his mind to completely black out. Lee's personal physician referred him to a nerve specialist in Galveston, but the businessman never made the appointment. One week later on the morning of November 23, 1951, a pajama-clad Lee shot himself through the heart in the bedroom of his home at 1561 Kirby Drive in the Houston suburb of River Oaks while his wife and workman were in another part of the house.

Leeds, Doris Theresa

Depressed by her recent estrangement from husband Martin Leeds, vice-president of Desilu Productions, the 38-year-old woman died on June 3, 1960, in Hollywood from an overdose of barbiturates in their home at 9451 Sunset Boulevard. Leeds' body, fully clothed and lying across a bed, was found by her 11-year-old son as he was leaving for school.

Lehman, Trent Lawson

As an 8-year-old, Lehman played the role of mischievous "Butch Everett" on the ABC television series *Nanny and the Professor* (1970–1971) starring Richard Long. After the program was cancelled, he made some commercials, but never again landed another television job. By 1982, the 20-year-old former child actor was hooked on drugs and unemployed, but trying to start a career as a cabinet maker. Depressed over the loss of some money in an unreported burglary and a recent breakup with his girlfriend, Lehman showed up on the doorstep of childhood friend, Joseph Allen, in Arleta, California, on January 17, 1982. Lehman asked Allen for a gun, threatened to take his own life, and refused his friend's offer to spend the night in his home, opting instead to sleep in his own van. After Lehman declined to join him for drinks with friends, Allen left him alone. Returning at 1:45 A.M. the next morning, Allen found Lehman hanging from a belt looped through an eight-foot chain-link fence behind the Vena Avenue Elementary School across the street from his home. A note in his pocket declared that he was leaving his possessions to his parents in Colorado Springs, Colorado.

Leigh, Megan

Leigh (born Michelle Maria Schei in Castro Valley, California, on March 2, 1964) danced in clubs in the Bay area, most notably stripping at the Mitchell Brothers' O'Farrell Theater in San Francisco, before entering the adult film business in late 1987 with a role in the triple-X feature *Secrets Behind the Green Door*. Initially adopting the "nom-de-porn" "Carolyn Chambers" (as an homage to porn star Marilyn Chambers), she later changed her stage name to Megan Leigh for billing purposes. Over the next three years, Leigh appeared in nearly 100 hardcore sex films, but despite an athletic body and girl-next-door looks, failed to achieve star status. By 1990 (except for an appearance in *Jail Babes*), the 26-year-old actress had been out of the business for ten months during which time she danced in clubs in New York, San Francisco, and Providence, Rhode Island. On June 16, 1990, Leigh was found dead from a self-inflicted gunshot wound to the head in her residence in Suisun City, California (55 miles east of San Francisco). In a note she alluded to a longstanding personal problem, unrelated to the porn world, that she could not resolve.

Lentz, Irene see *Irene*

Leonard, Harry

For three years 55-year-old film character actor Harry Leonard (*Ramona*, 1916) had longed to marry Anneska Frolik, 24. Shortly after dusk on August 31, 1917, Frolik's 24th birthday, Leonard arrived at her home at 1115½ South El Molino Street in Los Angeles carrying two packages. While waiting for the young woman to return home, Leonard spoke amiably with her sister-in-law and mother. Opening one of the packages to reveal a pile of unpublished screenplays tied with a red ribbon, Leonard declared that they would be valuable properties after the war. The women's patronizing smiles elicited a strange comment from the aging actor, "Ah, you laugh. Tragedy follows in the wake of laughter." Leonard fell into a dejected silence for the rest of the evening until Frolik returned at 9:00 P.M. The women left them alone in the parlor to talk. Whispers in the parlor were interrupted by three pistol shots fired in quick succession. Rushing into the room, Frolik's family saw her (bleeding from two shots to the chest and one in the stomach) grappling with the actor. Leonard produced a pint bottle of steaming sulfuric acid from his coat, tossed it in Frolik's eyes, and in the general direction of the horrified pair, before taking another bottle filled with carbolic acid from his pocket and drinking it. The actor staggered out of the house brandishing the automatic weapon.

He was found shortly afterward and returned to Frolik's home where he indicated two typewritten letters addressed to the girl's father lying near the manuscript before passing out from the pain. Both Anneska Frolik and her aged suitor later died. One of the letters, addressed "Not to be opened under any circumstances while I am in existence," willed the packaged screenplays to Frolik's father.

The other, also written to the man, intimated that while the young woman had once promised to marry him, she had experienced a change of heart. Leonard concluded: "I must show you I cannot live with her in this hell and I will try my best to live with her in Heaven, if there is one. I will take her with me through my act and I hope that you will forgive me. I hope we all will meet over there."

Leslie, Carole

Leslie (born Maureen Rippingale in Chelmsford, England, in 1935) first appeared in the 1947 British film *The Silver Darlings*. The actress was given the leading lady build-up in the late fifties (*These Dangerous Years*, 1957 [U.S. title *Dangerous Youth*]; *Woman in a Dressing Gown*, 1957; *No Trees in the Street*, 1958; *Operation Bullshine*, 1959), but by the sixties was relegated to co-starring in lower-case British films (*Doctor in Love*, 1960, with fellow suicide Virginia Maskell [see entry]; *What a Whopper!*, 1962; *The Pot Carriers*, 1962). On February 28, 1974, the 38-year-old actress took an overdose of barbiturates in her home at New Barnet. Michael Dalling, her film publicist husband, told authorities that Leslie often took anti-depressants. The Hornsey Coroner's Court recorded the death as a suicide.

Leslie, Lulu

Fearful that she would die among strangers and receive a pauper's burial in potter's field, the 75-year-old woman known to fellow boarding house tenants as "Mrs. Eva Smith" was in daily contact with a Staten Island undertaker. Once assured by the firm that she would be buried with her family in Philadelphia, the single woman gassed herself to death in her two-room basement apartment at 139 W. 101st Street in New York City on September 27, 1929. "Mrs. Smith" was found lying on the floor of her kitchen near a gas jet with one of its three jets wide open. A canvas bag strapped around her waist contained $720 in new bills. A letter from the Staten Island

funeral home confirming her burial plans was found atop one of several trunks filled with tattered costumes, press clippings, and handbills identifying the gas victim as former burlesque and vaudeville queen Lulu Leslie who, 50 years earlier, had danced in the musical extravaganzas *The Black Crook* and *King Cole the Second*, and with Billy Watson's *Beef Trust*.

Lessey, May Abbey

The 80-year-old widow of actor George Lessey had been in ill health for some time when she either jumped or fell from the window of her fourth floor apartment at 25 Tudor City Place in New York City on August 20, 1952. The former actress had appeared in the Broadway musicals *Anything Goes* (1934) and *Red, Hot and Blue* (1936), and for eight years was the president of the Professional Women's League, one of the oldest theatrical organizations for women in the country.

Levine, Hendrick

Badly crippled in a car accident two months earlier, the 44-year-old acrobat was no longer able to perform his part in the vaudeville act "The Levines," in which he co-billed with his wife, Elsie. Bookings dried up even though she continued to work as a single. On January 10, 1929, Elsie returned from a matinee performance in Chicago to their room at 123 West Ohio Street to discover that her husband had hanged himself. The note he left read: "Dear Wife Elsie: It is impossible to live any longer. I am very sorry. I am absolutely no good. Please forgive me.—Your loving husband."

Levitt, Robert D.

In December 1941, Levitt married musical comedy star Ethel Merman (her second marriage, his first) and after the war became eastern director of publicity for David O. Selznick's motion picture interests. He left Selznick to join the Hearst newspaper organization where he worked in a variety of executive positions before going to Columbia Screen Gems as director of national sales in the fifties. In 1952, Merman obtained a mutual-consent Mexican "quickie" divorce. He remarried that same year, but it too ended in divorce after four years. Levitt became president of California National Productions, Inc., a television film producing subsidiary of the National Broadcasting Company, but resigned on December 5, 1957, following a policy dispute with his superiors. On January 27, 1958, the 47-year-old former television executive's body was found by a maid in his country home in East Hampton, Long Island, New York. Levitt was lying, fully clothed, on a couch in the den on the second floor, his head resting on a folded topcoat. A note adressed "To Whom it May Concern" indicated that he had taken a massive overdose of barbiturates. Twenty bottles containing drugs and sleeping pills were found in the house. Levitt's short suicide note also directed the disposition of his estate.

FURTHER READING

Merman, Ethel, and Eells, George. *Merman.* New York: Simon and Schuster, 1978.

Levy, Adolph

Scheduled later in the day to appear at the Old Bailey to answer a charge of making a false statement in connection with his 1929 divorce, the 45-year-old film agent was found dead from gas poisoning on March 24, 1931, in a locked room in an apartment house in Oxford-Terrace, Hyde Park, W., in London where he was lodging under the name "Martin."

Levy, Raoul J.

Born in Antwerp, Belgium, on March 14, 1922, the producer-director who launched the meteoric career of Brigitte Bardot served as a pilot with the Royal Air Force during WWII before embarking on his own film career as a production assistant for his uncle at RKO on Mexican films after the war. Returning to Europe as a representative for an American producer, Levy formed his own production company in France in 1950. After a few undistinguished films, Levy produced *Et Dieu Créa la Femme* (*And God Created Woman*) in 1956, which unleashed sex kitten Brigitte Bardot and director Roger Vadim on the international film scene. Levy used the film's popularity to establish himself as the only French film producer to occupy a position in the industry comparable with that of major Hollywood producers. In 1962, Levy's attempt to make a big-budget Hollywood-type spectacular on the life of Marco Polo ended in financial ruin. The film, *La Fabuleuse Aventure de Marco Polo* (*Marco the Magnificent*), was eventually completed by another director and production company in 1965. Levy bounced back as a small independent producer-director and made Montgomery Clift's final movie, *The Defector*, in 1966.

On December 31, 1966, in the resort town of Saint-Tropez, the jilted 44 year old shot himself in the stomach with a rifle before the door of his 24-year-old girlfriend, script girl and textile heiress Isabelle Lons. He died before arriving at the hospital. Levy had attempted suicide with sleeping pills years earlier, but was saved when his secretary found him in his office.

Lewis, Gordon

Obsessed with the notion that someone was trying to kill him, the World War I veteran and Warner Bros. character actor walked into the middle of the Oracle Road in Tucson, Arizona, on March 17, 1933, turned to face his father's service station, and armed with a .38-caliber revolver borrowed minutes before from a nearby garage, fatally shot himself in the temple. Lewis, 43, reportedly had been ill since returning from California a few days prior to the suicide.

Lewis, Ronald

Born in Aberystwyth, Wales, on December 11, 1927, the veteran actor divided his career between stage and film work. In 1953, he made his film debut in the Ealing boxing film *The Square Ring*, recreating the part of "Eddie Lloyd," which he had played onstage at the Lyric, Hammersmith. Placed under contract by Sir Alexander Korda's London Films, Lewis became a well-known supporting character actor in several British films of the fifties and sixties including *The Prisoner* (1955), *The Wind Cannot Read* (1958), *Taste of Fear* (1961), *Billy Budd* (1962), *Mr. Sardonicus* (1963), and *The Brigand of Kandahar* (1965). Working little since appearing in the 1976 film *Anonymous Letters*, Lewis declared bankruptcy in 1980 with debts of £21,188. On January 11, 1982, the 53-year-old actor was found dead in a London boarding house with empty pill bottles and whiskey beside him. At the coroner's inquest, Lewis' brother testified that the actor was having financial difficulties and living on Social Security.

Lewis, Thurston Theodore

One day after slashing both wrists in the bathroom of his home at 310 South Massey Street in Watertown, New York, the 56-year-old cornetist died at Mercy Hospital on April 17, 1941. A musical prodigy, Lewis became a member of B. A. Rolfe's orchestra and in 1916 joined the Barnum & Bailey circus as assistant leader of the tent show's band. For 15 seasons, until 1931, Lewis served as musical director and manager of C. B. Maddock's musical acts on the B. F. Keith vaudeville circuit. While on the circuit, the musician scored a hit in the musical act "Rubeville," later recreating his role on film in a Pathé Studios short. Returning to his hometown of Watertown, New York, in 1931, Lewis became the director of both the high and junior high school bands. According to his surviving wife, Lewis had long been ill with a liver ailment.

Liddy, Lewis W.

Identified in press reports as a "screenwriter" and magazine editor, Liddy shot himself (after first taking a practice shot at the wall) on November 7, 1932, in his room at an apartment house located at 1109 Ingraham Street in Los Angeles. Friends reported that the 50-year-old writer was driven to the act by ill health.

Linder, Max

Born Gabriel-Maximilien Leuvielle on December 16, 1882 (some sources say 1883), in Caverne in the Bordeaux region of France, Linder was a true *auteur* who either wrote, produced, or directed many of the 150-plus feature films and shorts he appeared in during a 20 year film career extending from 1905 to 1925. Charlie Chaplin, whose career would surpass Linder's, referred to his colleague as "the Professor" and proudly considered himself to be among his disciples.

While Linder's wealthy parents expected him to one day manage their vineyards, his fascination with travelling shows and circuses led him to pursue an acting career. In 1899 he attended the famed Bordeaux Conservatoire where he won acting prizes for comedy and drama. Signing a contract with the Bordeaux Théâtre des Arts, Linder spent the next three years acting in the classic works of Moliere, Musset, and Corneille. A friendship with M. le Bargy of the Comédie-Française in the early 1900s led ultimately to roles in popular comic theatres like the Théâtre de l'Ambigu and the Olympia. Around this time he began calling himself Max Linder. In 1905, though still appearing in the Paris music halls at night, Linder spent his days acting in numerous Pathé studio shorts. Two years later, Linder introduced his comedic screen persona, a suave character in evening dress in a constant state of befuddlement, in director Louis Gasnier's *Les débuts d'un patineur* (*The Skater's Debut*). After the success of the film and subsequent shorts, the character was officially named "Max." The "Max" films, many co-written by Linder, made the actor an international star.

By May 1911, Linder was taking total control over his films as well as performing live in Europe for astronomical sums. In 1912, his $1 million franc income made him the

MAX LINDER—Although Charlie Chaplin considered himself a disciple of the French silent screen comic, Linder never achieved the level of artistic and commercial success in America realized by the "little tramp." After failing to find an audience in the States, a depressed Linder entered into a suicide pact with his wife. On October 31, 1925, the pair were found together near death in a Paris hotel room.

highest paid actor in the world. Declared unfit for military duty at the outbreak of World War I, Linder delivered dispatches between Paris and the front until forced out of the war by pneumonia. In the summer of 1916, George K. Spoor, president of the Essanay Company, lured Linder away from Pathé with an offer of $5,000 a week to make 12 three-reelers in Chicago. Brought in to replace Charlie Chaplin (who left the studio to work for Mutual), the filmmaker made three films in 1917: *Max Comes Across*, *Max Wants a Divorce*, and *Max and His Taxi*. Reception to the films was lukewarm at best, leading Spoor to cancel Linder's contract. Deeply depressed over the war and his failure in the States, the filmmaker established his own production company in Hollywood in 1921. However, the films *Seven Years Bad Luck* (1921), *Be My Wife* (1921), and *The Three Must-Get-Theres* (1922) all failed to make money.

Convinced that he was no longer funny and supremely aware that he would never achieve Chaplin's popularity, Linder returned to Europe where he made his last film, *Der Zirkuskönig* (*The King of the Circus*), in Vienna in 1925. As the film comic's depression deepened he spoke openly of suicide. In mid–1925 he purchased a revolver, but the weapon was instantly confiscated by a friend. Shortly afterward, Linder and his 21-year-old wife, the former Helene Peters, attended a performance of *Quo Vadis*. The show featured a scene in which some characters committed suicide by bleeding themselves to death. In a Paris hotel room at 88 bis Avenue Kléber near the Bois de Boulogne on October 31, 1925, the 41-year-old filmmaker with wife Helene consummated a suicide pact. After informing the hotel's porter that they were not to be disturbed, Linder and Helene drank large quantities of veronal, repeatedly injected themselves with morphine, then lay on the bed together and slit their wrists with a razor. The unconscious pair was discovered hours later after Helene's mother convinced hotel officials to force open the locked door of their room. Helene lingered for seven hours at a Paris hos-

pital before dying. Linder expired shortly after midnight. Both left suicide letters. After the couple's death it was revealed that in February 1924 the pair had been found together unconscious in a hotel room in Vienna. At the time, Linder dismissed the incident as an accidental overdose of a sleeping draught they often took.

FURTHER READING

Bottomore, Stephen. "Max Linder." In *World Film Directors: Volume I: 1890–1945*. Ed. by John Wakeman. New York: H. W. Wilson, 1987. pp. 671–677.

Lindsey, Ouida

Long active in Chicago's black community, Lindsey was an assistant dean at Columbia College and host of a Saturday morning television program, *Soul Searching*, on WFLD, Channel 32. With husband Paul in 1974, she published the book *Breaking the Bonds of Racism*, and from 1971 to 1978 contributed a column on the black experience, "For Real," for *The Chicago Sun-Times*." On August 6, 1981, Paul Lindsey contacted police after his wife phoned him at work threatening suicide. Police arrived at the Lindsey home at 7119 S. Luella Avenue on the city's South Side to find the 53-year-old woman lying on a basement sofa with a .38-caliber revolver nearby and a bullet wound in the head. A suicide note was found in the dining room. Paul Lindsey told authorities that his wife had been despondent over family problems.

Linkletter, Diane

Almost 25 years before actor Carroll O'-Connor's son, Hugh (see entry), took his life while under the influence of cocaine, television personality Art Linkletter lost his daughter to drugs at the height of the LSD craze in the late sixties. The youngest daughter of the popular *House Party* host was born on October 31, 1948. An aspiring actress, Linkletter had guest hosted on her father's show, but had done little else professionally. In 1969, the

DIANE LINKLETTER—While under the influence of LSD on October 5, 1969, Diane Linkletter, the 20-year-old daughter of television personality Art Linkletter, jumped from her sixth floor apartment at the Shoreham Towers, 8787 Shoreham Drive, in West Hollywood. Following her death, Art Linkletter became a vocal critic of drugs and people like Dr. Timothy Leary who advocated their use. *Photo 2000 by Jana Wells.*

20 year old was living in a 6th floor apartment at the Shoreham Towers at 8787 Shoreham Drive in West Hollywood, California. Linkletter ran with a fast Hollywood crowd and began experimenting with the mind-altering drug LSD then being promoted by counterculture guru Timothy Leary. According to Art Linkletter, he spoke candidly with Diane about her drug use six months prior to her death. She told her father that she used LSD to help cope with personal and professional problems. Though terrified of its effects, Diane told him that she was unable to stop using the drug.

In the late evening of October 4, 1969, Linkletter was on a bad LSD trip. Frightened, she phoned her boyfriend, Edward Durston, and asked him to come to her apartment at the Shoreham Towers. Durston, 27, arrived at 3:00 A.M. the following morning to find Linkletter despondent and depressed over her career and inability "to be her own person." Despite talking with her for hours, Durston was unable to calm Linkletter. In desperation, Linkletter phoned her brother Robert (father Art and mother Lois were away in Colorado) shortly before 9:00 A.M. at his Hollywood apartment to report that she had taken an overdose of LSD and was uncontrollably afraid. Robert told her to relax, that the drug would wear off, and that he would be right over. He spoke briefly with Durston who assured him that he would watch over her until he arrived.

Diane Linkletter was apparently calmer after hanging up the phone, but then suddenly dashed to the open kitchen window and climbed on top of the counter to jump. Durston managed to grab the belt loops of her dress as she fell from the sixth floor window, but the fabric tore loose in his hands. Suffering from massive contusions and multiple fractures, Linkletter was initially taken by ambulance to the Hollywood Receiving Hospital, but was immediately transferred to the County-USC Medical Center after the extent of her injuries had been assessed. She died there at 10:30 A.M. Linkletter was buried on October 7, 1969, at Forest Lawn Memorial Park in Hollywood under a simple flat marker inscribed with her name, year of birth and death, and the inscription "Darling, we loved you so much."

Following the death of his daughter, Art Linkletter became an outspoken critic of drugs and the people who advocated them. Of Diane's death, Linkletter remarked: "It wasn't suicide because she wasn't herself. It was murder. She was murdered by the people who manufacture and sell LSD.... I want her death to be a warning to the kids of this country that LSD can kill."

FURTHER READING

Linkletter, Art. *Hobo on the Way to Heaven*. 1st ed. Elgin, Ill.: D. C. Cook Pub. Co., 1980.

Little, "Little" Jack

Little (born John James Leonard in London, England, on May 28, 1900) came to the United States at an early age. Studying premed at the University of Iowa, he organized the university band before dropping out of school to form his own travelling big band. Throughout the twenties, Little toured the country fronting his own dance band at hotels, night clubs, and resorts. In the thirties, Little perfected a piano playing technique and intimate microphone hugging style of singing that would later set the stage for other "relaxed" crooners like Bing Crosby and Perry Como. On his 15 minute radio program (broadcast for many years on a nation-wide hook-up from Cincinnati), Little introduced his songs in a soft, whispering voice while executing a series of arpeggios on the piano. This "intimate personality technique" combined with his diminutive size earned him the radio nickname the "Cheerful Little Earful."

Little also composed and introduced many popular tunes of the day including "Jealous" (1924), "Ting-a-Ling" (a.k.a. "The Waltz of Bells") (1926), "In a Shanty in Old Shanty Town" (1932), "I Wouldn't Trade the Silver in My Mother's Hair (for All the Gold in the World)" (1932), "Hold Me," (1933), and "You're a Heavenly Thing" (1935). Several of his compositions were used in films: "Jealous" (*The Feminine Touch*, MGM, 1941; *Crazy House*, Universal, 1943; *Somebody Loves Me*, Paramount, 1952), "In a Shanty in Old Shanty Town" (*Roaring Twenties*, Warner Bros., 1939; *Lullaby of Broadway*, Warner Bros., 1951), "Hold Me" (*Peg O' My Heart*, MGM, 1933; *Three Faces of Eve*, 20th Century–Fox, 1957). At the end of the big band era, Little set a trend among former band leaders by forming a trio and performing in nightclubs, cafes, and cocktail lounges.

On April 9, 1956, the 55-year-old performer swallowed a lethal dose of sleeping pills in the bedroom of his home at 2549 Washington Street in Hollywood, Florida. Acquaintances told police that Little had recently been depressed over a lengthy bout with hepatitis and other ailments.

Livingston, Charlotte

A self-described screenwriter who was being treated for a broken right arm at Harbor Sanitarium, a private hospital in New York City, Livingston jumped to her death from the ninth floor window of her room on May 1, 1934. Earlier in the evening, Livingston, 35, had asked a nurse for a pencil and some paper. A note found in her room addressed to "Gertrude and Pete" asked for forgiveness and added: "No funeral please. Turn my body over to the medical examiner at Bellevue." Livingston was later identified as the former wife of Louis Livingston, a member of a prominent New York State family.

Llewellyn, Jacqueline

Described in press reports as a "former movie actress," the 25 year old was living in a San Francisco apartment house at 1103 Ellis Street with Russell Ransom, 20, a man whom she had met two months earlier in Long Beach, California, while her husband was away in Juarez, Mexico. On November 7, 1922, the destitute pair pawned one of

Llewellyn's rings and were returning to their apartment when the actress told Ransom she had just seen a man she feared would try to separate them. Upon retiring that night, Ransom placed a pistol under the pillow. Early the next morning, he was awakened by a shot. According to Ransom, the actress shot herself in the chest and then requested a paper and pencil with which to scribble the note, "I did," designed to exonerate him from any blame. Despite Ransom's last minute blood donation, Llewellyn died hours later on the operating table of the Central Emergency Hospital after issuing a dying statement further exonerating her lover of any involvement.

Loeb, Philip

Loeb (born in Philadelphia, Pennsylvania, in 1894) began his acting career in the early twenties through his association with New York City Theatre Guild productions like *Merchants of Glory* (1925), *Processional* (1925), *Juarez and Maximilian* (1926), *Ned McCobb's Daughter* (1926), *Merry-Go-Round* (1927), and *Right You Are* (1927). In 1934, Loeb joined Actors' Equity, becoming a member of the union's Executive Committee in 1937. As leader of the union's liberal faction, he was frequently accused of having Communist leanings due largely to his advocacy of controversial proposals like paid rehearsals for actors and the elimination of separate salary scales for junior members. The allegation was serious enough that in 1940 Loeb told congressional committee member Representative William P. Lambertson of Kansas: "I am not a Communist, Communist sympathizer or fellow-traveller and I have nothing to fear from an impartial inquiry."

Though primarily a stage actor prominent in character roles in the forties, Loeb also appeared in films including *The Mild West* (1933), the 1938 Marx Brothers comedy *Room Service*, *A Double Life* (1938), and *Molly* (1951), the movie version of the popular radio, and later, television program, *The Goldbergs*. Known on radio as *The Rise of the Goldbergs*, the long running show (1929–1945) was the brainchild of Gertrude Berg, who played "Molly Goldberg" in the series inspired by New York Jewish immigrants living on the Lower East Side. When *The Goldbergs* moved to CBS television in January 1949, Berg signed Loeb to play her husband, "Jake Goldberg," in the series. By 1951, however, Loeb's support of liberal causes within Actors' Equity had led to his blacklisting in the entertainment industry. Despite declaring under oath before a closed door session of the Senate Internal Security Committee that he was not, nor had ever been, a member of the Communist Party, Loeb was dropped from *The Goldbergs* over Berg's objection in 1951 by nervous executives of CBS and General Foods, the show's sponsor. Gertrude Berg reportedly paid her friend an $85,000 settlement after he was forced to leave the program. In January 1952, Loeb was attacked in *Red Channels*, an anti–Communist booklet designed by its publisher to expose "Reds." Effectively blacklisted, the "controversial" Loeb managed to find only occasional acting assignments.

Increasingly bitter and depressed, the 61-year-old actor registered as "Fred Lang" at the Taft Hotel in New York City on August 31, 1955. The next morning, September 1, a maid noticed a "Do Not Disturb" sign hanging from the door of Room 507. When she returned an hour later to clean the room, no one answered her repeated knocks on the door. The maid summoned the assistant manager who entered the room with a passkey. Loeb's pajama-clad body was found in bed. A bottle containing 14 sleeping pills was on a dresser next to a physician's prescription for 50 pills dated two days before.

Long, Ray

Long (born in Lebanon, Indiana, on March 23, 1878) worked on various Midwest newspapers before becoming editor-in-chief of *Cosmopolitan* in 1919. He retired from that position in 1931 and relocated to Hollywood where the next year he worked briefly on the

editorial board at Columbia studio and as a story scout for Fox. Leaving the studios, Long served as the editor of *Photoplay* and *Shadowplay* before transferring to a story scouting job on *Liberty* magazine. On July 9, 1935, the 53 year old complained of feeling ill and passed the day alone clad in silk pajamas in the bedroom of his home at 601 Camden Drive in Beverly Hills. Shortly after 6:00 P.M., Long sat on the edge of his bed, placed a shotgun between his knees, closed his mouth on the barrel, and shot himself. He died without regaining consciousness in the Beverly Hills Emergency Hospital.

Long Lance

In 1928 Chief Buffalo Child Long Lance published his autobiography, *Long Lance*, in which he colorfully recounted his childhood among the Blackfoot Indians of the Western Plains. The book received excellent reviews and made the former Wild West show performer and Carlisle Indian School graduate the most famous Native American of his day. Long Lance was so popular that he was signed to play the role of "Baluk, mighty hunter" of the Ojibwa tribe in the 1930 Paramount distributed film *The Silent Enemy*. Shot largely on the Temagamai Forest Reserve in northern Ontario, the film portrayed the Indians of Northern Canada before the coming of the white man. The film's success prompted the B. F. Goodrich Rubber Company to hire Long Lance, a former member of Olympic great Jim Thorpe's football team at Carlisle, to design a running shoe patterned on his mocassins.

At around 2:45 A.M. on Sunday, March 20, 1932, the 36-year-old actor-writer arrived drunk at the Los Angeles mansion of Anita Baldwin, a multi-millionaire friend. According to Baldwin, Long Lance seemed depressed and withdrawn as she tried to talk with him in the downstairs library. She soon left her uncommunicative friend alone in the library and retired to her bedroom upstairs. Moments later she heard a gunshot. Long Lance was found slumped on a leather settee by the library table bleeding profusely from a gaping wound in his head, his right hand still clutching a .45-caliber pistol. The noted Indian was buried on March 30, 1932 by members of the British Benevolent Society in the British Empire War Veterans' section of the Inglewood Cemetery in Los Angeles.

At the time the popular celebrity's suicide was inexplicable. Almost 50 years after his death, however, it was revealed that the Native American "Long Lance" was in reality Sylvester Clark Long, a black man born on December 1, 1890, in Winston-Salem, North Carolina. Long's father was black while his mother was apparently one-eighth Croatan Indian (which perhaps accounted for his high cheekbones and straight black hair). Fascinated by Indians and the West from an early age, Long was 13 when he joined a Wild West show. Away from his hometown, Long realized that he could "pass" for an Indian and escape being treated as "colored." Posing as a Cherokee, Long attended the prestigious Carlisle Indian School in Pennsylvania and upon graduation in 1912 changed his name to Sylvester Long Lance. Long attended St. John's Military School in Manilius, New York, for three years on scholarship before enlisting in the Canadian Army in 1916 to fight in World War I. Wounded in combat in 1917, he was discharged in 1919 and afterward worked as a reporter on several Canadian newspapers. Long's articles on the Indians of western Canada were regularly featured in top American magazines like *McClures, Cosmopolitan,* and *Good Housekeeping.* In 1922 he was formally adopted by the Blood Indians (members of the Blackfoot Confederacy) of southern Alberta and began using the name they gave him, Buffalo Child. Book and movie fame soon followed. Today, the suicide of "Long Lance" is attributed to what biographer Donald B. Smith called the man's inability "to resolve his inner conflict of being a black man masquerading as an Indian in a white man's world…."

FURTHER READING

Smith, Donald B. *Long Lance: The True Story of an Impostor.* Toronto, Canada: Macmillan of Canada, 1982.

Lorimer, Wright

After an unsuccessful career as a Baptist pastor in Watervliet, New York, Lorimer (real name Walter M. S. Lowell) began acting at the age of 25 in stock theatre in Chicago in 1899. Five years later he starred in a play he had written, *The Shepherd King,* when it opened on April 5, 1904, at the Knickerbocker Theatre in New York City. It ran for three seasons after which Lorimer performed in Henrik Ibsen's *The Wild Duck* and other plays. In March 1911, the 37-year-old actor filed a $48,400 lawsuit against theatrical manager William A. Brady for cancelling a contract that would have put *The Shepherd King* back on the stage. While waiting for the suit to come to trial, Lorimer worked sporadically as an actor, last appearing in a short-lived vaudeville sketch titled "The Crucifix."

Lorimer had been unemployed for four months when depression caused him to take his own life in his room at a boarding house on 124 West Sixty-fifth Street in New York City sometime between 10:00 P.M. on December 7 and the early morning of December 8, 1911. The lifeless actor was found on the kitchen floor next to the open baking oven in a seeping gas stove. Three letters were found near his body. In one addressed "To My Friends," Lorimer complained that Brady had driven him to suicide. Reacting to the actor's death, the theatrical manager surrendered all interests in *The Shepherd King* to Lorimer's ex-wife and her three children by the actor.

Lothrop, William H.

On May 2, 1913, moments before the curtain at the Boston Theatre was lifted on the first act of *The Round-Up,* the theatre's 38-year-old treasurer and assistant manager chatted amiably with a cast member. Lothrop retired to his office on the second balcony floor and soon afterward a shot rang out. He was found on a couch clutching a revolver in his left hand and bleeding profusely from a gunshot wound to the head. Lothrop died at Boston's Relief Hospital a half hour later without recognizing his wife of a year at his bedside. Shortly before shooting himself, Lothrop had phoned her and their conversation had sufficiently worried the woman to leave for the theatre. While no reason was publicly stated for the suicide, Lothrop's brother added an element of mystery to the affair when he stated that the man suffered from a paralysis of the left side that made it impossible for him to have committed the deed with his left hand.

Love, Robert

Known as a set designer under his real name, Abraham Levine, Love, 34, was a bit player in several films including the 1938 Norman Foster vehicle *I Cover Chinatown* in which he played an unnamed cop. According to his roommate, Daniel Harris, Love had been brooding for days over the suicide of actress Carole Landis (see entry), whom he had never met. On the morning of July 8, 1948, Harris entered the kitchen of the home he shared with Love at 1737 North Whitley Avenue in Los Angeles to find his roommate standing with his head over an open gas jet. When Harris turned off the gas, Love displayed a razor blade and, pointing to a minor cut on his neck, said: "This was too painful — I couldn't do it that way." Later that day, Harris took Love to visit a doctor with an office on the third floor of the Guaranty Building in downtown Hollywood. While waiting, Love suddenly jumped up (cutting his finger on a piece of overturned furniture) then ran up two flights of stairs to the fifth floor office of another doctor. According to the receptionist there, the actor muttered, "I'm brave, I'm brave, I can stand it," as he pushed through the crowded waiting room and dove through a half-opened window facing Ivar Street just off Hollywood Boulevard.

Lowers, Helen

Lowers, an 18-year-old chorister with a stock burlesque company appearing at the Palace Theatre in Buffalo, New York, was found on December 28, 1936, in an alley three stories below the open window of the Theatre Hotel room where she was staying. Earlier in the evening, the Greenville, Ohio, native had been drinking with a stagehand at the theatre before returning to the room she shared with another chorus girl. According to her roommate, Lowers "always became moody when she took a few drinks."

Lubetkin, Steven Roland

At 6:00 P.M. on June 1, 1979, the 30-year-old comedian jumped from the roof of the 14 floor Continental Hyatt House to his death on a concrete ramp leading to the Comedy Store parking lot on Hollywood's famed Sunset Boulevard. Lubetkin's suicide was the culmination of a career blighted by bad luck and self-doubt.

Born in Greenwich Village, Lubetkin regularly shared the bill at the Improv with best friend and fellow comedian Richard Lewis. Lubetkin was scheduled for a spot on *The Jack Paar Show* during its unsuccessful revival, when the program was cancelled before his appearance. In 1973, he moved to Los Angeles and struck up a close friendship with Mitzi Shore, owner of the Comedy Store and mother of comedian Pauly Shore. Months later he landed a spot on a Dean Martin comedy special, but his segment of the show was preempted by a news bulletin about President Nixon's trip to China. Lubetkin's biggest break came when he passed an audition for *The Tonight Show*, but after a pair of the show's talent scouts saw him working out new material in a club, they cancelled his appearance. Lubetkin quit performing, scraped together $15,000, and spent the next 18 months writing, starring in, producing, and directing the full-length movie *Dante Shocko*. The film was never released. Lubetkin became a semi-regular in comedy clubs throughout the Los Angeles area, but his career hit the skids after he became a leader in "CFC," Comedians for Compensation, a group of striking performers who sought payment for playing the

Comedy Store. Blackballed at the club, Lubetkin earned only $1,000 in the last 12 months of his life.

Weeks before his fatal plunge, the comedian became delusional, telling a former lover that he could see faces on blank sheets of paper and in rug patterns. In a crumpled note found on his body addressed to Richard Lewis, his family, and members of the CFC, Lubetkin wrote: "My name is Steve Lubetkin…. I used to work at the Comedy Store. Maybe this will help to bring about fairness. No revenge please. All my love." At a CFC memorial service for Lubetkin, Lewis summed up a prevailing show business sentiment when he tearfully said, "The business, by and large, is made up of wallets, not hearts."

Luciano, Ron

From 1968 to 1979 this American League umpire redefined the role of "the man in black" from that of an unobtrusive presence to that of a flashy showman who went about his work with theatrical flair and animation. The 6 foot, 4 inch, 300 pound former football lineman at Syracuse never backed down from on-field confrontations, and his chest-to-chest battles with fiery former Baltimore Orioles manager Earl Weaver were the stuff of baseball legend. In 1975 Luciano once ejected Weaver from both ends of a doubleheader. Retiring in 1980, the former ump worked as a sports commentator for NBC and co-authored with David Fisher several popular books of humorous baseball anecdotes: *The Umpire Strikes Back* (1982), *Strike Two* (1984), *The Fall of the Roman Umpire* (1986), *Remembrance of Swings Past* (1988), and *Baseball Lite* (1990).

On January 18, 1995, the 57-year-old Luciano was found dead from carbon monoxide poisoning in the garage of his home in Endicott, New York. While Weaver expressed sympathy for the dead man's family, Luciano's death did not alter the former manager's opinion about his umpiring: "He was a good minor league umpire. When he got to the major leagues, he lost his desire. I don't think he wanted to be there. I think he was looking for greener fields. He became a clown in the American League."

Ludwig, Charles "Zaza"

Born May 9, 1898, in Manchester, New Hampshire, Ludwig was one of the top dance band leaders in northern New England. On February 28, 1950, the musician's body was found hanging from a rafter in a barn adjacent to his house at 193 Massabesic Street in Manchester. Ludwig, 51, had been ill for the past two weeks.

Luftig, Charles "Chuck"

Until two months before inexplicably resigning his position, Luftig, the former personal manager for Red Skelton, had been a greeter at the MGM Grand in Las Vegas. In that capacity, the popular casino host was intimately acquainted with the nation's top gamblers, law enforcement officials, politicians, and show business personalities. In the mid-afternoon of August 22, 1975, a cleaning woman found Luftig's body, dressed in a silk bathrobe, on a couch in his Las Vegas apartment on Sands Road. He had been dead for some 24 to 36 hours. Several empty barbiturate vials were found on a coffee table adjacent to the couch along with a handwritten note indicating that he planned to kill himself.

Lygo, Mary

Lygo (born Irene Goodall in Akron, Ohio) joined the *Ziegfeld Follies* in 1918, and later worked for producers Simeon and Morris Gest in the New York stage production of *The Wanderer*. Madly in love with Chicago millionaire Gordon Thorne, son of one of the founders of Montgomery Ward & Company, Lygo wanted to marry the man, but was blocked by Thorne's mother who strongly disapproved of her. After the breakup, Lygo twice attempted to take her life. In May 1921 she slashed her wrists with a razor at the home of her plastic surgeon, and in 1922 she lay in a coma for a week after ingesting poison. One year later, Lygo filed a $100,000 breach of promise suit against Thorne, which was quietly settled out of court for $8,000.

In January 1927, Lygo travelled to the West Coast to play a nun in the Gest production of the *Miracle Play*. Hoping to break into films in Los Angeles, she took the name "Irene Fuller" to avoid any negative connotations associated with her true stage name. On May 31, 1927, "Fuller" was found unconscious by her roommate on the floor of their room in the Vivian Apartments at 637 North Bronson Avenue. A half-empty bottle of veronal tablets was found at the scene along with notes singed by "Fuller" in which she disposed of her possessions, requested that her mother not be told, and warned: "Be most careful as to the name 'M.L.' as it means so much to the press." Lygo's identity was subsequently established by a fellow actor who visited the comatose woman at the Receiving Hospital. Conjecture raged as to the reason for the act. Some ascribed the deed to her broken love affair with Thorne while others noted that she was despondent about not quickly breaking into films. The 25 year old died in the Receiving Hospital on June 2, 1927. A steamer trunk found after her death contained several tattered theatrical dresses and five pawn tickets.

McClelland, George F.

The former executive vice-president of the National Broadcasting Company left the radio giant in November 1933 to form a new radio chain, Broadcasting Stations Corporation, with an eye toward competing with NBC and CBS. On October 12, 1934, a cleaning woman entered McClelland's office at the BSC at 21 East Fortieth Street in New York City and found the 39-year-old businessman slumped over his desk with a pistol clutched in his hand. A bullet had passed through his head and stuck into the wall of the office. A blood-smeared note written in pencil to his secretary cited business troubles as the reason for the suicide.

McCoy, Charles "Kid"

McCoy, considered one of the greatest prizefighters in history and generally regarded as the inspiration for the term "the real McCoy," was born Norman Selby on a family farm in Moscow, Indiana, a small community 40 miles southeast of Indianapolis, on October 13, 1873. While much of McCoy's life is bound up in self-created fiction, he did run away from home in his mid-teens to become a hobo. He began his professional boxing career in Louisville, Kentucky, in 1890. By 1891, the fighter had dropped the sissy sounding name of Selby in favor of McCoy, the stage name of a ham actor he had once seen perform. According to legend, "the real McCoy" catch phrase was used both to distinguish him from other like-named pugilists and in recognition of his authentic boxing skills. Though tall, skinny, and pale, McCoy was a scientific boxer who amassed an incredible 36–2 record from 1891–1895. Nicknamed the "Corkscrew Kid" for a type of punch he twisted on impact, McCoy won his first world title on March 2, 1896, by knocking out welterweight Tommy Ryan in the 15th round. On December 17, 1897, he outpunched Don Creedon for the world middleweight title. McCoy retired in 1911 after 105 recorded bouts, posting a record of 81 wins, six losses, six draws, nine no-decisions, and three no-contests.

Outside the ring, McCoy was a flamboyant character with an eye for the ladies. He routinely carried up to $40,000 on his person and, though married ten times (including three times to Julia Woodruff Crosselmire), had no children. Shortly after retiring, the former fighter was arrested in Britain in 1912 on suspicion of stealing jewels from an Austrian princess in Belgium. Though the charges were eventually dropped, McCoy's reputation was permanently damaged. His post-fight career was filled with various unsuccessful business ventures. McCoy briefly opened a bar in New

York City (where he befriended future film directors D. W. Griffith and Mack Sennett), entered the diamond business, ran a detective agency, and launched a car dealership. In 1917, McCoy was cast as a detective investigating a jewelry robbery in *The House of Glass*, a silent film shot in New York by French film pioneer Emile Chautard. In 1919, D. W. Griffith picked the retired pugilist for the role of a prizefighter in the director's masterpiece *Broken Blossoms*. McCoy also appeared in *The Fourteenth Man* (1920) directed by Griffith assistant Joseph Henaberry, followed by *The Great Diamond Mystery*, released in 1924 shortly after McCoy had been arrested for murder.

By May 1924, McCoy (using the alias "Shields") had lived for three months with Theresa Mors, the 39-year-old divorced wife of art and antiques dealer Albert Mors, at the Nottingham Apartments at 2819 Leeward Avenue in Los Angeles. The divorced couple were locked in a bitter property settlement which, ironically for McCoy, centered around the disposition of some valuable jewels. While the events of the evening of August 12, 1924, remain somewhat confused, an argument over the divorce settlement between McCoy and Theresa Mors in their apartment left the woman fatally shot in the head. The next morning, a drunken and deranged McCoy appeared at the store of Albert Mors and wounded three people with a .32-caliber revolver before driving away from the scene. Later that day he turned himself in to police without incident. At his murder trial in December 1924, McCoy maintained that Mors shot herself in despair after he suggested that a property settlement could be reached if he were temporarily out of the picture. Deliberations lasted 78 hours, then a California record, before the jury on their 24th ballot found McCoy guilty of manslaughter and attempted murder. The ex-fighter was sentenced to 48 years in prison.

McCoy, a model prisoner at San Quentin, was paroled after eight years due largely to the efforts of car manufacturer Henry Ford. The multi-millionaire industrialist gave the 60 year old a job supervising 85 security guards charged with overseeing some 12,000 vegetable gardens established by Ford employees in Detroit during the Depression. The outbreak of armed hostilities in Europe deeply affected the 66-year-old McCoy. As the war news worsened, he became increasingly depressed, sleepless, and reliant on sleeping pills. On April 17, 1940, days after Nazi troops invaded Denmark and Norway, McCoy told his tenth wife, Sue Cobb Cowley, that he had to go to Chicago on business. Instead, late the next day McCoy checked himself into the Hotel Tuller in downtown Detroit and left a request for a 10:00 A.M. wakeup call for the next day. When McCoy failed to respond to the call on April 19, hotel officials forced entry into the room. They found him dead near an empty box of sleeping pills. A suicide note written in pen near the body read: "For the past eight years I have wanted to help humanity especially the youngsters who do not know Nature's Laws. That is, the proper carage of the body, or the right way to eat, etc. Everything in my possession I want to go to my dear wife Sue. To all my dear friends I wish you the best of luck. Sorry I could not endure this world's madness. The best to you all. Norman Selby. P.S. In my pockets you will find $17.78." In 1957, "Kid" McCoy was elected to *The Ring* Boxing Hall of Fame.

FURTHER READING

Cantwell, Robert. *The Real McCoy; The Life and Times of Norman Selby*. Princeton, N.J.: Auerbach Publishers, 1971.

McCullough, Paul

The straight man in the famous vaudeville comedy team of Clark & McCullough was born in Springfield, Ohio, in 1883. Five years older than his future partner, McCullough met Bobby Clark (later famous in the duo for sporting painted-on glasses) in grammar school, and also attended tumbling classes with him at the local YMCA. At

McCullough's suggestion, the pair became partners, and from 1906 to 1912 worked in a variety of minstrel shows and circuses as clowns and musical performers under the names of the Jazzbo Brothers, the Prosit Trio, and Sunshine and Roses.

On December 2, 1912, the comedy team of Clark & McCullough entered vaudeville at the Opera House in New Brunswick, New Jersey. They continued to tour vaudeville for five years until a strike against management in 1917 forced them to enter burlesque, where they achieved their greatest success featured in shows like *Puss Puss* in 1918. Following their London debut in *Chuckles of 1922*, the comedy team returned to America where their appearance in the 1922 edition of *The Music Box Revue* made them Broadway stars. From that time forward, Clark & McCullough were among the top comedy headliners in vaudeville. In 1928, Fox brought the team to Hollywood where they adapted their comedy routines for a series of 14 one-reelers that included two 1929 shorts, *The Bath Between* and *The Diplomats*. Dissatisfied with movies, they returned to Broadway, but were brought back to Hollywood in 1931 by RKO to star at $7,500 a week in some 15 two-reelers.

While in between tours in early 1936, McCullough suffered a nervous breakdown, and spent one month recuperating at the New England Sanitarium in Melrose, Massachusetts. Discharged just after 6:00 P.M. on March 23, 1936, McCullough, 52, was met at the sanitarium by a friend, Frank T. Ford, to drive him home to his wife in Brookline. As they were driving through the town square of Medford, McCullough asked Ford to stop at a barbershop so he could get a shave. Ford waited in the car while the comedian went into the shop. As the barber, Gaetano Cusolito, completed lathering McCullough's face, the straight man leaped from the chair, snatched the razor from Cusolito's hand, and slashed his own throat from ear to ear. After a brief rally, McCullough died shortly after 9:55 P.M. on March 25, 1936, in the Lawrence Memorial Hospital in Medford.

FURTHER READING

Slide, Anthony. *The Encyclopedia of Vaudeville.* Westport, Conn.: Greenwood Press, 1994.

McCutcheon, Wallace

The son of a Brooklyn, New York, stage manager, McCutcheon acted in some theatrical productions and also directed two films for Biograph in 1908 (*At the Crossroads of Life* and *At the French Ball*) before entering the British army as an ambulance driver at the outbreak of World War I. He later transferred to the British Royal Flying Corps where his battlefield heroics earned him the rank of major. Shortly after sustaining a severe head injury in combat, McCutcheon was dismissed from active service and returned to America with a metal plate in his skull. In 1917, the war hero married actress Pearl White, famous star of the 1914 Pathé serial *The Perils of Pauline*. Together they appeared in the 1919 serial *The Black Secret* and *The Thief* (1920). She divorced him in Providence, Rhode Island, in 1921.

Depressed and unemployed throughout most of the twenties, the 47-year-old actor shot himself through the right temple with a large caliber handgun in his room at 6326 Lexington Avenue in Hollywood on January 27, 1928. At the scene, authorities found two cents, several newspaper clippings related to Pearl White's activities abroad, and a note from McCutcheon that read, "Have a drink," under a half-filled gin bottle.

McDermott, Joseph A.

On March 6, 1923, one-half hour after the 33-year-old actor was found dying from asphyxiation in his gas-filled room at 1267 North Western Avenue in Hollywood, his landlady received a call instructing the out-of-work thespian to report for a role at a major studio. A one-time character actor with the Biograph Company, McDermott had fallen on hard professional times and was suffering from a lingering illness. Prior to ending his life, the actor had often spoke of suicide and had become deeply interested in various cult religions. The partially indecipherable note found in his room read, "Just couldn't make the grade. Feel my mind slipping away...."

McDonald, Sidney T.

On August 29, 1930, the assistant Northwest division manager of Fox–West Coast Theatres was in his office in the Skinner Building in Seattle, Washington, talking long distance to his wife, Olivette, in Dallas. After threatening to take poison, he drank a mixture of potassium cyanide. The woman heard the phone clatter to the floor and quickly notified the switchboard operator in the Skinner Building. The 50 year old was found lying unconscious beside his desk and died an hour later in Virginia Mason Hospital. Friends attributed the suicide to failing health.

McDowell, Nelson

In films since 1919 (*The Feud*), the veteran character actor appeared in scores of low-budget Westerns until ill health forced him to retire from the movies in the early forties. Since that time McDowell worked as a live-in caretaker of a property at 5302 Sunset Boulevard in Los Angeles. On November 3, 1947, the former actor's landlord found the 77 year old on the bedroom floor of his home mortally wounded from a single gunshot. On the floor next to McDowell lay an old-style pistol that he had carried in many of his cowboy roles. The actor died en route to Hollywood Receiving Hospital. While McDowell left a note directing the disposal of his belongings, he did not indicate a motive for his act.

McElroy, Gavin Blair

In 1918 McElroy, a former engineer on the Pennsylvania Railroad, formed a company with partner Kenneth S. Fitzpatrick. Fitzpatrick-McElroy started out as a booking agency for chorus girls and singers in small theatres, eventually expanding into a 32 theatre operation in Illinois, northern Indiana, and Michigan. Twelve years later, the 51-year-old Chicago-based theatre magnate was reputedly worth $6 million and (rebounding from a divorce) set to marry a 25 year old. On January 10, 1930, while his business partner was out of town, McElroy instructed his chauffeur to drive him to the vacant house of a friend. The driver waited outside in the car, but left after a five-hour wait, figuring that his employer had fallen asleep. Some time later, a 10-year-old boy shoveling snow discovered the front door of the house open and notified the janitor. McElroy, dead from a self-inflicted gunshot wound to the head, was found in the living room partially lying under a phonograph. A note addressed to the dead man's business partner "Fitz" found stuck inside McElroy's hatband read: "Take insurance and pay Blue Lagoon and Tebbe. They have both been too good to us to pass them by. Good-by." Letters in McElroy's pockets revealed that he owed more than $91,000, although a coroner's jury later concluded that loneliness, not financial worries, prompted the seemingly wealthy businessman to kill himself.

McFarland, Homer S.

In a combination of personal persistence and police ineptitude, the 27-year-old Walt Disney Studios artist was able to finally end his life on his second attempt. On February 18, 1937, a WPA worker in the Coldwater Canyon section of Los Angeles found McFarland slumped unconscious over the steering wheel of his car. The man pulled a piece of garden hose from the car's exhaust, opened the door, and summoned police. The groggy artist was taken to the Van Nuys station and questioned about the suicide attempt, which was apparently motivated by financial troubles. McFarland was ultimately released, but police retained the suicide note found in his car. The artist drove for some time before parking on Ventura Boulevard in front of the Encino

Country Club where he completed his inter-rupted carbon monoxide-induced suicide. The note left to his wife read: "Blanche, Am going to write with every grind of the motor. I am approaching death — terrible? — not so bad. My own, I love you, but I can't see the whole thing. I'm perspiring — HO! I wonder how long I can keep this up. I have got much time — no courage — terrible? What! Do you realize, my lamb, that I am bust? I'm perspir-ing like hell. Imagine what people think of me. Not much time left. I love you." And in an added postscript: "Bigger and better world I hope, O God. Will meet after the encore — heck! I need love — no sickness."

MacFarlane, Peter Clark

MacFarlane (born in St. Clair County, Missouri, in 1871) was a railroad man, acted on the San Francisco stage with the L. R. Stock-well repertory company, and served as the pas-tor of the First Church of the Disciples of Christ in Alameda from 1902 to 1908 before becoming a popular short story writer and nov-elist (*Those Who Have Come Back*, 1914; *Tongues of Flame*, 1924). MacFarlane also wrote the screenplays from his own original stories for the films *Guile of Women* (1921) starring Will Rogers and *A Pair of Hellions* (1924). On the morning of June 9, 1924, the 53-year-old writer applied for a gun permit in Pacific Grove, Cal-ifornia, telling the chief of police there that he needed the weapon for "home defense." Bid-ding his wife and children farewell, MacFar-lane travelled to San Francisco. That evening, he fired a bullet from a small caliber pistol into his temple on the steps of the San Francisco Morgue. He died minutes later en route to the Harbor Emergency Hospital. Long letters to his wife, children, the managing editor of the *San Francisco Examiner*, and his doctor were found on the body. The most telling, dated the day before the suicide, was addressed to his friend and physician, Dr. Rufus P. Rigdon. It read (in part):

> The long battle with ill health is at an end and it is a lost battle. It is just eleven years since you diagnosed diabetes in my case and told me that up to 40 it usually killed and beyond that it eventually dragged men out. That is what it has done for me. In-sulin seemed to do its work wonderfully so far as my body was concerned, but the mental vitality would not come back; or rather the nervous energy on which it de-pends. To a man of my calling, that makes me a physical bankrupt, without the power of sustaining concentrated thought or will force long enough to be effective for anything. I tried to delude myself with the belief that the old power was still hold-ing out, but it wasn't. It has been slipping for a year; it refuses to return. Nothing re-mains but to dynamite the ruins, as I shall have done before you receive this ... I go — realizing the grim humor that had I been run over by a Ford, my death would have been honorable, but that since I go of my own hand, it is an act of shame.

MacFarlane was interred at the Cypress Lawn Cemetery in San Francisco.

McIntire, Donald E.

Appointed by Fox president Harley L. Clark in May 1931 to recommend changes in the studio, McIntire's subsequent report so impressed the corporation's money men that by December he was installed as active head of the studio. McIntire quickly suffered a ner-vous breakdown and resigned in March 1932. On December 22, 1932, the 42-year-old for-mer studio head was receiving medical care in New York City's Hotel St. Moritz at 50 Cen-tral Park South when he leaped to his death from the window of his apartment on the 21st floor.

Mack, William

On November 22, 1931, two weeks after leaving his stagehand job at the Empress The-atre in Cincinnati, Mack climbed onto the railing of the Central Bridge between the Queen City and Newport, Kentucky. While hundreds watched from both banks, he leaped to his death into the Ohio River. Two wit-nesses obtained a rowboat and recovered the lifeless, fractured body, which was positively identified as the 65-year-old stagehand's by the name in his clothing. According to union officials, Mack had started a sick furlough two weeks before and was in generally bad health.

McKenna, Kyle

In a career lasting from 1997 to 2000, the gay porn star worked for every major company in the adult film industry including Centaur Films, Hot House Entertainment, Studio 2000, and Hollywood Sales. A fan favorite, McKenna was chosen as the "Best Bottom" in 1997, and the "Hottest Ass" in 1998. McKenna's films include *Invaders from Uranus, Das Butt, Ranger in the Wild*, and *Whatever You Say Sir!* Quiet and reclusive on the set, the 26-year-old performer broke up with his boyfriend in late 1999, and was experiencing bouts of depression. On February 16, 2000, McKenna packed up his belongings in a trash bag and left them outside the house he was sharing with friends in Salt Lake City, Utah. After writing a suicide note he took a lethal dose of sleeping pills. In accordance with his last wishes, McKenna's body was cremated and the ashes scattered in the desert.

FURTHER READING

Skee, Mickey. "Kyle McKenna Commits Suicide." *Adult Video News*, 16(6):62, June 2000.

Mackenzie, Billy

Born William MacArthur MacKenzie in Dundee, Scotland, on March 27, 1957, the singer has been variously called "a sinister Pavarotti" and "a monstrous madcap Bowie." With friend Alan Rankine he formed the postpunk group The Absorbic Ones, renamed The Associates in October 1979. Signing with Fiction Records, the band released the critically acclaimed album *The Affectionate Punch* in 1980. Thereafter, they formed their own Associates label, and enjoyed a string of Top 30 hits ("Party Fears Two," "Club Country," "18 Carat Love Affair"). In the mid-eighties a poor selling album, *Perhaps*, led MacKenzie and Rankine to revert to solo careers. They re-

formed the group in 1990 for one album, *Wild and Lonely*.

Although recording one solo album in the nineties (*Outernational*, 1992), MacKenzie spent most of the decade sliding into obscurity while appearing on other groups' records (Yello, Barry Adamson, and the German band Loom). In 1996, the unexpected death of MacKenzie's mother coincided with his signing a six-album deal with Nude Records. MacKenzie successfully hid his grief while finishing the album *Beyond the Sungoes*. However, on January 22, 1997, the 39-year-old singer took a fatal dose of pills in a garden shed behind his father's home in Auchterhouse near Dundee. In a note found at the scene, MacKenzie did not specify the reason for the act, but apologized to his family. *Beyond the Sungoes* was posthumously released to critical acclaim.

McNamara, Maggie

A petite brunette fashion model, McNamara was 23 years old when film director Otto Preminger picked her to replace Barbara Bel Geddes in the 1951 stage production of F. Hugh Herbert's *The Moon Is Blue*. Reprising the role in Preminger's 1953 film, McNamara was nominated for an Academy Award as Best Actress. Twentieth Century–Fox signed the young actress and she starred in two films, *Three Coins in the Fountain* (1954) and *Prince of Players* (1955), before inexplicably disappearing from the screen. She resurfaced briefly in 1963 with a supporting role in *The Cardinal*. Although appearing on the Broadway stage in *Step on a Crack* in 1962, McNamara apparently supported herself as a typist after divorcing film producer-director David Swift. On February 18, 1978, the 48-year-old former actress took an overdose of sleeping pills in New York City.

McNelley, Robert E. ("Bobby Gene")

A founding member of the Dayton, Ohio-based country-rock group McGuffey Lane, whose song "Long Time Lovin' You" reached 85 on the *Billboard* Top 100 chart in 1981, McNelley, 36, left the group in 1984 to pursue a songwriting career in Nashville, Tennessee, with little success. The musician was living with his 25-year-old girlfriend, Linda Sue Green, in a rented house at 5330 Linworth Road in Sharon Township near Columbus, Ohio, when, on January 7, 1987, a series of domestic arguments culminated in murder when McNelley shotgunned his lover in the head. Six hours later, McNelley turned the gun on himself.

McPhail, Allen

"I have worked hard to make good for eight years, but I have failed. Life is a joke," read the suicide note-cum-epitaph penned by the 28-year-old musician on October 22, 1909. A violinist at the Orpheum Theatre in Butte, Montana, McPhail played scores of theatres in the East before coming out West to try to win a soloist position. Failing, the frustrated musician cut the arteries of one wrist and hanged himself from the bedpost in his room at the Hotel Fair in Butte.

McPhail, Douglas

Described by Metropolitan Opera star Lawrence Tibbett as "one of the best young baritones I have heard," McPhail appeared with nightclub bands in South America before extra work in motion pictures led to romantic singing parts in features. Paired with Betty Jaynes in such films as *Sweethearts* (1938) and *Babes in Arms* (1939), McPhail secretly married the actress in 1938. When they divorced in 1941, Jaynes was awarded sole custody of their daughter. Shortly afterward, a distraught McPhail drank poison, but phoned his mother in time to be saved. The singer volunteered for the Army in 1943, but a fall incurred during basic training kept him bedridden for eight months. Medically discharged with the rank of private, the 30 year old worked four hours a day as a gardener while pursuing his musical studies in the hope of appearing in a concert. Suffering from acute nervous exhaustion, McPhail swallowed poison in his home at 1818 N. Vine in Hollywood on December 7, 1944. He died shortly afterward in General Hospital.

Maeno, Mitsuyasu

Maeno, a 29-year-old part-time pilot and bit player in some 20 Japanese porno movies, was fascinated by nationalist novelist Yukio Mishima, who committed ritual suicide on November 25, 1970, following an unsuccessful attempt to incite rebellion among troops of his country's Self Defense Force. Like Mishima, Maeno envisioned himself a Samurai warrior and longed for Japan to return to traditional imperial rule. In 1976, the porn actor became incensed after right-wing militarist Yoshio Kodama was caught accepting millions from Lockheed Aircraft Corporation to promote the sales of their planes in Japan. Maeno privately denounced Kodama as a "shameful person," and considered his bribes to Japanese politicians on Lockheed's behalf as a disgrace to the national cause.

Shortly before 9:00 A.M. on March 23, 1976, Maeno posed for photos garbed in a World War II aviator's shirt with a white scarf around his neck before taking off in a Piper Cherokee plane from a private airport on the western outskirts of Tokyo. The "star" of *Tokyo's Madame Emmanuelle*, in which he made love to porn star Kumi Tamaguchi while piloting his plane, flew the short distance to the western suburban residential district where Kodama lived. Maeno circled once above the politician's home while wrapping the white band of the kamikaze pilot around his head, then, shouting the traditional kamikaze cheer "Tenno hieka banzai" ("Ten thousand lives for His Majesty, the Emperor!"), dove the plane into the second floor veranda of Kodama's home. Maeno was killed instantly while the object of his assassination attempt escaped uninjured.

Mahan, Vivian L.

Depressed over lack of work and money, the 31-year-old film extra stabbed herself in the chest with a paring knife in her apartment at 1319 West First Street in Los Angeles on October 13, 1933. Mahan, the wife of actor Harry Bayfield, died a half hour later at the Georgia Street Receiving Hospital.

Major, John

The former manager of the Empire Theatre in Syracuse, New York, Major, 53, came to Rochester, New York, in mid–1921 to manage the Lyceum Theatre. Eighteen weeks before his death, painful and debilitating rheumatism forced him to give up the position and to spend six weeks in the spa at French Lick Springs, Indiana. The theatre manager returned to Rochester still wracked with unremitting pain and insomnia. On June 29, 1922, Major decided that he had endured enough. Leaving a note outlining his intention to do away with himself near his sleeping wife, Major slashed his throat and wrists with a razor, then jumped from a fourth floor window of a Scio Street apartment house.

Manker, Roy L.

The former newspaperman was the founder and president of the Palmer Photoplay Corporation until a physical and nervous breakdown in 1924 forced him to leave the company. Manker attempted a return to writing, but found himself unable to concentrate. Following several abortive attempts to secure employment, the one-time journalist was left penniless after a real estate deal in Florida turned sour. Fearing imminent mental collapse, Manker drew up a will leaving what was left of his possessions to his wife, Frances, and gave the document to neighbors. Two days later on the morning of November 4, 1926, the woman returned to their home at 2139 Holly Drive in Hollywood to find her 45-year-old husband slumped dead on the bathroom floor near a pipe oozing gas. Police determined that Manker had used a wrench to unscrew the cap covering the pipe.

Mann, Fred

Mann, 57, was the founder and propri-

etor of the Million Dollar Rainbo Garden at Clark Street and Lawrence Avenue, until Prohibition agents closed and padlocked the center of Chicago night life as a public nuisance in May 1928. The government allowed the club's pavilion to remain open for jai alai games, but ultimately denied Mann's petition to reopen the Rainbo as a restaurant. On October 18, 1930, Mann sat on a bench in Lincoln Park and, in full view of passing cars, fatally shot himself in the temple with a revolver. On a business card found in his partially closed left hand, the restaurateur had written in pencil, "Please remove my body to George Klaner's undertaking rooms, 4714 Broadway." On the reverse side was a farewell message to the undertaker, "Goodby [sic], George. Take care of everything. Notify Al [Mann's only son]." A second note addressed to Mann's widow was found in an inner pocket.

Mansfield, Edward

Elsie Orr, 24, and her sister, Helen Stolte, were known theatrically in the Bath Beach section of Brooklyn, New York, as the "Carr Sisters." Expert swimmers and divers since the age of 12, the pair were members of a water carnival show managed by Mansfield, and following a two year run, were together in the chorus of *Very Good, Eddie*. Mansfield became dangerously infatuated with Stolte, recently separated from her husband, but was opposed by Orr who warned her sister against having any involvement with him.

Orr had been married less than three weeks to Edward Orr, a member of the Canadian Flying Corps, when Mansfield invited Stolte to Metuchen, New Jersey, to pick up a car there he had promised to give her. Distrustful of his intentions, Orr accompanied her sister to Metuchen on June 15, 1918. Mansfield told the pair that the car was in a woods outside the town and drove them to a remote area near a rubber factory. Stolte waited in the car while Orr walked into the woods with the theatrical manager to retrieve the vehicle. Fifteen minutes later, Stolte heard moans coming from the woods. Investigating, she found the theatrical manager standing beside a stream holding a bloody pen knife, his throat gashed, and drinking from a bottle. Asked by Stolte where her sister was, Mansfield replied, "Where she will never go on the road again." Stolte fled the scene, returning minutes later with police. Mansfield lay unconscious on the ground from a near fatal dose of paris green while, nearby, Orr was found with her throat cut lodged in a clump of bushes. Mansfield died of the overdose later that night in Metuchen's St. Peter's Hospital.

Manuel, Richard

Known in his native Canada as "the white Ray Charles," the keyboardist and singer for The Band was born April 3, 1945, in Stratford, Ontario. Nicknamed "the Beak" because of his prominent nose, Manuel started piano lessons at 9, and by his teenage years was being heavily influenced by the blues of Charles and Bobby Bland. At 15 he co-founded a band called the Rebels (renamed the Rockin' Revols), but in the early sixties joined the Hawks, the backing band for rockabilly singer Ronnie Hawkins. Levon Helm already played drums for the Hawks, which would ultimately include other Band members — bassist Rich Danko, organist Garth Hudson, and guitarist Robbie Robertson.

In 1963, the quintet left Hawkins and toured small bars and dives throughout America billed as the Canadian Squires or Levon and the Hawks. By the time the group settled in New York City in 1964 they were well on their way to developing a trademark sound that blended R&B and gospel with country overtones. While backing blues singer John Hammond, Jr., in his Greenwich Village appearances, they were introduced to Bob Dylan in 1965. Dylan, who was just beginning to make his transition from acoustic to electric, signed the group (minus Helm) to back him on his 1965–1966 world tour. After a near fatal motorcycle crash in 1966, Dylan returned to

his home in Woodstock, New York, to recuperate. The group, reunited with Helm, joined Dylan in rural upstate New York and took up residence in a rambling house nicknamed Big Pink. The period of intense songwriting and recording that followed resulted in the group's rechristening themselves The Band. The highly regarded "sessions" were released in 1975 as *The Basement Tapes*. In 1968, The Band released their debut album, *Music from Big Pink*, a record containing the classic tracks "The Weight" and "This Wheel's on Fire." The equally critically acclaimed follow-up album *The Band* was released in 1969 and spawned the Robbie Robertson penned hits "The Night They Drove Old Dixie Down" and "Up on Cripple Creek."

The Band continued to record until 1976 when internal tensions in the group sparked by Robertson's refusal to continue touring and desire to pursue a solo career led to their breakup. Their farewell concert that year on Thanksgiving Day at San Francisco's Winterland was filmed by director Martin Scorsese as *The Last Waltz*. The concert featured the group with friends and admirers, which included Bob Dylan, Van Morrison, Neil Young, and Muddy Waters. After The Band's breakup, Manuel struggled for direction. A long-time abuser of drugs and alcohol, the singer-composer of The Band songs "In a Station," "We Can Talk," "Lonesome Suzie," and "Tears of Rage" (co-written with Dylan) desperately needed the group to reunite in order to focus his energy. It did so, at Helm's instigation, in 1984 with guitarist Jim Weider taking the place of Robbie Robertson. However, the inability of The Band to develop a songwriter in the group the caliber of the missing Robertson cast a pall over the subsequent tour.

On March 3, 1986, the newly reconstituted Band played two sets at the Cheek to Cheek lounge, an upscale art deco nightclub at the Villa Nova Restaurant in Winter Park, Florida, a suburb of Orlando. After the second show, the group retired to their rooms at the Quality Inn next door. Manuel visited Helm's room and, according to the drummer, spoke about songs and people. Manuel left in an up-beat mood around 2:30 A.M. on March 4, and returned to his room. Having forgotten his key, the 40-year-old keyboardist had to awaken his sleeping wife Arlie to let him in. "He was all pissed off about something," she said, and had complained earlier in the evening about the quality of the piano. Manuel finally laid on the bed with his clothes on, and Arlie went back to sleep.

Sometime between 2:30 and 3:30 A.M., he entered the bathroom, looped his belt around his neck, tied the other end to a shower curtain rod, and sat down hard. Arlie found her husband's body around noon. The medical examiner's report determined that Manuel had used cocaine sometime within the previous 24 hours and had a blood alcohol level of 0.15 percent at the time of his death, just slightly above the legal limit for intoxication. The musician was buried in the Avondale Cemetery in his hometown of Stratford, Ontario, on March 9, 1986. Commenting on his friend and bandmate's suicide, Levon Helm told Joe Forno, Jr., Manuel's personal manager, "God's thrown Richard back to us a lot of times. But this time he didn't."

FURTHER READING

Helm, Levon, and Davis, Stephen. *This Wheel's on Fire: Levon Helm and the Story of The Band.* 1st ed. New York: William Morrow & Co., 1993.

Marceline

Marceline Orbes (born in Saragossa, Spain, in 1873) ran away from home at age 7 to join a travelling circus. When a clown was unable to persuade the young boy to return, he found Orbes a job as a stableboy with the company. Orbes eventually became a tumbler with the show before exploiting his physicality in a sophisticated clown act where he was billed simply as "Marceline." In his Marceline persona, Orbes wore misfit evening clothes and achieved comic effects purely through pantomime. After delighting British audiences for five years at the London Hippodrome,

Marceline opened New York's Hippodrome in 1905. A smash hit, the "Prince of Clowns" played there for nine years before returning to London to perform. By 1920, however, the public's taste in entertainment was changing. After working with the Ringling Brothers Circus and on the Keith vaudeville circuit, Orbes left show business to open a restaurant in Greenwich Village and to speculate in Long Island and New Jersey real estate. When both ventures failed, the one-time internationally renowned vaudeville star was reduced to playing benefits, smokers, and local entertainments.

On November 5, 1927, two days after pawning a diamond ring for $15, Orbes was found kneeling beside his bed clutching a pistol, a fatal bullet wound in his right temple. Scattered on the floor around him were photographs taken of the 53-year-old headliner during his prime. Six dollars and a pawn ticket for a diamond ring were found nearby. He left no note. Days later, fewer than 50 show folk attended Marceline's funeral service in the Campbell Funeral Church on Broadway, although Charlie Chaplin did send flowers. In his eulogy, Harry Chesterfield, Secretary of the National Vaudeville Artists, lamented the fickleness of a public that could relegate a star of the magnitude of Marceline "to the ash heap of actors."

Markle, John

On November 16, 1987, three days after being fired from a brokerage house for embezzling funds, the 45-year-old investment banker son of Academy Award winning actress Mercedes McCambridge went on a murder-suicide spree in his home in Little Rock, Arkansas. Police found Markle's 45-year-old wife, Chris, in the third floor master bedroom, sprawled across a king-sized waterbed, shot three times. In the children's second floor bedroom, Markle's 12-year-old daughter, Amy, shot four times in the head and chest, lay in bed next to her 9-year-old sister, Suzanne, who had been shot five times. After killing his family, Markle descended to the first floor study, pointed a .38-caliber pistol to one temple and a .45-caliber gun to the other, and took his own life. A rubber "Freddy Krueger" mask (believed by authorities to have been worn by Markle during some of the shootings) was found near the body. A tape of *Nightmare on Elm Street* was in the VCR. A two line handwritten note stating that he had killed his wife and children was on a desk in the study.

McCambridge, an Oscar winner for her supporting performance in the 1950 film *All the King's Men*, and well-known as the demonic voice of the possessed little girl in *The Exorcist* (1973), was visibly moved at the funeral service in Little Rock attended by then Arkansas' first lady Hillary Clinton. Afterward, McCambridge quickly went on the legal offensive to block the publication of a bitter 13 page handwritten letter left to her by Markle. In April 1989 the Arkansas Supreme Court ruled against the actress and made the damning document part of the public police file. In the letter, dated October 1987, Markle exonerated McCambridge from any financial wrongdoing in his scheme to divert funds into her account, but indicted her as a mother. It read (in part): "I was essentially raised by live-in maids and relatives.... I was conceptualized to save a bad marriage.... I watched you try to kill yourself twice. You have never been there for me when the chips were down. When I cried on the phone you called me a 'snivelling wimp'.... Is this clear to you? That you have hurt every member of my family. That you have hurt me; that I stood by you under some really adverse conditions and that you have never done anything but manipulate me for your purposes.... You were never around much when I needed you so now I and my whole family are dead — so you can have the money. Funny how things work out, isn't it?"

Maroney, Robert N.

Unemployed for a month since last performing his magician's act in Hancock, Mary-land, Maroney (a.k.a "Willard the Wizard") with wife Othello and their 1-year-old daughter, Frances, moved to Cincinnati, Ohio, in November 1913. In the Queen City, the 27-year-old magician stayed on a month-long drinking binge, often consuming a quart of whiskey a day. In the early morning hours of December 29, 1913, a drunken Maroney returned to his room at the Hotel Walton and loudly accused his wife of being unfaithful. During the ensuing argument (according to Maroney's police statement), he saw the "devil" in Othello's eyes and in the sacred pictures on the walls of the hotel room. The crazed magician produced a gun and rapidly fired three shots into his wife, striking her in the stomach, right temple, and both ankles. Seeing similar devils in his child's eyes, Maroney shot Frances in the back of the head, then crushed the infant's fingers with the butt of the pistol. "I beat them like you beat meat and potatoes," he told sickened detectives. Maroney was apprehended one hour later running through the streets in his underwear. A court-ordered psychiatric evaluation of the double-murderer concluded: "Insanity due to excessive drink, taking the form of delusions of infidelity on the part of his wife."

Awaiting trial on two counts of first degree murder in the Central Station jail on June 21, 1914, Maroney climbed to the second floor tier of cells and shouted, "I said I was going to do it, and I'm going to!" and dove head-first to his death on the concrete courtyard 40 feet below.

Martin, Vallie Belasco

Not even being the second cousin of David Belasco, the world famous theatre impresario, could ensure the 25-year-old Milwaukee, Wisconsin-born Martin steady work on the boards although she had appeared to good notices in *Very Good, Eddie, My Lady Friends*, and in the road company of *Abie's Irish Rose*. Martin's literary aspirations were likewise thwarted. Weeks before taking her life, Martin's manuscript, *The Evolution of a*

Poetess, or, the Amusing Musings of a Misled Maid, had been rejected by a large publisher. The returned manuscript arrived by post the day after her death.

Discouraged by her stalled acting and writing careers, Martin was living with her mother in a seventh floor apartment at 260 Riverside Drive in New York City. On February 28, 1924, as her mother slept in another room, Martin swallowed a bottle of shoe polish containing a small, but sufficient, quantity of cyanide of potassium. The empty bottle was found under her pillow. A hastily penciled note on a bedside table read: "Mother Dear: As you know things have gone from bad to worse. At the beginning of the week I had several good prospects, but they have all gone bluey. I wish that theatrical managers and agents would realize that a girl's time is worth something. I hope they will realize it after this and not keep girls waiting. After reading Nietzsche's book I agree with his idea of the superfluity of life and so I am going to practice what he preaches. Goodbye and forgive me. Vallie." Ironically, after Martin's death several theatre people called the dead woman's mother to belatedly say that had they known of the actress' despair, they would have found a part for her.

Martorana, Samuel

In addition to organizing and conducting the Reading (Pennsylvania) Royal Italian Band, the 31-year-old Martorana played in the Federal Band, the Ringgold Band, and the Reading Symphony Orchestra. In the weeks before his suicide, colleagues noticed that Martorana was acting strangely. Despite having a pregnant wife at home, the conductor worked ceaselessly over the scores of operas and the creation of band music. At 6:30 A.M. on March 5, 1939, Martorana leaped headlong from the third floor window of his sister-in-law's West Reading home where his wife awaited the birth of their second child. Shortly afterward, the conductor's body was found outside on the pavement by his mother-in-

law. The coroner issued a certificate of death by suicide, blaming mental derangement brought on by excessive work and worry over his wife's condition.

Marvin, Mark

On March 7, 1958, Marvin's wife found the stage and film producer dead (apparently from an undetermined cause) in their New York City apartment at 280 Riverside Drive. A note beside the body revealed that he had incurable cancer. In a distinguished career, Marvin staged several plays in London, wrote a series of half-hour television films for Lexicon Films, Ltd., and co-produced *Child of Man*, a 1948 Danish film. Marvin's Broadway credits included *On Whitman Avenue*, a 1946 racial conflict drama featuring Canada Lee, and *Hide and Seek* in April 1957. At the time of his suicide, the 50-year-old producer was working with composer Harold Arlen on a production of Arlen's *The Blues Opera* (ultimately staged as *Free and Easy*.)

Maryott, Susan

The sister of Academy Award winning film director John Schlesinger (*Midnight Cowboy*, 1969), Maryott appeared with the Royal Shakespeare Company at Stratford-on-Avon during its 1962 season. Maryott fell hopelessly in love with a married playwright, but the affair ended. Later, when the dramatist was dying of cancer, his wife permitted the actress to sit at his bedside and nurse him. On July 19, 1963, three weeks after her lover's funeral, Maryott, 30, was found dead from an overdose of pills in her Chelsea flat in Beaufort Street, London. Police did not reveal the contents of a note found at the scene.

Maskell, Virginia

The British actress who began her film career opposite John Cassavetes and Sidney Poitier in the 1958 release *Virgin Island* was described in a *Times* obituary as possessing "talent and beauty, without that resolute urge to succeed which is a necessary part of star quality...." Though appearing in ten movies in the fifties and sixties, Maskell never seemed to find her niche in films and, during the end of her career, was frequently seen on stage and television.

Married to a company director in 1962, Maskell was treated for depression in 1966 following the birth of their second son. After suffering a nervous breakdown in late 1967, the 31-year-old actress spent nearly six weeks in Stoke Mandeville Hospital, Buckinghamshire, until she was allowed home three weeks before Christmas. Maskell disappeared from her home in Princes Risborough, Buckinghamshire, on January 24, 1968, after securing a fortnight's supply of sleeping pills from her doctor. She was found the next day unconscious from a barbiturate overdose and suffering from exposure in a woods only a mile from her home. The actress died later that day in the same hospital where she had been treated for depression. While contents of a note found on Maskell's bed on the day of her disappearance were not released, the coroner (who ruled that the actress took her life while the balance of her mind was disturbed) characterized it as "a hasty message of love and despair."

Mason, Lew

Mason, an assistant casting director for Edward Small, inhaled gas in his room at the Christie Hotel in Los Angeles on May 18, 1924. Friends found the unconscious film man next to an empty bottle of champagne and clinging to the picture of an unidentified woman. In a note filled with several postscripts, Mason left all his belongings to Marcella Daly, a young film actress. Prefacing the suicide letter with "This is the note. They always leave some kind of note," Mason observed that life was too fast paced for him, and advised his readers never "to lose their sense of humor." Mason was removed to the Hollywood Hospital, but died the next day after failing to respond to blood transfusions taken from two of his actor friends.

Massengale, Joseph

Massengale performed rodeo and cowboy stunts in the films *The Man Who Loved Cat Dancing* (1973), *The Frisco Kid* (1979), *Tom Horn* (1979), and *Stir Crazy* (1980). On television, the stuntman was seen in two made-for-television movies (*The Gambler*, 1980; *The Gambler II*, 1983), and on episodes of *Little House on the Prairie, How the West was Won*, and *Father Murphy*. Massengale, 36, and his wife, actress Kathleen O'Haco, were estranged and living apart when he phoned her from his Burbank, California, apartment on the afternoon of December 17, 1983, to plead for a reconciliation. During the course of the conversation, he threatened to kill himself if O'Haco would not return to him. Having heard similar threats before, the actress did not take Massengale seriously until she heard a gunshot over the line. Police found Massengale, still clutching the telephone in his left hand, dead from a bullet wound to his right temple inflicted by a 9mm automatic handgun.

Massey, Edward

The Harvard-educated playwright was a member of Professor George Baker's illustrious "Forty-Seven Workshop," and a former coach of that institution's dramatic club. In March 1917 his farce *Plots and Playwrights* was produced by the Washington Square Players. Another, *Box Seats*, was produced in April 1928 at the Little Theatre. As a director, Massey helmed the first American production of Chekhov's *The Cherry Orchard* in Boston. On Broadway he also directed *The Moon Is a Gong, The Belt*, and his last New York offering, *Michael Drops In*, in 1938. Depressed over world conditions, the 46-year-old dramatist gassed himself in his one room apartment at 1 Sheridan Square in New York City on February 8, 1942.

Massingham, Dorothy

Massingham (born in Highgate, London, on December 12, 1889) studied at the

Academy of Dramatic Art and made her stage debut with the Liverpool Repertory Theatre in February 1912 as "Kalleia" in *The Perplexed Husband*. After her first appearance in London at the Vaudeville Theatre on November 18, 1913, as "Claire" in *Great Catherine*, Massingham became a member of the Birmingham Repertory Company (1917–1919) where she gained renown as a top interpreter of Shakespeare. During the seasons of 1928–1929 and 1931–1932, she toured the United States and Canada with the Stratford-on-Avon-based New Shakespeare Company. As an actress, Massingham won critical recognition for combining emotional expressiveness with a rare power of intellectual perception. Also a playwright of great potential, Massingham wrote *Glass Houses* (1918), *The Goat* (1921), *Washed Ashore* (1922), *Not in Our Stars* (1924), and *The Haven* (1930).

In March 1933, the 43-year-old actress was placed in a nursing home after suffering a nervous breakdown brought on by overwork and aggravated by a severe case of influenza. On March 30, 1933, Massingham had been discharged for a week and was recuperating at a friend's home in Hampstead when her fully-clothed body was found on the floor of her bedroom near a fireplace with the gas ring turned fully on. She left no note. *The Lake*, her current play co-written with Murray Macdonald, was running in London at the time of her death. Ironically, one of its central themes was a young woman's thoughts of suicide.

Mastrocola, Enrico

Known professionally as "Henry Martin," the musician billed as a "one man band" had been appearing at the Two-Four Club in Philadelphia with his wife playing drums in the show. An argument between the pair in their room at the Hotel Leonard during the early morning hours of October 1, 1959, culminated with Mastrocola tying a 50 foot electric guitar cord around his neck, looping it over the door, and, while his wife tried to prevent the suicide, strangling himself to death.

Mathieson, Fiona

The daughter of the late Scottish film composer-conductor Muir Mathieson (1911–1975) appeared on stage and television before landing the part of "Clarrie" in BBC Radio's long running serial *The Archers* in 1985. On October 3, 1987, two days after being reported missing from their London home by her actor-husband Ian Brimble, the 36-year-old actress and mother of a 10-month-old son was found dead from an overdose of sleeping pills at the Royal Hotel in Tain, near Inverness, Scotland.

Matsumoto, Hideto

Born in Yokosuka, Kanagawa Prefecture, on December 13, 1964, "Hide" (as the lead guitarist was known to his legion of Japanese fans) joined a rock band known as X in 1987. The group released its first album, *Vanishing Vision*, in 1988 and followed the next year with *Blue Hood*. In 1992 the band changed its name to X Japan. Known for their wild hair and heavy makeup, the group dedicated themselves to several social causes including bone marrow transplants and AIDS activism. After announcing their disbandment in September 1997, X Japan performed its final live concert at the Tokyo Dome on New Year's Eve 1997.

On May 2, 1998, Matsumoto arrived at his Tokyo apartment at about 6:30 A.M. and went straight to bed. Shortly before 7:30 A.M. a family member entered the 33-year-old guitarist's room to find him seated and hanging from a torn towel attached to the bedroom doorknob á la Michael Hutchence (see entry) of the Australian rock group INXS. "Hide" was reportedly drunk when he committed the act. The guitarist died at a nearby hospital shortly before 9:00 A.M.

In the wake of the popular rock star's death, one teenaged Japanese girl destroyed herself in exactly the same manner. Another, wearing a bright orange-sleeved shirt with the word "Hide" scrawled across the back, was reported in critical condition after grief drove her to leap from a 30-foot-high pedestrian bridge. On May 7, 1998, a crowd estimated between 20,000 to 50,000 young people dressed in black and sporting the band's trademark red, orange, purple, and green-dyed hair jammed the streets outside the Tsukiji Hongaji temple in central Tokyo where funeral services were being conducted for the dead rock star. Web sites dedicated to the band were filled with messages of teen grief. One South Korean fan wrote, "I don't want to live anymore.... I loved him. Why did he leave me?"

Maynard, Claire

Maynard (born Marie McCarthy in Brooklyn, New York, in 1912) began her film career in 1931 with a small part in the Fox Film Corporation production *Good Sport* starring John Boles. When the Hollywood roles dried up, she moved to New York City and began modelling in gown shops. Her mother's death in 1939 prompted an unsuccessful suicide attempt that which left the former actress moody and withdrawn. On July 19, 1941, the body of the 29-year-old actress was found on the kitchen floor of her 16th floor apartment at 404 East Fifty-fifth Street by the building superintendent who broke down the door after smelling gas. After scribbling four notes (one to her dead mother and another to an unidentified person named "Ducky"), Maynard opened two gas jets on the kitchen stove.

Mayorova, Yelena

The 39-year-old Mayorova, described by one critic as the "most talented of the middle generation of actresses at the Chekhov Art Theatre," had electrified Russian audiences with her sensitive performance as the abandoned wife in the 1995 production of *Teibele and Her Demon*, Eve Friedman's play based on a story by Isaac Bashevis Singer. One week before she was to perform the role of "Masha" in the Moscow Art Theatre's production of Anton Chekhov's *Three Sisters*, Mayorova inexplicably took her life in a theatrical, but grisly, fashion. On August 23, 1997, the actress

doused herself with gasoline and set herself on fire in the stairway of her apartment building in central Moscow. Though firemen extinguished the blaze, which destroyed skin over 85 percent of her body, Mayorova died shortly afterward in a hospital without regaining consciousness.

Meek, Joe

Called the "Phil Spector of Britain," Meek (born 1929) became the premier independent record producer of the sixties after beginning his career in 1954 as an engineer with the IBC, the leading independent recording studio of the period. At the IBC, Meek worked with Lonnie Donegan, Frankie Vaughn, and Humphrey Lyttelton, and wrote "Put a Ring on Her Finger" for singer Tommy Steele in 1958. Meek went independent in 1960, ultimately setting up an apartment-studio above a shop in Holloway Road in London. It was in these cramped surroundings that the innovative producer pioneered the unusual sounds (ranging from electronic instruments to flushing toilets) that characterized much of his work.

In 1961, Meek founded The Tornados, an instrumental group he used as a house band at the Holloway Road studio to back solo performers like Billy Fury, John Leyton, and Don Charles. By 1962, their space aged instrumental, "Telstar," sold four million copies and was the first British rock record to reach Number 1 on the American charts. Co-written and produced by Meek, the tune's success established him as the top British independent producer of the era. In the mid-sixties, the move toward more melodic music spearheaded by The Beatles made Meek's music seem gimmicky. To accomodate the new trend, the producer countered with The Honeycombs' Top 5 hit "Have I the Right?" in 1964. This proved to be Meek's last hit, and following a string of musical flops he found himself largely unemployed and debt ridden.

Always a violent personality, Meek's erratic behavior (fueled by fear that he would be exposed as a homosexual) alienated many of his longtime friends. As he sank deeper into drug use and mental illness, Meek became convinced that his studio-living quarters had been bugged, and that unseen forces were trying to steal ideas directly from his mind. To thwart them, the 35-year-old producer burned all his notes and private documents except one that said: "I'm going now." On February 3, 1967, Meek argued with his landlady, who lived in the leather goods shop below his studio in Holloway Road. Fed up with the noise complaints of neighbors and Meek's slow rent payments, Violet Shenton was not going to renew his lease. As she was leaving his apartment, Meek fired a 12-gauge shotgun blast into her back, which knocked her down the stairs. The 54-year-old woman would die en route to a nearby hospital. Meek then reloaded, and ten seconds later, shot himself in the head. The murder-suicide occurred on the eighth anniversary of Buddy Holly's death near Mason City, Iowa, in 1959.

FURTHER READING

Repsch, John. *The Legendary Joe Meek: The Telstar Man.* London: Woodford House, 1989.

GUS MEINS — The German-born director helmed four ZaSu Pitts–Thelma Todd comedy shorts (*Sneak Easily*, 1932; *The Bargain of the Century*, 1933) for Hal Roach Studios in the early thirties. After Pitts left the studio in a salary dispute in 1933, Meins directed Todd and the comedienne's replacement, Patsy Kelly, in 12 shorts including *Beauty and the Bus* (1933), *Three Chumps Ahead* (1934), and *I'll Be Suing You* (1934). Arrested in July 1940 and charged with committing immoral acts against underaged boys, Meins, 45, jumped bail and was missing for four days when his decomposed body was found in his parked car in Los Angeles on August 4, 1940. *Courtesy of University of Southern California, on behalf of the USC Library Department of Special Collections.*

Meins, Gustave

The German-born Meins began his film career in 1919 as a scenarist and gag man at Fox Studios before stepping up to direct *Babes in Toyland* featuring Laurel & Hardy for Hal Roach Studios and MGM in 1934. From that date until his final film, *Scatterbrain* (Republic, 1940), the comedy specialist directed some 16 movies including *His Exciting Night* (Universal, 1938) and *Grandpa Goes to Town* (Republic, 1940). On Wednesday, July 31, 1940, police arrested Meins at his home at 3839 Carnavon Way in Los Angeles after the parents of six boys, ranging in age from 10 to 15 years, issued a complaint that the director had committed immoral acts against their sons in the basement workshop of his home. Freed later that evening after posting a $5,000 bond, Meins returned home just long enough to tell his 22-year-old son, "You probably won't see me again."

The 45-year-old director drove off in his green coupe and was missing for four days. In shock, his wife was admitted to a private hospital. As the day for Meins' court appearance passed and he forfeited his bond, his attorney and family suspected the worst. Their fears were realized on August 4, 1940, when the film man's decomposing remains were found in his parked car in the tall brush of a La Crescenta debris basin. Apparently dead from carbon monoxide poisoning since the time of his disappearance, Meins had fixed a rubber hose leading from the car's exhaust into the interior of the vehicle. No notes were found.

Melrose, Kitty

Melrose (real name Agnes Butterfield) last appeared onstage in *The Quaker Girl* during the early teens at the Adelphi Theatre in London. On June 3, 1912, the actress (age unknown) was found dead lying on her back with her head in a gas oven in her flat in St. Stephen's mansions, Smith-square, Westminster. Three months earlier, she had attempted to take her life with an overdose of veronal. Brought to self-destruction by her former lover's refusal to go against his family and marry her, Melrose left the man two letters. In one she wrote: "Eddie, my dear one, I cannot bear any more, and everyone has told me you won't, and have done with me. I am heartbroken, and cannot bear any more. Please forgive me, but I know as you do not love me, you will soon forget me. All my love, and good luck to you. Your Kit." And in a postscript: "It was wrong for every one to keep you from me. It has made it too impossible. I cannot fight alone, but I did believe in you, and did not think you would fail me.

But God's will. I know you thought you were doing right.— K." In the other: "Eddie — By leaving me alone you thought you were doing right, but it was all wrong and cruel. God forgive you, as I hope he will forgive me.— Kit."

Melrose, Percy C.

Melrose, 57, a former circus performer in a bicycle act, made a small fortune in the teens manufacturing patent medicine in the Columbus, Ohio, area. Married with two children, Melrose began an affair with his neighbor's wife, Eva Tootle, the 27-year-old mother of a small child. The affair ended in tragedy on May 16, 1918, with the discovery of their bullet-riddled bodies in the front seat of Melrose's car on a road near Lockbourne, just south of Columbus. A passing motorist found the pair when she noticed that the windshield of the car was covered over with newspapers and its curtains were drawn. Ballistics and a note found on the car's rear seat told the story of a murder-suicide. According to authorities, Melrose shot Tootle three times in the head during a struggle (as evidenced by defensive wounds on the woman's hands) then fired one bullet into his head just behind the right ear. A note found at the scene read, in part: "Facts: A ruined home and a ruined life, all because my wife was so extravagant. We have not loved each other for three or four years. I love little Eva because she is so pure. God have mercy on my soul and grant that my wife will rear my two children in the right way."

Mendelssohn, Eleonora

The great-granddaughter of composer Felix Mendelssohn, the 51-year-old actress established her name in German theatre under director Max Reinhardt prior to the rise of the Hitler regime. She wed actor Martin Kosleck in 1947 and the pair left Germany shortly after Hitler came to power. In America she was seen on Broadway in *Flight to the West*, *The Russian People*, and most recently in a road company production of *The Mad Woman of*

Chaillot. On January 4, 1951, Kosleck fractured his spine when he fell to the street from the window of their third floor apartment at 173 East Seventy-third Street in New York City. Despondent over her husband's hospitalization, Mendelssohn was found dead in her bed on the morning of January 24, 1951, from a deadly combination of sleeping pills and an ether-soaked cotton pad placed over her face and held secure with a towel and bath mat. Detectives found a partially empty can of ether and a syringe on a night table near her bed.

Merrige-Abrams, Salwa

Throughout her 19 year marriage to James Abrams, a 45-year-old National Airlines pilot, Merrige-Abrams had built her opera career around him and their children, Jack, 14, and Melisa Ann, 10. A talented mezzo soprano, the 43-year-old singer refused national roles in order to perform cameos in the Miami, Florida, area with the Greater Miami Opera Guild, the Civic Opera of the Palm Beaches, and the Miami Beach Symphony. Following the couple's separation in 1971, Merrige-Abrams underwent psychiatric counseling.

On the afternoon of July 14, 1973, one day after their divorce appeared to have become final, the singer phoned her ex-husband to come over to the home they once shared at 5450 SW Sixtieth Court in Miami to remove the remainder of his possessions. "I got a real surprise for you," she promised. Abrams, now living at a nearby residence with another woman, disregarded his attorney's advice to send a mover for the things and arrived at the house. There, Merrige-Abrams repeatedly shot the man with a .38-caliber revolver before reloading and systematically moving to other parts of the house to kill her two children. Apparently unable to shoot herself at the last minute, the singer downed several tranquilizers and barbiturates. Her unconscious body was found in the dining room near a piano covered with photos from her career and

a handwritten will. With three unserved first degree murder warrants still facing her, Merrige-Abrams died at the South Miami Hospital at 1:15 A.M. on July 19, 1973.

Merrill, Bob

Born H. Robert Merril Levan in Atlantic City, New Jersey, circa 1924, the one-time supper club singer wrote 25 hit songs including "If I Knew You Were Coming I'd Have Baked a Cake" (1950) and "(How Much is) That Doggie in the Window" (1952) before turning to Broadway in the late fifties. Originally hired by MGM to compose musicals, Merrill turned several of his film ideas into top Broadway hits. Shows featuring his Tony-nominated lyrics include *New Girl in Town* (1957), *Take Me Along* (1959), *Carnival* (1961; "Love Makes the World Go 'Round"), and *Funny Girl* (1964; "People" and "Don't Rain on My Parade.") In 1972, Merrill earned a Grammy nomination for his score to the musical *Sugar*, based on the 1959 Billy Wilder film *Some Like it Hot*. Merrill's screenplays include *Mahogany* (1975), *W.C. Fields & Me* (1976), and *Chu Chu and the Philly Flash* (1981). Depressed by prolonged gastrointestinal problems, the 74-year-old lyricist shot himself in the head while sitting in his car in Culver City, California, on February 17, 1998. According to his wife, Merrill "didn't want to be in a wheelchair. He wanted to be the master of his own fate."

Messenger, Frank

Messenger served as an assistant director on the 1920 Universal film *The Virgin of Stamboul* before moving to Metro-Goldwyn-Mayer in the early thirties. While continuing to assistant direct at MGM (*Eskimo*, 1934), Messenger became widely known as a production (or unit) manager for his work on *Maytime* (1937), *Rosalie* (1937), and his final film, *Northwest Passage*, released in 1940 after his death. Messenger also worked as unit manager on two films that featured future fellow suicides. In the 1938 historical drama *Marie*

Antoinette supporting actor Albert Dekker (see entry) played the role of the "Comte de Provence." Credited as "Albert van Dekker" in the film, the veteran character actor would die in 1968 under bizarre and mysterious circumstances. Richard Rosson (see entry), second unit director on the 1939 film *Stand Up and Fight*, committed suicide in 1953.

On December 19, 1939, the 48-year-old production manager was helping his wife, Dorothy, decorate the Christmas tree in their home at 6617 Maryland Drive in Hollywood when he suddenly left the room, went to the garage, and fatally shot himself in the head with a pistol. Messenger, according to authorities, had been unemployed for several months.

Metz, Henry

Billed as "Henry Hill" during the 50 years he toured in vaudeville, Metz also managed his producer-brother's theatrical company (the Gus Hill Minstrels) while occasionally performing in it. The 74-year-old actor had been retired from show business for nearly a decade when he hanged himself on April 29, 1940, in a rooming house in Rye, New York.

Midgley, Rex W.

Believed to have been despondent over financial worries, the former owner and manager of the American Theater in Oakland, California, drank poison in one of his apartment houses at Nineteenth and Jackson streets in that city on April 7, 1932. Midgley, 40, left two letters addressed to his wife and parents.

Mildwater, Justin

Devastated by the breakup of his four year marriage to *EastEnders* television star Nadia Sawalha, the 31-year-old record producer hanged himself with a nylon tow rope in the couple's rented house in Muswell Hill, North London, on Christmas Day in 1997. Sawalha, nightclub boss "Annie Palmer" on the popular British soap and sister of actress

Julia Sawalha ("Saffy" on *Absolutely Fabulous*), moved out of their home at the beginning of December 1997 amid rumors she was romantically involved with fellow *EastEnders* actor Marc Bannerman. Friends reported that two days before his death a drunken Mildwater phoned various acquaintances asking them for money to buy food and alcohol. Mildwater's father and brother who, with police, found the half-naked body at 12:50 P.M. on Christmas Day, maintained that they recovered two suicide notes at the scene. One was addressed to the family while the other, found beneath the couple's two wedding rings, was addressed to his estranged wife. According to the dead man's family, Sawalha never collected the rings or read the note. A coroner's inquest conducted in April 1998, however, stated that while no notes or drugs were found in Mildwater's house, there was vodka and an empty bottle of whiskey in the lounge. The record producer's blood contained traces of cannabis, heroin, and a level of alcohol 1½ times the legal limit.

Miller, Charles B.

A veteran character actor who appeared primarily in Westerns (*The Phantom Plainsman*, 1942; *The Lawless Breed*, 1952), Miller (born March 16, 1891) had been sick and out of work for some time when an argument with his wife ended in suicide in Burbank, California, on June 6, 1955. When informed by wife Marie that she planned to begin working that day to help support them, the 64-year-old unemployed actor threatened to shoot up the neighborhood with a .22-caliber rifle. She returned from work to find Miller dead from a self-inflicted gunshot wound in their trailer at 1004 Burbank Boulevard.

Miller, Wesley C.

Miller was the head sound engineer at MGM before retiring in 1959. On April 19, 1962, the 65 year old shot himself through the head with a .45-caliber automatic in the garage of his home at 200 Anita Drive in West

Los Angeles. His body was found by his wife, who heard the shot from the house.

Millington, Mary

The illegitimate daughter of Joan Quilter (daughter of noted Heraldic painter Edward Quilter) and a father about whom little is known, the woman who was to become Britain's best known porn star was born in London on May 5, 1945. Pretty, but considered too short to be a traditional model, 4 foot, 11 inch Mary Quilter was working as a veterinary assistant in Dorking when photographer and nudie filmmaker John Lindsay spotted her in a Kensington coffee bar in the mid-seventies. Married at 19 to Robert Maxted, a butcher's assistant, Quilter was an exhibitionist who eagerly accepted Lindsay's offer to photograph her for soft-core sex magazines. Around this time, Quilter borrowed the name Millington from a friend largely because she liked the "MM" initials of Marilyn Monroe.

In the mid-seventies, Lindsay took Millington to Germany to film the hard-core sex romp *Miss Bohrloch*. Millington's enthusiastic performance as a sex-loving prostitute earned the film the coveted Golden Phallus Award (porn's equivalent to an Oscar) at the German Wet Dream Festival. In Britain, Lindsay turned Millington over to David Sullivan, a newly emerging power in the world of soft-core pornography. Sullivan paid to have Millington's nose and teeth fixed, and featured her on the cover of his sex publications. Under Sullivan's relentless promotion, Millington became a one woman sex industry, even endorsing her own line of sex aids. As her fame soared on the back of several sex films (*Come Play with Me*, 1977; *What's Up Superdoc!*, 1978; *Queen of the Blues*, 1979), Millington fell into a life of prostitution with a client list that included the Shah of Persia, influential businessmen, visiting Saudi princes, trades union leaders, and well-known celebrities. Tiring of men, Millington began an affair with actress Diana Dors, with whose husband, Alan Lake, she had appeared in the 1979 British sex romp

Confessions from the David Galaxy Affair. Lake (see entry), devastated by the death of Dors on May 4, 1984, would commit suicide on October 10, 1984.

By her early 30s, the porn actress was a psychic wreck. Addicted to cocaine and antidepressants, Millington's unchecked kleptomania had led to several arrests for shoplifting, and a possible prison term loomed. On the evening of August 19, 1979, the 34-year-old porn star phoned her publicist, John East, from her home in Walton-on-the-Hill, Surrey, and asked him to sing her favorite song, "Goodnight Sweetheart." When East reached the line, "We'll meet tomorrow," Millington responded, "There ain't gonna be no tomorrow. Goodnight," and hung up the phone. The next day, authorities found Millington dead on her bed surrounded by pills and a half-empty bottle of vodka.

In a suicide note, she wrote: "I wish I had the chance to act but they never gave me a break. Not that I was offered a good part, but that was what I was looking forward to." Millington was buried alongside her mother in a churchyard in South Holmwood, near Dorking. Of her show business friends, only Diana Dors and husband Alan Lake attended the funeral.

Milocevic, Milos

Milocevic, an aspiring Yugoslavian actor known professionally as "Milos Milos," worked in Paris as Alain Delon's stand-in before a marriage to a Chicago socialite living in Los Angeles (followed by a hasty divorce) earned him U.S. citizenship. In Hollywood, Delon introduced the young actor to Mickey Rooney and his fifth wife, Barbara Ann Thomason, who were in the midst of marital difficulties brought on by the diminutive actor's drug abuse, overwork, and philandering. Milocevic, 24, and Thomason, 29, began an affair in 1965 while Rooney was in Beirut filming *24 Hours to Kill*, co-starring future suicide Walter Slezak. The affair deepened as Rooney, in serious tax trouble, was constantly on the road to generate income. While Rooney was in the Philippines shooting *Ambush Bay*, Thomason spent two weeks with her lover on location in Fort Bragg, California, where he had a small part as a submarine crewman in director Norman Jewison's *The Russians Are Coming! The Russians Are Coming!*. After the filming, Milosevic began spending nights with Thomason and her four children in Rooney's $200,000 home at 13030 Evanston Street in Brentwood. Rooney, back from the Philippines with a debilitating blood infection, was informed by Thomason that she wanted him out of the house. The couple officially separated on December 23, 1965.

A seasoned veteran of divorce court, the 44-year-old actor took the offensive. On January 24, 1966, he filed papers charging Thomason as an "unfit mother" and demanded sole custody of their children. Milocevic reacted by phoning Thomason's friends and threatening them not to testify in Rooney's behalf. When one friend refused, Milocevic allegedly said, "If Barbara even looks at another man I'll shoot her and myself in the bedroom or bathroom. It'll be like a film. We'll be sleeping like two lovers together. It'll be great. We'll be in the headlines."

Terrified of losing her children, Thomason visited Rooney in St. John's Hospital in Santa Monica on January 30, 1966. Unknown to the actor, she wore a wire that transmitted their conversation to a private detective parked outside the hospital who was taping the interview. During their talk, Thomason got Rooney to admit that she was not an unfit mother. Rooney offered to retract the statement in the press after they reconciled. As she was leaving, Thomason assured him, "If it makes you unhappy for me to see Milos, then I won't even see him as a friend." That same evening, Thomason played the tape at home for Milocevic, her private detective, and two friends who were staying in the guest house on the property. After hearing the tape, a seemingly calm Milocevic asked to speak with his lover in the master bedroom around 8:30 P.M.

Everyone else, except three of the four Rooney children who were asleep in the house at the time, left for the evening. The fourth child was staying with Rooney's mother.

The next afternoon, house guest Wilma Catania became alarmed when a maid informed her that neither Milocevic or Thomason had been seen that day. Catania secured a key and entered the bedroom. She found Thomason dead on the bathroom floor with the lifeless Milosevic sprawled atop her. A chrome-plated .38-caliber automatic registered to Rooney lay beside them. Police speculated that Thomason's statement about not seeing her lover again prompted Milosevic to shoot her once in the lower part of the jaw before firing a fatal shot into his temple.

FURTHER READING

Rooney, Mickey. *Life Is Too Short*. New York: Villard Books, 1991.

Minch, Conrad H.

Well-known and regarded as a band leader and orchestra player in central New York, Minch, a 69 year old in ill health, slashed his throat with a razor in his Amsterdam home on August 13, 1931.

Miroslava

With her family, Miroslava (born Miroslava Sternova in Prague) escaped from her native Czechoslovakia in 1940. In Mexican films since 1946, the actress also gained prominence in the theatre. In her most notable U.S. film appearance she played opposite Mel Ferrer as "Linda de Calderon" in the 1951 Columbia Pictures release *The Brave Bulls*, produced and directed by Robert Rossen (see entry). Ironically, a failed relationship with real-life bullfighter Luis Miguel Dominguin prompted her to commit suicide. On March 10, 1955, the beautiful 27-year-old actress was found dead from an overdose of sleeping pills in her apartment in Mexico City. Her tragic life inspired the 1993 Alejandro Pelayo-directed film *Miroslava*.

Mohamed, Hammed Ben

The 22-year-old Morroco-born acrobat was appearing with his troupe in the prologue to the film *Beau Geste* at the St. Francis Theatre in San Francisco when he committed suicide in his room at 34 Turk Street on October 23, 1926. Apparently despondent after a night of heavy drinking, the Arab slit his throat from ear to ear with a safety razor and bled to death on his bed. Mohamed's male friend and travelling companion could offer no reason for the suicide.

Moloney, Jay (James David)

In June 1983 Moloney, 20, was a student at the University of Southern California when he began interning in the mail room at the prestigious Creative Artists Agency in Beverly Hills. Tall, handsome, and brimming with boyish charm, Moloney rose from sorting mail to become the protégé of Michael Ovitz, the super-agent head of CAA. Under Ovitz's tutelage, Moloney became the ringleader of the "Young Turks," a group of rich, ambitious agents who stood to inherit the reigns of power at the talent firm. In his years at CAA, the young agent amassed a client list that included Steven Spielberg, Martin Scorsese, Mike Nichols, Bill Murray, Leonardo DiCaprio, Dustin Hoffman, David Letterman, and Tim Burton. Moloney, by age 30, was making more than $1 million a year and dating actresses Sherilynn Fenn, Gina Gershon, and Jennifer Grey. By 1994, however, the super-agent's world was starting to crumble.

The death of his alcoholic father in March of that year deeply affected Moloney. Cracks in his relationship with Ovitz, brought on by what his mentor described as his protégé's "cockiness," had already begun to show. When Ovitz left CAA in 1995 to become the president of the Walt Disney Company, Moloney was seemingly poised to become an even bigger force in the agency. By that time, however, Moloney's occasional weekend drug use (begun in 1995) had evolved into serious cocaine binges. Drug addiction coupled with a near fatal car crash prompted Moloney to leave CAA in May 1996. Although Ovitz and other friends staged an intervention and checked him into various drug rehab programs, Moloney struggled with his addiction.

In January 1999, Moloney was rehabbing at the Menninger Clinic in Topeka, Kansas, when fellow patients found him in his hotel bathroom with his throat and wrists slashed. He barely survived. The former agent had been out of the Hollywood mainstream for nearly four years when he attempted a comeback in early 1999. Hired as the president of Paradise Music & Entertainment, an LA-based management and production company involved in the production of music videos and television commercials run by rock star Bob Dylan's son, Jesse, Moloney assured his partners that he was drug-free. His contract was officially terminated by company officials in September 1999 after his ongoing drug use was discovered.

On November 16, 1999, two days after celebrating his 35th birthday, Moloney's body was found in the bathroom of his rented Mulholland Drive home hanging from a shower head by his friend Ben Taylor, son of singers James Taylor and Carly Simon. Three days later at an early afternoon memorial service held at the Paramount Theatre in Hollywood, some 1,000 guests from the entertainment industry heard Moloney eulogized by his surrogate father, Michael Ovitz, and client Bill Murray. At one point in his address, Murray quipped, "Because Jay would have wanted it that way, I'm going to waive my fee today. There are so many people here today that I would much rather be eulogizing." Richard Lovett, a managing partner at CAA, decried the media's attempt to present Moloney's death as the age-old story of Hollywood excess: "Jay had two real diseases — depression and drug addiction — that discovered each other." Moloney is buried in the Hollywood Memorial Park Cemetery.

Monroe, Marilyn

Although Marilyn Monroe made just 29 films in a life which ended with mysterious abruptness shortly after her 36th birthday, she continues to remain the most instantly recognizable movie star in the world. Her image is licensed by CMG Worldwide and is available on items as diverse as tee-shirts, coffee mugs, key chains, bed linen, and collector dolls. Her official website, www.marilynmonroe.com, is among the most popular of any movie star, living or dead. Since her death in 1962 more than 300 books have been published about this screen icon.

Today, nearly 40 years since her passing, the incidents surrounding Monroe's death continue to be the focus of endless conjecture. The star's connection with organized crime and the Kennedy brothers, John F. and Robert, has been well documented, as has the possible role her psychiatrist, Dr. Ralph Greenson, may have played in her death. The truth is that no writer knows with absolute certainty what exactly occurred in the late evening and early morning hours of August 4–5, 1962. What *is* known about Monroe paints a tragic story of a young, insecure woman who, while unable to find lasting love in three failed marriages, was nevertheless beloved by millions of fans who knew only her screen image as "the Blonde."

The future film goddess was born Norma Jeane Mortenson in Los Angeles on June 1, 1926, the illegitimate daughter of Gladys Pearl Monroe Mortenson and an unidentified man. While the identity of her father has never been positively established, Monroe believed it was the manager at the Consolidated Film Laboratories where her mother worked as a negative cutter. The Mortenson family had a history of mental illness. Monroe's grandmother died in a mental asylum in 1927. In January 1934 her mother, Gladys Mortenson (née Baker), was diagnosed as a paranoid schizophrenic and institutionalized for the remainder of her daughter's life. Her mother's institutionalization signalled the beginning of

lifelong feelings of insecurity and self-doubt for the 8-year-old child. Monroe was made a ward of the County of Los Angeles and placed with a series of foster parents who were given a stipend of $20 a month for her care. At one facility, she was molested by an elderly man who afterward gave her a nickel "not to tell." The child was not believed when she reported the incident.

Largely to avoid being placed with yet another set of foster parents, the 16-year-old Van Nuys High School student married James Edward Dougherty, a 21-year-old metal worker at Lockheed Aircraft, in Westwood on June 19, 1942. The couple had little in common and rarely spoke. Norma Jeane Dougherty dropped out of school and, after her husband joined the U.S. Merchant Marines in early 1944, took a $20 a week job as a parachute inspector at a defense plant in the San Fernando Valley. David Conover, an Army photographer assigned to shoot a feature on the women of the war for *Yank* magazine, "discovered" the alluring 18 year old working on the assembly line. Conover's photos of the teenager for *Yank* captured a sensually innocent young woman with a lush physique who was perfectly comfortable in front of a camera. After Norma Jeane confided to Conover that she longed to be a model, the photographer shot some studies of her in the Mojave Desert for her portfolio. Soon after the photos were seen, she quit her job at the defense plant and signed a contract with the Blue Book Model Agency in Hollywood. Under the direction of Emmeline Snively, head of the agency, she became a full-time model and began making cover appearances on second-tier magazines like *Click*, *See*, and *Laff*.

Through Snively's contacts in the motion picture business, Norma Jeane Dougherty came to the attention of studio casting executive Ben Lyon. Impressed by the curvaceous teenager, Lyon signed her to a $75 a week stock contract with 20th Century–Fox in September 1946. Lyon instantly changed the new contract player's name to "Marilyn Monroe." On October 2, 1946, just weeks after gaining finanical independence with her Fox contract, Monroe divorced James Dougherty while he was overseas. She continued to pose for cheesecake photographers while taking acting and diction lessons at the studio.

In 1948, the actress made her first film appearance in a microscopic part in *Scudda Hoo! Scudda Hay!* Later in the year she was cast as a waitress in the juvenile delinquency exploitation drama *Dangerous Years.* In 1948 she met the first of several powerful older men who were able to help her career. Joe Schenck, co-founder with Darryl Zanuck of 20th Century–Fox, was an executive producer in his seventies when he saw the sexy young Monroe walking on the studio lot. He invited her to the regular Sunday afternoon brunches at his home where she became a welcome fixture. Whether Monroe's relationship with the septuagenarian producer was sexual or platonic has long been debated. Schenck, however, did use his influence to get her signed with Columbia Pictures on March 9, 1948, after Fox dropped her contract. Monroe appeared in only one Columbia film, the ingénue lead in the 1948 musical *Ladies of the Chorus,* before the studio dropped her option six months later on September 8, 1948. According to Hollywood legend, the actress was let go after refusing to sleep with studio head Harry Cohn. However, a comparable Hollywood legend maintains that she did. Monroe fared better in a sexy walk-on role in the 1949 Marx Brothers romp *Love Happy,* but still could not find steady film work.

In the summer of 1949 following her dismissal from Columbia, Monroe was unemployed and desperate for money. Sporting long and curly reddish-brown hair, the out-of-work actress posed in a swimsuit for a Pabst Blue Ribbon billboard ad shot by photographer Tom Kelley. Initially declining his offer

MARILYN MONROE— Pictured here in a publicity shot for *Let's Make Love* (1960), Monroe remains the most instantly recognizable star ever produced by the Hollywood studio machine. An international sex symbol, the glamorous actress was in reality an insecure child-woman who suffered a string of three failed marriages, numerous unfulfilling love affairs, and chemical dependicies. The nature of her barbiturate overdose death (accidental, suicide, murder) at the age of 36 on August 5, 1962, remains Hollywood's greatest mystery. *Courtesy of University of Southern California, on behalf of the USC Library Department of Special Collections.*

to pose naked, Monroe returned a few days later and agreed to pose lying on red velvet because she needed the $50 fee to pay her rent. Kelley sold the color shots and complete reproduction rights to a lithographer who featured the nude Monroe on a calendar. Chicago-based publisher Hugh Hefner later featured the nude shot in the inaugural issue of *Playboy* in 1953. An upcoming star at the time of the provocative photo's publication, Monroe was not adversely affected by its publication. She explained, "I was hungry."

Around October 1949, the 22-year-old struggling actress was discovered by Johnny Hyde, executive vice-president of the William Morris Agency, who was taken by her cameo in *Love Happy*. The 53-year-old talent agent responsible for directing the careers of cinema sex queens Rita Hayworth and Veronica Lake fell madly in love with Monroe. Hyde, suffering from a bad heart, left his wife and family to devote his entire energy to building his young lover's career. The smitten agent transformed Monroe into "the Blonde" icon known today throughout the world. Under his direction, she learned how to dress and had plastic surgery done on her nose and jaw. In 1950 Hyde landed Monroe the second female lead in the Mickey Rooney film *The Fireball*. That same year Hyde convinced his client, director John Huston, to cast his protégé as the secretary-mistress to Louis Calhern's shady lawyer in MGM's crime drama *Asphalt Jungle*. On the strength of Monroe's sizzling portrayal in the film, Hyde negotiated a seven year contract for her with 20th Century–Fox in December 1950. Weeks after closing the deal, Hyde suffered a fatal heart attack on December 17, 1950, the day Monroe began filming *As Young as You Feel* (1951). Many in Hollywood felt that Hyde had literally worked himself to death promoting Monroe's career. Despite being requested by Hyde's family not to attend the funeral service at Forest Lawn, a distraught Monroe did so and threw herself screaming across his casket.

In his 1984 biography *Legend: The Life and Death of Marilyn Monroe*, Fred Lawrence Guiles reports that shortly after the funeral the young star attempted suicide while staying at the home of friend and drama coach Natasha Lytess. Returning early from a day of shopping, Lytess found a note pinned to Monroe's bedroom door that read, "Don't let Barbara [Lytess' four-year-old daughter] in." The drama coach found the actress unconscious in bed, her mouth filled with a purplish paste — some 30 half-dissolved Nembutal tablets.

In 1950, Monroe appeared in a small but memorable role as "Miss Caswell," the aspiring actress-girlfriend of theatre critic "Addison DeWitt" (George Sanders) in *All About Eve*. The Academy Award winning film featured three future suicides in its cast: Monroe, Sanders (see entry), and Barbara Bates (see entry). The studio carefully increased Monroe's duties in other films of the period including *Clash By Night* (1952), *We're Not Married* (1952), *Don't Bother to Knock* (1952), *Monkey Business* (1952), and *O'Henry's Full House*. In 1953, Monroe appeared in *Niagara*, the film that made her a star and cemented her image as the screen's quintessential sex goddess. Cast as an adulterous wife with murderous intent, Monroe stole the show undulating in a skin-tight red satin dress. *The New York Times* reviewer noted, "The producers are making full use of both the grandeur of the Falls and its adjacent areas as well as the grandeur that is Marilyn Monroe," adding, "The falls and Miss Monroe are something to see." The star's two 1953 follow-up films, the hugely successful *Gentlemen Prefer Blondes* and *How to Marry a Millionaire*, further typecast her as filmdom's "dumb blonde," a persona that rankled the actress and was at odds with her off-screen attempts to better herself through the study of literature.

During her suspension at Fox for refusing to star in the film *Heller in Pink Tights*, Monroe married New York Yankee baseball legend Joe DiMaggio in a civil ceremony in San Francisco on January 14, 1954. The "Yankee Clipper," then arguably the most popular player in baseball, was 12 years older than Monroe and insanely jealous of the star. Following a brief honeymoon in Paso Robles, the couple traveled to Japan where DiMaggio was regarded as a national idol. Cheering crowds at the airport, however, barely noticed the man on the arm of Marilyn Monroe. Angered over the slight, DiMaggio argued with his wife over her commitment to entertain U.S. Army troops stationed in Korea. As the baseball great fumed alone in Tokyo, Monroe was onstage in Korea provocatively performing in front of 100,000 screaming soldiers. Their marriage was already on the rocks when she agreed to do the Billy Wilder-directed comedy *The Seven Year Itch* (1955). An intensely private man, DiMaggio despised the show biz crowd and, in his unwillingness to accommodate Monroe's career in any fashion, wanted her to be his wife full time.

The situation reached its crisis during location shooting in New York City in September 1954. In order to shoot the film's most famous scene, Monroe standing over a Times Square subway grating, Wilder began filming the scene at 2:30 A.M. and closed down an entire city block around Lexington Avenue and Fifty-first Street. Even at that hour, a thousand raucous spectators had to be restrained behind police barricades. Blowers were installed under the grating to simulate the breeze generated by a passing subway train. Unknown to cast and crew, DiMaggio arrived unannounced from the coast to watch the filming. As the scene was shot, he watched in silent rage as Monroe's pleated crepe sundress was blown up around her waist to reveal a pair of scant ivory colored panties. The marriage was over nine months after it began. Shortly after the film wrapped, Monroe entered Cedars of Lebanon Hospital for gynecological surgery (some sources say to abort DiMaggio's baby). On October 3, 1954, she filed for divorce from the baseball legend, citing mental cruelty. At the hearing Monroe told the judge, "I was allowed to have no visitors: maybe three times in the nine months we were married. Once when I was sick he did allow someone to come and see me. The relationship was one of coldness and indifference." Monroe was granted an interlocutory divorce decree on October 27, 1954, although she and DiMaggio continued to remain close friends.

Dating from this period, Monroe began seeing a psychiatrist five times a week until her death in 1962. In January 1955, the popular actress walked out on Fox, defiantly resisting the studio's attempt to stereotype her in fluff like *The Revolt of Mamie Stover, How to Be Very, Very Popular*, and *The Girl in the Red Velvet Swing*. She went to New York, formed Marilyn Monroe Productions, and began to seriously study acting under Lee and Paula Strasberg at the Actors Studio. While mingling with the intellectual New York City set she became playwright Arthur Miller's unlikely lover. In January 1956, Monroe returned to Hollywood and signed a lucrative seven year non-exclusive, multi-picture deal with 20th Century–Fox. Under the terms of the contract, the actress was paid $100,000 a picture and given director, script, cameraman, and make-up man approval. In 1956, Monroe received good reviews for her sensitive performance in Joshua Logan's film version of *Bus Stop*, a play by fellow suicide William Inge (see entry). On June 29, 1956, shortly before leaving for England to star opposite Shakespearean acting great Laurence Olivier in *The Prince and the Showgirl*, the actress married Arthur Miller after converting to Judaism.

The Olivier-directed film was intended to expand Monroe's range as an actress. Instead, it proved to be a career and personal debacle. The classically trained Olivier was not sympathetic to the hours Monroe spent on-camera searching for her character's "motivation." At other times, the production stalled while cast and crew were forced to await the arrival of the chronically late actress. Olivier considered the popular American actress to be little more than a "troublesome bitch." Monroe, frustrated by Olivier, turned to Miller for support. He too, however, was disenchanted with the manner in which she interacted with Olivier and by her lack of professionalism on the set. Monroe went over the edge when she discovered a secret diary Miller was keeping about their marriage. In it, the playwright denigrated his wife and accused her of making "love a drudgery." Monroe suffered a nervous breakdown near the end of filming that necessitated that her psychiatrist be flown from New York to London so she could complete the film. Miller returned alone to New York. Frustrated, Monroe sharply increased her intake of champagne and sleeping pills to combat insomnia. Not surprisingly, given the conditions under which it was made, *The Prince and the Showgirl* received bad reviews. More strain was put on the faltering marriage when Monroe suffered a miscarriage on August 1, 1957.

In July 1958, the actress again teamed with Billy Wilder to begin shooting *Some Like It Hot* (1959) with Tony Curtis and Jack Lemmon. Unfailingly late to the set and usually unprepared when she got there, Monroe alienated everyone on the film. Tony Curtis, disgusted by his buxom costar's demands for multiple retakes, likened making love to her in the film to "kissing Hitler." Interviewed years later about Monroe, Curtis said that the sexy star created so much tension on the set that "nobody wanted to talk to her." Five days before filming ended on November 6, 1958, the 32-year-old actress collapsed on the set. Rushed to a hospital, she was told that she had again miscarried.

Trouble in the Monroe-Miller marriage became even more apparent while the star was filming *Let's Make Love* (1960) with French star Yves Montand, husband of actress Simone Signoret. Monroe, deeply in love with Montand, began an affair with the French actor during the film's production. Convinced that he would leave Signoret, Monroe was crushed when Montand refused to do so and further dismissed her affections for him as a "schoolgirl crush." Montand later ungallantly told the press that Monroe was a "sick lady" who "threw herself at me." Seventeen days after *Let's Make Love* wrapped, Monroe reported for work in Reno, Nevada, to begin filming Arthur Miller's *The Misfits*. Directed by John Huston and starring Monroe's idol, Clark Gable, the film was destined to be the final screen appearance for both megastars. Temperatures in the desert where most of the film was shot soared to more than 100 degrees daily and physically punished the cast and crew. By mutual agreement, Miller and Monroe decided to postpone their divorce until after the film was completed. Still, Monroe openly argued with Miller over the script, which he refused to change to accommodate the subtleties of her character. During the filming, the actress was hospitalized for an overdose of sleeping pills and exhaustion. On November 16, 1960, 12 days before the end of shooting, Clark Gable, 61, died of a fatal heart attack brought on by the physical demands of the film. Monroe divorced Miller in Juarez, Mexico, on January 20, 1961, one week before the opening of *The Misfits*.

Depressed, totally exhausted, and dangerously abusing alcohol and sedatives, Monroe required institutionalization less than one month after the film's premiere. Believing that her psychiatrist was only going to check her into a rest home, Monroe was floored when she was admitted under the name "Faye Miller" into New York's Payne-Whitney Hospital, a psychiatric facility for highly disturbed mental patients. In the hospital's atmosphere of locked down wards and padded walls, Monroe descended into hysteria and begged to be released. It took three days, but ex-husband Joe DiMaggio stepped in and had her transferred to a private room in the Neurological Institute, a unit of Columbia-Presbyterian Hospital. Monroe remained there for three weeks resting and withdrawing from pills. Shortly after being released, the actress was recuperating in her New York City apartment at East Fifty-seventh Street when she became suicidal after reading a newspaper interview with Clark Gable's widow. Kay Gable claimed that Monroe's erratic behavior on the set prolonged *The Misfits* for weeks, thereby contributing to her husband's death. Guilt-ridden, Monroe reportedly opened the window in her apartment and was seriously considering jumping when, at the last moment, she recognized someone on the street below she thought she knew. Friends hurriedly moved her out of the apartment and back to Hollywood where she purchased a one-story hacienda style bungalow at 12305 Fifth Helena Drive in Brentwood. Monroe's psychiatrist, Dr. Ralph Greenson, hired live-in housekeeper Eunice Murray to monitor his patient's condition.

In early April 1962 Fox scheduled Monroe to begin work on *Something's Got to Give* co-starring Dean Martin. Unhappy with the script, she delayed production until April 23, 1962. Claiming physical illness, the actress had spent only six partial days on the set by May 1962. Against studio orders, Monroe flew to New York City to appear at President John F. Kennedy's birthday party at Madison Square Garden on May 19, 1962. Dressed in a revealing skin-tight gown, Monroe sang "Happy Birthday" to the man with whom she had been secretly having an affair for some time. Kennedy, tired of the erratic actress and fearful of exposure, reportedly ended the affair and enlisted the aid of his younger brother, Attorney General Robert F. Kennedy, to provide damage control. Many writers on the case suggest that Robert Kennedy became sexually involved with Monroe as well and visited her on August 4, 1962, the day before her death. Rebuffed by the president, Monroe returned to Hollywood and the set of *Something's Got to Give* where she celebrated her 36th birthday on June 1, 1962. Still complaining of illness, the star managed to film a nude pool scene but little else. When she was a no-show after several days, Fox executives pulled the plug on the production and fired Marilyn Monroe on June 7, 1962, citing "willful violation of contract."

The actress continued to suffer from insomnia, deepening depression, and was now meeting almost daily with her psychiatrist, Dr. Ralph Greenson. Depending upon which of the 300 plus Monroe biographies one reads, the actress was also frantic to reestablish contact with President Kennedy and his brother, Robert. The final 24 hours of Monroe's life have been the subject of endless speculation. Numerous theories running the gamut from murder (a mob hit, a government conspiracy to protect the Kennedys) to accidental death (overdose by her psychiatrist) to suicide have been advanced to explain the untimely death of the 36-year-old movie queen. Sloppy police work, discrepancies in the autopsy and toxicology results, and the passage of time have conspired to render the true nature of Monroe's death unknowable.

On August 4, 1962, Monroe spent the day at her Brentwood home speaking to friends on the phone. Psychiatrist Ralph Greenson left at 7:00 P.M. after heavily tranquilizing the star. Around 8:00 P.M. friend Peter Lawford phoned to try to convince her to spend the evening with him and his wife, Pat. According to Lawford, the actress was despondent and tired, and her speech was slurred. As her voice became less and less audible, Lawford started yelling in an attempt to revive her. Monroe finally told him, "Say good-bye to Pat, say good-bye to Jack (President Kennedy), and say good-bye to yourself because you're a nice guy," then hung up. Around midnight companion-housekeeper Eunice Murray noticed a light under Monroe's bedroom door. Murray, however, became alarmed when the light was still on at 3:00 A.M. and a phone cord from Monroe's private line now led under the closed door of the room. Murray listened, heard nothing, then banged on Monroe's door. Unable to rouse the star, she went outside to look in through the bedroom window. She saw the nude Monroe lying motionless in the bed clutching a phone receiver. Hurrying inside, she phoned Dr. Greenson. When Greenson arrived around 3:30 A.M., he broke the bedroom window with a fireplace poker and entered the room. He notified Monroe's physician, Dr. Hyman Engelberg, who arrived around 3:50 A.M. to confirm that the star was dead. Police were not notified until around 4:30 A.M. An empty bottle of prescription Nembutal was found on a bedside table near the body, but no glass with which to wash them down.

Deputy Medical Examiner Dr. Thomas Noguchi conducted the Monroe autopsy, which was characterized by numerous discrepancies. Although there was a high concentration of barbiturates in her bloodstream, the equivalent of between 40 to 50 pills, her small intestine where the pills would be dissolved were not tested due to "lack of facilities." No pill residue was found in her stomach or any other internal organs. Some, suggesting that the lethal overdose of barbiturates was injected, pointed to a bruise on Monroe's hip as a possible injection site.

Noguchi, however, failed to make any note of needle marks in his report. Monroe's death was recorded as a "probable suicide." Joe DiMaggio took charge of his ex-wife's funeral at the Westwood Village Funeral Chapel on August 9, 1962. Per his instructions, Monroe's show biz friends were barred from the small private service. Actors Studio head Lee Strasberg delivered the eulogy, calling the star "a symbol of the eternal feminine." *The Los Angeles Herald-Examiner* reported that the funeral "ended with fans playing their usual roles of desecration as they stormed the vault after the mourners had departed, to ruthlessly rip to pieces the floral offerings for 'souvenirs.'" The world's greatest star was interred in a wall crypt in Westwood Memorial Park, Corridor of Memories, #24. A bronze identification plate reads simply, "Marilyn Monroe—1926–1962."

FURTHER READING (SELECTED)

Guiles, Fred Lawrence. *Legend: The Life and Death of Marilyn Monroe*. New York: Stein and Day, 1984.

———. *Norma Jean; The Life of Marilyn Monroe*. New York: McGraw-Hill, 1969.

Mailer, Norman. *Marilyn, a Biography*. New York: Grosset & Dunlap, 1973.

Monroe, Marilyn. *My Story*. New York: Stein and Day, 1974.

Shevey, Sandra. *The Marilyn Scandal: Her True Life Revealed by Those Who Knew Her*. 1st U.S. ed. New York: W. Morrow, 1987.

Spoto, Donald. *Marilyn Monroe: The Biography*. 1st ed. New York: HarperCollins Publishers, 1993.

Summers, Anthony. *Goddess: The Secret Lives of Marilyn Monroe*. New York: Macmillan, 1985.

Victor, Adam. *The Marilyn Encyclopedia*. 1st ed. Woodstock, N.Y.: Overlook Press, 1999.

Mont, Helen Kim

Prior to marrying interior decorator James Mont in March 1937, Helen Kim appeared in minor roles in Broadway productions like *Congai* (1928) and *Roar China* (1930). On April 24, 1937, the couple argued, and the 25-year-old actress returned alone to their fourth floor apartment at 480 Park Avenue in New York City. By coincidence, as

Mont was in her kitchen sucking deadly fumes through a tube connected to a gas range, some 200 persons were milling around in the lobby below drawn together by the promise of a "mystery party" in the building announced in an unsigned chain letter. Authorities worked over the former actress with a Pulmotor for more than half an hour before she died. Seven years before, while still Helen Kim, a 37-year-old poet named Robert Carroll Pew drank poison in her apartment and fell dead at her feet.

Moora, Robert L.

Moora was working as a rewrite man for *The New York Herald Tribune* when, at the outset of World War II, the Army sent him to Britain to assume the managing editorship of the London edition of the Army newspaper *Stars and Stripes*. After the war, Moora returned to the *Herald Tribune* where over the next 17 years he became the paper's Sunday editor and later news editor in its Washington Bureau. He left the newspaper in 1957 to join the public relations department of the Radio Corporation of America, later transferring from New York to Camden, New Jersey. On February 14, 1971, the 58-year-old public relations executive was found dead in his automobile near Medford Lakes, New Jersey. The State Police reported that the cancer-stricken Moora had run a hose from the exhaust into the sealed interior of the car.

Moore, Lotus

Long familiar to patrons of San Francisco's Tivoli Theatre as a musical comedy ingénue and previously as a leading member of the Jim Post beauty chorus, Moore was working in the "City by the Bay" as a cabaret entertainer at the Black Cat cafe at Eddy and Mason streets. Shortly before 7:00 A.M. on February 21, 1913, the semi-conscious woman was found writhing in agony in the rooms she shared at 1149 Divisadero Street with her mother and a 4-year-old daughter from a failed marriage. Clutched in Moore's hand was an empty bottle of cresoline that she used regularly as a throat balm. Moore was dead on arrival at Emergency Hospital. Accident or suicide? Three weeks before the popular entertainer had been severely burned about the face when an antiphlogistine preparation she was heating as an application for throat trouble exploded. The suicide theory advanced by the coroner that explained Moore's self-destruction as a reaction to her failing voice and lost beauty was discounted by her most intimate friends, who noted that she had fully recovered from the accident and was in excellent spirits.

Moorehead, Chester

Moorehead was 17 when he married 16-year-old future film star Constance Bennett (1904–1965), in Greenwich, Connecticut, in June 1921. The union was annulled in January 1923 after it was revealed that neither of the teens had married with parental consent and that Bennett had refused to live with him. Long unemployed due to illness and recently divorced, the 42-year-old former advertising copywriter had lived for five years in a room in Chicago's Wilmar Hotel at 11 W. Division Street. On December 12, 1945, Moorehead phoned the desk manager and informed the shaken man that he planned to commit suicide. The manager immediately notified Moorehead's neighbors, who entered his room just in time to see him down a handful of sleeping pills. "I'm going to sleep, and please don't try to stop me," muttered Moorehead as he tried to write a note to his mother. He collapsed and died after writing the salutation, "Dearest Mother —."

Moorey, Stefa

On February 3, 1972, the drowned body of the 38-year-old stage actress was found in Bourn Brook, Selly Oak, Birmingham, England. The coroner theorized that the actress' depression over being unable to conceive children was fatally exacerbated by the role of Queen Elizabeth I she was currently rehearsing for the Birmingham Repertory Theatre. In the play, parts of the dialogue spoken by Moorey touched on barrenness. Referring to a note that the actress left for her actor-husband, the coroner concluded: "It is quite clear that she badly wanted a baby, and there was evidence that she had taken an overdose of tablets."

Moriarty, Joanne

A former stewardess from the Chicago area, Moriarty, 25, had a bit part in the 1964 Universal film *Bedtime Story* starring Marlon Brando, David Niven, and Shirley Jones. On March 2, 1964, her husband of less than two months, actor Harry S. Parks, returned to their home in Los Angeles at 2:30 A.M. from a story conference with director Brian Hutton to find his wife unconscious in bed from an apparent overdose of sleeping pills. Empty bottles that had contained the prescribed medication were found at the scene. Moriarty was dead when an ambulance crew arrived.

Morphy, Lewis Harris

Apparently depressed over the death of his mother two years earlier and the recent failure of a resort he owned in Tennessee, show business sharpshooter and stuntman Morphy, 54, murdered his wife and mother-in-law in their Hollywood Hills home on November 7, 1958. One of the couple's three children present in the house at 2211 Stanley Hills Drive later told police that prior to the incident she heard Morphy mutter, "I've had enough. This is it." Around midnight, Morphy shot his wife, a 37-year-old former speedboat racing champion, in the head with a .25-caliber pistol. When her mother came to investigate the disturbance, the 70 year old was fatally wounded when she fractured her skull against a corner of a table during a struggle with Morphy. After phoning a friend to report that "I've lost everything," Morphy shot and killed himself at the foot of his wife's bed.

Morris, Chester

Born John Chester Brooks Morris in New York City on February 16, 1901, the future "Boston Blackie" of motion picture fame was the son of leading man stage actor William Morris and his wife, Etta Hawkins, the ingénue comedian for Charles Frohman's theatrical company. In 1917, Morris made his first film appearance as a college boy in *An Amateur Orphan*. While making his Broadway debut in February 1918 in *The Copperhead*, the young actor was also working in his second film, *The Beloved Traitor*, shot by Goldwyn at the Fort Lee Studios in New Jersey. Afterward, Morris appeared regularly on Broadway, in touring companies, and in stock theatre in Providence and Baltimore. In 1927, Morris was on Broadway in *Crime* when he was noticed by Hollywood talent scouts eager to find stage-trained actors for the talkies. Signed by D. W. Griffith to appear in the Roland West directed gangster film *Alibi*, Morris received an Academy Award nomination for Best Actor in 1928–1929 (he lost to Warner Baxter in *In Old Arizona*).

From that date on, the actor worked continually; first in a two-picture deal at MGM, then later in a series of action-filled stories with RKO in the thirties. In 1941, Morris played the title character in Columbia's *Meet Boston Blackie*, a role that would essentially relegate him to "B" pictures for the rest of his career. A reformed criminal turned detective, the Boston Blackie character was tailor-made for Morris, whose jut-jaw, hooked nose, and slicked back hair typified the determined, two-fisted hero. In all, Morris would portray the character in 14 films from 1941 through his bow in *Boston Blackie's Chinese Venture* in 1949. In between films in the series, Morris made numerous other movies and introduced the character on radio in 1944, where it was subsequently played by Richard Kollmar. Typecast in "B" movies, Morris returned to the stage in 1949 to headline a national touring company of *Detective Story*. Throughout the fifties he also appeared in several television shows including *Studio One*, *Suspense*, and *Lights Out*. Much in demand after the Boston Blackie series was broadcast on television, the actor continued to play in

CHESTER MORRIS— Best known to movie audiences as "Boston Blackie" in a series of 14 "B" movies in the forties, Morris was also an accomplished stage actor. Riddled with stomach cancer, the 69-year-old actor was found dead of a barbiturate overdose in his motel room in New Hope, Pennsylvania, on September 11, 1970.

summer stock and road shows. Morris returned to films in 1955 with *Unchained*, and the next year appeared as a sideshow hypnotist in the low-budget sci-fi feature *The She Creature*.

In 1970, Morris played his final film role, boxing commissioner "Pop Morris," in the 20th Century–Fox hit *The Great White Hope*. On September 11, 1970, days before the film was set to open, the 69-year-old actor was found dead of a barbiturate overdose in his room at the Holiday Inn in New Hope, Pennsylvania. Despite suffering from an advanced case of stomach cancer, Morris was in the area starring as "Captain Queeg" in *The Caine Mutiny Court-Martial* at the Bucks County Playhouse.

FURTHER READING

Bodeen, DeWitt. "Chester Morris." *Films in Review*, pp. 395–408, 412, Aug.–Sept. 1990.

Morris, Leonard

Spurned by Edith Creighton (real name Edith Simmons), part of a vaudeville act with her three sisters, stage electrician and former film projectionist Leonard Morris, 37, shot her to death inside a store in Theatrical City, New Jersey, near New Brunswick on July 17, 1917, before taking his own life. Creighton was in the store with her 6-year-old son when her rejected suitor entered, produced a pistol wrapped in a handkerchief from his pocket, then fired two shots as she fled from the rear of the store into a back yard. Morris pursued and, following Creighton back into the store, fired a lethal shot into her head. Declaring, "I am going to finish myself," the insanely jealous electrician fired once into his own head and fell beside Creighton's body. Morris died half an hour later as a doctor tried to remove him by stretcher to St. Peter's Hospital. Months prior to the murder-suicide Morris had become enamored with the performer after she moved into a rooming house where he resided.

Morrison, Fred R.

On August 6, 1961, Morrison, the father of screen star Janet Leigh, accompanied by his wife of 35 years, Helen, visited their daughter and her husband, actor Tony Curtis, at their Beverly Hills home. In her autobiography, Leigh observed that the couple had been arguing, a condition exacerbated when Curtis refused the 52-year-old insurance broker's request for a short term loan. Leigh and Jeannie Martin, wife of crooner Dean Martin, left the next day for the French Riviera to attend Princess Grace of Monaco's International Red Cross Ball on August 12, 1961. That same day, Morrison's body was found on a couch in his Beverly Hills business office in the Vollrath Building at 9835 Santa Monica Boulevard. A half empty bottle of barbiturates and a vitriolic note to his wife were found nearby. The note read: "Helen — I also just wanted to tell you one thing. You [deleted by press]. Now maybe you can be happy because you have to have a man dead before you could be happy. So — *I hate you.*" And in an odd postscript Morrison added: "And by the way — this time I didn't send a little man to market — this one is a big one."

FURTHER READING

Leigh, Janet. *There Really Was a Hollywood.* Garden City, N.Y.: Doubleday, 1984.

Mossman, James

After years of working as a journalist for newspapers in Australia and England, Mossman joined the British Broadcasting Corporation as a commentator on the network's *Panorama* public affairs program. His decade long tenure on the show was marked by an intelligent and easygoing manner. From 1969 until a few days before his death, Mossman edited and presented the BBC arts program *Review*. The newsman also authored three books: *Rebels in Paradise: Indonesia's Civil War* (1961), *Beggars on Horseback* (1966), and *Lifelines*, a novel published posthumously in 1971. On April 5, 1971, the 44-year-old Mossman was found by a housekeeper at his 300-year-old cottage in Gissing, Norfolk, dead from an overdose of tuinal barbiturate sleeping tablets.

In a manuscript found at the scene Mossman described how his mother had also taken her own life with the drug. Also recovered was a letter written in pencil to his brother that began: "Dear John, I cannot bear it anymore, but I don't know what it is."

Mottley, Eva

The Barbados-born black beauty turned to acting after serving 15 months in a British jail for possession of LSD. A former girlfriend of rock star David Bowie, Mottley's film credits included *Scrubbers* (1982) and a small role in *Superman III* (1983), although she was best known for her starring role as "Bella" in the British television series *Widows*. Upset over losing her job on the series in August 1984, the 31-year-old actress' allegations of sexual and racial prejudice among the show's production crew were lost amidst a swirl of alcohol and cocaine abuse that left her £25,000 in debt. On February 14, 1985, St. Valentine's Day, Mottley was found slumped on her knees by the telephone in her flat in Shirland Road, Maida Vale, West London. In her depression, Mottley had downed a deadly cocktail of barbiturates and alcohol. Two notes, one addressed to her parents and tucked in her bedclothes, and the other on a writing pad begun normally in blue ink and ending illegibly in red, were found at the scene.

Moult, Edward "Ted"

Moult parlayed a 1959 win in the "Brain of Britain" contest into a popular radio and later television career largely based on his image as the archetypal rustic wise man. A panelist on the British edition of radio's *What's My Line?*, Moult also appeared regularly on *Ask Me Another*, *Twenty Questions*, and as the gentleman farmer "Bill Insley" in the radio serial *The Archers*. Moult's television credits included *Blankety Blank*, *Play School*, and *Celebrity Squares*. Depressed over his deteriorating health and the poor summer weather that decimated the profits of his pick-your-own strawberry trade, the 60-year-old gentle-

man farmer entered the office of his 300 acre farm in Derbyshire on September 3, 1986, and took his life with a single shotgun blast.

Moyer, Helen Jean

Moyer, a 29-year-old native of Herkimer, New York, became a victim of technology after losing her job as assistant organist when the Loew's New York Theatre at Broadway and 45th streets converted from silent to sound motion pictures on June 9, 1929. Two days later, the unemployed musician tore up letters from her parents, carefully packed her personal belongings, then jumped to her death from the window of her 12th floor room at the Hotel Belvedere.

Mueller, Lawrence S.

Mueller, 32, a sign painter-artist from the California desert town of El Centro, married New York showgirl Evelyn Childs (real name Evelyn Pearl Tatum) on March 26, 1927. The 25-year-old actress soon tired of life away from the footlights and, on May 26, went to Los Angeles following a quarrel with her husband. Checking into the Rosegrove Hotel at 532 South Flower Street, Childs made the rounds of Hollywood studios and theatrical agencies looking for work. Distraught and anxious to save their marriage, Mueller sent a flurry of letters and telegrams addressed to his "golden girl" begging her to come back. She advised him not to come to Los Angeles as it might discourage producers from casting her. In a final letter before driving to Los Angeles, Mueller pleaded with his wife for "one week of happiness" together during which time he would look for work in the city and, if they still proved incompatible, he would accept a position in Chicago.

On the morning of May 30, 1927, the maid at the Rosegrove let herself into Childs' room to clean. The young showgirl, clad only in a flimsy pink nightgown, lay on the bed strangled to death with a bedsheet. Mueller's nude, lifeless body was found a few feet away suspended by a bedspread wound tightly about his neck attached to a closet door lintel. The record "All for Love" was on a rundown phonograph beside the bed. Among numerous letters chronicling the buildup to the tragedy was a picture of Mueller with the following written across the corner: "To Pearl, my perfect pal. Yesterday, today, and, I hope, forever."

Muller, Ben

The manager for many years of the Lodi and State theatres in Lodi, California, Muller, 42, had become increasingly depressed over business matters. Weeks before his death, he often threatened suicide to his wife and was never without a bottle of iodine laced with ant paste on his person. On January 3, 1938, Muller's wife and a friend found the theatre manager in the basement of his Lodi home at 710 South Street suspended from a cord attached to a ceiling joist. A note addressed to his wife and son found on the dining room table upstairs read: "Dear Ruth and Dickie: Forgive me for this act but I am going mad … sorry I made you both so much trouble…. Goodbye and good luck to you both." Evidence at the death scene suggested that Muller had eaten some of the deadly mixture before slipping a double noose around his neck and then kicking an 18 inch high box out from under his feet.

Mulligan, Griffin

Mulligan, employed for seven years as a stage electrician at the Loew's State theatre, ended his life with an army rifle in his Hollywood home on September 16, 1934, one day after his wife died in a hospital from injuries sustained three months before in a fall. The 39-year-old electrician left a brief note explaining that he was despondent over her death.

Munro, Viola Gordon

Viola, 55, a former stage actress, and husband Alfred, 75, a one-time theatrical representative of the Schubert organization in Boston, occupied a modest apartment over a two-car garage in Norfolk, Connecticut. On the morning of June 21, 1949, their downstairs neighbor noticed blood dripping from the ceiling as he went to get his car out of the garage. Police entered the Munros' apartment and found the former theatrical manager dead in bed from a gunshot wound to the head inflicted by his wife, who had then fired a fatal shot through her right ear. Facing imminent eviction from their apartment, the destitute pair had been unemployed for months and known to be drinking heavily.

Munrow, David

Credited with popularizing the music of the 16th Century, Munrow, 33, was the director of the Early Music Consort and presenter on the BBC Radio 3 program *Pied Piper*, which he began in 1971. An accomplished recorder player, Munrow and his consort were responsible for the music of several television series and films, among them *Henry VIII and His Six Wives* and *Elizabeth R.* Deeply depressed over the deaths of his father and father-in-law, the musician survived a pill overdose in 1975. On May 15, 1976, Munrow's wife found him hanging in the hayloft above the garage of their home at Long Park, Chesham Bois, Buckinghamshire. The coroner ruled that the act "was an impulsive suicide during a period of recovery from deep depression."

Munson, Ona

Born Ona Wolcott in Portland, Oregon, on June 16, 1906, Munson began her career in vaudeville in 1922. In 1925 an appearance in the title role of "Nanette" in the road show company of the musical *No, No Nanette* led to Munson replacing Louise Groody in the role on Broadway the next year. On the strength of that performance, Munson became recognized as a musical-comedy star on the New York stage and appeared in *Twinkle Twinkle*

(1926) opposite Joe E. Brown, *Manhattan Mary* (1927) with Ed Wynn, and *Hold Everything!* (1928) with Bert Lahr, better known as the "Cowardly Lion" in the 1939 MGM fantasy masterpiece *The Wizard of Oz*. After appearing in a few dramatic roles onstage, Munson went to Hollywood in 1931 and made the film comedies *Broadminded, The Hot Heiress,* and the Mervyn LeRoy directed drama *Five Star Final* starring Edward G. Robinson. Throughout the thirties, the actress divided her time between the stage (*Ghosts*, 1935, with Alla Nazimova) and movies (*Dramatic School* and *His Exciting Night*, 1938). In 1939, she landed the role of "Belle Watling," the prostitute-friend of "Rhett Butler" in the MGM Civil War epic *Gone with the Wind*. Following a memorable performance as "Madame Gin Sling" in Josef von Sternberg's *The Shanghai Gesture* (1942), Munson was relegated to low-budget Westerns like *Dakota* (1945). Her final screen appearance was in *The Red House* in 1947. During the fifties, Munson lived in New York City with her second husband, artist-designer Eugene Berman, while sporadically acting onstage. On February 11, 1955, Berman found his 48-year-old wife dead from an overdose of sleeping pills in her bedroom in their apartment at 225 West Eighty-sixth Street. On a table near the bed in which Munson was found was a note that read, "This is the only way I know to be free again…. Please don't follow me."

ONA MUNSON— A former musical star on Broadway, Munson relocated to Hollywood in 1931 and is best remembered as "Belle Watling" in *Gone with the Wind* (1939) and as "Madame Gin Sling" in *The Shanghai Gesture* (1942). Out of films after 1947, the 48-year-old actress took an overdose of sleeping pills in New York City on February 11, 1955, in order, according to her suicide note, "to be free again."

Murray, Oscar J.

In a career spanning 35 years, the 68-year-old operatic and theatrical manager was credited with bringing such celebrated actors as Sarah Bernhardt and Edwin Booth to Brooklyn, New York, when he managed that city's Academy of Music. Murray was the manager of the People's Bath, Ocean Parkway, and Brighton Beach Avenue, Coney Island, attractions when, despondent over the critical illness of his wife, he decided to end it all on October 13, 1929. Closing all the windows of his Coney Island apartment at 3044 Ocean Parkway, Murray opened three gas jets on his stove. He was found dead in his living room by the building superintendant after tenants complained of smelling gas.

Murray, Paul

Murray (real name McKay) entered show business in London in 1905 as a booker for the Stoll Circuit. In 1908, he became the British representative for the American William Morris Vaudeville Circuit. Though well-liked, Murray had no head for business and filed for bankruptcy at least twice in his career; the last was when his theatrical agency failed in 1948. Murray pinned his comeback hopes on a revival of Fred Duprez's farce, *My Wife's Family*, and was devastated when it closed in the second week of its run after backers withdrew their financial support. On October 17, 1949, the 60-year-old producer and his wife were found dead in the gas-filled bedroom of their London flat in Earls Court-Square West. Ironically, Murray needed only £200 to keep the show open, a sum several of his friends later said they would have given him had he but asked.

Nagle, Raymond

Forced by ill health to leave New York City and the vaudeville act of Mandel and Nagle, the 30-year-old actor checked into a San Francisco tuberculosis hospital. Days after his release, Nagle inhaled gas in his room at 719 Fillmore Street on March 3, 1917. Five cents was found in his pocket along with a letter from a woman in New York signed "Louise."

Nash, Marvin E.

Nash, the co-owner of the Harem Club at 10821 Long Beach Boulevard in Los Angeles, appeared in good spirits early on the evening of April 19, 1962. Later that night, a bartender found the 43-year-old club owner's body hanging from a necktie in the dressing room.

Neal, Sandra

A dancer in the floor show at the Club Alabam' in Chicago, the 22-year-old blonde left the Windy City in the fall of 1937 for New York City with dreams of making it big on Broadway. Neal knocked on booking agents' doors for five months, but never received a call back. On January 15, 1938, two friends took Neal to a Manhattan nightclub to cheer her up, but she burst into tears during the after-midnight show and went home. Later that morning she poisoned herself.

Nehoda, Ron

The former road manager for Frank Sinatra and rock stars Gary Wright and Peter Frampton, Nehoda, 30, had recently been hired in that same capacity for the 18 month Frank Zappa tour. On the morning of September 11, 1977, several hours after Zappa had made his Las Vegas debut before 4,000 at the Aladdin Theatre for the Performing Arts, Nehoda slit his wrists and groin with a razor blade in his room on the 24th floor of the Aladdin Hotel. Nehoda was found after a couple walking down the hall outside his room heard cries for help. In a handwritten note found at the scene, the road manager expressed his desire to die. Drugs were suspected as being the cause of the suicide.

Nelson, Evelyn

Often paired with Jack Hoxie in Western melodramas (*Cyclone Bliss*, 1921; *The Crow's Nest*, 1922; *Desert Rider*, 1923), Nelson was in her late teens when she met and fell in love with motion picture he-man Wallace Reid. The pair began an affair that continued until the married Reid, fearful that scandal might ruin his career, broke it off. The relationship resumed after Reid was granted an interlocutory divorce decree, but again fearing negative press, he finally called it quits. Ravaged by drug addiction, the so-called "King of Paramount" died in a sanitarium on January 18, 1923. Devastated by Reid's death, the 23-year-old actress tried to go on living, but as *The Los Angeles Examiner* reported on June 17, 1923, "heart broken, (she) gave up the struggle and embarked on the Great Adventure." The day before, Nelson's body was found in a gas-filled room in her luxuriously appointed bungalow at 6231 De Longpre Avenue in Hollywood. In a note addressed to her mother Nelson begged for forgiveness, adding that she had no reason for the suicide except that "I am tired." In another note penned moments before her death, the actress wrote: "I am just about gone, and will soon be with my friend, Wally Reid."

Nelson, William Hugh ("Billy"), Jr.

"Billy Nelson" (born in Fort Worth, Texas, on May 21, 1958) was the son of country music legend Willie Nelson and his first wife, Martha. Following his parents' divorce in 1963, Nelson was raised largely by relatives, friends, and the singer's second wife while his father was out on the road making a living. Plagued by alcohol and drug problems, Nelson was often in trouble with the law. From 1987 through 1989 he logged four DUI arrests and was charged with possession of marijuana. In early 1990, he underwent a 30-day in-patient treatment program for alcohol abuse. In June of that year after pleading guilty to a 1989 DUI charge, he was sentenced to 20 days in jail, stripped of his driver's license, fined $1,000, and ordered to perform 160 hours of community service. Described by a publicist as having "sparks" of talent, Nelson played guitar, wrote songs, sang at local clubs, and planned to release a gospel album of his own material. Mainly, however, he lived on an allowance from his famous father.

One week after a visit from him, Nelson, 33, was found on Christmas morning in 1991 hanging by a cord from a ceiling beam in his rural log cabin home in suburban Goodlettsville, Tennessee, outside Nashville. A coroner's report ruled that the sometime singer was legally drunk at the time of his death, which was estimated to have occurred sometime on Christmas Eve. According to a representative of Nelson's management company, "Willie is a firm believer in reincarnation and all of that ... so it makes it easier to take." Nelson buried his namesake in a private funeral in a small cemetery in Vaughn, Texas.

Nevius, Lynn

Joining WIS-TV in Columbia, South Carolina, after graduating from Columbia College in 1967, Nevius (married name Eve Lynn Nevius Sessions) co-hosted the station's popular *Today in Carolina* show, did interview segments on the *One O'Clock Report*, and was featured on the *Seven O'Clock Report*. On September 16, 1973, Nevius' husband found his 28-year-old wife lying at the top of the stairs in their home at 1401 Lorrick Avenue severely wounded from a self-inflicted gunshot. Nevius later died in Richland Memorial Hospital.

Newey, Murray George

One of New Zealand's most active movie producers, Newey began his career as first assistant director on New Zealand and Australian films like *Beyond Reasonable Doubt* (1979), *Race for the Yankee Zephyr* (1981), and *The Man from Snowy River* (1981). By the mid-eighties he was a full-time producer with a filmography that included New Zealand's first R-rated feature, *Death Warmed Up* (1984), along with *Never Say Die* (1988), *My Father Is a Vampire* (a.k.a. *Grampire*, 1991), and the 1995 exchange student romance *Bonjour Timothy*. Newey was also the New Zealand production manager for the 1987 Ron Howard directed film *Willow*. In 1995, the Newey-produced teen cancer drama *The Whole of the Moon* took Best Picture honors at the New Zealand Film Awards. On April 8, 1998, the 45-year-old producer took his own life (method unreported) at his home in Auckland. At the time of his death, Newey was working as a production executive and locations scout for the *Star Wars: Episode I— The Phantom Menace*.

Nirenska, Pola

Nirenska (born in Warsaw, Poland, to Jewish parents) began dancing as a young girl, ultimately travelling to Dresden, Germany, to study in the music and dance school run by Mary Wigman, a noted German Expressionist choreographer. After performing with Wigman's company during its 1932–33 tour of the U.S. and Germany, Nirenska embarked on a solo career throughout Europe as a dancer, teacher, and choreographer. At the International Dance Congress held in Vienna in 1934, the dancer won first prize for choreography and a second prize for performing. Forced to leave Europe at the outbreak of World War II, Nirenska emigrated to London where she gave solo recitals, choreographed musicals, worked as an artist's model, entertained the troops, and was briefly married to British RAF pilot and actor John Ledesma. By the end of the war, 74 members of Nirenska's family in Poland had been murdered in Nazi death camps. Only her father, who fled to Palestine, survived.

Coming to New York in 1949 to study under Doris Humphrey and others, Nirenska permanently settled in Washington, D.C., in 1951. That same year she married Jan Karski, a hero of the Polish underground who survived torture by the Gestapo to offer eyewitness testimony of the Nazi extermination camps. Deeply influenced by events of the war, Nirenska's major choreographic achievement was a tetralogy of works she created in Washington between 1981 and 1990 that were inspired by memories of Holocaust victims she had known. On July 25, 1992, the 81-year-old matriarch of modern dance leaped to her death from the balcony of her 11th floor apartment in Bethesda, Maryland. The Montgomery County medical examiner ruled the death a suicide.

Noel, Dawn Hope

Married to dance band leader Herbert James Noel, the 19-year-old stage actress was best known as the daughter of stage and film actress Adele Blood Hope (see entry) who committed suicide on September 13, 1936, after suffering business reversals. On the afternoon of Saturday, July 16, 1939, Herbert James Noel, 36, and his teen-aged wife checked into a nudist camp on Rancho Glassey, in Tunas Canyon, above Roscoe, California. From that day through Monday, the couple drank with others at the camp, returning periodically to their home at 13050 Riverside in North Hollywood to feed and walk their dogs. At 6:00 P.M. on Monday, July 18, the young actress left the camp to again feed the animals, and did not return for four hours. Noel and Dawn returned to their home later that night where he learned that two men and a woman who had been at the drinking party had been at their home with his wife during her extended absence from the camp. Noel refused to accept Dawn's explanation of her absence, and was angrily speaking with one of the men on the phone when he heard a sound "like the snap of a cap pistol" from the bedroom. The band leader dropped the phone, and ran to the bedroom where he found his wife splayed on the floor, bleeding from the right temple, with a .22-caliber rifle beside her.

Nordern, Cliff

Nordern (real name Robert Cleavanger) was formerly a ballet dancer, but in recent months the stunt actor had begun studying dramatics. On September 25, 1949, Nordern and his male roommate were entertaining friends in their home at 6718 Milner Road in Los Angeles when the 26-year-old student actor complained of not feeling well and refused food. Shortly before midnight, Nordern stopped breathing and could not be revived. Early findings from the assistant chief autopsy surgeon for the coroner suggested that Nordern had ingested arsenic fluoride. Investigators later found an empty container of ant paste in the kitchen.

Obee, Richard Rippon

Called "Obee Joyful" by friends, the 65-year-old former publicity director, actor, and theatrical road manager shot himself in San Francisco's Sutro Heights on August 27, 1932. In a note found at the scene, Obee explained that he was broke and unemployed. Two weeks before taking his life, the theatrical veteran let an insurance policy lapse, virtually ensuring that his surviving wife would be left penniless.

O'Brien, Pat Alva

Lt. O'Brien, a native-born American soldier of fortune who enlisted in the British Flying Corps at the beginning of World War I, was shot down in a dogfight, captured by the Germans, and placed in a prison camp in Belgium. While being transported to Germany, the aviator and a group of other prisoners broke away from their captors and, following an arduous 320 mile journey through three countries, ultimately escaped to freedom. The highly decorated war hero chronicled this adventure in his 1918 book *Outwitting the Hun*. In January 1920, the 30-year-old O'Brien married actress Virginia Dare, co-star of the 1917 Norma Talmadge vehicle *The Moth*. Dare, ascribing her husband's violent outbursts against her to a head injury suffered during the war, separated from O'Brien in late 1920. In an attempt at reconciliation, O'Brien checked into the Alexandria Hotel in Los Angeles where Dare was staying with her friend, Sarah Ottis.

When Dare refused to meet with him on the evening of December 17, 1920, O'Brien fatally shot himself in the head with his .45-caliber automatic service revolver in his suite at the Alexandria. One of the two notes found on a bedside table near O'Brien's body was addressed to his wife. It read (in part): "Only a coward would do what I am doing. But I guess I am one. With all my war record, I am just like the rest of the people in this world — a little bit of clay. And to you, my sweet little wife, I go thinking of you.... And bring trouble, sickness, disgrace and more bad luck than anyone in this world has ever had, and curse forever that awful woman, Sarah Ottis, that has broken our home and has taken you from me...." O'Brien was buried at the family homestead in Momence, Illinois.

FURTHER READING

O'Brien, Pat. *Outwitting the Hun; My Escape from a German Prison Camp*. New York: Harper & Brothers, 1918.

Ochs, Phil

Considered with Bob Dylan to be one of the foremost protest singers of the sixties, Philip David Ochs was born in El Paso, Texas, on December 19, 1940. Among the folk singer's earliest musical influences were country singers Hank Williams, fellow suicide Faron Young (see entry), and Johnny Cash, along with rock 'n' rollers Buddy Holly and the Everly Brothers. After graduating from Staunton Military Academy in Virginia, Ochs attended Ohio State University in 1958 as a journalism major. At OSU the 18 year old became widely known on campus for his pro–Castro and Che Guevara political commentaries in the school newspaper. Inspired by leftist politics and the music of Woody Guthrie, Pete Seeger, and the Weavers, Ochs formed the folk duo the Singing Socialists (a.k.a. the Sundowners) with his college roommate, Jim Glover, in the early sixties. The duo played coffeehouses and featured songs written by Ochs based on news accounts of political stories.

In early 1962, Ochs dropped out of school in his senior year after his unpopular political views caused him to be passed over for the editorship of the school newspaper. Relocating to New York City, he became a regular performer in the Greenwich Village folk clubs while contributing articles and eventually editing the folk music journal *Broadside*. At the *Broadside* office Ochs met Bob Dylan, the artist from whose shadow he would never be able to escape. Dylan and Ochs endured a stormy friendship that apparently ended when he bluntly told Dylan that he thought "Can You Please Crawl Out Your Window" would not be a hit for the folk singer. Dylan angrily told Ochs, "You're not a folk singer; you're just a journalist."

On the strength of his performance at the prestigious Newport Folk Festival in 1963,

Ochs signed a recording contract with Elektra the next year. His first album, *All the News That's Fit to Sing* (1964), contained topical songs about civil rights, Vietnam, and the Cuban crisis. His 1965 follow-up album, *I Ain't Marching Anymore*, firmly established him as the "Troubador of the New Left." Throughout the sixties Ochs continued to organize and perform at political events (most notably during the student demonstations at the 1968 Democratic National Convention in Chicago). Hoping to reach a wider audience, he released the autobiographical album *Rehearsals for Retirement* in 1969. The album's poor sales, however, prompted the folk singer to rethink his career.

In an effort to "wed Elvis Presley to the politics of Che Guevara," Ochs donned a gold lamé suit and played rock 'n' roll to a hostile crowd at Carnegie Hall in 1970. By 1972 musical tastes had changed to the extent that protest singers were no longer considered relevant. Dylan had moved on, but Ochs, a true child of the sixties, was unable or unwilling to change his music to suit popular tastes. With his career in sharp decline Ochs began to lose confidence in himself as a songwriter and performer. During a trip to Tanzania in 1973 he was mugged by three black men while walking on the beach at Dar es Salaam. One attacker held him around the neck while the other two rifled his pockets. The beating and strangulation ruptured Ochs' vocal chords, leaving him permanently unable to sing in the upper register.

Returning to New York City, Ochs began drinking heavily, acting erratically, and appearing deeply depressed. Though occasionally performing, most of his time was spent drifting aimlessly from one flophouse to another or staying with friends concerned about his drinking. What little confidence Ochs still possessed as an artist was totally destroyed in October 1975 when friend and longtime rival Bob Dylan, uneasy about Och's drinking and unpredictable behavior, failed to include him on his Rolling Thunder Revue. In December 1977, the 35-year-old folk singer

moved from Manhattan to live with his sister, Sonny Tanzman, in her house in Far Rockaway, Queens, New York. Although he had stopped drinking the confidence to write was gone. On April 9, 1976, the "singing journalist" hanged himself with a belt in the bathroom of his sister's home. Ochs was cremated the day after his death and his ashes were eventually scattered from the Queen's Post of Edinburgh Castle near the folk singer's ancestral home in Scotland.

FURTHER READING

Cohen, David. *Phil Ochs: A Bio-Bibliography*. Westport, Conn.: Greenwood Press, 1999.
Eliot, Marc. *Death of a Rebel*. Garden City, N.Y.: Anchor Press, 1979.
Schumacher, Michael. *There But for Fortune: The Life of Phil Ochs*. 1st ed. New York: Hyperion, 1996.

O'Connor, Hugh Edward Ralph

O'Connor (born April 7, 1962, in Rome, Italy) was adopted by Caroll O'Connor and his wife while the actor was in the country filming *Cleopatra* (1963). The 16 year old was a student at the Beverly Hills Preparatory school when doctors diagnosed him with Hodgkin's disease. O'Connor's neck tumor and spleen were removed in a successful series of three operations after which he underwent intensive radiation therapy at the John Wayne Cancer Center at UCLA. The teenager apparently began smoking marijuana to relieve the nausea caused by chemotherapy. However, by 1982–1983, when he was employed as a courier on his father's CBS series *Archie Bunker's Place* during its final season, O'Connor was abusing cocaine, amphetamines, alcohol, and prescription drugs. In 1984, O'Connor became the night manager at Carroll O'Connor's Place, his father's restaurant in Beverly Hills. Under his management, the eatery attracted a drug crowd and quickly went out of business. In 1989, following a stint in New York City as an assistant stage manager on Broadway, O'Connor joined the cast of his father's CBS television show *In the Heat of the Night* as "Lt. Lonnie Jamison." Drugs were rampant on the set and O'Connor and fellow addict and co-star Howard Rollins were often high. In the late eighties, the actor began the first of several attempts at drug rehabilitation with a stay at the Betty Ford Center in Rancho Mirage, California. Throughout the run of the series (1989–1995) O'Connor received regular treatment at an outpatient clinic in Atlanta. In 1994, he was a patient at the Springbrook Northwest medical facility in Newberg, Oregon, and one year before his death was treated at the Brotman Medical Center in Culver City, California. Nothing helped. On March 28, 1995, the third wedding anniversary of the 32-year-old actor and his wife, Angela, O'Connor was suffering from cocaine, vodka, and prescription pill-induced paranoia and delusions. Two weeks before in a dramatic demonstration of "tough love," Angela and 2-year-old son, Sean, had moved out of their hilltop home in the 200 block of Aderno Way in Pacific Palisades to take up residence in Carroll O'Connor's Malibu home. She gave her husband a simple ultimatum: immediately check into the St. John's Hospital detox center or else she would leave him permanently. Convinced that their conversation was being broadcast throughout the neighborhood, the delusional actor refused to consider any form of treatment.

At 6:30 A.M. on March 28, 1995, O'Connor phoned his father from the house on Aderno Way and told him, "This is a very dark day." In the early afternoon he phoned his father for the last time to announce that he had a gun and was going to "cap" himself. He flatly stated that he would rather die than do another six-month stint in rehab. The 71-year-old actor begged his son to call the doctor, but Hugh told him, "So long, I love you," before hanging up. Carroll O'Connor immediately notified police. They arrived at the young actor's home in the Pacific Palisades in full SWAT gear and secured the area. Three and a half hours later they tentatively entered the house to find O'Connor sitting on a sofa dead

from a .45-caliber semiautomatic gunshot wound to the head. The contents of a suicide note found nearby were not disclosed.

At a press conference held outside Carroll O'Connor's home later that night, the grieving father blamed drug pusher Harry Thomas Perzigian, 39, for selling his son the drugs that led to his death. Perzigian was arrested the next morning and charged with the possession and furnishing of cocaine. On January 11, 1996, Perzigian was convicted of the charges in a Santa Monica courtroom and sentenced to the maximum penalty of one year in county jail. In 1997, the convicted pusher sued Carroll O'Connor for $10 million, charging that the actor's description of him as a "sleazeball" and "partner in murder" after his son's death constituted slander. In July 1997 the jury rejected Perzigian's claim. That same year, a Los Angeles judge dismissed O'Connor's wrongful death suit against Perzigian, saying that it was filed after the expiration of the one-year statute of limitations. Hugh O'Connor's remains were cremated and interred after much controversy in a church in Rome.

FURTHER READING

O'Connor, Carroll. *I Think I'm Outta Here: A Memoir of All My Families.* New York: Pocket Books, 1998.

Odoms, Clifford R.

The sales manager for music publisher Leo Feist, Inc., for 18 years, Odoms retired in 1930 and opened a restaurant on Wilshire Boulevard in Los Angeles. Apparently worried over business matters, the 49-year-old restaurateur hanged himself in the garage of his home at 6101 Del Valle Drive on August 11, 1933.

O'Donnell, Helen

O'Donnell, a 40-year-old character actress on the New York stage, jumped nine stories to her death off the roof of the Hotel Richmond, 70 West Forty-sixth Street, on December 2, 1934. One of the two scrawled notes found in her eighth floor room was un-readable while the only legible phrases in the other, addressed to her 18-year-old daughter, were "I'm sorry" and "your loving mother." The manuscript of the play she had been studying, *Square Crooks*, was found opened in her room.

Ogden, William

Fearful that he had failed an audition for *Arthur Godfrey's Talent Scouts* television pro-gram, the 36-year-old guitarist phoned his ex-wife on September 7, 1953, and drunkenly told her that he wanted to "kill himself." Early the next morning, Ogden's body was found in his car at the rear of his rooming house at 85 E. First Avenue in Columbus, Ohio. The guitarist had taped a length of garden hose to the car's exhaust, placed the other end through a rear window, and laid down in the front seat with the engine running. Ironically, a spokesman for CBS-TV in New York reported that Ogden had not been rejected as a result of the audi-tion and was eligible for an appearance on an upcoming Godfrey talent show.

O'Hara, Brian

Born in the depressed Dingle area of Liv-erpool on March 12, 1941, O'Hara and school friend Billy Hatton taught themselves skiffle and rock 'n' roll songs in the mid-fifties. After performing around Liverpool dance halls and coffee clubs as the Two Jays, they added gui-tarist Joey Bower and drummer Brian Red-man to become the Four Jays in the early six-ties. In 1962 they placed tenth in a poll of local groups in *Mersey Beat*. Changing their name to Fourmost, the group (now with drummer Dave Lovelady) attracted the attention of Bea-tles manager Brian Epstein. After refusing Ep-stein's repeated request to turn professional, Fourmost finally accepted in 1963 when they saw the success of The Beatles.

Produced by Beatles super-producer George Martin, Fourmost scored several U.K. chart successes including the John Lennon-penned tune "Hello Little Girl" (No. 9),

Lennon and Paul McCartney's "I'm in Love" (No. 17), and "A Little Loving" (1964, No.6). In 1965 the group released their only album, *First and Fourmost*, a collection of country, comedy, and rock 'n' roll songs. Fourmost were part of a long-running variety show at the London Palladium and appeared in two 1965 British films, *Pop Gear* and *Ferry Cross the Mersey*. Ultimately giving up trying to make the charts, Fourmost settled into the well-pay-ing world of cabaret. The band fragmented in 1978 with several members forming Clouds. O'Hara continued as Fourmost with three local musicians, but sold them the name after a few years when he left to set up a used car business.

On June 27, 1999, the 58-year-old for-mer musician was found hanged at his home in Smithdown Road in the Wavetree area of Liverpool. Terence O'Hara, the dead man's brother, told an inquest that he found the gui-tarist in his underpants and shirt hanging from a ligature in an attic stairwell. In the absence of a suicide note, authorities estimated that O'Hara had been in that position for a num-ber of days. According to his brother, O'Hara had financial worries.

Okada, Yukiko

Awarded a prestigious prize in 1985 as Japan's top new pop singer of the year, Okada first came to prominence as a 15 year old after winning a national talent contest in 1983. Teen adulation, however, was no compensation for Okada's despair over a failed love affair. After earlier attempts to kill herself by slashing her wrists and filling her room with gas failed, the 18-year-old pop idol leaped from a seven story office building in downtown Tokyo on April 8, 1986. Devastated fans placed wreaths on the street corner where Okada landed and some, overcome by grief, ended their own lives. By mid–April 1986, two and a half weeks after the singer's death, some 33 persons ranging in age from 9 to their mid–20s committed sui-cide by jumping from buildings, hanging themselves, or self-immolation.

O'Keefe, Mildred

A *Ziegfeld Follies* dancer, the St. Paul, Minnesota, native performed on the New York stage in *Rio Rita* (1927) and with the Marx Brothers in *Animal Crackers* (1928). O'Keefe toured in Monte Carlo and Paris where she was credited with being among the first dancers to introduce the Black Bottom dance to the continent. O'Keefe was working as saleswoman in the gown department of New York City's Saks Fifth Avenue when she suffered a nervous breakdown in 1936. The 32-year-old former dancer returned to Minnesota and was visiting relatives in Minneapolis when she checked into the West Hotel as "M. Brown" on October 8, 1936. Two days later, O'Keefe's body was found in her room next to a pound can of potassium cyanide from which a teaspoon had been taken and dissolved into a nearby glass of water. An unsigned note expressed regret and said, "You will be better off without me."

Olmedo, Alberto

Olmedo (born August 24, 1933, in Rosario, Argentina) began his career as an actor in children's television in the sixties. Teamed with comic Jorge "el Gordo" Porcel, Olmedo appeared in more than a dozen hit comedies in Latin America throughout the seventies and eighties. Olmedo-Porcel films include *Los Doctores las prefieren desnudas* (1973), *Expertos en Pinchazos* (1979), *Los Fierecillos se divierten* (1983), and *Los Colimbas al ataque* (1986). In early 1988, the popular 54-year-old comedian was starring in a comedy revue in Mar del Plata, Argentina. Depressed by the show's poor reception, Olmedo told a magazine interviewer that "the public has abandoned me." On March 5, 1988, Olmedo jumped to his death from his 12th floor apartment in the seaside resort.

Olsen, John C.

Despondent over the death of his 5-year-old daughter from leukemia two years before, Olsen, the 38-year-old television actor and son of movie comedian Ole Oleson of Olsen and Johnson fame, was found dead in the attic of his apartment in Flushing, Queens, New York, on May 5, 1956. Last seen alive on April 13 when he apparently left home to work in Los Angeles, Olsen was reported missing by his wife five days later when she failed to hear from him. During his absence, the woman stayed with her sister, and together on May 5 they visited the apartment at 69-01 150th Street to pick up some draperies. They found Olsen in the attic, a narrow air space above the ceiling, surrounded by a pitcher of water, three empty bottles of sleeping pills, and a suitcase. A police examiner estimated that the actor had been dead about five days.

O'Neill, Peggy

O'Neill (real name Barbara Jeanne) was an aspiring film actress set to sign a long-term contract with Paramount on the day she committed suicide. On April 13, 1945, the pretty 21-year-old redhead arrived with a male friend in tow at the apartment of boyfriend-screenwriter Albert Mannheimer at 1014 N. Doheny Drive in Beverly Hills. Mannheimer, who wrote the screenplay for the popular Red Skelton comedy *DuBarry Was a Lady* in 1943, quarreled with O'Neill and left alone to attend the theatre. Arriving back at his apartment shortly before midnight, the screenwriter found O'Neill's fully clothed body slumped on the floor dead from an overdose of sleeping pills. In 1950, Mannheimer was nominated for an Academy Award for his screen adaption of *Born Yesterday* based on the original play by Garson Kanin.

Oram, Suzanne

The dancer trained with the London Festival Ballet and landed leading roles opposite Rudolf Nureyev in *Sleeping Beauty* and *Romeo and Juliet* before a foot injury forced her to retire. Oram then went into commercial theatre and worked in the first stage version of *Singing in the Rain* (1983) with Tommy

Steele. On January 29, 1987, the 30-year-old ballerina was found hanged in the bathroom of her flat in Victoria Square, Weston Super Mare.

Orbes, Marceline see *Marceline*

Osterman, Mary Dolores Daly

The former *Ziegfeld Follies* girl and widow of comedian Jack Osterman jumped or fell from her mother-in-law's 12th floor apartment window at 7 Park Avenue, New York, on September 7, 1950. According to her daughter and mother-in-law, the 42-year-old radio performer had not been depressed or worried about money.

Paine, William O.

Paine, 61, was a former president of the Hawaiian Association of Radio and Television Broadcasters and, since August 1969, had been the general manager and executive vice president of Maui Publishing Company where his duties included running the *Maui News* paper and KMVI-TV and radio. On October 29, 1975, the executive was found dead in his home in Spreckelsville, Maui, from an apparent self-inflicted gunshot wound.

Pascal, Christine

Pascal's work as an actress, scriptwriter, and director painted a particularly depressing view of French art and life.

Born in Lyons, France, on November 29, 1953, Pascal received her early education in a convent school, and was taking courses at the Lyons Conservatoire when she came to the attention of director Bernard Tavernier. In 1973, Tavernier cast her in his first film, *L'Horloger de Saint Paul*, thus marking the beginning a creative collaboration that saw the actress appear in several of the director's subsequent movies: *Que la fete commence* (1974), *Le Juge et l'assassin* (1976), and *Les Enfants gates* (1977 — her first screenplay with Tavernier).

As an actress, Pascal's breakthrough role came in director Michel Mitrani's 1973 feature, *Les Guichets de Louvre*, where she played a young student vainly trying to rescue Jews from the Nazis in Paris during 1942. Ironically, Pascal's first solo script and directorial effort, *Felicite* (1979), opened with a suicide scene. In 1992, Pascal earned her greatest critical and popular success directing *La Petit Prince a dit*. The story of a husband and wife dealing with the slow death of their daughter with a brain tumor earned her the Prix Louis-Delluc.

Irreverent and anti-social, Pascal told a film magazine interviewer in 1984: "I wish to die by my own hand when the right time comes." On August 30, 1996, the 42-year-old filmmaker jumped to her death from a window of a psychiatric clinic at Garches, in the suburbs of Paris, where she had been hospitalized for depression. Pascal was survived by Swiss producer-husband Robert Boner, whom she married in 1982.

Patrick, Warren A.

Patrick founded the theatrical trade paper *Show World* in Chicago in June 1907, but the impracticality of publishing such a paper in the Midwest forced him to suspend its publication in 1911 and take a position as a $10,000 a year western representative of the *Clipper*, a theatrical newspaper published in New York City. In June 1915, Patrick mysteriously disappeared from his home and for 11 days roamed the streets of Chicago in a daze before being found by a friend. On June 18, 1915, the 40-year-old newspaperman was being attended by a physician in his home at 686 East Fifty-first Street when he entered the bathroom in a highly nervous state. When Patrick failed to emerge after a considerable time, his half-brother opened the door to find him dead on the floor, an empty bottle of Lysol close at hand.

Patz, Louis

Patz, the division manager of the National Screen Service Corporation, had been missing for a couple of days when his body was found on the floor of his car in a parking lot near 4740 Roanoke Parkway in Kansas City, Missouri, on June 14, 1962. Two empty sleeping pill bottles were retrieved from the car along with a note to his wife in which the 63 year old expressed despair about being ill.

Pavley, Andreas

Pavley (real name Andreas Hendricus Theodorus van Dorp de Weyer) was born in Batavia, Java, on November 1, 1892, and raised in Amsterdam. He received his first formal dance training from Emil Jacques-Dalcroze in Geneva, Switzerland, during 1909–1911, afterward travelling to Paris and London to study with Ivan Clustine and Enrico Cecchetti. As "Andreas de Weyer," Pavley moved to London in 1912 and performed in a few ballets before being signed in early 1913 to dance in the company of Russian prima ballerina Anna Pavlova on her upcoming U.S. tour. As Andreas Pavley, the dancer remained with Pavlova for three years until leaving after the 1916 tour to form a studio and ballet company with fellow dancer Serge Oukrainsky. In 1919, the Pavley-Oukrainsky Company became associated with the prestigious Chicago Grand Opera. The association elevated the performer-choreographer to national renown and paved the way for his company to tour on the Keith-Orpheum Circuit.

Despite his popularity, however, by June 1931 the dancer was deeply in debt and the target of a blackmailer who called himself "Edward Walls." In a note to the 36-year-old Pavley, the extortionist threatened a scandalous exposure (possibly the dancer's homosexuality) unless he was paid $100. Unable or unwilling to meet the demand, Pavley broke out a window screen in his apartment on the 16th floor of the Hotel McCormick at 616 Rush Street in Chicago on June 26, 1931, and leaped to his death.

FURTHER READING

Corey, Arthur. *Danse Macabre: The Life and Death of Andreas Pavley.* Dallas: Bridwell Library, Southern Methodist University, 1977.

Payne, Donald Rollie

Payne, 45, an obstetrician-gynecologist in private practice in Washington, D.C., married NBC news correspondent Jessica Savitch in March 1981. In the mid-morning of August 3, 1981, Savitch found her husband hanging in the basement of their fashionable townhouse in Northwest Washington. According to the medical examiner, he had been dead for "three to five hours." Payne's act was attributed to acute depression over his chronic liver disease.

Peck, Jonathan G.

The firstborn son of actor Gregory Peck and divorced wife Greta Rice, Peck spent two years in the Peace Corps in Tanzania and six years in the U.S. Marine Corps Reserve after graduating from Occidental College. A former newsman at KNX radio in Los Angeles for nearly four years, the 30 year old joined Santa Maria, California, television station KCOY, Channel 12, as a reporter-cameraman in early 1975. Peck, expected to file three stories a day at the small, understaffed station, often complained to his father of overwork. Concurrently, he was suffering from medical and emotional problems. Doctors informed him that he had an enlarged heart, high blood pressure, and advanced arteriosclerosis. On the emotional front, Peck was depressed over the recent suicide of a close female friend and was crushed when a young divorcee with two children turned down his offer to live with him in his apartment in Santa Barbara.

The elder Peck was vacationing in Cap Ferrat, France, with his current wife, Veronique Passani, when he received word that his son had been found on June 28, 1975, in his Santa Barbara home dead from a single self-inflicted gunshot wound to the head. He left no note. The actor-father later admitted, "Whatever the other causes were, whatever the mistakes his mother and I may have made, whatever influences he was subjected to that made it apparently impossible for him to withstand that particular set of pressures at that particular time I don't know. But my regret that I'll live with for the rest of my life was that I was in France instead of here. I felt certain that had I been in Los Angeles he would have called me, because he often dropped in and talked things over with me." Peck is buried in Forest Lawn Cemetery under a simple headstone inscribed, "Beloved Son and Brother."

FURTHER READING

Freedland, Michael. *Gregory Peck: A Biography.* New York: W. Morrow, 1980.

Perkins, Frank

Known to Detroit's WJBK radio audience as "The Cynic," the 45-year-old commentator dispensed a diet of sound advice and curmudgeonly banter on his daily show. On October 14, 1940, Perkins was found dead from a drug overdose in his "Motor City" apartment at 630 Charlotte. Police ruled the sleeping pill overdose a suicide, adding that "The Cynic" had attempted self-destruction on a previous occasion. The secretary to the mayor of Detroit reportedly sponsored a collection to bury the penniless Perkins.

Perry, Geraldine

Perry, 27, the "Jari" of the Jari-Rene-Vic vaudeville team of female aerialists, swallowed poison in her room at the Hotel Fulton at 264 W. Forty-sixth Street in New York City on June 15, 1934. In January, Arthur Kay Hamlin, Perry's trapeze artist fiancé, had been killed in a fall in Jamaica, Long Island, after he crashed into a grand piano during an exit. Brooding over his death, Perry had earlier tried to destroy herself by intentionally slipping during a performance in Boston. She survived with a hip injury. Driven by despair, the aerialist's second attempt, committed during the week she was set to marry Hamlin, was successful. Following a matinee performance at Brooklyn's Albee Theatre, Perry returned to the hotel suite she shared with the others in the act. Perry excused herself and entered the bathroom where "Rene" and "Vic" heard the bathtub filling with water. Fifteen minutes later, the distraught woman emerged to announce, "I have taken poison. There's nothing you can do." Perry died shortly afterward in the Polyclinic Hospital.

Peters, Gleason G.

On May 23, 1939, the eve of a divorce hearing in which Mabel Peters, 40, was going to charge her husband, Gleason, with cruel and inhumane treatment, the 45-year-old proprietor of the Lafayette Club in Bradford, Pennsylvania, shot and killed his wife (the club's former hostess) in her room at the Emory Hotel and then turned the gun on himself.

Peterson, Frederick

On December 6, 1937, the 42-year-old film studio technician fatally shotgunned himself in the side in his home at 1218 South Cloverdale Avenue in Los Angeles.

Phillips, Genevieve

Unable to find film work after leaving a stage career in the East, the 23-year-old actress shot herself through the temple with a .22-caliber pistol in the bedroom of her home at 261 South Maple Drive in Beverly Hills, California, on March 18, 1938.

Phillips, Twila

Distraught over her relationship with Charles Richmond Stark, the 21-year-old radio and television actress opened four gas jets on the stove in her lover's apartment at 50 East Seventy-third Street in New York City on May 27, 1947. Stark returned home later in the evening to find Phillips dead on the kitchen floor and a note in which she declared her love for him.

Pierce, Jackie

Known in South Florida as the "First Lady of Television," Pierce hosted her own daytime show, *Jackie's House,* on WTVJ–Channel

4 in Miami from 1949 to 1956. Named the station's public service director in 1961, the popular personality thereafter limited her on-air appearances to the occasional interview. On August 1, 1967, a maid found the 49-year-old's body in the den of her home at 5301 SW Sixty-second Avenue in Miami. Dead from a self-inflicted .22-caliber gunshot wound to her right temple, Pierce left a suicide note in which she expressed concern over a number of problems.

Pierce, Justin

In 1995 director Larry Clark discovered Pierce, 20, skateboarding on the streets of Manhattan and cast him in the independent film *Kids*. Pierce's role as "Casper" earned him an Independent Spirit Award for Best Debut Performance. Over the next few years Pierce added to his film résumé with supporting roles in *A Brother's Kiss* (1997), *Black Male* (1999), and *Freak Weather* (1999). On television he appeared in two episodes of the Fox show *Malcolm in the Middle* in 2000. Pierce was in Las Vegas doing a video shoot for a fashion company when a violent confrontation between the 25-year-old actor and a family member at the Hard Rock Hotel prompted security officers there to ask him to leave in the early morning hours of July 10, 2000. Later that day at around 4:00 P.M., Pierce was found hanged in his room in the upscale Bellagio hotel-casino complex. The actor's death was reminiscent of that of *Suddenly Susan* television star David Strickland (see entry), who hanged himself in a Las Vegas motel room on March 22, 1999. Pierce took his life the day before the New York premiere of his latest film, *Pigeonholed*, co-starring Chris Noth and Rosanna Arquette.

Pike, Nita

A bit player in films since the thirties (*Palmy Days*, 1931; *Espionage*, 1937; *Suez*, 1938), Pike married veteran stage and film actor Alan Edwards in 1938 near the end of his career. Pike was inconsolable when Edwards,

61, died on May 8, 1954. Four hours before Edwards' funeral service on May 11, 1954, his 41-year-old wife's body was found in her bed at their apartment at 112¼ North Doheny Drive in Los Angeles. Clad in a pink embroidered nightgown, her head resting on a portrait of her husband of 16 years, Pike had ingested a lethal dose of sleeping pills. A note found beside the body read (in part): "Please cremate me in this nightgown with my darling Alan, at the same time." Joint funeral services were subsequently held at Forest Lawn Memorial Park in Glendale, California.

Pinchot, Rosamond see *Gaston, Rosamond Pinchot*

Piper, Franco

Known to music hall-goers throughout England as the "Banjo King," Piper, 52, had recently left the stage and placed his wife in a nursing home. On May 8, 1933, the entertainer's car was found parked alongside a lonely byroad near Edburton, England. In its front seat sat Piper, still clasping the revolver he had used to end his life. A pencilled note found lying on the driver's seat read: "My name is F. Piper. For any information go to my friend, Mr. Cyril Mawson, 25 Amesbury-Crescent, Hove." According to Mawson, "Mr. Piper had been depressed recently at having retired from the stage. He was independent, but he missed his work very much. When he went away this afternoon in the car we thought he was just going for a drive."

Pistilli, Luigi

Considered to be among Italy's foremost interpreters of the plays of Bertolt Brecht, Pistilli enjoyed stage successes in *The Threepenny Opera*, *St. Joan of the Stockyards*, *Lulu*, and in a 1995 production of Harold Pinter's *No Man's Land*. A veteran of several films, Pistilli appeared in small roles in two Clint Eastwood "Spaghetti Westerns" directed by Sergio Leone: *For a Few Dollars More* (1965, as

"Groggy") and *The Good, the Bad, and the Ugly* (1966, as "Padre Pablo Ramirez"). On television, Pistilli worked on the widely exported Mafia series *The Octopus*. Long subject to bouts of depression, the 66-year-old actor was appearing opposite actress-singer Milva in a brutally reviewed production of Terence Rattigan's *Tosca* at Milan's National Theatre in April 1996. Poor critical notices combined with Pistilli's own bitter press statements about the recent end of his four-year offstage relationship with Milva were believed to have driven the temperamental artist to take his life. On April 21, 1996, shortly before he was due to go onstage for one of the final performances of *Tosca*, Pistilli hanged himself in his Milan apartment. The actor reportedly left a note for his former companion, Milva.

Plato, Dana Michelle

The troubled star of television's *Diff'rent Strokes* was born to her 17-year-old mother, Linda Strain, on November 7, 1964, in Maywood, California. Strain, financially unable to support a child, put Plato up for adoption without ever seeing her. The young child was adopted by Dean and Kay Plato, owners of a trucking company in Montebello, California, and named Dana Michelle Plato. After the Platos divorced when she was 3, the young girl saw little of her father until he unsuccessfully tried to sue her for support in 1984.

Shortly after the breakup, Kay Plato was diagnosed with scleroderma, a rare blood disease that causes the skin to harden and thicken over time. She informed her 4-year-old daughter that the disease was ultimately fatal. Recognizing that Dana was a talented child, Kay Plato signed the 7 year old with a talent agency. During the next six years Dana appeared in more than 200 television commercials. In 1977, the 12 year old broke into films with a role in *Return to Boggy Creek*, a lackluster sequel to the 1972 cult hit *The Legend of Boggy Creek*. In 1978, Plato's career skyrocketed after she was signed by producer Al Burton to co-star with Gary Coleman and

Todd Bridges in the hit NBC comedy *Diff'rent Strokes*. As "Kimberly Drummond," Plato enjoyed instant recognition and celebrity status, but remained in the shadow of Coleman and Bridges.

According to her family, Plato was 12 when she began taking uppers and downers at school. Buckling under the pressures of too much fame too soon, the 13-year-old star began drinking to relax. The next year she overdosed on Valium. In 1980, the third season of *Diff'rent Strokes*, Plato's binge drinking was noticeably affecting her work. Kay Plato, concerned over her daughter's behavior, but physically weakened by her own losing battle with scleroderma, managed to get Dana drug counselling in 1981. By 1982, the fifth season of the popular sitcom, Plato was earning $22,000 an episode and in demand as a commercial spokeswoman for teen-oriented products. She was also an alcoholic and drug addict with a history of chronic eating disorders. In 1983, the 19-year-old actress stunned and angered NBC executives with the news that she was pregnant with boyfriend Lanny Lambert's baby. Asked by one cast member why she would jeopardize a lucrative career on the sitcom with a pregnancy, Plato replied, "When I get the baby, I will never be alone again." Shortly after being informed by NBC brass that they were dropping her from the series, Plato married Lambert in Las Vegas in June 1984. While writers were permanently sending "Kimberly" away to study in Paris, Plato gave birth to son Tyler on July 2, 1984. Freed from having to show up to work every day, Plato stayed drunk and high. Disgusted, Lambert walked out in 1985, taking his son to live with his mother in Tulsa, Oklahoma. After they divorced in 1990 the court awarded Lambert sole custody of the child.

For Plato, the years 1986 to 1991 were passed in an alcoholic and drug-induced haze. She was devastated when her mother finally passed away at age 49 on January 2, 1988. Inconsolable at the funeral, Plato screamed, "Why did you leave me?" and accused God of forsaking her. In an attempt to jumpstart her moribund career, the 25-year-old actress posed for *Playboy*. The nude pictorial featured in the June 1989 issue failed to generate any interest. By 1991, Plato was living in Las Vegas, working for $200 a week in a drive-thru cleaners, and drinking a gallon of vodka and two six-packs of beer a day. At 10:30 A.M. on February 28, 1991, Plato walked into Lake Video disguised in a hat, sunglasses, and a coat. Brandishing a pellet gun that resembled a 9mm pistol, the former child star demanded the video store clerk to empty the cash register. Moments after Plato fled with $160 in cash, the clerk dialed 911 to report that "Kimberly" from *Diff'rent Strokes* had just robbed the store. Twelve minutes later, Las Vegas police apprehended Plato. Unable to make her $13,000 bail, the actress languished in the Clark County Detention Center for five days until Las Vegas legend Wayne Newton (who did not know Plato) bailed her out. On August 8, 1991, Plato was given a six year suspended sentence, placed on five years' probation, enrolled in a drug program, and ordered to perform 400 hours of community service. In January 1992, she violated her parole by forging Valium prescriptions. Once again, however, the judge placed her on probation with no jail time.

In late 1991, Plato sought out her biological mother, Linda Strain, now living in Springfield, Missouri, with her children. In mid–1992, Plato landed a spot as a showgirl in a Las Vegas revue, but was fired after four months for drinking and poor attendance. Determined to have an acting career, Plato did two low-budget independent movies later that year, *The Sounds of Silence* and *Bikini Beach Race*. Still drinking heavily and popping pills, the 33-year-old unemployed actress signed on to do a lesbian role in the 1997 soft core porno film *Different Stroke: The Story of Jack & Jill ... and Jill*. By the end of 1998, Plato was down and out in Los Angeles scrounging for drug money and living in cheap hotels. In January 1999, she used money from a trust fund to buy a 37-foot Winnebago mobile home that she planned to drive cross country.

Plato was visiting her son in Tulsa, Oklahoma, when she met 28-year-old Robert Menchaca, Jr. The pair became lovers and spent three months together driving around the country. In May 1999, Plato was hired by Chicago publisher and rock promoter Shane Bugbee to emcee an adult entertainment expo in the Windy City. On May 7, 1999, Plato appeared on the Howard Stern radio show in New York City to promote the event. During the call-in portion of the program, a tearful Plato was viciously berated by many callers as a drugged-out alcoholic lesbian has-been. After the show, the 34-year-old actress returned to the home of Menchaca's parents in Moore, Oklahoma. The next day, May 8, 1999, Plato retreated into her Winnebago parked curbside outside the Menchaca home to rest. At 9:00 P.M. that evening fiancé-manager Menchaca found her face-up on the bed. Unable to wake her, he called 911. Plato was transported to the Southwest Medical Center in Oklahoma City were she was pronounced dead on arrival. The next day, the city's medical examiner recorded the death as an accidental overdose of the muscle relaxant Soma combined with the painkiller Loritab.

Inside the Winnebago, police found a digital camera with photos of Plato either passed out or already dead on the bed taken by Menchaca. According to Menchaca, he took the photos as a joke to show Plato when she woke up. However, on May 11, 1999, Menchaca showed up unannounced at Plato's wake with a video camera, but was blocked by her outraged family from filming the dead woman in her casket. According to published reports, Menchaca had been offered as much as $5,000 per photo for shots of the dead actress. On May 21, 1999, the Oklahoma City medical examiner amended the initial ruling of accidental death to suicide based on the large number and combination of pills ingested by Plato as well as her history of suicidal tendencies. Plato's remains were cremated and her ex-husband and son planned to scatter her ashes over the Pacific Ocean in accordance with her wishes.

Pollack, Ben

Popularly known as the "Father of Swing" during the big band era of the thirties and forties, Pollack broke into show business as a drummer with the New Orleans Rhythm Kings in the early twenties before forming his own band. Over the years, jazz luminaries like Benny Goodman, Jack Teagarden, Glenn Miller, and Harry James were all featured musicians in Pollack-led bands. Most were eventually sued by him in an attempt to share in their financial successes. Multi-talented, Pollack appeared in the film *The Benny Goodman Story* (1955) and wrote such songs as "Tin Roof Blues" (1923) and "Make Love to Me" (1953). Leaving show business in the mid-fifties, the band leader operated a Hollywood restaurant before moving to Palm Springs, California, around 1965 to run a bar with his sister. On June 7, 1971, a friend found the 67-year-old's body hanging in the bathroom of his Palm Springs home. In notes recovered at the scene, Pollack expressed despondency over financial and marital problems as well as concern that his rightful place in music history would be usurped by undeserving others.

Polyakov, Eugene

Polyakov (born in Moscow on April 27, 1943) began his formal dance training at Moscow's famed Bolshoi Ballet School at the age of 10. After graduating, he was sent to Siberia where, in addition to becoming the principal dancer of the Company of Novosibirsk, he also choreographed and produced ballet. In 1967, the 24-year-old dancer accompanied the Novosibirsk Ballet on a tour of Moscow and Paris. At the Festival du Marais, Polyakov distinguished himself in the roles of the "Bluebird" in *The Sleeping Beauty* and as the "Prince" in Oleg Vinogradov's staging of *Cinderella*. "Genia," as he was affectionately known, returned to Moscow in 1970 and taught at the Bolshoi Ballet until 1976. That same year he left Russia to become the ballet master at La Fenice in Venice. There Polyakov created the ballet *Francesca da Rimini*, his ver-

sion of *Spectra de la Rose*, and staged *Giselle* featuring Italian ballerina Elisabetta Terabust partnered by his longtime friend and colleague Rudolf Nureyev.

In 1977, Polyakov formed the Italian dance company Viva La Danza. The next year he accepted the post of director of dance as well as official ballet master and teacher at the Teatro Communale in Florence. During his five year tenure in Florence, the choreographer introduced several works including Stravinksy's *Baiser de la Free* and *Rossignol*. When Rudolf Nureyev accepted the post of artistic director at the Paris Opera Ballet in 1983, the internationally famed dancer invited Polyakov to join him as senior ballet master, in essence, his assistant. After Nureyev's departure in 1989, Polyakov with dancer Patrice Bart acted as caretaker directors of the ballet until replaced by Patrick Dupond in 1991. In 1992, Polyakov resumed his directorship of the Teatro Communale in Florence. After Nureyev's death in 1993, Polyakov spent the next few years conducting revivals of his friend's classic productions in Beijing, London, Berlin, Vienna, Stockholm, Milan, and Australia. In January 1996, the 53-year-old dancer went to the Paris Opera Ballet as its ballet master, but apparently fell into a deep depression. On October 25, 1996, Polyakov committed suicide by unreported means in Paris.

Pond, Lloyd

The director of the Albuquerque Mormon Choir and a band leader in the area, Pond, 52, was found hanged in the garage of his home at 3600 Colorado Court NE on May 11, 1962. Pond's body was discovered after his ex-wife returned to her home and found a note in her mailbox from the musician stating that he planned to kill himself.

Popescu, Stere

Popescu (born in Romania in 1920) defected to England in 1965 while working with the Romanian State Ballet. When the

Communist state officially refused the chore-ographer's request that his wife be permitted to join him, they were automatically divorced. Popescu's ballet, *Throughway*, part of a Ballet Rambert production at London's Jeannetta Cochrane Theatre, opened on March 5, 1968, but was taken off after only two performances. Depressed by the failure of his ballet and a savage *Times* review, Popescu, 47, returned to his home in Redcliffe Square, S.W., on March 7, 1968, wrote a letter in French expressing his feeling of hopelessness, then ingested a fatal dose of barbiturates.

Powell, Nicolette

Known to her friends as "Nico," the daughter of a Lloyd's of London insurance broker and a Latvian aristocrat, married the 9th Marquess of Londonderry in 1958 when she was only 17. The marriage ended in divorce in 1971 after blood tests suggested that British pop star Georgie Fame (real name Clive Powell), not the Marquess, was the father of a child born two years earlier. Days after her 31st birthday in February 1972, Nico married Fame in the Marylebone Register Office. By all accounts the pair were deeply in love and very happy. However, in 1988 Nico's fear of growing old was compounded by the necessity of placing her aged mother (suffering with Alzheimer's disease) in a nursing home. By 1991, the former debutante was on anti-depressants and, months later, withdrew from the world.

In April 1992, Nico attempted suicide by washing down 40 barbiturates with a half bottle of whiskey. She was found comatose in a car in a woods near her home and taken by helicopter to a hospital. Convinced that she had become "redundant" and unnecessary in the lives of her two grown sons (aged 24 and 20), the 52-year-old Powell drove her Ford Escort to the Clifton Suspension Bridge in Bristol on August 13, 1993. Walking out onto the bridge, she handed the car key and an envelope to two teenage girls who were enjoying the view, and asked, "Excuse me. Here's my address. Can

you raise the alarm?" The girls watched dumb-struck as Nico raised her right leg over the rail, then sat atop the railing to stare into the River Avon some 245 feet below. As the teens ran to alert the toll-keeper, Nico leaned forward headfirst and fell, still bent in a sitting position, to her death. A popular site for suicide, more than 1,000 people are thought to have fallen to their deaths from the Clifton Suspension Bridge since it was built in 1864. The Avon coroner recorded a verdict of suicide while suffering from depression, adding that he hoped bridge authorities would "take appropriate action to prevent a recurrence of such tragedies."

Powell, William David, Jr.

Born in 1925, the son of actor William Powell and his first wife, actress Eileen Wilson, was an associate producer for both Warner Bros. and Universal and, for three years, an executive of the National Broadcasting Company before turning to writing for television series. Powell wrote scripts for *Death Valley Days*, *Rawhide*, *77 Sunset Strip*, and *Bonanza*. Despondent over a chronic kidney condition and hepatitis, which had forced him to quit writing, Powell used a razor and a steak knife to slash his throat and wrists while in the shower of his garage apartment at 2542 Rinconia Drive in Hollywood. Powell's landlord found the body on March 13, 1968, after the 43-year-old scriptwriter had not picked up his mail for a week. The only part of a four page suicide note released to the press said, "Things aren't so good here. I'm going where it's better."

FURTHER READING

Francisco, Charles. *Gentleman: The William Powell Story.* 1st ed. New York: St. Martin's Press, 1985.

Preeman, Morse M.

On April 21, 1946, a business associate of Preeman's, the president of the Southern California Music Company, a sheet music jobbing house, arrived for an appointment at the 49 year old's Los Angeles home at 1270 S. Hauser Boulevard. A note pinned to the front door directed the man, Charles P. Mack, to the garage where he discovered Preeman dead from carbon monoxide poisoning beside his car. A hose attached to the car's exhaust pipe led into one of the windows. A note found near the body read: "Dear Charlie, Sorry. Letters to you and others on table in breakfast room." Preeman was survived by a wife, two daughters, a son, and a mother.

Presburg, Yolanda

The wife of a wealthy Chicago banker, Presburg, 41, sang for ten years in the chorus of the Chicago Civic Opera Company and was a member of the New York Grand Opera Choral Alliance. Obsessed with the notion that she had tuberculosis, the Hungarian-born singer checked into a sanitarium in Albuquerque, New Mexico. Despite being given a clean bill of health by specialists, she refused to accept their diagnosis. On August 20, 1926, Presburg boarded a North Shore Line train in Chicago bound for Milwaukee. Registering at the Wisconsin Hotel as "Yolanda Sugar," Presburg took a 7th floor room overlooking an inner court. At 2:05 P.M. guests heard a thunderous crash as the singer slammed into the roof of the hotel ballroom. Barely conscious, Presburg murmured, "I am from Chicago, my husband is not to blame," a phrase she reiterated during the five hours she clung to life in Milwaukee's Emergency Hospital. In her room at the hotel two notes were found, one in Hungarian to her husband, the other addressed to police. The message to authorities read: "Do not blame me for this act and do not blame my husband. I am sorry to do it. I have been suffering from what the doctors call T.B. My husband has done all he can do to cure me, sent me to sanitoria in the south, but it is no use."

Preston, Walter G., Jr.

Preston joined the National Broadcasting Company in 1935 as assistant to the vice-pres-

ident and treasurer after serving as assistant to the president of the University of Chicago from 1929 to 1932. Hard-working and well respected, Preston ultimately became the director of the public service division of the program department at NBC. In the early morning hours of December 6, 1941, the 39-year-old radio executive ended his life with an overdose of sleeping tablets in his apartment at 2 Beekman Place in Manhattan. Preston was clutching a pencil when he died and left several scrawled notes. His physician later told police that he had treated Preston for alcoholism.

Prevo, Alice Munn

Prevo, a dancer at the Midnight Follies Cafe in Chicago, was questioned with her husband by police in March 1926 regarding a Mrs. Carl Woods who was found slain in a bathtub in the Middleton Hotel at 1447 East 55th Street. Three months later, the 26-year-old entertainer drank poison and slashed her wrists. Though she survived, Prevo vowed to try again. On December 20, 1927, the entertainer shot and killed herself in her room at 6758 South Halsted Street in Chicago. In a note similar to that written at the time of her first suicide attempt, Prevo spoke of her disgust with the sordidness of her life, gave directions for her burial, and wished everyone a Merry Christmas.

Prince, Benjamin Sidney

A soldier in the Princess Pats, the first Canadian contingent to go overseas during World War I, Prince won every medal for bravery awarded by the British Army except the Victoria Cross. While serving as a member of a trench mortar crew at the battle of Ypres, he was only the man in his unit to survive a deadly gas attack. Prince sufficiently recovered from the gassing to serve with distinction in the British balloon service and after four years of near continuous combat ended the war with the rank of regimental Sergeant Major.

Nerves severely damaged by the wartime gassing and shell shock, Prince returned to civilian life as a real estate editor for the Memphis paper *Commercial Appeal* before leaving Tennessee to become the manager of the Washington Square Theatre in Quincy, Illinois, in 1924. He lasted six months before returning to Memphis to re-enter the newspaper business as an associate editor for the Associated Press. However, Prince quit after a few months when the click of the telegraph instruments aggravated his shattered nerves.

On the afternoon of June 15, 1925, the 30-year-old war hero waited until his wife was at work before ironically ending his life by the same means that ultimately drove him to the desperate act. Prince's body was found in the kitchen of his apartment at 211 North Third Street in Memphis in front of a gas stove with all its jets opened. A note found at the scene read: "What little I have I leave to the most wonderful girl in the world, my wife, Madge. Ben S. Prince. P.S. I want to be buried in my uniform."

Prinze, Freddie

Prinze, the popular star of the hit sitcom *Chico and the Man*, was the first entertainer of Hispanic descent to attain national prominence on television. Born into a poor and racially mixed section of Washington Heights, New York, on June 22, 1954, Prinze described himself as a "Hungarican." His father, Karl Pruetzel, was a Jewish-Hungarian immigrant while his mother, Maria, was a Puerto Rican immigrant and devout Catholic. Comedy early offered Prinze a means by which to cope with his confused racial identity and weight problem. As a kid, Prinze entertained his classmates at school while at home did his own make-believe radio show. At 14, he was selected to attend the prestigious New York High School for the Performing Arts, but proved to be a poor student. Instead of studying, Prinze (self-named because he wanted to be the "Prince of Comedy") nightly haunted comedy clubs like the Improvision on West

Forty-fourth Street waiting for a chance to hone his act during open mike nights. After famed talk show host Jack Paar caught Prinze's act at the Improvision, he gave the 18-year-old comedian his first big break.

On October 18, 1973, Prinze made his television debut on ABC's *Jack Paar Tonite*. Shortly after the appearance he dropped out of school and relocated to Hollywood to pursue a career full time. Prinze became a regular on the comedy circuit where his observations on, and stories about, people he knew in his Puerto Rican neighborhood marked him as an original comic. In December 1973, Prinze's career skyrocketed after a brilliant stand-up routine on *The Tonight Show*. Host Johnny Carson was so impressed with Prinze that he spontaneously invited the comedian over to the panel after his triumphant routine; it was the first time in the history of the show that anyone was invited to do so after their first appearance. Ironically, the second comedian that Carson so honored was Ray Combs (see entry), who would also commit suicide. The appearance caught the eye of television producer James Komack who (over the objections of NBC executives) hired Prinze to star opposite ex-vaudevillian and veteran character actor Jack Albertson, in *Chico and the Man*. Prinze, as the wisecracking Chicano "Chico Rodriquez," was the perfect foil for the grumpy Albertson who in the sitcom employed the young go-getter at his rundown garage in a Chicano barrio of East Los Angeles.

Debuting on September 13, 1974, *Chico and the Man* was an instant hit that continued to run until July 21, 1978 (more than six months after Prinze's death). The show, the first ever to star a Latino, added several of Prinze's catch phrases to popular speech ("Eees not mai yob" and "Looking good"), but also generated controversy in the Latino community. Several Latino organizations objected to Prinze, a Puerto Rican, playing a Chicano, especially one called "Chico," a name considered by many ethnics to be derogatory. Bowing to pressure, NBC hastily rewrote the character as a half-Puerto Rican and half-Chicano.

FREDDIE PRINZE—When Prinze, Puerto Rican on his mother's side, signed to star in the NBC sitcom *Chico and the Man* in 1974, he opened the professional doors for other entertainers of Hispanic descent. In a classic case of "too much too soon," however, the talented comic turned to drugs to escape the pressures of instant celebrity. On January 28, 1977, the 22-year-old Prinze shot himself in a Beverly Hills hotel room while under the influence of drugs. Freddie Prinze, Jr., 10 months old at the time of his father's death, has since appeared in films like *She's All That* (1999) and *Summer Catch* (2001).

By 1975, Prinze was on top of the show business world. A full-fledged television star, he was also making $25,000 a night doing stand-up in Las Vegas. Although living the "Hollywood Dream," Prinze was having trouble adjusting to the pressures of "too much stardom too soon." He confided to fellow comedian David Brenner that he often felt sui-cidal and was worried that he would be unable to maintain his current level of fame. To cope, the 20 year old began taking Quaaludes and cocaine and rapidly became addicted. Under the influence of drugs, Prinze's depression increased and was accompanied by erratic mood swings. According to friends, the stoned entertainer often threatened suicide and routinely held a gun to his head with the safety on and pulled the trigger. In November 1976, Prinze's struggle with drugs became public after he was charged with driving under the influence of methaqualone, the generic name for Quaaludes. Soon afterward, Katharine Elaine Cochran, his wife of 14 months, filed for divorce citing irreconcilable differences. Prinze moved into the Beverly Comstock Hotel where despite being isolated from his wife and 10-month-old son, Freddie, Jr., he continued his nonstop drug use.

In the early morning hours of January 28, 1977, the 22-year-old drugged-out superstar finally reached his limit. Unable to sleep, Prinze phoned his manager, Martin "Dusty" Snyder, from the Beverly Comstock. Alarmed by his client's bizarre phone manner, Snyder rushed over to the hotel. With Snyder in attendance, Prinze sat on the sofa and made calls to his mother, secretary, and wife in which he threatened to "end it all." Within moments of hanging up on his wife, the comedian pulled a .32-caliber pistol out from under a sofa cushion, placed it to his right temple, and fired. Rushed to the UCLA Medical Center, Prinze underwent emergency surgery later that morning. The next day at 1:00 P.M. he was removed from life support after his brain ceased functioning. Found at the scene, a suicide note dated January 28, 1977, read: "I must end it. There's no hope left. I'll be at peace. No one had any thing to do with this. My decision totally. Freddie Prinze."

On January 31, 1977, an estimated crowd of 1,000 fans and friends attended funeral services for Prinze at the Old North Church at Forest Lawn Memorial Park in the Hollywood Hills. Singer Tony Orlando eulogized his dead friend as "a man in turmoil" who "was in great pain." "Freddie Prinze is today exactly where he wants to be," Orlando said. "Rejoice in his heavenly breath." Seeking to exonerate her son's name and to collect his insurance, Prinze's mother took the insurance companies to court. In January 1983, a superior court judge ruled that Prinze had not intended to take his life, but was rather engaged in attention-getting behavior that resulted in his accidental death. Maria Pruetzel subsequently collected on two policies totalling some $200,000. The comedian's son, Freddie Prinze, Jr., has to date acted in several films including *I Know What You Did Last Summer* (1997) and *She's All That* (1999).

FURTHER READING

Pruetzel, Maria, and Barbour, John A. *The Freddie Prinze Story.* Kalamazoo, Mich.: Master's Press, 1978.

Purks, Thomas

A pianist and dance band leader in the Pittsburgh and Monongahela Valley districts, Purks, 32, committed suicide on July 26, 1940, in the home he shared with his mother in Charleroi, Pennsylvania. Dead from a single-barrelled shotgun blast to the heart, Purks was found by members of his family slumped in a kitchen chair. No motive for the suicide could be determined.

Putnam, J. Myles

On July 28, 1954, the 59-year-old former actor and manager was found dead in his New York City apartment at 312 West Seventy-fifth Street. Putnam had a gunshot wound under his chin and a .22-caliber rifle lay beside him.

Quigley, Jay

The most popular character actor on the Columbus, Ohio, stage, Quigley, 54, was hospitalized for a nervous breakdown and "general mental derangement" when he took his life on November 15, 1917. Shortly after his wife visited him, Quigley left the state hospital and took a streetcar to the Broad Street Bridge over the Scioto River. A witness saw the actor place a business card in his cap and leave it on the bridge before diving off the railing into the water and drowning.

Quine, Richard

An actor's son, Quine was born November 12, 1920, in Detroit, Michigan. He made his film debut in the 1933 Universal feature *Counsellor at Law*, starring John Barrymore and possible suicide Thelma Todd (see entry) in a bit part. As an actor, Quine also appeared in *Jane Eyre* (1934), *A Dog of Flanders* (1935), *King of the Underworld* (1939), and in the lead of *We've Never Been Licked* (1943). After World War II, Quine switched to directing and his first effort, *Leather Gloves* (a fight film co-directed and produced by William Asher) was released in 1948. Among Quine's more than two dozen movies as director are *Pushover* (1954), *The Solid Gold Cadillac, Bell, Book and Candle* (1958), *The World of Suzie Wong* (1960), *Sex and the Single Girl* (1964), and the hilarious 1965 Jack Lemmon comedy *How to Murder Your Wife*. With his career in decline in the late sixties, Quine directed his last feature, *The Prisoner of Zenda* starring Peter Sellers, in 1979. He was subsequently fired in 1980 from Sellers' final film, *The Fiendish Plot of Dr. Fu Manchu*.

Married four times, the director's first marriage to MGM starlet Susan Peters was marked by tragedy when she was paralyzed from the waist down after accidentally shooting herself while hunting. They divorced in 1948. Suffering for years from ill health and chronic depression, the 68-year-old director died on June 10, 1989, at the UCLA Medical Center hours after shooting himself in the head in his home. Of filmmaking, Quine once said, "Making a movie is a bit like having a baby. All you can hope for is that it won't have two heads and that it will be an entity in itself: who cares if it's a boy or a girl?"

Ramos, Flor Morales

"Ramito," born September 5, 1915, in the central Puerto Rican town of Caguas, was one of that country's most famous folk singers. In a career spanning 40 years and more than 50 records, Ramos became enduringly popular with the islanders and Puerto Ricans living in New York City (where he regularly performed) with songs like "El Apagon de Nueva York" ("New York Blackout") and "No Cambio A Puerto Rico" ("I Won't Change Puerto Rico"). At 12:50 A.M. on January 23, 1990, the 74-year-old six-time married father of 18 children shot himself in the right ear at the home of his in-laws in the southern coastal town of Salinas, Puerto Rico.

Rand, George

Though a veteran performer in stock theatre throughout New England under the professional names "Abner Slocum" and "Professor Thistlewaite," Rand (real name Schrand) is best remembered as the "Old Ranger" on the early NBC Blue radio Western adventure *Death Valley Days* (1930–1945). In the late thirties, Rand lost the high profile job and fell into a deep depression. On New Year's Eve 1938, the unemployed actor drank a bottle of poison in his home at 925 Thirty-sixth Avenue in Oakland, California. He died in the Alameda County Hospital on January 8, 1938.

Ransom, Edith

Unable to sustain the sudden fame she realized with her 1927 Broadway portrayal of "Tondelayo" in Leon Gordon's play *White Cargo*, Ransom wound up three years later playing small town opera houses in the Australian Outback. Nearly destitute, the actress returned to Seattle, Washington, around 1930 and launched a series of huge lawsuits calculated both to keep her name in the news and to recoup her lost fortune. Alone and living on a meager diet of bread and potatoes, Ransom filed a $1 million suit against a Pacific coast steamship company charging that she had been "shanghaied." In separate actions, she sued three local newspapers for libel as well as several city and welfare officials. On January 24, 1933, the 32-year-old actress overdosed on peraldehyde, a powerful sleeping drug, in her rooms at 814 Columbia Street. She died two days later at Seattle's Harborview Hospital. At the scene, investigators found a series of suicide notes in a room plastered with photos taken of the former star during her heyday.

Rapp, Danny

Rapp (born in Philadelphia, Pennsylvania, on May 10, 1941) founded the Italian-American vocal quartet "Danny and the Juniors" (initially called the "Juvenairs") in 1955. In 1957 the band's song "Do the Bop" came to the attention of Dick Clark, who convinced them to change its title to "At the Hop." After they performed it on Clark's television program *Bandstand*, the song rocketed to the top of the charts, eventually selling two million copies worldwide. A few other hits followed ("Rock 'n' Roll is Here to Stay," 1958; "Twistin' USA," 1960), but by the mid-seventies the group had become a fixture on the touring oldies circuits before ultimately degenerating into a lounge act. On April 1, 1983, Rapp disappeared without completing the last two nights of an engagement at the Silver Lining Lounge at Pointe Tapatio Resort in Phoenix, where the group had been performing since March 7.

Prior to his departure, Rapp's erratic behavior throughout the booking had forced a female band member to quit and resulted in the harassment of at least one hotel guest. Confronted by management over the incidents, the 42-year-old singer said, "That wasn't me." Three days later, a maid at the Yacht Club motel in the small desert town of Quartzsite, Arizona, found Rapp in his room dead from a self-inflicted gunshot wound to the right side of his head. Charlie Johnston, Rapp's booking agent, rather naively conjectured, "It's really too bad. To think he had reached the pinnacle of stardom in the 1950s and ends up in a little motel in Quartzsite, Arizona. He obviously was really despondent, I don't know over what."

Rappaport, David

The son of a London cab driver, Rappaport was born at Hackney on November 23, 1952, with achondroplasia, a form of dwarfism in which the trunk of the body grows, but arms and legs are stunted. When he reached his full height at age 8, Rappaport stood only 3 feet, 11 inches tall — one inch less than fellow actor and suicide Herve Villechaize (see entry) of *Fantasy Island* television fame.

After taking a degree in psychology from Bristol University and doing some teaching, Rappaport began acting. He scored his first theatrical success in 1976 in Ken Campbell's dramatic adaptation of the Robert Shea and Robert Anton Wilson *Illuminatus* novels for the science fiction theatre of Liverpool. Though other stage appearances followed, he would gain international recognition for his role in the 1981 fantasy film *The Time Bandits*. Rappaport also appeared in *The Bride* (1985) before moving to Hollywood in 1986 to star in the short-lived CBS television series *The Wizard*, about a toymaking genius who becomes involved in dangerous adventures.

While the program marked a first in television history, a dwarf starring in a series, Rappaport longed to escape being typecast as an anatomical anomaly. He once told an interviewer, "I look at boring people every day and I say, 'God, I wish I could be like that.' But my lot is to be unique, special, so I have to put up with it. It's a hard life." In 1989 his career received a temporary boost with his guest appearances as "Hamilton Schuyler," a high powered attorney and nemesis of "Victor Sifuentes" (Jimmy Smits) in the hit NBC television series *L.A. Law*.

By 1990, however, Rappaport's inability to land parts not based on his size combined with the death of a close friend from AIDS and the breakup of a love affair drove him to attempt suicide. On the night of March 4, 1990, the 37-year-old actor drove his Volkswagen to an isolated road below the "Hollywood" sign, ran a hose from the exhaust into the car, and lay down on the back seat. Paramedics found him unconsious and not breathing inside the idling auto. Although Rappaport survived and received psychiatric care, he was now a professional pariah. The suicide attempt made him uninsurable and no producer was willing to risk a potential cash loss by casting him. Unemployed and alone, Rappaport drove to Laurel Canyon Park about 200 yards off Mulholland Drive in the early evening of May 2, 1990. Leaving his dog in the car, he walked into some nearby bushes and fatally shot himself in the chest with a .38-caliber revolver.

Rawlins, Judy

Singer Vic Damone had the dubious distinction of marrying two women who were suspected of taking their lives. In 1954, Damone married Sardinian–born actress Pier Angeli (see entry). The couple divorced in 1958, but for years fought a bitter custody battle over their son. Angeli died of a barbiturate overdose in Beverly Hills on September 10, 1971. Damone married actress Judy Rawlins on October 24, 1963. The marriage lasted nearly eight years and produced three children before ending in divorce on June 28, 1971. The 45-year-old singer was scheduled to marry Becky Jones, a 26-year-old Houston oil heiress, on April 12, 1974, when he received news that Rawlins had been found dead in her Mandeville Canyon home in Los Angeles. On March 28, 1974, the couple's 5-year-old daughter, Daniella, entered her mother's bedroom around 10:00 A.M. to find Rawlins apparently in bed asleep. Unable to awaken her mother, the child informed a maid who summoned a fire department team. Rawlins, 36, was prononunced dead at 10:22 A.M. An empty pill bottle was found near the bed. The next day the Los Angeles County Coroner's Office listed the death as a "probable suicide." Damone temporarily postponed his wedding plans.

Ray, Margaret Mary

The psychologically troubled woman who stalked talk show host David Letterman from 1988 to 1992 gained a national celebrity of sorts by claiming to be the comedian's wife, and by repeatedly breaking into his home. Though once a punch line in one of Letterman's "Top Ten Lists," Ray's life was anything but funny. A diagnosed schizophrenic, she came from a family where two of her four siblings were also schizophrenic. Both brothers killed themselves as young men. Ray married in 1973, had four children, but divorced in 1983. Unable to hold a regular job, she lived on Social Security disability benefits for the mentally ill, and odd jobs like housesitting.

Ray's obsession with Letterman began in 1988. That year she was arrested at a toll booth in the Lincoln Tunnel driving the talk show host's Porsche. When unable to pay the toll, Ray identified herself as Letterman's wife and her son as David, Jr. During the next five years, she was arrested eight times for trespassing on Letterman's property in New Canaan, Connecticut, and on other charges. In all, she spent ten months in prison and 14 months in state mental institutions on various convictions. Released from a mental institution in 1993, Ray shifted her obsession to Story Musgrave, the astronaut who led the 1993 spacewalk to repair the Hubble Space

Telescope. She deluged him with letters, phone messages, and successfully posed as a journalist in 1994 and interviewed him at the Johnson Space Center in Houston. In September 1997, Ray showed up at his home in Osceola County, Florida, pounded on the doors and windows, and turned on the outside water faucets. Arrested for trespassing, the celebrity stalker spent most of 1998 in a mental hospital in Florida.

Released in August 1998, the 46 year old settled in Hotchkiss, Colorado, where she was known and liked. At 1:00 P.M. on October 5, 1998, Ray walked to the edge of town, stepped onto the railroad tracks, kneeled down, and let herself be run over by a 105 car coal train. A short note with the phone number of a friend who knew how to contact her family was found nearby. Letterman's statement to the press said: "This is a sad end to a confused life."

Raymond, Leslie Ray

Once familiar to Oakland, California, radio audiences as "Brother Bob," Raymond, 41, left the business, relocated to Los Angeles, and worked as a salesman in an air conditioning concern until his complicated personal life ultimately drove him to tragedy. On December 6, 1935, a motorist in the Palos Verdes Hills off Western Avenue noticed a parked car, engine running, with a 12-foot piece of rubber hose leading from the exhaust pipe in through a window of the vehicle. Investigators found Raymond's body in the car along with two scrapbooks filled with clippings chronicling his career as "Brother Bob." In his hat, lying on the seat beside him, was a note addressed to his wife expressing grief and shame over an affair he had been having with his young niece, Esther. The suicide note read: "Tubbsy Dear, I have done about every bad thing to you that any one person could — you are going to like Esther. She is a sweet, sweet girl — she is at a hotel in San Pedro — get her and start her on her way — give her a break — she, too, was wrong because she loved the wrong person — in my Dr. Jekyll and Mr. Hyde existence there has never been anyone like you — be a good gal — here is zero hour and nothing more to say...."

Redding, Earl

Redding, a 64-year-old veteran stage actor whose last Broadway appearance had been in *The Crucible* in 1933, died July 3, 1945, from a self-administered overdose of sleeping tablets in his room at the Langwell Hotel, 123 West Forty-fourth Street in midtown New York. Employed for the last eight months as a ticket taker at the Strand Theatre, Redding had suffered intense stomach pain for months. In four suicide notes (three to friends, one to the executive committee of the Actors' Equity Association) the supporting actor indicated that he "could not stand the pain any longer."

Reeves, George

The career of George "Superman" Reeves is Hollywood's most graphic example of an actor talented enough to perform in stronger material, but tragically typecast in a role from which the public would not let him escape. Whether the actor was driven to suicide by career frustrations or, as some have suggested, murdered as a direct result of his one-time involvement with the wife of a powerful studio executive, one essential fact remains — George Reeves will only be remembered because he played the "Man of Steel" on television.

Conceived out-of-wedlock, the future actor was born George Keefer Brewer in Woolstock, Iowa, on January 15, 1914. To

GEORGE REEVES— Reeves was poised to become a serious motion picture star with a standout performance opposite Claudette Colbert in *So Proudly We Hail!* (1943), but was unable to regain his career momentum after returning from military service in World War II. Several flop films later, Reeves gambled in 1950 that no one in the industry would notice if he briefly played "The Man of Steel" in the syndicated children's television show *The Adventures of Superman*. The program, a runaway hit that ran until 1957, hopelessly typecast Reeves and killed his chances for serious film work. Reeves, 45, reputedly shot himself in his Benedict Canyon home in the early morning hours of June 17, 1959. The star's unsettled personal life combined with sloppy police work has since given rise to intense speculation that he was murdered. *Courtesy of University of Southern California, on behalf of the USC Library Department of Special Collections.*

prevent her child's illegitimacy, mother Helen Lescher convinced the father, Don C. Brewer, to marry her. They divorced soon after the child's birth with Helen taking her infant son to live with her parents in Ashland, Kentucky. Mother and son moved to Pasadena, California, where she met and married Frank Joseph Bessolo. In 1927, the 13 year old was formally adopted by his stepfather and given the last name of Bessolo. The marriage, however, lasted only eight years. Frank Bessolo later fatally shot himself in the head. By all accounts, Helen Bessolo was an ultra-possessive mother who doted on her son. Over her objections, George excelled in boxing at Pasadena Junior College. He also received acting training at the Pasadena Community Playhouse where he performed Shakespeare with fellow players Victor Mature and Robert Preston.

In 1939, Warner Bros. studio head Jack Warner signed George Bessolo to a contract with an eye toward developing him as a B-unit player. Warner changed the actor's name to the more alluring box office monicker "George Reeves" and cast him in three 1939 shorts: *Pony Express Days*, *The Monroe Doctrine*, and *Ride, Cowboy, Ride*. That same year, Reeves made his full-length movie debut as "Stuart Tarleton," one of "Scarlett O'Hara's" suitors in the MGM Civil War epic *Gone with the Wind*. On September 22, 1940, Reeves married actress Eleanor Needles, his girlfriend of two years. The couple quietly divorced in 1949. After the box office success of *Gone with the Wind*, Reeves worked steadily in supporting roles in quality films like *Torrid Zone* (1940), *The Strawberry Blonde* (1941), *Blood and Sand* (1941), and *Lydia* (1941). In 1943, Reeves scored a solid hit as the male lead opposite Claudette Colbert in Paramount's World War II film *So Proudly We Hail!* Director Mark Sandrich was so impressed by Reeves' standout performance that he promised to make him a star after the war. Reeves, secure in the knowledge that he had a powerful ally in Hollywood, entered the Air Force Special Services shortly after the film was released. Unfortunately for the actor, Sandrich died in 1945.

After the war, Reeves struggled to restart his career and was briefly forced to work in radio in New York City. Relocating to Holly-wood, the actor landed a bit part in *Variety Girl* (1947) before starring in two low-budget jungle films in 1948 — *Jungle Goddess* and *Jungle Jim* featuring Johnny Weissmuller in the title role. In 1949, the fading actor reached the nadir of his film career when he starred in the title role of *Adventures of Sir Galahad*, a second-rate Columbia serial. With his career in motion pictures all but ended, Reeves turned to television as a last resort in 1950. Reeves, knowing that his jump to the small screen would in all likelihood signal the death knell to any future film opportunities, gambled that few would see his television performances. In 1950, he was chosen from among 200 other actors to star in the syndicated kiddie television show *The Adventures of Superman*. No one, let alone Reeves, felt that the half-hour program would last more than a few months. However, when the series debuted in July 1951 (backstopped by the low-budget film *Superman and the Mole Men*) it was an instant hit and continued to run until November 1957.

At the height of its popularity, the show was watched by 91 percent of all households with children under the age of 12. Reeves ultimately made $2,500 a week as the "Man of Steel," but was miserable. He once referred to acting in the series as "the bottom of the barrel." Though he continued to work in films (*Rancho Notorious*, 1952; *The Blue Gardenia*, 1953), his association with the Superman character proved too strong. The actor had a sizable supporting role in director Fred Zinneman's 1953 classic *From Here to Eternity*, but was all but edited out of the film after a preview audience started laughing and shouting "Superman!" when he appeared on screen. In his last film appearance, Walt Disney's 1956 *Westward Ho the Wagons!*, Reeves was forced to appear in whiskers and a broad-brimmed hat. The frustrated actor walked around the set telling anyone who would listen, "Here I am, wasting my life."

Shortly after divorcing wife Eleanor Needles in 1949, Reeves began a long affair with Toni Mannix, wife of Eddie Mannix, a vice-president at MGM who served as the "eyes and ears" of studio head Louis B. Mayer. The studio "fixer," Mannix specialized in cleaning up scandals like the possible suicide of producer Paul Bern (see entry) in 1932. The "Bulldog" reportedly helped circulate the vicious (and many say untrue) rumor that Bern, sex bomb Jean Harlow's husband at the time of his death, was impotent. Bern's suicide was sold to the public as the only way the producer could atone for his "sin" against the popular actress. Mannix suffered from heart trouble, knew of his wife's infidelity with Reeves, and apparently sanctioned it. As Catholics, divorce was not an option for either Eddie or Toni Mannix. Instead, he maintained a mistress while she focused on Reeves. Seven years older than Reeves when they met, 52-year-old Toni Mannix, like his mother, was incredibly possessive of the television star. She called him "the Boy" while he referred to her as "Mom." Mannix set Reeves up in a house at 1579 Benedict Canyon Drive and furnished it to the actor's taste.

Always a big drinker, Reeves began drinking even more as his television show continued to gain in popularity. By the mid-fifties alcohol had bloated "Superman" to the point where he was forced to wear a corset under his cape. Concerned that he might not have an acting career after the series ended, Reeves convinced the producers to let him direct three episodes during the show's final season in 1957. After seven years, 104 episodes, and one full-length film, *The Adventures of Superman* wrapped on November 27, 1957, amid talk that the show might be picked up in 1958.

In the fall of 1958 Reeves was in New York City on a promotional tour for the series when he met and fell in love with Lenore Lemmon, a sometime torch singer. Lemmon, twice married and 15 years younger than Toni Mannix, had a hard-earned reputation as a shady character with a history of writing bad checks. In the early forties she was barred from the Stork Club for brawling. Reeves unceremoniously dropped Mannix and installed Lemmon in his house on Benedict Canyon Drive. Toni Mannix, devastated and still pay-ing the bills on the house, became obsessed with the couple. Reeves alerted police that the woman was stalking him and making harassing phone calls. By mid–June 1959, the 45-year-old actor had not worked in two years and was living off residuals from the "Superman" series. Plans to set up a series of boxing exhibitions with prizefighter Archie Moore were cancelled due to poor ticket sales. Through it all, Reeves continued to spend $600 a month on liquor. One week before his death, however, he signed to do another season of *Superman* in which he would be allowed to direct several episodes. Additionally, he planned to marry Lemmon, 35, in Mexico on June 19, 1959.

What exactly happened during the early morning hours of June 16, 1959, in the star's house at 1579 Benedict Canyon Drive is now a matter of contention. Many believe that Reeves, depressed over his stalled career and not looking forward to playing "Superman" in another 26 television episodes, simply shot himself. Others (most notably Sam Kashner in his 1996 study of the case, *Hollywood Kryptonite*) believe that Reeves was murdered by underworld contacts of Eddie Mannix who was acting at the behest of his jilted wife Toni. According to the "official" version of the case, however, Reeves turned in early on the evening of June 15, 1959, leaving Lemmon alone downstairs with house guest Robert Condon, a writer doing a biographical piece on the actor. Sometime after midnight on June 17, friends William Bliss and Carol Van Ronkel dropped by the house for a drink, attracted by the glowing porch light. Friends of the couple knew that when the light was left on drinks were still being served. When switched off, they wished not to be disturbed. That night, Lemmon inadvertently left the porch light on. Lemmon, Condon, Bliss, and Van Ronkel were enjoying themselves when a sleepy and angry Reeves emerged from his upstairs bedroom clad in a dressing gown. The actor yelled at the new arrivals for calling "at this ungodly hour" and told them in no uncertain terms that he was in "no mood for a party." After threatening to physically throw Bliss out of the house, Reeves apologized, had a quick drink, and left to go back upstairs to bed.

According to published reports, Lemmon then "narrated" the events leading up to her lover's death. As she heard Reeves settling into his room over the garage, Lemmon announced, "That's George, he's going to shoot himself." As the sound of a drawer was heard opening she said, "See he's opening the drawers to get the gun out." Then as a shot rang out upstairs Lemmon shouted, "See there, I told you; he's shot himself." Bliss rushed up the stairs to find Reeves' nude body sprawled across the bed bleeding profusely from a gunshot wound through the right temple. The .30-caliber bullet fired from a 9mm German Luger found on the floor between the dead man's feet exited through the actor's left temple and lodged in the ceiling. The heavily oiled weapon yielded no fingerprints. An autopsy determined that Reeves' alcohol level was .27 percent. The legal level of intoxication in California in 1959 was .15. Lemmon later told police she was only "kidding" when she foretold Reeves' death.

According to Lemmon: "George couldn't exist in this kind of a world. That's why he killed himself. He died of a broken heart. From being Superman he couldn't get a job. He had been Superman on TELEVISION for eight years. A year and a half ago they stopped making them. George hadn't had a job since. His dignity was shattered. He was typed, and it was 'Sorry, George. We think you're great, but we can't use you.' He had been depressed for months and months, but he hid it. He was full of chuckles...." Amid ongoing controversy, the body of George Reeves was cremated and finally placed in the Mountain View Cemetery in Altadena, California. The urn reads: "My Beloved Son 'Superman'— George Bessolo Reeves — Jan. 6, 1914–June 16, 1959."

FURTHER READING

Henderson, Jan Alan. *George Reeves: The Man, the Myth, the Mystery.* Hollywood: Cult Movies, 1995.

_____. *Speeding Bullet: The Life and Bizarre Death of George Reeves.* Grand Rapids, Mich.: M. Bifulco, 1999.
Kashner, Sam, and Schoenburger, Nancy. *Hollywood Kryptonite: The Bulldog, the Lady, and the Death of Superman.* 1st ed. New York: St. Martin's Press, 1996.

Reilly, Catherine

Reilly, a fashion model-actress who played the "little blue nun" in television commercials for Blue Nun wine, shot her 34-year-old lover, New York City transit cop Michael Condon, then turned the gun on herself, ending a loud quarrel in her Manhattan apartment at 315 East Fifty-Fourth Street on July 7, 1982. Condon, separated from his wife and occasionally living with the 28-year-old actress, was shot once in the chest with his own .38-caliber sevice revolver before Reilly fired a round into her mouth. The fully clothed pair were found sprawled together in the living room with the .38 and Condon's unfired 9mm pistol lying nearby. Reilly had appeared in off-off Broadway plays, television soap operas, and in small roles in the films *Annie Hall* (1977) and *Superman* (1978).

Renaudin, Lester

Renaudin, a 21-year-old emcee at the Club Plantation in New Orleans, was married to his childhood sweetheart, Mary Lee Roberts, a 19-year-old dancer at the Club Avalon in Metairie Ridge, Louisiana, for two years when their recent estrangement exploded into a murder-suicide on January 26, 1933. Shortly before midnight, Renaudin waited in his car outside the Club Avalon for Roberts to report to work. When she arrived, he invited her into the car to talk. Minutes later, Renaudin pulled out a revolver, shot her through the heart, then fired a bullet into his brain. Roberts continued to scream, "Please don't let me die," until expiring (with her husband) en route to the hospital. A letter addressed to his father found on the dead emcee read: "I can't possibly live without Mary Lee and can do anything living with her. She is the only girl that could ever enter my life. I suppose I am crazy — I must be to do a thing like this. I would have gone crazy before the day was over. I never was happy in my life, so don't worry, my poor, good, sweet family. I loved you more than I ever could express. I would write more, but you know how I feel. Your downhearted son, Lester."

Rennie, Hugh

The English-born veteran stage actor appeared in various Theatre Guild productions on Broadway (*Ned McCobb's Daughter*, 1926; *Goodbye Again*, 1932; *Journey's End*, 1939 revival) as well as directing plays in several summer theatres. On September 28, 1953, the 50-year-old actor's pajama-clad body was discovered by his wife, stage actress Dortha Duckworth, hanging from a hall closet door in their five room apartment at 200 West Fifty-fourth Street in New York City. In four notes found at the scene, Rennie regretted that "he had caused so much trouble to everyone" and that he "had been in a terrible mess."

Reynolds, Florence

Reynolds (real name Walsh) fell in love with fellow vaudevillian Bruce Healy while acting with him in the Reynolds Trio. Despite learning that Healy was already married, she pawned $500 worth of her jewelry and borrowed money against a life insurance policy to post his bail on a bigamy charge. Healy repaid the kindness by leaving her. On May 25, 1928, a housekeeper found the young actress' body in her fourth-floor room at 148 West Seventy-eighth Street in New York City. Reynolds, clad in a nightgown, lay on the floor with her mouth pressed over an open floor board gas jet. Two notes found on a dresser in the sparsely furnished room asked that her family be notified and gave instructions for disposing of certain personal effects. Also lying on the dresser was a five page letter neatly written in green ink addressed "Dear Uncle Charlie." In it, Reynolds wrote: "I wish God would take me for I don't see how I can go on and on. My

faith in mankind gone, I am through with mankind forever."

Reynolds, Fred

Frustrated by his failure to make it as a headliner and disappointed over a love affair with chorus girl Ruth Bayliss, the 28-year-old dancing man of the *Lovely Lady* company leaped from a sixth floor window in Chicago's Berkshire Hotel on February 2, 1929. At the coroner's inquest, Bayliss testified that Reynolds entered her hotel room after their performance at the Garrick Theatre and discovered a letter she had written to another man. Telling the chorus girl not to forget to mail it in the morning, Reynolds asked permission to write a letter to his aunt. After doing so, the dancer jumped from the window. He died an hour later at the Henrotin Policlinic. The coroner's jury returned a verdict of "suicide while temporarily insane."

Reynolds, Lynn

Reynolds, a director-scenarist best known for Westerns like *The Deadwood Coach* (1924), *The Buckaroo Kid* (1926), and *Hey! Hey! Cowboy* (1927), had originally planned to spend only three days in the High Sierras shooting scenes for Universal's *Back to God's Country* starring Renée Adorée on loan-out from MGM at $3,500 a week. Instead, the company was snowed in for three weeks at Bishop, California, before Reynolds could complete the pivotal shots. Afterward, the 36-year-old director phoned his wife in Hollywood to let her know that he would not only be coming home on the evening of February 24, 1927, but would also like to have a dinner party with friends to mark the event.

Arriving at his home at 8281 Fountain Avenue, a tired and emotionally spent Reynolds was displeased to find only one couple, Mr. and Mrs. William H. White, had been invited by his wife, formerly known on screen as "Kathleen O'Connor." At dinner, the woman playfully "accused" Reynolds of having shared a lunch basket, which she had prepared for him, with Renée Adorée while on location. Shouting, "It's a lie!" Reynolds countered by accusing her of adultery. Enraged, the woman tossed an ashtray at Reynolds, prompting him to storm off to the sunroom at the rear of the house with his wife in pursuit. Mr. White followed the pair into the room and saw the woman, her eyes puffy from blows and pleading for her life, on the floor with Reynolds above her brandishing a .38-caliber pistol. The director then placed the pistol to his head and fired. He died the next day at Receiving Hospital. The film, *Back to God's Country*, was finished by director Irvin Willat and released on September 4, 1927.

Richards, (Margaret) Ann (Borden)

Richards (born October 1, 1935, in San Diego, California) began her career singing and playing piano with local groups in San Francisco and Oakland. In the fifties, she worked with Charlie Barnet and George Redman before joining the Stan Kenton band in 1955. She and Kenton married in October 1955. In 1956, Richards won the *Downbeat* poll as the number one band vocalist, but had already temporarily retired from singing to become a mother. Following the birth of her two children, she sang with Kenton's band until they divorced in 1961. During the sixties, Richards continued to sing in clubs in Los Angeles backed up by such jazz stalwarts as Jack Sheldon, Barney Kessel, Red Callender, and Larry Bunker. On April 1, 1982, William Botts, Richards' estranged second husband, became concerned after failing to hear from her for three weeks. Richards, 46, had recently ended a ten year engagement at the Bel-Air Hotel and was having trouble finding another job. Entering Richards' home in the Hollywood Hills, Botts found the singer in her bedroom dead from a gunshot wound to the right temple. A subsequent musical tribute for Richards held at the LA club Carmelo's benefited the surviving son of fellow musician and suicide Frank Rosolino (see entry).

Richert, Frederick

Richert, 51, formerly involved in the coal and ice business in Philadelphia, built a moving picture theatre in that city at Frankford Avenue and Rhawn Street in early 1914. As the theatre steadily lost vast sums of money, the frustrated theatre owner first attempted suicide by inhaling gas, but survived. Months passed before he tried again. On November 2, 1914, as his wife was busy on the first floor of their home at 7908 Frankford Avenue, Richert walked into a second floor bedroom and shot himself through the heart.

Ritchie, Adele

Once known as the "Dresden china doll of the musical comedy stage," Ritchie was born in Philadelphia in 1877. In 1893, she made her first public appearance in the light opera *The Algerian*. Leading roles in other operas ensued, followed by a stint in vaudeville. On November 3, 1916, the recently divorced actress married stage actor Guy Bates Post in Toronto shortly before his matinee performance as the lead in *Omar the Tentmaker*. After the marriage, Ritchie all but retired from the theatre although she did aid America's World War I recruiting effort by singing war songs in vaudeville in 1917. After the couple divorced in 1929, the 52-year-old actress relocated to the exclusive artist colony of Laguna Beach, California, where she directed plays for the Community Playhouse. There, Ritchie became close friends with Doris Murray Palmer, dubbed the "most beautiful woman in Laguna Beach," a wealthy divorcee some 20 years her junior. The pair were inseparable companions until Palmer's popularity in the community's closely knit social circle began to eclipse Ritchie's. A past collaborator with Ritchie in the Community Playhouse, Palmer had designed all the stage settings and scenery for the theatre's latest offering, *The Lady from Memphis*, and was set to direct alone.

The pair's relationship reached a crisis on April 24, 1930, at Palmer's hillside bungalow at 2337 Glenneyre Street in Laguna Beach. Ritchie was visiting her friend when she learned that Palmer had been invited to a luncheon and she had not. Ritchie insisted on attending, but Palmer was equally adamant that she was not invited, and angrily turning her back on the former actress, walked down a hallway leading to the garage. Ritchie pulled a nickel plated, pearl-handled .32-caliber revolver from her purse and shot the 35-year-old woman once in the back (the bullet entering under the left shoulder blade and piercing the heart) and once at close range in the back of the head. According to the police reconstruction of the crime, Ritchie then spent the next two hours driving around the community trying to decide a course of action. Finally, she returned to the scene of the crime and moved Palmer's body to a room adjoining the living room. Ritchie carefully arranged her friend's body: folded her arms across her chest, straightened out her clothes, combed her hair, placed a pillow beneath the head, then applied rouge, lipstick, and powder to Palmer's face. She then retired to the adjoining living room and, after first firing a shot at her head that missed, reclined on the sofa, placed the gun to her right ear, and pulled the trigger. In the throes of her death agony, the actress rolled to the floor. Their bodies were later discovered by a mutual friend who stopped by the bungalow to return Palmer's lost dog. Post, informed of his former wife's murder-suicide before a performance of *The Play's the Thing* in Hawaii, said, "We lived together fourteen years, but frankly I never felt I knew her. She was very proud."

Ritchie, Perry V.

Ritchie, a film actor with the Manchester, New Hampshire–based King-Lynch Players, relocated to Los Angeles where his offer of marriage to a film actress was refused. Fearful of the re-emergence of a debilitating mental disorder that had institutionalized him back East, the 30-year-old actor purchased four veronal tablets from a local pharmacy on July 27, 1918. Returning to his home at 1579 West Vernon Street, Ritchie downed the pills, then laid down beside an open baseboard gas jet.

Rivera, Carlos

A dancer with a vaudeville act headed by Senorita Alcaniz, the 32-year-old Rivera was fatally mangled and decapitated when he jumped in front of an eastbound New York Central passenger train in South Bend, Indiana, on February 15, 1930. A signed note found on a telegram in the dead man's pocket asked that his wife in Plainfield, Indiana, be notified of the "accident." The telegram, sent from New York to Plainfield two weeks before, read: "I have been looking for you every day. Let me know what's the matter. Much worried over your health."

Roberts, Albert G.

Peggy Shannon, a Broadway showgirl with the *Ziegfeld Follies* and *Earl Carroll's Vanities*, was brought to Hollywood by Paramount in the early thirties as a rival to Clara Bow. The shapely redhead made four films in 1931 (*The Secret Call*, *Silence*, *The Road to Reno*, *Touchdown*) and worked regularly throughout the decade in some 20 other films (*The Painted Woman*, 1932; *Night Life of the Gods*, 1935; *Youth on Parole*, 1937; *Girls on Probation*, 1938). By 1940, however, Shannon's career was in ruins due to her chronic alcoholism. In October 1940, three months after divorcing actor Alan Davis, the actress married Warner Bros. cameraman Albert G. Roberts in Mexico. Roberts, 39, operated second camera on two Bette Davis vehicles: *That Certain Woman* (1937) and director William Wyler's *Jezebel* (1938). On May 11, 1941, Roberts returned home from a fishing trip with a co-worker to find his 31-year-old wife's body slumped across the kitchen table of their home at 4318 Irvine Avenue in North Hollywood. Shannon was seated at a table strewn with empty liquor bottles and glasses, her head resting on her arms, with a cigarette burned down to the fingertips of her right hand. Her death was reportedly due to a liver ailment aggravated by years of heavy drinking.

Roberts was grief stricken. Just weeks later in the pre-dawn hours of May 30, 1941, the inconsolable cameraman visited Shannon's grave at Hollywood Memorial Park Cemetery with his police dog, Spec. Roberts returned to his North Hollywood home at dawn, phoned his sister Phoebe Genereux, and told her, "I'm going to join Peggy. I'm going to kill myself." Genereux screamed, "Al, don't do it!" to which Roberts replied, "Yes. It's all settled. I'll be with Peggy, now." Genereux heard a shot followed by Spec's barking.

Authorities arrived at Roberts' home to find that the cameraman had shot himself in the head with a .22-caliber rifle. Roberts was in the kitchen seated in the same chair and slumped across the same table where Shannon had died. In a corner of the room directly opposite the dead man hung a photo portrait of Shannon with a vase of flowers before it. Three notes were found on the bloodstained table beside the body. Two were for Genereux, and the other addressed to "Whom It May Concern," read: "It happens that I am very much in love with my wife, Peggy Shannon. In this spot she passed away. So in reverence to her you will find me in the same spot. No one will ever understand, as it should be. Why don't you all try a little harder? It wouldn't hurt. I can truthfully say for the both of us, Adios amigos.— Al Roberts."

Roberts, Jay Martin

The San Francisco–based composer had performed for several years in various clubs in the Canal Zone when he shot himself in the head in Panama City, Panama, on July 28, 1932. In a note to his mother, the 42-year-old Roberts wrote that he was "just tired of life and of the pain of insomnia, knotting muscles and nervousness."

Roberts, Nellie Brewster

Known in vaudeville and on the musical comedy stage as "Nellie Brewster," the 67-year-old retired actress and singer in such Broadway productions as *The Spring Chicken* and *Ninety in the Shade* was found by police on July 4, 1947, in her shabbily furnished room at 222 East Twenty-sixth Street in New York City. Despondent over her husband's death three weeks before, Roberts opened two gas jets on a range and died amid studio photographs and faded clippings dating back 30 years. In a note, the vaudevillian bequeathed a ring to her mother.

Roberts, Rachel

Born the daughter of a Baptist minister in Llanelli, Wales on September 20, 1927, Roberts overcame her parents' objections to become one of the finest stage and film actresses of the sixties. After studying at the Royal Academy of Dramatic Art, Roberts joined the Shakespeare Memorial Theatre in Stratford-on-Avon in 1951. Debuting on the London stage in 1953 in *The Buccaneer*, the actress joined the Old Vic company the next year and appeared in productions of *Macbeth* and *Othello*. In 1952, Roberts acted in her first film, *Valley of Song*, but would not become recognized as a top screen talent until her performance in director Karel Reisz's 1960 drama *Saturday Night and Sunday Morning*, for which she was presented the British Film Academy's best actress award. In 1963, she won the same award for her Oscar–nominated performance opposite Richard Harris in *This Sporting Life*, and was again honored by the British Film Academy with its best supporting actress award for her work in *Yanks* (1979).

While appearing opposite Rex Harrison in the play *Platonov* in London in 1960, Roberts, 33, fell in love with the 53-year-old actor. After their marriage (his fourth) on March 21, 1962, Roberts cut back on her career and tried to make a home for the globe-trotting actor. By the time they divorced in February 1971, Roberts was drinking heavily and subject to bouts of depression. Though continuing to work onstage and in films like Lindsay Anderson's *O Lucky Man!* (1973), and

Peter Weir's *Picnic at Hanging Rock* (1976), Roberts' unpredictable behavior, fuelled by alcohol, depression, and pills, made her largely unemployable. Her last regular work was from 1976–1978 on the television series *The Tony Randall Show*. On November 27, 1980, the 53-year-old stage and screen actress was found dead by her gardener in the back yard of her Bel Air home in West Los Angeles. The coroner ruled that Roberts, in addition to having taken a massive dose of barbiturates, had ingested a substance similar to lye or alkali, often found in weed killer or insecticide. A journal entry written by Roberts six days before her death read: "I've tried psychiatrists. I've tried Alcoholics Anonymous. I've tried Indian religion. I've been in and out of homes and clinics and health farms. I've tried sobriety. I've tried prayer. If God is there and would answer my prayer, what would I ask for? To be healed. To be able to live and enjoy life. To be able to act. To be able to give."

FURTHER READING

Roberts, Rachel. *No Bells on Sunday: The Journals of Rachel Roberts*. London: Pavilion, 1984.

Robertson, William T.

Robertson, 40, met his 17-year-old married girlfriend, Diane Stroud Provost, while managing the Bright Leaf Drive-In Theatre north of Kinston, North Carolina. Provost worked at the concession stand. Robertson lost his job at the theatre about the time his wife moved out of their house at 2504 Woodview Road in Kinston to live with her parents. On November 10, 1964, she returned to the house for some clothes to find a rental car parked in the carport. Afraid "she knew what had happened," the wife called the local police, who cut a screen door to gain entry. The sounds of a television set led an officer into the den where he found the murder-suicide. Provost was sitting on the couch with one bullet hole through her heart. Robertson lay at her feet dead from an identical wound. A Smith & Wesson .38-caliber pistol was lying

about three feet from his body. A coroner later ruled that the pair had been dead at least four days when they were found.

Robinson, Madeleine

In 1947 Robinson divorced filmmaker Edward Dmytryk, one of the so-called "Hollywood Ten." That same year the director of *Hitler's Children* (1943) was sentenced to a one year term for refusing to tell the House Un-American Activities Committee if he was a member of the Communist Party. Dmytryk was released in six months after admitting that while he had once been a Red, he now saw "the true motives of the Communist Party." At the time of the divorce, Robinson was awarded 25 percent of the director's gross income (not to exceed $25,000 or drop below $5,200 a year) and given another $100 a week for support of their one child. On June 6, 1952, Robinson's psychiatrist became alarmed when he was unable to reach her by phone for several hours. Beverly Hills police, dispatched to the attractive 39-year-old's apartment at 9361 W. Olympic Avenue, found her nightgown-clad body in bed. An empty whiskey glass lay near the bed while an empty bottle of prescription sleeping pills was discovered in the bathroom medicine chest. There was no note. While Robinson's mother insisted that the overdose was accidental, police suspected that a broken love affair with another of Hollywood's "Unfriendly Ten," producer-screenwriter Adrian Scott, prompted the fatal act. According to her psychiatrist, the woman had been "generally disappointed with life," and Scott, her former lover, admitted that she had twice before attempted to take her life.

Rocamora, Wynn

One of the top agents in Hollywood, the German–born Rocamora represented such stars as Gloria Swanson, Maureen O'Sullivan, Greer Garson, Dorothy Lamour, and gossip columnist Louella Parsons. In 1955, he became the artistic director of the Hollywood Bowl and was instrumental in bringing top flight European talent to America. Under his tenure, Swedish soprano Birgit Nilsson and Austrian conductor Herbert von Karajan made their debuts at the Bowl. He resigned the post at the end of the 1959 season. On December 2, 1959, the 52-year-old agent was found dead in the bedroom of his Hollywood Hills home at 6964 Los Tilos Road by his houseman who came to awaken him for breakfast. Police found three empty pill bottles in the bedroom and a suicide note addressed to his business partner propped up on an upstairs desk. It read in part: "I am sick physically and mentally — at the end of my rope. I can't go on."

Rockwell, George

On November 25, 1914, one day before their seventh wedding anniversary, Rockwell, 50, shot his wife, Amelia, and his 19-year-old stepdaughter, Flora Hollister, as they played cards with a friend at their luxurious home at 118 Malvern Place, in the Cincinnati, Ohio, suburb of Mt. Auburn. Rockwell, a former assistant general passenger agent of the Pennsylvania Line Railroad, had months before unsuccessfully convinced his wife to loan him money to buy stock in a motion picture company that was being promoted in Ohio. Over the objections of her daughter, Amelia Rockwell had given her husband $10,000 during the past two years for other failed get-rich-quick schemes. On this occasion she refused.

Rockwell moved into a small, unadorned room in the opulent house off the reception hall and slept on a cot. When he learned that his wife no longer trusted him to collect rent from her properties, Rockwell became enraged. On the night of the incident, the women had just settled down in the reception hall to play cards with a friend when Rockwell's bedroom door burst open and he emerged brandishing a pistol and shouting, "I will end it all." When the shooting stopped, Amelia Rockwell had been hit in the liver and chest. She died three hours later at Christ's Hospital. Her daughter, who sustained

wounds to the shoulder and thigh, survived. Authorities found Rockwell dead in a front room from a pistol shot to the right temple.

Rogers, Gustavus A.

In poor health since 1940, the prominent film industry attorney, philanthropist, and Democratic leader telephoned a stenographer on March 19, 1944, to meet him at his New York City office at 299 Broadway in order to perform "a special task." The worker arrived to find her 67-year-old employer hanging from the open door of an eight-foot-high steel cabinet.

Rogers, Will, Jr.

The son of famed humorist Will Rogers (1879–1935) was born in New York City on October 20, 1911, while his father was starring in the *Ziegfeld Follies*. A graduate of Stanford University, Rogers, 24, was working as a merchant seaman when his father was killed in an Alaskan plane crash along with aviator Wiley Post on August 15, 1935. Elected as a Democrat from a southern California district to the House of Representatives in 1942, Rogers resigned during World War II and joined the Army. As a member of the Tank Destroyer Corps, he was wounded at the Battle of the Bulge and decorated for bravery. After the war, Rogers lost a Senate race in 1946, but two years later became the southern California campaign manager for Harry Truman's reelection campaign.

In 1949, Rogers (who bore a striking physical resemblance to the humorist) portrayed his father in *Look for the Silver Lining*, the first of three such film characterizations. Rogers also played the title role in *The Story of Will Rogers* (1952) and impersonated his father again in the 1953 film biography *The Eddie Cantor Story*. His other films include *The Boy from Oklahoma* (1954) and *Wild Heritage* (1958). Capitalizing on *The Story of Will Rogers*, Rogers played a similar character, a folksy small town newspaper editor, on the CBS radio show *Rogers of the Gazette*

(1953–1954). From 1957 to 1958, he hosted the CBS television network's *Good Morning Show*. In addition to his numerous other activities, Rogers was also the editor-publisher of the *Beverly Hills Citizen* newspaper (1935–1953), chairman of the California State Park Commission from 1960 to 1962, and assistant to the U.S. Commissioner of Indian Affairs in the late sixties.

Retired and living on a ranch in Tubac, a small south central Arizona town some 140 miles southeast of Phoenix, the 81 year old had recently suffered a series of strokes and recurring heart problems, and was in constant pain from a hip replacement surgery. On July 9, 1993, Rogers was found beside his car near Tubac, the victim of a self-inflicted shotgun wound to the head. In a note found near the body, the former congressman, journalist, and actor (himself part Cherokee) asked that his two adoptive American Indian sons be notified of his death.

Rose, Joel

An icon in Cleveland, Rose co-hosted the popular show *The Morning Exchange* on WEWS-TV Channel 5 for 16 years. Known for his acerbic wit, the announcer co-anchored the noon news and was also heard on radio station WERE AM-1300 in Cleveland. Rose left broadcasting in 1983 to run Flagship Communications, his public relations and marketing firm.

On August 2, 2000, authorities searched the 64 year old's Brecksville, Ohio, home as part of a two-year ongoing investigation into complaints made by more than a dozen women throughout Ohio who had received anonymous mailings of underwear, pornography, and greetings cards. The women, ranging in ages from college students to women in their 60s, were typically blonde, thin, and had worked in local television and radio. Unnerved by the mailings, they formed a support group to compare their experiences and to meet with police and prosecutors. Rose denied the charges and, though not arrested, was com-

pelled to submit DNA blood and saliva samples to be compared with body fluids found on panties received by some of the women. Authorities also removed a computer hard drive and a typewriter from his house on Glen Valley Drive. Ironically, the beloved former broadcaster had only recently overseen the installation of new communications systems in the town's police and fire departments.

At 6:00 A.M. on August 4, 2000, two days after the police raid on his home, Rose told his wife, Lois, that he was going out for the newspaper. Instead, he walked into the woods near their home and shot himself in the right temple with a .38-caliber handgun. Rose left behind several notes, the contents of which were not disclosed.

An editorial in the August 5, 2000, edition of the *Plain Dealer*, the Cleveland newspaper many accused of provoking Rose's death with its front page story on the search of his home, commented: "And if it turns out that Rose was guilty of this strange and apparently petty perversion, his family nonetheless deserves the sympathy of a community that recalls his public persona fondly and will be saddened to learn of his private demons." Weeks later, preliminary DNA results were released that failed to link Rose to any of the sexually explicit mailings. Likewise, the typewriter confiscated from his home did not match the type found on many of the notes. Police, however, refused to rule Rose out as a suspect.

Rose, Monica

Born in London on February 11, 1948, the 4 foot, 9 inch tall Cockney was a 15-year-old junior accounts clerk when, in 1964, she was given tickets to Hughie Green's popular ITV quiz show *Double Your Money*. Selected as a contestant from the studio audience, Rose only won £8 but so impressed Green with her vibrant personality that he invited her back as a guest hostess six weeks later. She stayed on the show for three years, toured with Green in a stage act based on the program's format, and even gave a Royal Variety Performance before leaving to escape the pressures of stardom. She was reunited with Green in *Sky's the Limit* (1971–1974), a game show in which contestants could win free air miles plus spending money. After the show ended, the popular performer put together a song and dance cabaret act, but left show business for good in 1977.

Three years later, Rose was admitted to a hospital suffering from depression and nervous exhaustion. Shortly afterward, she married a Baptist lay minister, became a Christian, and took a job as a cashier in a supermarket near their home in Leicester. On February 8, 1994, after suffering ill health for many years, Rose killed herself with a combination of anti-depressants and painkillers in her home in Whetstone, Leicestershire.

Rosenberg, Edgar

As a child, Rosenberg (born in Bremerhaven, Germany, circa 1925) fled with his family to Denmark and later South Africa to escape Nazi oppression. Educated at Rugby and Cambridge in England, he came to New York in the late forties to work as an assistant for NBC entertainment vice-president Emmanual "Manny" Sachs. Rosenberg later became a producer on the prestigious cultural affairs program *Omnibus* (1953–1957), and also worked on entertainment programs like *The Pinky Lee Show*, *Your Hit Parade*, and *The Milton Berle Show*. In the late fifties he joined the top New York public and industrial relations firm Anna Rosenberg Associates (no relation). Taking a leave of absence from the company, Rosenberg worked with the Telsun Foundation, producers of the 1966 anti-drug film *The Poppy Is Also a Flower*, under the aegis of the United Nations. Through Telsun, Rosenberg became friends with British actor Peter Sellers. Faced with problems on a screenplay they were developing, Rosenberg hired Brooklyn–born comedienne Joan Rivers on the strength of her performances on *The Tonight Show* starring Johnny Carson. They flew to Jamaica to work on the script, fell in love, and following a four-day whirlwind courtship, married on July 15, 1965.

Rosenberg, the serious intellectual, and Rivers, the brash, street smart comic, were totally devoted to one another. Together they represented a formidable business partnership. While "Edgar" became the focus of much of Rivers' stand-up material, Rosenberg the producer was behind the scenes setting up movie and television deals for his wife. In 1978, he produced the film *Rabbit Test* directed by Rivers and starring Billy Crystal as a pregnant man. Rivers, a favorite of talk show host Johnny Carson, was named "permanent" guest host of *The Tonight Show* in 1983. The popular comedienne was the only host of the program until leaving in 1986 to host her own week night talk show, *The Late Show*, on the Fox Broadcasting Company. The breakup with Carson was both bitter and public. Carson felt betrayed by Rivers and never spoke to her again. Rosenberg was co-executive producer of *The Late Show* when it premiered on October 9, 1986.

As it became obvious that the program was never going to challenge Carson's late night ratings stranglehold, Rosenberg became increasingly more difficult to work with. In April 1987 Fox Broadcasting president Jamie Kellner barred him from the set. Host Joan Rivers was fired one month later after the May 15, 1987, telecast. Media pundits labelled Rosenberg as the prime cause for the show's failure. In 1984, the producer survived a massive heart attack and subsequent quadruple bypass surgery. Guilt over the failure of his wife's television show coupled with past and current health problems deeply depressed Rosenberg. While vacationing in Ireland in late July 1987, Rosenberg developed gastrointestinal bleeding and had to be hospitalized. The attack further affected his stamina and mental powers. At the time he told Rivers: "I get into bed and pray that I won't wake up in the morning."

In mid–August 1987, Rosenberg, 62, was in Philadelphia for real estate meetings with his business partner Thomas Pileggi. On the evening of August 13, he spoke with Pileggi on the phone and confessed that he was extremely depressed. After promising his business partner that he would not do any thing rash, Rosenberg called his 19-year-old daughter, Melissa, in Los Angeles and told her: "I've put everything in order for you. You must be an adult. Things are going to be difficult for you." Melissa and Joan Rivers hurriedly called Rosenberg's psychiatrist. Shortly afterward, Rosenberg called his family to assure them that he would meet with the doctor when he returned home the next day. He then called his psychiatrist to set up an appointment. A final phone call was made to arrange for a car to meet him at the airport to take him to Cedars-Sinai Medical Center.

The next morning, August 14, Pileggi worried when Rosenberg failed to answer the phone in his $450 a day suite at the downtown Four Seasons Hotel. He notified hotel security and they entered Room 425 when the producer failed to answer the door. Rosenberg's body was found sprawled on the bedroom floor, a victim of a lethal overdose of Valium washed down with scotch and cognac. He was officially pronounced dead at 11:45 A.M. Rosenberg left three cassette tapes: one for his wife, one for his daughter, and one for Pileggi. In the tape to his business partner, the producer explained that failing health made him feel he was a "burden to the people that he loved" and that he "couldn't go on." He asked Pileggi to deliver the remaining tapes to his family.

Rosolino, Frank

Rosolino (born August 20, 1926, in Detroit, Michigan) was a premier jazz trombonist who over the years performed with Gene Krupa, Stan Kenton, Dexter Gordon, and Quincy Jones. A staff musician in the early sixties on the *Steve Allen* television show, "Mr. West Coast Trombone" was also a talented comedian and scat singer. In a fit of depression on November 26, 1978, the 52-year-old musician shot his two sons (ages 11 and 7) with a

.38-caliber pistol as they lay asleep in separate bunk beds at their home on Nordhoff Street in Sepulveda, California. Rosolino was found fatally wounded on the living room floor. A note detailing his despondency was found at the scene. Seven-year-old Jason Rosolino survived. Of the bebop trombonist, renowned alto saxophonist and band leader Benny Carter said: "He was a fantastic musician, but behind that cut-up personality was a troubled man. He was like Pagliacci."

Ross, Albert H.

A Yale graduate, Ross, 36, was employed by NBC as a set designer and had assisted Jo Mielziner in designing sets for the television productions of *Mister Roberts* and *A Streetcar Named Desire*. On May 22, 1949, hours after telling a carpenter that he wanted to be left alone because he had a problem, Ross was found hanging from a pipe in the prop room in the sub-basement of Rockefeller Center. Days later, the sets he designed for the first television presentation of the Ballet Theatre were shown on the air.

Ross, Robin

The 33-year-old actress (also known as Wendy Ross) who once dated Burt Reynolds and John Wayne's son, Patrick, did guest shots on the hit television shows *Dallas*, *St. Elsewhere*, and *Charlie's Angels*. Ross was living in Canada when she lost $185,000, her entire life savings earned during a 15 year acting career, in the U.S. stock market crash in October 1987. Concerned over her daughter's mental health, Virginia Kent convinced the actress to come live with her at her home in Westgate, England. Although Ross was under a doctor's care and taking prescription sleeping pills and anti-depressants, she was still deeply troubled. According to Kent, her daughter kept repeating, "Mummy, we're poor now, we're poor." Kent later told a coroner's inquest, "I moved our beds together so I could reach out to her when she wept in the night."

On the morning of April 11, 1988, Ross told her mother that she was going shopping. Instead, the disturbed actress went to the Westgate Bay, near Margate, Kent. Witnesses saw the fully-clothed woman wade into the sea and then swim out about a quarter of a mile into a section of the water known for its treacherous tide. Ignoring the shouts of terrified onlookers, Ross calmly stretched out face-first in the water and let herself be taken under by the tow. Her lifeless body kept resurfacing every few moments until it was retrieved by a helicopter rescue crew.

Rosson, Richard

The brother of screenwriter-director Arthur and cinematographer Hal, Rosson broke into films as an actor in 1914 with supporting roles in *The Patchwork Girl of Oz* (Paramount) and *Richelieu* (Universal). After roles in some two dozen features, he made his directorial debut for Paramount in 1926 on the Gloria Swanson feature *Fine Manners*. Other films include *West Point of the Air* (1935), *Hideaway* (1937), and *Corvette K-255* (1943). During a 20 year association with MGM Rosson also did location-second unit directing for several of the studio's productions including Victor Fleming's *Captains Courageous* (1937), Julien Duvivier's *The Great Waltz* (1938), Compton Bennett and Andrew Marton's *King Solomon's Mines* (1950), and Mervyn LeRoy's *Quo Vadis* (1951).

In 1939, Rosson and his wife were in Austria shooting backgrounds for a film (later released as *Florian*) when World War II broke out. The Nazis confiscated their film and the pair spent 34 days in prison as suspected spies. In July 1941, Rosson photographed the historic Atlantic Conference of Roosevelt and Churchill aboard the American cruiser *Augusta* and the British battleship *Prince of Wales*.

In 1952, Rosson contracted a mysterious, undiagnosable fever while on location in South Africa filming scenes for the John Ford feature *Mogambo* (1953) starring Clark Gable and Ava Gardner. In failing health and unable to find medical relief, the 60-year-old director took his life on May 31, 1953, at his luxurious home at 797 South Amalfi Drive in Pacific Palisades, California. That morning, Rosson's wife, Vera, went to his room to find his bed undisturbed. A note on the night stand addressed to her read: "I cannot bear to go on. I love you very much." In the garage at the rear of the home, she found Rosson dead from carbon monoxide poisoning in the back seat of their car. A vacuum hose attached to the car's exhaust was inserted through a window.

Rovig, Melita Powell

During the years 1910–1912 Rovig sang with the New York Metropolitan Opera Company under the stage name "Horatia Powell." Relocating to Los Angeles, the retired singer began manufacturing an exclusive line of cosmetics targeted at an upscale clientele. In 1935, she married Charles Rovig, a 53-year-old sales manager for a liquor house. On the night of January 13, 1936, the pair was enjoying a quiet evening in their apartment at 706 South Mariposa Avenue when Rovig, 44, jealously accused her husband of numerous marital infidelities. A loud argument ensued in which Rovig, brandishing a revolver, threatened at one point to kill him. The liquor salesman disarmed the hysterical woman, hid the gun in a bureau drawer, and retired to bed. Shortly after daybreak, Rovig shot the sleeping man in the stomach and chest, then turned the gun on herself. He survived long enough to notify police and give a dying statement. In a note addressed to her sister, Rovig wrote that she feared her husband planned to leave her and that she was thinking of committing suicide.

Row, Harry

A Broadway theatrical producer, Row looped a rope around his neck, tied it to a transom, and jumped from a table in his room in the Emmett Hotel on 275 West Thirty-eighth Street in New York City on May 4,

1926. Friends told authorities that the 55-year-old producer had been depressed over his health for some time.

Rudolph, Mina

In her twenties, Rudolph had been a noted beauty and a musical comedy star of shows like *The Red Feather* at the Mason Opera House in Los Angeles. Now a 55-year-old former opera star beset by financial worries, Rudolph was rescued by police in the fall of 1936 after attempting to gas herself to death in the bathroom of her home at 508 North Bedford Drive in Beverly Hills. Weeks later on November 27, 1936, Rudolph registered at the exclusive Beverly Wilshire Hotel in Beverly Hills and requested a room on the upper floors where she could be away from street noise. Moments after being escorted to her room on the seventh floor, Rudolph wrote a note, removed her hat and glasses, then jumped from a window to her death.

The note, addressed to her former husband, Jefferson James Grove, read: "Dear Jeff: I have left a will giving everything to you, also the contents of my safety deposit box, which is under the name of Mrs. J. George Faber, Box No. 970. There is plenty of money to pay all expenses. Keep what you want here, and as to the rest, telephone the Goodwill. Well, I don't feel like retiring — much. Lovingly, Mina." In a postscript she added: "I don't want a minister, music nor praying at my funeral. Just one person to look at me. If I can't be put with Maude in 'Frisco, just scatter mine also. I'll be so glad when it's all over with." See entry Graves, Mina Rudolph.

Salmi, Albert

Salmi (born March 11, 1928, in the Coney Island section of Brooklyn, New York) took up acting following military service in World War II. From 1948 to 1954, the actor studied in New York with the Dramatic Workshop of the American Theatre Wing and the Actors Studio. Salmi appeared in several plays before achieving critical recognition as

"Bo Decker," the Montana Romeo, in the 1955 Broadway production of *Bus Stop*. He turned down the role in the film version because, like other actors in Lee Strasberg's Actors Studio, he did not want to be thought of as a "Hollywood sell-out." In 1956, Salmi (with Paul Newman and George Peppard) appeared on the early dramatic television program *The U.S. Steel Hour* in a highly regarded adaptation of "Bang the Drum Slowly." In 1958, Salmi overcame his feelings toward Hollywood and appeared as "Smerdyakov" in *The Brothers Karamazov*, director Richard Brooks' film adaptation for MGM of the Dostoyevsky novel. Many film Westerns followed (*The Bravados*, 1958; *The Unforgiven*, 1960; *Hour of the Gun*, 1967), but Salmi is probably best remembered for his 150–plus television credits on shows like *Rawhide*, *Bonanza*, *Wagon Train*, *The Big Valley*, and *The High Chaparral*. The beefy character actor was also a regular in two series: "Yadkin" from 1964 to 1965 in the NBC program *Daniel Boone* starring Fess Parker, and "Pete Ritter" in *Petrocelli*, the NBC series from 1974 to 1976 starring Barry Newman in the title role. In recognition of his realistic portrayal of cowboys on the small screen, Salmi was given the Western Heritage Award from the National Cowboy Hall of Fame.

The 62-year-old veteran of some 20 films was unemployed and living in Spokane, Washington, with his second wife, Roberta, when marital difficulties brought on by Salmi's drinking and physical abuse forced them to separate in February 1990. Salmi continued his abuse, this time by leaving her notes that read, "War of the Roses. You're a stupid girl. You're living out your fantasy.... We had a good thing going, too bad you tripped in the final straightaway." Fearful for her life after filing for divorce, the 55-year-old woman hired a private detective as a bodyguard, but dismissed him after family members convinced her that she was being foolish. On April 23, 1990, a neighbor dropped by the Salmi house to check on Roberta after not having seen her for two days. When no one answered the door, she peered through the kitchen window to see her friend lying in a pool of blood on the floor. When police entered the home, they found that Roberta Salmi had been shot to death with a .25-caliber handgun. In an upstairs den, Salmi had then fired a fatal .45-caliber pistol shot into his chest. Authorities estimated that the pair had been dead for less than 24 hours.

Sampson, Caleb

A classically trained keyboardist and composer, Sampson was the driving force behind Boston's Alloy Orchestra, a trio featuring synthesizers and percussion noted for scoring modern soundtracks to silent films. Sampson, with the Alloy Orchestra, created new music for two classic German silents (*Nosferatu*, 1922; *Metropolis*, 1926), often playing along with the films at various international film festivals. In addition to composing music for MTV, VH1, HBO, PBS, Showtime, and *Sesame Street*, Sampson also did the highly regarded soundtrack for the 1997 Errol Morris documentary *Fast, Cheap & Out of Control*.

Though happily married for five years to Kathleen Hickey and the father of a 19-month-old son, the 45-year-old composer had suffered for the last two years of his life from a severe sleep disorder. Often able to sleep for only two hours a night, Sampson was seeing a psychiatrist and taking anti-depressants and sleep aid medication. On June 8, 1998, Sampson kept an appointment with his psychiatrist in Cambridge, Massachusetts. Flatly refusing his doctor's suggestion that he be hospitalized for his acute depression, Sampson denied harboring any suicidal thoughts: "No, I'm safe. I would never do that to Kathy." Hours later, Sampson hanged himself in the studio he shared with writing and Alloy Orchestra partner Ken Winokur. According to Sampson's wife and friends, the composer had been unable to balance his creative life with worry over the more mundane demands of supporting and nurturing a family.

Sanders, George

Sanders, the consummate movie cad, was born in St. Petersburg, Russia, on July 3, 1906.

GEORGE SANDERS— No actor in the history of motion pictures ever played the cad or cynic better than George Sanders, pictured here in the 1956 RKO release *Death of a Scoundrel*. A veteran of 111 films and four marriages, the 65-year-old actor took his life with Nembutal and alcohol in Castelldefels, Spain, on April 24, 1972, but not before leaving one of the best suicide notes ever written.

During World War I his father, a Russian industrial manager of English descent, permanently moved the family to England. Sanders and his older brother Tom (later to be known in Hollywood as Tom Conway, star of the *Falcon* film series) were educated in British public schools (Dunhurst Preparatory School, Bedales School in Hampshire). At Brighton College in Sussex, Sanders excelled in sports and academics, but as a foreign-born student from a financially strapped family experienced the hostility and class snobbery of his native-born classmates. After college, Sanders went briefly into the textile business before going to Argentina in 1926 as a representative of the English and American Tobacco Company. He returned to England in the early thirties and, after making his London stage debut in the 1932 revue *Ballyhoo*, worked in British radio plays. In 1935, good reviews in his first leading stage role in *Further Outlook* led to a supporting part in the 1936 British film *The Man Who Could Work Miracles*. Sanders signed a long term contract with British and Dominion Films and was brought to Hollywood in 1936 after 20th Century–Fox bought that studio's assets.

Cast that same year as the aristocratic cad "Lord Everett Stacy" in director Henry King's *Lloyd's of London*, Sanders' suavely villainous portrayal in the film forever typecast him. It reached its apeothesis in his 1950 Best Supporting Actor Academy Award winning role as theatre critic "Addison DeWitt" in *All About Eve*. Notable among his 111 films are *Rebecca* (1940), *The Moon and Sixpence* (1942), *The Picture of Dorian Gray* (1945), *Forever Amber* (1947), two RKO "B" movie series (*The Saint*, five films; *The Falcon*, four films), *Death of a Scoundrel* (1956), *While the City Sleeps* (1956), *A Shot in the Dark* (1964), *The Quiller Memorandum* (1966), and the 1967 Disney animated feature *Jungle Book* with Sanders supplying the voice of the tiger "Shere Kahn." By the late sixties, Sanders was reduced to appearing in low-budget horror films like *The Body Stealers* (1969) and his final film, *Psychomania* (1972).

Though a success in films for many years, Sanders' off-screen life was marred by insecurity, depression, and years of psychoanalysis. As much a ladies' man offscreen as on, the suave, the suave actor was married four times: Susan Larson (1940–1947, divorce), Zsa Zsa Gabor (1949–1954, divorce), Benita Hume (1958–1967, she died), and Magda Gabor (1970–1971, divorce). In the sixties, Sanders' disastrous investment in a British sausage company (Cadco) led to bankruptcy and government censure. Physically debilitated and chronically depressed by a series of strokes, the 65-year-old actor checked into a suite at the seaside resort hotel Rey Don Jaime in Castelldefels, Spain, some ten miles north of Barcelona on April 23, 1972. Asking the desk clerk for a morning wake up call, Sanders retired early on the night of the 24th. When the actor failed to answer the next morning, the manager went to investigate and found Sanders dead, surrounded by five empty tubes of Nembutal. An autopsy revealed that he had washed down 60 30-milligram capsules with vodka.

Two notes were found at the scene. One, written in English, perfectly dovetailed with Sanders' screen persona as the eternal cynic. It read: "Dear World. I am leaving because I am bored. I feel I have lived long enough. I am leaving you with your worries in this sweet cesspool. Good luck." The other, in Spanish, asked that his sister, Margaret, be notified of his death in London. It was later revealed that on the night prior to his suicide, Sanders had written and posted a note to Margaret that read: "Dear Margoolinka. Don't be sad. I have only anticipated the inevitable by a few years."

FURTHER READING

Aherne, Brian. *A Dreadful Man*. New York: Simon and Schuster, 1979.
Sanders, George. *Memoirs of a Professional Cad*. New York: G. P. Putnam's Sons, 1960.
Vanderbeets, Richard. *George Sanders: An Exhausted Life*. Lanham, Md.: Madison Books, 1990.

Sanders, Scott

According to his friends, the 26-year-old drummer of the heavy metal band Castleblak went "psychotic" after Jennifer Lee Lilly, 23, ended their two-year relationship. Around 2:00 A.M. on April 4, 1991, Sanders tracked down a car Lilly and a group of her friends were driving in near Webster and Hayes streets in San Francisco. Shouting that he was "going to end this for once and all," the obsessed drummer forced Lilly into his car and sped away. Shortly afterward, a terrified Lilly phoned her roommate from an unknown location to report that Sanders had a gun. When asked where she was, the phone went dead. Authorities found Lilly's bullet-riddled body at 3:20 A.M. near a Bay Area Rapid Transit station in Lafayette, California. Three hours later, a motorist on State Road 29 near the Napa River watched as Sanders fired a round from a .38-caliber revolver point-blank into his chest and the car plunged down a 100–foot embankment.

Sanders, Steve

Sanders (born September 17, 1952, in Richland, Georgia) began his singing career as a child in gospel music where he was billed as "Little Stevie Sanders." He started acting at 12 when cast in the role of "Jody Baxter" in the Broadway musical *The Yearling*. After the show closed, Sanders appeared in Otto Preminger's 1967 movie *Hurry Sundown*, and was seen on the television series *Gunsmoke*. In 1981, Sanders caught his big break when he was hired to play rhythm guitar in the band backing the perennially popular country act The Oak Ridge Boys. In 1987, Sanders replaced the bearded, mountain man-garbed baritone, William Lee Golden, and sang lead vocals on several of the group's top singles ("Gonna Take a Lot of River," "No Matter How High," and "Lucky Moon").

Citing personal problems that were affecting the band, Sanders left the group in November 1995 and was replaced by William Lee Golden. The "personal problems" were a four-year court battle with first wife, Mary Milbourne Sanders, over child support. Through the years, Sanders and new wife, Janet, engaged in unending legal hassles with his ex involving charges and counter-charges

of malicious prosecution, slander, libel, assault, and criminal trespass. At about 1:00 A.M. on June 10, 1998, Sanders, 45, shot himself in the head in the bathroom of his home in a middle-class neighborhood of Cape Coral, Florida.

Saper, Marshall

Saper, a well-respected psychologist who collaborated with the police department and taught university classes, first established himself in 1980 as a popular radio talk show personality in Kansas City, Missouri. Over the next 11 years, "the old country psychologist" dispensed sound advice daily over KCMO-AM during a live three hour call-in show. The show, a consistent ratings winner, enjoyed a weekly audience of some 80,000 listeners from Chicago to Denver and from Minnesota to Oklahoma. When not on radio, Saper maintained a private practice, wrote books, and contributed an advice column for *The Squire*, a suburban weekly paper. In 1989, a former patient filed a civil suit against the psychologist alleging that he had coerced her into having a three year sexual relationship with him beginning in 1984. Saper, married with a 5-year-old child, vehemently denied the charge and prepared to meet the woman and her husband in court on November 4, 1991.

The day before the trial was scheduled to begin, the 52-year-old psychologist arose shortly after 6:00 A.M. in the suburban home in Overland Park, Kansas, he shared with his family, typed a note explaining his forthcoming actions, and armed himself with a .38-caliber pistol and some bullets. Saper drove his red Mazda convertible to the deserted parking lot of the Humana Hospital and Medical Center, and (according to official police reports) loaded the weapon. He got out of the car, stood next to it, and fired a shot into his chest. The bullet passed through a lung and exited through his back. About a minute later, Saper fired a second, fatal shot that severed his aorta. Saper once wrote that in rare cases suicide could be "a rational decision ... because of pressing, insurmountable realistic problems." The note he left expressed concern about the effect a lurid public trial would have had on his family and professional reputation. In April 1992, Saper's estate reached an out of court settlement with the woman and her husband.

Saunders, John Monk

Saunders (born November 22, 1897, in Hinckley, Minnesota) interrupted a brilliant undergraduate career at the University of Washington to serve in the U.S. Flying Corps during World War I. From 1914 to 1918, he saw action in Europe and the States as a flight instructor. After the war, Saunders finished his studies and was awarded a Rhodes Scholarship. In 1923, he earned a master's degree from Oxford. Saunders began his professional career as a reporter for *The Los Angeles Times*, and *New York Tribune*, and regularly contributed short stories to *Cosmopolitan* and *Liberty* magazine. In 1925, Famous Players–Lasky/Paramount bought the rights to two of his short stories and made *Too Many Kisses* (based on the *Cosmopolitan* story "The Maker of Gestures"), and *The Shock Punch*, both starring Richard Dix. Saunders utilized his experiences as a World War I aviator as grist for his stories, and later, screenplays. In 1927, Paramount Famous Lasky filmed Saunders' unfinished novel, *Wings*, the dramatic story of two American pilots serving in France during the Great War. Saunders wrote the screenplay for the film, which won the Academy Award for the Best Picture of 1927–1928, although it did not enjoy a wide release until 1929 when music and sound effects were added. Building on the success of *Wings*, Saunders wrote a sequel, *The Legion of the Condemned*, filmed in 1928.

During its shooting, the screenwriter met second wife Fay Wray, destined for fame as the "girl in the hairy paw" in the 1933 RKO classic *King Kong*. They married on June 15, 1928. A popular screenwriter for the next decade, films written or suggested by Saun-

ders' stories include *The Docks of New York* (1928), *The Dawn Patrol* (1930; for which he was awarded the Oscar for Best Original Story in 1931), *The Finger Points* (1931), *The Last Flight* (1931), *Ace of Aces* (1933), *West Point of the Air* (1935), *Devil Dogs of the Air* (1935), and *A Yank at Oxford* (1938).

By the summer of 1938, Wray could no longer endure Saunders' womanizing, drinking, and drug-taking. The pair divorced in early 1939. By all accounts, the divorce profoundly affected Saunders. In the fall of 1939 he was admitted to the Johns Hopkins Hospital in Baltimore for a nervous disorder. Upon his release, Saunders moved into a beach cottage on Estero Island, 15 miles from Fort Myers, Florida. Living as a recluse, except for the company of a private nurse, the Academy Award winner seldom left the cottage and was no longer writing. On March 11, 1940, three days after his nurse had left his employ, the fully-clothed body of the 42-year-old screenwriter was found by his housekeeper hanging in a closet. Saunders had fashioned the cord of a dressing gown into a noose, looped it around his neck, and tied the loose end to a hook. Death resulted from a broken neck. There was no note.

FURTHER READING

Slide, Anthony. "John Monk Saunders." In *American Screenwriters*, edited by Robert E. Morsberger. *Dictionary of Literary Biography*, v.26. Detroit: Gale, 1984. pp. 275–279.
Wray, Fay. *On the Other Hand: A Life Story.* New York: St. Martin's Press, 1989.

Savannah

Of the numerous porn stars who have committed suicide (see entries Shauna Grant, Fred Halsted, Alex Jordan, Megan Leigh, and Kyle McKenna), Savannah was the biggest name and the most well-known outside the narrow confines of the adult film industry. Savannah was born Shannon Michelle Wilsey on October 9, 1970, in Hawthorne, California, to Pamela, a 17-year-old unwed runaway, and Michael Wilsey, an 18-year-old postal clerk.

The couple married when Shannon was 18 months old, but divorced two months later. Relocating to a suburb of Houston, Texas, when Shannon was 2, Pamela was working at a grocery store when she met and married fellow clerk Joe Longoria, a father of four children by a previous marriage. Shannon took Longoria's name, but was not told that he was not her birth father. The family moved to Helton City, Texas, in 1976 where Shannon Longoria established herself as a popular, outgoing student who told classmates that her dream was to go to Hollywood and be a movie star. Shannon was 13 when middle school officials bluntly informed her that since she had never been formally adopted by Longoria it would be illegal to let her register for classes under that name. Shaken, the teenager was finally told by her mother that she was, in fact, a Wilsey. The revelation shattered the young girl.

Over night, Shannon changed from a happy child into a rebellious teen more interested in smoking dope, binge drinking, and cutting classes than attending school. Unable to cope, Shannon's mother shipped her off to live with an uncle in southern California. When he too failed to control her, Shannon spent the next three years shuffled between various family members. In 1986, the 16 year old moved in briefly with Michael Wilsey, her birth father, in Ventura, California. The arrangement quickly failed, and she returned to her uncle in southern California. At this time, Shannon reportedly told a relative that she had been raped by a family member, a charge her mother repeatedly denied.

By age 16, Shannon had developed into a beautiful young woman with a perfect body she knew could make her the center of attention. In 1986, Shannon went to a Gregg Allman concert at San Juan Capistrano. The 40-year-old, three time divorced musician then noted for his heavy drug use was immediately impressed by the curvaceous and scantily-clad teenager. The couple became instant lovers. Shannon had "Gregg" tattooed on her left ankle, and from 1986 to 1988 travelled and

did cocaine and heroin with the aging rock star. The 18 year old was crushed when Allman terminated the relationship in 1988.

In October 1989, Shannon was living with her father in Ventura and competing in bikini contests when she was approached by Mickey Ray, a photographer, to pose topless for some cheesecake photos he could peddle to men's magazines. She agreed and briefly lived with Ray until she began stealing his prescription medication. In 1989, the 19-year-old "model" began actively trying to meet and seduce rock stars. Provocatively attired, Shannon danced in front of the stage until she was noticed, then asked backstage to meet the band. That same year the "super groupie" met Billy Sheehan, bassist for the band Mr. Big, at a club in Ventura after she tossed her underwear on stage. They moved in together almost immediately. Shannon's topless photos led to small parts in two 1989 soft core films. In *Legal Tender* starring Morton Downey, Jr., she did a topless walk-on, and while billed as "Shannon Wilsey" in the slasher film *The Invisible Maniac*, she spoke her first lines on film. Unimpressive in both films, Shannon was not offerred additional work.

In 1990, Billy Sheehan was on tour with Mr. Big when his live-in girlfriend decided to pose, without his or her family's knowledge, for hard core sex magazines. That June, she was convicted for driving his Corvette while drunk. Weeks later, she succeeded in totalling the car. Shortly afterward, the couple split up after Sheehan saw a magazine at a newsstand featuring Shannon on the cover performing fellatio. The move from print to film hard core was a natural progression for the 19 year old. In 1990 she performed a lesbian sex scene with Raquel Darrian in the film *Raquel's Addiction*. That same year, billed as "Silver Kane," drug slang for a heroin syringe, she did another lesbian sex film, *No Boys Allowed*. In the fall of 1990, she signed a one year contract with Video Exclusives, a low-end company specializing in adult films with plotless sex scenes. Under the terms of the contract, the porn actress would do 25 sex scenes at $250 a scene with an additional $250 paid every time she was featured on a box cover. After signing the deal, Shannon rented a Hollywood apartment, had her breasts enlarged, and renamed herself "Savannah" after the title character in her favorite film, *Savannah Smiles*, a 1982 morality tale in which a rich little girl runs away from home and reforms criminals.

While making movies like *Trouble Maker*, *Nasty Reputation*, and *Sweet Cheeks* for Video Exclusives, Savannah was doing a gram of cocaine a day combined with the painkiller Percoset. Upon completion of her contract in the fall of 1991, Savannah signed a one year deal with Vivid Video, the most prestigious hard core producer in the industry. The girl with the angelic face framed in platinum hair with bangs, porcelain skin, and perfect body was paid $4,000 plus royalties for each of eight films. Under the company's tutelage, Savannah achieved the rank of a porn supermodel in such films as *On Trial 1: In Defense of Savannah* and *Indian Summer*. Though an unenthusiastic sexual performer (her orgasmic moans and groans had to be dubbed in), Savannah's presence in a video guaranteed huge sales. By mid–1991, Savannah was using her superstar status to meet and bed rock stars like Billy Idol and Mötley Crüe frontman Vince Neill. After Neill unceremoniously dumped her following a Hawaiian vacation in August 1991, Savannah entered into perhaps the only stable relationship in her life with comedian Pauly Shore. Shore, however, broke with her in 1992 when she refused to leave the porn world.

Savannah was already the biggest name in porn in January 1992 when she was honored as "Best New Starlet" for her work in *On Trial* at the 9th Annual *Adult Video News* Awards in Las Vegas. To celebrate, the starlet bought herself a white Corvette and began dating Slash, guitarist for the rock supergroup Guns n' Roses. The affair was short-lived. On April 3, 1992, a drunken Savannah fellated Slash in the middle of the Scrap Bar in New York City before collapsing senseless on a flight of stairs. Embarrassed by media attention to the inci-

dent, Slash married his former girlfriend within the week.

Heroin, added to the actress' laundry list of drugs, made her even more demanding, unpredictable, and impossible to deal with on the set. Savannah used the fact that her videos outsold all others five to six times over to haughtily demand script and cast approval. On the first day of filming *Sinderella* in 1992 she was five hours late to the set. When the star finally arrived, she pointed to a group of waiting actresses and loudly proclaimed, "I don't want ugly bitches like this in a scene with me!" Paul Thomas, who directed Savannah in the film and several others for Vivid, expressed the industry consensus toward the performer when he said: "She was a real bitch. A selfish, selfish bitch. She revelled in putting people down. She didn't like giving of herself in any way, shape or form. She was irresponsible and flaky and selfish and stupid."

By 1993, Savannah's body was showing the wear of a $200 a day heroin habit. Despite her popularity, Vivid fired her in 1993 when her erratic and insulting behavior became a liability. The dismissal signalled the beginning of the end for Savannah. In March 1993, a judge in Ventura issued an arrest warrant for her for failure to report to her probation officer on her 1990 drunk driving conviction. The IRS was also demanding back taxes. In a desperate bid to salvage her porn career, Savannah had her breasts enlarged to 34DD. The 22-year-old actress returned to her hard core roots in 1993 when she agreed to star in *Starbangers #1* for former employer Video Exclusives. Though Savannah was reportedly paid $9,000 for having sex with eight men at once, the film failed to revive her career.

A has-been in adult films by the end of 1993, Savannah turned to nude dancing in clubs to pay the bills and feed her drug habit. Much of the $5,000 a week she earned stripping was spent on so-called "dancing medicine." The cocaine, however, caused her to have wild mood swings. In May 1994 she turned down a lucrative dance gig in Canada because she could not get her drugs past customs. In June 1994 she was fired by a Florida nightclub for starting a brawl. Weeks later she was axed by a Las Vegas club for missing a scheduled performance. Savannah's latest boyfriend, Danny Boy of the white rap group House of Pain, was out of town on a European tour during the month of July 1994. On July 10, 1994, Savannah spent the evening drinking, drugging, and making the rounds of clubs with Jason Swing, a 22-year-old gofer for the band. Around 12:30 A.M. the next morning the pair was driving to Savannah's home on Valley Heart Drive near Coldwater Canyon when the 23-year-old porn star lost control of her Corvette and plowed into a fence and tree a few hundred yards from her house at 3502 Multiview Drive. Swing sustained a minor injury to his knee while Savannah suffered a cut and bump on her nose. They managed to drive the wrecked car home and park it in the garage.

As Swing walked back to the scene of the accident to assess the damage, Savannah hurried into the house to examine her bloody face. Although the damage to her nose would prove to be minor, she phoned her manager Nancy Pera in hysterics. "My face. It's ruined. How am I going to do my show?" she screamed in reference to an upcoming photo shoot and dancing engagement in Goldfinger's in Nyack, New York. Pera pleaded with Savannah to remain calm. She was on her way. Swing returned to the house to find a tearful Savannah lying on the concrete floor of the garage inspecting the front of the car. He tried to calm her and was leaving to get help when she suddenly produced a blue steel .40-caliber semiautomatic Beretta she had purchased in April 1994 for protection against a reported stalker. Swing turned back to Savannah just in time to hear her utter the words, "I'm so sorry," and see her shoot herself in the side of the head. The porn star was still alive when Nancy Pera arrived at the scene moments later at 2:15 A.M. In response to Pera's 911 call an ambulance transported the dying woman to St. Joseph's Medical Center in Burbank. Savannah languished on life support for nine hours before her father, Mike Wilsey, gave doctors permission to disconnect at 11:20 A.M.

Screw, the sex tabloid published by Al Goldstein, ran the headline "Ding Dong the Bitch is Dead" and reported that "Everyone knew that she was an airhead, and now she's got the hole in her dome to prove it." Savannah, a.k.a. Shannon Michelle Wilsey, was cremated and her ashes given to her father, who reportedly keeps them in a ceramic jar surrounded by her pictures in his home.

FURTHER READING

Wilkinson, Peter. "Dream Girl." *Rolling Stone*, 693:72–77, 79–80, 158, Oct. 20, 1994.
Sager, Mike. "Little Girl Lost." *GQ*, 64:218–221, November 1994.

Scala, Gia

Louis B. Mayer, head of MGM, once described glamour girl Gia Scala as a woman who "looks a little like Ingrid Bergman, a little like Grace Kelly, like Nancy Olson around the eyes and like four or five of those sexy Italian actresses below the neck." Born Giovanna Scoglio in Liverpool, England, on March 3, 1934, to an Italian nobleman father, Baron Pietro Scoglio, and an Irish mother, the future film star was 3 months old when her family moved to the seaport city of Messina, Sicily. Spending most of her early life in Rome, she left the "Eternal City" at 17 to study and pursue her dream of acting in America. In 1952, her mother arrived from Europe and they took an apartment together in New York City. Changing her name from Giovanna Scoglio to the more glamorous "Gia Scala," the aspiring actress studied drama with Stella Adler at the Actors Studio by night while spending her days behind a reservation counter at Scandinavian Airlines.

Scala was a contestant on a television game show when she was spotted by a New York talent scout of Universal-International, who brought her to the attention of the parent studio in Hollywood. The beautiful green-eyed brunette with the slinky figure was placed under contract in late 1954 and debuted the

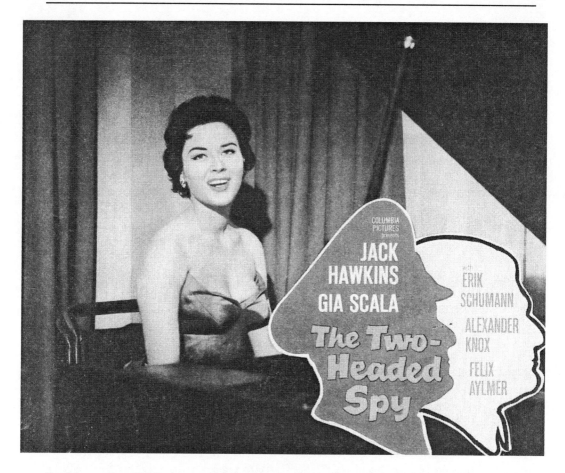

GIA SCALA— By 1957 Scala was enjoying comparable success with other foreign-born glamour girls like Sophia Loren and Anita Ekberg, but the death of her mother in 1958 sent her into an emotional tailspin. Deeply depressed, she attempted suicide in 1959 while filming *The Two-Headed Spy* in London. A has-been by the age of 38, Scala's alcoholism and depression led to her suspected suicide in Hollywood on April 20, 1972.

next year in a small role as a fisherman's daughter in the Rock Hudson film *All That Heaven Allows*. Scala received fourth billing in her follow-up film, *Price of Fear* (1956), and good reviews in *Four Girls in Town* (1956). Columbia and MGM, impressed by the sexy newcomer, bought up most of the rising star's contract from Universal-International and gave her the publicity build-up in films like *The Garment Jungle* (1957, Columbia), *Tip on a Dead Jockey* (1957, MGM), and *Don't Go Near the Water* (1957, MGM) opposite Glenn Ford.

By mid–1957, Scala was in the ranks with fellow foreign imports Sophia Loren and Anita Ekberg when her career was abruptly derailed by news that her beloved mother was suffering from inoperable lung cancer. Hours after meeting with a doctor at the Los Feliz Brown Derby to discuss her mother's terminal condition, the star was involved in a minor traffic accident and charged with drunken driving. The charge was dismissed, but the incident marked the beginning of a long series of public embarrassments and scandals that undermined Scala's career while offering glimpses into her steadily deteriorating mental state. Scala's mother died in 1958 following a Hawaiian vacation with her daughter. Devastated, the actress attempted to rebound emotionally and professionally. After becoming an American citizen in 1958, Scala travelled to England in 1959 to shoot *The Two-Headed Spy* for Columbia. The actress had turned down several choice roles during her mother's illness and this film was to be an important step in restarting her career. No one on the set, however, realized the extent of Scala's depression. While filming a scene on Waterloo Bridge, the actress jumped from the structure and tried to drown herself in the Thames River. Scala later dismissed the attempt as a publicity stunt.

Romantically linked over the years to actors Russ Tamblyn, John Saxon, and Earl Holliman, Scala married Don Burnett, an actor whom she had met in 1957 while filming *Don't Go Near the Water*, on August 21, 1959. In 1961, Scala earned strong reviews for her role as a Greek resistance fighter in the World War II box office smash *The Guns of Navarone*. Sadly, the biggest film of Scala's career proved to be her last significant work. In September 1970 Burnett ended the marriage on grounds of "incompatability." The next year he was forced to obtain a court order preventing his troubled ex-wife from "molesting, striking and harassing" him.

On April 22, 1971, a drunken Scala and her 22-year-old companion, Allen S. Bershin, were involved in a fist fight with a downtown Los Angeles parking lot attendant prompted by her refusal to pay a 50 cent overtime charge. Scala and Bershin pleaded "no contest" to charges of disturbing the peace and were placed on two years' probation. Amid an avalanche of unflattering press, Scala was ordered to undergo psychiatric observation on May 19, 1971, after collapsing in a Ventura County courtroom where she had been charged with drunken driving. Months before, the depressed actress had swallowed roach poison and last rites were administered by a priest after she learned that Burnett had married actress Barbara Anderson, police woman "Eve Whitfield" on the NBC series *Ironside*. She recovered, but her beauty was dissipated by years of heavy drinking. Scala

was injured in July 1971 when her sports car overturned on a winding road in the Hollywood Hills.

On April 20, 1972, the body of the 38-year-old actress was discovered in a second floor bedroom of her Hollywood Hills home at 7944 Woodrow Wilson Drive. One of three male friends staying with Scala found her body in a bedroom littered with several bottles of various medications and empty liquor bottles. While police listed her death as a "possible accidental liquor and drug overdose," those familiar with the actress' depressed and unstable mental state believed she had consciously taken her life. An autopsy revealed that she was suffering from severe coronary arteriosclerosis at the time of her alcohol and drug overdose, which may have contributed to her death. The actress is buried next to and shares a grave marker with her mother at the Holy Cross Cemetery in Culver City, California.

FURTHER READING

Crivello, Kirk. *Fallen Angels: The Lives and Untimely Deaths of Fourteen Hollywood Beauties*. Secaucus, N.J.: Citadel Press, 1988.

Scarboro, David

An original cast member on the popular British television soap opera *EastEnders*, the 20-year-old actor who portrayed the rebellious "Mark Fowler" in the BBC hit left the show for good on Christmas Day 1988 amid rumors of drink, drugs, and depression caused by his flagging popularity and turbulent love life. On April 27, 1988, Scarboro left his prized record collection with his recently estranged girlfriend. Hours later his body was found at the bottom of cliffs at Beachy Head, East Sussex. Well-known throughout Britain as a "popular" suicide spot, the area's reputation dated back to the 6th Century when St. Wilfred, arriving in East Sussex to convert the Anglo-Saxons to Christianity, found the locals sending volunteers drawn from the sick and elderly to plunge over the cliffs to placate the gods. According to Scarboro's manager, the young actor suffered from depression and had made an earlier attempt on his life. The East Sussex coroner recorded an open verdict on the death.

Schloss, Berrick

Born in New York City on January 3, 1883, Schloss' operatic career as "Berrick Van Norden" was in full bloom as a concert artist and soloist until he fell ill in 1911 while preparing to leave for Milan, Italy, to sing at the opera. Though forced to enter the family's millinery business in Providence, Rhode Island, Schloss continued his musical interests, founding and conducting that city's University Glee Club, while also serving on the faculties of the Providence College of Music and the Katharine Gibbs School. In addition, the tireless tenor was the soloist and musical director at the First Unitarian Church. In poor health for the past ten months, the 55-year-old Schloss took his life on August 28, 1938. A neighbor, detecting the odor of exhaust fumes coming from the closed garage behind Schloss' home at 120 Governor Street, entered to find the tenor slumped in the front seat of his running car.

Schoenstadt, Ralph

Leaving a note stating that he was tired of wine, women, and song, the manager of Chicago's People's Theater shot himself in the Picadilly Hotel at 5107 Blackstone Avenue on August 30, 1937. Schoenstadt, a 32-year-old bachelor, was the nephew of the man who introduced the nickelodeon to the Windy City and a cousin to the owners of a chain of motion picture houses.

Schuetze, Carl

A former member of the orchestras of the New York Philharmonic and Metropolitan Opera, the 52-year-old musician was brought to Hollywood by a concerned stepson who had received several letters from Schuetze in which he mentioned planning to end his life. Days after his arrival, Schuetze had to be bodily restrained from slashing his wrists by family members. Under a pretext, Schuetze's relatives brought him to the Hall of Records in Los Angeles on the afternoon of November 15, 1932. Taken to the ninth floor office of the County Lunacy Commission, Schuetze realized while speaking to the Commission's secretary that he was about to be declared insane. Whirling away from the attendants, Schuetze threw himself out of the open window and plunged to his death amid a crowd of horrified county workers leaving their offices for the day.

Schwartz, Adele

Despondent over the demise of her theatrical career and the loss of a $25,000 retirement fund in a bank crash, the 44-year-old actress who had often played light comedy roles on the Yiddish stage committed suicide on September 10, 1934, by inhaling gas in a ground floor room at 2926 West Thirty Second Street, Coney Island. In a note to her actor-husband, Schwartz explained that she did not want to become a burden to him.

Scoggin, Travis (Chic) Martin

Credited with giving actress Betty Hutton one of her first singing jobs before she hit it big with Vincent Lopez, Scoggin was a widely known band leader during the pre–World War II era. After disbanding his group, he headed the Chic Scoggin Theatrical Agency in Dallas, Texas, which specialized in booking popular bands and top singers throughout the Southwest. He had been in failing health for the past year when he shot himself in his hotel room in East Dallas on June 26, 1956. In three notes found at the scene (one addressed to band leader Hugh Fowler and another to a former police inspector), the 51-year-old veteran showman asked that his kin be notified and his remains taken to the Sparkman-Brand Funeral Home.

Scott, George (I)

The manager of London's Alhambra Theatre for five years prior to losing his job in mid–1908, Scott had been unemployed for eight months when he told a former music hall colleague that he was depressed over not finding work. On the morning of January 29, 1909, Scott stretched out on the bed in his room at the Tavistock Hotel, Covent Garden, and shot himself in the head with a rifle. Charles Dundas Slater (see entry), another former manager of the Alhambra Theatre, shot himself in a London taxi cab on July 8, 1912.

Scott, George (II)

The noted explorer and camera expert induced carbon monoxide poisoning in his Hollywood studio at 1658 North Vine Street on January 11, 1929. His body was found near open gas jets on a heater. At the time, it was widely believed that the 55-year-old cameraman's death meant the end of the Handscheikel process for coloring motion pictures. Scott was the brother-in-law of the late inventor and after the man's death the only person known to possess the secrets of the process.

Scott, Robert Crozier

Described by *Variety* as a "well-known author and scenario writer," Scott, 45, was served with divorce papers by his wife's attorney in Los Angeles on July 3, 1923. The next day the writer was found in bed with his throat cut at his home at 628 South Grand Avenue.

Scott, Russell

The one-time Chicago vaudeville actor murdered a 19-year-old pharmacy clerk in that city on April 2, 1924, and was sentenced to death with his accomplice-brother. As the debate over the killer's sanity raged in the courts for the next three years, Scott received three 11th hour stays of execution. To defray legal

costs, his wife wrote and circulated a pamphlet about his life and even formed a short-lived vaudeville act to sway public opinion. On October 8, 1927, Scott did what the state of Illinois had been unable to accomplish. During a routine cell block check, a guard in the Cook County Jail found Scott's lifeless body hanging by his belt from the top bars of his cell.

Seberg, Jean (Dorothy)

By the age of 12, Seberg (born November 13, 1938, in Marshalltown, Iowa) was reading Konstantin Stanislavsky's *An Actor Prepares* and writing letters to Marlon Brando inviting him to vacation with her family. Seberg was a 17-year-old freshman at the University of Iowa when her high school drama coach submitted her name (without her knowledge) to a nationwide talent search conducted by director Otto Preminger to cast an unknown in *Saint Joan*, his film adaptation of George Bernard Shaw's 1924 play *Saint Joan: A Chronicle Play in Six Scenes and an Epilogue*. She gained instant celebrity and industry scrutiny after she was selected from more than 18,000 contestants to play the title role in the 1957 United Artists film. Unfortunately, popular and critical reaction to her peformance was strongly negative. In a later interview, the actress admitted that "for a year or so, I couldn't walk in a room in which I knew more than three people were gathered."

In 1958, Preminger cast her in *Bonjour Tristesse*. Seberg's lukewarm reviews in the film seemingly spelled an end to her career in the States. However, after shooting the 1959 film *The Mouse That Roared* in England, Seberg made a decision that saved her acting career. While visiting France, she met first-time director Jean-Luc Godard who cast her opposite Jean-Paul Belmondo in his 1960 film *A Bout de Souffle* (*Breathless*). The film was an international hit with Seberg's performance as an American beatnik in Paris garnering strong critical acclaim. After making several forgettable films in France, she returned to America in 1964 to play a mental patient opposite Warren Beatty in director Robert Rossen's last film, *Lilith.* Never a large box office draw, the actress split her time between U.S. and French films. Seberg's American films include *Moment to Moment* (1966), *A Fine Madness* (1966), *Pendulum* (1969), *Paint Your Wagon* (1969), *Airport* (1970), and her final U.S. film, *Macho Callahan* (1970).

In the early sixties, Seberg's vocal and financial support of counterculture political groups like the Black Panthers prompted the FBI to wage a smear campaign against her. In 1970, the actress was in the process of divorcing the second of her three husbands, novelist and fellow suicide Romain Gary (see entry), when the FBI under the direction of Bureau chief J. Edgar Hoover fed *Los Angeles Times* entertainment columnist Joyce Haber information that Seberg was pregnant with the child of a Black Panther leader. Though the blind item referred to the actress in question as "Miss A," everyone in Hollywood knew it referred to Seberg. According to Gary, the six-months pregnant Seberg was so upset by the fabricated story that she attempted to kill herself in Majorca with sleeping pills. The baby, Gina Hart Gary, was delivered 63 days prematurely by Caesarean section in Geneva, Switzerland, on August 26, 1970. The infant died two days later. Seberg never emotionally recovered from the death of her child. Romain Gary later told reporters that "every year on the anniversary of this stillbirth, she tried to take her own life." In order to prove that the child was white, an open-casket funeral was conducted in Seberg's hometown of Marshalltown, Iowa.

Though under the care of a psychiatrist for severe depression and drinking heavily, Seberg continued to work in French films after 1970. On the evening of August 29, 1979, the 40-year-old actress and her 20-year-old Algerian lover, Ahmed Hasni, attended a showing of Romain Gary's *Clair de Femme* in Paris. The film, an account of a middle-aged man whose first wife is dying of cancer, depressed Seberg. Back at the second

floor studio apartment she shared with Hasni on the Avenue de Longchamp, Seberg left their bed sometime in the early morning of August 30. Hasni awoke later that morning, discovered her missing, and hurriedly notified police. Seberg, often institutionalized for depression, had two months earlier tried to kill herself by jumping in front of a subway train in Paris. Authorities conducted a systematic search of hospitals and clinics before focusing their investigation on the actress' missing white Renault.

On September 8, 1979, ten days after her disappearance, a night guard discovered Seberg's car parked in an upscale area on the right bank of the Seine near the couple's apartment. Seberg's badly decomposed nude body was found covered with a blanket curled up on the floor in the back seat of the car. An empty bottle of mineral water and prescription barbiturates were close at hand. A note left for her 16-year-old son read: "I can't live any longer with my nerves." An autopsy determined that she may have died on the day of her disappearance. Seberg was buried at the Cimitiere de Montparnasse in Paris.

Two days after the discovery of Seberg's body, Romain Gary held a news conference in Paris in which he forcefully alleged that the FBI had conspired to destroy the actress in retaliation for her support of the Black Panther Party. Responding to requests made under the Freedom of Information Act, the FBI admitted on September 15, 1979, that it was responsible for spreading the false rumor concerning the source of Seberg's pregnancy in a punitive attempt to discredit her in the eyes of the American people. Seberg's tragic life has since become the subject of a 1983 musical (*Jean Seberg*), a 1995 novel (Carlos Fuentes' *Diana: The Goddess Who Hunts Alone*), and a 1995 Mark Rappaport film (*From the Journals of Jean Seberg*).

FURTHER READING

Richards, David. *Played Out: The Jean Seberg Story.* 1st ed. New York: Random House, 1981.

Selby, Norman see McCoy, Charles "Kid"

Selkirk, Andres

A one-time cellist with various radio orchestras, Selkirk began a business arranging packaged radio programs until severe financial reverses left the 37 year old on the verge of bankruptcy. Forced to send his wife to live with her mother, Selkirk was scheduled to vacate their Chicago apartment at 180 East Delaware on September 7, 1934. That morning, he handed the bellboy two notes, one addressed to the manager of the building instructing him to break down the door of the apartment and to notify his wife, and the other to his wife explaining the deed. Selkirk then fired a bullet into his brain.

To his wife, he wrote: "Terese Dear: These are the last and honest words of a soul in turmoil. For what has happened to us I am entirely to blame. Living, I am of no use to anybody, not even myself. I want you to put all of this tangle out of your mind and begin anew. Good luck, and I wish you a new and better deal." In a message found at the scene dated August 7, Selkirk left a whimsical verse epitaph addressed to a female friend of the family: "Dear Honey: Since we got into this argument, let's have a lot of fun, shall we? What do you think of this paraphrase as an epitaph: 'Here lies the last work of Andy Selkirk; For him life held no terrors; He lived like a fool and died like a fool; No runs, no hits, some error. But no one left on bases.' To get the full significance of the above you should listen to two full baseball broadcasts from beginning to end. Yours in martyrdom, hi-de-hi, Andy."

Selznick, Mary Jennifer

The emotionally disturbed daughter of actress Jennifer Jones and film producer David O. Selznick (1902–1965) took acting lessons with Uta Hagen, but never appeared in any noteworthy production. Born on August 12, 1954, Selznick underwent extensive psycho-analysis, had an abortion, attempted suicide, and was placed for a time in a psychiatric ward. On May 11, 1976, the 21-year-old woman jumped to her death from the top floor of the Crown Towers at 10701 Wilshire Boulevard in Westwood.

FURTHER READING

Thomson, David. *Showman: The Life of David O. Selznick.* 1st ed. New York: Knopf, 1992.

Semenoff, Nikolai

Convinced that the influence of modern dance on traditional ballet was responsible for his financial ruin, the Russian-born Semenoff, 50, former master of the Imperial Theater of Moscow and a dance instructor in Cleveland, Ohio, hurled himself into the Niagra Falls in Buffalo, New York, on July 6, 1932. In a ten page letter written in Russian to his friend and former master Michel Fokine, ballet master of Buffalo, Semenoff protested the invasion of the field of classical dancing by modernistic expression.

Serkin, Robert

Brother of famed concert pianist Rudolf Serkin (1903–1991), the 48-year-old Jewish musician and Austrian refugee was recuperating from a nervous breakdown at the Firmin Desloge Hospital in St. Louis, Missouri, when he was found on September 3, 1943, hanging by the neck from a belt fastened to the top of a bathroom door.

Shannon, Del

Shannon (born Charles Weedon Westover in Coopersville, Michigan, on December 30, 1934) began playing guitar and singing while still in high school. During his pre–Shannon years, Westover patterned his playing off the country guitarists he saw in local bars while picking up his trademark falsetto singing style from the black vocal group the Ink Spots. Drafted immediately after graduation, Westover won a 7th Army amateur night talent show that earned him an appearance on the *Get Up and Go* radio show in Germany. Discharged in 1959, Westover worked as a carpet salesman in Battle Creek, Michigan, by day, while by night played guitar and sang as "Del Shannon" in the Charlie Johnson & The Big Little Show Band at the Hi-Lo Club in Grand Rapids. "Del" was a contraction of the "Coupe De Ville" car driven by his boss at the carpet store with "Shannon" chosen because he liked the name.

In 1960, Shannon signed with Detroit-based Embree Productions, which landed him a recording contract with Big Top Records in New York City. After an initial lackluster recording session, Shannon returned to the studio in early 1961 to record "Runaway," a tune co-written with The Big Little Show Band keyboardist Max Crook. The song, featuring Shannon's classic vocal and Creek's haunting musitron (electric organ) solo, reached Number 1 on the *Billboard* chart on March 6, 1961. "Runaway" remained on the chart for 17 weeks, reached Number 1 in 20 other countries, and to date has been covered more than 200 times by recording artists as diverse as Elvis Presley, Lawrence Welk, and Bonnie Raitt. The song was also prominently featured in the 1989 Tom Cruise film *Born on the Fourth of July* directed by Oliver Stone. Television producer Michael Mann commissioned Shannon to refashion some of the song's lyrics and used it as the theme of his NBC series *Crime Story* (1986–1988).

Shannon, who wrote most of his own material, followed up his smash debut single with several other solid chart hits. "Hats Off to Larry" (1961) reached Number 5 while "Little Town Flirt" (1962) peaked at Number 12. In early 1963, Shannon began his second tour of the United Kingdom, a country where he continued to retain his star status long after his popularity had waned in the States. While headlining a show at London's Royal Albert Hall he met The Beatles, who were a minor band on the program. As The Beatles had yet to invade America, Shannon convinced John

Lennon to let him record the Lennon-McCartney tune "From Me To You" as a way of generating more exposure for the band in the States. Shannon's version of The Beatles' tune debuted on the *Billboard* chart on June 29, 1963. Though the song peaked at Number 77 and lasted only four weeks on the survey, it represented the first time The Beatles charted in America. Ironically, after The Beatles' visit to New York City in February 1964 opened the floodgates of the British Invasion, fifties-style rockers like Shannon and Roy Orbison never again dominated the charts.

While enjoying a few more hits in the sixties with "Handy Man" (1964), "Keep Searchin' (We'll Follow the Sun)" (1964), and "Stranger in Town" (1965), Shannon would not crack the Top Fifty chart again until his Tom Petty-produced single "Sea of Love" peaked at Number 33 in 1981. Shannon spent the seventies as a fixture on the oldies circuit, often performing up to 100 shows a year. By the mid-seventies, the depressed singer was a full-blown alcoholic and spent his days alone drinking whiskey in the darkened recesses of the "mole hole," the name he gave to the windowless music studio in his garage. In 1979 Shannon joined Alcoholics Anonymous, quit drinking, and adopting the name "Charlie W" (Charles Westover), served as a dedicated and well-respected sponsor to other alcoholics in the program.

The eighties saw Shannon attempt a series of comebacks aided by a new generation of rockers who acknowledged their musical debt to him. Tom Petty of the Heartbreakers fame produced Shannon's 1981 album *Drop Down and Get Me*, but while yielding the modestly successful single "Sea of Love," the critically acclaimed record did not sell. In 1985 Shannon signed with Warner Bros. to record an album of country music in Nashville, but soon left the label after refusing to record more commercial music. Though financially secure through real estate investments, Shannon longed to escape from the cycle of rock 'n' roll revival shows he continued to play throughout the eighties. By 1989 Shannon's career was on the upswing thanks largely to Tom Petty. Roy Orbison's fatal heart attack on December 6, 1988, left an opening in the rock supergroup The Traveling Wilburys, which featured Petty, ex–Beatle George Harrison, Bob Dylan, and former Electric Light Orchestra member Jeff Lynne. Even as Shannon was actively under consideration as Orbison's replacement, the 55-year-old rocker was in a recording studio under the supervision of Petty and Lynne laying down new tracks with members of the Heartbreakers for his first album of new material in almost a decade.

Shannon's lifelong battle with depression, however, had been aggravated by the breakup of his 31-year marriage to wife Shirley in 1985. Although he married Bonnie Gutierrez in 1987, there were strained relations between Shannon and his children from his former marriage. On February 8, 1990, Shannon's body was found by his wife at about 11:25 P.M. in the den of their home in Santa Clarita, California. Shannon had placed the butt of a .22-caliber hunting rifle on the floor, pressed his cheek on the barrel, and pulled the trigger. He left no note. Shannon's Petty-Lynne produced album *Rock On* was posthumously released by MCA in 1991. Many reviewers considered it to be among the singer-guitarist-songwriter's best work.

Sheridan, Philip R.

A popular orchestra leader in the Pacific Northwest, Sheridan, 45, had been released from a tuberculosis sanitarium for less than a year when he single-mindedly set out to take his life. On November 30, 1937, Sheridan drove his automobile six miles south of Spokane, Washington, before he slashed his wrists and drank four ounces of Lysol. The unconscious orchestra leader was discovered by a passing motorist and transported to Spokane's Sacred Heart Hospital. Two notes found in the car were undecipherable. Days later on December 1, 1937, Sheridan fulfilled his death wish by jumping from the fourth-floor window of his hospital room.

Sherrin, Scott

Adopted in 1973 at the age of 1 month by a white family in Essex, Sherrin became one of Britain's leading black entertainers before mental illness and drug abuse led to his tragic death in 1996. Debuting at 8 on the children's television show *Minipops*, Sherrin was 11 when he became the youngest entertainer, black or white, to appear in a Royal Variety Performance. He portrayed "Fizzy" in the musical *Bugsy*. A high school dropout at 16, Sherrin was dancing in a West End production of *Cats* three years later when he was selected by Esther Rantzen to be the first black presenter on the BBC consumer television show *That's Life* in 1991. After the popular singer-dancer was signed for the lead role of "Tyrone" in the musical *Fame* at London's West End Cambridge Theatre in early 1995, Sherrin's future looked limitless. He was earning £2000 a week, dating a beautiful dancer in the show, Gina Lee Lincoln, and considering other professional offers.

Sherrin's personality, however, seemingly changed after a back injury sustained onstage forced the show's producers to replace him. In September 1995, shortly after breaking up with Lincoln, Sherrin attempted suicide by ingesting 150 paracetamol tablets and a bottle of gin. Barely surviving, the troubled entertainer rented an £800 a month flat in Soho where he spent his days alone chain-smoking cannabis and drinking. Following his botched suicide attempt, Sherrin began fantasizing that his real parents were Jimi Hendrix and Madonna. His adoptive parents were horrified when they visited their son in his new surroundings. Toilets in the flat had remained unflushed for weeks and shards of glass from broken mirrors littered the floor. Pictures, drawn by Sherrin in which he portrayed himself as God or Jesus Christ, were tacked onto the walls. He calmly told them that he would "put this world right by the year 2000," and announced that he was giving up the theatre to wander the world. Psychiatrists and social workers became involved in the case, but were ineffective.

In October 1995, Sherrin disappeared from his flat in Soho and his whereabouts remained a mystery until he was spotted tap dancing on the streets for money and sleeping rough under the Waterloo Station arches. At one point, he was found preaching with a group of evangelical Christians in London's Leicester Square. Shortly before Christmas, Sherrin paid £700 to be illegally smuggled into Germany, but was returned to England in January 1996 after he was unable to obtain a legal passport. Alarmed by their son's mental deterioration, Sherrin's parents persuaded him to stay with them at their home in Chelmsford, Essex. Convinced, however, that they were robots, Sherrin disappeared from their care on January 27, 1996. Three days later, the performer's rucksack containing a sleeping bag, clothes, passport application, £195 in cash, and his bank passbook was found floating in the Thames River at Wapping. Expecting the worst, Sherrin's family and friends awaited the inevitable bad news.

Five weeks later on March 1, 1996, the 23 year old's body was fished from the Thames River just below the Tower Bridge at Wapping in East London near the site where his personal effects had been found. An open verdict was returned at the Poplar's court, East London, based upon pathologist Dr. Stephen Chan's finding that he was not satisfied beyond a reasonable doubt that suicide had been Sherrin's stated objective at the time of his death.

Sherwood, Robert

A one-time radio announcer, Sherwood, 50, produced the Ingrid Bergman vehicle *Adam Had Four Sons* for Columbia in 1941. Failing to reconcile with his estranged wife in Hollywood on January 3, 1961, the former film producer returned to his bachelor apartment at the Sunset Sands, 8775 Sunset Boulevard, and fired a bullet into his head. Sherwood had recently been employed as an aircraft salesman.

Shibley, Nassib Abdullah

For months, the Syrian-born attorney and manager of Hungarian gypsy violinist Janczy Rigo had become increasingly jealous of the influence that the performer's wife, Katherine Emerson Rigo, exercised over his own wife, Leonore. Though husband and wife often argued over the intensely emotional relationship existing between the women, Leonore continued to see Mrs. Rigo. On the night of November 3, 1908, some three weeks after Leonore had consulted an attorney regarding a divorce, Shibley fatally chloroformed his wife in the bedroom of their spacious apartment at 508 W. 122nd Street in New York City. The young attorney placed her body in bed, and spent the next few hours writing letters. Shibley waited until a servant fed their 2-year-old son and left the apartment to take the child for a walk before re-entering the bedroom. There, he laid next to his dead wife, slit an artery in his left arm above the elbow with a razor blade, stabbed himself near the throat, and covered their bodies with a sheet.

A handwritten letter to Leonore's sister found on the dining room table read: "Better this than her life as exampled by the past few months. Take care of baby. I could not take him. You see why I took it all in and said nothing." In another letter, unaddressed, Shibley issued a warning to American men:

> Maybe I am insane; maybe not. I have loved my wife with a love that passeth human understanding. Let the men of America get out of their lives the artificial life — the restaurant life — smoking, drinking, especially among women, and such things as this will never be. Breed in your little girls the love of home so that they may see, and breed their children when women. I am happy. No temptation can now reach my loved wife. No stage, no restaurant, no automobile that I cannot provide, but peace — Goodbye, mother and brothers. By death I wipe out the sins of life. We prefer to be cremated or in one grave. This is only a parting. If men would only bring their wives to live within their means, and modestly, America would be a

Paradise and each woman could not set another an example. Oh, my people — I am, the first of you, a murderer and a suicide! How the words do burn! Forgive me!

In a statement to *The New York American*, Leonore's sister blamed Mrs. Rigo for the tragedy: "I feel convinced that my sister's death must be laid at the door of Mrs. Rigo. The violinist's wife seemed to exercise a strange fascination over my sister. The luxurious manner in which Rigo's wife lived undoubtedly had an effect on Mrs. Shibley. She had been perfectly happy at first in marrying a man who was devoted to her, but after she met Mrs. Rigo she at once began to show a distaste for domestic duties. Mrs. Rigo initiated her into all the hollow enjoyments of suppers at midnight restaurants and automobile rides to out-of-town inns. All that was out of keeping with her home environment." While Mrs. Rigo denied that any "unusual relationship" existed between them, she did admit that she "seemed to exercise a fascination" over Leonore, adding, "But if she wished to admire me, why should I object?" Mrs. Rigo also maintained that Shibley himself was "insanely infatuated" with her, but "met with no response."

Shields, Hugh M.

A former newspaperman, and for the last 20 years a live animation cartoonist with the Paul Terry Studios of New Rochelle, New York, Shields, 53, plunged to his death from his 11th floor apartment at 305 West Seventy-second Street in New York City on May 31, 1939. While in the absence of a note police were unable to determine whether Shields had jumped or fallen, his wife stated that he had suffered from a nervous condition.

Shields, Jimmie

The long-time gay companion of screen star William ("Billy") Haines was born James Shields Fickeisen in Pittsburgh, Pennsylvania, on May 24, 1905. He dropped Fickeisen after his parents divorced. Heeding his stepfather's advice that the military was a place where an effeminate boy could be made into a "man," Shields enlisted in the Navy in 1924 just days before his 19th birthday. One year into his enlistment, he was stricken with meningitis and honorably discharged in November 1925. Shields, 21, was cruising the streets and bathhouses of New York City for sex in early 1926 when he picked up William Haines, a popular film star who had appeared in several breezy roles (*A Slave of Fashion*, 1925; *Little Annie Rooney*, 1925). Shields followed Haines to Hollywood where the actor found him extra and stand-in work at MGM.

Shortly afterward, Haines and Shields openly moved in together and were recognized by the insular movie community as one of the most devoted couples in Hollywood (although both continued over the years to have numerous sexual liaisons). According to Hollywood legend, in early 1933 MGM studio head Louis B. Mayer called Haines into his office and threatened to fire the actor if he did not quit living with Shields and having homosexual affairs. Haines flatly refused and despite an 11 year association with MGM was summarily dismissed by the studio. In 1934, the actor made two films for Mascot (*Young and Beautiful* and *The Marines Are Coming*) before leaving show business to become one of Hollywood's top interior decorators. If Haines, however, contemplated a return to films the scandal at El Porto forever prevented it.

During the summer of 1936, Haines and Shields rented a beach house at 221 Moonstone Street in the seaside community of El Porto, California (part of the town of Manhattan Beach), 30 minutes south of Hollywood. A conservative community near Hermosa Beach with a large Ku Klux Klan membership, El Porto had an uneasy relationship with the show biz folks who frequently summered there. On Decoration Day weekend in 1936, Haines and Shields invited a large contingent of their mostly male friends from Hollywood to a party at their rented beach house. While accounts of the incident at El Porto vary, a general chronology of events can be broadly determined.

A few days before the party, Shields evidently gave Jimmy Walker, a 6-year-old neighbor boy, a few pennies. According to Kenneth Anger's account in *Hollywood Babylon II*, Walker was first attracted to the Moonstone Street address by the couple's pet poodle, Lord Peter Whimsy, apparently dyed purple for the party. El Porto residents, fueled by fan magazine innuendo that Haines and Shields were homosexuals, convinced themselves that the boy had been sexually molested.

On May 31, 1936, the couple entertained 17 male friends during a daylong house party. That night after the event had broken up, Haines and Shields ate at a local restaurant prior to driving back to Hollywood. As they were walking back to their house they were approached by several men. According to one published report, the couple was told: "We don't want you to live here. We'll give you just an hour to get out of town." When Haines tried to defuse the situation with humor one of the men knocked Shields to the ground. A mob, now 15 strong including some women, pushed and shoved the pair as they tried to get to their car to leave. When they finally did so, the vehicle had been smeared with tomatoes. Two days later, the parents of Jimmy Walker filed a morals complaint against Haines and one "James Doe." Haines refused to issue a complaint against his assailants. The charge against the couple was later dropped. Interviewed in the mid-eighties by author William J. Mann for his definitive biography of Haines, *Wisecracker*, Jimmy Walker, then 67, reported that Shields had fellated him.

While the incident spelled a finish to any possible film comeback, it did little to damage Haines' reputation as Hollywood's top interior decorator. Among the more than 400 clients he had during his lengthy career as president of the Beverly Hills-based William Haines, Inc., were several stars including Joan Crawford. Haines, 73, died from complications of lung cancer on December 26, 1973. The former actor was cremated and placed in

a small urn on a shelf at the Woodlawn Mausoleum in Santa Monica. A place next to Haines was reserved for Shields.

Haines' companion of nearly 50 years was devasted by his lover's death. On the evening of March 5, 1974, Shields, 69, telephoned several friends from the Brentwood home at 601 Lorna Lane he had shared with Haines for many years. After making the last call, he swallowed an entire bottle of sleeping pills, taped a note on his bedroom door instructing the maid not to enter, but rather to notify a family friend, then locked the door. Writing "Jimmie" in pen across the top of a legal-size notepad, Shields left a poignant suicide note: "Goodbye to all of you who have tried so hard to comfort me in my loss of William Haines, whom I have been with since 1926. I now find it impossible to go it alone — I am much too lonely." After finishing, he removed his clothes, laid down on his bed, and fell asleep at around 9:45 P.M. Shields was cremated without ceremony and placed in an urn beside Haines in Woodlawn Mausoleum.

FURTHER READING

Mann, William J. *Wisecracker: The Life and Times of William Haines, Hollywood's First Openly Gay Star.* New York: Viking, 1998.

Sidney, Carrie Webb

The wife of vaudeville comedian George Sidney and a member of the "Busy Izzy" Company that played the Stair and Havlin circuit was found dead by her husband in their home at 1658 North Western Avenue in Los Angeles on October 5, 1924. Sidney, 47, mixed cyanide of potassium in a soft drink, laid on a couch, then downed the deadly cocktail. A note left by the dead woman gave no motive for the suicide, but simply stated that she wanted to die.

Siegel, Norman

Siegel, 54, was a Scripps-Howard newspaper editor in Cleveland for almost 20 years before relocating to Hollywood in 1945 to ultimately become the publicity director at Paramount Studios. During his long tenure, Siegel organized and coordinated Hollywood troupes attending the Royal Command Performances in London and served as the public relations director for the Academy Award shows of 1951–52. At the time of his death on January 24, 1961, Siegel was the West Coast editor of *Photoplay*, a popular fan magazine focusing on the public and private lives of the stars. At 11:44 A.M. that day, the former studio publicity director was sitting near the ledge of the rooftop coffee shop atop the 13th floor of the Guaranty Building at 6331 Hollywood Boulevard when, according to a waitress, he jumped. The body landed on the second floor roof of the Bank of America branch at Hollywood Boulevard near Cahuenga. Although no note was found, police listed Siegel's death as a suicide.

Sire, Albert I.

During a half-century business career, the 75-year-old attorney and realtor owned several theatre properties in New York City including the Bijou, the Casino, the Madison Square Theatre, and the Loew's New York. In the early thirties financial reversals forced Sire to sell the properties to avoid foreclosure. On June 25, 1935, hours after losing the apartment he had occupied for 35 years in the San Jacinto Hotel, Sire leaped to his death from the roof of a 13 story apartment at 38 West Fifty-ninth Street, which he once owned. Unknown to Sire, earlier that morning his attorney had worked out a deal that would have allowed the failed businessman to retain the apartment. A note to his housekeeper scrawled in pencil outlining his burial plans and $6.75 in cash were found in his pockets. Once worth more than $10 million, Sire left an estate valued at less than $5,000 to his brother.

Skelton, Georgia

The former Georgia Maureen Davis was a photographer's model when she married radio and film comedian Red Skelton, then an Army private, on March 9, 1945. They had two children, Valentina and Richard Freeman. Richard was 9 years old when he died of leukemia at the UCLA Medical Center in 1958. In 1966, while husband Red was downstairs onstage at the Sands Hotel in Las Vegas, Georgia was wounded in the chest when, according to her statement to police, a .38-caliber pistol discharged after falling off a night stand in their room. The comedian filed suit for a dissolution of their 26 year marriage in 1971 citing "irreconcilable differences." Skelton later remarried. Georgia's health began to decline, and she was hospitalized at the Eisenhower Medical Center in 1972 for a rare blood disease. Later that year she suffered a heart attack. After eating dinner on May 10, 1976, the 18th anniversary of her son Richard's death, the troubled 54-year-old woman walked into the garden of her Rancho Mirage, California, home and shot herself.

Sklover, Theodora K.

A former dance and drama student at Bennington College, Sklover first used television as a teaching tool for preschoolers at the Bank Street College of Education in Manhattan. In the sixties, Sklover's interest in the educational aspects of television prompted her to organize Open Channel, a nonprofit organization that lobbied for greater community access to cable systems and public programming. When hired in 1979 as the director of the Governor's Office of Motion Picture and Television Development for the state of New York, Sklover was already a nationally recognized authority on public programming. She left the position after one year to develop Movie Makers, a series of evening classes in which she interviewed film personnel and screened their upcoming films.

By the nineties, however, Sklover owed the Internal Revenue Service more than $25,000 not including the 20 percent interest charges. In January 1992, the IRS froze her meager bank account, leaving her unable to pay the rent on her ninth floor apartment at

433 E. Fifty-first Street in New York City. On the night of May 11, 1992, after a druggist refused to sell her prescription pills, the 53-year-old woman returned to her apartment and washed down a bottle of over-the-counter pills with shots of Remy Martin brandy. She scrawled on a sheet of paper: "I was afraid that if I jumped I don't live high enough. The ninth floor might be too low. If I were to fail at this, too!" Awaking from a stupor several hours later, Sklover added to the note: "When I first moved here, young and innocent, someone jumped like this and gave me the courage to do it." She then leapt from her window, crashing into an air conditioner jutting out of an eighth floor window before landing on a plot of grass below. One of the first people at the scene heard Sklover utter, "I don't want to die," moments before she expired.

Skouras, Dionysia

At the request of her father, Spyros Skouras, president of 20th Century–Fox, the troubled 23 year old was indefinitely committed to the Hallbrooke Sanitarium in Westport, Connecticut, in January 1950. On July 17, 1950, Skouras was visiting her uncle, Charles P. Skouras, president of National Theatres, when she either leaped or fell to her death from the roof of the five story 20th Century–Fox office building at Washington Boulevard and Vermont Avenue in Hollywood. She died without regaining consciousness two hours later at the Georgia Street Receiving Hospital.

Slater, Charles Dundas

Connected with the management of London's Empire Theatre from 1889 to 1895, Slater was also the business manager of the Alhambra before leaving in 1907 to manage the London Coliseum music hall. Following years of faithful service, the 60 year old was dismissed on June 29, 1912 when his rheumatic gout and failing eyesight prevented him from discharging his business duties. At 4:30 P.M. on July 8, 1912, Slater flagged down a taxi cab

and told the driver to take him to Charing Cross Hospital. Minutes later, the cabbie heard what he believed was an exhaust backfire. Arriving at the hospital, the cabbie discovered Slater lying on the back seat with a gaping wound in his head and blood flowing from his mouth. A seven chamber revolver, with one spent round, was between his knees. He died two hours later.

In a letter found on his body, Slater wrote: "On the rocks. No hope. No daylight. God forgive me for this act, but I am hopeless, and if there is any one among my English and American friends who will have a friendly thought left for me let them now show it by doing all they can for my poor, faithful wife. I have led a white man's life, but this is a degraded dog's finish. I am broken-hearted, but not insane.— C.D.S." On September 10, 1912, a distinguished company of artists gave a performance at the London Coliseum for the benefit of Slater's widow and children. Years earlier on January 29, 1909, a former manager of the Alhambra Theatre, George Scott (I) (see entry), shot himself in a hotel room in London.

Slezak, Walter

Slezak, son of Leo Slezak (1873–1946), the famous operatic tenor and film comedian, was born in Vienna, Austria, on May 3, 1902. After studying chemistry and medicine for a year and a half at the University of Vienna, Slezak left school and became a bank clerk. In 1922 director Michael Kertesz (renamed Curtiz when he came to Hollywood in 1926) noticed Slezak drinking in a Viennese beer hall and signed him to play the romantic lead in the German film *Sodom und Gomorrah* (1922). Slezak established himself as a leading man on the German operatic stage and in films, but his inability to control his weight (280 pounds at his heaviest) relegated him to character parts.

In 1930, he made his U.S. debut on Broadway in the operetta *Meet My Sister* and for the next 12 years appeared in numerous plays and light opera. In 1942, director Leo McCarey brought the portly actor to Hollywood to appear as a Nazi in the Cary Grant–Ginger Rogers vehicle *Once Upon a Honeymoon*. Two years later, Alfred Hitchcock cast him as the incognito Nazi submarine commander in *Lifeboat*. In reprisal, Nazi authorities in Austria fined Slezak's father (who was singing Wagnerian opera in Vienna) 10,000 marks. Typecast as a heavy or a comedic bumbler, Slezak appeared in more than 35 films including *The Inspector General* (1949) and *Bedtime for Bonzo* (1951). During the 1954–1955 Broadway season, he won a Tony co-starring with Ezio Pinza in the musical *Fanny*. At the Metropolitan Opera in 1957 Slezak sang in the operetta *The Gypsy Baron*. In addition to film and stage work, the versatile actor also appeared in guest shots in numerous television series like *Rawhide*, *Batman*, and *Dr. Kildare*. Slezak retired in 1967, but returned briefly in 1974 to guest on the soap opera *One Life to Live*, which starred his daughter, Erica Slezak.

Retired with his wife of 40 years, Johanna, and living in Flower Hill, Long Island, New York, the 80-year-old actor was recuperating from prostate surgery and being treated several times a week for a nagging shoulder injury. On April 22, 1983, Slezak had just finished watching the late news on television with his wife when he walked into the back yard of their home and shot himself in the head with a .38-caliber pistol. According to her, just before ending his life the actor appeared to be crying and repeatedly stated that he "couldn't go on with this illness anymore."

FURTHER READING

Slezak, Walter. *What Time's the Next Swan?* Garden City, N.Y.: Doubleday, 1962.

Sloane, Everett

Sloane, one of Hollywood's best known character actors, once told an interviewer, "I never got the idea of becoming an actor until I was about 2 years old." Born in New York

City on October 1, 1909, Sloane made his stage debut at 7 as "Puck" in a school production of *A Midsummer Night's Dream*. He briefly attended the University of Pennsylvania, dropping out in 1927 to join a stock company in Moyland, Pennyslvania. When acting roles proved scarce, he became a stockbroker's runner at $17 a week. Within a year Sloane was earning $140 a week as an assistant to the manager, but left to do radio work when the stock market crash of 1929 cut his salary in half. During his first 15 years in radio, Sloane estimated that he played more than 15,000 roles in such dramas as *The Shadow*, *Buck Rogers*, *Pretty Kitty Kelly*, *Crime Doctor*, and an eight year run on *The Goldbergs*. In 1935, he made his Broadway debut in *Boy Meets Girl*.

Back on radio, Sloane joined Orson Welles' *Mercury Theatre on the Air* in 1938, and was part of the historic "The War of the Worlds" broadcast that made the "boy genius" a household name. Signed by RKO to direct *Citizen Kane* (1941), Welles brought Sloane with him to Hollywood and cast him as the "Bernstein" character in what many critics consider to be the greatest American film ever made. From that debut performance forward, Sloane established himself as one of the movies' premier character actors, appearing in such films as *The Lady from Shanghai* (1948), *The Men* (1950), *The Desert Fox* (1951), *Lust for Life* (1956), and two 1964 Jerry Lewis vehicles, *The Patsy* and *The Disorderly Orderly*. From the fifties on, Sloane also appeared in numerous television programs including a memorable performance in a 1960 *Twilight Zone* episode, "The Fever," in which he played a closeted compulsive gambler ultimately destroyed by a slot machine.

Increasingly depressed over his failing eyesight, the 55-year-old actor told his wife, Lillian, "You would be better off if I killed myself." On August 5, 1965, Sloane asked her for his sleeping pills and commented, "There are not enough," when she gave them to him. Shortly afterward, he left their Brentwood home at 13043 Sunset Boulevard for a doctor's appointment. Lillian Sloane filed a missing person's report with the West Los Angeles police when she learned that Sloane had failed to see his doctor, but had picked up a refill of 25 pills from the druggist. She cancelled the report when Sloane showed up hours later. The next morning at 10:15 A.M., Lillian found Sloane dead in bed from an overdose of sleeping pills. The contents of two notes left by the actor (one to his wife, the other to his agent) were not disclosed by authorities. Sloane is interred in Rosedale Memorial Park in Los Angeles.

Smith, Allen

Smith, a 28-year-old unemployed theatrical press agent formerly with the Paramount-Newark Theatre, pumped two rounds into his girlfriend, Mrs. Lois Duffy, then turned the .32-caliber gun on himself as the pair sat parked in a car on a lonely road outside the Mount Pleasant Cemetery in Newark, New Jersey, on April 18, 1937. Though Duffy, a 32-year-old telephone operator, had long been estranged from her husband, she had refused to divorce him and marry Smith because of her devout Catholic upbringing. Duffy was found slumped over the steering wheel with a bullet in her right temple and another in her right breast. On the seat beside her, Smith still held the gun in his right hand, dead from a single shot to his temple.

Smith, Edward J.

The 42-year-old Smith, treasurer of the Strand Theatre at Broadway and Forty-seventh Street for ten years, was found dead of gas poisoning in the kitchen of his New York City apartment on March 21, 1938, the first anniversary of his wife's death. A note addressed to his mother found near a photograph of his wife read: "Dear Mom, I can't go on any longer. I want to be buried with Margaret, my sweetheart, and my baby." The child had died some time before its mother.

Smith, Pete

The master of the comedy short was born in New York City on September 4, 1892.

Dropping out of school at 13 to work as a stenographer-typist, by 1912 Smith had become the secretary of a vaudeville performers' union, and later worked as a reviewer for *Billboard* magazine. Learning the fundamentals of press-agenting from Harry Reichenbach, Smith served as the publicity director for Famous Players–Lasky, Artcraft, and Mickey Neilan Productions before coming to Hollywood in the mid-twenties. By 1925 Smith was an established press agent with a client list that included Douglas Fairbanks, Sr., Conway Tearle, Milton Sills, and Corinne Griffith. That same year he signed an unprecedented $1,000 a week contract with MGM to tout that studio's galaxy of stars. In 1931 Smith began producing and narrating some ten to 18 humorous short films a year for MGM. In 1935 Smith introduced *Pete Smith Specialties*, a series of short subjects he produced and narrated that focused on the humorous side of life. The series was an instant hit with audiences, film distributors, and critics. From the mid-thirties to the mid-fifties, Smith cranked out some 300 shorts. Two, *Penny Wisdom* (1937) and *Quicker'n a Wink* (1940), won Academy Awards as best short subjects. Other Smith short subjects nominated for Academy Awards were *Wanted, A Master* (1936), *Romance of Radium* (1937), *Army Champions* (1941), *Sure Cures* (1946), *Now You See It* (1947), *You Can't Win* (1948), *Water Trix* (1949), and *Wrong Way Butch* (1950). In 1953 Smith was awarded an Honorary Oscar "for his witty and pungent observations on the American scene in his series of 'Pete Smith Specialties.'" Depressed over his deteriorating health, the 86-year-old producer jumped to his death from the roof of a convalescent hospital in Santa Monica, California, on the afternoon of January 12, 1979.

Smith, Worthington

Hours after his arrest on a drunk charge by Columbus, Ohio, police, Smith, a 34-year-old unemployed former manager of that city's Alhambra Theater, was found shortly after midnight on July 6, 1948, hanging by his shirt in a cell at City Prison.

Smitha, Silk

Considered the "Marilyn Monroe" of the South India film industry, the sex siren dubbed "Silk Smitha" because of her sensuous dancing was born Vijayalakshmi on December 2, 1960, in Elluru near Rajamundry in the southern state of Andhra Pradesh in India. Forced by poverty to drop out of school while still a child, the starstruck youngster went to Kodambakkam, South India's Hollywood, with the dream of breaking into movies. Not content to remain a make-up girl to an aspiring starlet, the young beauty quickly seduced the actress' manager-boyfriend who, renaming her Smitha, launched her into movies with an appearance in the 1979 Malayalam film, *Inaye Thedi*.

In 1980, Smitha got her big break with a major role in the Tamil film *Vandi Chakkram* (*The Wheel*). In it, she played a bar girl named "Silk" and established what was to become her trademark — a willingness to display her voluptuous figure just beyond what the censors would permit. The movie made Silk Smitha a star and in the next three years she appeared in more than 200 films, often in skimpy clothes performing provocative dances. During this period, she charged 5,000 rupees a dance and did as many as three sequences a day for as many films. In less than ten years in the industry, the seductive actress made more than 500 films.

However, much like the American porn star and fellow suicide Savannah (see entry), Smitha's abrasive personality made her one of the most unpopular performers in movies. As the public's taste in movie heroines began to change, Smitha found herself less in demand. Bad advice compounded a waning career. According to industry sources, her live-in lover lured Smitha into bankrolling two flop Telegu films. Twenty million rupees in debt and with another film halted in production due lack of funds, Smitha continued to work occasionally, but could not maintain her luxurious lifestyle.

On the morning of September 23, 1996, the 35-year-old South Indian actress was found hanging by a sari from the ceiling fan in the bedroom of her home in Saligramam, Madras' "Tinseltown." Unhappy over her stalled career and her boyfriend, Smitha's suicide note written in Telegu read, "I have no desire to live anymore" and contained allegations that those she trusted had turned out to be unworthy.

Smoller, Dorothy

Smoller, a one-time dancer in the company of Anna Pavlova, acted on Broadway in *Checkerboard* and *What's in a Name* in 1922 until a severe case of pulmonary tuberculosis exiled her to the Cragmore Sanitarium in Colorado Springs, Colorado, in 1923. There she met fellow patient Benjamin Strong, governor of the Federal Reserve Bank in New York, who (with others) helped subsidize the cost of Smoller's protracted stay at the facility. In 1925, Smoller left the sanitarium to live with her parents in California, but a chance to act in the Broadway play *Howdy, King* lured her back to New York in November 1926. Advised by her doctor that a return to stage work posed a significant health risk, the 25-year-old actress flatly stated that she would rather die than not make the attempt to fulfill her ambition.

One week before the start of the play, Smoller suffered a hemorrhage that effectively ended her acting career. On December 9, 1926, she drank a three ounce bottle of shoe polish containing cyanide of potassium as a base in her room on the 28th floor of the Hotel Shelton in New York City. She died fifteen minutes after the arrival of the hotel physician. Smoller left three notes. One was to Strong thanking him for his kindness and another was to a friend instructing him how to dispose of her property. In the note to her mother, the actress referred to her illness as a "chain of torture" that "pains all the time."

Snyder, Sadie

The daughter of Sarah Snyder, once known on the vaudeville stage as "Sara Sedalia," the 17-year-old vocalist assumed the name of "Sid Sedalia" when she began singing at Chicago's Delavan Cafe on North Clark Street in 1916. Snyder, described by her mother as a "good, straight girl," was concerned that "people might say bad things" about her because she was a cabaret singer. These feelings, amplified by a local newspaper exposé of the "sins" of cabaret life, further preyed on the young woman's mind. On the evening of February 16, 1916, Snyder locked herself in the bedroom of her home at 2125 North Clark Street, plugged the crack between two window sashes with a towel, then turned on the gas. Snyder's mother, with the aid of a boarder, later forced the door and found her daughter's lifeless body on the bed. Near at hand lay a newspaper folded to a story about the conduct of patrons in a Chicago cafe. On the wall beside the bed Snyder had scribbled, "Mama, I love you."

Soriero, Thomas D.

Soriero began in the theatre business in 1906 operating a nickelodeon, later graduating to managing theatres in Baltimore (1915), then rising to the position of mid-south division manager of RKO theatres. After accepting a post with the Skouras brothers in 1932, Soriero left in 1934 to work for MGM studio head Louis B. Mayer. On October 6, 1946, the 58 year old was the manager of downtown L.A.'s United Artists Theatre when he entered the Rives-Strong Building at 112 W. Ninth Street, went to the 12th floor, and jumped to his death into a light well below. No reason was given for the suicide.

Soundtracks, Epic see Epic Soundtracks

Southern, Dixie Lee

Southern (real name Florence Bridges) was a torch singer with the Georgia Ambassadors and vocalized on radio with Atlanta's WSB radio orchestra. Hours after appearing with the Georgia Ambassadors orchestra in a downtown Atlanta hotel on July 8, 1938, the 20

year old returned late to her parents' home at 1448 Glenwood Avenue in the company of the orchestra leader. Her parents scolded her for the lateness of the hour and Southern, threatening to kill herself, stormed off to her room. A female friend who spent the night with Southern in the same room later testified at the inquest that the singer appeared to have calmed down, but moments after turning out the light swallowed a bottle of poison. Southern died minutes after being admitted to a hospital.

Spears, Joseph

At one time, Spears, 60, managed the Murray and Mack show and was an agent with the company founded by George M. Cohan and Sam H. Harris. On April 20, 1929, Spears' body was found in the bathroom of his digs at the Hotel Flanders in New York City. Apparently, the unemployed theatrical manager had sat on the bath rug and slit his throat with a straight razor while gazing into a mirror. Years before he had attempted suicide by slashing his wrists. According to his brother-in-law, Spears was despondent over the death of his wife in December 1928. He left a fortune of nearly $400,000 from a family inheritance.

Spence, John Francis

In the summer of 1986, Spence (born February 3, 1969) formed the ska band No Doubt (his favorite expression) with Eric Stefani and his sister Gwen Stefani in Anaheim, California. The African-American lead singer's dynamic stage presence punctuated with backward flips made No Doubt stand out in conservative Orange County. On December 21, 1987, days before the fledgling band was set to play before record company executives at the Roxy in Los Angeles, the 18-year-old singer drove his car to a deserted lot in an Anaheim park. Shortly after 8:00 P.M. Spence fatally shot himself. A two-page letter found at the scene included the line, "I think I've felt too much pain and all I see in my future is more." It was signed, "I'm sorry. Goodbye."

Spirescu, Oscar

On September 7, 1918, the superintendent of a New York City apartment building at 305 W. Forty-fifth Street used a passkey to enter Spirescu's room after the musical director of Broadway's Strand Theatre failed to acknowledge the rings of numerous callers and messengers. He found Spirescu's body on the bed, a three ounce vial that had contained chloroform nearby. Although the police ruled the musical director's death as self-inflicted chloroform poisoning, friends denied that he had taken his life.

Spitzer, Henry M.

Spitzer, 54, president of a New York City-based music publishing business bearing his name, was formerly an executive with the Edward Morris Music Company and the Chappell Music Publishing Company as well as a member of the American Society of Composers, Authors and Publishers (ASCAP). Gone, however, were the days that spawned his one big song publishing hit, "Cruising Down the River" (1945), and by September 22, 1952, the veteran Tin Pan Alleyite was sick and financially ruined. That day, Spitzer committed suicide by inhaling illuminating gas in his Manhattan apartment at 333 West Fifty-seventh Street. The music publisher left four notes in which he attributed his self-destruction to illness and financial reverses.

Sprinkle, Arthur P., Jr.

Sprinkle, the station manager at NBC affiliate KONA-TV in Honolulu, appeared "happier than usual" to his secretary as he left the studios shortly before 1:00 P.M. on April 16, 1962. Moments later, a crane operator at a nearby construction site spotted the 41-year-old's body on the ground next to his convertible. He was shot once in the head and a single-barrel .410-gauge Iver Johnson shotgun was found near the body. A note, held by two rubber bands wound around his left wrist, asked that several people be notified, but did not give any motive for the suicide.

Stark, Peter

The 25-year-old son of producer Ray Stark (*The World of Suzie Wong*, 1960; *Funny Girl*, 1968; *The Sunshine Boys*, 1975) and grandson of *Ziegfeld Follies* star Fanny Brice (1891–1951) was working on a project at Columbia ironically titled "Death at an Early Age" when his broken body was found shortly after 8:00 A.M. on February 4, 1970, in a courtyard behind the building where he lived at 435 East Fifty-seventh Street in New York City. Stark placed a note on the front door informing his secretary to take the day off, then either fell or jumped from the bedroom window of his 14th floor apartment. Actor Kirk Douglas, a client of one-time agent Ray Stark, delivered the young producer's eulogy.

Steele, Ernest William

A trapeze artist with the Ringling Brothers Circus, Steele left the tour and returned to Boston after arguing with his partner. Soon afterward, the 37-year-old aerialist's marriage to wife Jenny, 28, dissolved under the strain of his jealousy and uncontrollable fits of melancholy. On January 31, 1915, the acrobat had not lived with his estranged wife and their two young children for 17 months. As was his custom, Steele picked up the older child every Sunday morning so the boy could spend the day with his grandmother.

While in the 4th floor apartment at 1366 Washington Street that his wife shared with her mother and three grown brothers, Steele took exception with the manner in which she was caring for their 20-month-old son, David. After making a few insulting remarks to his wife, Steele whipped out a homemade blackjack from his pocket and struck her three times in the head. A scuffle broke out between the acrobat and two of her brothers, but Steele wrenched himself free and, scooping up his infant son, stepped out of the window onto the ledge of the apartment building. Moments later, he threw the child 35 feet to the street below in full view of a crowd of worshippers leaving church after mass. Steele, brandishing a hunting knife, re-entered the apartment long enough to threaten, "I've got rid of one of them, and now I'll get the other," before retreating back onto the narrow ledge. When a policeman attempted to move toward him, Steele dropped the knife, put his arms to his side, and dove headfirst to his death. Both mother and child survived.

Steele, Murray M.

Three days after Mabel Foy, a vivacious 22-year-old divorcee and vaudeville actress, turned down his proposal of marriage, Steele, the 38-year-old former manager of San Francisco's Kinemacolor Motion Picture Company, sent a bunch of white roses to her apartment in that city on September 28, 1912. The accompanying note read, "I am going to the Park, sweetheart." Later that day, Steele was found under the bridge just inside the Stanyan Street entrance to the Golden Gate Park, a victim of a self-administered dose of cyanide of potassium. He died en route to Park Emergency Hospital. Inside the man's clothes, authorities found $114.92 in cash, a picture of his beloved, and notes to his father and Foy. To the actress he wrote: "My Dear Little Mabel: I am still so sorry and broken hearted about your not wanting to marry me, that I do not care to live any longer. I wish you good luck, and may God bless you. Your devoted friend, Murray M. Steele." Foy, who previously knew Steele back in his hometown of St. Louis, explained that the only reason she had not married him was that having been divorced for only three weeks she feared a bigamy charge.

Stegmeyer, Douglas Alan

The bass guitarist in, and former leader of, Billy Joel's band shot himself to death in his apartment in Smithtown, New York, on August 24, 1995. Joel commented on the 43-year-old musician's death: "I am just in shock…. He was with me from the 1970s through 1988 and was the leader of the nucleus of the group that was the band. We called him the 'Sergeant-at-Arms.'"

Stein, Solomon B.

Forced into bankruptcy by a $50,000 gem heist on October 8, 1928, the theatrical jeweler had recently been subpoenaed by the District Attorney's office to appear as a witness at trial for two men charged with the hold-up. Police speculate that the mental strain of the upcoming case combined with Stein's poor health drove the 36-year-old jeweler to take his life in the 12th floor office of the A. S. K. Jewelry Manufacturing Company at 74 West Forty-sixth Street in New York City on May 13, 1929. A salesman found Stein's body facedown in the office propped up on cushions against a chair. A tube leading from a gas jet attached to an open blow torch had fallen from his lips. A poetic note written in pencil found beside the body read: "Tired, he rests, and life's poor play is over. Approach thy grave like one who draws the draperies of death about him and lies down to dream, and so falls the curtain on the last act of my life. Good-bye, everybody." And in a postscript: "It takes a lot of gas to kill a man, but it is not so bad."

Steinberg, Jacob

The would-be Austrian-born motion picture impresario lost $60,000 over a two-year period immediately preceding his death in an unsuccessful bid to break into the film business. On September 21, 1914, Steinberg, 55, was found dead in the bathtub of his home at 85 Lenox Avenue, New York City. A tube in his mouth was connected to a running gas jet. On a nearby table he left a note in Hebrew explaining the suicide and $800 in cash to repay a debt he owed to a sister.

Sterling, Charles

Known throughout the music halls of Great Britain as "Sterling and His Dog," the vaudevillian was depressed over the dim prospect of obtaining more bookings when he bade goodbye to his wife, "Lillian the Beauty," and set sail March 16, 1912, from Liverpool aboard the Cunard Liner *Campania* bound for New York. Accompanied by his trick dog "Patsy," Sterling became so despondent that, unable to sleep, he had to be sedated by the ship's surgeon. On March 23, 1912, Sterling went berserk in the ship's hospital, screaming at an orderly: "I will kill every man on board. Go and bring me ten of the biggest men you have, and I will kill them first, and then send in the rest in batches. You shall remain to the last." When the frightened orderly returned with the doctor and six sailors to strap the vaudevillian into a straitjacket, they found the door barricaded. When they finally gained entry, Sterling's lifeless body was hanging from an iron pipe in the bathroom, a torn bedsheet twisted with rope fastened around his neck. Later that day he was buried at sea some 20 miles east of Nantucket. The ship's butcher reported great difficulty in preventing "Patsy" from jumping overboard to be with her master. The dog was subsequently returned to England under the immigration regulations.

Stern(ova), Miroslava see Miroslava

Stevens, Inger

Born Inger Stensland in Stockholm, Sweden, on October 18, 1934, the actress who would capture America's heart as "The Farmer's Daughter" on the popular sixties television show of the same name was 13 when she emigrated to the United States with her recently divorced father, who was studying at Harvard on a Fulbright scholarship. Although not knowing a word of English, Stevens quickly mastered the language and spoke without an accent. Deeply disturbed by her father's remarriage and relocation of the family to Manhattan, Kansas, the 16-year-old girl ran away and was working in a Kansas City, Missouri, burlesque revue

INGER STEVENS— Born in Stockholm, Sweden, Stevens parlayed a will to succeed and wholesome sexiness into a film career lasting from 1957 (*Man on Fire*) to 1969 (*A Dream of Kings*). Best known for her role as "Katy Holstrum" on the ABC television series *The Farmer's Daughter* (1963–1966), the 35-year-old actress was set to do another series when she took her life on April 30, 1970, with a combination of barbiturates and alcohol at her home in the Laurel Canyon section of Los Angeles.

under the name of "Kay Palmer" when she was found and returned home. Two years later upon graduating from high school, Stevens went alone to New York City where she supported herself as a chorus girl in the Latin Quarter while attending acting classes at the famed Actors Studio.

Statuesque, dimpled, and exuding a wholesome sexiness, Stevens landed several television commercials while also performing in summer stock theatre. In 1955, Stevens married her agent, Anthony Sogilo, but the couple separated after four months. They divorced in 1958. In 1956, her first Broadway appearance in the short-lived play *Debut* led to numerous television acting roles (*Philco Playhouse, Kraft Theatre, Zane Grey Theater*).

On the strength of a role in *Playhouse 90* Stevens was brought to Hollywood in 1957 to audition for a role in the film *The Tin Star*. Although judged too young for the part, Stevens was cast opposite Bing Crosby that year in her screen debut, *Man on Fire*. A highly publicized affair with her much older co-star ended when Crosby married actress Kathryn Grant later in 1957. In 1958, Stevens made two films, *Cry Terror* and *The Buccaneer*, before logging her first suicide attempt on New Year's Day 1959. Apparently distraught over a failed relationship, Stevens washed down 25 sleeping pills with ammonia, and remained blind for two weeks before recovering. In 1963, Stevens scored her biggest professional success when she landed the role of "Katrin 'Katy' Holstrum" in the ABC television series, *The Farmer's Daughter*. Based on the 1947 movie of the same name, the series ran until September 1966 and made Stevens a household name. From 1966 until her death, Stevens appeared in eight movies including *A Guide for the Married Man* (1967), *Firecreek* (1968), *Hang 'Em High* (1968), and *A Dream of Kings* (1969).

The 35-year-old actress was set to star in another television series, *The Most Deadly Game*, to begin filming in the summer of 1970 when years of personal unhappiness led her to take her life on April 30, 1970, in the house she shared with friend Lola Mae McNally in the Laurel Canyon section of Los Angeles. McNally returned home at 10:00 A.M. after spending the night out to find the negligee-clad Stevens face-down and semi-conscious on the kitchen floor. Stevens was pronounced dead on arrival at Hollywood Receiving Hospital. The autopsy revealed that the actress had swallowed a 2,000 milligram dose of the barbiturate Tedral, a prescription drug she kept for asthma relief, as well as a large amount of alcohol. It was revealed shortly after her death that Stevens had been secretly married to black musician Isaac "Ike" Jones since 1961.

Stewart, Iain Maxwell

Prominent in the Scottish shipbuilding industry, Stewart was also the director of Scottish Television, the central commercial station in Scotland. With actor and fellow countryman Sean Connery, the industrialist also helped set up the Scottish Educational Trust, an organization designed to help young Scots further their careers. Stewart, 69, was recuperating from two cancer-related operations at his country home in West Hoathly, Sussex, England, when he shot himself in the head on December 18, 1985. A shotgun was found near the body.

Stewart, Jay

During a career that spanned some 50 years in radio and then television, Stewart (real name Jay Fix) announced for numerous shows including *The Kate Smith Evening Hour* (1951–1952, NBC). Best known, however, as the popular announcer for the NBC game show *Let's Make a Deal*, which premiered on daytime television in 1963, Stewart was a fixture on the program until leaving in 1976. In one of the show's regular features, "Jay's Tray," Stewart carried a tray featuring a concealed prize into an audience dressed in wacky costumes. Often, Stewart would join the act as a booby prize by dressing up as a baby in a playpen during the show's climax when contestants were asked to choose one of three doors concealing prizes. After retiring from announcing, the 71 year old became an agent for emcees and announcers, specializing in game shows. On September 17, 1989, Stewart ended his life with a self-inflicted shotgun wound to the head outside the garage of his home on Grace Street in Hollywood. While contents of a suicide note were not released, Stewart's agent was quoted as saying that in the note, "Jay said he had been hurting for a long, long time."

Stierheim, Christopher

Despite lacking any formal training, Stierheim spent seven years acting in local theatre productions in the Pittsburgh, Pennsylvania, area. In early 1994, the 29-year-old actor starred in The Upstairs Theatre production of *The Normal Heart*, a serious drama about AIDS. The critically heralded performance was followed by a starring role in the theatre's production of *Jeffrey*, a humorous look at the epidemic. In the late afternoon of September 28, 1994, midway through the play's four-week run, Stierheim hanged himself from the door of his bedroom in his Shadyside apartment near Pittsburgh. He left no note.

According to friends, Stierheim (who was gay) was emotionally unaffected by the subject of the plays and did not suffer from the illness. Rather, he remained depressed over the unexpected death of his mother when he was a senior in high school while increasingly despondent over his failure to financially support himself as an actor. As an unpaid actor in community theatre, Stierheim supported himself by waiting tables and other odd jobs. Toward the end of his life the actor had been reduced to selling his clothes and jewelry to pay for rent and food. On the day of his death, Stierheim called his roommate to report that he had lost the key to a disabled man's apartment for whom he was working part time as a personal attendant. The key would cost $37 to replace, money he did not have. A distraught Stierheim told his roommate, "I'm no good. I'm worthless. I can't even hold on to

someone's key." One hour after calming Stierheim over the phone, the roommate returned to their apartment and discovered the actor's body. Stierheim was cremated and his ashes scattered in a grove of oak trees on the family farm in Adamsburg, Westmoreland County, Pennsylvania, near those of his mother.

Storer, Edna

The wife of radio program writer and producer Douglas F. Storer had been depressed for years over the mental illness of their 9-year-old son, John. On November 6, 1941, Douglas Storer returned home from work shortly before midnight to find a tragic scene of murder-suicide in the attached two-car garage of his home at 80 Barnard Road in the exclusive Beechmont Park section of New Rochelle, New York. Opening the door of the garage, the headlights from his car fell across the body of his son slumped on the floor. Nearby he found the body of his 44-year-old wife on the front seat of her car with its engine still running.

Storm, Rory

Storm (real name Alan Caldwell) founded the Hurricanes in 1957 and by 1960 they had established themselves as the most popular rock band in Liverpool, England. As lead singer for the band, Storm was an energetic performer whose onstage antics included climbing over the equipment and hanging from the rafters in clubs. In 1960–1961, the band signed drummer Richard Starkey who, as Ringo Starr, left the Hurricanes in 1962 to record with The Beatles. Though still a popular stage act throughout Britain, Rory Storm and the Hurricanes were overshadowed by the recording success of The Beatles.

The band broke up in 1967 after the death of bassist Ty Brian from complications following a recent appendectomy. Storm variously worked as a disc jockey in Benidorm, Spain, and reportedly as a ski instructor until chronic insomnia coupled with a chest condition led to his retirement in the early seventies. On September 28, 1972, shortly after the death of his father, the 33-year-old singer and his mother, Violet, committed suicide together by ingesting massive amounts of sleeping pills at their home in Broadgreen, Liverpool. A note was found near their bodies. Storm's sister later burned his extensive collection of memorabilia at the family home, "Stormsville."

Street, Mel

Born King Malachi Street near Grundy, West Virginia, on October 21, 1933, the popular country singer began performing on local radio in the fifties while supporting himself as a construction worker and auto mechanic. Street was 39 in 1972 when his 1970 song "Borrowed Angel" was re-released and became a country hit. Over the next six years, the singer recorded 12 Top 20 hits including some of the biggest "cheating songs" in country music history ("Lovin' on Back Streets," 1972; and "Forbidden Angel," 1974). Beset by personal problems and a crushing tour schedule of some 200 one night stands a year, Street became an alcoholic and sank into a dark depression.

On the morning of October 21, 1978, his 45th birthday, Street breakfasted with his wife and his brother and sister-in-law at his home at 268 Anderson Lane in Hendersonville, Tennessee. Suddenly excusing himself, he walked up the stairs to his bedroom, placed a .38-caliber revolver in his mouth, and pulled the trigger. The singer was rushed to Nashville Memorial Hospital where he died at 11:10 A.M. Ironically, his latest single written by Wayland Holyfield, "Just Hangin' On," was a ballad about a man near the end of his emotional rope. Country legend George Jones sang "Amazing Grace" at his friend's funeral in Woodlawn Memorial Park in Nashville on October 24, 1978. Three years after his death, a 1981 album advertised on television, *Mel Street's Greatest Hits*, sold 400,000 copies.

Strickland, David Gordon, Jr.

Strickland (born October 14, 1969, in Glen Cove, New York) was raised in Prince-

ton, New Jersey, until his family moved to Pacific Palisades, California, while he was in high school. At school Strickland devoted his energies to acting and binge drinking. After graduation, in lieu of college he wrote comedy sketches and acted with a theatre company in Los Angeles. To gain experience, Strickland acted for no pay in some 64 student films while supporting himself with odd jobs. Reportedly, he was fired from a part-time job at a health club for drinking. In 1995, Strickland struck paydirt with recurring roles in the television sitcoms *Roseanne, Sister, Sister,* and as "Hollis Pavelle," Paul Reiser's co-worker, in the NBC comedy hit *Mad About You.* In 1996, he landed the role of "Todd," a madcap music critic, on the NBC sitcom *Suddenly Susan* starring Brooke Shields.

Strickland, who played the role for three seasons and was set to return for a fourth, earned more than $35,000 a week on the hit series. Career success, however, did little to curb his manic depression and drinking. In October 1997, during the second season of *Suddenly Susan*, cast members noticed that their usually upbeat colleague was irritable. The next month, the actor disappeared overnight in a manic alcoholic episode that brought his binge drinking to light. In January 1998, Strickland was hospitalized after slashing his wrists in what doctors termed a "serious suicide attempt." Diagnosed as a manic depressive and placed on lithium to control his wild mood swings, the actor sought to counter the anti-depressant's side-effects (sluggishness and weight gain) by drinking. Alcohol only intensified the depression and during his manic episodes Strickland took to hanging out in the seedy parts of LA in search of cocaine. Soon he quit taking the medicine completely.

In October 1998, Strickland was arrested for possession of crack cocaine and sentenced to a three year drug diversion program. Despite religiously attending Alcoholics Anonymous meetings and receiving the suport of his fellow actors and girlfriend, *Beverly Hills, 90210* star Tiffani-Amber Thiessen, Strickland could only manage to remain sober for a few weeks at a time. In 1999, the sitcom star was looking forward to his appearance in the Dreamworks film *Forces of Nature* starring Ben Affleck and Sandra Bullock. While Strickland had appeared in the 1998 independent film *Delivered*, this was to be his first supporting role in a major motion picture. However, after viewing the final cut of the film Strickland was devastated to see that most of his screen time had been edited out of the finished product.

On Saturday, March 20, 1999, the 29-year-old actor was in what doctors call "rapid cycling," a state of increasing and uncontrollable mania in which extreme highs are followed rapidly by crushing lows. Following a night of nonstop crack smoking, cocaine snorting, and drinking, a sleepless Strickland left Los Angeles for Las Vegas on Sunday with newfound friend Andy Dick, a comedian and cast member of the sitcom *NewsRadio*. By late Sunday night the pair were in Vegas drinking beer chased with shots of tequila in the Girls of Glitter Gulch, a lap-dancing strip bar on Fremont Street. Shortly after 2:00 A.M. on Monday, March 22, Strickland and Dick moved to Cheetah's, another lap-dancing bar, where an employee later described them as "totally wasted." After the pair separated sometime after 4:00 A.M., Strickland paid $65 for a room in the Oasis Motel, an adult establishment with hourly rates in a sleazy area off the main Strip known locally as Sin City. Strickland walked to a nearby 7-Eleven, purchased a six pack of Coors, and chatted briefly with a prostitute before returning alone to his room.

Later that day around 11:00 A.M., the night manager's wife entered Room 20 to find Strickland (fully dressed in blue jeans, shirt, and running shoes) hanging by a knotted bedsheet from an exposed ceiling beam. After finishing off the six pack, the actor had lined up the bottles in a straight line on the floor, constructed a noose out of a queen-sized bedsheet, tied one end around his neck and the other to the beam, stepped up on a chair, then kicked it away. The morning of his death,

Strickland was scheduled to have appeared before a municipal court judge in Los Angeles to report his progress in a court-ordered narcotics education program stemming from his drug arrest in 1998.

FURTHER READING

Fleming, Charles. "Fallen Star." *TV Guide*, 47(23): 40–42, 48–49, June 5, 1999.

Styles, Patricia

On May 28, 1947, the pretty 23-year-old actress, radio singer, and daughter of West Coast radio producer-entertainer Hal Styles swallowed a handful of sleeping pills in Hollywood after Nate N. Sugarman, 44, terminated their stormy four year romance. Styles survived and continued to see the wealthy investment broker, but was shattered when Sugarman announced at a party in early December 1948 that he planned to marry a San Francisco radio singer. On December 13, 1948, Styles called Sugarman and asked him to drive her to a girlfriend's house in the San Fernando Valley.

During the drive through North Hollywood, they discussed Sugarman's upcoming wedding, and Styles told her former lover that she was engaged to marry a doctor. At her request, Sugarman stopped the car in front of a house at 11816 Riverside Drive. Styles produced a .32-caliber revolver, shot the businessman in the thigh and skimmed his head with a second shot. In the struggle for the gun, the pair fell into the street where Sugarman disentangled himself, and fled as Styles continued to fire after him. According to one witness, the actress then placed the pistol in her mouth, fired, and fell dead in the street next to the car.

A cryptic pencilled note found by authorities in the dead woman's purse read: "I'm going to lose any and all deep-rooted inhibitions and completely lose any self-consciousness that I might have…. And that I'm going to become rightfully self-confident so that I fear nothing or no one so that competition doesn't phase [*sic*] me in the least." Refusing to believe that his daughter had committed suicide, Hal Styles demanded a "full investigation." Despite conflicting eyewitness testimony, a coroner's jury ruled that Patricia Styles had taken her life after attempting to kill the man who had jilted her.

MARGARET SULLAVAN— An award winning stage actress who was equally accomplished in films like *Three Comrades* (1938) and *The Shop Around the Corner* (1940), Sullavan possessed a tempestuous personality that took a toll on her private life. Married four times, her first marriage to actor Henry Fonda in 1931 lasted less than two years. On January 1, 1960, Sullavan was found dead from an overdose of barbiturates in a New Haven, Connecticut, hotel room. Though the death of the 50-year-old actress was ruled accidental, Sullavan had recently been under a doctor's care for depression and a degenerative hearing loss.

Sullavan, Margaret Brooke

Born into a well-to-do society family in Norfolk, Virginia, on May 16, 1909, Sullavan attended the E. E. Clive Dramatic School in Boston. At 17 she made her professional stage debut with the University Players. On December 25, 1931, she married Henry Fonda, a fellow actor in the company, at the Kernan Hotel in Baltimore. The marriage ended in 1933 with Fonda later commenting that living with the mercurial Sullavan "was like living with lightning." Fonda's second wife, Frances Seymour Brokaw Fonda (see entry), would later cut her throat in a mental institution in Beacon, New York, on April 14, 1950.

After appearing in supporting roles in four Broadway flops, Sullavan took over the lead in *Dinner at Eight* in 1933. That same year, Universal signed her to a lucrative film contract initially casting her opposite John Boles in *Only Yesterday*. Sullavan's other films include *Little Man, What Now?* (1934), *The Good Fairy* (1935), *Next Time We Love* (1936), *The Shopworn Angel* (1938), *The Shop Around the Corner* (1940), *The Mortal Storm* (1940), *Back Street* (1941), *Cry Havoc* (1943), and *No Sad Songs for Me* (1950). In 1938, she won the New York Film Critics best actress award for her performance in *Three Comrades*. Though an excellent actress (especially in tearful melodramas), Sullavan's quick temper and obvious dislike of Hollywood continually put her at odds with the studio. During these periods, the actress returned to Broadway where she continued to deliver stand-out performances. In 1943, she was given the Donaldson Award for best lead performance in the John van Druten comedy *The Voice of the Turtle*.

Offstage, Sullavan's tempestuous personality took its toll in her private life. Marriages to film director William Wyler (1934–1936) and agent Leland Hayward (1936–1948), which produced three children, including actress-author Brooke Hayward, ended in divorce. In 1950 she married British industrialist Kenneth Wagg. While continuing to act onstage (*The Deep Blue Sea*, *Sabrina Fair*, *Janus*), Sullavan began experiencing degenerative hearing loss in the forties. Though she hid the condition from colleagues, her fear of missing cues made the actress even more nervous, moody, and withdrawn. On December 28, 1959, the 50-year-old actress opened in the play *Sweet Love Remembered* at the Shubert Theatre in New Haven, Connecticut. Broadway-bound, the play received lukewarm reviews, but Sullavan's performance was lauded. As the week progressed, the actress became increasingly nervous. At Sullavan's request, husband Kenneth Wagg arrived at her fifth floor room in New Haven's Taft Hotel to comfort her. A badly shaken Sullavan told him that she was "tired and exhausted" and "fed up with show business."

On the afternoon of January 1, 1960, Wagg conferred with the show's producers, Henry Margolis and Martin Gabel, at the Taft Hotel. At 5:30 P.M., he returned to Sullavan's room to wake her for the evening's performance. When she failed to respond, he summoned hotel staff to break down the locked and chained door. They found the actress lying in bed, unconscious, the open script of the play beside her. Sullavan was later pronounced dead on arrival at Grace–New Haven Community Hospital. Several half-filled bottles of Seconal were found in the room. There was no note, although a doctor who had treated her during the preceding week reported that Sullavan had been "nervous, depressed, and hysterical at the theatre." Sullavan's death from barbiturate poisoning was

officially ruled an "accidental death." According to the coroner, though the actress died of barbiturate poisoning it was "not such a massive overdose as one would expect in a suicide attempt."

Sullavan bequeathed her temporal bones (including the inner, middle, and outer ears) to the Lempert Institute of Otology for scientific study. The actress was cremated and her ashes interred in the White Chapel Protestant Episcopal Church Cemetery near Lively, Virginia. On October 18, 1960, Sullavan's 21-year-old daughter, Bridget Hayward, committed suicide with an overdose of sleeping pills in her three-room apartment at 135 East Fifty-fourth Street in New York City. Hayward left a note to her boyfriend saying, "This was the best way out."

FURTHER READING

Hayward, Brooke. *Haywire*. 1st ed. New York: Knopf, 1977.
Quirk, Lawrence J. *Margaret Sullavan: Child of Fate*. 1st ed. New York: St. Martin's Press, 1986.

Sutch, David Edward

Known in rock 'n' roll circles as "Screaming Lord Sutch," this true eccentric was a colorful fixture on the British political scene for nearly 40 years. Born in West Hampstead, England, on November 10, 1940, Sutch was 10 months old when his father, a Reserve policeman during World War II, was accidentally killed during a blackout. Though forced to raise her son in poverty in a flat on a dead-end street in Kilburn, Sutch's mother often took him to music halls and movies. After dropping out of school in 1956, Sutch took a job as a window cleaner while pursuing his real love of music. In 1959, the 18 year old fused his twin fascinations, horror movies and rock 'n' roll, into the group Screaming Lord Sutch and the Raving Savages. At one time or another, some of Britain's best young musicians (Jeff Beck, Jimmy Page, Nicky Hopkins) served their apprenticeship in his backup band.

As Screaming Lord Sutch, the young rocker based much of his over-the-top stage persona on "Screamin' Jay" Hawkins, a Cleveland-born blues shouter known for his provocative songs and wacky onstage antics. In 1961, Sutch was spotted by independent music producer Joe Meek, who recorded the performer's single "'Till the Following Night" and others ("I'm a Hog for You Baby") in his combination apartment and studio above a shop in London's Holloway Road. Meek (see entry) would later kill his landlady and then himself there on February 3, 1967.

Describing his act as "rock and roll vaudeville," Sutch crafted his show to be the ultimate in bad taste. After performing tunes like "My Big Black Coffin" and "All Black and Hairy," Screaming Lord Sutch often closed his show with his composition "Jack the Ripper." Outfitted in a black top hat, dark purple cloak, white opera gloves, and carrying a Gladstone bag filled with knives, scalpels, and syringes, Sutch chased a scantily clad girl around stage brandishing a knife. Stabbing the girl, he placed her "dead" body on an operating table, then dissected the cadaver removing previously purchased pig's hearts as his victim's vital organs.

In 1964, Sutch attempted to enter politics by standing for Parliament against Prime Minister Harold Wilson in the Huyton district. Running on a platform that promoted knighthood for The Beatles and an end to discrimination against long hair, Sutch's nomination papers were rejected. Shortly afterward, he launched the Official Monster Raving Loony Party famed in England for its campaign slogan "Vote for Insanity — You Know it Makes Sense." Though rejected for public office a record-setting 39 times over the next 30 years, Lord Sutch (he became one by deed poll) brought a much needed sense of humor to stodgy British politics. Campaigning in a grotesque top hat and gold lamé suit, the rocker cum politician broadcast his outrageous policies over a rusty bullhorn. While Loony proposals like forcing joggers and the unemployed to power a huge treadmill as a means to generate cheap electricity were dismissed as lunacy, the party was successful in realizing some of its agenda after its issues were embraced by the political mainstream. Loony policies voted into law included securing the vote for 18 year olds, all day Sunday pub openings, licensing for commercial radio, and passports for pets. In 1985, the government greatly increased the registration fees for British candidates in order to discourage zanies like Lord Sutch from running for office.

Over the years, he had lost hundreds of thousands of pounds by polling less votes than the minimum number required to retain his deposits. The rocker absorbed the massive losses by performing up to 250 shows a year. A lifelong manic depressive and insomniac who took Prozac for both conditions, Sutch was traumatized by the death of his mother in 1997, and more recently that of his beloved Yorkshire terrier, Rosie. Ten days before his suicide, the politician told his friend Cynthia Payne, a former brothelkeeper, not to worry about him. "I shall be on the front pages next week," he assured her. On June 16, 1999, the 58 year old was found by his fiancée, Yvonne Elwood, hanging by a multi-colored jump rope on the stairs of his late mother's home in South Harrow, northwest London. According to police Sgt. Stephen Burns, the house was so cluttered with old newspapers, suitcases, and litter that he had to clamber over several metal filing cases stored in the hallway to reach the body suspended from a staircase bannister. Two suicide notes dated June 14 and 15 signed "Lord David E. Sutch" were found; one was on a downstairs table, the other in a bedroom. Elwood, 41, testified at the inquest that Sutch had been "severely depressed" most of the time. The last entry in the musician's diary (written the day before his death) read: "Depression, depression, depression is too much."

Dr. William Dolman, the Hornsey coroner, officially ruled the death a suicide and commented: "He was a comedian with tragedy in his heart.... His life was a tragic comedy which came to a sudden end, [which] he obviously planned. The entertainment and fun he brought many, in what one might call the sometimes unsavoury world of politics, I hope will be remembered longer than the events of this June." At the time of his death, Lord Sutch was Britain's longest serving party leader. A spokesperson for Prime Minister Tony Blair's office issued the following statement: "Screaming Lord Sutch will be much missed. For many years he made a unique contribution to British politics. Our elections will never be quite the same without him." In a colorful funeral ceremony blending solemn hymns with a recording of Chuck Berry's "Roll Over Beethoven," Sutch was buried in St. Paul's Church in South Harrow on June 28, 1999.

FURTHER READING

Sutch, David, and Chippindale, Peter. *Life as Sutch: The Official Autobiography of a Monster Raving Loony.* London: HarperCollins, 1991.

Swift, Charles A.

Swift, 43, sports director for radio station WIP–Philadelphia since 1965, was the voice of the Philadelphia Eagles football team for nine years. One hour after wrecking his car on December 7, 1977, Swift shot himself with a .22-caliber pistol above his right ear in the dining room of his condominium in the Philadelphia suburb of Media. The veteran play-by-play man left no note. Friends who dined with Swift earlier in the evening said he did not appear depressed. Six months earlier, Swift had paid a $78 fine for wrecking his car under the influence of alcohol. He had recently contracted to broadcast Philadelphia 76ers basketball games on a New Jersey television network. According to Swift's widow, their 16-year-old daughter had awakened from a sound sleep the day before her father's suicide and announced, "Daddy's dead."

Taintor, Katherine Grey

Described by European police as "the mysterious American lady," the one-time New York City chorus girl was wanted in Brussels, Paris, Geneva, and Rome as part of an international gang that preyed on members of European royalty and high society. Taintor had previously served terms in French, German, and Belgian prisons for swindling when she was arrested in Zurich, Switzerland, in early 1924 on a charge of fraud involving $60,000. On May 31, 1924, days before her trial was set to begin, the ex-showgirl was found hanging from the window bar of her cell in Zurich Jail by a cord fashioned from her silken undergarments interwowen with strands of her own hair.

Tandler, Adolph

The Viennese-born Tandler moved to Los Angeles in 1908 and for several years played with a string quartet in the Alexandria Hotel. In November 1913 he became the conductor of the Los Angeles Symphony Orchestra, the forerunner of the Philharmonic, a position he held until the orchestra's dissolution in 1920. Professionally, Tandler returned to Germany to serve as the conductor of the International Music Festival in Salzburg, became the conductor of the American Chamber Symphony in 1934, and played viola with the Philharmonic Orchestra until retiring in 1951. On September 30, 1953, the bodies of Tandler, 78, and his 50-year-old daughter Hedwig, crippled by arthritis since age 14, were found in a parked car on a hillside in the Eagle Rock section of Los Angeles where the pair had often driven to enjoy the view. A hose led from the car's exhaust pipe into the closed interior of the auto. Tandler left three notes, one of which lamented that he was unable to make his wife happy.

Tannehill, Frank H.

A stage actor for more than half a century, Tannehill, 72, was also a playwright (*Nancy Hanks*) before retiring to manage theatres in the South and, more recently, to work for the Vaudeville Managers Protective Association. On February 5, 1932, he was in apparent good spirits when he entered the Elks

Club at 108 West Forty-third Street in New York City. Tannehill went to the roof solarium where shortly after 1:00 P.M. he plunged eight floors to his death, landing on a fourth floor roof extension. The medical examiner listed the death as a suicide.

Tasker, Robert Joyce

While serving a five-year sentence for robbery in San Quentin, Tasker (born 1903) wrote an account of prison life, *Grimhaven*, published by Knopf in 1928. Based on the book's success, he became a Hollywood screenwriter after his release. Tasker's screenplays include *Secrets of the French Police* (1932; starring suspected suicide Gwili Andre [see entry]), *Hell's Highway* (1932), *Doctor X* (1932; co-starring suicide Arthur Edmund Carew[e] [see entry]), *A Notorious Genteleman* (1935), *Back Door to Heaven* (1939), *The Secret Seven* (1940), *The Affairs of Jimmy Valentine* (1942), and *Secrets of the Underground* (1943). In 1942, he relocated to Mexico City to work for various film producers. Following a quarrel with his wife there on December 7, 1944, the 41-year-old screenwriter intentionally took an overdose of sleeping pills.

FURTHER READING

Tasker, Robert Joyce. *Grimhaven*. New York: A. A. Knopf, 1928.

Taylor, Donald F.

The sixth husband of want-to-be sex symbol Marie "The Body" McDonald, Taylor produced the 1963 sex farce *Promises! Promises!* starring his wife and Jayne Mansfield, who appeared nude in the Tommy Noonan-directed film. Despite a massive publicity campaign that touted McDonald's impressive physical dimensions, the blonde glamour girl never achieved star status. On October 21, 1965, Taylor found his 42-year-old wife's lifeless body slumped at her dressing table in their ranch-style home in the Hidden Hills section of Hollywood. An initial coroner's inconclusive finding of suicide or accidental death by

"acute drug intoxication" was later ruled "accidental" based on a review of McDonald's past life and normal pattern of living.

On January 3, 1966, Taylor, 47, was found dead in the same house at 5337 Jed Smith Road by his 16-year-old stepdaughter and her boyfriend. His fully-clothed body was discovered lying on the floor alongside his bed. An empty bottle of Seconal was found on the nightstand. Taylor left two handwritten suicide notes and a will instructing that his mother be given the remainder of his estate after the payment of all bills. In a note addressed to Robert N. Hirte, his business partner in the Marie McDonald, Inc., cosmetics firm, Taylor wrote: "Please go on with the cosmetics business. It was Marie's fervent desire to give women a product that would do them some good at a reasonable price." The fact that the note was dated two days before the discovery of his body led police to believe that Taylor actually took his life on January 1, 1966.

Taylor, Geneste ("Gene") R.

Educated in Oxford and known on radio for his courtly British vocal mannerisms, Taylor, 56, hosted a nightly 8:00 to midnight "middle-class music" show on KIKI–Honolulu. On September 24, 1957, the disc jockey, complaining of a cold, cut short his show and returned to his apartment at 2533-D Ala Wai Boulevard. One day earlier, Taylor's 26-year-old wife had followed the advice of her attorney and checked into a luxury hotel on the island following a quarrel with her husband of less than five months. Unable to reach him by phone, the woman returned to their apartment on September 25 to find Taylor dead from an overdose of sleeping pills slumped against the living room wall near a six foot rack containing hundreds of classical records. Though police did not release the contents of the disc jockey's suicide note, Mrs. Taylor told *The Honolulu Advertiser* that it read: "My own darling Jane: You said you don't love me, so I'm going to set you free. Please call my son. I'll be waiting for you on the other side."

Taylor, Mae Linnie

A grandchild of Blue Cloud, a Cherokee Indian war chief, and the daughter of Colonel R. Clay Crawford, commander of a negro regiment in the Civil War, Taylor was featured as "Blue Cloud" in her trick shooting act with the travelling 101 Ranch Show. She had also toured extensively in a one act piece called *A Child of the Prairie*. Depressed by a long illness, the 30-year-old performer laid on the bed of her New York City apartment at 247 West Thirty-eighth Street on July 18, 1916, and self-administered gas through a tube. In a note found at the scene, Taylor begged her husband of many years for forgiveness.

Tearle, Malcolm

Born into a renowned British acting family that had been continuously onstage since 1712, the youngest brother of Godfrey and Conway Tearle was unable to match their theatrical success. Though he recently appeared with brother Godfrey in the play *The Unguarded Moment*, Tearle was unemployed when the show closed and still smarting from a bitter divorce from film actress Roma Lynette. On December 7, 1935, the 47-year-old actor was found dead in a gas-filled room at Lamb's Conduit Street, Theobalds Road, London.

Teed, James

The former vaudevillian, who with wife Mary Lazell made up the team of Lazell and Teed, shot himself at his Bay Shore, Long Island, home at 36 O'Neil Avenue on March 18, 1938. Friends reported that Teed had been depressed ever since the death of his wife a year earlier.

Tellegen, Lou

Tellegen (born Isidor Louis Bernard Van Dammeler in Holland on November 26, 1881) first gained prominence on the Paris stage in 1909 as Sarah Bernhardt's leading man. He accompanied the actress on her highly lauded American tour and in 1911 starred opposite "the Divine Sarah" in his first film role, *La Dame aux Camelias*. Tellegen co-starred with her in two other films, *Adrienne Lecouvreur* (1912) and *Queen Elizabeth* (1912), before the latter helped launch him as a film star in America.

Known for his classic profile and Apollo-like physique, Tellegen was an early screen idol and a prototype of the ultra-sophisticated screen lover in such films as *Flame of the Desert* (1919), *The World and Its Woman* (1919), and *The Woman and the Puppet* (1920), all which co-starred his second wife, Geraldine Farrar. Other Tellegen films include *Let Not Man Put Asunder* (1924), *Parisian Love* (1925), *Womanpower* (1926), *Married Alive* (1927), and *No Other Woman* (1928, directed only). Tellegen's onscreen reputation as a lover (he starred in some 26 films in the thirties) mirrored his private life. He married four times and was estranged from his last wife, actress Eva Casanova, at the time of his death.

As the twenties ended, the aging actor's career hit the skids. Tellegen filed bankrupty in 1929 and, by the early thirties, was willing to accept any screen work. Despite enduring three operations in 1934, Tellegen was pinning his comeback hopes on a major role in the Fox film *Caravan*. Before he could report to work, however, ill health forced him back into the hospital. The lead in the film was ultimately given to fellow suicide Charles Boyer (see entry). On October 29, 1934, less than a month before his 53rd birthday, Tellegen was recuperating in the home of a lady friend at 1844 N. Vine Street in Hollywood. That morning, after refusing breakfast, Tellegen locked himself in the bathroom. Clad in a flannel robe, he carefully shaved, and applied makeup to his face. The faded star knelt down on a pillow and plunged a pair of three-inch sewing scissors seven times into his chest. According to friends, in addition to health and career woes, Tellegen feared that he was losing his mind. Informed of her late husband's death, Farrar responded, "It doesn't interest me in the least." Following a funeral reception

LOU TELLEGEN— The Dutch-born actor was one of Hollywood's first screen lovers, a role he also played off-screen in four failed marriages. A prototype of the ultra-sophisticated ladies' man in films of the teens and twenties, Tellegen saw his career end with the advent of the thirties. Broken in spirit and health, the 52-year-old actor stabbed himself to death with a pair of scissors in the Hollywood home of a lady friend on October 29, 1934.

paid for by his actor friends and attended by many women admirers of the former screen idol, Tellegen's body was cremated in accordance with his final wishes and the ashes scattered over the Pacific Ocean.

FURTHER READING

Tellegen, Lou. *Women Have Been Kind: The Memoirs of Lou Tellegen.* New York: The Vanguard Press, 1931.

Tembo, Biggie

Born Rodwell Marasha in Chinhoye, Mashonaland, on September 30, 1958, the composer-guitarist-singer formed the Bhundu Boys in Zimbabwe in 1980. Exponents of "Jit," a musical form described by *Los Angeles Times* pop music critic Robert Hilburn as a "roots-conscious form of Zimbabwe pop seasoned with a strong Caribbean lilt and Louisiana bayou R&B," the Bhundu Boys were "discovered" in 1986 by Gordon Muir, a Scots graphic artist who became enthralled by them after hearing advance tapes of their album *Shabini*. In mid–1986, Muir brought them to Scotland for a few small club dates where their dynamic live shows garnered them rave reviews by critics, underground radio play, and a legion of dedicated fans. The band subsequently toured extensively in England and in 1987, at Madonna's request, opened in front of 70,000 for the "Material Girl" at her Wembley Stadium show in London.

Just as international success seemed a certainty for the Bhundu Boys, Tembo, the group's primary composer and front man, was asked to leave by fellow band members fed up with his moodiness and inflated self-opinion. The dismissal spelled the end for both Tembo and the band. The Bhundu Boys fared badly without him, eventually losing three band members to AIDS-related diseases. Tembo returned to Zimbabwe and tried to regain his success with the veteran Harare group, the Ocean City Band. Though popular in Zimbabwe, Tembo was no longer an international celebrity. He slipped into bouts of depression, underwent psychiatric treatment for several years, and turned to Christianity. On July 30, 1995, Tembo hanged himself in a Harare hospital where he had been admitted for mental problems compounded by a stalled career and a catastrophic family crisis. As a suicide, Tembo forfeited his right to a customary traditional burial.

Tenco, Luigi

A former faculty member of the electronic engineering department at the University of Genoa, the protest singer was one of the few Italian composers of light music who had resisted the "beat" vogue. On January 26, 1967, Tenco and his performing partner, Dalida, presented his composition "Ciao, Amore, Ciao" ("So Long, My Love, So Long") on the opening day of the 17th San Remo Song Festival in Italy. One hour after a jury vote eliminated the protest ballad during the festival's first trial heat, the 28-year-old singer shot himself in the head with a pistol in his room in San Remo's luxurious Savoy Hotel. Dalida (see entry), herself a suicide in 1987, found his body at 2:30 A.M. the next day. A note near his body read: "I do this not because I'm tired of life but as an act of protest against a public that votes for 'Me, You and the Roses' as a finalist and against a commission re-selecting 'La Rivoluzione.'"

Theobald, Dolly

Dubbed the "smallest soubrette on the American Stage," the 36-year-old entertainer used a two-barrelled derringer to shoot herself through the heart in her room at the Star Hotel in Columbus, Ohio, on December 18, 1906. A player in *McFadden's Flats*, Theobald had quarreled earlier in the evening with her husband, Howard Powers, manager of the company, over his attentions to other women. Powers' attempt to placate his jealous wife with promises of a pony, a cart, and a diamond ring only made the tearful woman more despondent. Prostrated by the suicide, Powers was kept overnight in a sanitarium and released to friends the next day.

Thies, Henry R., Jr.

Thies (born in Chicago, Illinois, in 1893) became known in Detroit, Michigan, as a "boy wonder" on the violin and rapidly rose to lead his own orchestra in one of the city's top hotels. In 1926, the orchestra leader brought his stylish brand of symphonic jazz to Cincinnati where appearances at the Chatterbox Club led to a devoted following on local radio. Well known on the Ohio hotel circuit, Thies also toured on vaudeville and performed in theatres. In the early thirties, he left the road to become the orchestra leader for Cincinnati radio station WLW. Following a nervous breakdown in 1933, Thies took an overdose of sleeping pills and survived, but spent 15 months under observation in a sanitarium. Thies was apparently in good spirits after arriving at his home in the Phelps Apartment at 506 East Fourth Street in Cincinnati shortly after 6:00 P.M. on June 12, 1935. While his wife, 19-year-old son, and a musician-friend waited dinner for him in the dining room, Thies went to the bathroom to change. The 41-year-old orchestra leader stood in front of a long mirror, placed the muzzle of a .32-caliber pistol in his mouth, and pulled the trigger.

Thirkield, Robert Leeming

A stage actor who created roles in *Futz* and the Lanford Wilson plays *Balm in Gilead, Hot l Baltimore, The Mound Builders*, and *The Rimers of Eldritch*, Thirkield was best known in the theatrical world for co-founding (with producer Marshall Mason) Northwest Productions in 1964, and in 1969, the Circle Repertory Company with Mason, Wilson, and then wife Tanya Berezin. From 1982 to 1986, Thirkield was associate artistic director of River Arts Repertory in Woodstock, New York. On July 9, 1986, the 49-year-old actor jumped to his death from his Manhattan apartment.

FURTHER READING

Ryzuk, Mary S. *The Circle Repertory Company: The First Fifteen Years.* 1st ed. Ames: Iowa State University Press, 1989.

Thirsk, Jason Matthew

Original bassist and co-founder of the Hermosa Beach, California-based hard core punk combo Pennywise (named after the Stephen King killer-clown in the 1986 novel *It*), Thirsk, 27, left the band in early 1996 citing personal problems that left him reluctant to tour. On July 29, 1996, the former bassist's girlfriend found him dead from a gunshot wound to the head in his home in Hermosa Beach. Police estimated that he had been dead for a day. Although Thirsk had been deeply depressed for months over his estrangement from the band, a spokeswoman for Pennywise's label, Epitaph Records, put a different spin on his death. As an autopsy confirmed that the bassist had been drunk when he died, the label suggested that his death was accidental. The official press statement from Pennywise: "Although he was not performing with the band recently, his spirit was always with us & we hoped for him to return to the line-up soon. Jason's positive & uplifting lyrics are what defined our band, and attracted fans to Pennywise all over the world. We loved him very much & he will be greatly missed."

Thomas, Olive

The "world's most beautiful girl" was born Oliveretta Elaine Duffy in Charleroi, Pennsylvania, on October 20, 1898. Raised in an industrial section of Pittsburgh, she quit school at 14 and two years later on April 1, 1913, married Bernard McKee Thomas, a timekeeper in a local steel mill. The marriage ended in divorce on February 28, 1915, amid charges of cruelty and neglect directed by Olive Thomas against her husband. Shortly afterward, Thomas left Pittsburgh to pursue a modelling career in New York. To support herself, she worked as a $3.00 a week salesgirl at a department store in Harlem.

Stunningly attractive, Thomas also modelled for noted illustrator Harrison Fisher in 1915. Armed with a letter of introduction from Fisher, the 17-year-old beauty presented herself to Florenz Ziegfeld. Ever vigilant in his search for feminine pulchritude, the master showman signed the 17-year-old Thomas to a $75 a week contract and put her in his *Midnight Frolic* and *Follies*. Thomas was soon the toast of Broadway and hyped as the "world's most beautiful girl." In constant demand as an artist's model, the showgirl graced the covers of *Vogue* and *Vanity Fair,* and posed nude for Peruvian artist Alberto Vargas. In 1916 she left the *Follies* to appear in her first film, episode ten of the International/Wharton serial *Beatrice Fairfax.* Thomas signed a contract with Triangle Pictures and over the next couple of years established herself in films like *Madcap Madge* (1917), *An Even Break* (1917), *Limousine Life* (1918), *Betty Takes a Hand* (1918), *Heiress for a Day* (1918), and *Love's Prisoner* (1919). In 1919, the actress signed a lucrative contract with Myron Selznick (brother of David O. Selznick) to appear exclusively in films produced under the new Selznick Pictures banner. Thomas became a major star on the strength of *The Glorious Lady* (1919), *Upstairs and Down* (1919), *Everybody's Sweetheart* (1920), *The Flapper* (1920), *Footlights and Shadows* (1920), and *Youthful Folly* (1920).

At age 21, Thomas appeared to have a limitless future. Already acknowledged as one of the world's most beautiful women, it had taken her less than five years to establish herself as one of the most popular stars in all of movies. On the personal front, her April 1917 marriage to actor Jack Pickford, brother of top star Mary Pickford, was seemingly a happy one. Fan magazines dubbed them "The Ideal Couple." In reality, the marriage was marred by Jack Pickford's womanizing and drug and alcohol abuse. Donald Crisp, a fellow actor at Biograph, described Pickford as "a drunk before he was a man." In yet another attempt to fix their rocky marriage, the couple planned a second honeymoon in Paris in late 1920. Days before embarking on the *Imperator* from New

York harbor on August 12, Thomas took out a $300,000 life insurance policy on herself naming Pickford as the sole beneficiary. On their arrival in Paris, the couple checked into a luxurious suite in the Hotel Ritz and launched themselves into a nonstop whirlwind tour of decadent Montmartre nightlife.

Thomas evidently attended several parties with what *The Los Angeles Examiner* later called "the wildest of the Paris young set." Both Pickford, 24, and Thomas, 21, were well-known habitués of the Dead Rat, an after hours club in Montmarte where drug abuse and other forms of vice were the standard bill of fare. At around 4:00 A.M. on Monday, September 6, 1920, Thomas returned to their suite at the Ritz after a night of carousing. Pickford, who had remained at the hotel, was reportedly resentful and angry over his wife's activities. The couple argued and Thomas went into the bathroom. What occurred next is a matter of conjecture. The distraught actress drank three-quarters of a bottle of a liquid bichloride solution that was apparently clearly marked on the label as "for external use only." Thomas reportedly screamed, rushed to the bedroom, and told Pickford, "I've taken poison, goodbye, Jack." Pickford attempted to induce vomiting by forcing his wife to drink hot salt water and bicarbonate of soda until an ambulance arrived and took the poisoned actress to the American Hospital at Neuilly-sur-Seine.

Over the next five days, Thomas languished in a semi-coma interrupted by lucid moments of incredible pain. She died in Pickford's arms on September 10, 1920. In the ensuing media frenzy, Paris was condemned as a veritable Sodom and Gomorrah where a certain type of American came to give themselves over to corruption. Rumors swirled around Pickford's alleged drug use and the role, as sole beneficiary of his wife's large life insurance policy, he may have played in her death. The bereaved Pickford maintained that Thomas had mistakenly taken the poison thinking it was a sleeping solution. The death was officially ruled accidental. The "world's most

beautiful girl" was interred in the Pickford mausoleum in Woodlawn Cemetery, Bronx, New York. In 1922, Jack Pickford married former *Ziegfeld Follies* showgirl and Broadway musical star Marilyn Miller. She divorced him in 1927 claiming that he beat her. Pickford married his third *Ziegfeld Follies* girl, Mary Mulhern, in 1930. Terrified of his drunken and physically abusive moods, Mulhern ended the marriage in 1932. Pickford, 36, died either of neuritis, gastrointestinal problems, or a heart attack in Paris on January 3, 1933.

FURTHER READING

Whitfield, Eileen. *Pickford: The Woman Who Made Hollywood.* Lexington: University Press of Kentucky, 1997.

Thompson, Carlos

Thompson (real name Juan Carlos Mundin Shafter Thompson) was 16 years old in 1939 when he made his film debut in Argentina with *Y mañana serán hombres*. The handsome actor of German descent established himself as a lead in several important Argentinian films (*El crimen de Oribe*, 1950; and *El Tunel*, 1952) before his political opposition to dictator Juan Peron forced him to leave the country. In Hollywood from 1953, Thompson (with fellow actor Fernando Lamas) became the epitome of the suave Latin lover appearing opposite such screen beauties as Yvonne De Carlo (*Fort Algiers*, 1953), Lana Turner (*The Flame and the Flesh*, 1953), and Eleanor Parker (*Valley of the Kings*, 1954). In the mid-fifties, Thompson was working in European films when he met actress Lilli Palmer. They married in 1957 and settled in Switzerland. After appearing in his last film in 1966, *La Vie de Chateau*, Thompson turned to writing and television production. Following Palmer's death from a heart attack in 1986, the actor became increasingly withdrawn and depressed. Ending a four decade absence from his native Argentina, Thompson settled in the upscale neighborhood of Barrio Norte in Buenos Aires in September 1990. On October 10, 1990, the

67-year-old actor fatally shot himself in the head in his apartment. Two notes, one to his agent the other to his business partner, gave no reason for the action.

Thompson, Edith

The singer first gained public attention in 1910 when, with only six days' notice, she replaced an ill performer at a concert given by the Boston Symphony at the Sanders Theatre. Based on that success, the Newton, Massachusetts-based music teacher enjoyed a steady career as a concert artist and soloist with the Boston Symphony Orchestra. Thompson, 38, was busily preparing for an upcoming recital when overwork resulted in an apparent nervous breakdown. In Newton on August 13, 1925, the singer's drowned body was found a few feet offshore floating in a foot of water in an area known as Rubber Neck Cove on the Charles River, opposite Norumbega Park.

Thompson, Hallett

The veteran stage actor, also known as Frank Hallett Thompson, slashed his wrists and arms with two razors in his apartment at 552 Riverside Drive in New York City on August 12, 1938. Hallett, 67, was found unconscious in an easy chair facing a window overlooking the Hudson River. He died two days later in Harlem Hospital.

Thompson, Jack

Hobbled by a career-ending injury to a tendon in his right leg, the popular 32-year-old musical comedy and vaudeville dancer in shows like *Peggy Ann* and *A Connecticut Yankee* announced his decision to kill himself at a party in his Manhattan Towers apartment on the night of November 3, 1931. No one took the threat seriously and Thompson was permitted to leave the apartment. The dancer remained missing until December 5, 1931, when a badly decomposed body was fished out of the East River. A former roommate recognized the expensive imported shoes on the corpse's feet

as those of the dancer. Ironically, the "floater" was not positively identified until the surgeon who performed the unsuccessful surgery on Thompson's tendon confirmed the position of the scar on the body's right leg.

Thorne, Thomas

In a case of life imitating art, the 24-year-old stage actor presumably hanged himself in his room at the Alexandria Hotel in Chicago on March 11, 1910, because he was unduly influenced by a part he was playing in the production *The Fourth Estate* at the Studebaker Theatre. In the play, Thorne acted the role of a newspaper reporter who covered the suicide of a woman who could no longer bear the ghastliness of life.

Tibbetts, William Nelson

Known in the theatrical world as "William Stafford," the 45-year-old stage actor spent several years playing in stock companies and vaudeville throughout the country. During the summers, Tibbetts lived as a virtual recluse in Marblehead, Massachusetts. It was there on September 11, 1912, that the thespian's body was found in his room at 7 Hooper Street with a bullet wound over his heart and a .32-caliber pistol on the bed beside him. An opium kit was nearby. Authorities discovered an envelope containing $143 in cash and a note to his former mother-in-law asking her to bury him in Marblehead. Tibbetts' father, a well-known Boston stockbroker, had committed suicide 20 years earlier after losing $60,000 in a single day of speculation.

Todd, George M.

The body of the former manager of two Cleveland, Ohio, vaudeville theatres, the Lyceum and the Prospect, was found early on the morning of December 15, 1913, draped across his son's grave in Oak Grove Cemetery on the outskirts of Morenci, Michigan. Worried over financial and family matters, Todd drained an entire bottle of poison before shooting himself in the head.

Todd, Seumas

The youngest son from British actor Richard Todd's 22 year marriage to ex-model Virginia Mailer was a first year student at Northumbria University studying politics. Though his parents divorced in 1992, they still shared the same manor house at Little Ponton, near Grantham, Lincolnshire. On December 8, 1997, Todd, 20, returned home from the university for a weekend visit, left his bags in the hall, and went directly upstairs to his bedroom. After arriving home later that evening, Virginia Mailer noticed the bags, and went to her son's room. She found him dead on his bed from a head wound, the butt of a 12-gauge shotgun between his feet. A note simply stated that he "could not cope." In light of other suicides in Britain connected to the anti-acne drug Roac-cutane, Richard Todd, 78, was convinced that it was a strong factor in his son's death along with financial problems and school stress. Fearful of facial scarring after a severe case of chicken pox, the younger Todd was using the drug at the time of his death. Ironically, when the veteran actor was 19 his mother committed suicide while staying at her parents' home in Ireland. Clad only in a night-dress, she went out late one night and froze to death sitting on the bank of a river.

Todd, Thelma

In the dark history of Hollywood the un-natural death of screen star Thelma Todd in 1935 ranks with that of Jean Harlow's husband Paul Bern (see entry) in 1932 as one of Tinseltown's most enduring mysteries. Born the daughter of a corrupt civil servant father and an aggressive domineering mother, Alice, in Lawrence, Massachusetts, on July 29, 1906, Todd was by all accounts a strikingly beautiful child. By her teens, she was already well on her way to earning her Hollywood nickname "Hot Toddy" by dressing provocatively and "innocently" flirting with older men. After

graduating high school, she enrolled in 1923 in Lowell State Normal School, one of the most prestigious teachers' colleges in the East. During the summers, Todd worked as a part-time fashion model at a local theatre where her stunning good looks attracted much attention. In 1925, Alice Todd forced her 19-year-old daughter to enter the Miss Massachusetts beauty contest. Todd won and was instantly approached by a talent scout for Paramount and the Famous Players–Lasky studios. After passing a screen test, she signed a five year, $75 a week contract with Paramount, and took acting lessons at the studio in Astoria, New York.

In 1926 she made her film debut in the silent *Fascinating Youth* featuring Clara Bow. Later that year, she and her mother relocated to Hollywood where Paramount kept the actress busy in a variety of roles. By late 1928, Todd had appeared in more than a dozen films for Paramount and on loan-out to Warner Bros., First National, Columbia, and Hal Roach Studios. Though wanting to become a serious dramatic actress, Todd showed a flair for comedy unusual in such a beautiful woman. Hal Roach, after seeing her in the 1928 First National comedy *Vamping Venus*, signed her to a $75 a week deal in 1929. The king of motion picture comedy, Roach had Laurel & Hardy and Charlie Chase under contract and made the popular *Our Gang* series. While the contract with Roach permitted Todd to work for other studios with his approval, it also contained the bane of Hollywood actresses: the dreaded "potato clause." The contract option permitted the studio to unconditionally release an actress if her weight went up by more than five pounds over her original weight when she signed the contract. Todd was forced to starve herself and pop diet pills to fulfill her contractual obligation. The result — the beautiful young comedienne became addicted to amphetamines.

Under Roach, Todd blossomed into a comedienne with impeccable timing. Her first film for the comedy giant, the 1929 Laurel & Hardy talkie *Unaccustomed as We Are*,

Brother, MGM, 1933). In 1929, Todd was paired with comedian Charlie Chase in *Snappy Sneezer*. The duo clicked, on and off screen, and the actress was soon making $500 a week appearing with Chase in comedy shorts like *Crazy Feet* (1929), *The Real McCoy* (1930), *All Teed Up* (1930), *Dollar Dizzy* (1930), *Looser than Loose* (1930), *High C's* (1930), *The Pip from Pittsburgh* (1931), *Rough Seas* (1931), and *The Nickel Nurser* (1932).

Roach, however, wanted his studio to have a female comedy team that rivalled his success with Laurel & Hardy. In 1931 he teamed Todd, now making $2,000 a week, with ZaSu Pitts in *Let's Do Things*. The film's commercial success launched a series of Todd-Pitts shorts that included *Catch as Catch Can* (1931), *The Pajama Party* (1931), *War Mamas* (1931), *On the Loose* (1931), *Seal Skins* (1932), *Red Noses* (1932), *Strictly Unreliable* (1932), *The Old Bull* (1932), *Show Business* (1932), *Alum and Eve* (1932), *Sneak Easily* (1932), *Asleep at the Feet* (1933), *Maids A La Mode* (1933), *The Bargain of the Century* (1933), and *One Track Minds* (1933). Pitts left Roach in 1933 over a salary dispute and was replaced by comedienne Patsy Kelly in a series of shorts with Todd directed by suicide victim Gustave Meins (see entry). Todd-

THELMA TODD— Todd signed with Hal Roach in 1929 and became a first-rate comedienne in films with Charlie Chase, Laurel & Hardy, ZaSu Pitts, and Patsy Kelly. Known in thirties Hollywood as "Hot Toddy," the hard-partying actress purchased her own restaurant, "Thelma Todd's Sidewalk Cafe," in the Pacific Palisades section of Los Angeles in August 1934. When the 29-year-old actress resisted crime boss Lucky Luciano's efforts to establish a casino there, her body was found on December 16, 1935, in a car parked in a garage in the hills above the cafe. Though Todd's death from carbon monoxide poisoning was officially ruled "accidental," many now believe that she was murdered. *Courtesy of University of Southern California, on behalf of the USC Library Department of Special Collections.*

established Todd's physical look (dyed blonde hair) and screen persona (sexy, but tough). She made three other films with Stan and Ollie: *Another Fine Mess*, 1930; *Chickens Come Home*, 1931; and *Fra Diavolo* (a.k.a. *The Devil's*

Kelly pairings include *Beauty and the Bus*, 1933; *Back to Nature*, 1933; *Air Fright*, 1933; *Babes in the Goods*, 1934; *Soup and Fish*, 1934; *Man in Hollywood*, 1934; *I'll Be Suing You*, 1934; *Three Chumps Ahead*, 1934; *One Horse*

Farmers, 1934; and *Done in Oil*, 1934. In addition to her work with Roach, Todd also appeared in two Marx Brothers films for Paramount, *Monkey Business* (1931) and *Horse Feathers* (1932).

By the early thirties, "Hot Toddy" was well known in Hollywood as a hard working, hard drinking party girl who was always up for a good time. In 1931 she met Pasquale "Pat" DiCicco, an agent with mob connections, at a studio party at the Palace Theatre. Their marriage in July 1932 was marked by DiCicco's unexplained absences and his routine acts of physical violence against the popular actress. Through DiCicco, Todd met mob kingpin Charles "Lucky" Luciano who was in Los Angeles to oversee his interests in gambling, drugs, prostitution, and restaurant-union infiltration. By the time Todd divorced DiCicco in March 1934 on the grounds of mental cruelty, she was already deeply involved with Luciano. In August 1934, Todd and sometime lover Roland West purchased a three-story building on Roosevelt Highway (now Pacific Coast Highway) in Pacific Palisades. West, married to fading actress Jewel Carmen, had directed Todd in the 1931 dramatic flop *Corsair* starring suicide Chester Morris (see entry). West and Todd opened "Thelma Todd's Sidewalk Cafe" on the first floor of the building and maintained separate apartments on the second floor to hide their affair. The half-storied third floor was used as a storeroom. West and wife Carmen (who supplied the money for the cafe) lived in a house above the restaurant on Posetano Road. The couple's palatial home, Castillo del Mar, had a two car garage with an apartment above at 17531 Posetano Road situated below the house. On-foot access from the rear of the restaurant to the garage above where Todd and West kept their cars was gained by a flight of 270 cement steps snaking up the hillside.

Based on Todd's star power, the restaurant quickly became a favorite meeting place for celebrities, studio folk, and those interested in hobnobbing with the stars. As Hollywood legend goes, Luciano began putting pressure on Todd to force her to lease him the cafe's unused third floor as a site for a mob controlled gambling casino catering to the Tinseltown elite. Todd resisted even though the mob was already supplying the restaurant's liquor, steaks, and linen service at inflated prices. Despite overflow crowds of well-heeled customers, the cafe never turned a profit. By December 11, 1935, Luciano's insistence that the 29-year-old comedienne lease him the third-floor space for gambling reached the point where Todd called the office of Burton Fitts, the Los Angeles district attorney, for assistance. Proven by history to have been as corrupt as anyone he ever prosecuted, Fitts agreed to see Todd on December 17, 1935. In a bid to block Luciano, the actress publicly announced plans to convert the third floor area into a steakhouse.

Meanwhile, the Todd-West relationship had deteriorated to the extent that the jealous former director had taken to giving the hard partying actress a 2:00 A.M. curfew. If Todd failed to return to her second floor apartment by that hour West locked down the building. On Saturday, December 14, 1935, Todd and West argued about her plans to go alone to the Cafe Trocadero to attend a party for British comedian Stanley Lupino, father of film actress Ida Lupino. West sternly warned her that the building would be locked up at 2:00 A.M. whether she was home or not. Todd, dressed in a blue satin, sequined evening gown and mink stole, was chauffeured to the Trocadero by driver Ernest Peters. She arrived at 8:15 P.M. Ex-husband Pat DiCicco was there with a date, but Todd spoke with Ida Lupino instead about a wonderful new man in her life who lived in San Francisco. Todd was in high spirits the entire evening, but according to party-goers her mood changed dramatically after making a phone call to an unknown person shortly after 1:45 A.M.

Todd remained at the party until around 3:00 A.M. when Peters arrived to drive her back to her apartment. During the trip back, the terrified star urged Peters to drive faster. He later told authorities that he had reached speeds in excess of 70 miles per hour on the Roosevelt Highway. When they arrived at the cafe around 3:30 or 4:00 A.M., Todd dismissed Peters. As he drove away, he saw her walking in the direction of the cement steps leading up the hillside to the two-car garage above on Posetano Road.

At 10:00 A.M. on Monday, December 16, 1935, almost two days after the actress left for the party at the Trocadero, her maid, Mae Whitehead, arrived at the garage on Posetano Road to drive Todd's car to the rear of the cafe. Noticing that the right garage door was open about six inches, Whitehead entered the garage to find her employer's body wedged between the front seat and the steering wheel of her chocolate brown 1934 Lincoln Phaeton, the apparent victim of carbon monoxide poisoning. Todd, still dressed in the gown and mink she wore to the Trocadero, exhibited injuries not immediately associated with accidental or intentional carbon monoxide poisoning. Further examination revealed bruises on her neck, a broken nose, two cracked ribs on her right side, and a chipped front tooth. The coroner explained that the neck bruising was due to "post-mortem lividity" caused by the involuntary jerking of the neck immediately before death. The bloody lip and broken bones were the result of Todd's falling into the steering wheel and door during her death throes. A blood sample revealed a 70 percent carbon monoxide saturation and determined that the actress had been legally drunk at the time of her death.

The theory was advanced that Todd, after being dropped off at her locked apartment on Sunday morning, spent the rest of Sunday, December 15, somewhere before choosing to sleep in her car in the early morning hours of Monday. She apparently ran the car's engine to stay warm and, inebriated, died when overcome by exhaust fumes. However, Charles Smith, the cafe's treasurer who lived with his wife in the apartment above the death garage, testified at the inquest that he did not hear or smell anything during the hours she was supposed to have been dying of carbon

monoxide poisoning. Numerous people in different parts of Los Angeles spoke of seeing Todd at various times on Sunday in the company of a well-dressed male companion. A Christmas tree salesman in Santa Monica reported that he saw her around 11:45 P.M. that night.

Alice Todd, Thelma's stage door mother, initially claimed that her daughter had been murdered. Several other people took her view, but experienced mysterious memory lapses when called to testify at the inquest. Mae Whitehead flatly told officials that anonymous men had threatened her with harm if she chose to speak about any possible mob involvement in the cafe. Andy Edmonds, in her provocative book *Hot Toddy*, suggests that Todd was murdered on Luciano's orders and offers a plausible chronology of events and scenario that explains the movie star's untimely death. If nothing else, Edmonds points out the numerous inconsistencies in the official handling of the case.

On December 19, 1935, thousands of friends, fans, and curiosity seekers filed past Todd's open casket at Pierce Brothers Mortuary between 9:00 A.M. and 1:00 P.M. Later that afternoon, a private funeral service attended by close friends and family was conducted at the Wee Kirk o' the Heather Chapel at Forest Lawn Cemetery in Glendale. The remains of the "Ice Cream Blonde" were cremated and presented to her mother, Alice. Following Alice's death in 1969, the funeral urn containing the actress' ashes was placed in her mother's coffin and buried in the Bellevue Cemetery in Lawrence, Massachusetts.

FURTHER READING

Edmonds, Andy. *Hot Toddy: The True Story of Hollywood's Most Sensational Murder.* 1st ed. New York: William Morrow, 1989.

Townsend, William H.

On March 28, 1933, Townsend, a 60-year-old English actor and radio performer, wrote a note to his landlord apologizing for "causing trouble," then turned on the gas in his one room apartment at 62 West Sixty-ninth Street in New York City. Friends of the actor reported that he had been depressed since the death of his wife a year and a half earlier.

Toye, John

After ten years in the theatre, Toye joined Scottish Television (STV) in 1976 as anchor for the evening news program *Scotland Today*. Ten years and some 3,000 programs later, the newscaster was removed when network executives decided to revamp the show in 1986. Toye briefly remained with STV presenting *What's Your Problem*, a weekly consumer program. As his career declined, Toye began to drink, once even admitting himself to a hospital for a month to control his addiction. Fined for drunk driving and threatened with jail time should he be convicted again, Toye tried to rebuild his life in Scotland's West Country. In 1990, he moved into a flat above a charity shop in the Devon village of South Molton and started to look for work. In two years, the 56-year-old former anchorman landed only occasional work in news programs and a voice-over assignment for a television documentary.

On the afternoon of April 29, 1992, the rector of the church where Toye sang in the choir received a letter from him stating that he intended to kill himself. The rector hurried to Toye's flat, which was already jammed with police who had been summoned there by a concerned friend of the former newscaster. Breaking into the flat, authorities found Toye in a sitting position with a gunshot wound to his head and a double-barreled shotgun beside him. Near the body was a glass and an empty bottle of wine. Copies of a recently drafted will, a handwritten note, a sealed package for a friend, and a bundle of sheet music were also recovered. Once asked how he would like to be remembered, Toye had responded: "Just as a nice guy who tried to do a good job."

Traina, Nicholas John Steel

The adopted son of best-selling romance writer Danielle Steel, Traina suffered neurological damage from birth, was lithium dependent, and had been in and out of hospitals for mental illness and attention deficit disorder since he was 11. Despite being under the daily care of Julie Campbell, the former director of the adolescent program at Newbridge Foundation in Berkeley (a chemical dependency program), Traina worked for a season as a television reporter and was lead singer of the punk band Link 80 for two and a half years. Recently, he had started a new band called Knowledge. A manic depressive, the 19-year-old singer had attempted to overdose on heroin three times since October 1997. On September 20, 1997, Traina's body, clad only in boxer shorts, was found leaning against the bed in the apartment he shared with full-time therapist Campbell in Pleasant Hill, a suburb of San Francisco, California. A syringe, a cotton ball, and a spoon containing burnt heroin residue were found nearby. An autopsy report concluded that Traina's blood, in addition to containing normal ranges of the prescribed antidepressant Prozac, also exhibited a level of morphine, a heroin byproduct, within the "toxic to fatal range." Apparently the singer had not been taking the prescribed level of lithium for his manic depression. While Steel characterized the incident as an accidental drug overdose, Campbell believed it was intentional: "I think he knew no matter how good today is, he would always have the pain of tomorrow because he was depressed. I think his life was a suicide note. His songs, his tapes, they all had pain in them."

FURTHER READING

Steel, Danielle. *His Bright Light: The Story of Nick Traina*. New York: Delacorte Press, 1998.

Troutman, Larry

The Hamilton, Ohio, native, with brothers Roger, Lester, and Tony, co-founded the funk band Zapp in Dayton, Ohio, in

1978. Though not performing on the band's 1980 Warner Bros. release *Zapp*, Troutman did play congas on their second album, *Zapp II*, in 1982. The first album produced the popular single "More Bounce to the Ounce" and marked Troutman's younger brother, Roger, as the band's star performer and creative force. In that 1980 hit, Roger Troutman's vocals were sung through a vocoder or talkbox, a voice distorting device that had already been used effectively in rock music by Joe Walsh ("Rocky Mountain Way," 1973) and by Peter Frampton ("Do You Feel Like We Do," 1976).

Roger Troutman continued his influential funk career throughout the eighties and nineties. Recording as "Roger," Troutman reached Number 3 on the *Billboard* singles chart in 1987 with "I Want to be Your Man." In the mid-eighties, older brother Larry essentially left performing to manage Zapp and to assume the presidency of the brothers' Dayton-based company. Troutman Enterprises, formed in 1980 to train unskilled workers and to create jobs for them in Dayton, was composed of three recording studios, real estate ventures, and contracting businesses. Nicknamed "Dollars," Larry Troutman was at the helm of the company when it filed for bankruptcy in 1992 seeking relief from a $3.8 million debt and more than $400,000 in delinquent taxes. In 1996, a judge issued a preliminary ruling stating that the case should be switched from bankruptcy reorganization to a liquidation. As Troutman Enterprises crumbled around its president, Roger Troutman's career was resurging. In 1996, he added his vocoder sound to the Dr. Dre–produced Tupac Shakur hit "California Love." That same year, Warner Bros. released a second greatest hits album of Zapp material under the band name Zapp & Roger. Troutman also sang back-up to rapper Nature on Dr. Dre's 1997 multi-act disc, *The Firm*, and in 1998 appeared on the track "No Man's Land" on Gerald Levert's CD *Love & Consequences*. He planned to tour in the summer of 1999.

At about 7:20 A.M. on April 25, 1999, Roger Troutman, 47, was found lying in an alley behind Catalpa Drive near the recording studio his family owned in northwest Dayton, Ohio. Four gunshot wounds, two in the front and two in the back, riddled the singer's body. He died shortly afterward at Good Samaritan Hospital and Health Center. A few blocks away in the 2100 block of Harvard Boulevard, police found Larry Troutman's car crashed into a tree. Inside, Troutman, 54, was dead from a single self-inflicted gunshot wound to the head from a .357 Magnum pistol found on the front seat next to his body. Police later determined the weapon had been used to kill Roger Troutman.

While none of the surviving brothers could supply a motive for the murder-suicide, police speculated that business problems combined with friction over Roger's desire to pursue a solo career might have prompted Larry to commit the act. On May 1, 1999, a single funeral service attended by an estimated 4,000 mourners was held for both brothers at the nondenominational Solid Rock Church in Monroe, Ohio. Rufus Troutman, III, a nephew of the brothers who had performed with Zapp, sang a variation of "Amazing Grace" using Roger Troutman's trademark vocoder. The brothers were buried in Greenwood Cemetery in their hometown of Hamilton, Ohio.

Tucker, E. William

Tucker, an accomplished guitarist, songwriter, producer, and remixer who collaborated with groups and individuals like Foetus, Chris Connelly, Revolting Cocks, Ween, Pigface, and My Life with the Thrill Cult, was best known as a member of the Chicago-based industrial music band Ministry from 1989 to 1991. He played keyboards during the group's "The Mind Is a Terrible Thing to Taste" tour in 1989, and in 1999 signed on as a guitarist for their "Dark Side of the Spoon" tour. On May 14, 1999, weeks before the tour was scheduled to begin, the 38-year-old musician was found dead in his Chicago apartment by a roommate. Tucker apparently took an

HELEN TWELVETREES—A stage actress, Twelvetrees received star billing in her first Hollywood film, *The Ghost Talks* (1929). Typecast in a series of weepy thirties melodramas, the actress ended her career as a headliner in 1939 with a star turn opposite Buck Jones in *Unmarried.* Twelvetrees continued to work sporadically onstage in the forties. On February 13, 1958, the 49-year-old actress ingested a fatal dose of sedatives possibly prompted by a painful kidney condition.

overdose of pills and then slit his throat (although some reports listed the cause of death as a self-inflicted gunshot wound). Contents of a ten page suicide note were not revealed. Tucker's associates speculated that the musician took his life to escape years of pain from an undisclosed illness.

Tuckner, Howard

The native New Yorker had been the anchorman and senior correspondent for *The 51st State*, a WNET–New York television news and public affairs program before leaving the station for ABC News. A specialist in foreign affairs, Tuckner filed reports from Southeast Asia and Bangladesh, served as bureau chief in Hong Kong, and was the network's chief correspondent in Johannesburg, South Africa, prior to leaving ABC several months before his death. On June 4, 1980, while under treatment for acute depression, the 48-year-old news journalist jumped to his death from the window of his parents' apartment in the Bronx.

Turner, Irene Laura

Since the 1938 death of her husband, Frank Turner, a theatrical producer, the musical comedy player of 35 years before had little to look forward to except her niece's wedding. On the morning of May 20, 1939, with the wedding only a few hours away, Turner, 58, swallowed poison in her home at 215 Mineola Boulevard in Mineola, New York. She left a note saying that she "only wanted to see the day my niece got married." The bride and groom were not told of the tragedy until after the wedding.

Twelvetrees, Helen

Born Helen Marie Jurgens in Brooklyn, New York, on Christmas Day 1908, Twelvetrees trained for the stage at the American Academy of Dramatic Arts.

Following a brief career as an artist's model, she joined the stock company of the Stuart Walker Players and appeared in *An American Tragedy*, *Elmer Gantry*, and *Roulette*. Unlike most fledgling actresses, Twelvetrees (who took her stage name from her first husband, actor Clark Twelvetrees) received star billing in her first Hollywood film, the 1929 Fox comedy-melodrama *The Ghost Talks*. Typecast in weepy melodramas, the actress jerked tears in *Young Bride* (1932), *Disgraced* (1933), *She Was a Lady* (1934), and *She Gets Her Man* (1935). After performing in some 35 films, Twelvetrees last enjoyed star billing opposite Buck Jones in the 1939 Paramount drama *Unmarried*. She later appeared on stage as "Blanche" in a successful stock company production of Tennessee Williams' *A Streetcar Named Desire*. Twelvetrees was married to her third husband, Air Force Captain Conrad Payne, when she began suffering from a painful kidney condition. On February 13, 1958, the 49-year-old actress was rushed to the hospital on the Olmstead Air Force Base in Harrisburg, Pennsylvania, after she was found comatose in her home from an overdose of sedatives. Twelvetrees' death later that day was ruled a suicide, although she had been taking pills to control her pain.

Utrera, Adolf

"'Just Sang My Last Song' sounds good for a song title…. It is just a plain suicide. I have needed a long rest. And this is probably the longest one I will get." So read the note left by the 30-year-old Cuban pianist and singer-songwriter on December 3, 1931, shortly before he stuffed towels around the doors and windows of his Manhattan apartment at 176 West Eighty-sixth Street and then opened the gas jets on a kitchen range. According to friends, although Utrera had a contract with the Columbia Phonograph Company to make Spanish language records, he was concerned over a recent lack of work and an impending operation.

Van Cott, J. Marston

Van Cott, the son of an assistant Los Angeles district attorney, was the secretary of the Bakersfield Musicians' Union and an insurance salesman. On the morning of October 23, 1937, friends of the 40-year-old musician received two cryptic notes from him indicating that he planned to take his life. In one he wrote, "Ill health got me. My pay checks will take care of everything." In the other he asked that a portion of his money be turned over to his landlady. Hours later, police were called to a knoll overlooking an East Bakersfield, California, residential district by two small boys who reported finding a man slumped over the wheel of an automobile. Van Cott had run a garden hose from the car's exhaust in through a window of the sedan and propped the throttle open until the gas tank went dry.

Van Dyke, Kelly Jean

The daughter of television star Jerry Van Dyke ("Luther Van Dam" in the ABC series *Coach*) and niece of Dick Van Dyke had a long history of drinking and drug abuse. Unknown to her father, she appeared as "Nancee Kellee" in two pornographic videos — *The Coach's Daughter* (1991) and *Club Josephine* (1992). The 33-year-old woman was estranged from her husband, actor Jack Nance, and sharing an apartment on Bellingham Avenue in North Hollywood with friend Lisa Loring, the former child actress who played "Wednesday" on *The Addams Family* television series in the mid-sixties. On November 17, 1991, Van Dyke phoned her husband on location in Madera County, California, threatening to kill herself. Nance notified the Madera County Sheriff's Department who in turn contacted the Los Angeles Police Department. When officers arrived at the Bellingham Avenue apartment 20 minutes later, Lisa Loring had already discovered Van Dyke's body hanging from a rope plant hanger in her bedroom.

Van Norden, Berrick see Schloss, Berrick

Van Riper, Kay

After graduating from the University of Minnesota in 1929, Van Riper came to Los Angeles that same year and landed a job writing scripts for a local radio station. While there, an interest in writing historical novels found expression in her creation of the series *English Coronets*, in which she wrote, directed, and acted. From 1936 until 1944, Van Riper was under contract at MGM as a screenwriter. Eventually, she earned $1,500 a week writing several installments of the studio's popular *Andy Hardy* series; *Judge Hardy's Children* (1937), *Out West with the Hardys* (1938), *Andy Hardy Gets Spring Fever* (1939), and *The Hardys Ride High* (1939). In addition to the Hardy films, the talented scenarist also wrote or collaborated on *Babes in Arms* (1939), *The Harvey Girls* (1946), and others. For 20 years, Van Riper's body had been wracked with spinal arthritis and a sciatic condition of the legs that eventually became unendurable. Forced into semi-retirement by her maladies, the writer tried to end it all with pills on September 14, 1948, but an inhalator squad managed to save her life. On December 31 of that same year, Van Riper's mother found her pajama-clad daughter dead from an overdose of sleeping pills slumped in front of her bed in her home at 1237 Valley View Road in Glendale, California. Authorities listed her death as a suicide although the 40 year old had not left a note.

Van Zandt, Philip

Van Zandt (born in Amsterdam, Holland, on October 3, 1904) began his stage career in New York in 1927 before coming to Hollywood in 1939 to act in the Columbia Pictures prison drama *Those High Grey Walls*. Over the next 20 years, the veteran character actor appeared in some 400 films including *Citizen Kane* (1941), *Cyrano de Bergerac* (1950), the Lon Chaney bio-pic *Man of a Thousand Faces* (1957), and his final film, *The Crooked Circle*, in 1958. On February 16, 1958, Van Zandt, 53, was found dead in his Hollywood apartment at 1225 N. Gower Street. A bottle of sleeping pills was located near his bed.

Varnadore, Thurman and Beulah

On the afternoon of July 20, 1927, occupants of a rooming house at 3832 West Pine Boulevard in St. Louis, Missouri, notified police after smelling gas seeping from a locked third floor apartment. Kicking in the door, police discovered the emaciated, shabbily dressed bodies of Thurman Varnadore, 38, and his 37-year-old wife, Beulah, on the floor near a rubber hose attached to an open gas jet on the stove. The keyhole, windows, and other openings in the sparsely furnished room had been stuffed with rags and paper. The couple, in the final stages of drug addiction, each weighed less than 100 pounds and, according to their landlady, could not walk without supporting one another. In the room, authorities found several hypodermic syringes, a quantity of morphine, and an undated *Variety* clipping announcing that Varnadore, known onstage as "Bud Varn," was presenting a new blackface vaudeville act. The clipping further identified him as a doctor of divinity and an evangelist, a claim substantiated by Varnadore's landlady.

Shortly before the double suicide, Varnadore told the woman that his promising career as an ordained Baptist minister had been devastated when chronic asthma ruined his voice. Turning to morphine to ease the pain, he quickly became addicted as had his wife. Before becoming too weak to walk, Varnadore had tried to make a living selling books door-to-door. At the morgue, a search of Varnadore's pockets uncovered a one cent piece and a wedding ring.

Vega, Carlos

For many years the drummer for singer-songwriter James Taylor, the Cuban-born session musician also recorded and performed with Boz Scaggs, Joni Mitchell, Vince Gill,

Linda Ronstadt, and Olivia Newton-John (including the *Grease* soundtrack). Vega was also a member of keyboardist David Garfield's fusion band Karizma. The 41-year-old drummer had long been battling a drug problem when on April 7, 1998 (one day before he was scheduled to appear live with Taylor on *The Oprah Winfrey Show*), he fatally shotgunned himself in the chest at his suburban home in Los Angeles. Taylor, in a written statement, said: "It has been a great privilege and delight working with Carlos for the past 13 years and wonderful to have collaborated with so talented a player. I miss him terribly as a friend and an artist."

Velez, Lupe

While the probable suicide of cinema sex queen Marilyn Monroe (see entry) in 1962 endures in the public mind as the epitome of Hollywood tragedy, the spectacular death of the tempestuous Lupe Velez nearly two decades earlier is the true stuff of Tinseltown legend.

Velez (born Maria Guadaloupe Velez de Villalobos in San Luis Potosi, Mexico, on July 18, 1908) was the product of the union between a colonel in dictator Porfirio Diaz's army and a one-time diva with the Mexico City Opera. A high spirited youth, Velez was 13 when her parents sent her to Our Lady of the Lake convent in San Antonio, Texas, to be educated. She returned to Mexico two years later following the death of her father in a military action and worked as a salesgirl in a department store to help support her family. Velez was taking dance lessons when she was noticed by a Mexican producer who offered her a feature role at a salary of $350 a week in the musical revue *Ra-Ta-Plan*. Though only 17 and barely 5 feet tall, Velez sported a 37-26-35 figure combined with a fiery and flirtatious personality that made her irresistible to men. She appeared in some Mexican short films and stripped in burlesque before coming to Hollywood in 1925 to audition for a stage production. Though she failed to get the part,

Velez was hired as the feature dancer in the 1927 New York stage production of *The Music Box Revue* starring Fanny Brice. Impressed by the dancer's figure and stage presence, Hal Roach signed her as a "bathing beauty" and cast her in the 1927 Charlie Chase comedy short *What Women Did for Me* and with Laurel & Hardy in *Sailors Beware*. That same year the 19 year old was signed by United Artists to appear opposite Douglas Fairbanks in *The Gaucho*. Velez won rave reviews for her earthy love scenes with Fairbanks and was subsequently signed to a five year contract with the studio.

Cast in a series of fiery and temperamental roles, Velez's most passionate scenes were played out in real life. Variously nicknamed the "Hot Tamale," the "Mexican Wildcat," and the "Mexican Hurricane," Velez cut a wide sexual swath through Hollywood. The list of her lovers reads like a "Who's Who of Hollywood" and included Douglas Fairbanks, Tom Mix, Charlie Chaplin, singer Russ Columbo, Gary Cooper, director Victor Fleming, boxer Jack Dempsey, Fox production chief Winfield Sheehan, Bruce Cabot, Henry Wilcoxon, Red Skelton, Guinn "Big Boy" Williams, Clayton Moore, and writer Erich Maria Remarque. In 1929, Velez met the great love of her life, Gary Cooper, when they starred together in the Paramount film *Wolf Song*. The couple's torrid affair, punctuated by embarrassing public set-tos, ended in 1930 after the physically exhausted Cooper was sent out of the country by the studio to escape the actress. She reportedly fired a gunshot at the actor as his train left the station.

In 1932, Velez met Olympic swimming sensation and *Tarzan* star Johnny Weissmuller while starring on Broadway in Ziegfeld's *Hot-Cha!* opposite Bert Lahr. At the time, the 25-year-old, 6'3" Adonis had already won five gold medals in two separate Olympics. Weissmuller quickly divorced socialite wife Bobbe Arnst and secretly married Velez in Las Vegas on October 8, 1933. In a portent of things to come, she presented Weissmuller with a pair of boxing gloves inscribed, "Darling, so you

LUPE VELEZ— The star of the popular RKO *Mexican Spitfire* series, Velez was one of Hollywood's sexiest and most mercurial women during the thirties and forties. In addition to celebrated dalliances with Gary Cooper, Tom Mix, and singer Ross Columbo, the Mexican-born actress was once married to Johnny "Tarzan" Weissmuller. Velez's suicide in her Beverly Hills home on December 14, 1944, has since become show business legend.

can punch me if I leave you." He needed them. Their stormy marriage lasted until August 15, 1938, and was characterized by public bickering followed by intense reconciliations. Make-up artists on the *Tarzan* set reportedly worked for hours on Weissmuller's body to cover the bruises, scratches, hickeys, and love bites inflicted on him by the passionate Velez.

In 1934, Velez signed a new contract with MGM, but after deciding to no longer target films at the Spanish speaking market, the studio dropped the Mexican star after she completed *Hollywood Party*. Without a contract for the first time in her Hollywood career, Velez went to England in 1935 where she still enjoyed star status. She completed three films (*The Morals of Marcus*, 1935; *Gypsy Melody*, 1936; *Mad About Money*, 1936) and starred in a musical revue (*Transatlantic*

Rhythm) before returning to the U.S. in 1936 to tour vaudeville with Weissmuller. Finding jobs scarce in Hollywood after making the Wheeler and Woolsey vehicle *High Flyers* for RKO in 1937, Velez returned to Mexico where she was still regarded as a national hero. While there she made *La Zandunga* for Film Selectos in 1938. Following her divorce from Weissmuller in 1938, Velez went to Broadway to jumpstart her career in Cole Porter's musical *You Never Know* co-starring Clifton Webb. The show bombed and Velez returned to Hollywood, no longer among the town's top box office draws. In 1939 she made a programmer for RKO, *The Girl from Mexico*, which launched her in the highly popular *Mexican Spitfire* series. As the volatile character "Carmelita" opposite vaudeville-trained Leon Errol as "Uncle Matt," Velez essentially engaged in self-parody in eight films ending with the tragically titled *Mexican Spitfire's Blessed Event* in 1943.

Although RKO signed Velez to a $1,500 a week contract she was still painfully aware that she was now making only a third of the salary she used to command and that in a B-movie series. After completing *Redhead from Manhattan* for Columbia in 1943, Velez announced that she was leaving Hollywood forever to make movies in Mexico. Ironically, the actress would posthumously receive her best reviews for the 1944 Santanda Producers release *Nana* filmed at the Aztec Studio in Mexico City.

In 1943, Velez took 27-year-old French bit player Harald Ramond (Maresch) as her lover. The 36-year-old actress was three months pregnant with Ramond's child when on November 27, 1944, she announced, without his knowledge, that they were engaged to be married. Ramond at first flatly refused to marry his lover, then agreed to a "fake" marriage that would last just long enough to legitimize the child followed by a quick annullment. Velez was stunned and humiliated yet acutely aware that being an unwed mother in Hollywood could spell career suicide. Despite her active sex life, the actress was a devout Roman Catholic who refused to consider abortion as a way out of her predicament. On December 10, 1944, Velez publicly broke off her engagement with Ramond. Three days later, she attended the Hollywood premiere of *Nana* with Estelle Taylor and Benita (Mrs. Jack) Oakie. Afterward, the group returned to Velez's mansion, Casa Felicitas ("Happy Home"), at 732 N. Rodeo Drive in Beverly Hills where the actress served them a spicy Mexican meal. When her guests departed around 3:00 on the morning of December 14, Velez retired to her all-white bedroom that she had filled earlier with bouquets of gardenias, tuberoses, and dozens of lit candles. Her hair and nails already done to perfection, Velez changed into her finest blue satin pajamas, placed two suicide notes on a bedside table, washed down 75 Seconal tablets with brandy, slipped into bed under an eiderdown quilt,

placed her hands across her breasts, and waited for death.

According to the "official" version of events, Velez was found later that morning in this striking movie star tableau by her housekeeper. Noted gossip columnist Louella Parson's wrote, "Lupe was never lovelier as she lay there, as if slumbering ... like a child taking nappy." The "unofficial" story that has since passed into Hollywood legend records a far different final scene. In it, Velez became nauseous from the combination of the spicy meal, Seconal, and brandy and staggered from her bed to the bathroom leaving a trail of vomit across the white carpet. The heavily drugged actress slipped on the bathroom tiles and fell headfirst into the toilet bowl where she was found later that morning.

One suicide note addressed to Harald Ramond effectively killed the Hollywood hopeful's acting career. It read: "May God forgive you and forgive me, too, but I prefer to take my life away and our baby's before I bring him shame or kill him. How could you, Harald, fake such a great love for me and our baby when all the time you didn't want us? I see no other way out for me so goodbye and good luck to you. Love, Lupe." In the other addressed to friend and housekeeper Beulah Kinder, Velez wrote: "My faithful friend, you and only you know the fact for the reason I am taking my life. May God forgive me, and don't think bad of me. I love you many. Take care of your mother, so goodbye and try to forgive me. Say goodbye to all my friends and the American press that were always so nice to me. P.S. Take care of Chips and Chops [her dogs]."

With public opinion firmly against him, Ramond tried to create a cover story that did not make him look like a heel. According to Ramond, he could not marry her immediately because of pressing business engagements. While initially denying that he asked Velez to sign an agreement that would later let him annul the marriage, Ramond admitted that he did so out of momentary anger. The actor further suggested that his unfamiliarity with the English language led the Mexican actress to mistakenly believe he did not intend to marry her. Ramond finally contended that he thought Velez was joking with him when she told him that she was pregnant. Hollywood and the public refused to buy any of Ramond's explanations. His career was ruined.

On the morning of December 21, 1944, the body of Lupe Velez, dressed in a white crepe gown with the chain of a gold crucifix entwined in her fingers, lay in state at the Church of the Recessional at Forest Lawn in Glendale while 4,000 people filed by her open casket. That afternoon, an additional 5,000 mourners, fans, and curiosity seekers repeated the ritual at the Cunningham & O'Connor Mortuary chapel. The body was flown to Mexico City where a crowd of 10,000 mourners (three-quarters men) passed by the casket. Amid a near riot generated by thousands of the star's grief-stricken fans, the "Mexican Spitfire" was buried in the Panteon de Dolores ("graveyard of sorrows") in Mexico City on December 27, 1944. Johnny Weissmuller, Arturo de Cordova, and Gilbert Roland served as honorary pallbearers. Harald Ramond also attended, but kept a low profile. In her will, Velez left half her estate (valued at $160,000) to Beulah Kinder with the remainder to be equally divided among her family. On June 21, 1945, Velez's possessions were disposed of at public auction. The 12 room Spanish style Beverly Hills suicide house fetched $41,750 while the dead star's jewelry went for more than $100,000.

FURTHER READING

Conner, Floyd. *Lupe Velez and Her Lovers.* New York: Barricade Books, 1993.

Vidot, Charlotte

The actress-wife of comedian Clarence C. Kolb, star of the Kolb and Dill vaudeville show *A Peck o' Pickles*, inexplicably swallowed a glass of cyanide of potassium in her room at the St. Dominic Apartments, 980 Bush Street, in San Francisco, California, on March 5, 1915. While Vidot, 37, had been under a doc-

tor's care for nervousness and depression, she never intimated that she was suicidal. Kolb, who cut short his performance at LA's Morosco Theatre, maintained that she had inadvertently taken a fatal dose of the sedative to make her sleep. The pair married in 1902 while playing together in the *Fiddle Dee Dee* company.

Villasenor, Edgar Ricardo

A native of El Salvador, Villasenor moved to Las Vegas in the early sixties, became a naturalized American citizen, and founded the *Weekly Reviewer*. The entertainment-oriented publication evolved into the four-color slick magazine *Las Vegas Star*, which in later years was published as the *Star International*. The publication targeted the entertainment and gambling industries in Las Vegas, Reno, Lake Tahoe, and Atlantic City, New Jersey. Apparently despondent over business problems in recent weeks, the 57-year-old magazine publisher shot himself in the head on April 14, 1990, in his Las Vegas home. Villasenor's body was found by his brother on a couch with the revolver still clutched in his right hand.

Villechaize, Herve

From 1978 to 1983, the diminutive 3 foot, 11 inch actor's shout, "De Plane! De Plane!" signalled the beginning of the popular ABC television series *Fantasy Island*. As "Tattoo," star Ricardo Montalban's cherubic sidekick, Villechaize was a fixture on the show until quitting over a salary dispute a year before the show was cancelled in 1984.

Born in Paris on April 23, 1943, Villechaize was one of four sons of a surgeon and his British wife. Only Villechaize suffered from dwarfism and his early years were spent vainly searching for a cure. In a 1983 proposal for his never published autobiography, the actor wrote: "I was injected with bone marrow from sheep in Germany; I was studied at the Mayo Clinic in America. Then one day when I was 13, I said, 'That's it. I don't want anything done to me ever again.'" After attending the prestigious Beaux-Arts School in Paris, a 20-year-old Villechaize came to New York to continue his art studies. Making little headway as a painter, he answered a newspaper ad seeking "a small person for workshop theatre." This led to off-Broadway acting roles, but Villechaize (despairing that he would forever be typecast by his size) had a card printed that read: "I am not available for Santa's helper or Baby New Year elves. Thank you."

By 1974, Villechaize had been reduced to living in his car when he landed his first major film role as Christopher Lee's sidekick "Nick Nack" in the James Bond adventure *The Man with the Golden Gun*. The picture's success brought the actor to the attention of producers who cast him in *Fantasy Island*. Predictably, Villechaize found little work after leaving the series except for the occasional television guest shot (*The Larry Sanders Show*, *The Ben Stiller Show*) and commercials for Coors beer and Dunkin' Donuts that traded on his past fame as "Tattoo."

As the actor's career disintegrated into parody, his personal life unravelled. During a 1982 divorce from actress Camille Hagan, his second and last wife, she accused the actor of shoving her into a fireplace and firing a pistol at her. In 1985, he was fined $425 after pleading no contest on a gun charge. The next year he was arrested for kicking and threatening a 6'3" man who tried to serve him with legal papers in a court action brought by his ex-wife. In 1988, the actor was sued by his landlord for $3,300 in unpaid rent. The dispute was settled when Villechaize agreed to move out in exchange for not having to pay back rent. Born with undersized lungs, Villechaize endured a lifelong battle with respiratory problems. In 1992, he nearly died during a bout with pneumonia while also suffering from ulcers and a spastic colon.

On September 4, 1993, the 50-year-old actor and his common-law wife, Kathy Self, returned to his North Hollywood home after dining with friends. Self was in bed asleep at 3:00 A.M. when Villechaize walked out onto the back porch, pressed a gun into a pillow covering his chest to muffle the sound, and shot himself. Villechaize tape recorded the event and left a note to Self explaining that although he "loved everybody" he could no longer endure his ongoing medical difficulties. In accordance with the former television star's wishes, no memorial service was performed, and his body was cremated and his ashes scattered at sea.

Vincent, James

Vincent, 53, was the New York stage manager for actress Katherine Cornell and appeared opposite her on Broadway in *The Letter* before coming to Hollywood in the mid-thirties to work as a dialogue director. Though primarily employed by Paramount to work with Bing Crosby, Bob Hope, and Cecil B. De Mille, Vincent was also engaged by MGM in 1936 to act in an "advisory capacity" during the filming of *Romeo and Juliet* starring Leslie Howard and Norma Shearer as the star-crossed lovers. On June 10, 1953, Vincent's body was found floating in the Hudson River near Yonkers, New York. In the water for at least three days, the body bore no marks of violence and was identified through a California driver's license, a Social Security card, and a withdrawal card from the Screen Actors Guild dated April 1952. According to his long-time friend, director George Cukor, Vincent had intimated to him three weeks earlier that he planned to enter a religious institution in up-state New York.

Visaria, Ravi

Visaria, 13, a weekend student at London's Sylvia Young Theatre School where Spice Girl Emma Bunton was groomed for stardom, had appeared in several BBC television and radio productions before landing a small, but coveted, speaking part in the 1995 London Palladium production of *Oliver!* A model teen, the young actor's life began to nosedive in early 1997 after he began sniffing lighter fluid for thrills at his school in Kettering, Northamptonshire. Visaria's parents, concerned over the marked deterioration in their son's appearance and his rebellious attitude, removed all the solvents from their home. Visaria assured them that he had quit, then used his dinner money to buy lighters. On March 29, 1997, 24 hours after angrily walking out during an argument with his parents over his behavior, Visaria's body was found by a passer-by hanging in a woods in Kettering near his home.

Vogel, Patricia F.

Estranged from her husband, film cameraman Paul C. Vogel, the 32-year-old former actress hanged herself with a noose fashioned from two bathroom cords in her apartment at 210-A South Arnez Drive in Beverly Hills on June 25, 1941. In a poignant note to her husband and two young children Vogel explained: "I have struggled so long for health that I'm so tired I can't go on. Everyone has been so kind and helpful and has tried to give me the courage I needed. But I am certain I'll never get better. God keep you all and forgive me."

Vogelsang, Roland F.

A ticket taker for Delmar Garden amusement places, the 25-year-old ex-theatre treasurer and assistant manager swallowed carbolic acid in his St. Louis, Missouri, home on June 27, 1909. Found unconscious in bed by his wife, Vogelsang died in the ambulance en route to the City Hospital. Family and friends could ascribe no reason for the act.

Vollman, William

On March 28, 1941, the 67-year-old president and treasurer of the Cincinnati-based Strand Enterprises, Inc., entered his fourth floor office at 529 Walnut Street and fired two practice shots from a .32-caliber pistol before sending a single shot into his right temple. Conscious when found by an elevator operator, Vollman told authorities that he had shot himself because of ill health and financial stress. Hours later, the manager of the Strand Theatre died on an operating table in the Queen City's General Hospital.

Von Erich Family

The history of America's first family of professional wrestling reads like a Shakespearean tragedy or, more accurately, the *Book of Job*. The family's patriarch, Fritz Von Erich, born Jack Adkisson in Leon County, Texas, in 1931 (some sources report 1929), was a football lineman for Southern Methodist University and briefly played professionally for the Dallas Texans of the National Football League. At 6'4" and 260 pounds, Adkisson was a natural for professional wrestling. Adopting the Teutonic name "Fritz Von Erich," he capitalized on the post–World War II dislike of all things German by fashioning the bad guy image of a goose-stepping, Iron Cross wearing Nazi. Von Erich fashioned his incredible forearm and hand strength into a trademark hold called the "Iron Claw." Once clamped over the face of an opponent, the claw hold induced full-body paralysis. From the late fifties until his retirement from the ring on June 14, 1982, Fritz Von Erich was one of the most popular draws in professional wrestling. Though no longer performing, Von Erich continued to promote wrestling events and oversaw the careers of his sons who followed their father into the "square circle." His tragedy, the so-called "Von Erich curse," would be to live to see five of his six sons die unnatural deaths, three by suicide.

In 1959, seven-year-old Jack Barton Adkisson, Jr., was electrocuted in a freak accident near Niagra Falls, New York while playing in the family trailer. Twenty-five-year-old third born son David Von Erich (David Adkisson), the 6'7" "Yellow Rose of Texas," was wrestling in Tokyo, Japan, when he died of acute enteritis, an intestinal inflammation, on February 10, 1984. Three of his brothers would subsequently commit suicide in the space of six years.

Von Erich, Michael

The fifth son of Fritz Von Erich was born Michael Brett Adkisson in Denton County, Texas, on March 2, 1966. Michael began wrestling in November 1983, and was voted Rookie of the Year in 1984 and Most Inspirational Athlete in 1985 by the readers of *Pro Wrestling Illustrated*. In 1985, the 19-year-old wrestler contracted toxic shock syndrome following a routine operation for a separated shoulder at the Baylor University Medical Center. Michael's temperature spiked to 107 degrees and remained high for hours. Not initially expected to live, Von Erich lost 70 pounds during his month-long hospitalization.

Though recovering, the young wrestler was never again the same either physically or mentally. Depressed by his slow recovery, constant pain, and diminished physical skills, Michael began abusing the tranquilizer Placidyl. Unknown to his family he was obtaining the prescription from two doctors. The 21-year-old wrestler's career and marriage were crumbling when he was arrested in Argyle, Texas, on Saturday, April 11, 1987, and charged with driving while intoxicated, possession of a controlled substance, and misdemeanor possession of less than two ounces of marijuana. He disappeared later that day after posting a $3,500 bond.

Concerned, the Von Erich family visited Michael's apartment in Roanoke and found a handwritten note there telling his brother Chris that he could have his scuba gear. On Wednesday, April 15, 1987, Michael's abandoned 1986 grey Mercury Marquis was discovered on a dirt side road near the entrance of Pilot Knoll Park on Lewisville Lake in Denton County, Texas. An unsigned note on the front seat read: "Mom and Dad, I am in a better place. I'll be watching." At 9:20 A.M. the next day a dog from the Grand Prairie canine corps sniffed out the wrestler's body zipped inside a navy blue sleeping bag in thick underbrush about 600 yards from where his car had been found. A small red canvas bag re-covered at the scene contained his driver's license, billfold, $48 in cash, an asthma inhalator, and other personal possessions. An autopsy determined that Michael committed suicide sometime on Sunday, April 12, 1987, from an acute overdose of Placidyl. Michael Von Erich is buried in Grove Hill Memorial Park in Dallas, Texas.

Von Erich, Chris

According to Dave Meltzer of *The Wrestling Observer*, a national newsletter devoted to the sport, Chris Von Erich felt extreme pressure to live up to the standards of his brothers (Kerry, Kevin, and David) despite lacking their size. The smallest of the Von Erichs at 5'5" and 175 pounds, Chris (born Chris Adkisson in Denton County, Texas, on September 30, 1969) suffered from severe asthma since childhood. Though he worked hard to develop his body through rigorous workouts, the youngest of the Von Erich sons was just too small to compete at the championship level. Plagued by brittle bones, Chris suffered a broken elbow in a match in Dallas in 1991 that was slow to heal. The 21-year-old wrestler, however, continued to compete on small cards.

Early in the evening of September 12, 1991, Chris' older brother, Kevin, and their mother, Doris, tried to comfort the depressed athlete on the grounds of the family ranch near Edom in East Texas. The spot, 100 yards north of the ranch house, was near a mound of Indian relics the family had gathered years before. Kevin and his mother returned home after Chris told them to leave him alone. They returned a couple of hours later around 9:00 P.M. to find that Chris had shot himself in the head with a 9mm pistol. The contents of a suicide note found at the scene were not released. Still clinging to life, the young wrestler was helicoptered to the East Texas Medical Center in Tyler where he died 20 minutes later. An autopsy revealed traces of cocaine and Valium in his system.

Von Erich, Kerry

Von Erich's fourth son (born Kerry Gene Adkisson on February 3, 1960) was known on the wrestling circuit as "The Texas Tornado." Kerry combined a relentless weight room regimen with anabolic steroids to create a musclebound 6'4", 290 pound body. On May 6, 1984, he won the National Wrestling Alliance World Heavyweight Championship, but lost it later that month. On June 4, 1986, the wrestler severely injured his ankle in a motorcycle accident. His right foot was amputated one year later after the bones failed to bond. Fearful that news of the injury would end his career, Von Erich continued to wrestle wearing a prosthetic foot. To maintain the fiction, he arrived at the arena dressed, and after bouts showered with his boots on. Though noticeably limping, the wrestler controlled the constant pain with Novocaine injections. By 1991 Kerry Von Erich's life was falling apart. Addicted to cocaine and painkillers, he was no longer a top wrestling attraction. That year, Von Erich's wife of ten years divorced him, and he was struggling to pay $2,500 a month in support of his two young children. To make matters worse he was in trouble with the Internal Revenue Service. On February 9, 1992, Von Erich was arrested in Richardson, Texas, with six forged prescriptions for the painkiller Vicodin and tranquilizer Valium. Von Erich checked into the Betty Ford Center, pleaded no contest in October 1992, and was sentenced to ten years' probation. On January 13, 1993, he was placed under arrest in Irving, Texas, after police found a syringe and cocaine under the seat of the car he was driving. Indicted on drug possession charges, Von Erich was released on bond and scheduled to attend a probation violation hearing on February 18, 1993. He never made it.

The morning of the hearing, he called his older brother Kevin and announced his intention to commit suicide, but not right away. Later that day, Von Erich met his ex-wife, Cathy, for lunch in Dallas and told her of his plan. During the drug-riddled years of their marriage Kerry had often threatened suicide to his wife. At one point, she removed all the guns from their house. Today, however, she did not believe him even after he gave her a list of the pallbearers he wanted at his funeral. After Von Erich left the restaurant, Cathy noticed some words that he had scrawled on the tablecloth. They read, "Tonight I walk with my brothers."

Kerry Von Erich drove directly to his father's ranch in Denton, Texas. He spoke briefly with his father in the yard and then entered the house alone. Unknown to the elder Von Erich, his troubled son took the .44-caliber Smith & Wesson revolver he had given his father as a Christmas present two years before. Outside, Kerry hugged his father and said, "I really love you, Dad. I just want to go out and drive for a while. I need to be alone, to think about some things." When Kerry failed to return after 45 minutes Von Erich and a family friend drove around the ranch until they found his parked Jeep. Nearby, they discovered the 33-year-old wrestler lying in a patch of mesquite, the gun clenched in his left hand, dead from a bullet fired directly into his heart. The Tarrant County Medical Examiner's Office later ruled that the wrestler had been legally intoxicated and under the influence of cocaine at the time of his suicide.

Fritz Von Erich, 68, died of brain cancer on September 10, 1997. He shares a grave marker with his son, Kerry, in the Grove Hill Memorial Park cemetery in Dallas. Von Erich's inscription reads, "Beloved Father," Kerry's, "'Walking With My Brothers.'"

FURTHER READING

Dooley, Kirk. *Tragedies and Triumphs of America's First Family of Wrestling.* Dallas, Tex.: Taylor Pub. Co., 1987.

von Kreisler, Alexander

Prior to joining the music faculty of the University of Texas at Austin in 1945 as a professor of advanced score reading and orchestration, the Russian-born von Kreisler had conducted weekly symphony concerts in

Cincinnati broadcast over CBS radio and had also batoned the CBS Symphony in New York. On August 23, 1969, von Kreisler's wife found her 75-year-old husband's lifeless body slumped over a low rock wall circling the patio in the rear of their home at 4608 Horseshoe Bend in northwest Austin. A single-shot .22-caliber rifle lay nearby.

Wade, Richard

On the night of August 6, 1933, the 29-year-old MGM cameraman entered the bathroom of his home at 4058 Lincoln Avenue in Culver City, California, and fired a bullet into his head. The bullet passed through Wade's head, ripped through a partition and into an adjoining bedroom where it barely missed the cameraman's sleeping 1-year-old child. In the absence of a note, Wade's friends were at a loss to explain the action, although the studio had been on strike for two weeks.

Wagner, George E.

"Clown Dons Mask of Death After Wife Divorces Him" was the *Milwaukee Sentinel* headline on August 26, 1934, the day after the popular clown-juggler was found hanged in his room in Milwaukee, Wisconsin. Known in the Ringling Bros. and Barnum & Bailey Circus world as the "Jolly Jenaro," the 55 year old Wagner had been divorced by his wife four months earlier on grounds that the wealthy performer's frugality amounted to stinginess. Ever the clown, Wagner had told the judge, "I've tamed lions and managed unruly cats in a show, but I couldn't handle her." A week prior to his death, Wagner threatened suicide during a visit with his sister. When she failed to hear from him for several days, she went to the clown's room at 1212 W. Hadley Street. Through a side window she saw her brother's body hanging by a bathrobe cord from a light fixture. Wagner had been dead for 48 hours. A handwritten will dividing about $15,000 in cash and government bonds among his family was found on a table.

Walcamp, Marie

In pre–World War I America three women reigned as the most popular female stars in serials: Pearl White, Ruth Roland, and

MARIE WALCAMP— One of the most popular female serial stars during the teens in such chapter plays as *Liberty, A Daughter of the U.S.A.* (1916), *The Red Ace* (1917), *The Lion's Claws* (1918), and *The Red Glove* (1919), Walcamp was through in films by 1927. Ill and depressed, the 42-year-old former actress gassed herself to death in Los Angeles on November 17, 1936.

Marie Walcamp. Born in Dennison, Ohio, on July 27, 1894, Walcamp acted in stock theatre on both coasts before signing with Universal Film Company in 1913–1914. In 1914, she was teamed with William Clifford in a series of two-reelers that included *Olana of the South Seas*, *Rescued by the Wireless*, *The Law of the Lumberjack*, and at least eight other melodramas. The next year she was paired with actor William Clifford in *The Blood of the Children*, *Custer's Last Scout*, and *The Terrors of the Jungle*. In 1916, Walcamp became a star doing her own stunts in the action-packed serial *Liberty, A Daughter of the U.S.A.* The "Daredevil of the Movies" solidified her star status in five other serials: *Patria* (1917), *The Red Ace* (1917), *The Lion's Claws* (1918), *The Red Glove* (1919), *The Dragon's Nest* (1920). Shortly after returning from the Orient where *The Dragon's Nest* was shot, she married her co-star in the film, Harland Tucker, and retired. In 1924, Walcamp attempted a minor comeback in two Westerns, *Treasure Canyon* and *Western Vengeance*, and the spy thriller *A Desperate Adventure*. Failing to regain her popularity, the former star made her last movie, *In a Moment of Temptation*, in 1927. In the credits, Walcamp received fourth billing behind its star, Grant Withers (see entry), who took his life with sleeping pills on March 27, 1959.

On November 17, 1936, Harland Tucker returned from a business trip to find his 42-year-old wife dead in a gas-filled room of their home in Los Angeles. According to Tucker, Walcamp had been ill and depressed for months.

Waldman, Josef

Waldman, 40, former first violinist of the Philadelphia Symphony Orchestra between 1912 and 1915, was killed instantly on December 11, 1933, when he jumped from the fifth floor bedroom window of his New York City apartment at 505 West 164th Street. According to Waldman's mother, with whom he lived, the musician had been depressed and unhappy since suffering a severe nervous breakdown 11 years earlier.

Walker, E. Clarke

Walker, the manager of the Pantages Theatre in Spokane, Washington, since October 7, 1907, suffered from diabetes in the last two years of his life. Aggravating the condition, he had been unable to sleep during the two weeks prior to his suicide on November 12, 1922. Amid conflicting reports that he was to be investigated for account shortages and ticket fraud, Walker locked the door of his second floor office in the theatre following a conference with a Pantages executive from Portland, Oregon. Using a .32-caliber Harrington & Richards revolver he purchased on October 2, the 44-year-old theatre manager fatally shot himself through the right temple. Afterward, the Pantages representative denied that Walker was being investigated for business irregularities.

Wallace, Ray Charles

Legendary cinema sex queen Mae West (1892–1980) was appearing in a nightclub in Chicago when Wallace, her chauffeur, drove the actress' car to a farm near Patoka, Indiana, on February 15, 1955. There, he ran a hose from the exhaust pipe to the interior of the car and asphyxiated himself. According to West's manager, the 44-year-old chauffeur recently appeared to have developed a persecution complex.

Walsh, May

Stagestruck early in life, the young woman graduated from the chorus to vaudeville, but her popularity soon waned. Walsh had been supporting herself by singing in Chicago nightclubs when early on the morning of October 19, 1913, she asked her chauffeur sweetheart if he would marry her. When informed that he would not due to other family commitments, Walsh calmly walked to a cabinet, drank from a bottle of carbolic acid, and died at the the the feet of her lover.

Walters, Homer M.

Walters and Lillian Tyler, both 32, played together in the orchestra at the Loew's

Park Theatre in Cleveland, Ohio. During his 12 year courtship of Tyler, Walters had spent $15,000 on the organist in an unsuccessful bid to marry her. In early March 1925, Walters struck the woman after he caught her entertaining a young college boy in her apartment. He was arrested for assault and battery, but released after Tyler refused to testify against him. On March 25, 1925, a frightened Tyler phoned authorities to report that Walters had repeatedly threatened her life. At a meeting before the police prosecutor, Lillian Tyler intimated to her frustrated suitor that she "might" put him on probation and, if he behaved himself, possibly marry him later.

At 5:30 P.M. on March 28, 1925, Tyler was sitting alone in the front row of the Loew's Park Theatre during a non-musical interlude in the comedy film *The Burglar*. Walters, who had recently quit the orchestra to become the treasurer of his father's coal company, sat down beside her. Although an estimated 200 patrons were in the theatre, no one was seated in the next ten rows behind the couple. During an action scene in the film punctuated by some 50 sound effect shots, Walters produced a revolver and pumped four rounds into Tyler's cheek, temple, neck, and eye. Afterward, he shot himself in the head. Unaware that the pistol reports they heard were not part of the movie, the audience laughed and applauded as two people lay dead in the front row. Their bodies, Tyler's slumped in her seat and Walters' splayed on the floor at her feet, were found by an usher ten minutes later.

Ward, Jeff

A veteran Chicago-based session drummer, Ward, 30, played on several successful records including Ministry's *The Mind Is a Terrible Thing to Taste*, the Revolting Cocks' *Beers, Steers + Queers*, and was tour drummer with the Nine Inch Nails during Lollapalooza '91. Ward was drummer for the industrial rock band Low Pop Suicide when he died from self-inflicted carbon monoxide poisoning in his West Side Chicago home on March 19, 1993.

According to one-time bandmate Dan McGuinness of Coven, Ward was disillusioned with rock and had struggled unsuccessfully to kick a heroin habit. McGuinness said: "There are people in the business who dissed Jeff. Jeff wasn't the kind of guy who would hold a grudge against people; he would still show up and play on a session if he was asked. But he'd say, 'I can't believe I have to call and ask for royalties.'"

Warfel, Jack

Apparently despondent over the sale of his family home, the 49-year-old assistant film-drama reviewer for the *Cleveland Press* took his life on November 15, 1958. Warfel's body was found on the floor of a closed garage next to a running car at his home in Cleveland.

Waring, Peter

Waring (real name John Peter Roderick Mainwaring) was among Britain's most popular radio comedians until the BBC discharged him in 1948 after learning that he was charged with obtaining credit under false pretenses. On July 9, 1949, one day after being sentenced to nine months imprisonment for fraud, the 30-year-old comedian used a length of mailbag cord to hang himself in his cell at London's Pentonville Prison.

Warner, Jewel see *Leavy, Adelaide M.*

Weaver, Howard E.

Depressed over the loss of his managerial position at New York City's Henry Miller Theatre and fearful that he had contracted tuberculosis, Weaver, 45, hanged himself from an electric light fixture in the bath at his room at the Hotel Woodstock, 127 West Forty-third Street, in that city on September 16, 1924. Authorities found three neatly typed notes at the scene variously addressed to the hotel manager, a theatrical friend, and his wife. To his wife he asked forgiveness for having been a "disappointment and a failure."

Weaver, Winstead Sheffield ("Doodles")

The uncle of film actress Sigourney Weaver, "Doodles" performed with the madcap Spike Jones band and scored a hit in the fifties with their novelty song "Beedlebaum." A versatile character actor, Weaver became hopelessly typecast in films as the goofy, hayseed hick based on his early screen appearances in two 1937 movies, *Behind the Headlines* and *Topper*. Weaver's many film credits include *Gentleman Prefer Blondes* (1953), *The Errand Boy* (1961), *That Darn Cat!* (1965), and *Road to Nashville* (1967). On television, the comedian starred in *Doodles Weaver*, a half-hour comedy-variety program that intermittently ran on NBC for three months in 1951.

Concerned that he had been unable to contact his father by phone for several days, Weaver's son, Winstead, visited the actor's home in Burbank, California, on January 15, 1983. He discovered the 71 year old's body in the living room dead from two .22-caliber pistol wounds to the chest. The gun and about $54 in cash were found nearby. Winstead Weaver told police that his father had been despondent for some time over a heart ailment. Weaver was buried on Santa Catalina Island.

Webb, Richard

Webb (born September 9, 1915, in Bloomington, Illinois) began his career on the New York stage before coming to Hollywood in 1941 to briefly appear in the Preston Sturges classic *Sullivan's Travels*. After serving in the military during World War II, the actor returned to Hollywood and appeared in some 60 films. These include *Sands of Iwo Jima* (1949), *I Was a Communist for the FBI* (1951), *The Nebraskan* (1953), *Three Hours to Kill* (1954), *Hillbillys in a Haunted House* (1967), *The Gay Deceivers* (1969), and *Mulefeathers* (1977).

It was on television, however, that Webb achieved his greatest recognition. From 1954 to 1956, he appeared as the title character on

RICHARD WEBB—Webb appeared in more than 60 films in an acting career that spanned the forties through the seventies, but gained an immortality of sorts on television playing the title role in the CBS kid series *Captain Midnight* from 1954 to 1956. After leaving acting in the seventies and writing a few books on the supernatural, the physically ailing 77 year old shot himself at his home in Van Nuys, California on June 10, 1993.

the popular CBS kid action adventure *Captain Midnight* sponsored by Ovaltine. In 1958–1959, Webb starred as "Don Jagger" in the short-lived syndicated police drama *U.S. Border Patrol*. In all, the durable character actor made some 260 television appearances in shows like *Maverick*, *Perry Mason*, and *Lassie*.

As Webb's acting career began to wane in the late sixties he turned an interest in the supernatural and reincarnation into a second career as a writer. In 1971 he published *Great Ghosts of the West* and *Voices from Another World: True Tales of the Occult* followed in 1974 with *They Came Back*. Despondent over a debilitating respiratory illness, the 77-year-old actor shot himself in his home in Van Nuys, California, on June 10, 1993.

Webster, George Hopkinson

Webster broke into pictures in 1919 and for the next 30 years served as an assistant director at Universal, Monogram, Warner Bros., and Republic studios where he specialized in Western films like *Prairie Trails* (1920), *Blazing the Way* (1920), *Cowboys from Texas* (1939), and *Ghost Valley Raiders* (1940) starring fellow suicide Don "Red" Barry (see entry). Unable to find steady film work since leaving Republic in 1946, Webster, 60, was reported missing by his wife on November 14, 1949. She told authorities: "He hadn't been able to get work for three years. We had hit rock bottom and he was very despondent." A week later, Webster's body washed ashore on the beach in Santa Monica.

Wegefarth, Gustavus A.

Business worries and poor health were cited as the reasons the 55-year-old manager and lessee of Philadelphia's Grand Opera House went into the bedroom of his home at 2218 Venango Street on November 3, 1907, and pumped three bullets into his head. Although the bullets were removed at the Samaritan Hospital, Wegefarth never regained consciousness and died three days later with most of his family at his bedside. The day of his death, the company Stair & Haviland announced that they had secretly purchased the Grand Opera House from Wegefarth the week before. A new theatrical project also added to his anxiety. As promoter and principal stockholder in the new William Penn Theatre in West Philadelphia, Wegefarth continually fretted over the costly construction delays that threatened to push back the house's proposed opening.

Wehle, Billy

Known as the "King of the Tent Shows," Wehle was born in Louisville, Kentucky, on July 26, 1894, and began his nearly 25 year show business career in Atlanta in 1910 as a song plugger in a dime store. In 1920, he opened his own show "Billy Wehle's Bluegrass Belles," and three years later teamed with comedian Roy Hughes to open the tent show "Billroy's Comedians." With his profits, Wehle bought out Hughes after only two weeks. In 1941, he opened a new tent show and briefly teamed up with the Grand Ole Opry in Nashville before folding in 1944. Afterward, Wehle entered the insurance business in Miami and retired following his wife's death. In failing health and living in an extended care facility in Miami, Wehle, 73, went with a friend on March 6, 1968, to the Taj Apartments at 33 SW Second Avenue on the pretext of letting a room. While the manager was answering the phone, Wehle slipped into an elevator, rode to the seventh floor, and jumped to his death from a fire escape.

Weiss, Lewis Allen

Weiss, 59, helped build the Don Lee Broadcasting System into America's largest regional radio network. Joining the firm in 1930 as vice president and general manager, he left after four years to manage the Detroit radio station WJR. After Don Lee's death, Weiss returned to the organization as its president in 1936. During his tenure, Weiss allied it with the Mutual Broadcasting System, and saw it grow to national prominence. The radio executive retired in 1950 as board chairman of the Mutual System and vice-president and general manager of Don Lee. Weiss, the victim of a series of light strokes and progressive muscular atrophy, was given six months to live by his doctor. A week before his death on June 15, 1953, he told intimates that he was "getting his house in order." On that date, Weiss shot himself in the forehead with a .32-caliber pistol in the bedroom of his home at 627 Alpine Drive in Beverly Hills. Two guns, a .38-caliber pistol and the fatal .32, were found near his body.

Weiss, Phillip

After suffering financial losses, the 37-year-old former manager of the Equity Ticket Agency hanged himself in the kitchen of his apartment on the seventh floor of 230 West Seventy-ninth Street in New York City on October 23, 1933.

Wells, Jake

Known as the "Father of Vaudeville in Atlanta," Wells managed the Richmond Bluebirds of the Atlantic League to three pennants before purchasing his first theatre in Richmond, Virginia, in the late 1890s. In his nearly 30 year career as the "Dean of Southern Vaudeville," the showman purchased several other theatres and opened a chain of summer amusement parks throughout North Carolina, Virginia, and Georgia. Five weeks before committing suicide on March 16, 1927, the 63-year-old promoter suffered a nervous breakdown precipitated by concern over his own ill health and that of his wife. On the fatal day, Wells, accompanied by Betty Schaeffner, manager of his Park Hill Inn, was driving near Hendersonville, North Carolina, when they stopped to pick wild flowers. Schaeffner began picking flowers while Wells leaned against a pine tree. Moments after uttering, "It'll all be over soon," the promoter drew a revolver from a pocket and shot himself under the chin. The woman vainly tried to wrest the gun from Wells before he fired a second deadly bullet into his head.

Wells, Marie Edith

Wells, a former musical star on the New York stage who often appeared in Flo Ziegfeld productions, entered silent films in 1915 after a throat condition forced her to give up singing. In her first film, *The Builder of Bridges* (Frohman Amusement Corporation, 1915), she starred opposite British actor C. Aubrey Smith, also making his film debut. Wells co-starred in several silent films (*The Conquest of Canaan*, 1916; *The Love Brand*, 1923), but when talkies arrived she was relegated to an occasional extra role. In Hollywood on July 3, 1949, the faded silent movie queen was found dead in her room at 1114 Coronado Terrace, the victim of a lethal dose of sleeping pills. Her suicide note read: "Dear Eloise and Billy, forgive me please but my health is so bad and I just can't go on. I love you. Lots of happiness and good health. God bless you all. Aunt Re." Wells was 55.

West, Vera

West became the head costume designer at Universal in 1926 after studying under Lady Duff Gordon at the Philadelphia School of Design. During her 20 year tenure at the studio, West designed clothes for more than 90 films. Among the best known are *Destry Rides Again* (1939), *Son of Frankenstein* (1939), *My Little Chickadee* (1940), *Phantom of the Opera* (1943), *Cobra Woman* (1944) and *The Killers* (1946). After completing work on her last film, *Pirates of Monterey*, she left the studio in 1947 to become associated with a custom gown shop in the Beverly Wilshire Hotel in Beverly Hills.

On Saturday night, June 28, 1947, the 47-year-old costume designer quarreled with her husband, Jack C. West, head of a cosmetics firm in Hollywood. After she threatened to divorce him, Jack West left "West Manor," their lavish ranch home at 5119 Bluebell Avenue in North Hollywood, and checked into the Beverly Hills Hotel. At 3:30 A.M. the next morning, Robert T. Landry, a former news magazine photographer who was staying in the guest house at the rear of the West home, returned to West Manor to find all the lights on, but no signs of movement in the main house. As Landry walked past the pool to the guest house, his attention was drawn by West's two Scotties, Duffie and Tammie, whimpering at the water's edge. Investigating, he found West's nightgown-clad body floating face down in the pool. Inside the house, authorities recovered an empty bottle of sleeping pills, and two hastily pencilled messages. One read: "This is the only way. I am tired of being blackmailed." The other, written on the back of a torn greeting card, read: "The Fortune Teller told me there was only one way to duck the blackmail I've paid for 23 years. Death."

Questioned by police, Jack West stated that while his wife had been ill and nervous, she had never been a victim of blackmail. According to her husband, who was intimately familiar with West's financial affairs, the suicide notes that pointed to blackmail were merely "gremlins of my wife's imagination." The death was officially ruled as "asphyxia due to drowning." West is buried in Forest Lawn Memorial Park in Glendale, California.

Westmore, George

Descended from a long line of bootmakers, bakers, and barrelmakers, the patriarch of the most famous family of make-up artists in motion picture history was born on the Isle of Wight in England on June 27, 1879. After being mustered out of the British Army as "medically unfit" in 1901, Westmore opened up a hair dressing salon in Newport on the Isle of Wight. His subsequent marriage to Ada Savage resulted in 19 children, many of whom died in childbirth. Westmore taught six of his sons (Mont, Perc, Ern, Wally, Bud, and Frank) the craft of hairstyling, wigmaking, and make-up. The tragedy of Westmore's life would be that each of them would ultimately surpass him in the profession.

After years of travelling in Canada and the U.S., Westmore opened a wigmaking shop in Cleveland, Ohio, where he also per-

fected his make-up techniques on area prostitutes. In the hope of breaking into motion pictures, Westmore moved the clan to Hollywood in March 1917. While working at Maison Cesare, the top hair salon in Los Angeles, Westmore talked the Selig Studio into hiring him in 1917. There, in a small cubicle off the main silent stage, Westmore created the first film studio make-up department. Still using the Maison Cesare as his home base, the make-up artist slowly built up a show business clientele. Triangle Studio star Billie Burke was so impressed by Westmore's work that she brought him to the attention of studio vice-president Thomas Ince, who hired Westmore at $150 a week to create a make-up department at the studio. Working with Triangle's stable of stars (Douglas Fairbanks, Nita Naldi, Anita Stewart, Theda Bara), Westmore pioneered the use of false eyelashes and layered haircuts. When both studios went out of existence in the late teens, Westmore freelanced on films like *Smilin' Through* (1922) and *Secrets* (1924).

By the early twenties, however, Westmore's sons were getting jobs that he felt should have been his. In 1923, Mont Westmore, 21, was named head of the make-up department at First National (later Warner Bros.). In 1926, Wally, 20, was selected over his father to helm the make-up department at Paramount, a post he would hold for 43 years. Two years later, Ern Westmore, 24, was chosen to run the make-up department at RKO. After working on Cecil B. DeMille's 1926 epic *The King of Kings*, the family patriarch opened a trendy new salon on Hollywood Boulevard and waited in vain for his show business friends to arrive. They all, however, preferred his sons. The final insult to Westmore's dignity occurred in 1931 when the Motion Picture Academy awarded its Cup (the forerunner of the Oscar) to Ern Westmore for his work on the Richard Dix classic *Cimarron*. Weeks after his eldest son won the coveted award, the 52-year-old makeup artist died on July 12, 1931, four days after drinking bichloride of mercury.

FURTHER READING

Westmore, Frank, and Davidson, Muriel. *The Westmores of Hollywood.* 1st ed. Philadelphia: Lippincott, 1976.

Weston, Charles H.

Weston formerly managed actress Maude Adams and at one time conducted American tours for the legendary Sarah Bernhardt. Long out of show business and alternately living in Newark, New Jersey, and in a cheap rooming house in Harlem, Weston, 50, waited until after office hours on August 15, 1919, to enter the Aeolian Building at 27 West Forty-second Street in New York City. The former theatrical manager took an elevator to the 17th floor, opened a window, tossed his straw hat on the floor, then jumped. Weston's body struck the roof of a four story building below, partially crashing through its tin and board covering. Among the items found on the body were a letter to theatrical managers Cohan & Harris, a "To Whom It May Concern" letter, and a permit from the Board of Health authorizing Weston to use drugs.

Whale, James

The director who infused the American horror film with taste, pathos, and humor was born in the small mining village of Dudley, England, on July 22, 1889. The son of a local blast furnacemen, Whale was the sixth of seven children, and one of only three to survive past infancy. An artistic child, he enrolled at 21 as an evening student at the Dudley School of Arts and Crafts where he distinguished himself as an excellent artist. At the outbreak of World War I Whale entered officer's training school and was commissioned as a Second Lieutenant in the 2/7th Worcestershire Infantry in August 1914. On August 25, 1917, the 28-year-old officer was captured by Germans during night reconnaissance on the Western Front and sent to a POW camp in Holzminden, Germany. Largely to kill boredom, Whale spent the 15 months of his incarceration sketching theatrical scenes,

JAMES WHALE— British director James Whale brought a level of sophistication and wit to Universal horror films like *Frankenstein* (1931), *The Invisible Man* (1933), and *The Bride of Frankenstein* (1935). In 1998 the film *Gods and Monsters* starring Ian McKellen as Whale focused on the director's last days with a particular emphasis on his homosexuality and mental and physical decline. Pictured here after a fire at his Pacific Palisades home in 1954, the director had not made a movie since the laughable *Green Hell* in 1940. For years, Whale's death in 1957 at the age of 67 was believed to have been accidental. However, the director's longtime companion, David Lewis, released Whale's suicide note shortly before his own death in 1987. *Courtesy of University of Southern California, on behalf of the USC Library Department of Special Collections.*

designing sets, and directing original stage productions using the camp's 1,400 prisoners as cast and crew.

After the Armistice, Whale returned to England in 1918 and joined the Birmingham Repertory Company as a bit actor. During the early twenties he worked with various repertory companies learning every facet of the theatre from costume and scenery design to stage management. In 1925 Whale made his London acting debut in a production of *A Comedy of Good and Evil* at the Ambassadors Theatre. After directing a few small-scale productions, Whale established himself with playwright R. C. Sherriff's World War I play *Journey's End* starring Colin Clive in 1928. In 1929, Whale brought the play to New York City where it recreated its West End success and brought him to the attention of Hollywood.

In the wake of the transition from silent to talking pictures, studios were vying to hire actors and directors comfortable with dialog. They naturally turned to the legitimate stage. In 1929, Paramount signed Whale, 39, to a $500-a-week contract and relocated him to Hollywood to learn about the picture business.In the close-knit picture community, Whale lived an openly gay lifestyle with his lover, film producer David Lewis, 15 years his junior. In 1937 they built a house together at 788 S. Amalfi Drive in Pacific Palisades. While waiting to direct the film version of *Journey's End*, Whale was assigned to direct the dialog on *The Love Doctor* (1929), and Howard Hughes' World War I airplane epic *Hell's Angels* (1930). Whale's first directorial effort, *Journey's End* (1930), was a critical and commercial success. Now established as a bankable director, Whale signed a lucrative five year contract with Universal in 1931. The contract not only guaranteed the director a $2,500 a week salary, but gave him the freedom to choose to direct any property owned by the studio. After scoring a huge box office hit with the 1931 melodrama *Waterloo Bridge*, Whale chose to direct a screen version of Mary Shelley's gothic novel *Frankenstein, or the Modern*

Prometheus. The film version, *Frankenstein*, starring Colin Clive as "Dr. Henry Frankenstein" and unknown British actor Boris Karloff as the "monster," cost a hefty $291,000 to make, but grossed a staggering $5 million in its initial theatrical release in 1931. Garrett Fort (see entry), a screenwriter on the film, later took his life with sleeping pills on October 26, 1945.

Whale followed up his *Frankenstein* success with a series of atmospheric films that not only defined him as the top director in the genre, but also helped to make Universal synonymous with movie horror. *The Old Dark House* (1932), *The Invisible Man* (1933), and his masterpiece, *The Bride of Frankenstein* (1935), were all box office hits. After directing *Remember Last Night* (1935) and the popular musical *Showboat* in 1936, Whale was earning the top salary of $75,000 a film. In late 1936, amid a top management shake-up at Universal, Whale contracted to make *The Road Back*, the film version of exiled German writer Erich Maria Remarque's anti-war novel follow-up to his classic *All Quiet on the Western Front*.

After the start of filming in 1937, the Nazi government in Germany called a meeting with the studio manager at Universal and a representative of the German consulate in Los Angeles to voice concern over the possible manner in which Germans might be portrayed in the film. The consulate official bluntly pointed out that foreign markets accounted for almost 40 percent of a U.S. film's earnings and that *The Road Back* would almost certainly be banned in Germany. The German government also sent letters to the actors informing them that their future films would be boycotted in Germany. Whale's new bosses at Universal forced him to reshoot battle scenes that might offend the Germans and ordered 21 cuts be made to placate the Nazis. Outraged, Whale refused to make the cuts. Universal edited the film and brought in Edward Sloman to direct several scenes of comic relief to dilute the film's anti-war intensity. In June 1937, the studio supplied a print of the newly edited *The Road Back* to the German ambassador, Hans Luther, who refused to view it, giving as his reason a lack of authority to pass judgement on movies for German consumption. Whale refused to attend the film's premiere on June 17, 1937. Not surprisingly, *The Road Back* was critically panned as an "approximation" of Remarque's novel. The furor ended Whale's contract with Universal and marked the beginning of the end of his film career.

Other films directed by Whale include *The Great Garrick* (1937, featuring fellow suicide Albert Dekker [see entry] in a small role), *Port of Seven Seas* (1938), *Sinners in Paradise* (1938), *Wives Under Suspicion* (1938), *The Man in the Iron Mask* (1939), and *Green Hell* (1940). Few of the films made money and by the early forties Whale was all but unemployable. In 1941, friends got Whale a job directing *They Dare Not Love* at Columbia for $30,000, a pittance of his former salary, but he was quickly replaced by Charles Vidor after the film's star, George Brent, complained about not liking him. Whale would never direct another film. Though financially secure, the 53-year-old-director wanted to work. To kill the boredom while awaiting the job offers that never came, Whale resumed painting. He converted an outbuilding on his Amalfi Drive property into a studio and spent several hours a day there working. In 1951, Whale directed the play *Pagan in the Parlor* at the Pasadena Playhouse. The comedy was a modest success and Whale travelled to Europe in 1952 to make arrangements to direct the play in England.

Whale, 63, was vacationing in Paris after the show's brief run when he met 25-year-old Strasbourg-born Pierre Foegel in a gay bar. Infatuated with the younger man, Whale hired Foegel as his "chauffeur" and returned to the States with him in tow. Shortly after Foegel moved into the house on Amalfi Drive, David Lewis, Whale's live-in companion and lover for more than 24 years, moved out. Whale and Lewis, however, remained cordial. Over Whale's strong objections, a homesick Foegel returned to France five months later in mid–1953. Alone except for a small live-in

staff, Whale (who did not swim and hated the water) built a pool in his back yard. Lured by free food and drinks, many attractive young men attended Whale's frequent "pool parties." The director began keeping a pornographic diary from which he often read aloud to his guests. Foegel returned to Whale in early 1954 and in gratitude the director purchased him a gas station to manage.

In the spring of 1956 Whale suffered the first of a series of debilitating strokes that left him unable to paint or drive. Broken in health and spirit, he turned to sleeping pills and tranquilizers to deaden his jangled nerves and depression. On the morning of May 29, 1957 the 67-year-old director gave his nurse the day off, leaving himself alone in the house except for the maid. Sometime between the hours of 8:00 A.M. and 1:00 P.M. Whale, dressed in his favorite suit and tie, dove headfirst into the shallow end of the pool, knocking himself unconscious when his forehead struck the concrete bottom. Later that day, Whale's maid called Foegel at the gas station after discovering her employer's body resting on the bottom of the pool. Foegel hurriedly picked up George Lovett, Whale's personal business manager, and drove to the house where he managed to fish his lover's lifeless body out of the pool moments before the police arrived. Whale's death was officially ruled an "accidental drowning." Following a funeral service conducted at the Wayside Chapel in Westwood on June 3, 1957, Whale's remains were cremated and placed in a niche in the Columbarium of Memory at Forest Lawn Memorial Park in Glendale.

Shortly before his death in 1987, David Lewis revealed the existence of a suicide note that Whale had left in his studio–pool house prior to jumping in the water. Found at the time by Whale's maid, she gave it to George Lovett who, instead of turning it over to police, entrusted it to Lewis. Rapidly written by Whale in blue ink on a half-sheet of personal stationery folded booklike, the front of the document read, "James Whale, 788 Amalfi Drive, Pacific, Palisades, California, EXbrook 5-5844." Inside, Whale wrote:

To ALL I LOVE, Do not grieve for me. My nerves are all shot and for the last year I have been in agony day and night — except when I sleep with sleeping pills — and any peace I have by day is when I am drugged by pills. I have had a wonderful life but it is over and my nerves get worse and I am afraid they will have to take me away. So please forgive me, all those I love and may God forgive me too, but I cannot bear the agony and it [is] best for everyone this way. The future is just old age and illness and pain. Goodbye all and thank you for all your love. I must have peace and this is the only way. Jimmy.

And in a post script on the back:

Do not let my family come — my last wish is to be cremated so nobody will grieve over my grave. No one is to blame — I have wonderful friends and they do all they can for me, but my heart is in my mouth all the time and I have no peace. I cannot keep still and the future would be worse. My financial affairs are all in order and I hope will help my loved ones to forget a little. It will be a great shock, but I pray they will be given strength to come through and be happy for my release from this constant fear. I've tried very hard all I know for a year and it gets worse inside, so please take comfort in knowing I will not suffer any more. J.

David Lewis, 83 at the time of his death, was subsequently cremated and his ashes placed in a niche in the Columbarium of Memory almost directly opposite those of Whale's, his companion for so many years.

FURTHER READING

Curtis, James. *James Whale: A New World of Gods and Monsters.* Boston: Faber and Faber, 1998.

Wildberg, Constance

In 1949, the former Constance Bennett of Atlanta married John Wildberg, the Broadway producer of *One Touch of Venus* (1943), *Porgy and Bess* (1943), *Anna Lucasta* (1944), and *Black Chiffon* (1950). The pair were staying in a suite in the Beverly Hills Hotel during a visit to Los Angeles when the 25-year-

old woman, brooding over her inability to stop drinking, became suicidal. According to the 48-year-old producer, they attended a cocktail party on December 17, 1950, and returned to the hotel at 10:15 P.M. He went to sleep in a twin bed while she sat beside her bed. Wildberg awakened at 6:45 A.M. to find his fully-clothed wife dead. A box of sleeping pills, with 22 of its 24 tablets gone, was found in a medicine chest. A note to her father found in the bedroom read: "Pappy dearest, I hope you will forgive me. I cannot stand it any longer. I always loved you very much. I hope that you understand this life is unbearable. There is no remedy but what I am doing right now. Much love to all of you for always."

Wilder, Mildred Havican

A graduate of the Boston Conservatory of Music, Wilder came to Reno, Nevada, in 1931 and made a local name as a nightclub pianist and singer. On April 24, 1939, in Carson City, Nevada, the 34-year-old performer broke down on the stand during divorce proceedings against her third husband. The next day, Wilder's body was found on the dump of the Black Panther mine five miles north of Reno, an area in which she often took long solitary walks. At the scene, police recovered two empty bottles of pills from the dead woman's purse. A coroner's jury ascribed Wilder's death as due to "an overdose of sleeping tablets taken while she was in a state of extreme nervousness."

Wilkinson, Kevin Michael

Universally regarded as one of the finest British drummers in rock music, Wilkinson (born in Stoke-on-Trent, Staffordshire, on June 11, 1958) played with China Crisis (1982–1989), Marillion (1991–1993), and Squeeze (1995–1998). During the summer of 1998, Wilkinson undertook an eighties revival tour of the U.S. featuring acts of the decade, which included Howard Jones (for whom he drummed), Culture Club, and Human League. Concerned over the human tragedy in

Kosovo, Wilkinson convinced several of his colleagues to perform at KosovAid, a Live-Aid style charity concert held at the Oasis Leisure Centre in Swindon in mid–1999. Seven weeks later on July 17, 1999, the body of the 41-year-old father of three was found by his wife hanging in their country home at Baydon near Swindon, Wiltshire. Friends reported that Wilkinson had recently complained of depression and spoke of how touring was negatively affecting his family life.

Williams, Gertrude

The smartly dressed body of the former showgirl was found in the basement room of a cheap New York City rooming house at 364 West Fifty-fifth Street on March 8, 1934. The day before, Williams had checked in as "Rita Jones" and, opting not to gas herself with a length of hose, took her life with half a box of pills found near her body. Police found 60 cents in the room.

Williams, Paul

Williams (born July 2, 1939 in Birmingham, Alabama) and Eddie Kendricks were singing with the Detroit-based R&B group The Primes when they formed The Elgins with Otis Williams (no relation), Melvin Franklin, and Eldridge Bryant of The Distants in the early sixties. Berry Gordy renamed the group The Temptations after signing them to Motown in 1961. Paul Williams, the acknowledged "Soul of the Temptations," was the creative force behind the group's distinctive choreography and sang lead vocals on many of their hits. After David Ruffin replaced Bryant in 1963 the group became one of Motown's top acts. Their numerous hits included "The Way You Do the Things You Do" (1964), "My Girl" (1965), "Get Ready" (1966), "I Wish it Would Rain" (1968), and "I Can't Get Next to You" (1969).

By mid–1967, however, Williams' failing marriage exacerbated by his undiagnosed sickle cell anemia and unchecked drinking were affecting his work. In less than two years,

the baritone's health deteriorated to the point where he could not travel or perform without a tank of oxygen at the ready. In 1971, the group hired Richard Street of The Monitors to stand backstage behind the curtains during live performances and sing Williams' harmony parts. Later that year, a doctor ordered the ailing Williams to stop touring, although he continued to create new dance steps for the group. Depressed by his lack of involvement with The Temptations, Williams tried to convince Motown to feature him as a solo artist. While the label did record him on two songs, including the strangely prophetic "I Feel Like Giving Up," neither was released.

On August 17, 1973, the body of the 34-year-old "Soul of the Temptations" was found slumped in the front seat of his car at 14th and West Grand Boulevard in Detroit, Michigan. Dressed only in a swimsuit, Williams had shot himself with a pistol (still clutched in his hand) in the left side of the head. While many, including his family, continue to maintain that Williams was murdered, Temptations co-founder Otis Williams believes unhappiness and depression prompted his bandmate to commit suicide.

FURTHER READING

Williams, Otis. *Temptations*. New York: G. P. Putnam's Sons, 1988.

Williams, Rozz

Born Roger Alan Painter, the "King of Gothic Rock" was only 16 years old when he founded Christian Death in 1982, the same year their influential debut album, *Only Theatre of Pain*, was released. Cited as an inspiration by Trent Reznor (Nine Inch Nails) and Marilyn Manson, the vocalist dabbled in bisexuality, cross-dressing, and satanism, and ranted against organized religion. These themes were darkly chronicled in several of the band's subsequent albums: *Theatre of Hate* (1983), *Catastrophe Ballet* (1984), and *Ashes* (1985). Shunning the goth label, Williams left the band in 1985 with then wife Eva O. to form Shadow Project. He rejoined Christian Death in 1990 and remained for four years. Although manic depressive and addicted to heroin and alcohol, Williams worked tirelessly throughout his career on a variety of musical projects with Heltir, Premature Ejaculation, Dream Home Heartache, Bloodflag, Mephisto Waltz, Daucus Karota, and Pompeii 99. In 1997 he released his final work, *The Whorses' Mouth*, a spoken word piece that explored his long battle with heroin and other addictions.

According to a former lover, Williams was fixated on the year 1334 (the height of the Black Death), which might explain his decision to take his life at age 34. On April Fool's Day 1998, Williams was found hanging by a roommate in the bedroom of his West Hollywood apartment. Bandmate William Faith released this statement: "No one close to him knows why, and no note was left…. Know in your hearts that the world lost one of the most brilliant and wonderful people who ever bothered to walk its ground — I will miss him in a way I can never hope to explain to any of you."

Williams, Wendy Orleans

The Plasmatics, founded by Williams and her manager-lover Rod Swenson in New York City in 1978, was a radical and influential punk metal band that rode to prominence on its frenetic stage shows featuring the mohawk-adorned lead vocalist Williams chainsawing guitars and blowing up speaker cabinets and cars. Born in Webster, New York, in 1949, Williams dropped out of school in the ninth grade and knocked around Europe for a while before settling in New York City where Swenson (a.k.a. "Captain Kink") put her to work in live sex shows. Onstage with the Plasmatics, the "Queen of Shock Rock" wore provocatively ripped clothes, covered her nipples with tape, and was constantly in trouble with the law. In 1981, Williams and Swenson were arrested in Milwaukee after the singer allegedly simulated a sex act in a nightclub con-

cert. Later that year, Wendy O. (appearing on the stage covered only in shaving cream) was acquitted of an obscenity charge in Cleveland for again simulating sex onstage. At the height of the band's popularity in 1985, Williams was nominated for a Grammy in the best Female Rock Vocal category.

After the Plasmatics quit touring in 1988, Williams enjoyed a moderately successful solo career. In 1991 she moved with Swenson to Storrs, Connecticut, and built a geodesic dome house in the woods outside of town. Disillusioned with show business, the tattoo-covered singer worked in near-anonymity at a local health food store and as a licensed wildlife rehabilitator. Frustrated and depressed over having to lead a conventional life, Williams attempted suicide in 1993 by banging a knife into her chest with a hammer. In the summer of 1997, she overdosed on ephedrine, a synthetic version of the health-food store product Herbal Ectasy. Swenson, who vowed to Williams that he would never intervene if she chose to end her life, sat with his lover in their garden so she would not die alone. He finally called poison control, however, after Williams revived and spent days being sick and sleepless.

In the spring of 1998, the 48-year-old former rock star separated from Swenson and was living with a tattoo artist, Steve Gabriel, over his shop in East Hartford. By April 6, 1998, Williams had cancelled phone service and was having her mail forwarded to Swenson's home. That day, she took Gabriel's .38-caliber pistol, a few pieces of clothing, a teapot, an address book, and some photos of squirrels she had raised, and drove to Swenson's home in Storrs. Swenson was not at home, but when he returned he found that Williams had left him a package of buckwheat noodles that he liked, a packet of seeds, oriental massage balm, and sealed letters. The documents included a "living will" denying life support and a love letter to her long-time companion.

One of the letters read: "The act of taking my own life is not something I am doing without a lot of thought. I don't believe that people should take their own lives without deep and thoughtful reflection over a considerable period of time. I do believe strongly, however, that the right to do so is one of the most fundamental rights that anyone in a free society should have. For me much of the world makes no sense, but my feelings about what I am doing ring loud and clear to an inner ear and a place where there is no self, only calm. Love always, Wendy."

Swenson searched the surrounding woods for an hour before finding her body. After feeding the squirrels, Williams had placed a plastic bag over her head as a courtesy to the person who would find the body, put the gun to her head, then fired.

FURTHER READING

Williams, Joy. "The Love Song of Wendy O. Williams." *Spin*, 14(9):134–138, Sept. 1998.

Willis, Debbie

The attractive 15-year-old Welsh red-haired model appeared in three episodes of the story "Who Stole the Bloater?" dramatized for the BBC children's program *Jackanory* and was featured in a popular television commercial for Jacobs biscuits. Willis, who according to a friend, "could pass for a girl of 20 when she was made up and in her best clothes," was confronted by her father on the evening of October 24, 1994, after returning to their home in Tanywern Road, Ystalyfera, near Swansea, West Glamorgan, Wales, from a night spent drinking with friends at a local pub. Reprimanded by her father, Willis stormed upstairs and apparently took tablets from a bathroom cabinet. Willis' body was found in her bed the next day by an older brother.

Willmott, Lee

Although Willmott and his wife were vaudeville headliners, the 40-year-old comedian and dance man was unable to find work in pictures following the heyday of live enter-tainment. The pair divorced in 1936 after six years of marriage. Willmott had lived for only a few days in a rooming house at 308 South Flower Street in Los Angeles when on March 9, 1938, he entered the Taft Building at Hollywood Boulevard and Vine Street. According to a police report, it took the unemployed comic less than a minute to enter a seventh floor rest room, clamber out onto the sill of a window, and leap to his death. In the dead man's wallet, police found a clipped newspaper picture of his divorced wife and his discharge papers from the United States Marines.

Wills, Lynn Alfred

Willis, the 30-year-old chief announcer for Philadelphia radio station KYW, was recovering from an appendicitis operation when in delirium he jumped from his bed in that city's Presbyterian Hospital on September 21, 1937. With a nurse in hot pursuit, Willis hobbled up the stairs to a second floor landing, tore out a window screen, jumped to the street below, and died from a skull fracture an hour later. Months before, the announcer had suffered a nervous breakdown.

Wilson, Alan ("Blind Owl")

Wilson (born in Boston, Massachusetts, on July 4, 1943) met fellow blues aficionado Bob "the Bear" Hite in 1965, and one year later formed the highly regarded white blues band Canned Heat. A bespectacled introvert who majored in music at Boston University, "Blind Owl" Wilson played slide guitar and was described by guitar legend Mike Bloomfield as "the best goddamn harp player there is." Best remembered for the pair of hits in 1968, "On the Road Again" and "Going Up the Country," Canned Heat played both the Monterey Pop Festival (1967) and Woodstock (1969). A committed ecologist who never owned a house, Wilson, 27, was living in a van in the back yard of Bob Hite's Topanga Canyon home prior to joining the band on a six-week European tour when Hite's wife found the guitarist dead in a sleeping bag on

September 3, 1970. Four barbiturate tablets were found in his pocket. A spokesman for the group's label, Liberty Records, said that Wilson had been depressed recently. Canned Heat co-founder and singer Bob Hite subsequently died of a heart attack in April 1981 at the age of 36.

Wilson, Jack

Wilson, 50, had played blackface roles in vaudeville for nearly 25 years when he was set to appear in a new act at the Scollay Square Theatre in Boston. On November 1, 1931, while two of his fellow performers in the upcoming show waited for him in the lobby of New York City's Hotel Marie Antoinette at Sixty-sixth Street and Broadway, Wilson had already shot himself in the head with a .22-caliber target pistol in his room. Police learned from Wilson's friends that the comedian had been in constant pain from injuries sustained in an automobile accident a year before and recently was unusually depressed over his inability to get backing for a radio act.

Wilson, Read

Poor health forced the popular chief announcer of Asheville, North Carolina, radio station WWNC to retire in November 1963 after nearly 25 years on the air. His potpourri program *Top O' the Morning* was a western North Carolina institution. The show's trademark chime (made by striking a suspended frying pan lid with a pencil ferrule) was instantly familiar to thousands of early morning listeners. Scheduled to enter a local hospital earlier in the day on May 1, 1964, Wilson's body was found that afternoon by his wife in their home at 36 Forest Hill Drive in Asheville. The 49-year-old retired announcer, a past president of the Asheville Rifle and Pistol Club, had fired a pistol shot into his heart.

Winchell, Jennie

On October 25, 1949, the 77-year-old mother of Broadway newspaper columnist Walter Winchell (1897–1972) was admitted to the Doctors Hospital in New York City suffering from a heart ailment. At 5:45 P.M. on November 14, 1949, Winchell was being attended by a nurse, Kathleen Carton, in her private room on the tenth floor of the hospital. According to Carton, she noticed the window was open about 12 inches from the sill when she left to fetch Winchell's supper tray. When she returned, the bed was empty and the window was open about two and a half feet. The old woman's body was splayed on the Eighty-seventh Street sidewalk. Authorities were uncertain whether Winchell fell or jumped to her death.

Winkler, Alexander

A dancing instructor and manager of the vaudeville act Winkler's Madcaps, the 42-year-old divorced father of an 18-year-old daughter violently opposed the young woman's upcoming marriage to a waiter when, he argued, a prominent artist wished to marry her. Following a quarrel with his ex-wife over the proposed nuptials, Winkler inhaled gas at his apartment at 342 West Forty-fifth Street in New York City on November 18, 1916. Winkler was found holding a picture of his mother in one hand and a miniature of his wife in the other. He left several letters and in one, addressed "To the Public," wrote: "He died without leaving one cent of debt." Prior to taking his life, Winkler decided to leave his daughter a macabre wedding gift. In a telegram sent to his wife shortly before inhaling the fatal gas, he wrote: "Lilly's wedding present will be ready for shipment when you receive this." The shaken woman vowed, "Even his death will not prevent her from marrying the man she loves."

Winter, Julian

On December 23, 1930, the day he was set to open on Broadway in the role of the health inspector in *The Inspector General*, the 325 pound comic actor jumped naked to his death from the window of his eighth floor apartment at 205 West Fifty-seventh Street in New York City. As a crowd gathered below the window, Winter's wife and father struggled with the 39 year old, but fearing his weight would drag them down with him, released their holds. The veteran of such Broadway shows as *The Cocoanuts*, *The Vagabond King*, and *Loud Speaker* had recently been suffering from a nervous ailment brought on by worry about business troubles. A doctor had been summoned moments before Winter ran to the window and took the deadly plunge.

Wise, Fred

Wise (born May 27, 1915, in New York City) began writing song lyrics for the annual Varsity Show while a student in Columbia College. After graduating in 1935 he worked in the publicity department at MGM for the next four years. During World War II, Wise served as a radio operator at General Dwight D. Eisenhower's headquarters in Europe. After the war, he stepped up his songwriting output. Already credited with writing the English lyrics for "Bells of San Raquel" (1934) and "Nightingale" (1942), Wise contributed the words for "The Best Man" (1946), "Roses in the Rain" (1947), "The Melancholy Minstrel" (1948), "You, You, You are the One" (1948), "The Slider" (1949), the well-known 1948 tune "'A'—You're Adorable" ("The Alphabet Song"), and many others.

In 1957, the lyricist received his doctorate in psychology from Columbia University, opened up a Park Avenue office, and established the Bronx Consultation Clinic, a low-cost psychiatric outpatient facility. The next year, Wise wrote the lyrics for "Don't Ask Me Why," a song introduced by Elvis Presley in his 1958 film *King Creole*. Other Wise-Presley collaborations included "Fame and Fortune" (1960), "Wooden Heart" in the 1960 film *G. I. Blues*, "Rock-A-Hula Baby" in the 1961 feature *Blue Hawaii*, and "Kissin' Cousins," the title track from the 1964 film.

On January 18, 1966, the 50-year-old psychiatrist-songwriter quarreled with his wife, Elaine, over a television set in their seventh floor apartment at 322 Central Park West in New York City. Leaving their 12-year-old daughter asleep in another room, Elaine Wise left the apartment to take a short walk while her husband settled down. Rounding the corner of 92nd Street, the woman saw her husband's crumpled body, clad in shorts and a tee-shirt, on the sidewalk below their apartment window. Mrs. Wise told authorities that while her husband had often threatened suicide, she never took him seriously.

Wiswell, Louis C.

In a long career in the theatre, Wiswell produced many plays starring his late wife Zelda Sears (1873–1935) and was associated with some of the giants of American theatrical production including David Belasco, Homer F. Curran, and Henry W. Savage. Wiswell was retired and living in Beverly Hills, California, when a friend of his daughter's dropped by his apartment at 215 S. Spalding Drive on January 29, 1942. A note tacked to the front door warned: "Do not enter. Call the police." When authorities entered the apartment, they found the 78-year-old theatrical producer dead, a bullet through his heart, and numerous notes at his bedside. In them, Wiswell stated that he took his life so that he "no longer would be a burden to those around me."

Withers, Grant

Born Granville G. Withers in Pueblo, Colorado, on January 17, 1904, the veteran film actor came to California in the early twenties as a newspaper reporter for *The Los Angeles Record*. In films since 1926 (*Fighting Hearts*, *The Gentle Cyclone*), Withers was a leading man in silents, but with the advent of sound was relegated to roles in B-films and serials (*The Red Rider*, 1934; *Fighting Marines*, 1935; *Jungle Jim*, 1937). In a career spanning more than 30 years, Withers appeared in nearly 200 films (including many Westerns) and in guest spots on several television shows

(*Gunsmoke, Cheyenne, Zane Grey Theater*). Withers' last screen role was a bit part, "Paul Moran," in director Roger Corman's 1958 low-budget gangster film *I, Mobster.*

Married five times, Withers caused a scandal in 1930 when he eloped to Yuma, Arizona with a 17-year-old Loretta Young, a "Wampas Baby Star" in 1929. The marriage was annulled the same year. On the evening of March 27, 1959, the 55-year-old actor was found dead from an overdose of prescription sleeping pills in the bedroom of his North Hollywood bachelor apartment at 4817 Ben Avenue. Withers, wearing eyeglasses, was in bed holding a phone receiver. A note on a bedside table read: "Please forgive me — my family — I was so unhappy. It's better this way. Thanks to all my friends. Sorry I let them down." Informed of her first husband's death, Loretta Young appeared shaken and repeatedly uttered, "Oh, I'm so sorry." According to friends, Withers had recently been despondent over financial matters. His death came on the first anniversary of his mother's passing in 1958.

Wolf, Jutta

Last seen professionally in an off Broadway production of James Joyce's *Exiles* a year before, Wolf swallowed two bottles of sleeping pills in her New York city apartment at 51 Fifth Avenue on February 24, 1958. The actress was 33.

Woodson, Mary

Soul singer Al Green had already logged seven Top Ten hits with "Let's Stay Together" (1971), "Look What You've Done for Me" (1972), "I'm Still in Love with You" (1972), "You Ought to Be with Me" (1972), "Call Me" (1973), "Here I Am" (1973), and "Sha-La-La (Make me Happy)" (1974) when scandal and tragedy touched his life in the early morning hours of October 18, 1974. Minutes after Green informed Mary Woodson, his 29-year-old married girlfriend, that he would not marry her, the singer went upstairs in his house at 1404 St. Paul in northwest Shelby County outside of Memphis, Tennessee to take a bath.

In an act that has since become the stuff of show biz legend, Woodson (who had been receiving psychiatric treatment for suicidal depression) entered the bathroom and flung a pot of boiling grits on Green, inflicting second degree burns on his back, arms, and stomach. Green fled to the bedroom of Carlotta Beth Williams, his married 21-year-old houseguest, and barricaded the door. The frightened couple remained there for half an hour after hearing two gunshots from another part of the house. When the couple emerged they found Woodson lying in a hallway near her bedroom dead from a single shot to the head from a .38-caliber Rossi revolver found on the floor near her body. Police described the second bullet found in a nearby wall as a "courage shot" probably fired by Woodson to "test" the weapon and to build up her nerve. Woodson's purse contained a three-page handwritten note to Green. It read (in part): "All I wanted to do was to be with you and love you until I die. I love you, Al. I'm not mad just unhappy because I can't be with you." Green's press statement released through his public relations consultant said: "I am deeply hurt because of Mary Woodson's disastrous action — not because of what she did to me, but because of taking her own life.... I pray that God will forgive her."

FURTHER READING

Green, Al, and Seay, Davin. *Take Me to the River.* New York: HarperEntertainment, 2000.

Yamamota, Tojo

Yamamota (real name Harold Watanabe) was a villainous fixture in the Nashville, Tennessee, wrestling circuit for three decades. The 5'7", 230 pound grappler began wrestling in 1953 and, with Alex Perez, won the Southern Tag Team Title in 1964. In the seventies, Yamamota teamed with George Gulas to win the Mid-America Tag Team Title in 1977.

Although the wrestler teamed with Jerry Jarrett to hold the Mid-America Title in 1980, he spent most of the decade as a manager overseeing the careers of Phil Hickerson, Akio Sato, and Tarzan Goto. In late 1991, Yamamota was forced to retire after being diagnosed with kidney disease and diabetes. On February 19, 1992, the 51-year-old wrestler shot himself in the right temple with a .25-caliber automatic pistol in his apartment on Lebanon Road in Nashville, Tennessee. In a handwritten note found next to his body, Yamamota thanked the apartment manager for the man's kindness to him during his illness.

York, Duke

York, in films since 1933 with an uncredited role in *Roman Scandals*, was a stuntman and bit player in more than 60 films until his death in 1952. While largely uncredited, York often appeared as a tough (*Sworn Enemy*, 1936; *Never Give a Sucker an Even Break*, 1941), a minor functionary (a guard in the 1952 James Stewart bio-pic *Carbine Williams*), and in many Westerns (*Silver Canyon*, 1951). In 1936 York played "King Kala," ruler of an underwater kingdom of shark-men, in Universal's *Flash Gordon* serial starring Buster Crabbe in the title role. On January 24, 1952, the 43-year-old character actor phoned his ex-fiancée, Catherine Moench, from his Los Angeles apartment at 1771 North Sycamore Avenue. During their three hour conversation he repeatedly threatened to kill himself. Alone across town in her Beverly Hills apartment, Moench tried to keep York on the line while trying to summon outside aid. Finally, Moench heard a gunshot. She notified a friend of York's who hurriedly dropped by his apartment. York was found sprawled on the floor, the phone receiver across his chest, a gun nearby. When the authorities arrived, a detective hung up the phone. It instantly rang and after the officer identified himself, Moench responded, "So he did it." York (real name Charles E. Sinsabaugh) is interred in Foyer F of the Abbey of the Psalms in the Hollywood Forever Cemetery.

Young, Faron

Variously known throughout his 40–plus year career as the "Hillbilly Heartthrob" and the "Singing Sheriff," Young was born the son of a dairy farmer in Shreveport, Louisiana, on February 25, 1932. He briefly attended Shreveport's Centenary College, but dropped out to become a regular on the "Louisiana Hayride." While on the show, Young teamed with Webb Pierce and the duo performed in honky-tonks and nightclubs throughout the South. Shortly after Capitol Records signed him in 1952, the country singer was drafted into the Army, where he spent the Korean War in the Special Services division singing for troops in Asia and appearing in recruitment shows. While on leave in 1952, Young recorded his first Capitol single "Goin' Steady." Released on January 10, 1953, the tune peaked at Number 2 and stayed on the charts for 18 weeks. Discharged from the Army in November 1954, Young released the Top Ten hit "If You Ain't Lovin'" followed quickly in 1955 by his first Number 1 single, "Live Fast, Love Hard, Die Young."

The singer's unique meld of gritty honky-tonk *a la* Hank Williams with smooth pop vocalizing *a la* Jim Reeves kept him on the charts for 36 years, including four other Number 1 hits: "Alone With You" (1958), "Country Girl" (1959), "Hello Walls" (1961, written by Willie Nelson), and "It's Four in the Morning" (1971). Young also appeared in several television shows and films including *Hidden Heart* (1956), *Daniel Boone, Trail Blazer* (1957), *Raiders of Old California* (1957), *Country Music Holiday* (1958), *Second Fiddle to a Steel Guitar* (1965), *Nashville Rebel* (1966), and *What am I Bid?* (1967). In 1963, Young cofounded the country music publication *Music City News*. In 1965 he left the Grand Ole Opry for the more lucrative private tour circuit. Though he continued to chart throughout the period, by the late seventies (his last Top Ten hit, "Some Kind of Woman," came in 1974) and early eighties Young's career had noticeably slowed.

Offstage, Young's behavior often rivalled the lyrics of his songs. In the eighties two women filed physical abuse charges against the singer and he was twice arrested in 1983 for drunk driving. In an October 1986 divorce proceeding from his wife, Young admitted that during a heated argument with the woman he fired gunshots into the ceiling of his home. "I figure it's my house," Young told the judge. In the early nineties, crippled by emphysema and prostate cancer, Young unofficially retired from performing and limited his appearances to occasional spots on the TNN talk show *Nashville Now*. In 1996 Young sold his tour bus, ceased all personal appearances, and openly criticized Nashville's musical establishment for its disregard of the older country stars. Young complained that they were not only underappreciated, but ill paid in comparison to the current crop of younger Nashville performers who had yet to "pay their dues" in the business.

Depressed over his declining health and feeling abandoned by Music Row, the 64-year-old "Singing Sheriff" penned a suicide note and then shot himself in the head with a .38-caliber revolver in his home on Montchanin Road outside Nashville, Tennessee, on December 9, 1996. A friend found the mortally wounded singer around 1:40 A.M. the following day. Surrounded by his four children from a past marriage, the country legend died later that afternoon at the Columbia-Summit Medical Center in Nashville. Young was cremated and his ashes scattered over Old Hickory Lake near Hendersonville, Tennessee. Asked to comment on his friend's death, Waylon Jennings said, "It's just too sad to talk about."

Young, Gig

Born Byron Ellsworth Barr in St. Cloud, Minnesota, on November 4, 1913, the future Gig Young moved to Washington, D.C., in 1932 after his family lost their canning business during the Depression. In D.C., Young worked on a used car lot by day and took act-

ing classes at night. The classes led to his first semi-professional theatrical experience with the local Phil Hayden Players and to some screen appearances in non-union industrial films. Telling his parents that he was sharing gas expenses with a friend driving to Hollywood, the 25 year old in fact hitchhiked to the film capital in 1938. Young pumped gas, waited tables, cut grass, and finally built scenery to pay his weekly tuition at the prestigious Pasadena Community Playhouse.

Young acted in nine plays there from February 1939 through May 1940 before being spotted by a Warner Bros. talent scout. Impressed by the newcomer's striking good looks, winning smile, easygoing manner, and obvious appeal to women, the studio signed Young to a long term contract at $75 a week on March 29, 1941. As "Bryon Barr" (his real name), the fledgling actor appeared in several small parts (*The Man Who Came to Dinner*, 1941; *Sergeant York*, 1941; *Dive Bomber*, 1941; *Captains of the Clouds*; 1942) before landing the feature role that would launch his career and rename him. In 1942, he played the character "Gig Young" opposite Barbara Stanwyck in *The Gay Sisters*. At studio head Jack Warner's insistence, Byron Barr was rechristened Gig Young. The Warner publicity department played up the gimmick of an actor being named after his screen character in the film's promotion. Young followed this critically acclaimed performance with another strong role in the 1943 Bette Davis film *Old Acquaintance*.

The actor's career momentum was halted by World War II. After his discharge from the Coast Guard in 1945, Young returned to Hollywood and a succession of weak roles in minor films (*Escape Me Never*, 1947; *The Woman in White*, 1948), which set the stage for the frustrated actor to be forever typecast as a perennial second lead, bon vivant, or unsuccessful suitor in a string of sophisticated comedies. Dropped by Warners in 1948, Young free-lanced at various studios before signing a contract with MGM in 1951. That year he was nominated for a Supporting Actor Oscar for his true-to-life role as an alcoholic in MGM's *Come Fill the Cup* starring James Cagney. Although Young lost the Oscar to Karl Malden (*A Streetcar Named Desire*), he had every reason to believe that he would now be cast in stronger roles. He was not. After appearing in the mediocre *Holiday for Sinners* (1952), Young performed with distinction on Broadway in *Oh Men! Oh Women!* from December 1953 through mid–June 1954.

While continuing to make films (*The Desperate Hours*, 1955), Young became the host of the ABC television show *Warner Brothers Presents* for its entire 1955–1956 run. In 1958, Young received another Best Supporting Actor Academy Award nomination for his performance in the Paramount comedy *Teacher's Pet* starring Clark Gable. He lost to Burl Ives in *The Big Country*. Young was well cast as a charming con artist in the NBC television series *The Rogues* co-starring fellow suicide Charles Boyer (see entry), but the program only lasted the 1964–1965 season. On his third try, the aging actor won a Best Supporting Actor Oscar in 1969 for his brilliant portrayal of the Depression-era dance marathon promoter "Rocky Gravo" in *They Shoot Horses, Don't They?*

GIG YOUNG— Young's suave and debonair screen persona belied a complex true-life personality plagued by deep-seated self-doubt fuelled by drug and alcohol addictions. Typecast as the perennial second lead in a series of sophisticated comedies, the actor was at his best playing tormented characters like the alcoholic in *Come Fill the Cup* (1951). In 1969 he was awarded the Oscar for Best Supporting Actor for his riveting portrayal of a Depression-era dance marathon promoter in *They Shoot Horses, Don't They?* On October 19, 1978, the 64-year-old actor murdered his fifth wife, Kim Schmidt, in their New York City apartment before turning the gun on himself.

By this point in his career, however, years of alcoholism and addiction to sedatives had left Young physically and emotionally ravaged. While he continued to get supporting roles in interesting films like director Sam Peckinpah's *Bring Me the Head of Alfredo Garcia* (1974) and *The Killer Elite* (1975), Young's

career was essentially over after his Oscar win. In late 1977, the actor was brought to Hong Kong to work on his 55th and final film, the prophetically titled *The Game of Death*. Filming was originally suspended in 1973 after the death of its star, Kung fu master Bruce Lee, but Golden Harvest studio, attempting to cash in on the star's enduring popularity, scrapped all the scenes except Lee's and reshot a new story around them.

On the set, Young met German-born Kim Schmidt, an attractive 30-year-old script girl whose lifelong dream was to marry a film star and come to America. At 63, Young had already been to the altar on four previous occasions. His first marriage to actress Sheila Stapler on August 2, 1940, ended in divorce on October 6, 1949. Young married Sophie Rosenstein, a Warner Bros. drama coach six years his senior, on January 1, 1951. Deeply in love, Young remained devoted to Rosenstein until her death from cervical cancer on November 10, 1952. Marriage three, to Elizabeth Montgomery, daughter of actor Robert Montgomery who was destined to become famous as "Samantha" on the popular television show *Bewitched*, occurred in Las Vegas on December 28, 1956. They divorced in 1963. A fourth marriage, to Beverly Hills real estate broker Elaine Whitman in 1963, produced one child and ended in a rancorous divorce in 1967.

Determined to make his marriage to Kim Schmidt work, Young moved into apartment 1BB in the Osborne at 205 West Fifty-seventh Street in New York City and valiantly struggled to kick his alcohol and drug addictions. On October 19, 1978, between the hours of 2:30 and 3:30 P.M., the building manager heard what sounded like two gunshots issuing from the couple's apartment. He did not notify authorities, however, until becoming suspicious after groceries delivered to the apartment stood outside the door for hours. Police entered the apartment at 7:30 P.M. to find the fully-clothed pair dead on the bedroom floor. Schmidt had been killed instantly by a single pistol shot to the base of the skull. Near her on the floor lay Young with a .38-caliber snub-nosed Smith & Wesson pistol clenched in his hand. The actor known for his sophisticated charm had placed the gun in his mouth and fired.

A diary written in Young's hand and opened to September 27, 1978, was found on a desk in the sitting room. The entry read, "We Were Married Today." A search of the premises yielded 350 rounds of ammunition and three other handguns in addition to the murder weapon. Also found at the scene were explicit snapshots taken with an automatic timer of Young and his wife of three weeks engaged in various sexual positions. When the autopsy revealed no sign of alcohol or barbiturates in the actor's system, authorities offered a theory of the murder-suicide based upon available evidence. According to the police theory of the crime, Young was already acutely stressed out by money problems and his withdrawal from drugs and alcohol when the couple began arguing. Schmidt, a U.S. citizen since their marriage, may have threatened to leave him to work as a publicist for her old boyfriend. As evidenced by the existence of the sex photos (ostensibly used to excite the dissipated actor), she may have mentioned his periodic impotence. Young's remains were cremated and interred under his real name, Byron Barr, in the Green Hills Cemetery in Waynesville, North Carolina.

FURTHER READING

Eells, George. *Final Gig: The Man Behind the Murder*. San Diego: Harcourt Brace Jovanovich, 1991.

Younger, A. (Andrew) P.

In Hollywood since the mid-to-late teens, Younger either contributed the story, adapted, or wrote more than 50 films. These included *Fair and Warmer* (1919), *Desperate Youth* (1921), *The Torrent* (1924, also directed), *The Devil's Cargo* (1925), *In Old Kentucky* (1927), and *Five and Ten* (1931). At the height of his career as a scenarist-screenwriter for Metro-Goldwyn-Mayer, Younger was earning $1,500 a week plus bonuses. In the late evening of November 29, 1931 (according to Younger's stepson, Frank Deering), the 41-year-old screenwriter was awakened from sleep by a dog barking in the back yard of his luxurious home at 145 South Beachwood Avenue in Los Angeles. Fearing a prowler, Younger found his .38-caliber automatic pistol and went into the bathroom to examine the weapon. The gun accidentally discharged, fatally striking him in the right temple. Younger died soon afterward at the Georgia Street Receiving Hospital.

Initial police reports differed from Deering's account. According to the investigating officer's report: "Younger stood in front of a mirror in the bathroom, held the gun in his right hand and shot himself in the right temple." Forensics confirmed that the gun had been placed tightly against his head when fired. An investigation conducted for the coroner's jury uncovered two possible motives that supported a ruling of suicide. Although Younger had $30,000 in the bank, his lucrative contract with MGM had been terminated the week before his death. That same week, Younger had been arrested during a police liquor raid at his home. The screenwriter's death was officially ruled a suicide.

"Yvonnek" see *Jullion, M. Arthur*

Zegart, Arthur

A three-time Emmy nominee, Zegart was involved in the production of some 125 documentaries, many of which were shown on such television series as *NBC White Paper*, *Du Pont Show of the Week*, *Directions*, and *N.E.T. Journal*. During World War II, Zegart led an Air Force photography unit and in the late forties was chief of the United Nations film division. In 1956 he received the Albert Lasker Award for writing and directing *Wassaic Story*, a CBS exposé focusing on the care of retarded children at an upstate New York mental hospital. Zegart, 72, suffered for several years with a blood disease when, on February 2, 1989, he

leaped to his death off the Tappan Zee Bridge near his home in Nyack, New York.

Zimmerman, Frank G.

The son of the so-called "dean of theatrical managers" in Philadelphia and New York, Zimmerman, 45, inherited a large share of his father's $3 million estate. Several months prior to his suicide, the widely-known Philadelphia-based theatrical man underwent a minor operation and, although fully recovered, became morose and nervous. On the morning of July 12, 1927, Zimmerman locked himself in the bathroom of his apartment at Forty-sixth and Pine Streets and shot himself in the head. His wife heard the shot, summoned help, and after the door was forced, found her partially dressed husband lying in the tub clutching a revolver.

Zinn, A. M.

A former vaudeville director and musical comedy lyricist, Zinn brooded for ten years over the death of his wife, known professionally as Frances Vanita Grey. Fearing insanity, the 55 year old shot himself in the head as he sat in the lobby of the Hotel LaSalle in Chicago on November 19, 1928. Among the numerous notes left by Zinn was a request that Al Jolson and Leon Errol be notified of his death and that he be buried in potter's field.

Zoltai, Stephen

A 49-year-old music editor employed by Carl Fischer, Inc., Zoltai fired a .22-caliber rifle shot into his chest while in the bedroom of his home at 33-35 Seventieth Street, Jackson Heights, Queens, on May 9, 1949. Zoltai's sister told police that her brother had been depressed over poor health for some time.

BIBLIOGRAPHY

Books

Aherne, Brian. *A Dreadful Man*. New York: Simon and Schuster, 1979.

American Film Institute Catalog of Motion Pictures Produced in the United States. Berkeley: University of California Press, 1971–.

American National Biography. New York: Oxford University Press, 1999.

Anger, Kenneth. *Hollywood Babylon*. San Francisco: Straight Arrow Books, 1975.

_____. *Hollywood Babylon II*. 1st ed. New York: Dutton, 1984.

ASCAP Biographical Dictionary. 4th ed. New York: R. R. Bowker Co., 1980.

Azerrad, Michael. *Come as You Are: The Story of Nirvana*. 1st ed. New York: Doubleday, 1993.

Baker, Carlos. *Ernest Hemingway: A Life Story*. New York: Scribner, 1989.

Barrymore, Diana, and Frank, Gerold. *Too Much, Too Soon*. 1st ed. New York: Holt, 1957.

Bebbington, Warren, ed. *The Oxford Companion to Australian Music*. Melbourne and New York: Oxford University Press, 1997.

Bennett, Jill, and Goodwin, Suzanne. *Godfrey: A Special Time Remembered*. London: Houghton and Stoughton, 1983.

Bessy, Maurice, and Chardans, Jean-Louis. *Dictionnaire du Cinéma et de la Télévision*. 4 vols. Paris: J.J. Pauvert, 1965–1971.

Birkos, Alexander S., comp. *Soviet Cinema: Directors and Films*. Hamden, Conn.: Archon Books, 1976.

Black, Suzi. *Nirvana Tribute: The Life and Death of Kurt Cobain, the Full Story*. London: Omnibus, 1994.

Blanch, Tony, and Schreiber, Brad. *Death in Paradise: An Illustrated History of the Los Angeles County Department of Coroner*. Los Angeles: General Publishing Group, 1998.

Bogle, Donald. *Dorothy Dandridge: A Biography*. New York: Amistad, 1997.

Boussinot, Roger. *L'encyclopédie du Cinéma*. 2 vols. Paris: Bordas, 1995.

Bradshaw, Jon. *Dreams That Money Can Buy: The Tragic Life of Libby Holman*. 1st ed. New York: W. Morrow, 1985.

Brayer, Elizabeth. *George Eastman: A Biography*. Baltimore: Johns Hopkins University Press, 1996.

Brown, Kelly R. *Florence Lawrence, the Biograph Girl: America's First Movie Star*. Jefferson, N.C.: McFarland, 1999.

Buffalo Child Long Lance. *Long Lance*. New York: Cosmopolitan Book Corp., 1928.

Canadian Encyclopedia. 2nd ed. 4 vols. Edmonton: Hurtig Publishers, 1988.

Cantwell, Robert. *The Real McCoy; The Life and Times of Norman Selby*. Princeton, N.J.: Auerbach Publishers, 1971.

Castleman, Harry, and Podrazik, Walter J. *Harry and Wally's Favorite TV Shows*. 1st ed. New York: Prentice Hall Press, 1989.

Clarke, Martin, and Woods, Paul, ed. *Kurt Cobain: The Cobain Dossier*. London: Plexus, 1999.

Cohen, David. *Phil Ochs: A Bio-Bibliography*. Westport, Conn.: Greenwood Press, 1999.

Cohen-Stratnyer, Barbara Naomi. *Biographical Dictionary of Dance*. New York: Schirmer Books; London: Collier Macmillan, 1982.

Collier, Peter. *The Fondas: A Hollywood Dynasty*. New York: Putnam's Sons, 1991.

Conner, Floyd. *Lupe Velez and Her Lovers*. New York: Barricade Books, 1993.

Copeland, Bobby J. *B-Western Boot Hill: A Final Tribute to the Cowboys and Cowgirls Who Rode the Saturday Matinee Movie Range*. Madison, N.C.: Empire Publishing, 1999.

Corey, Arthur. *Danse Macabre: The Life and Death of Andreas Pavley*. Dallas: Bridwell Library, Southern Methodist University, 1977.

Crivello, Kirk. *Fallen Angels: The Lives and Untimely Deaths of Fourteen Hollywood Beauties.* Secaucus, N.J.: Citadel Press, 1988.

Crosby, Gary, and Firestone, Ross. *Going My Own Way.* 1st ed. Garden City, N.Y.: Doubleday, 1983.

Curtis, Deborah. *Touching from a Distance: Ian Curtis and Joy Division.* London and Boston: Faber and Faber, 1995.

Curtis, James. *James Whale: A New World of Gods and Monsters.* Boston: Faber and Faber, 1998.

Dalton, David. *James Dean: The Mutant King.* New York: St. Martin's Press, 1983.

Dandridge, Dorothy, and Conrad, Earl. *Everything and Nothing; The Dorothy Dandridge Tragedy.* New York: Abelard-Schuman, 1970.

Dannemann, Monika. *The Inner Worlds of Jimi Hendrix.* 1st U.S. ed. New York: St. Martin's Press, 1995.

Dictionary of American Biography. 22 vols. New York: C. Scribner's Sons, 1928–1944 (with additional supplements).

Doherty, Eddie. *The Rain Girl: The Tragic Story of Jeanne Eagels.* 1st ed. Philadelphia: Macrae Smith Company, 1930.

Dooley, Kirk. *Tragedies and Triumphs of America's First Family of Wrestling.* Dallas, Tex.: Taylor Pub. Co., 1987.

Doyle, Billy H. *The Ultimate Directory of Film Technicians: A Necrology of Dates and Places of Births and Deaths of More Than 9,000 Producers, Screenwriters, Composers, Cinematographers, Art Directors, Costume Designers, Choreographers, Executives, and Publicists.* Lanham, Md.: Scarecrow Press, 1999.

Edmonds, Andy. *Hot Toddy: The True Story of Hollywood's Most Sensational Murder.* New York: Morrow, 1989.

Eells, George. *Final Gig: The Man Behind the Murder.* San Diego: Harcourt Brace Jovanovich, 1991.

Eliot, Marc. *Death of a Rebel.* Garden City, N.Y.: Anchor Press, 1979.

Etkind, Marc. *—Or Not to Be: A Collection of Suicide Notes.* New York: Riverhead Books, 1997.

Fleischer, Richard. *Just Tell Me When to Cry: A Memoir.* 1st Carroll & Graf ed. New York: Carroll & Graf, 1993.

Flowers, Claude. *Dreams Never End: New Order + Joy Division.* London: Omnibus, 1995.

Fonda, Henry, and Teichmann, Howard. *Fonda: My Life.* New York: New American Library, 1981.

Francisco, Charles. *Gentleman: The William Powell Story.* 1st ed. New York: St. Martin's Press, 1985.

Franklin, Joe. *Joe Franklin's Encyclopedia of Comedians.* 1st ed. Secaucus, N.J.: Citadel Press, 1979.

Freedland, Michael. *Gregory Peck: A Biography.* New York: W. Morrow, 1980.

Gammond, Peter. *The Oxford Companion to Popular Music.* Oxford (England) and New York: Oxford University Press, 1991.

Garner, Joe. *We Interrupt This Broadcast: The 47 Events That Stopped Our Lives.* Naperville, Ill.: Sourcebooks, 1998.

Garraty, John A., and Carnes, Mark C. *American National Biography.* 24 vols. New York: Oxford University Press, 1999.

Gee, Michael. *The Final Days of Michael Hutchence.* London: Omnibus Press, 1998.

Gilmore, John. *Laid Bare: A Memoir of Wrecked Lives and the Hollywood Death Trip.* Los Angeles: Amok, 1997.

Goble, Alan, ed. *The Complete Index to British Sound Film Since 1928.* New Providence, N.J.: Bowker Saur, 1999.

Golden, Eve. *Platinum Girl: The Life and Legends of Jean Harlow.* New York: Abbeville Press, 1991.

Goodwin, Cliff. *When the Wind Changed: The Life and Death of Tony Hancock.* London: Century, 1999.

Green, Al, and Seay, Davin. *Take Me to the River.* New York: HarperEntertainment, 2000.

Guiles, Fred Lawrence. *Legend: The Life and Death of Marilyn Monroe.* New York: Stein and Day, 1984.

_____. *Norma Jean; The Life of Marilyn Monroe.* New York: McGraw-Hill, 1969.

Harvey, Diana Karanikas, and Harvey, Jackson. *Dead Before Their Time.* New York: MetroBooks, 1996.

Hayward, Brooke. *Haywire.* 1st ed. New York: Knopf, 1977.

Helm, Levon, and Davis, Stephen. *This Wheel's on Fire: Levon Helm and the Story of The Band.* 1st ed. New York: William Morrow & Co., 1993.

Hemingway, Gregory H. *Papa: A Personal Memoir.* Boston: Houghton Mifflin, 1976.

Henderson, Jan Alan. *George Reeves: The Man, the Myth, the Mystery.* Hollywood: Cult Movies, 1995.

_____. *Speeding Bullet: The Life and Bizarre Death of George Reeves.* Grand Rapids, Mich.: M. Bifulco, 1999.

Henry, Marilyn, and DeSourdis, Ron. *The Films of Alan Ladd.* 1st ed. Secaucus, N.J.: Citadel Press, 1981.

Hitchcock, H. Wiley, and Sadie, Stanley, eds. *The New Grove Dictionary of American Music.* 4 vols. London: Macmillan, 1986.

Hotchner, A. E. *Papa Hemingway; A Personal Memoir.* New York: Random House, 1966.

Houseman, John. *Final Dress.* New York: Simon and Schuster, 1983.

Humphries, Patrick. *Nick Drake.* London: Bloomsbury, 1997.

International Dictionary of Films and Filmakers. 3rd ed. 4 vols. Detroit: St. James Press, 1997.

International Encyclopedia of Dance. 6 vols. New York: Oxford University Press, 1998.

Jackson, Kenneth T., ed. *The Scribner Encyclopedia of American Lives.* 2 vols. New York: Charles Scribner's Sons, 1998.

Jacobson, Laurie, and Wanamaker, Marc. *Hollywood Haunted: A Ghostly Tour of Filmland.* 1st ed. Santa Monica: Angel City Press, 1984.

_____. *Hollywood Heartbreak: The Tragic and Mysterious Deaths of Hollywood's Most Remarkable Legends.* New York: Simon & Schuster, 1984.

Jason, Rick. *Scrapbooks of My Mind: A Hollywood Autobiography.* [Moorpark, Calif.?]: Argoe Publishing, 2000.

Johnson, Mark. *An Ideal for Living: An History of Joy Division: From Their Mythical Origins as the Stiff Kittens to the Programmed Future as New Order.* London and New York: Bobcat Books, 1986.

Kashner, Sam, and Schoenberger, Nancy. *Hollywood Kryptonite: The Bulldog, the Lady, and the Death of Superman.* 1st ed. New York: St. Martin's Press, 1996.

Katchmer, George A. *Eighty Silent Film Stars: Biographies and Filmographies of the Obscure to the Well Known.* Jefferson, N.C.: McFarland, 1991.

Katz, Ephraim. *The Film Encyclopedia.* 2nd ed. New York: HarperCollins Publishers, 1994.

Kernfeld, Barry, ed. *The New Grove Dictionary of Jazz.* 2 vols. London: Macmillan, 1988.

Keyes, Evelyn. *Scarlett O'Hara's Younger Sister: My Lively Life In and Out of Hollywood.* 1st ed. Secaucus, N.J.: L. Stuart, 1977.

Kingsbury, Paul, ed. *The Encyclopedia of Country Music: The Ultimate Guide to the Music.* New York: Oxford University Press, 1998.

Langman, Larry. *Encyclopedia of American Film Comedy.* New York: Garland, 1987.

_____. *A Guide to American Screenwriters: The Sound Era, 1929–1982.* New York: Garland Pub., 1984.

Larkin, Colin, ed. *The Guinness Encyclopedia of Popular Music.* 3rd ed. London and New York: Muze, 1998.

Leigh, Janet. *There Really Was a Hollywood.* Garden City, N.Y.: Doubleday, 1984.

Lentz, Harris M. *Biographical Dictionary of Professional Wrestling.* Jefferson, N.C.: McFarland, 1997.

_____. *Western and Frontier Film and Television Credits 1903–1995.* Jefferson, N.C.: McFarland, 1996.

Linet, Beverly. *Ladd: The Life, the Legend, the Legacy of Alan Ladd: A Biography.* New York: Arbor House, 1979.

Linkletter, Art. *Hobo on the Way to Heaven.* 1st ed. Elgin, Ill.: D. C. Cook Pub. Co., 1980.

Lynn, Kenneth S. *Hemingway.* New York: Simon and Schuster, 1987.

Lyons, Len, and Perlo, Don. *Jazz Portraits: The Lives and Music of the Jazz Masters.* New York: Morrow, 1989.

McClintick, David. *Indecent Exposure: A True Story of Hollywood and Wall Street.* New York: Morrow, 1982.

Machlin, Milt. *Libby.* New York: Dorchester Pub. Co., 1980.

McKinney, Grange B. *Art Acord and the Movies: A Biography and Filmography.* Raleigh, N.C.: Wyatt Classics, 2000.

Mailer, Norman. *Marilyn, a Biography.* New York: Grosset & Dunlap, 1973.

Maltin, Leonard, ed. *Leonard Maltin's 2000 Movie & Video Guide.* New York: Signet, 1999.

_____, and Bann, Richard W. *Our Gang: The Life and Times of the Little Rascals.* New York: Crown Publishers, 1976.

Mank, Gregory William. *Women in Horror Films, 1940s.* Jefferson, N.C.: McFarland, 1999.

Mann, William J. *Wisecracker: The Life and Times of William Haines, Hollywood's First Openly Gay Star.* New York: Viking, 1998.

Manso, Peter. *Brando: The Biography.* 1st ed. New York: Hyperion, 1994.

The Marshall Cavendish Illustrated History of Popular Music. Reference ed. 21 vols. New York: M. Cavendish, 1989–1990.

Marx, Samuel, and Vanderveen, Joyce. *Deadly Illusions: Jean Harlow and the Murder of Paul Bern.* New York: Random House, 1990.

Matovina, Dan. *Without You: The Tragic Story of Badfinger.* San Mateo, Calif.: Frances Glover Books, 1997.

Meade, Marion. *Buster Keaton: Cut to the Chase.* New York: HarperCollins, 1995.

Mellow, James R. *Hemingway: A Life Without Consequences.* Boston: Houghton Mifflin, 1992.

Merman, Ethel, and Eells, George. *Merman.* New York: Simon and Schuster, 1978.

Meyers, Jeffrey. *Hemingway, a Biography.* 1st ed. New York: Harper & Row, 1985.

Mills, Earl. *Dorothy Dandridge: A Portrait in Black.* Los Angeles: Holloway House, 1970 (Reprinted 1999).

Monroe, Marilyn. *My Story.* New York: Stein and Day, 1974.

Morsberger, Robert E., ed. *American Screenwriters.* Detroit, Mich.: Gale Research Co., 1984.

Moseley, Rex. *Rex Harrison: The First Biography.* Kent, England: New English Library, 1987.

Mosley, Leonard. *Zanuck: The Rise and Fall of Hollywood's Last Tycoon.* 1st ed. Boston: Little, Brown, 1984.

Newcomb, Horace, ed. *Museum of Broadcast Communications Encyclopedia of Television.* 3 vols. Chicago: Fitzroy Dearborn Publishers, 1997.

Notable Names in the American Theatre. New and Rev. ed. Clifton, N.J.: J. T. White, 1976.

Oakes, Philip. *Tony Hancock*. London: Woburn Press, 1975.

O'Brien, Pat. *Outwitting the Hun; My Escape from a German Prison Camp*. New York: Harper & Brothers, 1918.

O'Connor, Carroll. *I Think I'm Outta Here: A Memoir of All My Families*. New York: Pocket Books, 1998.

Oliver, Charles M. *Ernest Hemingway A to Z: The Essential Reference to the Life and Work*. New York: Facts on File, 1999.

Palmer, Scott. *British Film Actors' Credits, 1895–1987*. Jefferson, N.C.: McFarland, 1988.

Parish, James Robert. *The Hollywood Celebrity Death Book: From Theda Bara and Rudolph Valentino to Marilyn Monroe and James Dean*. Las Vegas, Nev.: Pioneer Books, 1993.

Perry, Hamilton Darby. *Libby Holman: Body and Soul*. 1st ed. Boston: Little, Brown, 1983.

Perry, Jeb H. *Variety Obits: An Index to Obituaries in Variety, 1905–1978*. Metuchen, N.J.: Scarecrow Press, 1980.

Pike, Jeff. *Death of Rock and Roll: Untimely Demises, Morbid Preoccupations, and Forecasts of Doom in Rock Music*. Boston: Faber and Faber, 1993.

Porter, David L., ed. *Biographical Dictionary of American Sports: Basketball and Other Indoor Sports*. New York: Greenwood Press, 1989.

Powell, William S., ed. *Dictionary of North Carolina Biography*. 6 vols. Chapel Hill: University of North Carolina Press, 1979–1996.

Pruetzel, Maria, and Barbour, John A. *The Freddie Prinze Story*. Kalamazoo, Mich.: Master's Press, 1978.

Quirk, Lawrence J. *Fasten Your Seat Belts: The Passionate Life of Bette Davis*. 1st ed. New York: Morrow, 1990.

_____. *Margaret Sullavan: Child of Fate*. 1st ed. New York: St. Martin's Press, 1986.

Rajadhyaksha, Ashish. *Encyclopaedia of Indian Cinema*. New rev. ed. Chicago: Fitzroy Dearborn, 1999.

Repsch, John. *The Legendary Joe Meek: The Telstar Man*. London: Woodford House, 1989.

Reynolds, Patrick. *The Gilded Leaf: Triumph, Tragedy, and Tobacco: Three Generations of the R. J. Reynolds Family and Fortune*. 1st ed. Boston: Little, Brown, 1989.

Richards, David. *Played Out: The Jean Seberg Story*. 1st ed. New York: Random House, 1981.

Riese, Randall. *Nashville Babylon: The Uncensored Truth and Private Lives of Country Music's Stars*. New York: Congdon & Weed, 1988.

Rigdon, Walter. *The Biographical Encyclopedia & Who's Who of the American Theatre*. 1st ed. New York: J. H. Heineman, 1966.

Roberts, Rachel. *No Bells on Sunday: The Journals of Rachel Roberts*. London: Pavilion, 1984.

Rooney, Mickey. *Life Is Too Short*. New York: Villard Books, 1991.

Rosenthal, Eric, ed. *Encyclopaedia of Southern Africa* 6th ed. London; New York: F. Warne, 1973.

Rovin, Jeff. *TV Babylon*. Updated ed. New York: Signet, 1987.

Ryzuk, Mary S. *The Circle Repertory Company: The First Fifteen Years*. 1st ed. Ames: Iowa State University Press, 1989.

Sanders, George. *Memoirs of a Professional Cad*. New York: G. P. Putnam's Sons, 1960.

Sandford, Christopher. *Kurt Cobain*. 1st Carroll & Graf ed. New York: Carroll & Graf, 1995.

Schessler, Kenneth. *This Is Hollywood: An Unusual Movieland Guide*. 6th ed. La Verne, Calif.: Ken Schessler Publishing, 1987.

Schumacher, Michael. *There But for Fortune: The Life of Phil Ochs*. 1st ed. New York: Hyperion, 1996.

Seinfelt, Mark. *Final Drafts: Suicides of World-Famous Authors*. Amherst, N.Y.: Prometheus Books, 1999.

Shale, Richard. *The Academy Awards Index: The Complete Categorical and Chronological Record*. Westport, Conn.: Greenwood Press, 1993.

Shapiro, Harry. *Graham Bond: The Mighty Shadow*. Enfield: Guinness Publishing, 1992.

Shevey, Sandra. *The Marilyn Scandal: Her True Life Revealed by Those Who Knew Her*. 1st U.S. ed. New York: W. Morrow, 1987.

Shulman, Irving. *Harlow, an Intimate Biography*. New York: Bernard Geis Associates, 1964.

Siebenand, Paul Alcuin. *The Beginnings of Gay Cinema in Los Angeles: The Industry and the Audience*. Thesis (Ph.D.): University of Southern California, 1975.

Slezak, Walter. *What Time's the Next Swan?* Garden City, N.Y.: Doubleday, 1962.

Slide, Anthony. *The Encyclopedia of Vaudeville*. Westport, Conn.: Greenwood Press, 1994.

Sloan, James Park. *Jerzy Kosinski: A Biography*. New York: Dutton, 1996.

Smith, Donald B. *Long Lance: The True Story of an Impostor*. Toronto, Canada: Macmillan of Canada, 1982.

Spoto, Donald. *Marilyn Monroe: The Biography*. 1st ed. New York: HarperCollins Publishers, 1993.

Steel, Danielle. *His Bright Light: The Story of Nick Traina*. New York: Delacorte Press, 1998.

Stenn, David. *Bombshell: The Life and Death of Jean Harlow*. 1st ed. New York: Doubleday, 1993.

Summers, Anthony. *Goddess: The Secret Lives of Marilyn Monroe*. New York: Macmillan, 1985.

Sutch, David, and Chippindale, Peter. *Life as Sutch: The Official Autobiography of a Monster Raving Loony*. London: HarperCollins, 1991.

Sweeney, Kevin. *Henry Fonda: A Bio-Bibliography*. New York: Greenwood Press, 1992.

Swindell, Larry. *Charles Boyer: The Reluctant Lover.* 1st ed. Garden City, N.Y.: Doubleday, 1983.

Tasker, Robert Joyce. *Grimhaven.* New York: A. A. Knopf, 1928.

Tellegen, Lou. *Women Have Been Kind: The Memoirs of Lou Tellegen.* New York: The Vanguard Press, 1931.

Thomas, Bob. *Golden Boy: The Untold Story of William Holden.* New York: St. Martin's Press, 1983.

_____. *Walt Disney: An American Original.* New York: Simon and Schuster, 1976.

Thompson, Dave. *Better to Burn Out: The Cult of Death in Rock 'n' Roll.* New York: Thunder's Mouth Press, 1999.

_____. *Never Fade Away: The Kurt Cobain Story.* St. Martin's paperbacks ed. New York: St. Martin's Paperbacks, 1994.

Thomson, David. *Showman: The Life of David O. Selznick.* 1st ed. New York: Knopf, 1992.

Towell, Garv, and Keates, Wayne E. *Saddle Pals.* Madison, N.C.: Empire Publishing, 1994.

Uglow, Jennifer S., ed. *The Continuum Dictionary of Women's Biography.* New expanded ed. New York: Continuum, 1989.

Vanderbeets, Richard. *George Sanders: An Exhausted Life.* Lanham, Md.: Madison Books, 1990.

Vazzana, Eugene Michael. *Silent Film Necrology: Births and Deaths of Over 9000 Performers, Directors, Producers and Other Filmmakers of the Silent Era, Through 1993.* Jefferson, N.C.: McFarland, 1995.

Victor, Adam. *The Marilyn Encyclopedia.* 1st ed. Woodstock, N.Y.: Overlook Press, 1999.

Vincendeau, Ginette, ed. *Encyclopedia of European Cinema.* London: Cassell: British Film Institute, 1995.

Voss, Ralph F. *A Life of William Inge: The Strains of Triumph.* Lawrence: University of Kansas Press, 1989.

Wakeman, John, ed. *World Film Directors: Volume I: 1890–1945.* New York: H. W. Wilson, 1987.

_____, ed. *World Film Directors: Volume II: 1945–1985.* New York: H. W. Wilson, 1988.

West, Mike. *Joy Division.* Todmorden, England: Babylon Books, 1984.

Westmore, Frank, and Davidson, Muriel. *The Westmores of Hollywood.* 1st ed. Philadelphia: Lippincott, 1976.

Whissen, Thomas. *Guide to American Cinema, 1930–1965.* Westport, Conn.: Greenwood Press, 1998.

Whitburn, Joel. *Joel Whitburn's Top Country Singles, 1943–1993.* Menomonee Falls, Wis.: Record Research, 1994.

_____. *Joel Whitburn's Top Pop Singles, 1955–1990.* Menomonee Falls, Wis.: Record Research Inc., 1991.

Whitfield, Eileen. *Pickford: The Woman Who Made Hollywood.* Lexington: University Press of Kentucky, 1997.

Who Was Who in the Theatre, 1912–1976: A Biographical Dictionary of Actors, Actresses, Directors, Playwrights, and Producers of the English-Speaking Theatre. 4 vols. Detroit: Gale Research Co., 1978.

Williams, Otis. *Temptations.* New York: G. P. Putnam's Sons, 1988.

Wilmut, Roger. *The Illustrated Hancock: with a Commentary.* London: Macdonald Queen Anne Press, 1986.

_____. *Tony Hancock "Artiste": A Tony Hancock Companion.* London: Eyre Methuen, 1978.

Wray, Fay. *On the Other Hand: A Life Story.* New York: St. Martin's Press, 1989.

Ziegfeld, Richard E., and Ziegfeld, Paulette. *The Ziegfeld Touch: The Life and Times of Florenz Ziegfeld, Jr.* New York: H. N. Abrams, 1993.

Publications

Adult Video News
The Advocate
Billboard
Classic Images
Crime Beat
Current Biography
Entertainment Weekly
Facts on File
Film Comment
Films in Review
GQ
Hollywood Reporter

Los Angeles Magazine
Mojo
New Yorker
Newsweek
People Weekly
Rolling Stone
Saturday Review
Spin
Time
TV Guide
Wrestling Observer

Newspapers

Albuquerque Journal
Arizona Daily Star
Arizona Republic
Asheville Citizen (Asheville, N.C.)
Atlanta Journal and Constitution
Austin-American
Austin Statesman
Australian Financial Review
Bakersfield Californian
Baltimore Sun
Beaumont Enterprise
Birmingham Post (England)
Boston Daily Globe
Boston Evening Transcript
Boston Globe
Boston Herald
Bridgeport Post (Connecticut)

Buffalo Courier Express
Buffalo News
Butte Inter Mountain
Charleston Gazette
Chicago Daily Herald
Chicago Daily Tribune
Chicago Tribune
Cincinnati Enquirer
Cleveland Plain Dealer
Columbus Dispatch
Commercial Appeal (Memphis, Tenn.)
Courier-Journal (Louisville, Ky.)
Courier-Post (Camden, N.J.)
Daily Home News (New Brunswick, N.J.)
Daily Mail (London)
Daily Mirror (London)
Daily News (Los Angeles)
Daily Telegraph (London)
Daily Yomiuri (Tokyo, Japan)
Dallas Morning News
Dayton Daily News
Des Moines Register
Detroit Free Press
Erie Daily Times
Evening Standard (London)
Ft. Wayne Journal-Gazette
Ft. Worth Star-Telegram
Fresno Bee
Gazette (Montreal)
Globe and Mail
Grand Rapids Press
Greensboro Daily News
Greenville News (South Carolina)
Guardian (London)
Hartford Courant
The Herald (Glasgow)
Honolulu Advertiser
Houston Chronicle
Houston Post
Independent (London)
Indianapolis Star
Irish Times
Jerusalem Post
Kansas City Star
Kinston Daily Free Press (Kinston, N.C.)
Las Vegas Review-Journal
Las Vegas Sun
Lodi News-Sentinel (Lodi, Calif.)
Los Angeles Daily News
Los Angeles Examiner
Los Angeles Herald-Examiner
Los Angeles Times
Mainichi Daily News
Miami Herald
Miami Herald Record
Milwaukee Journal
Milwaukee Sentinel
Minneapolis Tribune

Le Monde
Nashville Banner
National Enquirer
New Hampshire Morning Union (Manchester, N.H.)
New Orleans Times-Picayune
New York American
New York Daily News
New York Journal-American
New York Post
New York Times
Newsday
Norfolk Virginian-Pilot
Oakland Tribune
Omaha World-Herald
Orange County Register
Orlando Sentinel
Ottawa Citizen
Peoria Journal Star
Philadelphia Inquirer
Phoenix Gazette
Pittsburgh Post-Gazette
Pittsburgh Press
Portland Oregonian
Portland Press Herald
Providence Journal
Reading Eagle (Reading, Penn.)
Reno Evening Gazette
Sacramento Bee
St. Louis Post-Dispatch
San Diego Union
San Diego Union-Tribune
San Francisco Chronicle
San Francisco Examiner
San Jose Mercury Herald
Santa Fe New Mexican
Savannah Morning News
The Scotsman
Seattle Post Intelligencer
Seattle Times
SF Weekly
South Bend Tribune
Spokesman-Review (Spokane, Wash.)
The State (Columbia, S.C.)
Straits Times (Singapore)
Tampa Tribune
Le Temps
The Tennessean (Nashville, Tenn.)
Times (London)
Toledo Blade
Toronto Star
Tucson Daily Citizen
Warrensburg-Lake George News (Warrensburg, N.Y.)
Washington Post
Watertown Daily News (Watertown, N.Y.)

Websites

All Music Guide — www.allmusic.com
Find A Grave — www.findagrave.com
Findadeath — www.findadeath.com
Internet Movie Database — http://us.imdb.com

Appendix I: Occupations

Actors, Motion Picture and Stage

Abingdon, William L. 5; Acord, Art 6–7; Adams, Nick 8; Albertson, Arthur 9; Alexander, Aleta Freel 9; Alexander, Ross 9–10; Allen, Chet R. 10; Andre, Gwili 11; Angeli, Pier 11–13; Ardell, John E. 13; Armedariz, Pedro 13–14; Armitage, Pauline 14–15; Austin, Anne 15–16; Aye, Maryon (Marion) 16; Aylmer, David 17; Ayres, Dudley 17–18; Bacon, Faith 18; Bantchevsky, Bantcho 21–22; Barnet, Boris Vasilievich 22–23; Barron, Donna 23; Barry, Don "Red" 23–24; Barrymore, Diana (Blanche) 24–25; Bates, Barbara 26–27; Battles, Marjorie Ann 27; Beckett, Scott Hastings 28; Bell, Stanley 30; Benda, Marion 31; Benet, Brenda 31; Bennett, Jill 32–33; Bennison, Louis 33; Bergman, Mary Kay 33–34; Bern, Paul 34–37; Bing, Herman 38; Blandick, Clara 39; Bloodgood, Clara 40; Bowers, John 42–43; Boyer, Charles 44–45; Bradbury, James, Jr. 45; Brand, Marlon 46; Brody, Lee 49; Brooke, Tyler 49; Buckley, Helen Curry 52; Burton, Sam J. 52; Canada, Tressie J. 54; Capucine 54–56; Carew(e), Arthur Edmund 56; Charle, Tamara 58; Charters, Spencer 59; Collins, Etta Stewart 63–64; Cooksey, Curtis 65; Cotton, Lucy 66–67; Crosby, Dennis Michael 70; Crosby, Lindsay 71; Cuneo, Lester H. 72; Cutts, Patricia 73; Dalida 74; Dandridge, Dorothy Jean 75–77; Dane, Karl 77–78; Darvi, Bella 79–80; Davies, Lynette 81; Davis, Peggy 81–82; Dekker, Albert 83–84; Dewaère, Patrick 85; Dolly, Jenny 87–88; Donnelly, Cornelius 88; Doonan, Patric 88; Dougherty, Virgil "Jack" 88; Dowling, Joan 89; Drew, Lillian 90; Du Cello, Countess (Mary) 91; Duel, Peter 91–92; Du Fragnne, Jacques 93; Dunville, T. E. (Thomas Edward) 93; Eagels, Jeanne 94–95; Edwards, Jeannie 97; Eichelberger, Ethyl 97; Entwistle, Peg 99–100; Eustache, Jean 102; Farnsworth, Richard 103–5; Farrar, Margaret 105; Finch, Mark 106–7; Finley, Ned 107; Flanders, Edward Paul 108–9; Flather, Charlotte Carter 109; Flory, Regine 109–10; Fluellen, Joel 110; Fox, Grace 112; Frazin, Gladys 112; Freeman, Max 112; Gaby, Frank 114; Gaston, Rosamond Pinchot 116–17; Gildo, Rex 119–20; Gillingwater, Claude, Sr. 120; Gleason, Russell 120–21; Gold, Cecil 121–22; Gottlieb, Betty Montague 124; Graham, Juliann 125; Greene, Winifred 127; Grey, Marion 127–28; Hale, Dorothy 128–29; Hall, Jon 129–30; Hall-Davis, Lillian 130; Hamer, Rusty 131; Hancock, Tony 132–33; Hanley, Evelyn 133; Hartman, Brynn 134–35; Hartman, Elizabeth 135–36; Hassall, Imogen 136; Hastings, Cuyler 136; Haver, Phyllis 137–38;

Art Directors, Designers, and Make-Up Artists

Artists, Animators, and Cartoonists

Cameramen and Editors, Film

Celebrity Spouses, Relatives, and Lovers

Circus Performers and Executives

Clowns and Mimes

Comedians

Composers and Songwriters

Producers and Directors, Theatre

Producers, Directors, and Managers, Television and Radio

Record Executives and Producers

Restaurateurs and Nightclub Managers

Rodeo Performers and Promoters

Screenwriters, Playwrights, and Novelists

Showgirls

Television and Radio Personalities

Adams, Nick 8; Allard, Bob 10; Allen, Chet R. 10; Ayres, Dudley 17–18; Barry, Don "Red" 23–24; Baxter, Dale 27–28; Beckett, Scott Hastings 28; Bergman, Mary Kay 33–34; Boyer, Charles 44–45; Brody, Lee 49; Chubbuck, Christine 59–60; Collins, Sid 64; Combs, Raymond Neil, Jr. 64–65; Common, Tommy 65; Crockett, Clarence 69; Crofoot, Alan 69; Cutts, Patricia 73; Davies, Lynette 81; Desmonde, Jerry 85; Douglas, Barbara L. 89; Duel, Peter 91–92; Fluellen, Joel 110; Fox, Grace 112; Garroway, Dave 115; Gillott, Jacky 120; Greene, Gilbert Clayton 127; Hall, Jon 129–30; Hamer, Rusty 131; Hancock, Tony 132–33; Hanley, Evelyn 133; Hansen, Vern 133; Hassall, Imogen 136; Hemingway, Margaux 140–41; Henry, John 141; Hoegler, Albert 144; Holland, Anthony 144; Hollenbeck, Don 144; Holliday, Michael 145; Howard, Lisa 150; Howden, Victoria 150–51; Huet, Jacqueline 151; Jackson, Glenn E. 158; Jason, Rick 161; Jerome, Suzie 162; Jones, Kenneth Bruce 163; Justice, Barry Norval Bannatyne 165; Keats, Steven 168; Keith, Brian 169–70; Kennedy, Pat 171–72; Kenney, Charles Elbert 172; Kent, Kay 172; Korsten, Georg (Ge) 174; Ladd, Alan Walbridge 176–78; Lehman, Trent Lawson 188–89; Lindsey, Ouida 194; Linkletter, Diane 194–96; Loeb, Philip 197–98; Luciano, Ron 201; Massengale, Joseph 214; Mathieson, Fiona 215; Mossman, James 233–34; Mottley, Eva 234; Moult, Edward "Ted" 234; Munrow, David 235; Nevius, Lynn 238; O'Connor, Hugh Edward 241–42; Olmedo, Alberto 244; Olsen, John C. 244; Phillips, Twila 247; Pierce, Jackie 247–48; Pierce, Justin 248; Pistilli, Luigi 249; Plato, Dana 249–50; Prinze, Freddie 254–56; Quine, Richard 256–57; Rand, George 257; Rappaport, David 258; Raymond, Leslie Ray 259–60; Reeves, George 260–63; Reilly, Catherine 263; Roberts, Rachel 267–68; Rogers, Will, Jr. 269–70; Rose, Joel 270; Rose, Monica 270–71; Ross, Robin 272–73; Salmi, Albert 274–75; Sanders, Steve 277; Saper, Marshall 277–78; Scarboro, David 283–84; Sherrin, Scott 289–90; Slezak, Walter 294–95; Sloane, Everett 295–96; Stevens, Inger 301–2; Stewart, Jay 302–3; Strickland, David Gordon, Jr. 304–5; Swift, Charles A. 309; Thies, Henry R., Jr. 313–14; Townsend, William H. 320–21; Toye, John 321; Villechaize, Herve 329–30; Waring, Peter 336; Weaver, Winstead Sheffield ("Doodles") 337; Webb, Richard 337–38; Willis, Debbie 347; Wilson, Read 348; Withers, Grant 349–50; Young, Faron 351–52; Young, Gig 352–54

Theatre Owners, Managers, and Architects

Barraco, Paul 23; Bettelheim, Spencer D. 38; Beyfuss, Alexander 38; Bishop, Robert Hamilton, III 39; Blattner, Ludwig 39–40; Brady, James Kelvin 45–46; Brill, Peter 48–49; Canow, William 54; Carr, Joseph L. 57; Casady, Weir 57; Crandall, Harry M. 67–68; Croft, Lee D. 69–70; Daniels, Roy G. 78; Dimmitt, Charles Ridgley 86; Dittrich, Frederick A. 86; Dusenbury, Will J. 93–94; Falke, Charles H. 103; Geare, Reginald Wyckliffe 118; Goerlitz, Ernest 121; Goldsmith, Arthur 122; Greenfield, Louis R. 127; Hamilton, Harry Lud 131–32; Handley, Frank 133; Hanley, Michael Edward 133–34; Hendon, Rigby D. 141; Hoppe, William H., Jr. 148; Ingersoll, Fred 156; Israel, Richard 157–58; Kaimann, William J. 166; Kaliski, Louis 166; Kelly, George Augustus 171; Kinney, Anthony 174; Klaw, Joseph 174; Krause, Benjamin 176; Lashley, H. T. (Dick) 183; Laughlin, Leo C. 183; Lothrop, William H. 199–200; McDonald, Sidney T. 205; McElroy, Gavin Blair 205; Major, John 209; Mansfield, Edward 209–10; Midgley, Rex W. 220; Muller, Ben 235; Murray, Oscar J. 236; Prince, Benjamin Sidney 253–54; Putnam, J. Myles 256; Richert, Frederick 265; Robertson, William T. 268; Rockwell, George 269; Schoenstadt, Ralph 284; Scott, George (I) 285; Sire, Albert I. 293; Slater, Charles Dundas 294; Smith, Edward J. 296; Smith, Worthington 296; Soriero, Thomas D. 298; Spears, Joseph 298; Steele,

APPENDIX II:
METHODS OF SUICIDE

Airplane

Maeno, Mitsuyasu 208

Automobile

Davis, Peggy 81–82; Koenig, Frank 174

Carbon Monoxide

Allard, Bob 10; Andre, Rene 11; Ardell, John E. 13; Austin, John Van "Tex" 16; Bates, Barbara 26–27; Best, Don 37–38; Brandstatter, Adolph "Eddie" 47–48; Brooke, Tyler 49; Chic, Charles J. 59; Dannemann, Monika 78–79; Dougherty, Virgil "Jack" 88; Douglas, Barbara L. 89; Dreyfuss, Doris 90; Dreyfuss, Henry 90; Eberhardt, Walter F. 96; Ellison, Jim 98; Espe, Geraldine Soles 101–2; Fabris, Pasqual 102–3; Fletcher, Stoughton J. 109; Gaston, Rosamond Pinchot 116–17; Greenacre, Fern 127; Hammond, Charles P. 132; Henshaw, Roger Dale 141; Holman, Libby 145–47; Inge, William Motter 155–56; King, Edward L. 173; Klaw, Joseph 174; Lazarus, Sidney 187; Luciano, Ron 201; McFarland, Homer S. 205–6; Meins, Gustave 217–18; Moora, Robert L. 230; Ogden, William 243; Preeman, Morse M. 252–53; Raymond, Leslie Ray 259–60; Rosson, Richard 273; Schloss, Berrick 284; Storer, Edna 303; Tandler, Adolph 309; Todd, Thelma 317–20; Van Cott, J. Marston 324; Wallace, Ray Charles 335; Ward, Jeff 336; Warfel, Jack 336

Drowning

Ayler, Albert 16–17; Bowers, John 42–43; Davies, Lynette 81; Dunville, T. E. (Thomas Edward) 93; Dusenbury, Will J. 93–94; Eisenberg, Emanuel 98; Fillmore, Russell 106; Hamilton, Harry Lud 131–32; Moorey, Stefa 231; Quigley, Jay 256; Ross, Robin 272–73; Sherrin, Scott 289–90; Thompson, Edith 316; Thompson, Jack 316; Vincent, James 330; Webster, George Hopkinson 338; West, Vera 339–40; Whale, James 341–44

Drugs/Pills

Adams, Nick 8; Allen, Chet R. 10; Angeli, Pier 11–13; Austin, Anne 15–16; Aylmer, David 17; Barrymore, Diana (Blanche) 24–25; Beckett, Scott Hastings 28; Bellamy, Peter Franklyn 30–31; Benda, Marion 31; Bennett, Jill 32–33; Bondshu, Neil 41; Borneman, Ernest 42; Boyer, Charles 44–45; Breen, Benita 48; Cady, Jerome 53; Charters, Spencer 59; Cory, George 66; Cotton, Lucy 66–67; Crane, Vincent 68; Crash, Darby 68–69; Cutts, Patricia 73; Dalida 74; Dandridge, Dorothy Jean 75–77; Deckers, Jeanine 82; Desmonde, Jerry

Electrocution

Exposure

Fire

Gas

Gasoline ingestion/inhalation

Gun

Hanging

Collins, Sid 64; Combs, Raymond Neil, Jr. 64–65; Cooper, Courtney Ryley 65–66; Curtis, Ian 72–73; Dekker, Albert 83–84; Dolly, Jenny 87–88; Evans, Tom (Badfinger) 18–20; Fisher, Fred 108; Freeman, Max 112; Gaby, Frank 114; Goldsmith, Arthur 122; Grant, Arthur J. 125; Greenfield, Louis R. 127; Ham, Peter William (Badfinger) 18–20; Hansen, Vern 134; Hoegler, Albert 144; Holliday, Frank, Jr. 145; Hutchence, Michael Kelland Frank 151–53; Jackson, Charles 158; Jacobs, David 158–59; Johannesson, Cary Jon 162–63; Jordan, Alex 163; Lehman, Trent Lawson 188–89; Levine, Hendrick 190; Ludwig, Charles "Zaza" 201; McPhail, Allen 208; Manuel, Richard 210–11; Mastrocola, Enrico 215; Matsumoto, Hideto 215–16; Metz, Henry 220; Mildwater, Justin 220; Moloney, Jay (James David) 223; Mueller, Lawrence S. 234–35; Muller, Ben 235; Munrow, David 235; Nash, Marvin E. 237; Nelson, William Hugh ("Billy"), Jr. 238; Ochs, Phil 240–41; Odoms, Clifford R. 242; O'Hara, Brian 243; Oram, Suzanne 244–45; Payne, Donald Rollie 246; Pierce, Justin 248; Pistilli, Luigi 248–49; Pollack, Ben 251; Pond, Lloyd 251; Rennie, Hugh 264; Rogers, Gustavus A. 269; Ross, Albert H. 272; Row, Harry 273–74; Sampson, Caleb 275; Saunders, John Monk 278; Scott, Russell 285; Serkin, Robert 287; Smith, Worthington 296; Smitha, Silk 297; Sterling, Charles 300–1; Stierheim, Christopher 303; Strickland, David Gordon, Jr. 304–5; Sutch, David Edward 307–9; Taintor, Katherine Grey 309; Tembo, Biggie 312–13; Thorne, Thomas 316; Van Dyke, Kelly Jean 324; Visaria, Ravi 330; Vogel, Patricia F. 331; Wagner, George E. 334; Waring, Peter 336; Weaver, Howard E. 336–37; Weiss, Phillip 339; Wilkinson, Kevin Michael 344–45; Williams, Rozz 345–46

Jumping

Alban, Jean-Pierre 8; Armitage, Pauline 14–15; Bacon, Faith 18; Bantchevsky, Bantcho 21–22; Barron, Donna 23; Bell, Stanley 30; Brody, Lee 49; Brooks, Joseph 49; Canada, Tressie J. 54; Capucine 54–56; Carroll, James 57; Chavez, Dolores Lila Bettua 59; Creelman, James A. 69; Crofoot, Alan 69; Desai, Manmohan 84–85; Dobritch, Alexander Anthony 86–87; Donley, Katherine 88; Duell, Joseph 93; Ecker, Murray 96; Entwistle, Peg 99–100; Falke, Charles H. 103; Finch, Mark 106–7; Fox, Grace 112; Fritz, Ward C. 113; Furst, Anton 114; Gardner, Frank 114–15; Gates, Ivan R. 117; Geng, Nian Mei 118; Gildo, Rex 119–20; Gleason, Russell 120–21; Graves, Mina Rudolph 127; Hale, Dorothy 128–29; Hammell, John A. 132; Hartman, Elizabeth 135–36; Hathaway, Donny 137; Hayes, Ray 138; Irene 156–57; Israel, Richard 157–58; Itami, Juzo 158; Judd, Terence 164; Jullion, M. Arthur 165; Jutra, Claude 165–66; Kean, Norman 166–67; Keim, Adrienne LaChamp 168–69; Kennedy, Kevin J. 171; King, Allyn 173; Lancer, Martin 180; Laszlo, Lola 183; Lavrova, Vera 183–84; Lee, Harry 187–88; Lee, Thomas Stewart 188; Lessey, May Abbey 190; Linkletter, Diane 194–96; Livingston, Charlotte 197; Love, Robert 200; Lowers, Helen 200; Lubetkin, Steven Roland 200–1; McIntire, Donald E. 206; Mack, William 206–7; Major, John 209; Maroney, Robert N. 212; Martorana, Samuel 213; Moyer, Helen Jean 234; Nirenska, Pola 238–39; O'Donnell, Helen 242–43; Okada, Yukiko 243; Olmedo, Alberto 244; Osterman, Mary Dolores Daly 245; Pascal, Christine 245; Pavley, Andreas 246; Powell, Nicolette 252; Presburg, Yolanda 253; Reynolds, Fred 264; Rudolph, Mina 274; Scarboro, David 283–84; Schuetze, Carl 284; Selznick, Mary Jennifer 287; Semenoff, Nikolai 287; Sheridan, Philip R. 289; Shields, Hugh M. 292; Siegel, Norman 292–93; Sire, Albert I. 293; Sklover, Theodora K. 293–94; Skouras, Dionysia 294; Smith, Pete 296; Soriero, Thomas D. 298; Stark, Peter 299; Steele, Ernest William 299–300; Tannehill, Frank H. 309–10; Thirkield, Robert Leeming 313; Tuckner, Howard 323; Waldman, Josef 335; Wehle, Billy 338; Weston, Charles H. 341; Willmott, Lee 347; Wills, Lynn Alfred 347; Winchell, Jennie 348; Winter, Julian 348–49; Wise, Fred 349; Zegart, Arthur 355

Knife/Razor/Scissors

Abingdon, William L. 5; Brower, James "Jay" Delano 49; Carnevale, Luigi 56–57; Eichelberger, Ethyl 97; Flynn, J. Thornton 110; Fonda, Frances Seymour Brokaw 110–11; Hall-Davis, Lillian 130; Jerome, Suzie 162; Kauter, William 166; King, Edwin 173–74; Lewis, Thurston Theodore 192; Linder, Max 192–94; McCullough, Paul 203–4; Mahan, Vivian L. 208–9; Mansfield, Edward 209–10; Minch, Conrad H. 222; Mohamed, Hammed Ben 223; Nehoda, Ron 237; Powell, William David, Jr. 252; Scott, Robert Crozier 285; Shibley, Nassib Abdullah 290–91; Spears, Joseph 298; Tellegen, Lou 311–12; Thompson, Hallett 316

Murder/Suicide

Behrmann, Dimitri 30; Bennison, Louis 33; Buckland, Wilfred, Sr. 51–52; Canow, William 54; Donley, Katherine 88; Duarte, Pablo 91; Gonzalez, Israel Chappa 122–23; Gottlieb, Betty Montague 124; Hartman, Brynn 134–35; Harvey, Gerald 136; Heckler, Herbert 138–39; Howden, Victoria 150–51; Jones, Kenneth Bruce 163; Kean, Norman 166–67; Kelly, George Augustus 171; Leonard, Harry 189–90; McNelley, Robert E. ("Bobby Gene") 207–8; Mansfield, Edward 209–10; Markle, John 211–12; Maroney, Robert N. 212; Melrose, Percy C. 218; Merrige-Abrams, Salwa 219; Milocevic, Milos 221–22; Morris, Leonard 233; Mueller, Lawrence S. 234–35; Munro, Viola Gordon 235; Peters, Gleason G. 247; Reilly, Catherine 263; Renaudin, Lester 263–64; Ritchie, Adele 265–66; Robertson, William T. 268; Rockwell, George 269; Rosolino, Frank 272; Rovig, Melita Powell 273; Salmi, Albert 274–75; Sanders, Scott 276–77; Shibley, Nassib Adbullah 290–91; Storer, Edna 303; Troutman, Larry 321–22; Walters, Homer M. 335–36; Young, Gig 352–54

Poison

Acord, Art 6–7; Albertson, Arthur 9; Anderson, Charles 10–11; Ash, Ernest A. 15; Auer, Norma 15; Aye, Maryon (Marion) 16; Baucus, Frank M. 27; Bengston, Elmer L. 31–32; Boyce, St. Elmo 43; Brown, Susan 49; Carr, Joseph L. 57; Daly, Anna 74–75; DeBerg, Adolph 82; Drew, Lillian 90; Du Fragnne, Jacques 93; Dupree, Maida 93; Edwards, Jeannie 97; Farrar, Margaret 105; Fay, Florence 105; Finley, Ned 107; Flather, Charlotte Carter 109; Fletcher, John W. 109; Frazier, Brenda 112; Freeman, Max 112; Goerlitz, Ernest 121; Gold, Cecil 121–22; Grant, Isabella 125–26; Greene, Gilbert Clayton 127; Greene, Winifred 127; Grey, Marion 127–28; Hanley, Evelyn 133; Horton, Murray 148; Hurst, Ronald S. 151; Hyde, George R. 153; Keenan, Geraldine 168; Krause, Benjamin 176; LaGrange, Vivian 179; Lawrence, Florence 184–87; Leonard, Harry 189–90; Linder, Max 192–94; McDonald, Sidney T. 205; McPhail, Douglas 208; Mansfield, Edward 209–10; Martin, Vallie Belasco 212–13; Midgley, Rex W. 220; Moore, Lotus 230–31; Neal, Sandra 237; Nordern, Cliff 239; O'Keefe, Mildred 244; Patrick, Warren A. 245; Perry, Geraldine 247; Rand, George 257; Roberts, Rachel 267–68; Sidney, Carrie Webb 292; Smoller, Dorothy 297; Southern, Dixie Lee 298; Spirescu, Oscar 299; Steele, Murray M. 300; Thomas, Olive 314–15; Turner, Irene Laura 323; Vidot, Charlotte 329; Vogelsang, Roland F. 331; Walsh, May 335; Westmore, George 340–41

Suffocation

Blandick, Clara 39; Kosinski, Jerzy 175

Suicide Pacts

Deckers, Jeanine 82; Dimsdale, Howard 86; Dreyfuss, Henry 90; Giaconni, Ernesto 119; Henshaw, Roger Dale 141; Lazarus, Sidney 187; Leavy, Adelaide M. 187; Linder, Max 192–94; Storm, Rory 303–4; Varnadore, Thurman 325; Warner, Jewel 187

Train/Subway

Battles, Marjorie Ann 27; Bond, Graham 40–41; Borland, Adrian 41–42; Brennan, Louis Kelso 48; Davis, Rose 82; Ray, Margaret Mary 259; Rivera, Carlos 266

INDEX

Names and page numbers in **boldface** *refer to main entries.*